Inside
the Machine

An Illustrated Introduction to
Microprocessors and Computer Architecture

Jon Stokes

**NO STARCH
PRESS**

San Francisco

Printed in Canada

10 09 08 07   2 3 4 5 6 7 8 9

ISBN-10: 1-59327-104-2
ISBN-13: 978-1-59327-104-6

Publisher: William Pollock
Production Editor: Elizabeth Campbell
Cover Design: Octopod Studios
Developmental Editor: William Pollock
Copyeditors: Sarah Lemaire, Megan Dunchak
Compositor: Riley Hoffman
Proofreader: Stephanie Provines
Indexer: Nancy Guenther

For information on book distributors or translations, please contact No Starch Press, Inc. directly:

No Starch Press, Inc.
555 De Haro Street, Suite 250, San Francisco, CA 94107
phone: 415.863.9900; fax: 415.863.9950; info@nostarch.com; www.nostarch.com

Library of Congress Cataloging-in-Publication Data

Stokes, Jon
  Inside the machine : an illustrated introduction to microprocessors and computer architecture / Jon
Stokes.
       p. cm.
  Includes index.
  ISBN-13: 978-1-59327-104-6
  ISBN-10: 1-59327-104-2
 1. Computer architecture. 2. Microprocessors--Design and construction. I. Title.
  TK7895.M5S76 2006
  621.39'2--dc22
                                         2005037262

The photograph in the center of the cover shows a small portion of an Intel 80486DX2 microprocessor die at 200x optical magnification. Most of the visible features are the top metal interconnect layers which wire most of the on-die components together.

Cover photo by Matt Britt and Matt Gibbs.

To my parents, who instilled in me a love of learning and education, and to my grandparents, who footed the bill.

BRIEF CONTENTS

CONTENTS IN DETAIL

3
PIPELINED EXECUTION

35

4
SUPERSCALAR EXECUTION

61

5
THE INTEL PENTIUM AND PENTIUM PRO

79

6
POWERPC PROCESSORS: 600 SERIES, 700 SERIES, AND 7400   111

7
INTEL'S PENTIUM 4 VS. MOTOROLA'S G4E: APPROACHES AND DESIGN PHILOSOPHIES   137

8
INTEL'S PENTIUM 4 VS. MOTOROLA'S G4E: THE BACK END — 161

9
64-BIT COMPUTING AND X86-64 — 179

12
INTEL'S PENTIUM M, CORE DUO, AND CORE 2 DUO   235

BIBLIOGRAPHY AND SUGGESTED READING   271

INDEX   275

PREFACE

"The purpose of computing is insight, not numbers."
—Richard W. Hamming (1915–1998)

When mathematician and computing pioneer Richard Hamming penned this maxim in 1962, the era of digital computing was still very much in its infancy. There were only about 10,000 computers in existence worldwide; each one was large and expensive, and each required teams of engineers for maintenance and operation. Getting results out of these mammoth machines was a matter of laboriously inputting long strings of numbers, waiting for the machine to perform its calculations, and then interpreting the resulting mass of ones and zeros. This tedious and painstaking process prompted Hamming to remind his colleagues that the reams of numbers they worked with on a daily basis were only a means to a much higher and often non-numerical end: keener insight into the world around them.

In today's post-Internet age, hundreds of millions of people regularly use computers not just to gain insight, but to book airline tickets, to play poker, to assemble photo albums, to find companionship, and to do every other sort of human activity from the mundane to the sublime. In stark contrast to the way things were 40 years ago, the experience of using a computer to do math on large sets of numbers is fairly foreign to many users, who spend only a very small fraction of their computer time explicitly performing arithmetic operations. In popular operating systems from Microsoft and Apple, a small calculator application is tucked away somewhere in a folder and accessed only infrequently, if at all, by the majority of users. This small, seldom-used calculator application is the perfect metaphor for the modern computer's hidden identity as a shuffler of numbers.

This book is aimed at reintroducing the computer as a calculating device that performs layer upon layer of miraculous sleights of hand in order to hide from the user the rapid flow of numbers inside the machine. The first few chapters introduce basic computing concepts, and subsequent chapters work through a series of more advanced explanations, rooted in real-world hardware, that show how instructions, data, and numerical results move through the computers people use every day. In the end, *Inside the Machine* aims to give the reader an intermediate to advanced knowledge of how a variety of microprocessors function and how they stack up to each other from multiple design and performance perspectives.

Ultimately, I have tried to write the book that I would have wanted to read as an undergraduate computer engineering student: a book that puts the pieces together in a big-picture sort of way, while still containing enough detailed information to offer a firm grasp of the major design principles underlying modern microprocessors. It is my hope that *Inside the Machine*'s blend of exposition, history, and architectural "comparative anatomy" will accomplish that goal.

ACKNOWLEDGMENTS

This book is a distillation and adaptation of over eight years' worth of my technical articles and news reporting for *Ars Technica*, and as such, it reflects the insights and information offered to me by the many thousands of readers who've taken the time to contact me with their feedback. Journalists, professors, students, industry professionals, and, in many cases, some of the scientists and engineers who've worked on the processors covered in this book have all contributed to the text within these pages, and I want to thank these correspondents for their corrections, clarifications, and patient explanations. In particular, I'd like to thank the folks at IBM for their help with the articles that provided the material for the part of the book dealing with the PowerPC 970. I'd also like to thank Intel Corp., and George Alfs in particular, for answering my questions about the processors covered in Chapter 12. (All errors are my own.)

I want to thank Bill Pollock at No Starch Press for agreeing to publish *Inside the Machine*, and for patiently guiding me through my first book. Other No Starch Press staff for whom thanks are in order include Elizabeth Campbell (production editor), Sarah Lemaire (copyeditor), Riley Hoffman (compositor), Stephanie Provines (proofreader), and Megan Dunchak.

I would like to give special thanks to the staff of *Ars Technica* and to the site's forum participants, many of whom have provided me with the constructive criticism, encouragement, and education without which this book would not have been possible. Thanks are also in order for my technical prereaders, especially Lee Harrison and Holger Bettag, both of whom furnished invaluable advice and feedback on earlier drafts of this text. Finally, I would like to thank my wife, Christina, for her patience and loving support in helping me finish this project.

Jon Stokes
Chicago, 2006

INTRODUCTION

Inside the Machine is an introduction to computers that is intended to fill the gap that exists between classic but more challenging introductions to computer architecture, like John L. Hennessy's and David A. Patterson's popular textbooks, and the growing mass of works that are simply too basic for motivated non-specialist readers. Readers with some experience using computers and with even the most minimal scripting or programming experience should finish *Inside the Machine* with a thorough and advanced understanding of the high-level organization of modern computers. Should they so choose, such readers would then be well equipped to tackle more advanced works like the aforementioned classics, either on their own or as part of formal curriculum.

The book's comparative approach, described below, introduces new design features by comparing them with earlier features intended to solve the same problem(s). Thus, beginning and intermediate readers are encouraged to read the chapters in order, because each chapter assumes a familiarity with the concepts and processor designs introduced in the chapters prior to it.

More advanced readers who are already familiar with some of the processors covered will find that the individual chapters can stand alone. The book's extensive use of headings and subheadings means that it can also be employed as a general reference for the processors described, though that is not the purpose for which it was designed.

The first four chapters of *Inside the Machine* are dedicated to laying the conceptual groundwork for later chapters' studies of real-world microprocessors. These chapters use a simplified example processor, the DLW, to illustrate basic and intermediate concepts like the instructions/data distinction, assembly language programming, superscalar execution, pipelining, the programming model, machine language, and so on.

The middle portion of the book consists of detailed studies of two popular desktop processor lines: the Pentium line from Intel and the PowerPC line from IBM and Motorola. These chapters walk the reader through the chronological development of each processor line, describing the evolution of the microarchitectures and instruction set architectures under discussion. Along the way, more advanced concepts like speculative execution, vector processing, and instruction set translation are introduced and explored via a discussion of one or more real-world processors.

Throughout the middle part of the book, the overall approach is what might be called "comparative anatomy," in which each new processor's novel features are explained in terms of how they differ from analogous features found in predecessors and/or competitors. The comparative part of the book culminates in Chapters 7 and 8, which consist of detailed comparisons of two starkly different and very important processors: Intel's Pentium 4 and Motorola's MPC7450 (popularly known as the G4e).

After a brief introduction to 64-bit computing and the 64-bit extensions to the popular *x*86 instruction set architecture in Chapter 9, the microarchitecture of the first mass-market 64-bit processor, the IBM PowerPC 970, is treated in Chapter 10. This study of the 970, the majority of which is also directly applicable to IBM's POWER4 mainframe processor, concludes the book's coverage of PowerPC processors.

Chapter 11 covers the organization and functioning of the memory hierarchy found in almost all modern computers.

Inside the Machine's concluding chapter is given over to an in-depth examination of the latest generation of processors from Intel: the Pentium M, Core Duo, and Core 2 Duo. This chapter contains the most detailed discussion of these processors available online or in print, and it includes some new information that has not been publicly released prior to the printing of this book.

1

BASIC COMPUTING CONCEPTS

Modern computers come in all shapes and sizes, and they aid us in a million different types of tasks ranging from the serious, like air traffic control and cancer research, to the not-so-serious, like computer gaming and photograph retouching. But as diverse as computers are in their outward forms and in the uses to which they're put, they're all amazingly similar in basic function. All of them rely on a limited repertoire of technologies that enable them do the myriad kinds of miracles we've come to expect from them.

At the heart of the modern computer is the *microprocessor*—also commonly called the *central processing unit (CPU)*—a tiny, square sliver of silicon that's etched with a microscopic network of gates and channels through which electricity flows. This network of gates (*transistors*) and channels (*wires* or *lines*) is a very small version of the kind of circuitry that we've all seen when cracking open a television remote or an old radio. In short, the microprocessor isn't just the "heart" of a modern computer—it's a computer in and of itself. Once you understand how this tiny computer works, you'll have a thorough grasp of the fundamental concepts that underlie all of modern computing, from the aforementioned air traffic control system to the silicon brain that controls the brakes on a luxury car.

This chapter will introduce you to the microprocessor, and you'll begin to get a feel for just how straightforward computers really are. You need master only a few fundamental concepts before you explore the microprocessor technologies detailed in the later chapters of this book.

To that end, this chapter builds the general conceptual framework on which I'll hang the technical details covered in the rest of the book. Both newcomers to the study of computer architecture and more advanced readers are encouraged to read this chapter all the way through, because its abstractions and generalizations furnish the large conceptual "boxes" in which I'll later place the specifics of particular architectures.

The Calculator Model of Computing

Figure 1-1 is an abstract graphical representation of what a computer does. In a nutshell, a computer takes a stream of instructions (code) and a stream of data as input, and it produces a stream of results as output. For the purposes of our initial discussion, we can generalize by saying that the *code stream* consists of different types of arithmetic operations and the *data stream* consists of the data on which those operations operate. The *results stream*, then, is made up of the results of these operations. You could also say that the results stream begins to flow when the operators in the code stream are carried out on the operands in the data stream.

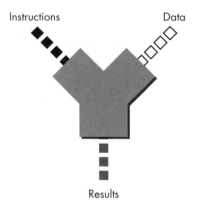

Figure 1-1: A simple representation of a general-purpose computer

NOTE *Figure 1-1 is my own variation on the traditional way of representing a processor's* arithmetic logic unit (ALU), *which is the part of the processor that does the addition, subtraction, and so on, of numbers. However, instead of showing two operands entering the top ports and a result exiting the bottom port (as is the custom in the literature), I've depicted code and data streams entering the top ports and a* results stream *leaving the bottom port.*

To illustrate this point, imagine that one of those little black boxes in the code stream of Figure 1-1 is an addition operator (a + sign) and that two of the white data boxes contain two integers to be added together, as shown in Figure 1-2.

Figure 1-2: Instructions are combined with data to produce results

You might think of these black-and-white boxes as the keys on a calculator—with the white keys being numbers and the black keys being operators—the gray boxes are the results that appear on the calculator's screen. Thus the two input streams (the code stream and the data stream) represent sequences of key presses (arithmetic operator keys and number keys), while the output stream represents the resulting sequence of numbers displayed on the calculator's screen.

The kind of simple calculation described above represents the sort of thing that we intuitively think computers do: like a pocket calculator, the computer takes numbers and arithmetic operators (such as +, −, ÷, ×, etc.) as input, performs the requested operation, and then displays the results. These results might be in the form of pixel values that make up a rendered scene in a computer game, or they might be dollar values in a financial spreadsheet.

The File-Clerk Model of Computing

The "calculator" model of computing, while useful in many respects, isn't the only or even the best way to think about what computers do. As an alternative, consider the following definition of a computer:

> A *computer* is a device that shuffles numbers around from place to place, reading, writing, erasing, and rewriting different numbers in different locations according to a set of inputs, a fixed set of rules for processing those inputs, and the prior history of all the inputs that the computer has seen since it was last reset, until a predefined set of criteria are met that cause the computer to halt.

We might, after Richard Feynman, call this idea of a computer as a reader, writer, and modifier of numbers the "file-clerk" model of computing (as opposed to the aforementioned calculator model). In the file-clerk model, the computer accesses a large (theoretically infinite) store of sequentially arranged numbers for the purpose of altering that store to achieve a desired result. Once this desired result is achieved, the computer halts so that the now-modified store of numbers can be read and interpreted by humans.

The file-clerk model of computing might not initially strike you as all that useful, but as this chapter progresses, you'll begin to understand how important it is. This way of looking at computers is powerful because it emphasizes the end product of computation rather than the computation itself. After all, the purpose of computers isn't just to compute in the abstract, but to produce usable results from a given data set.

NOTE   *Those who've studied computer science will recognize in the preceding description the beginnings of a discussion of a Turing machine. The Turing machine is, however, too abstract for our purposes here, so I won't actually describe one. The description that I develop here sticks closer to the classic Reduced Instruction Set Computing (RISC) load-store model, where the computer is "fixed" along with the storage. The Turing model of a computer as a movable read-write head (with a state table) traversing a linear "tape" is too far from real-life hardware organization to be anything but confusing in this discussion.*

In other words, what matters in computing is not that you did some math, but that you started with a body of numbers, applied a sequence of operations to it, and got a body of results. Those results could, again, represent pixel values for a rendered scene or an environmental snapshot in a weather simulation. Indeed, the idea that a computer is a device that transforms one set of numbers into another should be intuitively obvious to anyone who has ever used a Photoshop filter. Once we understand computers not in terms of the math they do, but in terms of the numbers they move and modify, we can begin to get a fuller picture of how they operate.

In a nutshell, a computer is a device that reads, modifies, and writes sequences of numbers. These three functions—read, modify, and write—are the three most fundamental functions that a computer performs, and all of the machine's components are designed to aid in carrying them out. This read-modify-write sequence is actually inherent in the three central bullet points of our initial file-clerk definition of a computer. Here is the sequence mapped explicitly onto the file-clerk definition:

> A computer is a device that shuffles numbers around from place to place, reading, writing, erasing, and rewriting different numbers in different locations according to a set of inputs [*read*], a fixed set of rules for processing those inputs [*modify*], and the prior history of all the inputs that the computer has seen since it was last reset [*write*], until a predefined set of criteria are met that cause the computer to halt.

That sums up what a computer does. And, in fact, that's *all* a computer does. Whether you're playing a game or listening to music, everything that's going on under the computer's hood fits into this model.

NOTE   *All of this is fairly simple so far, and I've even been a bit repetitive with the explanations to drive home the basic read-modify-write structure of all computer operations. It's important to grasp this structure in its simplicity, because as we increase our computing model's level of complexity, we'll see this structure repeated at every level.*

The Stored-Program Computer

All computers consist of at least three fundamental types of structures needed to carry out the read-modify-write sequence:

Storage

To say that a computer "reads" and "writes" numbers implies that there is at least one number-holding structure that it reads from and writes to. All computers have a place to put numbers—a storage area that can be read from and written to.

Arithmetic logic unit (ALU)

Similarly, to say that a computer "modifies" numbers implies that the computer contains a device for performing operations on numbers. This device is the ALU, and it's the part of the computer that performs arithmetic operations (addition, subtraction, and so on), on numbers from the storage area. First, numbers are read from storage into the ALU's data input port. Once inside the ALU, they're modified by means of an arithmetic calculation, and then they're written back to storage via the ALU's output port.

The ALU is actually the green, three-port device at the center of Figure 1-1. Note that ALUs aren't normally understood as having a code input port along with their data input port and results output port. They do, of course, have command input lines that let the computer specify which operation the ALU is to carry out on the data arriving at its data input port, so while the depiction of a code input port on the ALU in Figure 1-1 is unique, it is not misleading.

Bus

In order to move numbers between the ALU and storage, some means of transmitting numbers is required. Thus, the ALU reads from and writes to the data storage area by means of the *data bus*, which is a network of transmission lines for shuttling numbers around inside the computer. Instructions travel into the ALU via the *instruction bus*, but we won't cover how instructions arrive at the ALU until Chapter 2. For now, the data bus is the only bus that concerns us.

The code stream in Figure 1-1 flows into the ALU in the form of a sequence of arithmetic instructions (add, subtract, multiply, and so on). The operands for these instructions make up the data stream, which flows over the data bus from the storage area into the ALU. As the ALU carries out operations on the incoming operands, the results stream flows out of the ALU and back into the storage area via the data bus. This process continues until the code stream stops coming into the ALU. Figure 1-3 expands on Figure 1-1 and shows the storage area.

The data enters the ALU from a special storage area, but where does the code stream come from? One might imagine that it comes from the keypad of some person standing at the computer and entering a sequence of instructions, each of which is then transmitted to the code input port of the ALU, or perhaps that the code stream is a prerecorded list of instructions that is fed into the ALU, one instruction at a time, by some manual or automated mechanism. Figure 1-3 depicts the code stream as a prerecorded list of instructions that is stored in a special storage area just like the data stream, and modern computers do store the code stream in just such a manner.

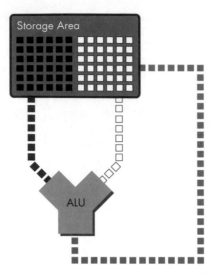

Figure 1-3: A simple computer, with an ALU
and a region for storing instructions and data

NOTE   *More advanced readers might notice that in Figure 1-3 (and in Figure 1-4 later)
I've separated the code and data in main memory after the manner of a Harvard
architecture level-one cache. In reality, blocks of code and data are mixed together in
main memory, but for now I've chosen to illustrate them as logically separated.*

The modern computer's ability to store and reuse prerecorded sequences
of commands makes it fundamentally different from the simpler calculating
machines that preceded it. Prior to the invention of the first *stored-program
computer*,[1] all computing devices, from the abacus to the earliest electronic
computing machines, had to be manipulated by an operator or group of
operators who manually entered a particular sequence of commands each
time they wanted to make a particular calculation. In contrast, modern computers store and reuse such command sequences, and as such they have a
level of flexibility and usefulness that sets them apart from everything that
has come before. In the rest of this chapter, you'll get a first-hand look at the
many ways that the stored-program concept affects the design and capabilities of the modern computer.

Refining the File-Clerk Model

Let's take a closer look at the relationship between the code, data, and
results streams by means of a quick example. In this example, the code
stream consists of a single instruction, an add, which tells the ALU to add
two numbers together.

---

[1] In 1944 J. Presper Eckert, John Mauchly, and John von Neumann proposed the first stored-
program computer, the EDVAC (Electronic Discrete Variable Automatic Computer), and in
1949 such a machine, the EDSAC, was built by Maurice Wilkes of Cambridge University.

The add instruction travels from code storage to the ALU. For now, let's not concern ourselves with how the instruction gets from code storage to the ALU; let's just assume that it shows up at the ALU's code input port announcing that there is an addition to be carried out immediately. The ALU goes through the following sequence of steps:

1. Obtain the two numbers to be added (the input operands) from data storage.
2. Add the numbers.
3. Place the results back into data storage.

The preceding example probably sounds simple, but it conveys the basic manner in which computers—*all* computers—operate. Computers are fed a sequence of instructions one by one, and in order to execute them, the computer must first obtain the necessary data, then perform the calculation specified by the instruction, and finally write the result into a place where the end user can find it. Those three steps are carried out billions of times per second on a modern CPU, again and again and again. It's only because the computer executes these steps so rapidly that it's able to present the illusion that something much more conceptually complex is going on.

To return to our file-clerk analogy, a computer is like a file clerk who sits at his desk all day waiting for messages from his boss. Eventually, the boss sends him a message telling him to perform a calculation on a pair of numbers. The message tells him which calculation to perform, and where in his personal filing cabinet the necessary numbers are located. So the clerk first retrieves the numbers from his filing cabinet, then performs the calculation, and finally places the results back into the filing cabinet. It's a boring, mindless, repetitive task that's repeated endlessly, day in and day out, which is precisely why we've invented a machine that can do it efficiently and not complain.

The Register File

Since numbers must first be fetched from storage before they can be added, we want our data storage space to be as fast as possible so that the operation can be carried out quickly. Since the ALU is the part of the processor that does the actual addition, we'd like to place the data storage as close as possible to the ALU so it can read the operands almost instantaneously. However, practical considerations, such as a CPU's limited surface area, constrain the size of the storage area that we can stick next to the ALU. This means that in real life, most computers have a relatively small number of very fast data storage locations attached to the ALU. These storage locations are called *registers*, and the first *x*86 computers only had eight of them to work with. These registers, which are arrayed in a storage structure called a *register file*, store only a small subset of the data that the code stream needs (and we'll talk about where the rest of that data lives shortly).

Building on our previous, three-step description of what goes on when a computer's ALU is commanded to add two numbers, we can modify it as follows. To execute an add instruction, the ALU must perform these steps:

1. Obtain the two numbers to be added (the *input operands*) from two *source registers.*
2. Add the numbers.
3. Place the results back in a *destination register.*

For a concrete example, let's look at addition on a simple computer with only four registers, named A, B, C, and D. Suppose each of these registers contains a number, and we want to add the contents of two registers together and overwrite the contents of a third register with the resulting sum, as in the following operation:

Code	Comments
A + B = C	Add the contents of registers A and B, and place the result in C, overwriting whatever was there.

Upon receiving an instruction commanding it to perform this addition operation, the ALU in our simple computer would carry out the following three familiar steps:

1. Read the contents of registers A and B.
2. Add the contents of A and B.
3. Write the result to register C.

NOTE *You should recognize these three steps as a more specific form of the read-modify-write sequence from earlier, where the generic modify step is replaced with an addition operation.*

This three-step sequence is quite simple, but it's at the very core of how a microprocessor really works. In fact, if you glance ahead to Chapter 10's discussion of the PowerPC 970's pipeline, you'll see that it actually has separate stages for each of these three operations: stage 12 is the register read step, stage 13 is the actual execute step, and stage 14 is the write-back step. (Don't worry if you don't know what a pipeline is, because that's a topic for Chapter 3.) So the 970's ALU reads two operands from the register file, adds them together, and writes the sum back to the register file. If we were to stop our discussion right here, you'd already understand the three core stages of the 970's main integer pipeline—all the other stages are either just preparation to get to this point or they're cleanup work after it.

RAM: When Registers Alone Won't Cut It

Obviously, four (or even eight) registers aren't even close to the theoretically infinite storage space I mentioned earlier in this chapter. In order to make a viable computer that does useful work, you need to be able to store very large data sets. This is where the computer's *main memory* comes in. Main memory, which in modern computers is always some type of *random access memory (RAM)*, stores the data set on which the computer operates, and only a small portion of that data set at a time is moved to the registers for easy access from the ALU (as shown in Figure 1-4).

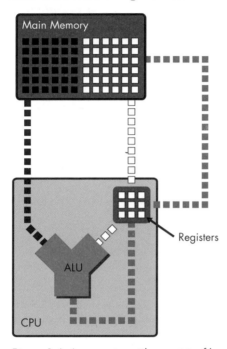

Figure 1-4: A computer with a register file

Figure 1-4 gives only the slightest indication of it, but main memory is situated quite a bit farther away from the ALU than are the registers. In fact, the ALU and the registers are internal parts of the microprocessor, but main memory is a completely separate component of the computer system that is connected to the processor via the *memory bus*. Transferring data between main memory and the registers via the memory bus takes a significant amount of time. Thus, if there were no registers and the ALU had to read data directly from main memory for each calculation, computers would run very slowly. However, because the registers enable the computer to store data near the ALU, where it can be accessed nearly instantaneously, the computer's computational speed is decoupled somewhat from the speed of main memory. (We'll discuss the problem of memory access speeds and computational performance in more detail in Chapter 11, when we talk about caches.)

The File-Clerk Model Revisited and Expanded

To return to our file-clerk metaphor, we can think of main memory as a document storage room located on another floor and the registers as a small, personal filing cabinet where the file clerk places the papers on which he's currently working. The clerk doesn't really know anything about the document storage room—what it is or where it's located—because his desk and his personal filing cabinet are all he concerns himself with. For documents that are in the storage room, there's another office worker, the office secretary, whose job it is to locate files in the storage room and retrieve them for the clerk.

This secretary represents a few different units within the processor, all of which we'll meet Chapter 4. For now, suffice it to say that when the boss wants the clerk to work on a file that's not in the clerk's personal filing cabinet, the secretary must first be ordered, via a message from the boss, to retrieve the file from the storage room and place it in the clerk's cabinet so that the clerk can access it when he gets the order to begin working on it.

An Example: Adding Two Numbers

To translate this office example into computing terms, let's look at how the computer uses main memory, the register file, and the ALU to add two numbers.

To add two numbers stored in main memory, the computer must perform these steps:

1. Load the two operands from main memory into the two source registers.
2. Add the contents of the source registers and place the results in the destination register, using the ALU. To do so, the ALU must perform these steps:
    a. Read the contents of registers A and B into the ALU's input ports.
    b. Add the contents of A and B in the ALU.
    c. Write the result to register C via the ALU's output port.
3. Store the contents of the destination register in main memory.

Since steps 2a, 2b, and 2c all take a trivial amount of time to complete, relative to steps 1 and 3, we can ignore them. Hence our addition looks like this:

1. Load the two operands from main memory into the two source registers.
2. Add the contents of the source registers, and place the results in the destination register, using the ALU.
3. Store the contents of the destination register in main memory.

The existence of main memory means that the user—the boss in our filing-clerk analogy—must manage the flow of information between main memory and the CPU's registers. This means that the user must issue instructions to more than just the processor's ALU; he or she must also issue instructions to the parts of the CPU that handle memory traffic. Thus, the preceding three steps are representative of the kinds of instructions you find when you take a close look at the code stream.

A Closer Look at the Code Stream: The Program

At the beginning of this chapter, I defined the code stream as consisting of "an ordered sequence of operations," and this definition is fine as far as it goes. But in order to dig deeper, we need a more detailed picture of what the code stream is and how it works.

The term *operations* suggests a series of simple arithmetic operations like addition or subtraction, but the code stream consists of more than just arithmetic operations. Therefore, it would be better to say that the code stream consists of an ordered sequence of *instructions*. Instructions, generally speaking, are commands that tell the whole computer—not just the ALU, but multiple parts of the machine—exactly what actions to perform. As we've seen, a computer's list of potential actions encompasses more than just simple arithmetic operations.

General Instruction Types

Instructions are grouped into ordered lists that, when taken as a whole, tell the different parts of the computer how to work together to perform a specific task, like grayscaling an image or playing a media file. These ordered lists of instructions are called *programs*, and they consist of a few basic types of instructions.

In modern RISC microprocessors, the act of moving data between memory and the registers is under the explicit control of the code stream, or program. So if a programmer wants to add two numbers that are located in main memory and then store the result back in main memory, he or she must write a list of instructions (a program) to tell the computer exactly what to do. The program must consist of:

- a load instruction to move the two numbers from memory into the registers
- an add instruction to tell the ALU to add the two numbers
- a store instruction to tell the computer to place the result of the addition back into memory, overwriting whatever was previously there

These operations fall into two main categories:

Arithmetic instructions
These instructions tell the ALU to perform an arithmetic calculation (for example, add, sub, mul, div).

Memory-access instructions
These instructions tell the parts of the processor that deal with main memory to move data from and to main memory (for example, load and store).

NOTE   *We'll discuss a third type of instruction, the branch instruction, shortly. Branch instructions are technically a special type of memory-access instruction, but they access code storage instead of data storage. Still, it's easier to treat branches as a third category of instruction.*

The *arithmetic instruction* fits with our calculator metaphor and is the type of instruction most familiar to anyone who's worked with computers. Instructions like integer and floating-point addition, subtraction, multiplication, and division all fall under this general category.

NOTE *In order to simplify the discussion and reduce the number of terms, I'm temporarily including logical operations like* AND, OR, NOT, NOR, *and so on, under the general heading of arithmetic instructions. The difference between arithmetic and logical operations will be introduced in Chapter 2.*

The *memory-access instruction* is just as important as the arithmetic instruction, because without access to main memory's data storage regions, the computer would have no way to get data into or out of the register file.

To show you how memory-access and arithmetic operations work together within the context of the code stream, the remainder of this chapter will use a series of increasingly detailed examples. All of the examples are based on a simple, hypothetical computer, which I'll call the DLW-1.[2]

The DLW-1's Basic Architecture and Arithmetic Instruction Format

The DLW-1 microprocessor consists of an ALU (along with a few other units that I'll describe later) attached to four registers, named A, B, C, and D for convenience. The DLW-1 is attached to a bank of main memory that's laid out as a line of 256 memory cells, numbered #0 to #255. (The number that identifies an individual memory cell is called an *address*.)

The DLW-1's Arithmetic Instruction Format

All of the DLW-1's arithmetic instructions are in the following *instruction format*:

```
instruction source1, source2, destination
```

There are four parts to this instruction format, each of which is called a *field*. The *instruction* field specifies the type of operation being performed (for example, an addition, a subtraction, a multiplication, and so on). The two *source* fields tell the computer which registers hold the two numbers being operated on, or the *operands*. Finally, the *destination* field tells the computer which register to place the result in.

As a quick illustration, an addition instruction that adds the numbers in registers A and B (the two source registers) and places the result in register C (the destination register) would look like this:

Code	Comments
add A, B, C	Add the contents of registers A and B and place the result in C, overwriting whatever was previously there.

---

[2] "DLW" in honor of the DLX architecture used by Hennessy and Patterson in their books on computer architecture.

The DLW-1's Memory Instruction Format

In order to get the processor to move two operands from main memory into the source registers so they can be added, you need to tell the processor explicitly that you want to move the data in two specific memory cells to two specific registers. This "filing" operation is done via a memory-access instruction called the load.

As its name suggests, the load instruction loads the appropriate data from main memory into the appropriate registers so that the data will be available for subsequent arithmetic instructions. The store instruction is the reverse of the load instruction, and it takes data from a register and stores it in a location in main memory, overwriting whatever was there previously.

All of the memory-access instructions for the DLW-1 have the following instruction format:

```
instruction source, destination
```

For all memory accesses, the instruction field specifies the type of memory operation to be performed (either a load or a store). In the case of a load, the source field tells the computer which memory address to fetch the data from, while the destination field specifies which register to put it in. Conversely, in the case of a store, the source field tells the computer which register to take the data from, and the destination field specifies which memory address to write the data to.

An Example DLW-1 Program

Now consider Program 1-1, which is a piece of DLW-1 code. Each of the lines in the program must be executed in sequence to achieve the desired result.

Line	Code	Comments
1	load #12, A	Read the contents of memory cell #12 into register A.
2	load #13, B	Read the contents of memory cell #13 into register B.
3	add A, B, C	Add the numbers in registers A and B and store the result in C.
4	store C, #14	Write the result of the addition from register C into memory cell #14.

Program 1-1: Program to add two numbers from main memory

Suppose the main memory looked like the following before running Program 1-1:

#11 #12 #13 #14

12	6	2	3

After doing our addition and storing the results, the memory would be changed so that the contents of cell #14 would be overwritten by the sum of cells #12 and #13, as shown here:

```
#11   #12   #13   #14
┌─────┬─────┬─────┬─────┐
│ 12  │  6  │  2  │  8  │
└─────┴─────┴─────┴─────┘
```

A Closer Look at Memory Accesses: Register vs. Immediate

The examples so far presume that the programmer knows the exact memory location of every number that he or she wants to load and store. In other words, it presumes that in composing each program, the programmer has at his or her disposal a list of the contents of memory cells #0 through #255.

While such an accurate snapshot of the initial state of main memory may be feasible for a small example computer with only 256 memory locations, such snapshots almost never exist in the real world. Real computers have billions of possible locations in which data can be stored, so programmers need a more flexible way to access memory, a way that doesn't require each memory access to specify numerically an exact memory address.

Modern computers allow the *contents* of a register to be used as a memory address, a move that provides the programmer with the desired flexibility. But before discussing the effects of this move in more detail, let's take one more look at the basic add instruction.

Immediate Values

All of the arithmetic instructions so far have required two source registers as input. However, it's possible to replace one or both of the source registers with an explicit numerical value, called an *immediate value*. For instance, to increase whatever number is in register A by 2, we don't need to load the value 2 into a second source register, like B, from some cell in main memory that contains that value. Rather, we can just tell the computer to add 2 to A directly, as follows:

Code	Comments
add A, 2, A	Add 2 to the contents of register A and place the result back into A, overwriting whatever was there.

I've actually been using immediate values all along in my examples, but just not in any arithmetic instructions. In all of the preceding examples, each load and store uses an immediate value in order to specify a memory address. So the #12 in the load instruction in line 1 of Program 1-1 is just an immediate value (a regular whole number) prefixed by a # sign to let the computer know that this particular immediate value is a memory address that designates a cell in memory.

Memory addresses are just regular whole numbers that are specially marked with the # sign. Because they're regular whole numbers, they can be stored in registers—and stored in memory—just like any other number. Thus, the whole-number contents of a register, like D, could be construed by the computer as representing a memory address.

For example, say that we've stored the number 12 in register D, and that we intend to use the contents of D as the address of a memory cell in Program 1-2.

Line	Code	Comments
1	load #D, A	Read the contents of the memory cell designated by the number stored in D (where D = 12) into register A.
2	load #13, B	Read the contents of memory cell #13 into register B.
3	add A, B, C	Add the numbers in registers A and B and store the result in C.
4	store C, #14	Write the result of the addition from register C into memory cell #14.

Program 1-2: Program to add two numbers from main memory using an address stored in a register

Program 1-2 is essentially the same as Program 1-1, and given the same input, it yields the same results. The only difference is in line 1:

Program 1-1, Line 1	Program 1-2, Line 1
load #12, A	load #D, A

Since the content of D is the number 12, we can tell the computer to look in D for the memory cell address by substituting the register name (this time marked with a # sign for use as an address), for the actual memory cell number in line 1's load instruction. Thus, the first lines of Programs 1-1 and 1-2 are functionally equivalent.

This same trick works for store instructions, as well. For example, if we place the number 14 in D we can modify the store command in line 4 of Program 1-1 to read as follows: store C, #D. Again, this modification would not change the program's output.

Because memory addresses are just regular numbers, they can be stored in memory cells as well as in registers. Program 1-3 illustrates the use of a memory address that's stored in another memory cell. If we take the input for Program 1-1 and apply it to Program 1-3, we get the same output as if we'd just run Program 1-1 without modification:

Line	Code	Comments
1	load #11, D	Read the contents of memory cell #11 into D.
2	load #D, A	Read the contents of the memory cell designated by the number in D (where D = 12) into register A.
3	load #13, B	Read the contents of memory cell #13 into register B.
4	add A, B, C	Add the numbers in registers A and B and store the result in C.
5	store C, #14	Write the result of the addition from register C into memory cell #14.

Program 1-3: Program to add two numbers from memory using an address stored in a memory cell.

The first instruction in Program 1-3 loads the number 12 from memory cell #11 into register D. The second instruction then uses the content of D (which is the value 12) as a memory address in order to load register A into memory location #12.

But why go to the trouble of storing memory addresses in memory cells and then loading the addresses from main memory into the registers before they're finally ready to be used to access memory again? Isn't this an overly complicated way to do things?

Actually, these capabilities are designed to make programmers' lives easier, because when used with the register-relative addressing technique described next they make managing code and data traffic between the processor and massive amounts of main memory much less complex.

Register-Relative Addressing

In real-world programs, loads and stores most often use *register-relative addressing*, which is a way of specifying memory addresses relative to a register that contains a fixed *base address*.

For example, we've been using D to store memory addresses, so let's say that on the DLW-1 we can assume that, unless it is explicitly told to do otherwise, the operating system always loads the starting address (or base address) of a program's data segment into D. Remember that code and data are logically separated in main memory, and that data flows into the processor from a data storage area, while code flows into the processor from a special code storage area. Main memory itself is just one long row of undifferentiated memory cells, each one *byte* in width, that store numbers. The computer carves up this long row of bytes into multiple segments, some of which store code and some of which store data.

A *data segment* is a block of contiguous memory cells that a program stores all of its data in, so if a programmer knows a data segment's starting address (base address) in memory, he or she can access all of the other memory locations in that segment using this formula:

```
base address + offset
```

where *offset* is the distance in bytes of the desired memory location from the data segment's base address.

Thus, `load` and `store` instructions in DLW-1 assembly would normally look something like this:

Code	Comments
load #(D + 108), A	Read the contents of the memory cell at location #(D + 108) into A.
store B, #(D + 108)	Write the contents of B into the memory cell at location #(D + 108).

In the case of the `load`, the processor takes the number in D, which is the base address of the data segment, adds 108 to it, and uses the result as the `load`'s destination memory address. The `store` works in the exact same way.

Of course, this technique requires that a quick addition operation (called an *address calculation*) be part of the execution of the `load` instruction, so this is why the *load-store units* on modern processors contain very fast integer addition hardware. (As we'll learn in Chapter 4, the load-store unit is the execution unit responsible for executing `load` and `store` instructions, just like the arithmetic-logic unit is responsible for executing arithmetic instructions.)

By using register-relative addressing instead of *absolute addressing* (in which memory addresses are given as immediate values), a programmer can write programs without knowing the exact location of data in memory. All the programmer needs to know is which register the operating system will place the data segment's base address in, and he or she can do all memory accesses relative to that base address. In situations where a programmer uses absolute addressing, when the operating system loads the program into memory, all of the program's immediate address values have to be changed to reflect the data segment's actual location in memory.

Because both memory addresses and regular integer numbers are stored in the same registers, these registers are called *general-purpose registers (GPRs)*. On the DLW-1, A, B, C, and D are all GPRs.

2

THE MECHANICS OF PROGRAM EXECUTION

Now that we understand the basics of computer organization, it's time to take a closer look at the nuts and bolts of how stored programs are actually executed by the computer. To that end, this chapter will cover core programming concepts like machine language, the programming model, the instruction set architecture, branch instructions, and the fetch-execute loop.

Opcodes and Machine Language

If you've been following the discussion so far, it shouldn't surprise you to learn that both memory addresses and instructions are ordinary numbers that can be stored in memory. All of the instructions in a program like Program 1-1 are represented inside the computer as strings of numbers. Indeed, a program is one long string of numbers stored in a series of memory locations.

How is a program like Program 1-1 rendered in numerical notation so that it can be stored in memory and executed by the computer? The answer is simpler than you might think.

As you may already know, a computer actually only understands 1s and 0s (or "high" and "low" electric voltages), not English words like *add*, *load*, and *store*, or letters and base-10 numbers like A, B, 12, and 13. In order for the computer to run a program, therefore, all of its instructions must be rendered in *binary notation*. Think of translating English words into Morse code's dots and dashes and you'll have some idea of what I'm talking about.

Machine Language on the DLW-1

The translation of programs of any complexity into this binary-based *machine language* is a massive undertaking that's meant to be done by a computer, but I'll show you the basics of how it works so you can understand what's going on. The following example is simplified, but useful nonetheless.

The English words in a program, like *add*, *load*, and *store*, are *mnemonics* (meaning they're easy for people to remember), and they're all mapped to strings of binary numbers, called *opcodes*, that the computer can understand. Each opcode designates a different operation that the processor can perform. Table 2-1 maps each of the mnemonics used in Chapter 1 to a 3-bit opcode for the hypothetical DLW-1 microprocessor. We can also map the four register names to 2-bit binary codes, as shown in Table 2-2.

Table 2-1: Mapping of Mnemonics to Opcodes for the DLW-1

Mnemonic	Opcode
add	000
sub	001
load	010
store	011

Table 2-2: Mapping of Registers to Binary Codes for the DLW-1

Register	Binary Code
A	00
B	01
C	10
D	11

The binary values representing both the opcodes and the register codes are arranged in one of a number of 16-bit (or 2-byte) formats to get a complete *machine language instruction*, which is a binary number that can be stored in RAM and used by the processor.

Because programmer-written instructions must be translated into binary codes before a computer can read them, it is common to see programs in any format—binary, assembly, or a high-level language like BASIC or C, referred to generically as "code" or "codes." So programmers sometimes speak of "assembler code," "binary code," or "C code," when referring to programs written in assembly, binary, or C language. Programmers also will often describe the act of programming as "writing code" or "coding." I have adopted this terminology in this book, and will henceforth use the term "code" regularly to refer generically to instruction sequences and programs.

Binary Encoding of Arithmetic Instructions

Arithmetic instructions have the simplest machine language instruction formats, so we'll start with them. Figure 2-1 shows the format for the machine language encoding of a *register-type* arithmetic instruction.

0	1	2	3	4	5	6	7
mode	opcode			source1		source2	

Byte 1

8	9	10	11	12	13	14	15
destination		000000					

Byte 2

Figure 2-1: Machine language format for a register-type instruction

In a register-type arithmetic instruction (that is, an arithmetic instruction that uses only registers and no immediate values), the first bit of the instruction is the *mode bit*. If the mode bit is set to 0, then the instruction is a register-type instruction; if it's set to 1, then the instruction is of the immediate type.

Bits 1–3 of the instruction specify the opcode, which tells the computer what type of operation the instruction represents. Bits 4–5 specify the instruction's first source register, 6–7 specify the second source register, and 8–9 specify the destination register. The last six bits are not needed by register-to-register arithmetic instructions, so they're padded with 0s (they're *zeroed out* in computer jargon) and ignored.

Now, let's use the binary values in Tables 2-1 and 2-2 to translate the add instruction in line 3 of Program 1-1 into a 2-byte (or 16-bit) machine language instruction:

Assembly Language Instruction	Machine Language Instruction
add A, B, C	00000001 10000000

Here are a few more examples of arithmetic instructions, just so you can get the hang of it:

Assembly Language Instruction	Machine Language Instruction
add C, D, A	00001011 00000000
add D, B, C	00001101 10000000
sub A, D, C	00010011 10000000

Increasing the number of binary digits in the opcode and register fields increases the total number of instructions the machine can use and the number of registers it can have. For example, if you know something about binary notation, then you probably know that a 3-bit opcode allows the processor to map up to 2^3 mnemonics, which means that it can have up to 2^3, or 8, instructions in its *instruction set*; increasing the opcode size to 8 bits would allow the processor's instruction set to contain up to 2^8, or 256, instructions. Similarly, increasing the number of bits in the register field increases the possible number of registers that the machine can have.

Arithmetic instructions containing an immediate value use an *immediate-type* instruction format, which is slightly different from the register-type format we just saw. In an immediate-type instruction, the first byte contains the opcode, the source register, and the destination register, while the second byte contains the immediate value, as shown in Figure 2-2.

0	1	2	3	4	5	6	7
mode	opcode			source		destination	

Byte 1

8	9	10	11	12	13	14	15
8-bit immediate value							

Byte 2

Figure 2-2: Machine language format for an immediate-type instruction

Here are a few immediate-type arithmetic instructions translated from assembly language to machine language:

Assembly Language Instruction	Machine Language Instruction
add C, 8, A	10001000 00001000
add 5, A, C	10000010 00000101
sub 25, D, C	10011110 00011001

Binary Encoding of Memory Access Instructions

Memory-access instructions use both register- and immediate-type instruction formats exactly like those shown for arithmetic instructions. The only difference lies in how they use them. Let's take the case of a load first.

The load Instruction

We've previously seen two types of load, the first of which was the immediate type. An immediate-type load (see Figure 2-3) uses the immediate-type instruction format, but because the load's source is an immediate value (a memory address) and not a register, the source field is unneeded and must be zeroed out. (The source field is not ignored, though, and in a moment we'll see what happens if it isn't zeroed out.)

0	1	2	3	4	5	6	7
mode	opcode			00		destination	

Byte 1

8	9	10	11	12	13	14	15
8-bit immediate source address							

Byte 2

Figure 2-3: Machine language format for an immediate-type load

Now let's translate the immediate-type load in line 1 of Program 1-1 (12 is 1100 in binary notation):

Assembly Language Instruction	Machine Language Instruction
load #12, A	10100000 00001100

The 2-byte machine language instruction on the right is a binary representation of the assembly language instruction on the left. The first byte corresponds to an immediate-type load instruction that takes register A as its destination. The second byte is the binary representation of the number 12, which is the source address in memory that the data is to be loaded from.

The second type of load we've seen is the register type. A register-type load uses the register-type instruction format, but with the source2 field zeroed out and ignored, as shown in Figure 2-4.

In Figure 2-4, the source1 field specifies the register containing the memory address that the processor is to load data from, and the destination field specifies the register that the loaded data is to be placed in.

0	1	2	3	4	5	6	7
mode	opcode			source1		00	

Byte 1

8	9	10	11	12	13	14	15
destination		000000					

Byte 2

Figure 2-4: Machine language format for a register-type load

For a register-relative addressed load, we use a version of the immediate-type instruction format, shown in Figure 2-5, with the base field specifying the register that contains the base address and the offset stored in the second byte of the instruction.

0	1	2	3	4	5	6	7
mode	opcode			base		destination	

Byte 1

8	9	10	11	12	13	14	15
8-bit immediate offset							

Byte 2

Figure 2-5: Machine language format for a register-relative load

Recall from Table 2-2 that 00 is the binary number that designates register A. Therefore, as a result of the DLW-1's particular machine language encoding scheme, any register but A could theoretically be used to store the base address for a register-relative load.

The store Instruction

The register-type binary format for a store instruction is the same as it is for a load, except that the destination field specifies a register containing a destination memory address, and the source1 field specifies the register containing the data to be stored to memory.

The immediate-type machine language format for a store, pictured in Figure 2-6, is also similar to the immediate-type format for a load, except that since the destination register is not needed (the destination is the immediate memory address) the destination field is zeroed out, while the source field specifies which register holds the data to be stored.

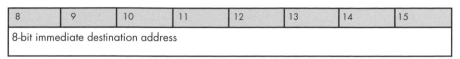

0	1	2	3	4	5	6	7
mode	opcode			source		00	

Byte 1

8	9	10	11	12	13	14	15
8-bit immediate destination address							

Byte 2

Figure 2-6: Machine language format for an immediate-type store

The register-relative store, on the other hand, uses the same immediate-type instruction format used for the register-relative load (Figure 2-5), but the destination field is set to a nonzero value, and the offset is stored in the second byte. Again, the base address for a register-relative store can theoretically be stored in any register other than A, although by convention it's stored in D.

Translating an Example Program into Machine Language

For our simple computer with four registers, three instructions, and 256 memory cells, it's tedious but trivial to translate Program 1-1 into machine-readable binary representation using the previous tables and instruction formats. Program 2-1 shows the translation.

Line	Assembly Language	Machine Language
1	load #12, A	10100000 00001100
2	load #13, B	10100001 00001101
3	add A, B, C	00000001 10000000
4	store C, #14	10111000 00001110

Program 2-1: A translation of Program 1-1 into machine language

The 1s and 0s in the rightmost column of Program 2-1 represent the high and low voltages that the computer "thinks" in.

Real machine language instructions are usually longer and more complex than the simple ones I've given here, but the basic idea is exactly the same. Program instructions are translated into machine language in a mechanical, predefined manner, and even in the case of a fully modern microprocessor, doing such translations by hand is merely a matter of knowing the instruction formats and having access to the right charts and tables.

Of course, for the most part the only people who do such translations by hand are computer engineering or computer science undergraduates who've been assigned them for homework. This wasn't always the case, though.

The Programming Model and the ISA

Back in the bad old days, programmers had to enter programs into the computer directly in machine language (after having walked five miles in the snow uphill to work). In the very early stages of computing, this was done by flipping switches. The programmer toggled strings of 1s and 0s into the computer's very limited memory, ran the program, and then pored over the resulting strings of 1s and 0s to decode the answer.

Once memory sizes and processing power increased to the point where programmer time and effort were valuable enough relative to computing time and memory space, computer scientists devised ways of allowing the computer to use a portion of its power and memory to take on some of the burden of making its cryptic input and output a little more human-friendly.

In short, the tedious task of converting human-readable programs into machine-readable binary code was automated; hence the birth of *assembly language* programming. Programs could now be written using mnemonics, register names, and memory locations, before being converted by an *assembler* into machine language for processing.

In order to write assembly language programs for a machine, you have to understand the machine's available resources: how many registers it has, what instructions it supports, and so on. In other words, you need a well-defined model of the machine you're trying to program.

The Programming Model

The *programming model* is the programmer's interface to the microprocessor. It hides all of the processor's complex implementation details behind a relatively simple, clean layer of abstraction that exposes to the programmer all of the processor's functionality. (See Chapter 4 for more on the history and development of the programming model.)

Figure 2-7 shows a diagram of a programming model for an eight-register machine. By now, most of the parts of the diagram should be familiar to you. The ALU performs arithmetic, the registers store numbers, and the *input-output unit (I/O unit)* is responsible for interacting with memory and the rest of the system (via loads and stores). The parts of the processor that we haven't yet met lie in the *control unit*. Of these, we'll cover the *program counter* and the *instruction register* now.

The Instruction Register and Program Counter

Because programs are stored in memory as ordered sequences of instructions and memory is arranged as a linear series of addresses, each instruction in a program lives at its own memory address. In order to step through and execute the lines of a program, the computer simply begins at the program's starting address and then steps through each successive memory location, fetching each successive instruction from memory, placing it in a special register, and executing it as shown in Figure 2-8.

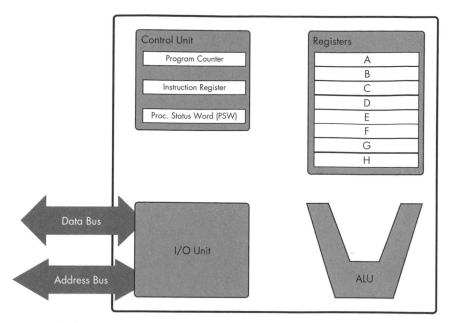

Figure 2-7: The programming model for a simple eight-register machine

The instructions in our DLW-1 computer are two bytes long. If we assume that each memory cell holds one byte, then the DLW-1 must step through memory by fetching instructions from two cells at a time.

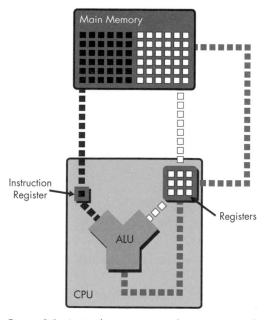

Figure 2-8: A simple computer with instruction and data registers

For example, if the starting address in Program 1-1 were #500, it would look like Figure 2-9 in memory (with the instructions rendered in machine language, not assembly language, of course).

#500 #501 #502 #503 #504 #505 #506 #507

| load #12, A | load #13, B | add A, B, C | store C, #14 |

Figure 2-9: An illustration of Program 1-1 in memory, starting at address #500

The Instruction Fetch: Loading the Instruction Register

An *instruction fetch* is a special type of load that happens automatically for every instruction. It always takes the address that's currently in the program counter register as its source and the instruction register as its destination. The control unit uses a fetch to load each instruction of a program from memory into the instruction register, where that instruction is *decoded* before being executed; and while that instruction is being decoded, the processor places the address of the next instruction into the program counter by incrementing the address that's currently in the program counter, so that the newly incremented address points to the next instruction the sequence. In the case of our DLW-1, the program counter is incremented by two every time an instruction is fetched, because the two-byte instructions begin at every other byte in memory.

Running a Simple Program: The Fetch-Execute Loop

In Chapter 1 we discussed the steps a processor takes to perform calculations on numbers using the ALU in combination with a fetched arithmetic instruction. Now let's look at the steps the processor takes in order to fetch a series of instructions—a program—and feed them to either the ALU (in the case of arithmetic instructions) or the memory access hardware (in the case of loads and stores):

1. *Fetch* the next instruction from the address stored in the program counter, and load that instruction into the instruction register. Increment the program counter.
2. *Decode* the instruction in the instruction register.
3. *Execute* the instruction in the instruction register, using the following rules:
    a. If the instruction is an arithmetic instruction, execute it using the ALU and register file.
    b. If the instruction is a memory access instruction, execute it using the memory-access hardware.

These three steps are fairly straightforward, and with one modification they describe the way that microprocessors execute programs (as we'll see in the section "Branch Instructions" on page 30). Computer scientists often refer to these steps as the *fetch-execute loop* or the *fetch-execute cycle*. The fetch-execute loop is repeated for as long as the computer is powered on. The machine iterates through the entire loop, from step 1 to step 3, over and over again many millions or billions of times per second in order to run programs.

Let's run through the three steps with our example program as shown in Figure 2-9. (This example presumes that #500 is already in the program counter.) Here's what the processor does, in order:

1. Fetch the instruction beginning at #500, and load `load #12, A` into the instruction register. Increment the program counter to #502.

2. Decode `load #12, A` in the instruction register.

3. Execute `load #12, A` from the instruction register, using the memory-access hardware.

4. Fetch the instruction beginning at #502, and load `load #13, B` in the instruction register. Increment the program counter to #504.

5. Decode `load #13, B` in the instruction register.

6. Execute `load #13, B` from the instruction register, using the memory-access hardware.

7. Fetch the instruction beginning at #504, and load `add A, B, C` into the instruction register. Increment the program counter to #506.

8. Decode `add A, B, C` in the instruction register.

9. Execute `add A, B, C` from the instruction register, using the ALU and register file.

10. Fetch the instruction at #506, and load `store C, #14` in the instruction register. Increment the program counter to #508.

11. Decode `store C, #14` in the instruction register.

12. Execute `store C, #14` from the instruction register, using the memory-access hardware.

NOTE *To zoom in on the execute steps of the preceding sequence, revisit Chapter 1, and particularly the sections "Refining the File-Clerk Model" on page 6 and "RAM: When Registers Alone Won't Cut It" on page 8. If you do, you'll gain a pretty good understanding of what's involved in executing a program on any machine. Sure, there are important machine-specific variations for most of what I've presented here, but the general outlines (and even a decent number of the specifics) are the same.*

The Clock

Steps 1 through 12 in the previous section don't take an arbitrary amount of time to complete. Rather, they're performed according to the pulse of the clock that governs every action the processor takes.

This clock pulse, which is generated by a *clock generator* module on the motherboard and is fed into the processor from the outside, times the functioning of the processor so that, on the DLW-1 at least, all three steps of the fetch-execute loop are completed in exactly one beat of the clock. Thus, the program in Figure 2-9, as I've traced its execution in the preceding section, takes exactly four clock beats to finish execution, because a new instruction is fetched on each beat of the clock.

One obvious way to speed up the execution of programs on the DLW-1 would be to speed up its clock generator so that each step takes less time to complete. This is generally true of all microprocessors, hence the race among microprocessor designers to build and market chips with ever-higher clock speeds. (We'll talk more about the relationship between clock speed and performance in Chapter 3.)

Branch Instructions

As I've presented it so far, the processor moves through each line in a program in sequence until it reaches the end of the program, at which point the program's output is available to the user.

There are certain instructions in the instruction stream, however, that allow the processor to jump to a program line that is out of sequence. For instance, by inserting a *branch instruction* into line 5 of a program, we could cause the processor's control unit to jump all the way down to line 20 and begin executing there (a *forward branch*), or we could cause it to jump back up to line 1 (a *backward branch*). Because a program is an ordered sequence of instructions, by including forward and backward branch instructions, we can arbitrarily move about in the program. This is a powerful ability, and branches are an essential part of computing.

Rather than thinking about forward or backward branches, it's more useful for our present purposes to categorize all branches as being one of the following two types: conditional branches or unconditional branches.

Unconditional Branch

An *unconditional branch* instruction consists of two parts: the branch instruction and the target address.

```
jump #target
```

For an unconditional branch, #target can be either an immediate value, like #12, or an address stored in a register, like #D.

Unconditional branches are fairly easy to execute, since all that the computer needs to do upon decoding such a branch in the instruction register is to have the control unit replace the address currently in the program counter with branch's target address. Then the next time the processor goes to fetch the instruction at the address given by the program counter, it'll fetch the address at the branch target instead.

Conditional Branch

Though it has the same basic instruction format as the unconditional branch (instruction #target), the *conditional branch* instruction is a little more complicated, because it involves jumping to the target address only if a certain condition is met.

For example, say we want to jump to a new line of the program only if the previous arithmetic instruction's result is zero; if the result is nonzero, we want to continue executing normally. We would use a conditional branch instruction that first checks to see if the previously executed arithmetic instruction yielded a zero result, and then writes the branch target into the program counter if it did.

Because of such conditional jumps, we need a special register or set of registers in which to store information about the results of arithmetic instructions—information such as whether the previous result was zero or nonzero, positive or negative, and so on.

Different architectures handle this in different ways, but in our DLW-1, this is the function of the *processor status word (PSW)* register. On the DLW-1, every arithmetic operation stores different types of data about its outcome in the PSW upon completion. To execute a conditional branch, the DLW-1 must first *evaluate* the condition on which the branch depends (e.g., "is the previous arithmetic instruction's result zero?" in the preceding example) by checking the appropriate bit in the PSW to see if that condition is true or false. If the branch condition evaluates to true, then the control unit replaces the address in the program counter with the branch target address. If the branch condition evaluates to false, then the program counter is left as-is, and the next instruction in the normal program sequence is fetched on the next cycle.

For example, suppose we had just subtracted the number in A from the number in B, and if the result was zero (that is, if the two numbers were equal), we want to jump to the instruction at memory address #106. Program 2-2 shows what assembler code for such a conditional branch might look like.

Line	Code	Comments
16	sub A, B, C	Subtract the number in register A from the number in register B and store the result in C.
17	jumpz #106	Check the PSW, and if the result of the previous instruction was zero, jump to the instruction at address #106. If the result was nonzero, continue on to line 18.
18	add A, B, C	Add the numbers in registers A and B and store the result in C.

Program 2-2: Assembler code for a conditional branch

The jumpz instruction causes the processor to check the PSW to determine whether a certain bit is 1 (true) or 0 (false). If the bit is 1, the result of the subtraction instruction was 0 and the program counter must be loaded with the branch target address. If the bit is 0, the program counter is incremented to point to the next instruction in sequence (which is the add instruction in line 18).

There are other bits in the PSW that specify other types of information about the result of the previous operation (whether it is positive or negative, is too large for the registers to hold, and so on). As such, there are also other types of conditional branch instructions that check these bits. For instance, the jumpn instruction jumps to the target address if the result of the preceding arithmetic operation was negative; the jumpo instruction jumps to the target address if the result of the previous operation was too large and overflowed the register. If the machine language instruction format of the DLW-1 could accommodate more than eight possible instructions, we could add more types of conditional jumps.

Branch Instructions and the Fetch-Execute Loop

Now that we have looked at the basics of branching, we can modify our three-step summary of program execution to include the possibility of a branch instruction:

1. *Fetch* the next instruction from the address stored in the program counter, and load that instruction into the instruction register. Increment the program counter.
2. *Decode* the instruction in the instruction register.
3. *Execute* the instruction in the instruction register, using the following rules:
    a. If the instruction is an arithmetic instruction, then execute it using the ALU and register file.
    b. If the instruction is a memory-access instruction, then execute it using the memory hardware.
    c. If the instruction is a branch instruction, then execute it using the control unit and the program counter. (For a taken branch, write the branch target address into the program counter.)

In short, you might say that branch instructions allow the programmer to redirect the processor as it travels through the instruction stream. Branches point the processor to different sections of the code stream by manipulating its control unit, which, because it contains the instruction register and program counter, is the rudder of the CPU.

The Branch Instruction as a Special Type of Load

Recall that an instruction fetch is a special type of load that happens automatically for every instruction and that always takes the address in the program counter as its source and the instruction register as its destination. With that in mind, you might think of a branch instruction as a similar kind of load, but under the control of the programmer instead of the CPU. The branch instruction is a load that takes the address specified by #target as its source and the instruction register as its destination.

Like a regular load, a branch instruction can take as its target an address stored in a register. In other words, branch instructions can use register-relative addressing just like regular load instructions. This capability is useful because it allows the computer to store blocks of code at arbitrary places in memory. The programmer doesn't need to know the address where the block of code will wind up before writing a branch instruction that jumps to that particular block; all he or she needs is a way to get to the memory location where the operating system, which is responsible for managing memory, has stored the starting address of the desired block of code.

Consider Program 2-3, in which the programmer knows that the operating system has placed the address of the branch target in line 17 in register C. Upon reaching line 17, the computer jumps to the address stored in C by copying the contents of C into the instruction register.

Line	Code	Comments
16	sub A, B, A	Subtract the number in register A from the number in register B and store the result in A.
17	jumpz #C	Check the PSW, and if the result of the previous instruction was zero, jump to the instruction at the address stored in C. If the result was nonzero, continue on to line 18.
18	add A, 15, A	Add 15 to the number in A and store the result in A.

Program 2-3: A conditional branch that uses an address stored in a register

When a programmer uses register-relative addressing with a branch instruction, the operating system must load a certain register with the base address of the *code segment* in which the program resides. Like the data segment, the code segment is a contiguous block of memory cells, but its cells store instructions instead of data. So to jump to line 15 in the currently running program, assuming that the operating system has placed the base address of the code segment in C, the programmer could use the following instruction:

Code	Comments
jump #(C + 30)	Jump to the instruction located 30 bytes away from the start of the code segment. (Each instruction is 2 bytes in length, so this puts us at the 15 instruction.)

Branch Instructions and Labels

In programs written for real-world architectures, branch targets don't usually take the form of either immediate values or register-relative values. Rather, the programmer places a *label* on the line of code to which he or she wants to jump, and then puts that label in the branch's target field. Program 2-4 shows a portion of assembly language code that uses labels.

```
      sub A, B, A
      jumpz LBL1
      add A, 15, A
      store A, #(D + 16)
LBL1: add A, B, B
      store B, #(D + 16)
```

Program 2-4: Assembly language code that uses labels

In this example, if the contents of A and B are equal, the computer will jump to the instruction with the label LBL1 and begin executing there, skipping the instructions between the jump and the labeled add. Just as the absolute memory addresses used in load and store instructions are modified at load time to fit the location in memory of the program's data segment, labels like LBL1 are changed at load time into memory addresses that reflect the location in memory of the program's code segment.

Excursus: Booting Up

If you've been around computers for any length of time, you've heard the terms *reboot* or *boot up* used in connection with either resetting the computer to its initial state or powering it on initially. The term boot is a shortened version of the term bootstrap, which is itself a reference to the seemingly impossible task a computer must perform on start-up, namely, "pulling itself up by its own bootstraps."

I say "seemingly impossible," because when a computer is first powered on there is no program in memory, but programs contain the instructions that make the computer run. If the processor has no program running when it's first powered on, then how does it know where to fetch the first instruction from?

The solution to this dilemma is that the microprocessor, in its power-on default state, is hard-wired to fetch that first instruction from a predetermined address in memory. This first instruction, which is loaded into the processor's instruction register, is the first line of a program called the BIOS that lives in a special set of storage locations—a small read-only memory (ROM) module attached to the computer's motherboard. It's the job of the BIOS to perform basic tests of the RAM and peripherals in order to verify that everything is working properly. Then the boot process can continue.

At the end of the BIOS program lies a jump instruction, the target of which is the location of a *bootloader* program. By using a jump, the BIOS hands off control of the system to this second program, whose job it is to search for and load the computer's operating system from the hard disk. The operating system (OS) loads and unloads all of the other programs that run on the computer, so once the OS is up and running the computer is ready to interact with the user.

3

PIPELINED EXECUTION

All of the processor architectures that you've looked at so far are relatively simple, and they reflect the earliest stages of computer evolution. This chapter will bring you closer to the modern computing era by introducing one of the key innovations that underlies the rapid performance increases that have characterized the past few decades of microprocessor development: *pipelined execution.*

Pipelined execution is a technique that enables microprocessor designers to increase the speed at which a processor operates, thereby decreasing the amount of time that the processor takes to execute a program. This chapter will first introduce the concept of pipelining by means of a factory analogy, and it will then apply the analogy to microprocessors. You'll then learn how to evaluate the benefits of pipelining, before I conclude with a discussion of the technique's limitations and costs.

This chapter's discussion of pipelined execution focuses solely on the execution of arithmetic instructions. Memory instructions and branch instructions are pipelined using the same fundamental principles as arithmetic instructions, and later chapters will cover the peculiarities of the actual execution process of each of these two types of instruction.

The Lifecycle of an Instruction

In the previous chapter, you learned that a computer repeats three basic steps over and over again in order to execute a program:

1. *Fetch* the next instruction from the address stored in the program counter and load that instruction into the instruction register. Increment the program counter.
2. *Decode* the instruction in the instruction register.
3. *Execute* the instruction in the instruction register.

You should also recall that step 3, the execute step, itself can consist of multiple sub-steps, depending on the type of instruction being executed (arithmetic, memory access, or branch). In the case of the arithmetic instruction add A, B, C, the example we used last time, the three sub-steps are as follows:

1. *Read* the contents of registers A and B.
2. *Add* the contents of A and B.
3. *Write* the result back to register C.

Thus the expanded list of actions required to execute an arithmetic instruction is as follows (substitute any other arithmetic instruction for *add* in the following list to see how it's executed):

1. *Fetch* the next instruction from the address stored in the program counter and load that instruction into the instruction register. Increment the program counter.
2. *Decode* the instruction in the instruction register.
3. *Execute* the instruction in the instruction register. Because the instruction is not a branch instruction but an arithmetic instruction, send it to the arithmetic logic unit (ALU).
   a. *Read* the contents of registers A and B.
   b. *Add* the contents of A and B.
   c. *Write* the result back to register C.

At this point, I need to make a modification to the preceding list. For reasons we'll discuss in detail when we talk about the instruction window in Chapter 5, most modern microprocessors treat sub-steps 3a and 3b as a group, while they treat step 3c, the register write, separately. To reflect this conceptual and architectural division, this list should be modified to look as follows:

1. *Fetch* the next instruction from the address stored in the program counter, and load that instruction into the instruction register. Increment the program counter.
2. *Decode* the instruction in the instruction register.
3. *Execute* the instruction in the instruction register. Because the instruction is not a branch instruction but an arithmetic instruction, send it to the ALU.
   a. *Read* the contents of registers A and B.
   b. *Add* the contents of A and B.
4. *Write* the result back to register C.

In a modern processor, these four steps are repeated over and over again until the program is finished executing. These are, in fact, the four stages in a classic RISC[1] pipeline. (I'll define the term *pipeline* shortly; for now, just think of a pipeline as a series of stages that each instruction in the code stream must pass through when the code stream is being executed.) Here are the four stages in their abbreviated form, the form in which you'll most often see them:

1. Fetch
2. Decode
3. Execute
4. Write (or "write-back")

Each of these stages could be said to represent one *phase* in the *lifecycle* of an instruction. An instruction starts out in the *fetch phase*, moves to the *decode phase*, then to the *execute phase*, and finally to the *write phase*. As I mentioned in "The Clock" on page 29, each phase takes a fixed, but by no means equal, amount of time. In most of the example processors with which you'll be working in this chapter, all four phases take an equal amount of time; this is not usually the case in real-world processors. In any case, if the DLW-1 takes exactly 1 nanosecond (ns) to complete each phase, then the DLW-1 can finish one instruction every 4 ns.

---

[1] The term *RISC* is an acronym for *Reduced Instruction Set Computing*. I'll cover this term in more detail in Chapter 5.

Basic Instruction Flow

One useful division that computer architects often employ when talking about CPUs is that of *front end* versus *back end*. As you already know, when instructions are fetched from main memory, they must be decoded for execution. This fetching and decoding takes place in the processor's front end.

You can see in Figure 3-1 that the front end roughly corresponds to the control and I/O units in the previous chapter's diagram of the DLW-1's programming model. The ALU and registers constitute the back end of the DLW-1. Instructions make their way from the front end down through the back end, where the work of number crunching gets done.

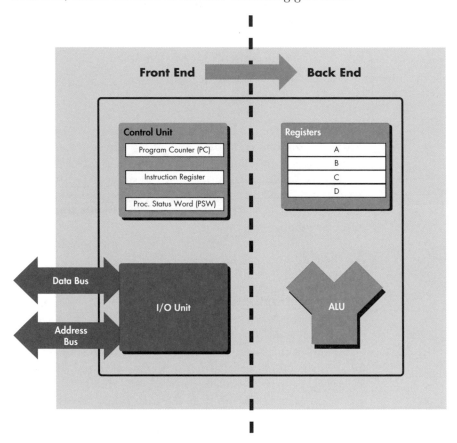

Figure 3-1: Front end versus back end

We can now modify Figure 1-4 to show all four phases of execution (see Figure 3-2).

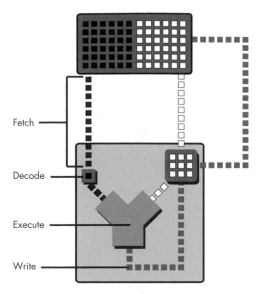

Figure 3-2: Four phases of execution

From here on out, we're going to focus primarily on the code stream, and more specifically, on how instructions enter and flow through the microprocessor, so the diagrams will need to leave out the data and results streams entirely. Figure 3-3 presents a microprocessor's basic instruction flow in a manner that's straightforward, yet easily elaborated upon.

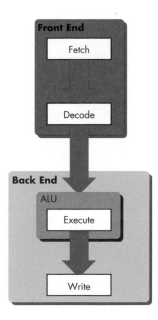

Figure 3-3: Basic instruction flow

In Figure 3-3, instructions flow from the front end's fetch and decode phases into the back end's execute and write phases. (Don't worry if this seems too simple. As the level of complexity of the architectures under discussion increases, so will the complexity of the diagrams.)

Pipelining Explained

Let's say my friends and I have decided to go into the automotive manufacturing business and that our first product is to be a sport utility vehicle (SUV). After some research, we determine that there are five stages in the SUV-building process:

Stage 1: Build the chassis.

Stage 2: Drop the engine into the chassis.

Stage 3: Put the doors, a hood, and coverings on the chassis.

Stage 4: Attach the wheels.

Stage 5: Paint the SUV.

Each of these stages requires the use of highly trained workers with very specialized skill sets—workers who are good at building chasses don't know much about engines, bodywork, wheels, or painting, and likewise for engine builders, painters, and the other crews. So when we make our first attempt to put together an SUV factory, we hire and train five crews of specialists, one for each stage of the SUV-building process. There's one crew to build the chassis, one to drop the engines, one to put the doors, hood, and coverings on the chassis, another for the wheels, and a painting crew. Finally, because the crews are so specialized and efficient, each stage of the SUV-building process takes a crew exactly one hour to complete.

Now, since my friends and I are computer types and not industrial engineers, we had a lot to learn about making efficient use of factory resources. We based the functioning of our first factory on the following plan: Place all five crews in a line on the factory floor, and have the first crew start an SUV at Stage 1. After Stage 1 is complete, the Stage 1 crew passes the partially finished SUV off to the Stage 2 crew and then hits the break room to play some foosball, while the Stage 2 crew builds the engine and drops it in. Once the Stage 2 crew is done, the SUV moves down to Stage 3, and the Stage 3 crew takes over, while the Stage 2 crew joins the Stage 1 crew in the break room.

The SUV moves on down the line through all five stages in this way, with only one crew working on one stage at any given time while the rest of the crews sit idle. Once the completed SUV finishes Stage 5, the crew at Stage 1 starts on another SUV. At this rate, it takes exactly five hours to finish a single SUV, and our factory completes one SUV every five hours.

In Figure 3-4, you can see the SUV pass through all five stages. The SUV enters the factory floor at the beginning of the first hour, where the Stage 1 crew begins work on it. Notice that all of the other crews are sitting idle while the Stage 1 crew does its work. At the beginning of the second hour, the Stage 2 crew takes over, and the other four crews sit idle while waiting on

Stage 2. This process continues as the SUV moves down the line, until at the beginning of the sixth hour, one SUV stands completed and while another has entered Stage 1.

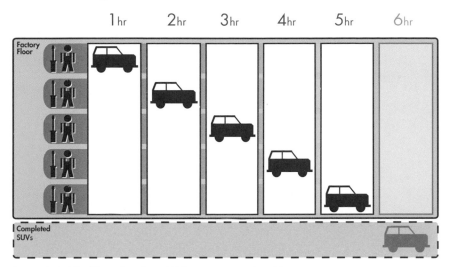

Figure 3-4: The lifecycle of an SUV in a non-pipelined factory

Fast-forward one year. Our SUV, the Extinction LE, is selling like . . . well, it's selling like an SUV, which means it's doing pretty well. In fact, our SUV is selling so well that we've attracted the attention of the military and have been offered a contract to provide SUVs to the U.S. Army on an ongoing basis. The Army likes to order multiple SUVs at a time; one order might come in for 10 SUVs, and another order might come in for 500 SUVs. The more of these orders that we can fill each fiscal year, the more money we can make during that same period and the better our balance sheet looks. This, of course, means that we need to find a way to increase the number of SUVs that our factory can complete per hour, known as our factory's *SUV completion rate*. By completing more SUVs per hour, we can fill the Army's orders faster and make more money each year.

The most intuitive way to go about increasing our factory's SUV completion rate is to try and decrease the production time of each SUV. If we can get the crews to work twice as fast, our factory can produce twice as many SUVs in the same amount of time. Our crews are already working as hard as they can, though, so unless there's a technological breakthrough that increases their productivity, this option is off the table for now.

Since we can't speed up our crews, we can always use the brute-force approach and just throw money at the problem by building a second assembly line. If we hire and train five new crews to form a second assembly line, also capable of producing one car every five hours, we can complete a grand total of two SUVs every five hours from the factory floor—double the SUV completion rate of our present factory. This doesn't seem like a very efficient use of factory resources, though, since not only do we have twice as many crews working at once but we also have twice as many crews in the break room at once. There has to be a better way.

Faced with a lack of options, we hire a team of consultants to figure out a clever way to increase overall factory productivity without either doubling the number of crews or increasing each individual crew's productivity. One year and thousands of billable hours later, the consultants hit upon a solution. Why let our crews spend four-fifths of their work day in the break room, when they could be doing useful work during that time? With proper scheduling of the existing five crews, our factory can complete *one SUV each hour,* thus drastically improving both the efficiency and the output of our assembly line. The revised workflow would look as follows:

1. The Stage 1 crew builds a chassis.
2. Once the chassis is complete, they send it on to the Stage 2 crew.
3. The Stage 2 crew receives the chassis and begins dropping the engine in, while the Stage 1 crew starts on a new chassis.
4. When both Stage 1 and Stage 2 crews are finished, the Stage 2 crew's work advances to Stage 3, the Stage 1 crew's work advances to Stage 2, and the Stage 1 crew starts on a new chassis.

Figure 3-5 illustrates this workflow in action. Notice that multiple crews have multiple SUVs simultaneously in progress on the factory floor. Compare this figure to Figure 3-4, where only one crew is active at a time and only one SUV is on the factory floor at a time.

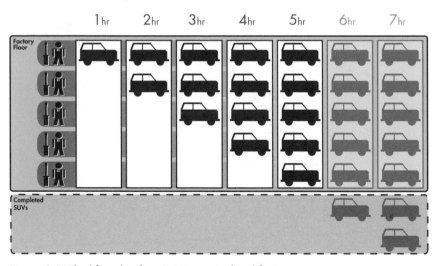

Figure 3-5: The lifecycle of an SUV in a pipelined factory

So as the assembly line begins to fill up with SUVs in various stages of production, more of the crews are put to work simultaneously until all of the crews are working on a different vehicle in a different stage of production. (Of course, this is how most of us nowadays in the post-Ford era expect a good, efficient assembly line to work.) If we can keep the assembly line full and keep all five crews working at once, we can produce one SUV every hour: a fivefold improvement in SUV completion rate over the previous completion rate of one SUV every five hours. That, in a nutshell, is pipelining.

While the total amount of time that each individual SUV spends in production has not changed from the original five hours, the rate at which the factory as a whole completes SUVs has increased drastically. Furthermore, the rate at which the factory can fulfill the Army's orders for batches of SUVs has increased drastically, as well. Pipelining works its magic by making optimal use of already existing resources. We don't need to speed up each individual stage of the production process, nor do we need to drastically increase the amount of resources that we throw at the problem; all that's necessary is that we get more work out of resources that are already there.

WHY THE SUV FACTORY?

The preceding discussion uses a factory analogy to explain pipelining. Other books use simpler analogies, like doing laundry, for instance, to explain this technique, but there are a few reasons why I chose a more elaborate and lengthy analogy to illustrate what is a relatively simple concept. First, I use factory analogies throughout this book, because assembly line-based factories are easy for readers to visualize and there's plenty of room for filling out the mental image in interesting ways in order to make a variety of related points. Second, and perhaps even more importantly, the many scheduling-, queuing- and resource management–related problems that factory designers face have direct analogies in computer architecture. In many cases, the problems and solutions are exactly the same, simply translated into a different domain. (Similar queuing-related problem/solution pairs also crop up in the service industry, which is why analogies involving supermarkets and fast food restaurants are also favorites of mine.)

Applying the Analogy

Bringing our discussion back to microprocessors, it should be easy to see how this concept applies to the four phases of an instruction's lifecycle. Just as the owners of the factory in our analogy wanted to increase the number of SUVs that the factory could finish in a given period of time, microprocessor designers are always looking for ways to increase the number of instructions that a CPU can complete in a given period of time. When you recall that a program is an ordered sequence of instructions, it becomes clear that increasing the number of instructions executed per unit time is one way to decrease the total amount of time that it takes to execute a program. (The other way to decrease a program's execution time is to decrease the number of instructions in the program, but this chapter won't address that approach until later.) In terms of our analogy, a program is like an order of SUVs from the military; just like increasing our factory's output of SUVs per hour enabled us to fill orders faster, increasing a processor's *instruction completion rate* (the number of instructions completed per unit time) enables it to run programs faster.

A Non-Pipelined Processor

The previous chapter briefly described how the simple processors described so far (e.g., the DLW-1) use the clock to time its internal operations. These non-pipelined processors work on one instruction at a time, moving each instruction through all four phases of its lifecycle during the course of one clock cycle. Thus non-pipelined processors are also called *single-cycle* processors, because all instructions take exactly one clock cycle to execute fully (i.e., to pass through all four phases of their lifecycles).

Because the processor completes instructions at a rate of one per clock cycle, you want the CPU's clock to run as fast as possible so that the processor's instruction completion rate can be as high as possible.

Thus you need to calculate the maximum amount of time that it takes to complete an instruction and make the clock cycle time equivalent to that length of time. It just so happens that on the hypothetical example CPU, the four phases of the instruction's lifecycle take a total of 4 ns to complete. Therefore, you should set the duration of the CPU clock cycle to 4 ns, so that the CPU can complete the instruction's lifecycle—from *fetch* to *write-back*—in a single clock. (A CPU clock cycle is often just called a *clock* for short.)

In Figure 3-6, the blue instruction leaves the code storage area, enters the processor, and then advances through the phases of its lifecycle over the course of the 4 ns clock period, until at the end of the fourth nanosecond, it completes the last phase and its lifecycle is over. The end of the fourth nanosecond is also the end of the first clock cycle, so now that the first clock cycle is finished and the blue instruction has completed its execution, the red instruction can enter the processor at the start of a new clock cycle and go through the same process. This 4 ns sequence of steps is repeated until, after a total of 16 ns (or four clock cycles), the processor has completed all four instructions at a completion rate of 0.25 instructions/ns (= 4 instructions/ 16 ns).

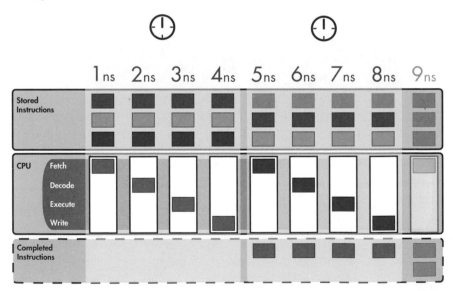

Figure 3-6: A single-cycle processor

Single-cycle processors like the one in Figure 3-6 are simple to design, but they waste a lot of hardware resources. All of that white space in the diagram represents processor hardware that's sitting idle while it waits for the instruction that's currently in the processor to finish executing. By pipelining the processor in this figure, you can put more of that hardware to work every nanosecond, thereby increasing the processor's efficiency and its performance on executing programs.

Before moving on, I should clarify a few concepts illustrated in Figure 3-6. At the bottom is a region labeled "Completed Instructions." Completed instructions don't actually go anywhere when they're finished executing; once they've done their job of telling the processor how to modify the data stream, they're simply deleted from the processor. So the "Completed Instructions" box does not represent a real part of the computer, which is why I've placed a dotted line around it. This area is just a place for you to keep track of how many instructions the processor has completed in a certain amount of time, or the processor's instruction completion rate (or *completion rate*, for short), so that when you compare different types of processors, you'll have a place where you can quickly see which processor performs better. The more instructions a processor completes in a set amount of time, the better it performs on programs, which are an ordered sequence of instructions. Think of the "Completed Instructions" box as a sort of scoreboard for tracking each processor's completion rate, and check the box in each of the subsequent figures to see how long it takes for the processor to populate this box.

Following on the preceding point, you may be curious as to why the blue instruction that has completed in the fourth nanosecond does not appear in the "Completed Instructions" box until the fifth nanosecond. The reason is straightforward and stems from the nature of the diagram. Because an instruction spends *one complete nanosecond*, from start to finish, in each stage of execution, the blue instruction enters the write phase at the *beginning* of the fourth nanosecond and exits the write phase at the *end* of the fourth nanosecond. This means that the fifth nanosecond is the first full nanosecond in which the blue instruction stands completed. Thus at the beginning of the fifth nanosecond (which coincides with the end of the fourth nanosecond), the processor has completed one instruction.

A Pipelined Processor

Pipelining a processor means breaking down its instruction execution process—what I've been calling the instruction's lifecycle—into a series of discrete *pipeline stages* that can be completed in sequence by specialized hardware. Recall the way that we broke down the SUV assembly process into five discrete steps—with one dedicated crew assigned to complete each step—and you'll get the idea.

Because an instruction's lifecycle consists of four fairly distinct phases, you can start by breaking down the single-cycle processor's instruction execution process into a sequence of four discrete pipeline stages, where each pipeline stage corresponds to a phase in the standard instruction lifecycle:

Stage 1: Fetch the instruction from code storage.

Stage 2: Decode the instruction.

Stage 3: Execute the instruction.

Stage 4: Write the results of the instruction back to the register file.

Note that the number of pipeline stages is called the *pipeline depth*. So the four-stage pipeline has a pipeline depth of four.

For convenience's sake, let's say that each of these four pipeline stages takes exactly 1 ns to finish its work on an instruction, just like each crew in our assembly line analogy takes one hour to finish its portion of the work on an SUV. So the original single-cycle processor's 4 ns execution process is now broken down into four discrete, sequential pipeline stages of 1 ns each in length.

Now let's step through another diagram together to see how a pipelined CPU would execute the four instructions depicted in Figure 3-7.

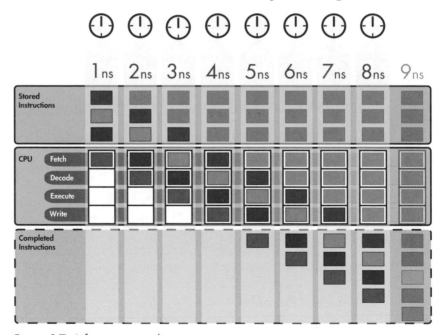

Figure 3-7: A four-stage pipeline

At the beginning of the first nanosecond, the blue instruction enters the fetch stage. After that nanosecond is complete, the second nanosecond begins and the blue instruction moves on to the decode stage, while the next instruction, the red one, starts to make its way from code storage to the processor (i.e., it enters the fetch stage). At the start of the third nanosecond, the blue instruction advances to the execute stage, the red instruction advances to the decode stage, and the green instruction enters the fetch stage. At the fourth nanosecond, the blue instruction advances to the write stage, the red instruction advances to the execute stage, the green instruction advances to the decode stage, and the purple instruction advances to the fetch stage. After the fourth nanosecond has fully elapsed and the fifth nanosecond starts, the blue instruction has passed from the pipeline and is now finished executing. Thus we can say that at the end of 4 ns (= four clock cycles), the pipelined processor depicted in Figure 3-7 has completed one instruction.

At start of the fifth nanosecond, the pipeline is now full and the processor can begin completing instructions at a rate of one instruction per nanosecond. This one instruction/ns completion rate is a fourfold improvement over the single-cycle processor's completion rate of 0.25 instructions/ns (or four instructions every 16 ns).

Shrinking the Clock

You can see from Figure 3-7 that the role of the CPU clock changes slightly in a pipelined processor, compared to the single-cycle processor shown in Figure 3-6. Because all of the pipeline stages must now work together simultaneously and be ready at the start of each new nanosecond to hand over the results of their work to the next pipeline stage, the clock is needed to coordinate the activity of the whole pipeline. The way this is done is simple: Shrink the clock cycle time to match the time it takes each stage to complete its work so that at the start of each clock cycle, each pipeline stage hands off the instruction it was working on to the next stage in the pipeline. Because each pipeline stage in the example processor takes 1 ns to complete its work, you can set the clock cycle to be 1 ns in duration.

This new method of clocking the processor means that a new instruction will not necessarily be completed at the close of each clock cycle, as was the case with the single-cycle processor. Instead, a new instruction will be completed at the close of only those clock cycles in which the write stage has been working on an instruction. Any clock cycle with an empty write stage will add no new instructions to the "Completed Instructions" box, and any clock cycle with an active write stage will add one new instruction to the box. Of course, this means that when the pipeline first starts to work on a program, there will be a few clock cycles—three to be exact—during which no instructions are completed. But once the fourth clock cycle starts, the first instruction enters the write stage and the pipeline can then begin completing new instructions on each clock cycle, which, because each clock cycle is 1 ns, translates into a completion rate of one instruction per nanosecond.

Shrinking Program Execution Time

Note that the total execution time for each individual instruction is not changed by pipelining. It still takes an instruction 4 ns to make it all the way through the processor; that 4 ns can be split up into four clock cycles of 1 ns each, or it can cover one longer clock cycle, but it's still the same 4 ns. Thus pipelining doesn't speed up instruction execution time, but it does speed up *program execution time* (the number of nanoseconds that it takes to execute an entire program) by increasing the number of instructions finished per unit of time. Just like pipelining our hypothetical SUV assembly line allowed us to fill the Army's orders in a shorter span of time, even though each individual SUV still spent a total of five hours in the assembly line, so does pipelining allow a processor to execute programs in a shorter amount of time, even though each individual instruction still spends the same amount of time traveling through the CPU. Pipelining makes more efficient use of the CPU's existing resources by putting all of its units to work simultaneously, thereby allowing it to do more total work each nanosecond.

The Speedup from Pipelining

In general, the speedup in completion rate versus a single-cycle implementation that's gained from pipelining is ideally equal to the number of pipeline stages. A four-stage pipeline yields a fourfold speedup in the completion rate versus a single-cycle pipeline, a five-stage pipeline yields a fivefold speedup, a twelve-stage pipeline yields a twelvefold speedup, and so on. This speedup is possible because the more pipeline stages there are in a processor, the more instructions the processor can work on simultaneously, and the more instructions it can complete in a given period of time. So the more finely you can slice those four phases of the instruction's lifecycle, the more of the hardware that's used to implement those phases you can put to work at any given moment.

To return to our assembly line analogy, let's say that each crew is made up of six workers, and that each of the hour-long tasks that each crew performs can be readily subdivided into two shorter, 30-minute tasks. So we can double our factory's throughput by splitting each crew into two smaller, more specialized crews of three workers each, and then having each smaller crew perform one of the shorter tasks on one SUV per 30 minutes.

Stage 1: Build the chassis.

- **Crew 1a:** Fit the parts of the chassis together and spot-weld the joints.
- **Crew 1b:** Fully weld all the parts of the chassis.

Stage 2: Drop the engine into the chassis.

- **Crew 2a:** Place the engine into the chassis and mount it in place.
- **Crew 2b:** Connect the engine to the moving parts of the car.

Stage 3: Put the doors, a hood, and coverings on the chassis.

- **Crew 3a:** Put the doors and hood on the chassis.
- **Crew 3b:** Put the other coverings on the chassis.

Stage 4: Attach the wheels.

- **Crew 4a:** Attach the two front wheels.
- **Crew 4b:** Attach the two rear wheels.

Stage 5: Paint the SUV.

- **Crew 5a:** Paint the sides of the SUV.
- **Crew 5b:** Paint the top of the SUV.

After the modifications described here, the 10 smaller crews in our factory now have a collective total of 10 SUVs in progress during the course of any given 30-minute period. Furthermore, our factory can now complete a new SUV every 30 minutes, a tenfold improvement over our first factory's completion rate of one SUV every five hours. So by pipelining our assembly line even more deeply, we've put even more of its workers to work concurrently, thereby increasing the number of SUVs that can be worked on simultaneously and increasing the number of SUVs that can be completed within a given period of time.

Deepening the pipeline of the four-stage processor works on similar principles and has a similar effect on completion rates. Just as the five stages in our SUV assembly line could be broken down further into a longer sequence of more specialized stages, the execution process that each instruction goes through can be broken down into a series of much more than just four discrete stages. By breaking the processor's four-stage pipeline down into a longer series of shorter, more specialized stages, even more of the processor's specialized hardware can work simultaneously on more instructions and thereby increase the number of instructions that the pipeline completes each nanosecond.

We first moved from a single-cycle processor to a pipelined processor by taking the 4 ns time period that the instruction spent traveling through the processor and slicing it into four discrete pipeline stages of 1 ns each in length. These four discrete pipeline stages corresponded to the four phases of an instruction's lifecycle. A processor's pipeline stages aren't always going to correspond exactly to the four phases of a processor's lifecycle, though. Some processors have a five-stage pipeline, some have a six-stage pipeline, and many have pipelines deeper than 10 or 20 stages. In such cases, the CPU designer must slice up the instruction's lifecycle into the desired number of stages in such a way that all the stages are equal in length.

Now let's take that 4 ns execution process and slice it into eight discrete stages. Because all eight pipeline stages must be of exactly the same duration for pipelining to work, the eight pipeline stages must each be 4 ns ÷ 8 = 0.5 ns in length. Since we're presently working with an idealized example, let's pretend that splitting up the processor's four-phase lifecycle into eight equally long (0.5 ns) pipeline stages is a trivial matter, and that the results look like what you see in Figure 3-8. (In reality, this task is not trivial and involves a number of trade-offs. As a concession to that reality, I've chosen to use the eight stages of a real-world pipeline—the MIPS pipeline—in Figure 3-8, instead of just splitting each of the four traditional stages in two.)

Because pipelining requires that each pipeline stage take exactly one clock cycle to complete, the clock cycle can now be shortened to 0.5 ns in order to fit the lengths of the eight pipeline stages. At the bottom of Figure 3-8, you can see the impact that this increased number of pipeline stages has on the number of instructions completed per unit time.

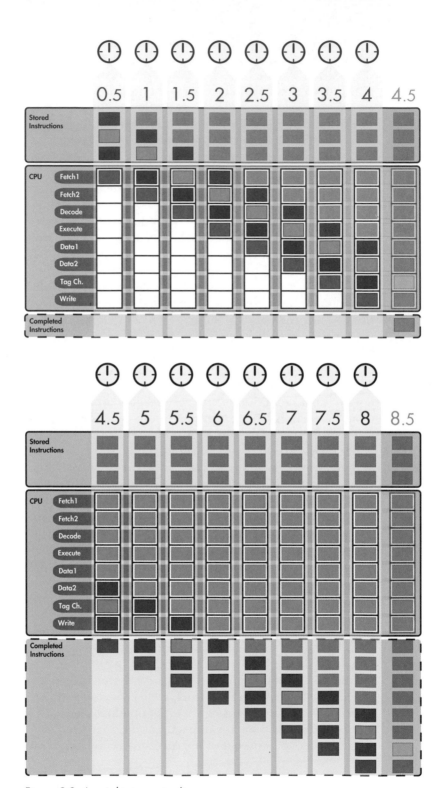

Figure 3-8: An eight-stage pipeline

The single-cycle processor can complete one instruction every 4 ns, for a completion rate of 0.25 instructions/ns, and the four-stage pipelined processor can complete one instruction every nanosecond for a completion rate of one instructions/ns. The eight-stage processor depicted in Figure 3-8 improves on both of these by completing one instruction every 0.5 ns, for a completion rate of two instructions/ns. Note that because each instruction still takes 4 ns to execute, the first 4 ns of the eight-stage processor are still dedicated to filling up the pipeline. But once the pipeline is full, the processor can begin completing instructions twice as fast as the four-stage processor and eight times as fast as the single-stage processor.

This eightfold increase in completion rate versus a single-cycle design means that the eight-stage processor can execute programs much faster than either a single-cycle or a four-stage processor. But does the eightfold increase in completion rate translate into an eightfold increase in processor performance? Not exactly.

Program Execution Time and Completion Rate

If the program that the single-cycle processor in Figure 3-6 is running consisted of only the four instructions depicted, that program would have a program execution time of 16 ns, or 4 instructions ÷ 0.25 instructions/ns. If the program consisted of, say, seven instructions, it would have a program execution time of 7 instructions ÷ 0.25 instructions/ns = 28 ns. In general, a program's execution time is equal to the total number of instructions in the program divided by the processor's instruction completion rate (number of instructions completed per nanosecond), as in the following equation:

```
program execution time = number of instructions in program / instruction
completion rate
```

Most of the time, when I talk about processor *performance* in this book, I'm talking about program execution time. One processor performs better than another if it executes all of a program's instructions in a shorter amount of time, so reducing program execution time is the key to increasing processor performance.

From the preceding equation, it should be clear that program execution time can be reduced in one of two ways: by a reduction in the number of instructions per program or by an increase in the processor's completion rate. For now, let's assume that the number of instructions in a program is fixed and that there's nothing that can be done about this term of the equation. As such, our focus in this chapter will be on increasing instruction completion rates.

In the case of a non-pipelined, single-cycle processor, the instruction completion rate (x instructions per 1 ns) is simply the inverse of the instruction execution time (y ns per 1 instruction), where x and y have different numerical values. Because the relationship between completion rate and instruction execution time is simple and direct in a single-cycle processor, an *n*fold improvement in one is an *n*fold improvement in the other. So improving the performance of a single-cycle processor is really about reducing instruction execution times.

With pipelined processors, the relationship between instruction execution time and completion rate is more complex. As discussed previously, pipelined processors allow you to increase the processor's completion rate without altering the instruction execution time. Of course, a reduction in instruction execution time still translates into a completion rate improvement, but the reverse is not necessarily true. In fact, as you'll learn later on, pipelining's improvements to completion rate often come at the price of *increased* instruction execution times. This means that for pipelining to improve performance, the processor's completion rate must be as high as possible over the course of a program's execution.

The Relationship Between Completion Rate and Program Execution Time

If you look at the "Completed Instructions" box of the four-stage processor back in Figure 3-7, you'll see that a total of five instructions have been completed at the start of the ninth nanosecond. In contrast, the non-pipelined processor illustrated in Figure 3-6 sports two completed instructions at the start of the ninth nanosecond. Five completed instructions in the span of 8 ns is obviously not a fourfold improvement over two completed instructions in the same time period, so what gives?

Remember that it took the pipelined processor 4 ns initially to fill up with instructions; the pipelined processor did not complete its first instruction until the end of the fourth nanosecond. Therefore, it completed fewer instructions over the first 8 ns of that program's execution than it would have had the pipeline been full for the entire 8 ns.

When the processor is executing programs that consist of thousands of instructions, then as the number of nanoseconds stretches into the thousands, the impact on program execution time of those four initial nanoseconds, during which only one instruction was completed, begins to vanish and the pipelined processor's advantage begins to approach the fourfold mark. For example, after 1,000 ns, the non-pipelined processor will have completed 250 instructions (1000 ns ÷ 0.25 instructions/ns = 250 instructions), while the pipelined processor will have completed 996 instructions [(1000 ns − 4 ns) ÷ 1 instructions/ns]—a 3.984-fold improvement.

What I've just described using this concrete example is the difference between a pipeline's *maximum theoretical completion rate* and its real-world *average completion rate*. In the previous example, the four-stage processor's maximum theoretical completion rate, i.e., its completion rate on cycles when its entire pipeline is full, is one instruction/ns. However, the processor's average completion rate during its first 8 ns is 5 instructions/8 ns = 0.625 instructions/ns. The processor's average completion rate improves as it passes more clock cycles with its pipeline full, until at 1,000 ns, its average completion rate is 996 instructions/1000 ns = 0.996 instructions/ns.

At this point, it might help to look at a graph of the four-stage pipeline's average completion rate as the number of nanoseconds increases, illustrated in Figure 3-9.

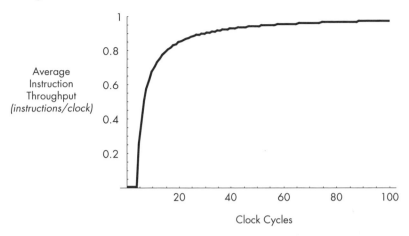

Figure 3-9: Average completion rate of a four-stage pipeline

You can see how the processor's average completion rate stays at zero until the 4 ns mark, after which point the pipeline is full and the processor can begin completing a new instruction on each nanosecond, causing the average completion rate for the entire program to curve upward and eventually to approach the maximum completion rate of one instruction/ns.

So in conclusion, a pipelined processor can only approach its ideal completion rate if it can go for long stretches with its pipeline full on every clock cycle.

Instruction Throughput and Pipeline Stalls

Pipelining isn't totally "free," however. Pipelining adds some complexity to the microprocessor's control logic, because all of these stages have to be kept in sync. Even more important for the present discussion, though, is the fact that pipelining adds some complexity to the ways in which you assess the processor's performance.

Instruction Throughput

Up until now, we've talked about microprocessor performance mainly in terms of instruction completion rate, or the number of instructions that the processor's pipeline can complete each nanosecond. A more common performance metric in the real world is a pipeline's *instruction throughput,* or the number of instructions that the processor completes *each clock cycle.* You might be thinking that a pipeline's instruction throughput should always be one instruction/clock, because I stated previously that a pipelined processor completes a new instruction at the end of each clock cycle *in which the write stage has been active.* But notice how the emphasized part of that definition qualifies it a bit; you've already seen that the write stage is inactive during clock cycles in which the pipeline is being filled, so on those clock cycles, the processor's instruction throughput is 0 instructions/clock. In contrast, when the instruction's pipeline is full and the write stage is active, the pipelined processor has an instruction throughput of 1 instruction/clock.

So just like there was a difference between a processor's maximum theoretical completion rate and its average completion rate, there's also a difference between a processor's maximum theoretical instruction throughput and its average instruction throughput:

Instruction throughput

The number of instructions that the processor finishes executing on each clock cycle. You'll also see instruction throughput referred to as instructions per clock (IPC).

Maximum theoretical instruction throughput

The theoretical maximum number of instructions that the processor can finish executing on each clock cycle. For the simple kinds of pipelined and non-pipelined processors described so far, this number is always one instruction per cycle (one instruction/clock or one IPC).

Average instruction throughput

The average number of instructions per clock (IPC) that the processor has actually completed over a certain number of cycles.

A processor's instruction throughput is closely tied to its instruction completion rate—the more instructions that the processor completes each clock cycle (instructions/clock), the more instructions it also completes over a given period of time (instructions/ns).

We'll talk more about the relationship between these two metrics in a moment, but for now just remember that a higher instruction throughput translates into a higher instruction completion rate, and hence better performance.

Pipeline Stalls

In the real world, a processor's pipeline can be found in more conditions than just the two described so far: a full pipeline or a pipeline that's being filled. Sometimes, instructions get hung up in one pipeline stage for multiple cycles. There are a number of reasons why this might happen—we'll discuss many of them throughout this book—but when it happens, the pipeline is said to *stall*. When the pipeline stalls, or gets hung in a certain stage, all of the instructions in the stages below the one where the stall happened continue advancing normally, while the stalled instruction just sits in its stage, and all the instructions behind it back up.

In Figure 3-10, the orange instruction is stalled for two extra cycles in the fetch stage. Because the instruction is stalled, a new gap opens ahead of it in the pipeline for each cycle that it stalls. Once the instruction starts advancing through the pipeline again, the gaps in the pipeline that were created by the stall—gaps that are commonly called "pipeline bubbles"—travel down the pipeline ahead of the formerly stalled instruction until they eventually leave the pipeline.

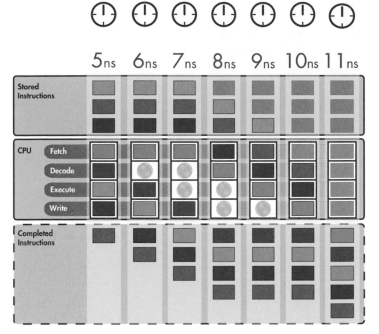

Figure 3-10: Pipeline stalls in a four-stage pipeline would look different without the effect of the "bubbles."

Pipeline stalls—or bubbles—reduce a pipeline's average instruction throughput, because they prevent the pipeline from attaining the maximum throughput of one finished instruction per cycle. In Figure 3-10, the orange instruction has stalled in the fetch stage for two extra cycles, creating two bubbles that will propagate through the pipeline. (Again, the bubble is simply a way of signifying that the pipeline stage in which the bubble sits is doing no work during that cycle.) Once the instructions below the bubble have completed, the processor will complete no new instructions until the bubbles move out of the pipeline. So at the ends of clock cycles 9 and 10, no new instructions are added to the "Completed Instructions" region; normally, two new instructions would be added to the region at the ends of these two cycles. Because of the bubbles, though, the processor is two instructions behind schedule when it hits the 11th clock cycle and begins racking up completed instructions again.

The more of these bubbles that crop up in the pipeline, the farther away the processor's actual instruction throughput is from its maximum instruction throughput. In the preceding example, the processor should ideally have completed seven instructions by the time it finishes the 10th clock cycle, for an average instruction throughput of 0.7 instructions per clock. (Remember, the maximum instruction throughput possible under ideal conditions is one instruction per clock, but many more cycles with no bubbles would be needed to approach that maximum.) But because of the pipeline stall, the processor only completes five instructions in 10 clocks, for an average instruction throughput of 0.5 instructions per clock. 0.5 instructions per clock is half the theoretical maximum instruction throughput, but of course the processor spent a few clocks filling the pipeline, so it couldn't have achieved that after 10 clocks, even under ideal conditions. More important is the fact that 0.5 instructions per clock is only 71 percent of the throughput that it could have achieved were there no stall (i.e., 0.7 instructions per clock). Because pipeline stalls decrease the processor's average instruction throughput, they increase the amount of time that it takes to execute the currently running program. If the program in the preceding example consisted of only the seven instructions pictured, then the pipeline stall would have resulted in a 29 percent program execution time increase.

Look at the graph in Figure 3-11; it shows what that two-cycle stall does to the average instruction throughput.

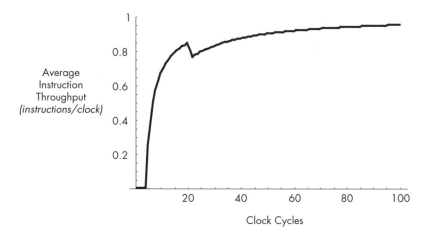

Figure 3-11: Average instruction throughput of a four-stage pipeline with a two-cycle stall

The processor's average instruction throughput stops rising and begins to plummet when the first bubble hits the write stage, and it doesn't recover until the bubbles have left the pipeline.

To get an even better picture of the impact that stalls can have on a pipeline's average instruction throughput, let's now look at the impact that a stall of 10 cycles (starting in the fetch stage of the 18th cycle) would have over the course of 100 cycles in the four-stage pipeline described so far. Look at the graph in Figure 3-12.

After the first bubble of the stall hits the write stage in the 20th clock, the average instruction throughput stops increasing and begins to decrease. For each clock in which there's a bubble in the write stage, the pipeline's instruction throughput is 0 instructions/clock, so its average instruction throughput for the whole period continues to decline. After the last bubble has worked its way out of the write stage, then the pipeline begins completing new instructions again at a rate of one instruction/cycle and its average instruction throughput begins to climb. And when the processor's instruction throughput begins to climb, so does its completion rate and its performance on programs.

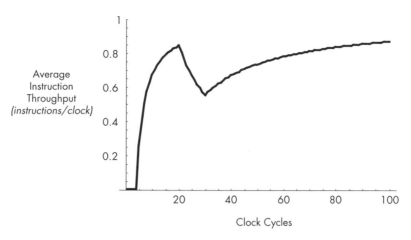

Figure 3-12: Average instruction throughput of a four-stage pipeline with a 10-cycle stall

Now, 10 or 20 cycles worth of stalls here and there may not seem like much, but they do add up. Even more important, though, is the fact that the numbers in the preceding examples would be increased by a factor of 30 or more in real-world execution scenarios. As of this writing, a processor can spend from 50 to 120 nanoseconds waiting on data from main memory. For a 3 GHz processor that has a clock cycle time of a fraction of a nanosecond, a 100 ns main memory access translates into a few thousand clock cycles worth of bubbles—and that's just for one main memory access out of the many millions that a program might make over the course of its execution.

In later chapters, we'll look at the causes of pipeline stalls and the many tricks that computer architects use to overcome them.

Instruction Latency and Pipeline Stalls

Before closing out our discussion of pipeline stalls, I should introduce another term that you'll be seeing periodically throughout the rest of the book: *instruction latency*. An instruction's latency is the number of clock cycles it takes for the instruction to pass through the pipeline. For a single-cycle processor, all instructions have a latency of one clock cycle. In contrast, for the simple four-stage pipeline described so far, all instructions have a latency of four cycles. To get a visual image of this, take one more look at the blue instruction in Figure 3-6 earlier in this chapter; this instruction takes four clock cycles to advance, at a rate of one clock cycle per stage, through each of the four stages of the pipeline. Likewise, instructions have a latency of eight cycles on an eight-stage pipeline, 12 cycles on a 12-stage pipeline, and so on.

In real-world processors, instruction latency is not necessarily a fixed number that's equal to the number of pipeline stages. Because instructions can get hung up in one or more pipeline stages for multiple cycles, each extra cycle that they spend waiting in a pipeline stage adds one more cycle to their latency. So the instruction latencies given in the previous paragraph (i.e., four cycles for a four-stage pipeline, eight cycles for an eight-stage pipeline, and so on) represent *minimum* instruction latencies. Actual instruction latencies in pipelines of any length can be longer than the depth of the pipeline, depending on whether or not the instruction stalls in one or more stages.

Limits to Pipelining

As you can probably guess, there are some practical limits to how deeply you can pipeline an assembly line or a processor before the actual speedup in completion rate that you gain from pipelining starts to become significantly less than the ideal speedup that you might expect. In the real world, the different phases of an instruction's lifecycle don't easily break down into an arbitrarily high number of shorter stages of perfectly equal duration. Some stages are inherently more complex and take longer than others.

But because each pipeline stage must take exactly one clock cycle to complete, the clock pulse that coordinates all the stages can be no faster than the pipeline's slowest stage. In other words, the amount of time it takes for the slowest stage in the pipeline to complete will determine the length of the CPU's clock cycle and thus the length of every pipeline stage. This means that the pipeline's slowest stage will spend the entire clock cycle working, while the faster stages will spend part of the clock cycle idle. Not only does this waste resources, but it increases each instruction's overall execution time by dragging out some phases of the lifecycle to take up more time than they would if the processor was not pipelined—all of the other stages must wait a little extra time each cycle while the slowest stage plays catch-up.

So, as you slice the pipeline more finely in order to add stages and increase throughput, the individual stages get less and less uniform in length and complexity, with the result that the processor's overall instruction execution time gets longer. Because of this feature of pipelining, one of the most difficult and important challenges that the CPU designer faces is that of balancing the pipeline so that no one stage has to do more work to do than any other. The designer must distribute the work of processing an instruction evenly to each stage, so that no one stage takes up too much time and thus slows down the entire pipeline.

Clock Period and Completion Rate

If the pipelined processor's clock cycle time, or *clock period*, is longer than its ideal length (i.e., non-pipelined instruction execution time/pipeline depth), and it always is, then the processor's completion rate will suffer. If the instruction throughput stays fixed at, say, one instruction/clock, then as the clock period increases, the completion rate decreases. Because new instructions can be completed only at the end of each clock cycle, a longer clock cycle translates into fewer instructions completed per nanosecond, which in turn translates into longer program execution times.

To get a better feel for the relationship between completion rate, instruction throughput, and clock cycle time, let's take the eight-stage pipeline from Figure 3-8 and increase its clock cycle time to 1 ns instead of 0.5 ns. Its first 9 ns of execution would then look as in Figure 3-13.

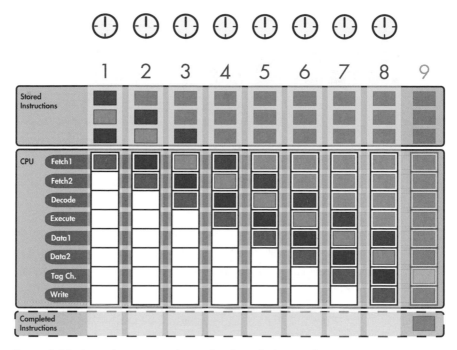

Figure 3-13: An eight-stage pipeline with a 1 ns clock period

As you can see, the instruction execution time has now increased from an original time of 4 ns to a new time of 8 ns, which means that the eight-stage pipeline does not complete its first instruction until the end of the eighth nanosecond. Once the pipeline is full, the processor pictured in Figure 3-13 begins completing instructions at a rate of one instruction per nanosecond. This completion rate is half the completion rate of the ideal eight-stage pipeline with the 0.5 ns clock cycle time. It's also the exact same completion rate as the one instruction/ns completion rate of the ideal four-stage pipeline. In short, the longer clock cycle time of the new eight-stage pipeline has robbed the deeper pipeline of its completion rate advantage. Furthermore, the eight-stage pipeline now takes twice as long to fill.

Take a look at the graph in Figure 3-14 to see what this doubled execution time does to the eight-stage pipeline's average completion rate curve versus the same curve for a four-stage pipeline.

It takes longer for the slower eight-stage pipeline to fill up, which means that its average completion rate—and hence its performance—ramps up more slowly when the pipeline is first filled with instructions. There are many situations in which a processor that's executing a program must flush its pipeline entirely and then begin refilling it from a different point in the code stream. In such instances, that slower-ramping completion rate curve causes a performance hit.

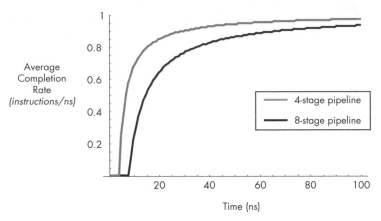

Figure 3-14: Average instruction completion rate for four- and eight-stage pipelines with a 1 ns clock period

In the end, the performance gains brought about by pipelining depend on two things:

1. Pipeline stalls must be avoided. As you've seen earlier, pipeline stalls cause the processor's completion rate and performance to drop. Main memory accesses are a major cause of pipeline stalls, but this problem can be alleviated significantly by the use of caching. We'll cover caching in detail in Chapter 11. Other causes of stalls, like the various types of hazards, will be covered at the end of Chapter 4.

2. Pipeline refills must be avoided. Flushing the pipeline and refilling it again takes a serious toll on both completion rate and performance. Once the pipeline is full, it must remain full for as long as possible if the average completion rate is to be kept up.

When we look more closely at real-world pipelined processors in later chapters, you'll see these two issues come up again and again. In fact, much of the rest of the book will be about how the different architectures under discussion work to keep their pipelines full by preventing stalls and ensuring a continuous and uninterrupted flow of instructions into the processor from the code storage area.

The Cost of Pipelining

In addition to the inherent limits to performance improvement that we've just looked at, pipelining requires a nontrivial amount of extra bookkeeping and buffering logic to implement, so it incurs an overhead cost in transistors and die space. Furthermore, this overhead cost increases with pipeline depth, so that a processor with a very deep pipeline (for example, Intel's Pentium 4) spends a significant amount of its transistor budget on pipeline-related logic. These overhead costs place some practical constraints on how deeply you can pipeline a processor. I'll say a lot more about such constraints in the chapters covering the Pentium line and the Pentium 4.

4

SUPERSCALAR EXECUTION

Chapters 1 and 2 described the processor as it is visible to the programmer. The register files, the processor status word (PSW), the arithmetic logic unit (ALU), and other parts of the programming model are all there to provide a means for the programmer to manipulate the processor and make it do useful work. In other words, the programming model is essentially a user interface for the CPU.

Much like the graphical user interfaces on modern computer systems, there's a lot more going on under the hood of a microprocessor than the simplicity of the programming model would imply. In Chapter 12, I'll talk about the various ways in which the operating system and processor collaborate to fool the user into thinking that he or she is executing multiple programs at once. There's a similar sort of trickery that goes on beneath the programming model in a modern microprocessor, but it's intended to fool the programmer into thinking that there's only one thing going on at a time, when really there are multiple things happening simultaneously. Let me explain.

Back in the days when computer designers could fit relatively few transistors on a single piece of silicon, many parts of the programming model actually resided on separate chips attached to a single circuit board. For instance, one chip contained the ALU, another chip contained the control unit, still another chip contained the registers, and so on. Such computers were relatively slow, and the fact that they were made of multiple chips made them expensive. Each chip had its own manufacturing and packaging costs, so the more chips you put on a board, the more expensive the overall system was. (Note that this is still true today. The cost of producing systems and components can be drastically reduced by packing the functionality of multiple chips into a single chip.)

With the advent of the Intel 4004 in 1971, all of that changed. The 4004 was the world's first microprocessor on a chip. Designed to be the brains of a calculator manufactured by a now defunct company named Busicom, the 4004 had 16 four-bit registers, an ALU, and decoding and control logic all packed onto a single, 2,300-transistor chip. The 4004 was quite a feat for its day, and it paved the way for the PC revolution. However, it wasn't until Intel released the 8080 four years later that the world saw the first true general-purpose CPU.

During the decades following the 8080, the number of transistors that could be packed onto a single chip increased at a stunning pace. As CPU designers had more and more transistors to work with when designing new chips, they began to think up novel ways for using those transistors to increase computing performance on application code. One of the first things that occurred to designers was that they could put more than one ALU on a chip and have both ALUs working in parallel to process code faster. Since these designs could do more than one scalar (or *integer*, for our purposes) operation at once, they were called *superscalar* computers. The RS6000 from IBM was released in 1990 and was the world's first commercially available superscalar CPU. Intel followed in 1993 with the Pentium, which, with its two ALUs, brought the *x*86 world into the superscalar era.

For illustrative purposes, I'll now introduce a *two-way superscalar* version of the DLW-1, called the DLW-2 and illustrated in Figure 4-1. The DLW-2 has two ALUs, so it's able to execute two arithmetic instructions in parallel (hence the term *two-way* superscalar). These two ALUs share a single register file, a situation that in terms of our file clerk analogy would correspond to the file clerk sharing his personal filing cabinet with a second file clerk.

As you can probably guess from looking at Figure 4-1, superscalar processing adds a bit of complexity to the DLW-2's design, because it needs new circuitry that enables it to reorder the linear instruction stream so that some of the stream's instructions can execute in parallel. This circuitry has to ensure that it's "safe" to dispatch two instructions in parallel to the two execution units. But before I go on to discuss some reasons why it might not be safe to execute two instructions in parallel, I should define the term I just used—*dispatch*.

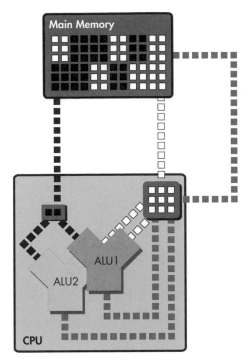

Figure 4-1: The superscalar DLW-2

Notice that in Figure 4-2 I've renamed the second pipeline stage *decode/ dispatch*. This is because attached to the latter part of the decode stage is a bit of dispatch circuitry whose job it is to determine whether or not two instructions can be executed in parallel, in other words, on the same clock cycle. If they can be executed in parallel, the dispatch unit sends one instruction to the first integer ALU and one to the second integer ALU. If they can't be dispatched in parallel, the dispatch unit sends them in program order to the first of the two ALUs. There are a few reasons why the dispatcher might decide that two instructions can't be executed in parallel, and we'll cover those in the following sections.

It's important to note that even though the processor has multiple ALUs, the programming model does not change. The programmer still writes to the same interface, even though that interface now represents a fundamentally different type of machine than the processor actually is; the interface represents a sequential execution machine, but the processor is actually a parallel execution machine. So even though the superscalar CPU executes instructions in parallel, the illusion of sequential execution absolutely must be maintained for the sake of the programmer. We'll see some reasons why this is so later on, but for now the important thing to remember is that main memory still sees one sequential code stream, one data stream, and one results stream, even though the code and data streams are carved up inside the computer and pushed through the two ALUs in parallel.

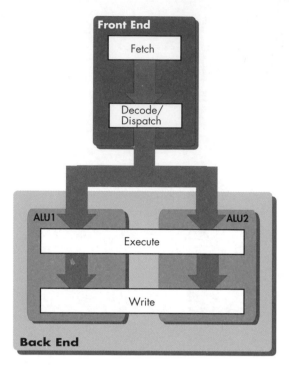

Figure 4-2: The pipeline of the superscalar DLW-2

If the processor is to execute multiple instructions at once, it must be able to fetch and decode multiple instructions at once. A two-way superscalar processor like the DLW-2 can fetch two instructions at once from memory on each clock cycle, and it can also decode and dispatch two instructions each clock cycle. So the DLW-2 fetches instructions from memory in groups of two, starting at the memory address that marks the beginning of the current program's code segment and incrementing the program counter to point four bytes ahead each time a new instruction is fetched. (Remember, the DLW-2's instructions are two bytes wide.)

As you might guess, fetching and decoding two instructions at a time complicates the way the DLW-2 deals with branch instructions. What if the first instruction in a fetched pair happens to be a branch instruction that has the processor jump directly to another part of memory? In this case, the second instruction in the pair has to be discarded. This wastes fetch bandwidth and introduces a bubble into the pipeline. There are other issues relating to superscalar execution and branch instructions, and I'll say more about them in the section on control hazards.

Superscalar Computing and IPC

Superscalar computing allows a microprocessor to increase the number of instructions per clock that it completes beyond one instruction per clock. Recall that one instruction per clock was the maximum theoretical instruction throughput for a pipelined processor, as described in "Instruction Throughput" on page 53. Because a superscalar machine can have multiple instructions in multiple write stages on each clock cycle, the superscalar machine can complete multiple instructions per cycle. If we adapt Chapter 3's pipeline diagrams to take account of superscalar execution, they look like Figure 4-3.

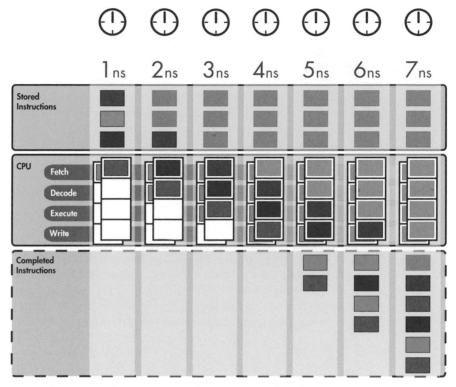

Figure 4-3: Superscalar execution and pipelining combined

In Figure 4-3, two instructions are added to the *Completed Instructions* box on each cycle once the pipeline is full. The more ALU pipelines that a processor has operating in parallel, the more instructions it can add to that box on each cycle. Thus superscalar computing allows you to increase a processor's IPC by adding more hardware. There are some practical limits to how many instructions can be executed in parallel, and we'll discuss those later.

Expanding Superscalar Processing with Execution Units

Most modern processors do more with superscalar execution than just adding a second ALU. Rather, they distribute the work of handling different types of instructions among different types of execution units. An *execution unit* is a block of circuitry in the processor's back end that executes a certain category of instruction. For instance, you've already met the arithmetic logic unit (ALU), an execution unit that performs arithmetic and logical operations on integers. In this section we'll take a closer look at the ALU, and you'll learn about some other types of execution units for non-integer arithmetic operations, memory accesses, and branch instructions.

Basic Number Formats and Computer Arithmetic

The kinds of numbers on which modern microprocessors operate can be divided into two main types: integers (aka fixed-point numbers) and floating-point numbers. *Integers* are simply whole numbers of the type with which you first learn to count in grade school. An integer can be positive, negative, or zero, but it cannot, of course, be a fraction. Integers are also called *fixed-point numbers* because an integer's decimal point does not move. Examples of integers are 1, 0, 500, 27, and 42. Arithmetic and logical operations involving integers are among the simplest and fastest operations that a microprocessor performs. Applications like compilers, databases, and word processors make heavy use of integer operations, because the numbers they deal with are usually whole numbers.

A *floating-point number* is a decimal number that represents a fraction. Examples of floating-point numbers are 56.5, 901.688, and 41.9999. As you can see from these three numbers, the decimal point "floats" around and isn't fixed in once place, hence the name. The number of places behind the decimal point determines a floating-point number's accuracy, so floating-point numbers are often *approximations* of fractional values. Arithmetic and logical operations performed on floating-point numbers are more complex and, hence, slower than their integer counterparts. Because floating-point numbers are approximations of fractional values, and the real world is kind of approximate and fractional, floating-point arithmetic is commonly found in real world–oriented applications like simulations, games, and signal-processing applications.

Both integer and floating-point numbers can themselves be divided into one of two types: scalars and vectors. *Scalars* are values that have only one numerical component, and they're best understood in contrast with *vectors*. Briefly, a vector is a multicomponent value, most often seen as an ordered sequence or array of numbers. (Vectors are covered in detail in "The Vector Execution Units" on page 168.) Here are some examples of different types of vectors and scalars:

	Integer	Floating-Point
Scalar	14 –500 37	1.01 15.234 –0.0023
Vector	{5, –7, –9, 8} {1,003, 42, 97, 86, 97} {234, 7, 6, 1, 3, 10, 11}	{0.99, –1.1, 3.31} {50.01, 0.002, –1.4, 1.4} {5.6, 22.3, 44.444, 76.01, 9.9}

Returning to the code/data distinction, we can say that the data stream consists of four types of numbers: scalar integers, scalar floating-point numbers, vector integers, and vector floating-point numbers. (Note that even memory addresses fall into one of these four categories—scalar integers.) The code stream, then, consists of instructions that operate on all four types of numbers.

The kinds of operations that can be performed on the four types of numbers fall into two main categories: arithmetic operations and logical operations. When I first introduced arithmetic operations in Chapter 1, I lumped them together with logical operations for the sake of convenience. At this point, though, it's useful to distinguish the two types of operations from one another:

- Arithmetic operations are operations like addition, subtraction, multiplication, and division, all of which can be performed on any type of number.

- Logical operations are Boolean operations like AND, OR, NOT, and XOR, along with bit shifts and rotates. Such operations are performed on scalar and vector integers, as well as on the contents of special-purpose registers like the processor status word (PSW).

The types of operations performed on these types of numbers can be broken down as illustrated in Figure 4-4.

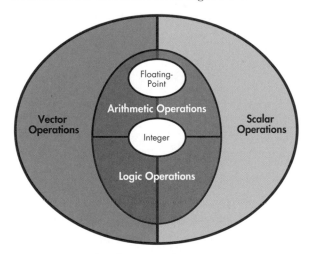

Figure 4-4: Number formats and operation types

As you make your way through the rest of the book, you may want to refer back to this section occasionally. Different microprocessors divide these operations among different execution units in a variety of ways, and things can easily get confusing.

Arithmetic Logic Units

On early microprocessors, as on the DLW-1 and DLW-2, all integer arithmetic and logical operations were handled by the ALU. Floating-point operations were executed by a companion chip, commonly called an *arithmetic coprocessor*, that was attached to the motherboard and designed to work in conjunction with the microprocessor. Eventually, floating-point capabilities were integrated onto the CPU as a separate execution unit alongside the ALU.

Consider the Intel Pentium processor depicted in Figure 4-5, which contains two integer ALUs and a floating-point ALU, along with some other units that we'll describe shortly.

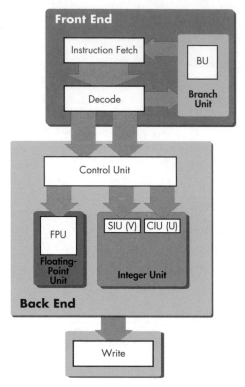

Figure 4-5: The Intel Pentium

This diagram is a variation on Figure 4-2, with the execute stage replaced by labeled white boxes (SIU, CIU, FPU, BU, etc.) that designate the type of execution unit that's modifying the code stream during the execution phase. Notice also that the figure contains a slight shift in terminology that I should clarify before we move on.

Until now, I've been using the term *ALU* as synonymous with *integer execution unit*. After the previous section, however, we know that a microprocessor does arithmetic and logical operations on more than just integer data, so we have to be more precise in our terminology. From now on, *ALU* is a general term for any execution unit that performs arithmetic and logical operations on any type of data. More specific labels will be used to identify the ALUs that handle specific types of instructions and numerical data. For instance, an *integer execution unit (IU)* is an ALU that executes integer arithmetic and logical instructions, a *floating-point execution unit (FPU)* is an ALU that executes floating-point arithmetic and logical instructions, and so on. Figure 4-5 shows that the Pentium has two IUs—a simple integer unit (SIU) and a complex integer unit (CIU)—and a single FPU.

Execution units can be organized logically into functional blocks for ease of reference, so the two integer execution units can be referred to collectively as the Pentium's *integer unit*. The Pentium's *floating-point unit* consists of only a single FPU, but some processors have more than one FPU; likewise with the load-store unit (LSU). The floating-point unit can consist of two FPUs—FPU1 and FPU2—and the load-store unit can consist of LSU1 and LSU2. In both cases, we'll often refer to "the FPU" or "the LSU" when we mean all of the execution units in that functional block, taken as a group.

Many modern microprocessors also feature vector execution units, which perform arithmetic and logical operations on vectors. I won't describe vector computing in detail here, however, because that discussion belongs in another chapter.

Memory-Access Units

In almost all of the processors that we'll cover in later chapters, you'll see a pair of execution units that execute memory-access instructions: the load-store unit and the branch execution unit. The *load-store unit (LSU)* is responsible for the execution of load and store instructions, as well as for *address generation*. As mentioned in Chapter 1, LSUs have small, stripped-down integer addition hardware that can quickly perform the addition required to compute an address.

The *branch execution unit (BEU)* is responsible for executing conditional and unconditional branch instructions. The BEU of the DLW series reads the processor status word as described in Chapter 1 and decides whether or not to replace the program counter with the branch target. The BEU also often has its own address generation unit for performing quick address calculations as needed. We'll talk more about the branch units of real-world processors later on.

Microarchitecture and the ISA

In the preceding discussion of superscalar execution, I made a number of references to the discrepancy between the linear-execution, single-ALU programming model that the programmer sees and what the superscalar processor's hardware actually does. It's now time to flesh out that distinction between the programming model and the actual hardware by introducing some concepts and vocabulary that will allow us to talk with more precision about the divisions between the apparent and the actual in computer architecture.

Chapter 1 introduced the concept of the programming model as an abstract representation of the microprocessor that exposes to the programmer the microprocessor's functionality. The DLW-1's programming model consisted of a single, integer-only ALU, four general-purpose registers, a program counter, an instruction register, a processor status word, and a control unit. The DLW-1's *instruction set* consisted of a few instructions for working with different parts of the programming model: arithmetic instructions (e.g., add and sub) for the ALU and general-purpose registers (GPRs), load and store instructions for manipulating the control unit and filling the GPRs with data, and branch instructions for checking the PSW and changing the PC. We can call this programmer-centric combination of programming model and instruction set an *instruction set architecture (ISA)*.

The DLW-1's ISA was a straightforward reflection of its hardware, which consisted of a single ALU, four GPRs, a PC, a PSW, and a control unit. In contrast, the successor to the DLW-1, the DLW-2, contained a second ALU that was invisible to the programmer and accessible only to the DLW-2's decode/dispatch logic. The DLW-2's decode/dispatch logic would examine pairs of integer arithmetic instructions to determine if they could safely be executed in parallel (and hence out of sequential program order). If they could, it would send them off to the two integer ALUs to be executed simultaneously. Now, the DLW-2 has the same instruction set architecture as the DLW-1—the instruction set and programming model remain unchanged—but the DLW-2's *hardware implementation* of that ISA is significantly different in that the DLW-2 is superscalar.

A particular processor's hardware implementation of an ISA is generally referred to as that processor's *microarchitecture*. We might call the ISA introduced with the DLW-1 the *DLW ISA*. Each successive iteration of our hypothetical DLW line of computers—the DLW-1 and DLW-2—implements the DLW ISA using a different microarchitecture. The DLW-1 has only one ALU, while the DLW-2 is a two-way superscalar implementation of the DLW-ISA.

Intel's *x*86 hardware followed the same sort of evolution, with each successive generation becoming more complex while the ISA stayed largely unchanged. Regarding the Pentium's inclusion of floating-point hardware, you might be wondering how the programmer was able to use the floating-point hardware (i.e., the FPU plus a floating-point register file) if the original *x*86 ISA didn't include any floating-point operations or specify any floating-point registers. The Pentium's designers had to make the following changes to the ISA to accommodate the new functionality:

- First, they had to modify the programming model by adding an FPU and floating-point–specific registers.
- Second, they had to extend the instruction set by adding a new group of floating-point arithmetic instructions.

These types of *ISA extensions* are fairly common in the computing world. Intel extended the original *x*86 instruction set to include the *x*87 floating-point extensions. The *x*87 included an FPU and a stack-based floating-point register file, but we'll talk in more detail about the *x*87's stack-based architecture in the next chapter. Intel later extended *x*86 again with the introduction of a vector-processing instruction set called *MMX (multimedia extensions)*, and again with the introduction of the *SSE (streaming SIMD extensions)* and SSE2 instruction sets. (*SIMD* stands for *single instruction, multiple data* and is another way of describing vector computing. We'll cover this in more detail in "The Vector Execution Units" on page 168.) Similarly, Apple, Motorola, and IBM added a set of vector extensions to the PowerPC ISA in the form of AltiVec, as the extensions are called by Motorola, or VMX, as they're called by IBM.

A Brief History of the ISA

Back in the early days of computing, computer makers like IBM didn't build a whole line of software-compatible computer systems and aim each system at a different price/performance point. Instead, each of a manufacturer's systems was like each of today's game consoles, at least from a programmer's perspective—programmers wrote directly to the machine's unique hardware, with the result that a program written for one machine would run neither on competing machines nor on other machines from a different product line put out by the manufacturer's own company. Just like a Nintendo 64 will run neither PlayStation games nor older SNES games, programs written for one circa-1960 machine wouldn't run on any machine but that one particular product from that one particular manufacturer. The programming model was different for each machine, and the code was fitted directly to the hardware like a key fits a lock (see Figure 4-6).

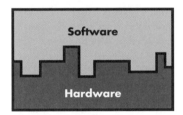

Figure 4-6: Software was custom-fitted
to each generation of hardware

The problems this situation posed are obvious. Every time a new machine came out, software developers had to start from scratch. You couldn't reuse programs, and programmers had to learn the intricacies of each new piece of hardware in order to code for it. This cost quite a bit of time and money, making software development a very expensive undertaking. This situation presented computer system designers with the following problem: How do you *expose* (make available) the functionality of a range of related hardware systems in a way that allows software to be easily developed for and ported between those systems? IBM solved this problem in the 1960s with the launch of the IBM System/360, which ushered in the era of modern computer architecture. The System/360 introduced the concept of the ISA as a layer of abstraction—or an interface, if you will—separated from a particular processor's microarchitecture (see Figure 4-7). This means that the information the programmer needed to know to program the machine was abstracted from the actual hardware implementation of that machine. Once the design and specification of the instruction set, or the set of instructions available to a programmer for writing programs, was separated from the low-level details of a particular machine's design, programs written for a particular ISA could run on any machine that implemented that ISA.

Thus the ISA provided a standardized way to expose the features of a system's hardware that allowed manufacturers to innovate and fine-tune that hardware for performance without worrying about breaking the existing software base. You could release a first-generation product with a particular

ISA, and then work on speeding up the implementation of that same ISA for the second-generation product, which would be backward-compatible with the first generation. We take all this for granted now, but before the IBM System/360, binary compatibility between different machines of different generations didn't exist.

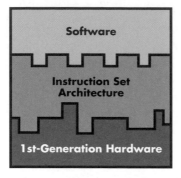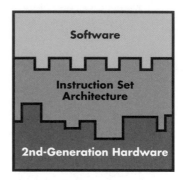

Figure 4-7: The ISA sits between the software and the hardware, providing a consistent interface to the software across hardware generations.

The blue layer in Figure 4-7 simply represents the ISA as an abstract model of a machine for which a programmer writes programs. As mentioned earlier, the technical innovation that made this abstract layer possible was something called the microcode engine. A *microcode engine* is sort of like a CPU within a CPU. It consists of a tiny bit of storage, the *microcode ROM*, which holds *microcode programs*, and an execution unit that executes those programs. The job of each of these microcode programs is to translate a particular instruction into a series of commands that controls the internal parts of the chip. When a System/360 instruction is executed, the microcode unit reads the instruction in, accesses the portion of the microcode ROM where that instruction's corresponding microcode program is located, and then produces a sequence of *machine instructions*, in the processor's internal instruction format, that orchestrates the dance of memory accesses and functional unit activations that actually does the number crunching (or whatever else) the architectural instruction has commanded the machine to do.

By decoding instructions this way, all programs are effectively running in *emulation*. This means that the ISA represents a sort of idealized model, emulated by the underlying hardware, on the basis of which programmers can design applications. This emulation means that between iterations of a product line, a vendor can change the way their CPU executes a program, and all they have to do is rewrite the microcode program each time so the programmer will never have to be aware of the hardware differences because the ISA hasn't changed a bit. Microcode engines still show up in modern CPUs. AMD's Athlon processor uses one for the part of its decoding path that decodes the larger *x*86 instructions, as do Intel's Pentium III and Pentium 4.

The key to understanding Figure 4-7 is that the blue layer represents a layer of abstraction that hides the complexity of the underlying hardware from the programmer. The blue layer is not a hardware layer (that's the gray one) and it's not a software layer (that's the peach one), but it's a *conceptual layer*. Think of it like a user interface that hides the complexity of an operating system from the user. All the user needs to know to use the machine is how to close windows, launch programs, find files, and so on. The UI (and by this I mean the WIMP conceptual paradigm—windows, icons, menus, pointer—not the software that implements the UI) exposes the machine's power and functionality to the user in a way that he or she can understand and use. And whether that UI appears on a PDA or on a desktop machine, the user still knows how to use it to control the machine.

The main drawback to using microcode to implement an ISA is that the microcode engine was, in the beginning, slower than direct decoding. (Modern microcode engines are about 99 percent as fast as direct execution.) However, the ability to separate ISA design from microarchitectural implementation was so significant for the development of modern computing that the small speed hit incurred was well worth it.

The advent of the *reduced instruction set computing (RISC)* movement in the 1970s saw a couple of changes to the scheme described previously. First and foremost, RISC was all about throwing stuff overboard in the name of speed. So the first thing to go was the microcode engine. Microcode had allowed ISA designers to get elaborate with instruction sets, adding in all sorts of complex and specialized instructions that were intended to make programmers' lives easier but that were in reality rarely used. More instructions meant that you needed more microcode ROM, which in turn meant larger CPU die sizes, higher power consumption, and so on. Since RISC was more about less, the microcode engine got the ax. RISC reduced the number of instructions in the instruction set and reduced the size and complexity of each individual instruction so that this smaller, faster, and more lightweight instruction set could be more easily implemented directly in hardware, without a bulky microcode engine.

While RISC designs went back to the old method of direct execution of instructions, they kept the concept of the ISA intact. Computer architects had by this time learned the immense value of not breaking backward compatibility with old software, and they weren't about to go back to the bad old days of marrying software to a single product. So the ISA stayed, but in a stripped-down, much simplified form that enabled designers to implement directly in hardware the same lightweight ISA over a variety of different hardware types.

NOTE *Because the older, non-RISC ISAs featured richer, more complex instruction sets, they were labeled* complex instruction set computing (CISC) *ISAs in order to distinguish them from the new RISC ISAs. The* x86 *ISA is the most popular example of a CISC ISA, while PowerPC, MIPS, and Arm are all examples of popular RISC ISAs.*

Moving Complexity from Hardware to Software

RISC machines were able to get rid of the microcode engine and still retain the benefits of the ISA by moving complexity from hardware to software. Where the microcode engine made CISC programming easier by providing programmers with a rich variety of complex instructions, RISC programmers depended on high-level languages, like C, and on compilers to ease the burden of writing code for RISC ISAs' restricted instruction sets.

Because a RISC ISA's instruction set is more limited, it's harder to write long programs in assembly language for a RISC processor. (Imagine trying to write a novel while restricting yourself to a fifth grade vocabulary, and you'll get the idea.) A RISC assembly language programmer may have to use many instructions to achieve the same result that a CISC assembly language programmer can get with one or two instructions. The advent of high-level languages (HLLs), like C, and the increasing sophistication of compiler technology combined to effectively eliminate this programmer-unfriendly aspect of RISC computing.

The ISA was and is still the optimal solution to the problem of easily and consistently exposing hardware functionality to programmers so that software can be used across a wide range of machines. The greatest testament to the power and flexibility of the ISA is the longevity and ubiquity of the world's most popular and successful ISA: the *x*86 ISA. Programs written for the Intel 8086, a chip released in 1978, can run with relatively little modification on the latest Pentium 4. However, on a microarchitectural level, the 8086 and the Pentium 4 are as different as the Ford Model T and the Ford Mustang Cobra.

Challenges to Pipelining and Superscalar Design

I noted previously that there are conditions under which two arithmetic instructions cannot be "safely" dispatched in parallel for simultaneous execution by the DLW-2's two ALUs. Such conditions are called *hazards*, and they can all be placed in one of three categories:

- Data hazards
- Structural hazards
- Control hazards

Because pipelining is a form of parallel execution, these three types of hazards can also hinder pipelined execution, causing bubbles to occur in the pipeline. In the following three sections, I'll discuss each of these types of hazards. I won't go into a huge amount of detail about the tricks that computer architects use to eliminate them or alleviate their affects, because we'll discuss those when we look at specific microprocessors in the next few chapters.

Data Hazards

The best way to explain what a *data hazard* is to illustrate one. Consider Program 4-1:

Line #	Code	Comments
1	add A, B, C	Add the numbers in registers A and B and store the result in C.
2	add C, D, D	Add the numbers in registers C and D and store the result in D.

Program 4-1: A data hazard

Because the second instruction in Program 4-1 depends on the outcome of the first instruction, the two instructions cannot be executed simultaneously. Rather, the add in line 1 *must* finish first, so that the result is available in C for the add in line 2.

Data hazards are a problem for both superscalar and pipelined execution. If Program 4-1 is run on a superscalar processor with two integer ALUs, the two add instructions cannot be executed simultaneously by the two ALUs. Rather, the ALU executing the add in line 1 has to finish first, and then the other ALU can execute the add in line 2. Similarly, if Program 4-1 is run on a pipelined processor, the second add has to wait until the first add completes the write stage before it can enter the execute phase. Thus the dispatch circuitry has to recognize the add in line 2's dependence on the add in line 1, and keep the add in line 2 from entering the execute stage until the add in line 1's result is available in register C.

Most pipelined processors can do a trick called *forwarding* that's aimed at alleviating the effects of this problem. With forwarding, the processor takes the result of the first add from the ALU's output port and feeds it directly back into the ALU's input port, bypassing the register-file write stage. Thus the second add has to wait for the first add to finish only the execute stage, and not the execute and write stages, before it's able to move into the execute stage itself.

Register renaming is a trick that helps overcome data hazards on superscalar machines. Since any given machine's programming model often specifies fewer registers than can be implemented in hardware, a given microprocessor implementation often has more registers than the number specified in the programming model. To get an idea of how this group of additional registers is used, take a look at Figure 4-8.

In Figure 4-8, the DLW-2's programmer thinks that he or she is using a single ALU with four architectural general-purpose registers—A, B, C, and D—attached to it, because four registers and one ALU are all that the DLW architecture's programming model specifies. However, the actual superscalar DLW-2 hardware has two ALUs and 16 microarchitectural GPRs implemented in hardware. Thus the DLW-2's register rename logic can map the four architectural registers to the available microarchitectural registers in such a way as to prevent false register name conflicts.

In Figure 4-8, an instruction that's being executed by IU1 might think that it's the only instruction executing and that it's using registers A, B, and C, but it's actually using rename registers 2, 5, and 10. Likewise, a second instruction executing simultaneously with the first instruction but in IU2 might also think that it's the only instruction executing and that it has a monopoly on the register file, but in reality, it's using registers 3, 7, 12, and 16. Once both IUs have finished executing their respective instructions, the DLW-2's writeback logic takes care of transferring the contents of the rename registers back to the four architectural registers in the proper order so that the program's state can be changed.

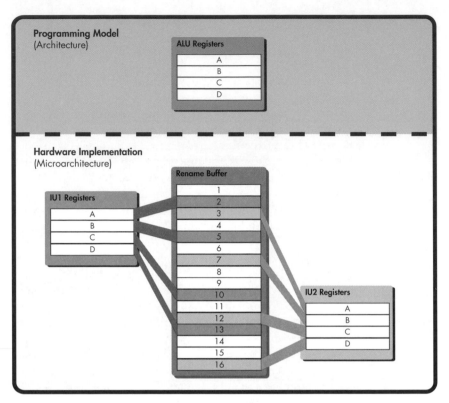

Figure 4-8: Register renaming

Let's take a quick look at a false register name conflict in Program 4-2.

Line #	Code	Comments
1	add A, B, C	Add the numbers in registers A and B and store the result in C.
2	add D, B, A	Add the numbers in registers B and D and store the result in A.

Program 4-2: A false register name conflict

In Program 4-2, there is no data dependency, and both add instructions can take place simultaneously except for one problem: the first add reads the contents of A for its input, while the second add writes a new value into A as its output. Therefore, the first add's read absolutely must take place *before* the second add's write. Register renaming solves this register name conflict by allowing the second add to write its output to a temporary register; after both adds have executed in parallel, the result of the second add is written from that temporary register into the architectural register A after the first add has finished executing and written back its own results.

Structural Hazards

Program 4-3 contains a short code example that shows superscalar execution in action. Assuming the programming model presented for the DLW-2, consider the following snippet of code.

Line #	Code	Comments
15	add A, B, B	Add the numbers in registers A and B and store the result in B.
16	add C, D, D	Add the numbers in registers C and D and store the result in D.

Program 4-3: A structural hazard

At first glance, there appears to be nothing wrong with Program 4-3. There's no data hazard, because the two instructions don't depend on each other. So it should be possible to execute them in parallel. However, this example presumes that both ALUs share the same group of four registers. But in order for the DLW-2's register file to accommodate multiple ALUs accessing it at once, it needs to be different from the DLW-1's register file in one important way: it must be able to accommodate two simultaneous writes. Otherwise, executing Program 4-3's two instructions in parallel would trigger what's called a *structural hazard*, where the processor doesn't have enough resources to execute both instructions at once.

The Register File

In a superscalar design with multiple ALUs, it would take an enormous number of wires to connect each register directly to each ALU. This problem gets worse as the number of registers and ALUs increases. Hence, in super-scalar designs with a large number of registers, a CPU's registers are grouped together into a special unit called a *register file*. This unit is a memory array, much like the array of cells that makes up a computer's main memory, and it's accessed through a special interface that allows the ALU to read from or write to specific registers. This interface consists of a data bus and two types of ports: the *read ports* and the *write ports*. In order to read a value from a single register in the register file, the ALU accesses the register file's read port and requests that the data from a specific register be placed on the special internal data bus that the register file shares with the ALU. Likewise, writing to the register file is done through the file's write port.

A single read port allows the ALU to access a single register at a time, so in order for an ALU to read from two registers simultaneously (as in the case of a three-operand add instruction), the register file must have two read ports. Likewise, a write port allows the ALU to write to only one register at a time, so a single ALU needs a single write port in order to be able to write the results of an operation back to a register. Therefore, the register file needs two read ports and one write port for each ALU. So for the two-ALU superscalar design, the register file needs a total of four read ports and two write ports.

It so happens that the amount of die space that the register file takes up increases approximately with the square of the number of ports, so there is a practical limit on the number of ports that a given register file can support. This is one of the reasons why modern CPUs use separate register files to store integer, floating-point, and vector numbers. Since each type of math (integer, floating-point, and vector) uses a different type of execution unit, attaching multiple integer, floating-point, and vector execution units to a single register file would result in quite a large file.

There's also another reason for using multiple register files to accommodate different types of execution units. As the size of the register file increases, so does the amount of time it takes to access it. You might recall from "The File-Clerk Model Revisited and Expanded" on page 9 that we assume that register reads and writes happen instantaneously. If a register file gets too large and the register file access latency gets too high, this can slow down register accesses to the point where such access takes up a noticeable amount of time. So instead of using one massive register file for each type of numerical data, computer architects use two or three register files connected to a few different types of execution units.

Incidentally, if you'll recall "Opcodes and Machine Language" on page 19, the DLW-1 used a series of binary numbers to designate which of the four registers an instruction was accessing. Well, in the case of a register file read, these numbers are fed into the register file's interface in order to specify which of the registers should place its data on the data bus. Taking our two-bit register designations as an example, a port on our four-register file would have two lines that would be held at either high or low voltages (depending on whether the bit placed on each line was a 1 or a 0), and these lines would tell the file which of its registers should have its data placed on the data bus.

Control Hazards

Control hazards, also known as *branch hazards*, are hazards that arise when the processor arrives at a conditional branch and has to decide which instruction to fetch next. In more primitive processors, the pipeline stalls while the branch condition is evaluated and the branch target is calculated. This stall inserts a few cycles of bubbles into the pipeline, depending on how long it takes the processor to identify and locate the branch target instruction.

Modern processors use a technique called *branch prediction* to get around these branch-related stalls. We'll discuss branch prediction in more detail in the next chapter.

Another potential problem associated with branches lies in the fact that once the branch condition is evaluated and the address of the next instruction is loaded into the program counter, it then takes a number of cycles to actually fetch the next instruction from storage. This *instruction load latency* is added to the branch condition evaluation latency discussed earlier in this section. Depending on where the next instruction is located—such as in a nearby cache, in main memory, or on a hard disk—it can take anywhere from a few cycles to thousands of cycles to fetch the instruction. The cycles that the processor spends waiting on that instruction to show up are dead, wasted cycles that show up as bubbles in the processor's pipeline and kill performance. Computer architects use *instruction caching* to alleviate the effects of load latency, and we'll talk more about this technique in the next chapter.

5

THE INTEL PENTIUM AND PENTIUM PRO

Now that you've got the basics of microprocessor architecture down, let's look at some real hardware to see how manufacturers implement the two main concepts covered in the previous two chapters—pipelining and superscalar execution—and introduce an entirely new concept: the instruction window. First, we'll wrap up our discussion of the fundamentals of microprocessors by taking a look at the Pentium. Then we'll explore in detail the P6 microarchitecture that forms the heart of the Pentium Pro, Pentium II, and Pentium III. The P6 microarchitecture represents a fundamental departure from the microprocessor designs we've studied so far, and an understanding of how it works will give you a solid grasp of the most important concepts in modern microprocessor architecture.

The Original Pentium

The original Pentium is an extremely modest design by today's standards. Transistor budgets were smaller when the chip was introduced in 1993, so the Pentium doesn't pack nearly as much hardware onto its die as a modern microprocessor. Table 5-1 summarizes its features.

Table 5-1: Summary of Pentium Features

Introduction Date	March 22, 1993
Manufacturing Process	0.8 micron
Transistor Count	3.1 million
Clock Speed at Introduction	60 and 66 MHz
Cache Sizes	L1: 8KB instruction, 8KB data
*x*86 ISA Extensions	MMX added in 1997

A glance at a diagram of the Pentium (see Figure 5-1) shows that it has two integer ALUs and a floating-point ALU, along with some other units that I'll describe later. The Pentium also has a *level 1 cache*—a component of the microprocessor that you haven't yet seen. Before moving on, let's take a moment to look in more detail at this new component, which acts as a code and data storage area for the processor.

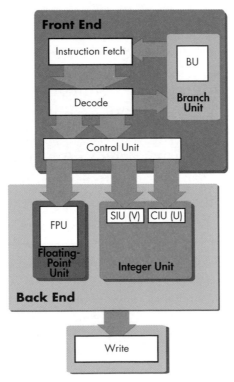

Figure 5-1: The basic microarchitecture of the original Intel Pentium

Caches

So far, I've talked about code and data as if they were all stored in main memory. While this may be true in a limited sense, it doesn't tell the whole story. Though processor speeds have increased dramatically over the past two decades, the speed of main memory has not been able to keep pace. In every computer system currently on the market, there's a yawning speed gap between the processor and main memory. It takes such a huge number of processor clock cycles to transfer code and data between main memory and the registers and execution units that if no solution were available to alleviate this bottleneck, it would kill most of the performance gains brought on by the increase in processor clock speeds.

Very fast memory that could close some of the speed gap is indeed available, but it's too expensive to be widely used in a PC system's main memory. In fact, as a general rule of thumb, the faster the memory technology, the more it costs per unit of storage. As a result, computer system designers fill the speed gap by placing smaller amounts of faster, more expensive memory, called *cache memory*, in between main memory and the registers. These caches, which are depicted in Figure 5-2, hold chunks of frequently used code and data, keeping them within easy reach of the processor's front end.

In most systems, there are multiple levels of cache between main memory and the registers. The level 1 cache (called *L1 cache* or just *L1* for short) is the smallest, most expensive bit of cache, so it's located the closest to the processor's back end. Most PC systems have another level of cache, called *level 2 cache* (*L2 cache* or just *L2*), located between the L1 cache and main memory, and some systems even have a third cache level, *L3 cache*, located between the L2 cache and main memory. In fact, as Figure 5-2 shows, main memory itself is really just a cache for the hard disk drive.

When the processor needs a particular piece of code or data, it first checks the L1 cache to see if the desired item is present. If it is—a situation called a *cache hit*—it moves that item directly to either the fetch stage (in the case of code) or the register file (in the case of data). If the item is not present—a *cache miss*—the processor checks the slower but larger L2 cache. If the item is present in the L2, it's copied into the L1 and passed along to the front end or back end. If there's a cache miss in the L2, the processor checks the L3, and so on, until there's either a cache hit, or the cache miss propagates all the way out to main memory.

One popular way of laying out the L1 cache is to have code and data stored in separate halves of the cache. The code half of the cache is often referred to as the *instruction cache* or *I-cache*, and the data half of the cache is referred to as the *data cache* or *D-cache*. This kind of split cache design has certain performance advantages and is used in the all of the processors discussed in this book.

NOTE   *The split L1 cache design is often called the* Harvard architecture *as an homage to the Harvard Mark I. The Mark I was a relay-based computer designed by IBM and shipped to Harvard in 1944, and it was the first machine to incorporate the conceptual split between code and data explicitly into its architecture.*

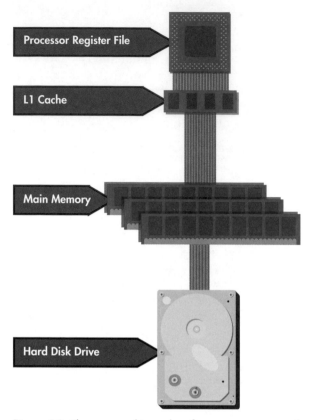

Figure 5-2: The memory hierarchy of a computer system, from the smallest, fastest, and most expensive memory (the register file) to the largest, slowest, and least expensive (the hard disk)

Back when transistor budgets were much tighter than they are today, all caches were located somewhere on the computer's system bus between the CPU and main memory. Today, however, the L1 and L2 caches are commonly integrated onto the CPU die itself, along with the rest of the CPU's circuitry. An on-die cache has significant performance advantages over an off-die cache and is essential for keeping today's deeply pipelined superscalar machines full of code and data.

The Pentium's Pipeline

As you've probably already guessed, a superscalar processor doesn't have just one pipeline. Because its execute stage is split up among multiple execution units that operate in parallel, a processor like the Pentium can be said to have multiple pipelines—one for each execution unit. Figure 5-3 illustrates the Pentium's multiple pipelines.

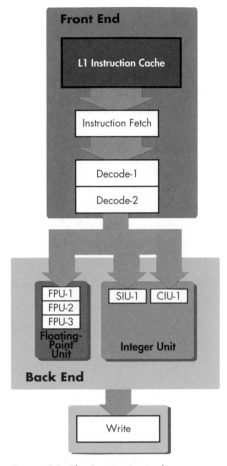

Figure 5-3: The Pentium's pipelines

As you can see, each of the Pentium's pipelines shares four stages in common:

- Fetch
- Decode-1
- Decode-2
- Write

It's when an instruction reaches the execute phase of its lifecycle that it enters a more specialized pipeline, specific to the execution unit.

A processor's various execution units can have different pipeline depths, with the integer pipeline usually being the shortest and the floating-point pipeline usually being the longest. In Figure 5-3, you can see that the Pentium's two integer ALUs have single-stage pipelines, while the floating-point unit has a three-stage pipeline.

Because the integer pipeline is the shortest, it's normally taken to be the default pipeline in discussions of a processor's microarchitecture. So when you see a reference, either in this text or in another text, to a superscalar processor's *pipeline* or *basic pipeline*, you should assume it's referring to the processor's integer pipeline.

The Pentium's basic integer pipeline is five stages long, with the stages broken down as follows:

1. **Prefetch/Fetch** Instructions are fetched from the instruction cache and aligned in prefetch buffers for decoding.

2. **Decode-1** Instructions are decoded into the Pentium's internal instruction format using a fast set of hardware-based rules. Branch prediction also takes place at this stage.

3. **Decode-2** Instructions that require the microcode ROM are decoded here. Also, address computations take place at this stage.

4. **Execute** The integer hardware ALU executes the instruction.

5. **Write-back** The results of the computation are written back to the register file.

These stages should be familiar to you, although the first three stages are slightly different from those of the simple four-stage pipelines described so far. Let's take a quick trip through the Pentium's pipeline stages, so that you can examine each one in a bit more detail.

The *prefetch/fetch* stage corresponds to the fetch phase of the standard instruction lifecycle. Unlike the simple, uniformly sized two-byte instructions of our example DLW architecture, x86 instructions can range in size from 1 to 17 bytes in length, though the average instruction length is a little under 3 bytes. x86's widely variable instruction length complicates the Pentium's fetch stage, because instructions cannot simply be fetched and then fed directly into the decode stage. Instead, x86 instructions are first fetched into a buffer, where each instruction's boundaries are detected and marked. From this buffer, the marked instructions are then aligned and sent to the Pentium's decode hardware.

The decode phase of the Pentium's execution process is split into two pipeline stages, the first of which corresponds most closely to the decode pipeline stage with which you're already familiar. The *decode-1* stage takes the newly fetched instruction and decodes it into the Pentium's internal instruction format, so that it can be used to tell the processor's execution units how to manipulate the data stream. The decode-1 stage also involves the Pentium's branch unit, which checks the currently decoding instruction to see if it's a branch, and if it is a branch, to determine its type. It's at this point that *branch prediction* takes place, but we'll cover branch prediction in more detail in a moment.

The main difference between the Pentium's five-stage pipeline and the four-stage pipelines discussed in Chapter 3 lies in the second decode stage. RISC ISAs, like the primitive DLW ISA of Chapters 1 and 2, support only a few simple, load-store addressing modes. In contrast, the x86 ISA supports multiple complex addressing modes, which were originally designed to make assembly language programmers' lives easier but ended up making everyone's lives more difficult. These addressing modes require extra address computations, and these computations are relegated to the *decode-2* stage, where dedicated address computation hardware handles them before dispatching the instruction to the execution units.

The decode-2 stage is also where the Pentium's microcode ROM kicks in. The Pentium decodes many *x*86 instructions directly in its decoding hardware, but the longer instructions are decoded by means of a microcode ROM, as described in the section "A Brief History of the ISA" on page 71.

Once instructions have been decoded, the Pentium's control unit determines when they can be dispatched to the back end and to which execution unit. So the control unit's job is to coordinate the movement of instructions from the processor's front end to its back end, so that they can enter the execute and write-back phases of the execution process.

The last two pipeline stages—execute and write-back—should be familiar to you by now. The next major section will describe the Pentium's execution units, so think of it as a more detailed discussion of the execute stage.

The Branch Unit and Branch Prediction

Before we take a closer look at the back end of the Pentium, let's look at one aspect of the Pentium's front end in a bit more detail: the *branch unit (BU)*.

On the right side of the Pentium's front end, shown earlier in Figure 5-1, notice a branch unit attached to the instruction fetch and decode/dispatch pipeline stages. I've depicted the branch unit as part of the front end of the machine—even though it technically still counts as a *memory access unit*—because the BU works closely with the instruction fetcher, steering it by means of the program counter to different sections of the code stream.

The branch unit contains the *branch execution unit (BEU)* and the *branch prediction unit (BPU)*, and whenever the front end's decoder encounters a conditional branch instruction, it sends it to the BU to be executed. The BU in turn usually needs to send it off to one of the other execution units to have the instruction's branch condition evaluated, so that the BU can determine if the branch is *taken* or *not taken*. Once the BU determines that the branch has been taken, it has to get the starting address of the next block of code to be executed. This address, the *branch target*, must be calculated, and the front end must be told to begin fetching code at the new address.

In older processors, the entire processor just sort of sat idle and waited for the branch condition to be evaluated, a wait that could be quite long if the evaluation involved a complex calculation of some sort. Modern processors use a technique called *speculative execution*, which involves making an educated guess at which direction the branch will ultimately take and then beginning execution at the new branch target *before* the branch's condition is actually evaluated. This educated guess is made using one of a variety of branch prediction techniques, about which I'll talk more in a moment. Speculative execution is used to keep the delays associated with evaluating branches from introducing bubbles into the pipeline.

Instructions that are speculatively executed cannot write their results back to the register file until the branch condition is evaluated. If the BPU predicted the branch correctly, those speculative instructions can then be marked as non-speculative and have their results written back just like regular instructions.

Branch prediction can backfire when the processor incorrectly predicts a branch. Such mispredictions are bad, because if all of those instructions that the processor has loaded into the pipeline and begun speculatively executing turn out to be from the wrong branch target, the pipeline must be flushed of the erroneous, speculative instructions and their attendant results. After this pipeline flush, the front end must then fetch the correct branch target address so that the processor can begin executing at the right place in the code stream.

As you learned in Chapter 3, flushing the pipeline of instructions and then refilling it again causes a huge hit to the processor's average completion rate and overall performance. Furthermore, there's a delay (and therefore a few cycles worth of pipeline bubbles) associated with calculating the correct branch target and loading the new instruction stream into the front end. This delay can degrade performance significantly, especially on branch-intensive code. It is therefore imperative that a processor's branch prediction hardware be as accurate as possible.

There are two main types of branch prediction: static prediction and dynamic prediction. *Static branch prediction* is simple and relies on the assumption that the majority of backward-pointing branches occur in the context of repetitive loops, where the branch instruction is used to determine whether or not to repeat the loop again. Most of the time, a loop's exit condition will be false, which means that the loop's branch will evaluate to taken, thereby instructing the machine to repeat the loop's code one more time. This being the case, static branch prediction merely assumes that all backward branches are taken. For a branch that points forward to a block of code that comes later in the program, the static predictor assumes that the branch is not taken.

Static prediction is very fast because it doesn't involve any table lookups or calculations, but its success rate varies widely with the program's instruction mix. If the program is full of loops, static prediction works fairly well; if it's not full of loops, static branch prediction performs quite poorly.

To get around the problems associated with static prediction, computer architects use a variety of algorithms for predicting branches based on a program's past behavior. These *dynamic branch prediction* algorithms usually involve the use of both of two types of tables—the *branch history table (BHT)* and the *branch target buffer (BTB)*—to record information about the outcomes of branches that have already been executed. The BHT creates an entry for each conditional branch that the BU has encountered on its last few cycles. This entry includes some bits that indicate the likelihood that the branch will be taken based on its past history. When the front end encounters a branch instruction that has an entry in its BHT, the branch predictor uses this branch history information to decide whether or not to speculatively execute the branch.

Should the branch predictor decide to execute the branch speculatively, it needs to know exactly where in memory the branch is pointing—in other words, it needs a branch target. The BTB stores the branch targets of previously executed branches, so when a branch is taken, the BPU grabs the speculative branch target from the BTB and tells the front end to begin fetching instructions from that address. Hopefully, the BTB contains an entry for the branch you're trying to execute, and hopefully that entry is correct. If the branch target either isn't there or is wrong, you've got a problem. I won't get into the issues surrounding BTB performance, but suffice it to say that a larger BTB is usually better, because it can store more branch targets and thus lower the chances of a BTB miss.

The Pentium uses both static and dynamic branch prediction techniques to prevent mispredictions and branch delays. If a branch instruction does not have an entry in the BHT, the Pentium uses static prediction to decide which path to take. If the instruction does have a BHT entry, dynamic prediction is used. The Pentium's BHT holds 256 entries, which means that it does not have enough space to store information on most of the branches in an average program. Nonetheless, the BHT allows the Pentium to predict branches with a much higher success rate, from 75 to 85 percent, according to Intel, than if it used static prediction alone. The Pentium also uses a BTB to store predicted branch targets. In most of Intel's literature and diagrams, the BTB and BHT are combined under the label the *front-end BTB* and are considered a single structure.

The Pentium's Back End

The Pentium's superscalar back end is fairly straightforward. It has two five-stage integer pipelines, which Intel has designated U and V, and one six-stage floating-point pipeline. This section will take a closer look at each of these ALUs.

The Integer ALUs

The Pentium's U and V integer pipes are not fully symmetric. U, as the default pipe, is slightly more capable and contains a shifter, which V lacks. For this reason, in Figure 5-1, I've labeled the U pipe *simple integer unit (SIU)* and the V pipe *complex integer unit (CIU)*. Most of the designs that we'll study throughout this book have asymmetrical integer units, where one integer unit is more complex and capable of handling more types of instructions than the other, simpler unit.

The Pentium's integer units aren't fully independent. There is a set of restrictions, which I won't take time to outline, that places limits on which combinations of integer instructions can be issued in parallel. All told, though, the Pentium's two integer units initially provided solid enough integer performance for it to be competitive in its day, especially for integer-intensive office apps.

The final thing worth noting about the Pentium's two integer ALUs is that they are responsible for many of the processor's address calculations.

More recently designed processors have specialized hardware for handling the address calculations associated with loads and stores, but on the Pentium these calculations are done in the integer ALUs.

The Floating-Point ALU

Floating-point operations are usually more complex to implement than integer operations, so floating-point pipelines often feature more stages than integer pipelines. The Pentium's six-stage floating-point pipeline is no exception to this rule. The Pentium's floating-point performance is limited by two main factors. First, the processor can only dispatch both a floating-point and an integer operation simultaneously under extremely restrictive circumstances. This isn't too bad, though, because floating-point and integer code are rarely mixed. The second factor, the unfortunate design of the *x*87 floating-point architecture, is more important.

In contrast to the average RISC ISA's *flat* floating-point register file, the *x*87 register file contains eight 80-bit registers arranged in the form of a stack. A *stack* is a simple data storage structure commonly used by programmers and some scientific calculators to perform arithmetic.

NOTE   *Flat is an adjective that programmers use to describe an array of elements that is logically laid out so that any element is accessible via a simple address. For instance, all of the register files that we've seen so far are flat, because a programmer needs to know only the name of the register in order to access that register. Contrast the flat file with the stack structure described next, in which elements that are inside the data structure are not immediately and directly accessible to the programmer.*

As Figure 5-4 illustrates, a programmer writes data to the stack by *pushing* it onto the top of the stack via the push instruction. The stack therefore grows with each new piece of data that is pushed onto its top. To read data from the stack, the programmer issues a pop instruction, which returns the topmost piece of data and removes that data from the stack, causing the stack to shrink.

As the stack grows and shrinks, the variable ST, which stands for the *stack top*, always points to the top element of the stack. In the most basic type of stack, ST is the only element of the stack that can be directly accessed by the programmer—it is read using the pop command, and it is written to using the push command. This being the case, if you want to read the blue element from the stack in Figure 5-4, you have to pop all of the elements above it, and then you have to pop the blue element itself. Similarly, if you want to alter the blue element, you first have to pop all of the elements above it. Then you pop the blue element itself, alter it, and then push the modified element back onto the stack.

Because the first item that you place in a stack is not accessible until you've removed all the items above it, a stack is often called a *FILO (first in, last out)* data structure. Contrast this with a traditional queue structure, like a supermarket checkout line, which is a *FIFO (first in, first out)* structure.

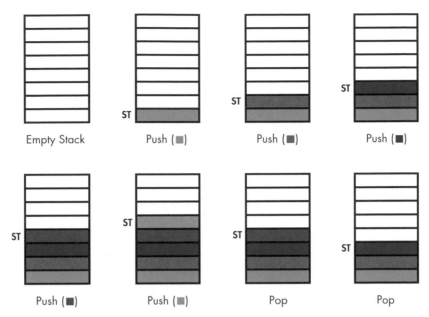

Figure 5-4: Pushing and popping data on a simple stack

All of this pushing and popping sounds like a lot of work, and you might wonder why anyone would use such a data structure. As it turns out, a stack is ideal for certain specialized types of applications, like parsing natural language, keeping track of nested procedure calls, and evaluating postfix arithmetic expressions. It was the stack's utility for evaluating postfix arithmetic expressions that recommended it to the designers of the *x*87 floating-point unit (FPU), so they arranged the FPU's eight floating-point registers as a stack.

NOTE   *Normal arithmetic expressions, like 5 + 2 − 1 = 6, are called* infix *expressions, because the arithmetic operators (+ and −) are situated in between the numbers on which they operate.* Postfix *expressions, in contrast, have the operators affixed to the end of the expression, e.g. 521−+ = 6. You could evaluate this expression from left to right using a stack by pushing the numbers 5, 2, and 1 onto the stack (in that order), and then popping them back off (first 1, then 2, and finally 5) as the operators at the end of the expression are encountered. The operators would be applied to the popped numbers as they appear, and the running result would be stored in the top of the stack.*

The *x*87 register file is a little different than the simple stack described two paragraphs ago, because ST is not the only variable through which the stack elements can be accessed. Instead, the programmer can read and write the lower elements of the stack by using ST with an index value that designates the desired element's position relative to the top of the stack. For example, in Figure 5-5, the stack is at its tallest when the green value has just been pushed onto it. This green value is accessed via the variable ST(0), because it occupies the top of the stack. The blue value, because it is three elements down from the top of the stack, is accessed via ST(3).

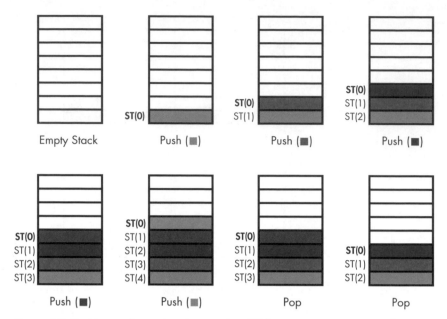

Figure 5-5: Pushing and popping data on the x87 floating-point register stack

In general, to read from or write to a specific register in the stack, you can just use the form ST(i), where i is the number of registers from the top of the stack.

Programming purists might suggest that since you can access its stack elements arbitrarily, it's kind of pointless to still call the *x*87 register file a stack. This would be true except for one catch: For every floating-point arithmetic instruction, at least one of the operands must be the stack top. For instance, if you want to add two floating-point numbers, one of the numbers must be in the stack top and the other can be in any of the other registers. For example, the instruction

```
fadd ST, ST(5)
```

performs the operation

```
ST = ST + ST(5)
```

Though the stack-based nature of *x*87's floating-point register file was originally a boon to assembly language programmers, it soon began to become an obstacle to floating-point performance as compilers saw more widespread use. A flat register file is easier for a compiler to manage, and the newer RISC ISAs featured not only large, flat register files but also three-operand floating-point instructions.

While compiler tricks are arguably enough to make up for *x*87's two-operand limit under most circumstances, they're not quite able to overcome both the two-operand limit and the stack-based limit. So compiler tricks alone won't eliminate the performance penalties associated with both of these quirks combined. The stack-based register file is bad enough that a microarchitectural hack is needed in order simulate a flat register file and thereby keep the *x*87's design from hobbling floating-point performance.

This microarchitectural hack involves turbocharging a single instruction: fxch. The fxch instruction is an ordinary *x*87 instruction that allows you to swap any element of the stack with the stack top. For example, if you wanted to calculate ST(2) = ST(2) + ST(6), you might execute the code shown in Program 5-1:

Line #	Code	Comments
1	fxch ST(2)	Place the contents of ST(2) into ST and the contents of ST into ST(2).
2	fadd ST, ST(6)	Add the contents of ST to ST(6).
3	fxch ST(2)	Place the contents of ST(2) into ST and the contents of ST into ST(2).

Program 5-1: Using the fxch instruction

Now, here's where the microarchitectural hack comes in. On all modern *x*86 designs, from the original Pentium up to but not including the Pentium 4, the fxch instruction can be executed in zero cycles. This means that for all intents and purposes, fxch is "free of charge" and can therefore be used when needed without a performance hit. (Note, however, that the fxch instruction still takes up decode bandwidth, so even when it's "free," it's not entirely "free.") If you stop and think about the fact that, before executing any floating-point instruction (which has to involve the stack top), you can instantaneously swap ST with any other register, you'll realize that a zero-cycle fxch instruction gives programmers the functional equivalent of a flat register file.

To revisit the previous example, the fact that the first instruction in Program 5-1 executes "instantaneously," as it were, means that the series of operations effectively looks as follows:

```
fadd ST(2), ST(6)
```

There are in fact some limitations on the use of the "free" fxch instruction, but the overall result is that by using this trick, both the Pentium and its successors get the effective benefits of a flat register file, but with the aforementioned hit to decode bandwidth.

x86 Overhead on the Pentium

There are a number of places, like the Pentium's decode-2 stage, where legacy *x*86 support adds significant overhead to the Pentium's design. Intel has estimated that a whopping 30 percent of the Pentium's transistors are dedicated solely to providing *x*86 legacy support. When you consider the fact that the Pentium's RISC competitors with comparable transistor counts could spend those transistors on performance-enhancing hardware like execution units and cache, it's no wonder that the Pentium lagged behind some of its contemporaries when it was first introduced.

A large chunk of the Pentium's legacy-supporting transistors are eaten up by its microcode ROM. Chapter 4 explained that one of the big benefits of RISC processors is that they don't need the microcode ROMs that CISC designs require for decoding large, complex instructions. (For more on *x*86 as a CISC ISA, see the section "CISC, RISC, and Instruction Set Translation" on page 103.)

The front end of the Pentium also suffers from *x*86-related bloat, in that its prefetch logic has to take account of the fact that *x*86 instructions are not a uniform size and hence can straddle cache lines. The Pentium's decode logic also has to support *x*86's segmented memory model, which means checking for and enforcing code segment limits; such checking requires its own dedicated address calculation hardware, in addition to the Pentium's other address hardware.

Summary: The Pentium in Historical Context

The primary factor constraining the Pentium's performance versus its RISC competitors was the fact that its entire front end was bloated with hardware that was there solely to support *x*86 features which, even at the time of the processor's introduction, were rapidly falling out of use. With transistor budgets as tight as they were in 1993, each of those extra address adders and prefetch buffers—not to mention the microcode ROM—represented a painful expenditure of scarce resources that did nothing to enhance the Pentium's performance.

Fortunately for Intel, Pentium's legacy support headaches weren't the end of the story. There were a few facts and trends working in the favor of Intel and the *x*86 ISA. If we momentarily forget about ISA extensions like MMX, SSE, and so on, and the odd handful of special-purpose instructions, like Intel's CPU identifier instruction, that get added to the *x*86 ISA every so often, the core legacy *x*86 ISA is fixed in size and has not grown over the years. Similarly, with one exception (the P6, covered next), the amount of hardware that it takes to support such instructions has not tended to grow either.

Transistors, on the other hand, have shrunk rapidly since the Pentium was introduced. When you put these two facts together, this means that the relative cost (in transistors) of *x*86 support, a cost that is mostly concentrated in an *x*86 CPU's front end, has dropped as CPU transistor counts have increased.

*x*86 support accounts for well under 10 percent of the transistors on the Pentium 4, and this percentage is even smaller for the very latest Intel processors. This steady and dramatic decrease in the relative cost of legacy support has contributed significantly to the ability of *x*86 hardware to catch up to and even surpass its RISC competitors in both integer and floating-point performance. In other words, Moore's Curves have been extremely kind to the *x*86 ISA.

In spite of the high price it paid for *x*86 support, the Pentium was commercially successful, and it furthered Intel's dominance in the *x*86 market that the company had invented. But for Intel to take *x*86 performance to the next level, it needed to take a series of radical steps with the follow-on to the Pentium, the Pentium Pro.

NOTE *Here and throughout this book, I use the term* Moore's Curves *in place of the more popular phrase* Moore's Law. *For a detailed explanation of the phenomenon referred to by both of these terms, see my article at Ars Technica entitled "Understanding Moore's Law" (http://arstechnica.com/paedia/m/moore/moore-1.html).*

The Intel P6 Microarchitecture: The Pentium Pro

Intel's P6 microarchitecture, first implemented in the Pentium Pro, was by any reasonable metric a resounding success. Its performance was significantly better than that of the Pentium, and the market rewarded Intel handsomely for it. The microarchitecture also proved extremely scalable, furnishing Intel with a good half-decade of desktop dominance and paving the way for *x*86 systems to compete with RISC in the workstation and server markets. Table 5-2 summarizes the evolution of the P6 microarchitecture's features.

Table 5-2: The Evolution of the P6

	Pentium Pro Vitals	Pentium II Vitals	Pentium III Vitals
Introduction Date	November 1, 1995	May 7, 1997	February 26, 1999
Process	0.60/0.35 micron	0.35 micron	0.25 micron
Transistor Count	5.5 million	7.5 million	9.5 million
Clock Speed at Introduction	150, 166, 180, and 200 MHz	233, 266, and 300 MHz	450 and 500 MHz
L1 Cache Size	8KB instruction, 8KB data	16KB instruction, 16KB data	16KB instruction, 16KB data
L2 Cache Size	256KB or 512KB (on-die)	512KB (off-die)	512KB (on-die)
*x*86 ISA Extensions		MMX	SSE added in 1999

What was the P6's secret, and how did it offer such a quantum leap in performance? The answer is complex and involves the contribution of numerous technologies and techniques, the most important of which had already been introduced into the *x*86 world by Intel's smaller *x*86 competitors (most notably, AMD's K5): the decoupling of the front end's fetching and decoding functions from the back end's execution function by means of an instruction window.

Figure 5-6 illustrates the basic P6 microarchitecture. As you can see, this microarchitecture sports a quite a few prominent features that distinguish it fundamentally from the designs we've studied thus far.

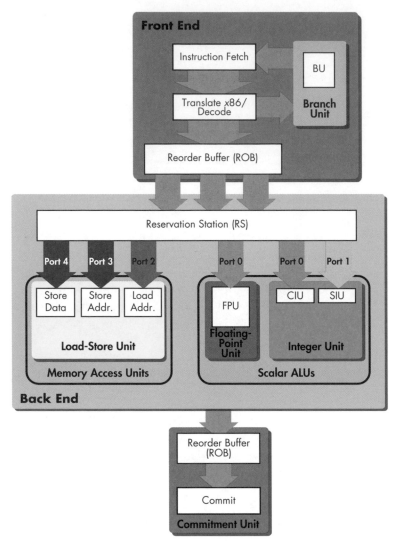

Figure 5-6: The Pentium Pro

Decoupling the Front End from the Back End

In the Pentium and its predecessors, instructions travel directly from the decoding hardware to the execution hardware, as depicted in Figure 5-7. In this simple processor, instructions are *statically scheduled* by the dispatch logic for execution by the two ALUs. First, instructions are fetched and decoded. Next, the control unit's dispatch logic examines a pair of instructions using a set of hardwired rules to determine whether or not they can be executed in parallel. If the two instructions can be executed in parallel, the control unit sends them to the two ALUs, where they're simultaneously executed on the same clock cycle. When the two instructions have *completed* their execution phase (i.e., their results are available on the data bus), they're put back in program order, and their results are written back to the register file in the proper sequence.

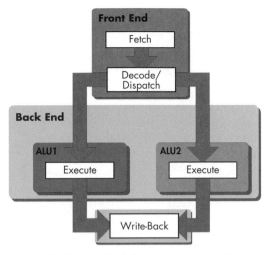

Figure 5-7: Static scheduling in the original Pentium

This static, rules-based approach to dispatching instructions is rigid and simplistic, and it has two major drawbacks, both stemming from the fact that although the code stream is inherently sequential, a superscalar processor attempts to execute parts of it in parallel. Specifically, static scheduling

- adapts poorly to the dynamic and ever-changing code stream;
- makes poor use of wider superscalar hardware.

Because the Pentium can dispatch at most two operations simultaneously from its decode hardware to its execution hardware on each clock cycle, its dispatch rules look at only two instructions at a time to see if they can or cannot be dispatched simultaneously. If more execution hardware were added to the Pentium, and the dispatch width were increased to three instructions per cycle (as it is in the P6), the rules for determining which instructions go where would need to be able to account for various possible combinations of two and three instructions at a time in order to get those instructions to the right execution unit at the right time. Furthermore, such rules would inevitably be difficult for programmers to optimize for, and if they weren't overly complex, there would necessarily exist many common instruction sequences that would perform suboptimally under the default rule set. In plain English, the makeup of the code stream would change from application to application and from moment to moment, but the rules responsible for scheduling the code stream's execution on the Pentium's back end would be forever fixed.

The Issue Phase

The solution to the dilemma posed by static execution is to dispatch newly decoded instructions into a special buffer that sits between the front end and the execution units. Once this buffer collects a handful of instructions that are waiting to execute, the processor's *dynamic scheduling* logic can examine the instructions and, after taking into account the state of the processor and the resources currently available for execution, *issue* instructions from the buffer to the execution units at the most opportune time and in the optimal order. The dynamic scheduling logic has quite a bit of freedom to reorder the code stream so that instructions execute optimally, even if it means that two (or more) instructions must be executed not just in parallel but in reverse order. With dynamic scheduling, the current context in which a particular instruction finds itself executing can have much more of an impact on when and how it's executed. In replacing the Pentium's control unit with the combination of a buffer and a dynamic scheduler, the P6 microarchitecture replaces fixed rules with flexibility.

Of course, instructions that have been issued from the buffer to the execution units out of program order must be put back in program order once they've completed their execution phase, so another buffer is needed to catch the instructions that have completed execution and to place them back in program order. We'll discuss that second buffer more in a moment.

Figure 5-8 shows the two new buffers, both of which work together to decouple the execute phase from the rest of the instruction's lifecycle.

In the processor depicted in Figure 5-8, instructions flow in program order from the decode stage into the first buffer, the *issue buffer*, where they sit until the processor's dynamic scheduler determines that they're ready to execute. Once the instructions are ready to execute, they flow from the issue buffer into the execution unit. This move, when instructions travel from the issue buffer where they're scheduled for optimal execution into the execution units themselves, is called *issuing*.

There are a number of factors that can prevent an instruction from executing out of order in the manner described earlier. The instruction may depend for input on the results of an as-yet-unexecuted instruction, or it may be waiting on data to be loaded from memory, or it may be waiting for a busy execution unit to become available, or any one of a number of other conditions may need to be met before the decoded instruction is ready to be sent off to the proper execution unit. But once the instruction is ready, the scheduler sees that it is issued to the execution unit, where it will be executed.

This new twist on the standard instruction lifecycle is called *out-of-order execution*, or *dynamic execution*, and it requires the addition of two new phases to our instruction's lifecycle, as shown in Table 5-3. The first new phase is the *issue phase*, and it encompasses the buffering and reordering of the code stream that I've just described.

The issue phase is implemented in different ways by different processors. It may take multiple pipeline stages, and it may involve the use of multiple buffers arranged in different configurations. What all of the different implementations have in common, though, is that instructions enter the issue phase and then wait there for an unspecified amount of time until the moment is right for them to execute. When they execute, they may do so out of program order.

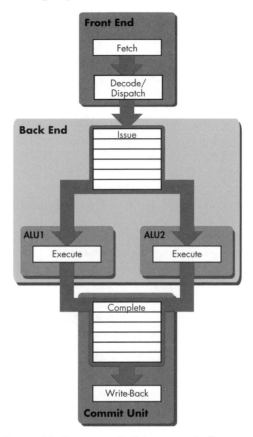

Figure 5-8: Dynamic scheduling using buffers

Aside from its use in dynamic scheduling, another important function of the issue buffer is that it allows the processor to "squeeze" bubbles out of the pipeline prior to the execution phase. The buffer is a queue, and instructions that enter it drop down into the bottommost available entry.

Table 5-3: Phases of a Dynamically Scheduled Instruction's Lifecycle

1	Fetch	In order
2	Decode/dispatch	
3	Issue	Reorder
4	Execute	Out of order
5	Complete	Reorder
6	Write-back (commit)	In order

So if an instruction is preceded by a pipeline bubble, when it enters the issue buffer, it will drop down into the empty space directly behind the instruction ahead of it, thereby eliminating the bubble.

Of course, the issue buffer's ability to squeeze out pipeline bubbles depends on the front end's ability to produce more instructions per cycle than the back end can consume. If the back end and front end move in lock step, the pipeline bubbles will propagate through the issue queues into the back end.

The Completion Phase

The second phase that out-of-order execution adds to an instruction's lifecycle is the *completion phase*. In this phase, instructions that have finished executing, or *completed execution*, wait in a second buffer to have their results written back to the register file *in program order*. When an instruction's results are written back to the register file and the programmer-visible machine state is permanently altered, that instruction is said to *commit*. Instructions must commit in program order if the illusion of sequential execution is to be maintained. This means that no instruction can commit until all of the instructions that were originally ahead of it in the code stream have committed.

The requirement that all instructions must commit in their original program order is what necessitates the second buffer shown in Figure 5-8. The processor needs a place to collect instructions as they complete the out-of-order execution phase of their lifecycle, so that they can be put back in their original order before being sent to the final write stage, where they're committed. Like the issue buffer described earlier, this completion buffer can take a number of forms. We'll look at the form that this buffer takes in the P6 shortly.

I stated previously that an instruction sits in the completion phase's buffer, which I'll call the *completion buffer* for now, and waits to have its result written back to the register file. But where does the instruction's result wait during this interim period? When an instruction is executed out of order, its result goes into a special rename register that has been allocated especially for use by that instruction. Note that this rename register is part of the processor's internal bookkeeping apparatus, which means it is not a part of the programming model and is therefore not visible to the programmer. The result waits in this hidden rename register until the instruction commits, at which time the result is written from the rename register into the programmer-visible architectural register file. After the instruction's result is committed, the rename register then goes back into the pool of available rename registers, where it can be assigned to another instruction on a later cycle.

The P6's Issue Phase: The Reservation Station

The P6 microarchitecture feeds each newly decoded instruction into a buffer called the *reservation station (RS)*, where it waits until all of its execution requirements are met. Once they've been met, the instruction then moves out of the reservation station into an execution unit (i.e., it is issued), where it executes.

A glance at the P6 diagram (Figure 5-6) shows that up to three instructions per cycle can be dispatched from the decoders into the reservation station. And as you'll see shortly, up to five instructions per cycle can be issued from the reservation station into the execution units. Thus the Pentium's original superscalar design, in which two instructions per cycle could dispatch from the decoders directly into the back end, has been replaced with a buffered design in which three instructions can dispatch into the buffer and five instructions can issue out of it on any given cycle.

This buffering action, and the decoupling of the front end's fetch/decode bandwidth from the back end's execution bandwidth that it enables, are at the heart of the P6's performance gains.

The P6's Completion Phase: The Reorder Buffer

Because the P6 microarchitecture must commit its instructions in order, it needs a place to keep track of the original program order of each instruction that enters the reservation station. Therefore, after the instructions are decoded, they must travel through the *reorder buffer (ROB)* before flowing into the reservation station. The ROB is like a large logbook in which the P6 can record all the essential information about each instruction that enters the out-of-order back end. The primary function of the ROB is to ensure that instructions come out the other side of the out-of-order back end in the same order in which they entered it. In other words, it's the reservation station's job to see that instructions are executed in the most optimal order, even if that means executing them out of program order. It's the reorder buffer's job to ensure that the finished instructions get put back in program order and that their results are written to the architectural register file in the proper sequence. To this end, the ROB stores data about each instruction's status, operands, register needs, original place in the program, and so on.

So newly decoded instructions flow into the ROB, where their relevant information is logged in one of 40 available entries. From there, they pass on to the reservation station, and then on to the back end. Once they're done executing, they wait in the ROB until they're ready to be committed.

The role I've just described for the reorder buffer should be familiar to you at this point. The reorder buffer corresponds to the structure that I called the *completion buffer* earlier, but with a few extra duties assigned to it.

If you look at my diagram of the P6 microarchitecture, you'll notice that the reorder buffer is depicted in two spots: the front end and the commit unit. This is because the ROB is active in both of these phases of the instruction's lifecycle. The ROB is tasked with tracking instructions as they move through the phases of their lifecycle and with putting the instructions back in program order at the end of their lifecycle. So newly decoded instructions must be given a tracking entry in the ROB and have a temporary rename register allocated for their private use. Similarly, newly executed instructions must wait in the ROB before they can commit by having the contents of the temporary rename register that holds their result permanently written to the architectural register file.

As implied in the previous sentence, not only does the P6's ROB act as a completion buffer and an instruction tracker, but it also handles register renaming. Each of the P6 microarchitecture's 40 ROB entries has a *data field* that holds program data just like an *x*86 register. These fields give the P6's back end 40 microarchitectural rename registers to work with, and they're used in combination with the P6's *register allocation table (RAT)* to implement register renaming in the P6 microarchitecture.

The Instruction Window

The reservation station and the reorder buffer together make up the heart of the P6's out-of-order back end, and they account for its drastic clock-for-clock performance advantage over the original Pentium. These two buffers—the one for reshuffling and optimizing the code stream (the RS) and the other for unshuffling and reordering the code stream (the ROB)—enable the P6 processor to dynamically and intelligently adapt its operation to fit the needs of the ever-changing code stream.

A common metaphor for thinking about and talking about the P6's RS + ROB combination, or analogous structures on other processors, is that of an instruction window. The P6's ROB can track up to 40 instructions in various stages of execution, and its reservation station can hold and examine up to 20 instructions to determine the optimal time for them to execute. Think of the reservation station's 20-instruction buffer as a window that moves along the sequentially ordered code stream; on any given cycle, the P6 is looking through this window at that visible segment of the code stream and thinking about how its hardware can optimally execute the 20 or so instructions that it sees there.

A good analogy for this is the game of Tetris, where a small preview window shows you the next piece that will come your way while you're deciding how best to place the currently falling piece. Thus at any given moment, you can see a total of two Tetris pieces and think about how those two should fit with the pieces that have gone before and those that might come after.

The P6 microarchitecture's job is a little harder than the average Tetris player's, because it must maneuver and optimally place as many as three falling pieces at a time; hence it needs to be able to see farther ahead into the future in order to make the best decisions about what to place where and when. The P6's wider instruction window allows the processor to look further ahead in the code stream and to juggle its instructions so that they fit together with the currently available execution resources in the optimal manner.

The P6 Pipeline

The P6 has a 12-stage pipeline that's considerably longer than the Pentium's five-stage pipeline. I won't enumerate and describe all 12 stages individually, but I will give a general overview of the phases that the P6's pipeline passes through.

BTB access and instruction fetch

The first three-and-a-half pipeline stages are dedicated to accessing the branch target buffer and fetching the next instruction. The P6's two-cycle instruction fetch phase is longer than the Pentium's one-cycle fetch phase, but it keeps the L1 cache access latency from holding back the clock speed of the processor as a whole.

Decode

The next two-and-a-half stages are dedicated to decoding x86 instructions and breaking them down into the P6's internal, RISC-like instruction format. We'll discuss this instruction set translation, which takes place in all modern x86 processors and even in some RISC processors, in more detail shortly.

Register rename

This stage takes care of register renaming and logging instructions in the ROB.

Write to RS

Writing instructions from the ROB into the RS takes one cycle, and it occurs in this stage.

Read from RS

At this point, the issue phase of the instruction's lifecycle is under way. Instructions can sit in the RS for an unspecified number of cycles before being read from the RS. Even if they're read from the RS immediately after entering it, it takes one cycle to move instructions out of the RS, through the *issue ports* and into the execution units.

Execute

Instruction execution can take one cycle, as in the case of simple integer instructions, or multiple cycles, as in the case of floating-point instructions.

Commit

These two final cycles are dedicated to writing the results of the instruction execution back into the ROB, and then committing the instructions by writing their results from the ROB into the architectural register file.

Lengthening the P6's pipeline as described in this chapter has two primary beneficial effects. First, it allows Intel to crank up the processor's clock speed, since each of the stages is shorter and simpler and can be completed quicker. The second effect is a little more subtle and less widely appreciated.

The P6's longer pipeline, when combined with its buffered decoupling of fetch/decode bandwidth from execution bandwidth, allows the processor to hide hiccups in the fetch and decode stages. In short, the nine pipeline stages that lie ahead of the execute stage combine with the RS to form a deep buffer for instructions. This buffer can hide gaps and hang-ups in the flow of instructions in much the same way that a large water reservoir can hide interruptions in the flow of water to a facility.

But on the downside (to continue the water reservoir example), when one dead animal is spotted floating in the reservoir, the whole thing has to be flushed. This is sort of the case with the P6 and a branch misprediction.

Branch Prediction on the P6

The P6's architects expended considerably more resources than its predecessor on branch prediction and managed to boost dynamic branch prediction accuracy from the Pentium's approximately 75 percent rate to upwards of 90 percent. The P6 has a 512-entry BHT + BTB, and it uses four bits to record branch history information (compared to the Pentium's two-bit predictor). The four-bit prediction scheme allows the Pentium to store more of each branch's history, thereby increasing its ability to correctly predict branch outcomes.

As you learned in Chapter 2, branch prediction gets more important as pipelines get longer, because a pipeline flush due to a misprediction means more lost cycles and a longer recovery time for the processor's instruction throughput and completion rate.

Consider the case of a conditional branch whose outcome depends on the result of an integer calculation. On the original Pentium, the calculation happens in the fourth pipeline stage, and if the branch prediction unit (BPU) has guessed incorrectly, only three cycles worth of work would be lost in the pipeline flush. On the P6, though, the conditional calculation isn't performed until stage 10, which means 10 cycles worth of work get flushed if the BPU guesses incorrectly.

When a dynamically scheduled processor executes instructions speculatively, those speculative instructions and their results are stored in the ROB just like non-speculative instructions. However, the ROB entries for the speculative instructions are marked as speculative and prevented from committing until the branch condition is evaluated. When the branch condition has been evaluated, if the BPU guessed correctly, the speculative instructions' ROB entries are marked as non-speculative, and the instructions are committed in order. If the BPU guessed incorrectly, the speculative instructions and their results are deleted from the ROB without being committed.

The P6 Back End

The P6's back end (illustrated in Figure 5-9) is significantly wider than that of the Pentium. Like the Pentium, it contains two asymmetrical integer ALUs and a separate floating-point unit, but its load-store capabilities have been beefed up to include three execution units devoted solely to memory accesses: a *load address unit*, a *store address unit*, and a *store data unit*. The load address and store address units each contain a pair of four-input adders for calculating addresses and checking segment limits; these are the adders that show up in the decode-1 stage of the original Pentium.

The asymmetrical integer ALUs on the P6 have single-cycle throughput and latency for most operations, with multiplication having single-cycle throughput but four-cycle latency. Thus, multiply instructions execute faster on the P6 than on the Pentium.

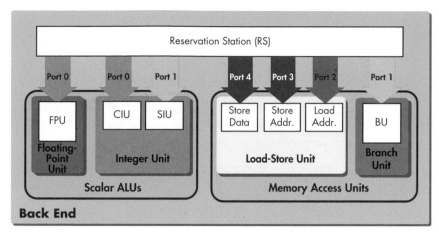

Figure 5-9: The P6 back end

The P6's floating-point unit executes most single- and double-precision operations in three cycles, with five cycles needed for multiply instructions. The FPU is fully pipelined for most instructions, so that most instructions execute with a single-cycle throughput. Some instructions, like floating-point division and square root, are not pipelined and take 18 to 38 and 29 to 69 cycles, respectively.

From the present overview's perspective, the most noteworthy feature of the P6's back end is that its execution units are attached to the reservation station via five issue ports, as shown in Figure 5-9.

This means that up to five instructions per cycle can pass from the reservation station through the issue ports and into the execution units. This five–issue port structure is one of the most recognizable features of the P6, and when later designs (like the PII) added execution units to the microarchitecture (like MMX units), they had to be added on the existing issue ports.

If you looked closely at the Pentium Pro diagram, you probably noticed that there were already two units that shared a single port in the original Pentium Pro: the simple integer unit and the floating-point unit. This means that there are some restrictions on issuing a second integer computation and a floating-point computation, but these restrictions rarely affect performance.

CISC, RISC, and Instruction Set Translation

Like the original Pentium, the P6 spends extra time in the decode phase, but this time, the extra cycle and a half goes not to address calculations but to *instruction set translation*. ISA translation is an important technique used in many modern processors, but before you can understand how it works you must first become acquainted with two terms that often show up in computer architecture discussions: RISC and CISC.

One of the most important ways in which the *x*86 ISA differs from that of both the PowerPC ISA (described in the next chapter) and the hypothetical DLW ISA presented in Chapter 2 is that it supports register-to-memory and memory-to-memory format arithmetic instructions. On the DLW architecture, source and destination operands for every arithmetic instruction had to be either registers or immediate values, and it was the programmer's responsibility to include in the program the load and store instructions necessary to ensure that the arithmetic instructions' source registers were populated with the correct values from memory and their results written back to memory. On the *x86* architecture, the programmer can voluntarily surrender control of most load-store traffic to the processor by using source and/or destination operands that are memory locations. If the DLW architecture supported such operations, they might look like Program 5-2:

Line #	Code	Comments
1	add #12, #13, A	Add the contents of memory locations #12 and #13 and place the result in register A.
2	sub A, #15, #16	Subtract the contents of register A from the contents of memory location #15 and store the result in memory location #16.
3	sub A, #B, #100	Subtract the contents of register A from the contents of the memory location pointed to by #B and store the result in memory location #100.

Program 5-2: Arithmetic instructions using memory-to-memory and memory-to-register formats

Adding the contents of two memory locations, as in line 1 of Program 5-2, still requires the processor to load the necessary values into registers and store the results. However, in memory-to-register and memory-to-memory format instructions, these load and store operations are *implicit* in the instruction. The processor must look at the instruction and figure out that it needs to perform the necessary memory accesses; then it must perform them before and/or after it executes the arithmetic part of the instruction. So for the add in line 1 of Program 5-2, the processor would have to perform two loads before executing the addition. Similarly, for the subtractions in lines 2 and 3, the processor would have to perform one load before executing the subtraction and one store afterwards.

The use of such register-to-memory and memory-to-memory format instructions shifts the burden of scheduling memory traffic from the programmer to the processor, freeing the programmer to focus on other aspects of coding. It also has the effect of reducing the number of instructions that a programmer must write (or *code density*) in order to perform most tasks. In the days when programmers programmed primarily in assembly language, compilers for *high-level languages (HLLs)* like C and FORTRAN were primitive, and main memories were small and expensive, ISA qualities like programmer ease-of-use and high code density were very attractive.

A further technique that ISAs like *x86* use to lessen the burden on programmers and increase code density is the inclusion of ISA-level support for complex data types like *strings*. A string is simply a series, or "string," of contiguous memory locations of a certain length. Strings are often used to store ASCII text, so a short string might store a word, or a longer string might store a whole sentence. If an ISA includes instructions for working with strings—and the x86 ISA does—assembly language programmers can write programs like text editors and terminal applications in a much shorter length of time and with significantly fewer instructions than they could if the ISA lacked such support.

Complex instructions, like the x86 string manipulation instructions, carry out complex, multistep tasks and therefore stand in for what would otherwise be many lines of RISC assembler code. These types of instructions have serious drawbacks, though, when it comes to performing the kind of dynamic scheduling and out-of-order execution described earlier in this chapter. String instructions, for instance, have latencies that can vary with the length of the string being manipulated—the longer the string, the more cycles the instruction takes to execute. Because their latencies are not predictable, it's difficult for the processor to schedule them optimally using the dynamic scheduling mechanisms described previously.

Finally, complex instructions often vary in the number of bytes they need in order to be rendered in machine language. Such variable-length instructions are more difficult to fetch and decode, and once they're decoded, they're more difficult to schedule.

Because of its use of multiple instruction formats (register-to-memory and memory-to-memory) and complex, variable-length instructions, x86 is an example of an approach to processor and ISA design called complex instruction set computing (CISC). Both DLW and PowerPC, in contrast, represent an approach called reduced instruction set computing (RISC), in which all machine language instructions are the same length, fewer instruction formats are supported, and complex instructions are eliminated entirely. RISC ISAs are harder to program for in assembly language, so they assume the existence and widespread use of high-level languages and sophisticated compilers. For RISC programmers who use a high-level language like C, the burden of scheduling memory traffic and handling complex data types shifts from the processor to the compiler. By shifting the burden of scheduling memory accesses and other types of code to the compiler, processors that implement RISC ISAs can be made less complex, and because they're less complex, they can be faster and more efficient.

It would be nice if x86, which is far and away the world's most popular ISA, were RISC, but it isn't. The x86 ISA is a textbook example of a CISC ISA, and that means processors that implement x86 require more complicated microarchitectures. At some point, x86 processor designers realized that in order to use the latest RISC-oriented dynamic scheduling techniques to speed x86-based architectures without the processor's complexity spinning out of control, they'd have to limit the added complexity to the front end by translating x86 CISC operations into smaller, faster, more uniform RISC-like operations for use in the back end. AMD's K6 and Intel's P6 were two early x86 designs that used this type of instruction set translation to great advantage. The technique was so successful that all subsequent x86 processors from both Intel and AMD have used instruction set translation, as have some RISC processors like IBM's PowerPC 970.

The P6 Microarchitecture's Instruction Decoding Unit

The P6 microarchitecture breaks down complex, variable-length *x*86 instructions into one or more smaller, fixed-length *micro-operations* (aka *micro-ops*, *μops*, or *uops*) using a decoding unit that consists of three separate decoders, depicted in Figure 5-10: two simple/fast decoders, which handle simple *x*86 instructions and can produce one decoded micro-op per cycle; and one complex/slow decoder, which handles the more complex *x*86 instructions and can produce up to four decoded micro-ops per cycle.

Sixteen-byte groups of architected *x*86 instructions are fetched from the I-cache into the front end's 32-byte instruction queue, where predecoding logic first identifies each instruction's boundaries and type before aligning the instructions for entry into the decoding hardware. Up to three *x*86 instructions per cycle can then move from the instruction queue into the decoders, where they're converted to micro-ops and passed into a micro-op queue before going to the ROB. Together, the P6's three decoders are capable of producing up to six decoded micro-ops per cycle (four from the complex/slow decoder plus one from each of the two simple/fast decoders) for consumption by the micro-op queue. The micro-op queue, in turn, is capable of passing up to three micro-ops per cycle into the P6's instruction window.

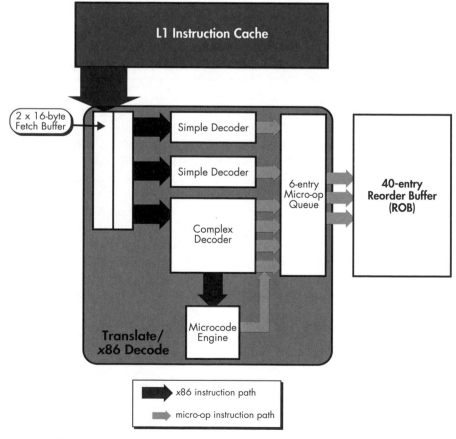

Figure 5-10: The P6 microarchitecture's decoding hardware

Simple *x86* instructions, which can be decoded very rapidly and which break down into only one or two micro-ops, are by far the most common type of instruction found in an average *x86* program. So the P6 dedicates most of its decoding hardware to these types of instructions. More complex *x86* instructions, like string manipulation instructions, are less common and take longer to decode. The P6's complex/slow decoder works in conjunction with the microcode ROM to handle the really complex legacy instructions, which are translated into sequences of micro-ops that are read directly from the ROM.

The Cost of x86 Legacy Support on the P6

All of this decoding and translation hardware takes up a lot of transistors. MDR estimates that close to 40 percent of the P6's transistor budget is spent on *x86* legacy support. If correct, that's even higher than the astonishing 30 percent estimate for the original Pentium, and even if it's incorrect, it still suggests that the cost of legacy support is quite high.

At this point, you're probably thinking back to the conclusion of the first part of this chapter, in which I suggested that the relative cost of *x86* support has decreased with successive generations of the Pentium. This is still true, but the trend didn't hold for the first instantiation of the P6 microarchitecture: the original 133 MHz Pentium Pro. The Pentium Pro's L1 cache was a modest 16KB, which was small even by 1995 standards. The chip's designers had to skimp on on-die cache, because they'd spent so much of their transistor budget on the decoding and translation hardware. Comparable RISC processors had two to four times that amount of cache, because less of the die was taken up with front-end logic, so they could use the space for cache.

When the P6 microarchitecture was originally launched in its Pentium Pro incarnation, transistor counts were still relatively low by today's standards. But as Moore's Curves marched on, microprocessor designers went from thinking, "How do we squeeze all the hardware that we'd like to put on the chip into our transistor budget?" to "Now our generous transistor budget will let us do some really nice things!" to "How on earth do we get this many transistors to do useful, performance-enhancing work?"

What really drove the decrease in subsequent generations' costs for *x86* support was the increase in L1 cache sizes and the L2 cache's move onto the die, because the answer to that last question has—until recently—been, "Let's add cache."

Summary: The P6 Microarchitecture in Historical Context

This concluding section provides an overview of the P6 microarchitecture in its various incarnations. The main focus here is on fitting everything together and giving you a sense of the big picture of how the P6 evolved. The historical narrative outlined in this section seems, in retrospect, to have unfolded over a much longer length of time than the seven years that it actually took to go from the Pentium Pro to the Pentium 4, but seven years is an eternity in computer time.

The Pentium Pro

The processor described in the preceding section under the name *P6* is the original, 133 MHz Pentium Pro. As you can see from the processor comparison in Table 5-2, the Pentium Pro was relatively short on transistors, short on cache, and short on features. In fact, the original Pentium eventually got rudimentary SIMD computing support in the form of Intel's MMX (Multimedia Extensions), but the Pentium Pro didn't have enough room for that, so SIMD got jettisoned in favor of all that fancy decoding logic described earlier.

In spite of all its shortcomings, though, the Pentium Pro did manage to raise the *x*86 performance bar significantly. Its out-of-order execution engine, dual integer pipelines, and improved floating-point unit gave it enough oomph to get the *x*86 ISA into the commodity server market.

The Pentium II

MMX didn't make a return to the Intel product line until the Pentium II. Introduced in 1997, this next generation of the P6 microarchitecture debuted at speeds ranging from 233 to 300 MHz and sported a number of performance-enhancing improvements over its predecessor.

First among these improvements was an on-die, split L1 cache that was doubled in size to 32KB. This larger L1 helped boost performance across the board by keeping the PII's lengthy pipeline full of code and data.

The P6's basic pipeline stayed the same in the PII, but Intel widened the back end as depicted in Figure 5-11 by adding the aforementioned MMX support in the form of two new MMX execution units: one on issue port 0 and the other on issue port 1. MMX provided vector support for integers only, though. It wasn't until the introduction of Streaming SIMD Extensions (SSE) with the PIII that the P6 microarchitecture got support for floating-point vector processing.

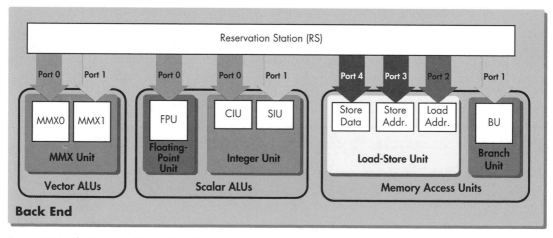

Figure 5-11: The Pentium II's back end

The Pentium II's integer and floating-point performance was relatively good compared to its CISC competitors, and it helped further the trend, started by the Pentium Pro, of x86 commodity hardware's migration into the server and workstation realms. However, the PII still couldn't stand up to RISC designs built on the same process with similar transistor counts. Its main advantage was in bang for the buck, whereas the more expensive RISC chips specialized in pure bang.

The Pentium III

Intel introduced its next P6 derivative, the Pentium III (PIII), in 1999 at 450 MHz on a 0.25 micron manufacturing process. The first version of the Pentium III, code-named *Katmai*, had a 512KB off-die L2 cache that shared a small piece of circuit board (called a *daughtercard*) with the PIII. While this design offered fair performance, the PIII didn't really begin to take off from a performance standpoint until the introduction of the next version of the PIII, code-named *Coppermine*, in early 2000.

Coppermine was produced on a 0.18 micron manufacturing process, which means that Intel could pack more transistors onto the processor die. Intel took advantage of this capability by reducing the PIII's L2 cache size to 256KB and moving the cache onto the CPU die itself. Having the L2 on the same die as both the CPU and the L1 cache dramatically reduced the L2 cache's access time, a fact that more than made up for the reduction in cache size. Coppermine's performance scaled well with increases in clock speed, eventually passing the 1 GHz milestone shortly after AMD's Athlon.

The Pentium III processor introduced two significant additions to the x86 ISA, the most important of which was a set of floating-point SIMD extensions to the x86 architecture called Streaming SIMD Extensions (SSE). With the addition of SSE's 70 new instructions, the x86 architecture completed much more of what had been lacking in its support for vector computing, making it more attractive for applications like games and digital signal processing. I'll cover the MMX and SSE extensions in more detail in Chapter 8, but for now it's necessary to say a word about how the extensions were implemented in hardware.

The Pentium III's designers added the majority of the new SSE hardware on issue port 1 (see the back end in Figure 5-12). The new SSE units attached to port 1 handle vector SIMD addition, shuffle, and reciprocal arithmetic functions. Intel also modified the FPU on port 0 to handle SSE multiplies. Thus the Pentium III's main FPU functional block is responsible for both scalar and vector operations.

The PIII also introduced the infamous *processor serial number (PSN)*, along with new x86 instructions aimed at reading the number. The PSN was a unique serial number that marked each processor, and it was intended for use in securing online commercial transactions. However, due to concerns from privacy advocates, the PSN was eventually dropped from the Pentium line.

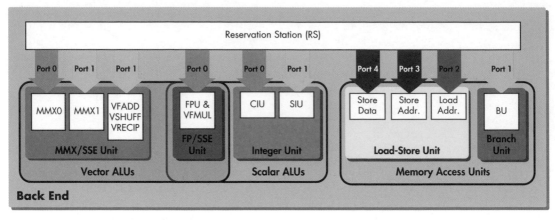

Figure 5-12: The Pentium III's back end

Conclusion

The Pentium may not have outperformed its RISC contemporaries, but it was superior enough to its *x*86-based competition to keep Intel comfortably in command of the commodity PC market. Indeed, prior to the rise of Advanced Micro Devices (AMD) as a serious competitor, Intel had the luxury of setting the pace of progress in the *x*86 PC space. Products were released when Intel was ready to release them, and clock speeds climbed when Intel was ready for them to climb. Intel's competitors were left to respond to what the larger chipmaker was doing, with their own *x*86 products always lagging significantly behind Intel's in performance and popularity.

AMD's Athlon was the first *x*86 processor to pose any sort of threat to Intel's technical dominance, and by the time the PIII made its debut in 1999, it was clear that Intel and AMD were locked in a "gigahertz race" to see who would be the first to introduce a processor with a 1 GHz clock speed. The P6 microarchitecture in its PIII incarnation was Intel's horse in this race, and that basic design eventually reached the 1 GHz mark shortly after AMD's Athlon. Thus a microarchitecture that started out at 150 MHz eventually carried *x*86 beyond 1 GHz and into the lucrative server and workstation markets that RISC architectures had traditionally dominated.

The gigahertz race had a profound effect not only on the commodity PC market but also on the Pentium line itself, insofar as the next chip to bear the Pentium name—the Pentium 4—bore the marks of the gigahertz race stamped into its very architecture. If Intel learned anything in those last few years of the P6's life, it learned that clock speed sells, and it kept that lesson foremost in its mind when it designed the Pentium 4's NetBurst microarchitecture. (For more on the Pentium 4, see Chapters 7 and 8.)

6

POWERPC PROCESSORS: 600 SERIES, 700 SERIES, AND 7400

Now that you've been introduced to the first half of Intel's Pentium line in the previous chapter, this chapter will focus on the origins and development of another popular family of microprocessors: the PowerPC (or PPC) line of processors produced from the joint efforts of Apple, IBM, and Motorola. Because the PowerPC family of processors is extremely large and can be found in an array of applications that ranges from mainframes to desktop PCs to routers to game consoles, this chapter's coverage of PowerPC will present only a small and limited sample of the processors that implement the PowerPC ISA. Specifically, this chapter will focus exclusively on a subset of the PowerPC chips that have been shipped in Apple products, because these chips are the most directly comparable to the Pentium line in that they're aimed at the "personal computer" market.

A Brief History of PowerPC

The PowerPC architecture has its roots in two separate architectures. The first of these is an architecture called POWER (Performance Optimization With Enhanced RISC), IBM's RISC architecture developed for use in mainframes and servers. The second is Motorola's 68000 (aka the 68K) processor, which prior to PowerPC, formed the core of Apple's desktop computing line.

To make a long story very short, IBM needed a way to turn POWER into a wider range of computing products for use outside the server closet, Motorola needed a high-end RISC microprocessor in order to compete in the RISC workstation market, and Apple needed a CPU for its personal computers that would be both cutting-edge and backward compatible with the 68K.

Thus the AIM (Apple, IBM, Motorola) alliance was born, and with it was also born a subset of the POWER architecture dubbed PowerPC. PowerPC processors were to be jointly designed and produced by IBM and Motorola with input from Apple, and were to be used in Apple computers and in the embedded market. The AIM alliance has since passed into history, but PowerPC lives on, not only in Apple computers but in a whole host of different products that use PowerPC-based chips from Motorola and IBM.

The PowerPC 601

In 1993, AIM kicked off the PowerPC party by releasing the 32-bit PowerPC 601 at an initial speed of 66 MHz. The 601, which was based on IBM's older RISC Single Chip (RSC) processor and was originally designed to serve as a "bridge" between POWER and PowerPC, combines parts of IBM's POWER architecture with the 60*x* bus developed by Motorola for use with their 88000. As a bridge, the 601 supports a union of the POWER and PowerPC instruction sets, and it enabled the first PowerPC application writers to easily make the transition from the older ISA to the newer.

NOTE   *The term* 32-bit *may be unfamiliar to you at this point. If you're curious about what it means, you might want to skip ahead and skim the chapter on 64-bit computing, Chapter 9.*

Table 6-1 summarizes the features of the PowerPC 601.

Table 6-1: Features of the PowerPC 601

Introduction Date	March 14, 1994
Process	0.60 micron
Transistor Count	2.8 million
Die Size	121 mm^2
Clock Speed at Introduction	60–80 MHz
Cache Sizes	32KB unified L1
First Appeared In	Power Macintosh 6100/60

Even though the joint IBM-Motorola team in Austin, Texas had only 12 months to get this chip off the ground, it was a very nice and full-featured RISC design for its time.

The 601's Pipeline and Front End

In the previous chapter, you learned how complex the different Pentiums' front ends and pipelines tend to be. There is none of that with the 601, which has a classic four-stage RISC integer pipeline:

1. Fetch
2. Decode/dispatch
3. Execute
4. Write-back

The fact that PowerPC's RISC instructions are all the same size means that the 601's instruction fetch logic doesn't have the instruction alignment headaches that plague *x*86 designs, and thus the fetch hardware is simpler and faster. Back when transistor budgets were tight, this kind of thing could make a big difference in performance, power consumption, and cost.

The PowerPC Instruction Queue

As you can see in Figure 6-1, up to eight instructions per cycle can be fetched directly into an eight-entry *instruction queue (IQ)*, where they are decoded before being dispatched to the back end. Get used to seeing the instruction queue, because it shows up in some form in every single PPC model that we'll discuss in this book, all the way down to the PPC 970.

The instruction queue is used mainly for detecting and dealing with branches. The 601's branch unit scans the bottom four entries of the queue, identifying branch instructions and determining what type they are (conditional, unconditional, etc.). In cases where the branch unit has enough information to resolve the branch immediately (e.g., in the case of an unconditional branch, or a conditional branch whose condition depends on information that's already in the condition register), the branch instruction is simply deleted from the instruction queue and replaced with the instruction located at the branch target.

NOTE *The PowerPC condition register is the analog of the processor status word on the Pentium. We'll discuss the condition register in more detail in Chapter 10.*

This branch-elimination technique, called *branch folding*, speeds performance in two ways. First, it eliminates an instruction (the branch) from the code stream, which frees up dispatch bandwidth for other instructions. Second, it eliminates the single-cycle pipeline bubble that usually occurs immediately after a branch. All of the PowerPC processors covered in this chapter perform branch folding.

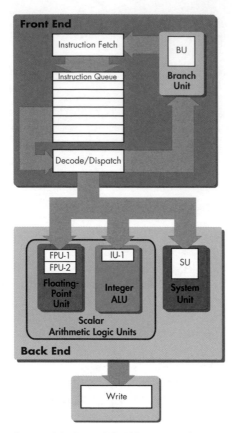

Figure 6-1: PowerPC 601 microarchitecture

If the branch unit determines that the branch is not taken, it allows the branch to propagate to the bottom of the queue, where the dispatch logic simply deletes it from the code stream. The act of allowing not-taken branches to fall out of the instruction queue is called *fall-through*, and it happens on all the PowerPC processors covered in this book.

Non-branch instructions and branch instructions that are not folded sit in the instruction queue while the dispatch logic examines the four bottommost entries to see which three of them it can send off to the back end on the next cycle. The dispatch logic can dispatch up to three instructions per cycle out of order from the bottom four queue entries, with a few restrictions, of which one is the most important for our immediate purposes: Integer instructions can be dispatched only from the bottommost queue entry.

Instruction Scheduling on the 601

Notice that the 601 has no equivalent to the Pentium Pro's reorder buffer (ROB) for keeping track of the original program order. Instead, instructions are tagged with what amounts to metadata so that the write-back logic can commit the results to the register file in program order. This technique of tagging instructions with program-order metadata works fine for a simple, statically scheduled design like the 601 with a very small number of in-flight instructions. But later, dynamically scheduled PPC designs would require dedicated structures for tracking larger numbers of in-flight instructions and making sure that they commit their results in order.

The 601's Back End

From the dispatch stage, instructions go into the 601's back end, where they're executed by each of three different execution units: the integer unit, the floating-point unit, or the branch unit. Let's take a look at each of these units in turn.

The Integer Unit

The 601's 32-bit integer unit is a straightforward fixed-point ALU that is responsible for all of the integer math—including address calculations—on the chip. While x86 designs, like the original Pentium, need extra address adders to keep all of the address calculations associated with x86's multiplicity of addressing modes from tying up the back end's integer hardware, the 601's RISC, load-store memory model means that it can feasibly handle memory traffic and regular ALU traffic with a single integer execution unit.

So the 601's integer unit handles the following memory-related functions, most of which are moved off into a dedicated load-store unit in subsequent PPC designs:

- integer and floating-point load-address calculations
- integer and floating-point store-address calculations
- integer and floating-point load-data operations
- integer store-data operations

Cramming all of these load-store functions into the 601's single integer ALU doesn't exactly help the chip's integer performance, but it is good enough to keep up with the Pentium in this area, even though the Pentium has two integer ALUs. Most of this integer performance parity probably comes from the 601's huge 32KB unified L1 cache (compare that to the Pentium's 8KB split L1), a luxury afforded the 601 by the relative simplicity of its front-end decoding hardware.

A final point worth noting about the 601's integer unit is that multi-cycle integer instructions (e.g., integer multiplies and divides) are not fully pipelined. When an instruction that takes, say, five cycles to execute entered the IU, it ties up the entire IU for the whole five cycles. Thankfully, the most common integer instructions are single-cycle instructions.

The Floating-Point Unit

With its single floating-point unit, which handles all floating-point calculations and store-address operations, the 601 was a very strong performer when it was first launched.

The 601's floating-point pipeline is six stages long, and includes the four basic stages outlined earlier in this chapter, but with an extra decode stage and an extra execute stage. What really sets the chip's floating-point hardware apart when compared to its contemporaries is the fact that not only are almost all single-precision operations fully pipelined, but most double-precision (64-bit) floating-point operations are as well. This means that for single-precision operations (with the exception of divides) and most double-precision operations, the 601's floating-point hardware can turn out one instruction per cycle with a two-cycle latency.

Another great feature of the 601's FPU is its ability to do single-precision fused multiply-add (`fmadd`) instructions with single-cycle throughput. The `fmadd` is a core digital signal processing (DSP) and scientific computing function, so the 601's fast `fmadd` capabilities make it well suited to these types of applications. This single-cycle `fmadd` capability is actually a significant feature of the entire PowerPC computing line, from the 601 on down to the present day, and it is one reason why these processors have been so popular for media and scientific applications.

Another factor in the 601's floating-point dominance is that its integer unit handles all of the memory traffic (with the FPU providing the data for floating-point stores). This means that during long stretches of floating-point–only code, the integer unit acts like a dedicated load-store unit (LSU), whose sole purpose is to keep the FPU fed with data.

Such an FPU + LSU combination performs well for two reasons: First, integer and floating-point code are rarely mixed, so it doesn't matter for performance if the integer unit is tied up with floating-point–related memory traffic. Second, floating-point code is often data-intensive, with lots of loads and stores, and thus high levels of memory traffic to keep a dedicated LSU busy.

When you combine both of these factors with the 601's hefty 32KB L1 cache and its ability to do single-cycle fused multiply-adds at a rate of one per clock, you have a floating-point force to be reckoned with in 1994 terms.

The Branch Execution Unit

The 601's branch unit (BU) works in combination with the instruction fetcher and the instruction queue to steer the front end of the processor through the code stream by executing branch instructions and predicting branches. Regarding the latter function, the 601's BU uses a simple static branch predictor to predict conditional branches. I'll talk a bit more about branch prediction and speculative execution in covering the 603e in "The PowerPC 603 and 603e" on page 118.

The Sequencer Unit

The 601 contains a peculiar holdover from the IBM RSC called the sequencer unit. The *sequencer unit*, which I'll admit is a bit of a mystery to me, appears to be a small, CISC-like processor with its own 18-bit instruction set, 32-word RAM, microcode ROM, register file, and execution unit, all of which are embedded on the 601. Its purpose is to execute some legacy instructions particular to the older RSC; to take care of housekeeping chores like self-test, reset, and initialization functions; and to handle exceptions, interrupts, and errors.

The inclusion of the sequencer unit on the 601 is quite obviously the result of the time crunch that the 601 team faced in bringing the first PowerPC chip to market; IBM admitted this much in its 601 white paper. The team started with IBM's RSC as its basis and began redesigning it to implement the PowerPC ISA. Instead of throwing out the sequencer unit, a component that played a major role in the functioning of the original RSC, IBM simply scaled back its size and functionality for use in the 601.

I don't have any exact figures, but I think it's safe to say that this embedded subprocessor unit took up a decent amount of die space on the 601 and that the design team would have thrown it out if it had had more time. Subsequent PowerPC processors, which didn't have to worry about RSC legacy support, implemented all of the (non–RSC-related) functions of the 601's sequencer unit by spreading them out into other functional blocks.

Latency and Throughput Revisited

On superscalar processors like the 601 and its more modern counterparts, different instructions take different numbers of cycles to pass through the processor. Different execution units often have different pipeline depths, and even within one execution unit, different instructions sometimes take different numbers of cycles. Regarding this latter case, one instruction can take longer to pass through an ALU than another instruction, either because the instruction has a mandatory stall in a certain stage or because the particular *subunit* that is handling the instruction has a longer pipeline than the other subunits that together make up the ALU. This being the case, it no longer makes sense for us to simplistically treat instruction latency as a property of the processor as a whole. Rather, instruction latency is actually a matter of the individual instruction, so our discussion will reflect that from now on.

Earlier, we defined an instruction's latency as the minimum number of cycles that an instruction must spend in the execution phase. Here are the latencies of some commonly used PowerPC instructions on the PowerPC G4, a processor that we'll discuss in "The PowerPC 7400 (aka the G4)" on page 133:

Mnemonic	Cycles to Execute
add	1
and	1
cmp	1
divw	19
mul	6

Notice that most of the instructions take only one cycle to execute, while a few, like division and multiplication, take more. An integer division for a full word, for example, takes 19 cycles to execute, while a 32-bit multiply takes 6 cycles. This means that the division instruction sits in IU1's integer pipeline for 19 cycles, and during this time, no other instruction can execute in IU1.

Now let's look at the floating-point instruction latencies for the G4:

Mnemonic	Cycles to Execute
fabs	1-1-1
fadd	1-1-1
fdiv	32
fmadd	1-1-1
fmul	1-1-1
fsub	1-1-1

These latencies are listed a bit differently than the integer instruction latencies. The numbers separated by dashes tell how long the instruction spends in each of the FPU's three pipeline stages. Most of the instructions listed spend one cycle in each stage, for a total of three cycles in the G4's FPU pipeline, so if a program is using only these instructions, the FPU can start and finish one instruction on each cycle.

A few instructions, like floating-point division, have only a single number in the latency column. This is because an fdiv ties up the entire floating-point pipeline when executing. While an fdiv is grinding out its 32 cycles in the FPU, no other instructions can execute along with it in the floating-point pipeline. This means that any floating-point instructions that come immediately after the fdiv in the code stream must wait in the instruction queue because they cannot be dispatched while the fdiv is executing.

Summary: The 601 in Historical Context

The 601 could spend a ton of transistors (at least, a ton for its day) on a 32KB cache, because its front end was so much simpler than that of its x86 counterpart, the Intel Pentium. This was a significant advantage to using RISC at that time. The chip made its debut in the PowerMac 6100 to good reviews, and it put Apple in the performance lead over its x86 competition. The 601 was definitive in firmly establishing the cult of Apple as a high-end computer maker.

Nonetheless, the 601 did leave some room for improvement. The sequencer unit that it inherited from its mainframe ancestor took up valuable die space that could have been put to better use. With a little more time to tweak it, the 601 could have been closer to perfect. But near perfection would have to wait for the one-two punch of the 603e and 604.

The PowerPC 603 and 603e

While one team was putting the finishing touches on the 601, another team at IBM's Sommerset Design Center in Austin had already begun working on the 601's successor—the 603. The 603 was a significantly different design than the 601, so it was less of an evolutionary shift than it was a completely different processor. Table 6-2 summarizes the features of the PowerPC 603 and 603e.

Table 6-2: Features of the PowerPC 603 and 603e

	PowerPC 603 Vitals	PowerPC 603e Vitals
Introduction Date	May 1, 1995	October 16, 1995
Process	0.50 micron	0.50 micron
Transistor Count	1.6 million	2.6 million
Die Size	81 mm^2	98 mm^2
Clock Speed at Introduction	75 MHz	100 MHz
L1 Cache Size	16KB split L1	32KB split L1
First Appeared In	Macintosh Performa 5200CD	Macintosh Performa 6300CD

The 603 was designed to run on very little power, because Apple needed a chip for its PowerBook line of laptop computers. As a result, the processor had a very good performance-per-watt ratio on native PowerPC code, and in fact was able to match the 601 in clock-for-clock performance even though it had about half the number of transistors as the older processor. But the 603's smaller 16KB split L1 cache meant that it was pretty bad at emulating the legacy 68K code that formed a large part of Apple's OS and application base.

As a result, the 603 was relegated to the very lowest end of Apple's product line (the Performas, beginning with the 6200, and the all-in-ones designed for the education market, beginning with the 5200), until a tweaked version (the 603e) with an enlarged, 32KB split cache was released. The 603e performed better on emulated 68K code, so it saw widespread use in the PowerBook line.

This section will take a quick look at the microarchitecture of the 603e, illustrated in Figure 6-2, because it was the version of the 603 that saw the most widespread use.

NOTE *The 604 was also released at the same time as the original 603. The 604, which was intended for Apple's high-end products just like the 603e was intended for its low-end products, was yet another brand new design. We'll cover the 604 in "The PowerPC 604" on page 123.*

The 603e's Back End

Like the 601, the 603e sports the classic RISC four-stage pipeline. But unlike the 601, which can decode and dispatch up to three instructions per cycle to any of its execution units—including its branch unit—the 603e has one important restriction that constrains how it uses its dispatch bandwidth of three instructions per cycle.

On the 603e, and on all processors derived from it (the 750 and the 7400/7410), branches that aren't folded or don't fall through are dispatched from the instruction queue to the branch unit over a *dispatch bus* that isn't connected to any of the other execution units. This way, branch instructions don't take up any of the available dispatch bandwidth that feeds the main part of the back end. The 603e and its derivatives can dispatch one branch instruction per cycle to the branch unit over this particular bus.

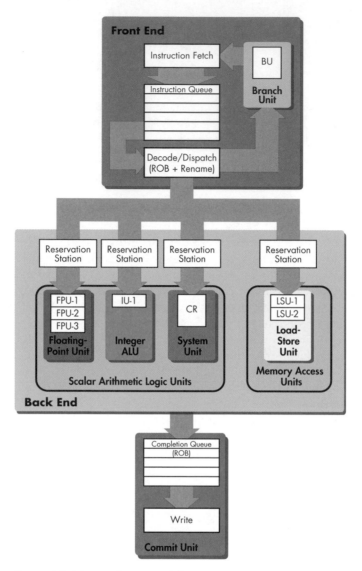

Figure 6-2: Microarchitecture of the PowerPC 603e

Non-branch instructions can dispatch at a rate of up to two instructions per cycle to the back end, which means that the 603 has a maximum dispatch rate of three instructions per cycle (two non-branch + one branch). However, because two non-branch instructions per cycle can dispatch, branch instructions are often ignored when discussing the dispatch rate of the 603 and its successors. Therefore, these processors are often said to have a dispatch rate of up to two instructions per cycle, even though the dispatch rate is *technically* three instructions per cycle.

The 603e's dispatch logic takes a maximum of two non-branch instructions per cycle from the bottom of the instruction queue and passes them to the back end, where they are executed by one of five execution units:

- Integer unit
- Floating-point unit
- Branch unit
- Load-store unit
- System unit

Notice that this list contains two more units than the analogous list for the 601: the load-store unit (LSU) and the *system unit*. The 603e's load-store unit takes over all of the address-calculating labors that the older 601 foisted onto its lone integer ALU. Because the 603e has a dedicated LSU for performing address calculations and executing store-data operations, its integer unit is freed up from having to handle memory traffic and can therefore focus solely on integer arithmetic. This helps improve the 603e's performance on integer code.

The 603e's dedicated system unit also takes over some of the functions of the 601's integer unit, in that it handles updates to the PowerPC condition register. We'll talk more about the condition register in Chapter 10, so don't worry if you don't know what it is. The 603e's system unit also contains a limited integer adder, which can take some of the burden off the integer ALU by doing certain types of addition. (The original 603's system unit lacked this feature.)

The 603e's basic floating-point pipeline differs from that of the 601 in that it has one more execute stage and one less decode stage. Most floating-point instructions have a three-cycle latency (and a one-cycle throughput) on the 603e, compared to a two-cycle latency on the 601. This three-cycle latency/one-cycle throughput design wouldn't be bad at all if it weren't for one serious problem: At its very fastest, the 603e's FPU can only execute three instructions every four cycles. In other words, after every third single-cycle floating-point instruction, there is a mandatory pipeline bubble. I won't get into the reason for this, but the 603e's FPU took a nontrivial hit to performance for this three-instruction/four-cycle design.

The other, perhaps more serious, flaw in the 603e's FPU is that it is not fully pipelined for multiply operations. Double-precision multiplies—and this includes double-precision fmadds—spend two cycles in the execute stage, which means that the 603e's FPU can complete only one double-precision multiply every two cycles.

603e's floating-point unit isn't all bad news, though. It still has the standard PPC ability to do single-precision fmadd operations, with a four-cycle latency and a one-cycle throughput. This fast fmadd ability helped the architecture retain much of its usefulness for DSP, scientific, and media applications, in spite of the aforementioned drawbacks.

The 603e's Front End, Instruction Window, and Branch Prediction

Up to two instructions per cycle can be fetched into the 603e's six-entry instruction queue. From there, a maximum of two instructions per cycle (one fewer than the 601) can be dispatched from the two bottom entries in the IQ to the reservation stations in the 603e's back end.

Not only does the 603e dispatch one fewer instruction per cycle to its back end than the 601 does, but its overall approach to superscalar and out-of-order execution differs from that of the 601 in another way, as well. The 603e uses a dedicated *commit unit*, which contains a five-entry *completion queue* (analogous to the P6's ROB) for keeping track of the program order of in-flight instructions. When instructions execute out of order, the commit unit refers to the information stored in the completion queue and puts the instructions back in program order before committing them.

To use a term that figured prominently in our discussion of the Pentium, the 603 is the first PowerPC processor to feature dynamic scheduling via a full-blown instruction window, complete with a ROB and reservation stations. We'll talk more about the concept of the instruction window and about the structures that make it up (the ROB and the reservation stations) in the next section on the 604. For now, it suffices to say that the 603's instruction window is quite small compared to that of its successors—three of its four reservation stations are only single-entry, and one is double-entry (the one attached to the load-store unit). Because the 603's instruction window is so small, it needs relatively few rename registers to temporarily hold execution results prior to commitment. The 603 has five general-purpose rename registers, four floating-point rename registers, and one rename register each for the condition register (CR), link register (LR), and count register (CTR).

The 603 and 603e follow the 601 in their ability to do speculative execution by means of a simple, static branch predictor. Like the static predictor on the 601, the 603e's predictor marks forward branches as not taken and backward branches as taken. This static branch predictor is simple and fast, but it is only mildly effective compared to even a weakly designed dynamic branch predictor. If PPC users in the 603e/604 era wanted dynamic branch prediction, they had to upgrade to the 604.

Summary: The 603 and 603e in Historical Context

With its stellar performance-per-watt ratio, the 603 was a great little processor, and it would have made a good low- to midrange desktop processor as well if it weren't for Apple's legacy 68K code base. The 603e's tweaks and larger cache size helped with the legacy problems somewhat, but the updated chip still played second fiddle in Apple's product line to the larger, much more powerful 604.

You haven't seen the last of the 603e, though. The 603e's design formed the basis for what would eventually become Motorola's PowerPC 7400—aka the G4—which we'll cover in "The PowerPC 7400 (aka the G4)" on page 133.

The PowerPC 604

At the same time the 603 was making its way toward the market, the 604 was in the works as well. The 604 was to be Apple's high-end PPC desktop processor, so its power and transistor budgets were much higher than that of the 603. Table 6-3 summarizes the 604's features, and a quick glance at a diagram of the 604 (see Figure 6-3) shows some obvious ways that it differs from its lower-end sibling. For example, in the front end, the length of the instruction queue has been increased by two entries. In the back end, two more integer units have been added, and the CR logical unit has been removed. These changes reflect some important differences in the overall approach of the 604, differences that will be examined in greater detail shortly.

Table 6-3: Features of the PowerPC 604 and 604e

	PowerPC 604	PowerPC 604e
Introduction Date	May 1, 1995	July 19, 1996
Process	0.50 micron	0.35 micron
Transistor Count	3.6 million	5.1 million
Die Size	197 mm^2	148 mm^2
Clock Speed at Introduction	120 MHz	180–200 MHz
L1 Cache Size	32KB split L1	64KB split L1
First Appeared In	PowerMac 9500/120	Power Computing PowerTower Pro 200 (PowerMac 9500/180 on August 7, 1996)

The 604's Pipeline and Back End

The 604's pipeline is deeper than that of the 601 and the 603, and it consists of the following six stages:

Four Phases of the Standard RISC Pipeline	Six Stages of the 604's Pipeline
Fetch	1. Fetch
Decode/dispatch	2. Decode
	3. Dispatch (ROB and rename)
Execute	4. Execute
Write-back	5. Complete
	6. Write-back

In the 604, the standard RISC decode/dispatch phase is split into two stages, as is the write-back phase. I'll explain just how these two new pipeline stages work in the section on the instruction window, but for now all you need to understand is that this lengthened pipeline enables the 604 to reach higher clock speeds than its predecessors. Because each pipeline stage is simpler, it takes less time to complete, which means that the CPU's clock cycle time can be shortened.

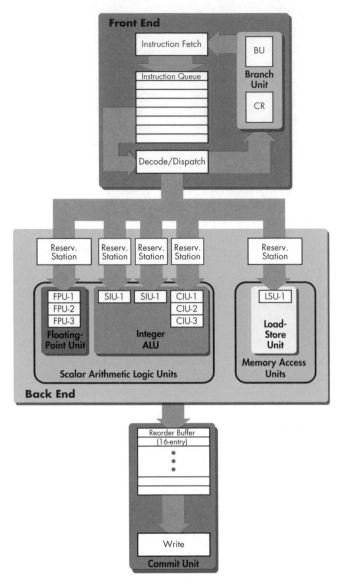

Figure 6-3: PowerPC 604 microarchitecture

Aside from the longer pipeline, another factor that really sets the 604 apart from the other 600-series PPC designs discussed so far is its wider back end. The 604 can execute up to six instructions per clock cycle in the following six execution units:

- Branch unit (BU)/condition register unit (CRU)
- Load-store unit (LSU)
- Floating-point unit (FPU)

- Three integer units (IU)
  - Two simple integer units (SIUs)
  - One complex integer unit (CIU)

Unlike the other 600-series processors, the 604 has multiple integer units. This division of labor, where multiple fast integer units executed simple integer instructions and one slower integer unit execute complex integer instructions, will be discussed in more detail in Chapter 8. Any integer instruction that takes only a single cycle to execute can pass through one of the two SIUs. On the other hand, integer instructions that take multiple cycles to execute, like integer divides, have to pass through the slower CIU.

Like the 603e, the 604 has *register renaming*, a technique that is facilitated by the 12-entry register rename file attached to the 32-entry general-purpose register file. These rename buffers allow the 604's execution units more options for avoiding false dependencies and register-related stalls.

The 604's floating-point unit does most single- and double-precision operations with a three-cycle latency, just like the 603e. Unlike the 603e, though, the 604's floating-point unit is fully pipelined for double-precision multiplies. Floating-point division and two other instructions take from 18 to 33 cycles on the 604, as on the 603e. Finally, the 604's 32-entry floating-point register file is attached to an 8-entry floating-point rename register buffer.

The 604's load-store unit (LSU) is also similar to that of the 603e. Like the 603e's LSU, it contains an adder for doing address calculations and handles all load-store traffic, but unlike the 603e, it's connected to deeper load and store queues and allows a little more flexibility for the optimal reordering of memory operations.

The 604's branch unit also features a dynamic branch prediction scheme that's a vast improvement over the 603e's static branch predictor. The 604 has a large, 512-entry branch history table (BHT) with two bits per entry for tracking branches, coupled with a 64-entry *branch target address cache (BTAC)*, which is the equivalent of the Pentium's BTB.

As always, the more transistors you spend on branch prediction, the better performance is, so the 604's more advanced branch unit helps it quite a bit. Still, in the case of a misprediction, the 604's longer pipeline has to pay a higher price than its shorter-pipelined predecessors in terms of performance. Of course, the bigger performance loss associated with a misprediction is also the reason the 604 needs to spend those extra resources on branch prediction.

Notice that the list of execution units on page 124 is missing a unit that is present on the 603e: the system unit. The 603e's system unit handled updates to the PPC condition register, a function that was handled by the integer execution unit on the older 601. The 604 moves the responsibility of dealing with the condition register onto the branch unit. So the 604's branch unit contains a separate execution unit that handles all logical operations that involve the PowerPC condition register. This condition register unit (CRU) shares a dispatch bus and some other resources with the branch execution unit, so it's not a fully independent execution unit like the 603e's system unit. What does this BU/CRU combination do for performance? It probably doesn't have a huge impact, but whatever impact it does have is significant enough to where the 604's immediate successor—the 604e—adds an independent execution unit to the back end for CR logical operations.

The 604's Front End and Instruction Window

The 604's front end and instruction window look like a combination of the best features of the 601 and the 603e. Like the 601, the 604's instruction queue is eight entries deep. Instructions are fetched from the L1 cache into the instruction queue, where they're decoded before being dispatched to the back end. Branches that can be folded are folded, and the 604's dispatch logic can dispatch up to four instructions per cycle (up from two on the 603e and three on the 601) from the bottom four entries of the instruction queue to the back end's execution units.

During the 604's dispatch stage, rename registers and a reorder buffer entry are assigned to each dispatching instruction. When the instruction is ready to dispatch, it's sent either directly to an execution unit or to an execution unit's reservation station, depending on whether or not its operands are available at the time of dispatch. Note that the 604 can dispatch at most one instruction to each execution unit, and there are certain rules that govern when the dispatch logic can dispatch an instruction to the back end. We'll cover these rules in more detail in a moment, but for now you need to be aware of one of the rules: An instruction cannot dispatch if the execution unit that it needs is not available.

The Issue Phase: The 604's Reservation Stations

In Figure 6-3, you probably noticed that each of the 604's execution units has a reservation station attached to it; this includes a reservation station each (not depicted) for the branch execution and condition register units that make up the branch unit. The 604's reservation stations are relatively small, two-entry (the CIU's reservation station is single-entry), first-in first-out (FIFO) affairs, but they make up the heart of the 604's instruction window, because they allow the instructions assigned to one execution unit to issue out of program order with respect to the instructions that are assigned to the other execution units.

This works as follows: The dispatch stage sends instructions into the reservation stations (i.e., the issue phase) in program order, and, with one important exception (described in the next paragraph), the instructions pass through their respective reservation stations in order. An instruction enters the top of a reservation station, and as the instructions ahead of it issue, it moves down the queue, until it eventually exits through the bottom (i.e., it issues).

Therefore, we can say each instruction issues in order with respect to the other instructions in its same reservation station. However, the various reservation stations can issue instructions at different times, with the result that instructions issue out of order from the perspective of the overall program flow.

The simple integer units function a little differently than described earlier, because they allow instructions to issue from their two-entry reservation stations out of order with respect to the other instructions in their own execution unit. So unlike other types of instructions described previously, integer instructions can move through their respective reservation stations and pipelines out of program order, not just with respect to the overall program flow, but with respect to the other instructions in their own reservation station.

The reservation stations in the 604 and its architectural successors exist to keep instructions that lack their input operand data but are otherwise ready to dispatch from tying up the instruction queue. If an instruction meets all of the other dispatch requirements (see "The Four Rules of Instruction Dispatch"), and if its assigned execution unit is available but it just doesn't yet have access to the part of the data stream that it needs, it dispatches to the appropriate execution unit's reservation station so that the instructions behind it in the instruction queue can move up and be dispatched.

The small size of the 604's reservation stations compared to similar structures on the P6 is due to the fact that the 604's pipeline is relatively short. Pipeline stalls aren't quite as devastating for performance on a machine with a 6-stage pipeline as they are on a machine with a 12-stage pipeline, so the 604 doesn't need as large of an instruction window as its super-pipelined counterparts.

The Four Rules of Instruction Dispatch

Here are the four most important rules governing instruction dispatch on the 604:

The in-order dispatch rule

Before an instruction can dispatch, all of the instructions preceding that instruction must have dispatched. In other words, instructions dispatch from the instruction queue in program order. It is not until instructions have arrived at the reservation stations, where they may issue out of order to the execution units, that the original program order is disrupted.

The issue buffer/execution unit availability rule

Before the dispatch logic can send an instruction to an execution unit's reservation station, that reservation station must have an entry available. If an instruction doesn't need to go to a reservation station because its inputs are available at the time of dispatch, the required execution unit must have a pipeline slot available, and the unit's reservation station must be empty (i.e., there are no older instructions waiting to execute) before the instruction can be sent to the execution unit. (This rule is modified on the PowerPC 7450—aka G4e—and we'll cover the modification in "The PowerPC 7400 (aka the G4)" on page 133.)

The completion buffer availability rule

For an instruction to dispatch, there must be space available in the completion queue so that a new entry can be created for the instruction. Remember, the completion queue (or ROB) keeps track of the program order of each in-flight instruction, so any instruction that enters the out-of-order back end must be logged in the completion queue first.

The rename register availability rule

There must be enough rename registers available to temporarily store the results for each register that the instruction will modify.

If a dispatched instruction meets the requirements imposed by these rules, and if it meets the other more instruction-specific dispatch rules not listed here, it can dispatch from the instruction queue to the back end.

All of the PowerPC processors discussed in this chapter that have reservation stations are subject to (at least) these four dispatch rules, so keep these rules in mind as we talk about instruction dispatch throughout the rest of this chapter. Note that all of the processors—including the 604—have additional rules that govern the dispatch of specific types of instructions, but these four general dispatch rules are the most important.

The Completion Phase: The 604's Reorder Buffer

As with the P6 microarchitecture, the reservation stations aren't the only structures that make up the 604's instruction window. The 604 has a 16-entry reorder buffer (ROB) that performs the same function as the P6 microarchitecture's much larger 40-entry ROB.

The ROB corresponds to the simpler completion queue on older PPC processors. In the dispatch stage, not only are instructions sent to the back end's reservation stations, but entries for the dispatched instructions are allocated an entry in the ROB and a set of rename registers. In the completion stage, the instructions are put back in program order so that their results can be written back to the register file in the subsequent write-back stage. The completion stage corresponds to what I've called the completion phase of an instruction's lifecycle, and the write-back stage corresponds to what I've called the *commit phase*.

The 604's ROB is much smaller than the P6's ROB for the same reason that the 604's reservation stations are fewer: the 604 has a much shallower pipeline, which means that it needs a much smaller instruction window for tracking fewer in-flight instructions in order to achieve the same performance.

The trade-off for this lack of complexity and lower pipeline depth is a lower clock speed. The 6-stage 604 debuted in May 1995 at 120 MHz, while the 12-stage Pentium Pro debuted later that year (November 1995) at speeds ranging from 150 to 200 MHz.

Summary: The 604 in Historical Context

With a 32KB split L1 cache, the 604 had a much heftier cache than its predecessors, which it needed to help keep its deeper pipeline fed. The larger cache, higher dispatch and issue rate, wider back end, and deeper pipeline made for a solid RISC performer that was easily able to keep pace with its *x*86 competitors.

Still, the Pentium Pro was no slouch, and its performance was scaling well with improvements in processor manufacturing techniques. Apple needed more power from AIM to keep the pace, and more power is what they got with a minor microarchitectural revision that came to be called the 604e.

The PowerPC 604e

The 604e built on gains made by the 604 with a few core changes that included a doubling of the L1 cache size (to 32KB instruction/32KB data) and the addition of a new independent execution unit: the *condition register unit (CRU)*.

The previous 600-series processors had moved the responsibility for handling condition register logical operations back and forth among various units (the integer unit in the 601, the system unit in the 603/603e, and the branch unit in the 604). Now with the 604e, these operations got an execution unit of their own. The 604e sported a functional block in its back end that was dedicated to handling condition register logical operations, which meant that these not uncommon operations didn't tie up other execution units—like the integer unit or the branch unit—that had more serious work to do.

The 604e's branch unit, now that it was free from having to handle CR logical operations, got a few expanded capabilities that I won't detail here. The 604e's caches, in addition to being enlarged, also got additional copyback buffers and a handful of other enhancements.

The 604e was ultimately able to scale up to 350 MHz once it moved from a 0.35 to a 0.25 micron manufacturing process, making it a successful part for Apple's budding RISC media workstation line.

The PowerPC 750 (aka the G3)

The PowerPC 750—known to Apple users as the G3—is a design based heavily on the 603/603e. Its four-stage pipeline is the same as that of the 603/603e, and many of the features of its front end and back end will be familiar to you from our discussion of the older processor. Nonetheless, the 750 sports a few very powerful improvements over the 603e that make it faster than even the 604e, as you can see in Table 6-4.

Table 6-4: Features of the PowerPC 750

Introduction Date	September 1997
Process	0.25 micron
Transistor Count	6.35 million
Die Size	67 mm^2
Clock Speed at Introduction	200–300 MHz
Cache Sizes	64KB split L1, 1MB L2
First Appeared In	Power Macintosh G3

The 750's significant improvement in performance over the 603/603e is the result of a number of factors, not the least of which are the improvements that IBM made to the 750's integer and floating-point capabilities.

A quick glance at the 750's layout (see Figure 6-4) reveals that its back end is wider than that of the 603. More specifically, where the 603 has a single integer unit, the 750 has two—a simple integer unit (SIU) and complex integer unit (CIU). The 750's complex integer unit handles all integer instructions, while the simple integer unit handles all integer instructions except multiply and divide. Most of the integer instructions that execute in the SIU are single-cycle instructions.

Like the 603 (and the 604), the 750's floating-point unit can execute all single-precision floating-point operations—including multiply—with a latency of three cycles. And like the 603, early versions of the 750 had to insert a pipeline bubble after every third floating-point instruction in its pipeline; this is fixed in later IBM-produced versions of the 750. Double-precision floating-point operations, with the exception of operations involving multiplication, also take three cycles on the 750. Double-precision multiply and multiply-add operations take four cycles, because the 750 doesn't have a full double-precision FPU.

The 750's load-store unit and system register unit perform the same functions described in the preceding section for the 603, so they don't merit further comment.

The 750's Front End, Instruction Window, and Branch Instruction

The 750 fetches up to four instructions per cycle into its six-entry instruction queue, and it dispatches up to two non-branch instructions per cycle from the IQ's two bottom entries. The dispatch logic follows the four dispatch rules described earlier when deciding when an instruction is eligible to dispatch, and each dispatched instruction is assigned an entry in the 750's six-entry ROB (compare the 603's five-entry ROB).

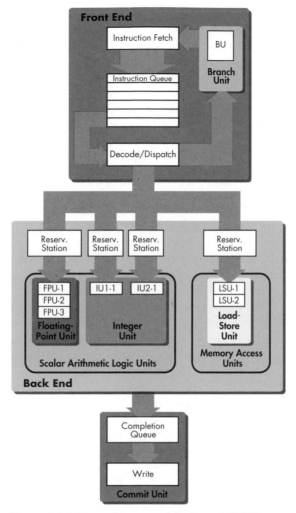

Figure 6-4: Microarchitecture of the PowerPC 750

As on the 603 and 604, newly dispatched instructions enter the reservation station of the execution unit to which they have been dispatched, where they wait for their operands to become available so that they can issue. The 750's reservation station configuration is similar to that of the 603 in that, with the exception of the two-entry reservation station attached to the 750's LSU, all of the execution units have single-entry reservation stations. And like the 603, the 750's branch unit has no reservation station.

Because the 750's instruction window is so small, it has half the rename registers of the 604. Nonetheless, the 750's six general-purpose and six floating-point rename registers still put it ahead of the 603's number of rename registers (five GPRs and four FPRs). Like the 603, the 750 has one rename register each for the CR, LR, and CTR.

You would think that the 750's smaller reservation stations and shorter ROB would put it at a disadvantage with respect to the 604, which has a larger instruction window. But the 750's pipeline is shorter than that of the 604, so it needs fewer buffers to track fewer in-flight instructions. More importantly, though, the 750 has one very clever trick up its sleeve that it uses to keep its pipeline full.

Recall that standard dynamic branch prediction schemes generally use a branch history table (BHT) in combination with a branch target buffer (BTB) to speculate on the outcome of branch instructions and to redirect the processor's front end to a different point in the code stream based on this speculation. The BHT stores information on the past behavior (taken or not taken) of the most recently executes branch instructions, so that the processor can determine whether or not it should take these branches if it encounters them again. The target addresses of recently taken branches are stored in the BTB, so that when the branch prediction hardware decides to speculatively take a branch, it has immediate access to that branch's target address without having to recalculate it. The target address of the speculatively taken branch is loaded from the BTB into the instruction register, so that on the next fetch cycle, the processor can begin fetching and speculatively executing instructions from the target address.

The 750 improves on this standard scheme in a very clever way. Instead of storing only the target addresses of recently taken branches in a BTB, the 750's 64-entry *branch target instruction cache (BTIC)* stores the instruction that is located at the branch's target address. When the 750's branch prediction unit examines the 512-entry BHT and decides to speculatively take a branch, it doesn't have to go to code storage to fetch the first instruction from that branch's target address. Instead, the BPU loads the branch's target instruction directly from the BTIC into the instruction queue, which means that the processor doesn't have to wait around for the fetch logic to go out and fetch the target instruction from code storage. This scheme saves valuable cycles, and it helps keep performance-killing bubbles out of the 750's pipeline.

Summary: The PowerPC 750 in Historical Context

In spite of its short pipeline and small instruction window, the 750 packed quite a punch. It managed to outperform the 604, partially because of a dedicated back-side L2 cache interface that allowed it to offload L2 traffic from the front-side bus. It was so successful that a 604 derivative was scrapped in favor of just building on the 750. The 750 and its immediate successors, all of which went under the name of *G3*, eventually found widespread use both as embedded devices and across Apple's entire product line, from its portables to its workstations.

The G3 lacked one important feature that separated it from the *x*86 competition, though: vector computing capabilities. While comparable PC processors supported SIMD in the form of Intel's and AMD's vector extensions to the *x*86 instruction set, the G3 was stuck in the world of scalar computing. So when Motorola decided to develop the G3 into an even more capable embedded and media workstation chip, this lack was the first thing it addressed.

The PowerPC 7400 (aka the G4)

The Motorola MPC7400 (aka the G4) was designed as a media processing powerhouse for desktops and portables. Apple Computer used the 7400 as the CPU in the first version of their G4 workstation line, and this processor was later replaced by a lower-power version—the 7410—before the 7450 (aka the G4+ or G4e) was introduced. Today, the successors to the 7400/7410 have seen widespread use as *embedded processors*, which means that they're used in routers and other non-PC devices that need a microprocessor with low power consumption and strong DSP capabilities. Table 6-5 lists the features of the PowerPC 7400.

Table 6-5: Features of the PowerPC 7400

Introduction Date	September 1999
Process	0.20 micron
Transistor Count	10.5 million
Die Size	83 mm^2
Clock Speed at Introduction	400–600 MHz
Cache Sizes	64KB split L1, 2MB L2 supported via on-chip tags
First Appeared In	Power Macintosh G4

Figure 6-5 illustrates the PowerPC 7400 microarchitecture.

Except for the addition of SIMD capabilities, which we'll discuss in the next chapter, the G4 is essentially the same as the 750. Motorola's technical summary of the G4 has this to say about the G4 compared to the 750:

> The design philosophy on the MPC7410 (and the MPC7400) is to change from the MPC750 base only where required to gain compelling multimedia and multiprocessor performance. The MPC7410's core is essentially the same as the MPC750's, except that whereas the MPC750 has a 6-entry completion queue and has slower performance on some floating-point double-precision operations, the MPC7410 has an 8-entry completion queue and a full double-precision FPU. The MPC7410 also adds the AltiVec instruction set, has a new memory subsystem, and can interface to the improved MPX bus.
>
> —*MPC7410 RISC Microprocessor Technical Summary, section 3.11.*

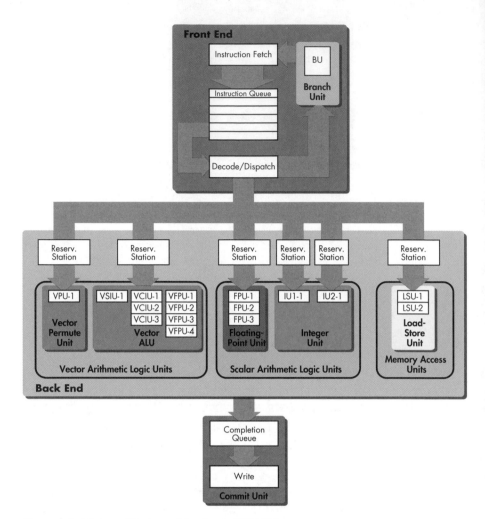

Figure 6-5: Microarchitecture of the PowerPC 7400

Aside from the vector execution unit, the most important difference in the back ends of the two units lies in the G4's improved FPU. The G4's FPU is a full-blown double-precision FPU, and it does single- and double-precision floating-point operations, including multiply and multiply-add, in three fully-pipelined cycles.

With respect to the instruction window, the G4 has the same number and configuration of reservation stations as the 750. (Note that the G4's two vector execution units, which were not present on the 750, each have a one-entry reservation station.) The only difference is that the G4's instruction queue has been lengthened to eight entries from the 750's original six as a way of reducing dispatch bottlenecks.

The G4's Vector Unit

In the late 1990s, Apple, Motorola, and IBM jointly developed a set of SIMD extensions to the PowerPC instruction set for use in the PowerPC processor series. These SIMD extensions went by different names: IBM called them VMX, and Motorola called them AltiVec. This book will refer to these extensions using Motorola's AltiVec label.

The new AltiVec instructions, which I'll cover in detail in Chapter 8, were first introduced in the G4. The G4 executes these instructions in its vector unit, which consists of two vector execution units: the *vector ALU (VALU)* and the *vector permute unit (VPU)*. The VALU performs vector arithmetic and logical operations, while the VPU performs permute and shift operations on vectors.

To support the AltiVec instructions, which can operate on up to 128 bits of data at a time, 32 new 128-bit vector registers were added to the PowerPC ISA. On the G4, these 32 architectural registers are accompanied by 6 vector rename registers.

Summary: The PowerPC G4 in Historical Context

The G4's AltiVec instruction set was a hit, and it began to see widespread use by Apple and by Motorola's embedded customers. But there was still much room for improvement to the G4's AltiVec implementation. In particular, the vector unit's single VALU was tasked with handling all integer and floating-point vector operations. Just like scalar code benefits from the presence of multiple specialized scalar ALUs, vector performance could be improved by splitting the burden of vector computation among multiple specialized VALUs operating in parallel. Such an improvement would have to wait for the successor to the G4—the G4e.

The major problem with the G4 was that its short, four-stage pipeline severely limited the upward scalability of its clock rate. While Intel and AMD were locked in the gigahertz race, Motorola's G4 was stuck around the 500 MHz mark for quite a long time. As a result, Apple's *x*86 competitors soon surpassed it in both clock speed and performance, leaving what was once the most powerful commodity RISC workstation line in serious trouble with the market.

Conclusion

The 600 series saw the PPC line go from the new kid on the block to a mature RISC alternative that brought Apple's PowerMac workstation to the forefront of personal computing performance. While the initial 601 had a few teething problems, the line was in great shape after the 603e and 604e made it to market. The 603e was a superb mobile chip that worked well in Apple's laptops, and even though it had a more limited instruction dispatch/commit bandwidth and a smaller cache than the 601, it still managed to beat its predecessor because of its more efficient use of transistors.

The 604 doubled the 603's instruction dispatch and commit bandwidth, and it sported a wider back end and a larger instruction window that enabled its back end to grind through more instructions per clock. Furthermore, its pipeline was deepened in order to increase the number of instructions per clock and to allow for better clock speed scaling. The end result was that the 604 was a strong enough desktop chip to keep the PowerMac comfortably in the performance game.

It's important to remember, though, that the 600 series reigned at a time when transistor budgets were still relatively small by today's standards, so the PowerPC architecture's RISC nature gave it a definite cost, performance, and power consumption edge over the *x*86 competition. This is not to say that the 600 series was always in the performance lead; it wasn't. The performance crown changed hands a number of time during this period.

During the heyday of the 600 series and into the dawn of the G3 era, the fact that PowerPC was a RISC ISA was a strong mark in the platform's favor. But as Moore's Curves drove transistor counts and MHz numbers ever higher, the relative cost of legacy *x*86 support began to go down and the PowerPC ISA's RISC advantage started to wane. By the time the 7400 hit the market, *x*86 processors from Intel and AMD were already catching up to it in performance, and by the time the gigahertz race was over, Apple's flagship workstation line was in trouble. The 7400's clock speed and performance had stagnated for too long during a period when Intel and AMD were locked in a heated price/performance competition.

Apple's stop-gap solution to this problem was to turn to *symmetric multiprocessing (SMP)* in order to increase the performance of its desktop line. (See Chapter 12 for a more detailed discussion of SMP.) By offering computers in which two G4s worked together to execute code and process data, Apple hoped to pack more processing power into its computers in a way that didn't rely on Motorola to ramp up clock speeds. The dual G4 met with mixed success in the market, and it wasn't until the debut of the significantly redesigned PowerPC 7450 (aka G4+ or G4e) that Apple saw the per-processor performance of its workstations improve. The introduction of the G4e into its workstation line enabled Apple to recover some ground in its race with its primary competitor in the PC space—systems based on Intel's Pentium 4.

7

INTEL'S PENTIUM 4 VS. MOTOROLA'S G4E: APPROACHES AND DESIGN PHILOSOPHIES

Now that we've covered not only the microprocessor basics but also the development of two popular *x*86 and PowerPC processor lines, you're equipped to compare and to understand two of the processors that have been among the most popular examples of these two lines: Intel's Pentium 4 and Motorola's G4e.

When the Pentium 4 hit the market in November 2000, it was the first major new *x*86 microarchitecture from Intel since the 1995 introduction of the Pentium Pro. In the years prior to the Pentium 4's launch, the Pentium Pro's P6 core dominated the market in its incarnations as the Pentium II and Pentium III, and anyone who was paying attention during that time learned at least one major lesson: Clock speed sells. Intel was definitely paying attention, and as the Willamette team members labored away in Hillsboro, Oregon, they kept MHz foremost in their minds. This singular focus is evident in everything from Intel's Pentium 4 promotional and technical literature down to the very last detail of the processor's design. As this chapter will show, the successor to the most successful *x86* microarchitecture of all time was a machine built from the ground up for stratospheric clock speed.

NOTE Willamette *was Intel's code name for the Pentium 4 while the project was in development. Intel's projects are usually code-named after rivers in Oregon. Many companies use code names that follow a certain convention, like Apple's use of the names of large cats for versions of OS X.*

Motorola introduced MPC7450 in January 2001, and Apple quickly adopted it under the *G4* moniker. Because the 7450 represented a significant departure from the 7400, the 7450 was often referred to as the G4e or the G4+, so throughout this chapter we'll call it the G4e. The new processor had a slightly deeper pipeline, which allowed it to scale to higher clock speeds, and both its front end and back ends boasted a whole host of improvements that set it apart from the original G4. It also continued the excellent performance/power consumption ratio of its predecessors. These features combined to make it an excellent chip for portables, and Apple has exploited derivatives of this basic architecture under the G4 name in a series of innovative desktop enclosure designs and portables. The G4e also brought enhanced vector computing performance to the table, which made it a great platform for DSP and media applications.

This chapter will examine the trade-offs and design decisions that the Pentium 4's architects made in their effort to build a MHz monster, paying special attention to the innovative features that the Pentium 4 sported and the ways that those features fit with the processor's overall design philosophy and target application domain. We'll cover the Pentium 4's ultradeep pipeline, its trace cache, its double-pumped ALUs, and a host of other aspects of its design, all with an eye to their impact on performance. As a point of comparison, we'll also look at the microarchitecture of Motorola's G4e. By examining two microprocessor designs side by side, you'll gain a deeper understanding of how the concepts outlined in the previous chapters play out in a pair of popular, real-world designs.

The Pentium 4's Speed Addiction

Table 7-1 lists the features of the Pentium 4.

Table 7-1: Features of the Pentium 4

Introduction Date	April 23, 2001
Process	0.18 micron
Transistor Count	42 million
Clock Speed at Introduction	1.7 GHz
Cache Sizes	L1: Approximately 16KB instruction, 16KB data
Features	Simultaneous Multithreading (SMT, aka "hyperthreading") added in 2003. 64-bit support (EM64T) and SSE3 added in 2004. Virtualization Technology (VT) added in 2005.

While some processors still have the classic, four-stage pipeline, described in Chapter 1, most modern CPUs are more complicated. You've already seen how the original Pentium had a second decode stage, and the P6 core tripled the standard four-stage pipeline to 12 stages. The Pentium 4, with a whopping 20 stages in its basic pipeline, takes this tactic to the extreme. Take a look at Figure 7-1. The chart shows the relative clock frequencies of Intel's last six *x*86 designs. (This picture assumes the same manufacturing process for all six cores.) The vertical axis shows the relative clock frequency, and the horizontal axis shows the various processors relative to each other.

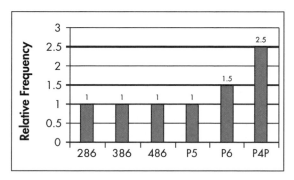

Figure 7-1: The relative frequencies of Intel's processors

Intel's explanation of this diagram and the history it illustrates is enlightening, as it shows where their design priorities were:

> Figure [3.2] shows that the 286, Intel386™, Intel486™, and Pentium® (P5) processors had similar pipeline depths—they would run at similar clock rates if they were all implemented on the same silicon process technology. They all have a similar number of gates of logic per clock cycle. The P6 microarchitecture lengthened the processor pipelines, allowing fewer gates of logic per pipeline stage, which delivered significantly higher frequency and performance. The P6 microarchitecture approximately doubled the number of pipeline stages compared to the earlier processors and was able to achieve about a 1.5 times higher frequency on the same process technology. The NetBurst microarchitecture was designed to have an even deeper pipeline (about two times the P6 micro-architecture) with even fewer gates of logic per clock cycle to allow an industry-leading clock rate.
>
> —*The Microarchitecture of the Pentium 4 Processor, p. 3.*

As you learned in Chapter 2, there are limits to how deeply you can pipeline an architecture before you begin to reach a point of diminishing returns. Deeper pipelining results in an increase in instruction execution time; this increase can be quite damaging to instruction completion rates if the pipeline has to be flushed and refilled often. Furthermore, in order to realize the throughput gains that deep pipelining promises, the processor's clock speed must increase in proportion to its pipeline depth. But in the real world, speeding up the clock of a deeply pipelined processor to match its pipeline depth is not all that easy.

Because of these drawbacks to deep pipelining, many critics of the Pentium 4's microarchitecture, dubbed NetBurst by Intel, have suggested that its staggeringly long pipeline was a gimmick—a poor design choice made for reasons of marketing and not performance and scalability. Intel knew that the public naïvely equated higher MHz numbers with higher performance, or so the argument went, so they designed the Pentium 4 to run at stratospheric clock speeds and in the process, made design trade-offs that would prove detrimental to real-world performance and long-term scalability.

As it turns out, the Pentium 4's critics were both wrong and right. In spite of the predictions of its most ardent detractors, the Pentium 4's performance has scaled fairly well with its clock rate, a phenomenon that readers of this book would expect given the section "Pipelining Explained" on page 40. But though they were wrong about its performance, the Pentium 4's critics were right about the origins of the processor's deeply pipelined approach. Revelations from former members of the Pentium 4's design team, as well as my own off-the-record conversations with Intel folks, all indicate that the Pentium 4's design was the result of a marketing-driven focus on clock speeds at the expense of actual performance and long-term scalability.

It's my understanding that this fact was widely known within Intel, even though it was not, and probably never will be, publicly acknowledged. We now know that during the course of the Pentium 4's design, the design team was under pressure from the marketing folks to turn out a chip that would give Intel a massive MHz lead over its rivals. The reasoning apparently went that MHz was a single number that the general public understood, and they knew that, just like with everything in the world—except for golf scores—higher numbers are somehow better.

When it comes to processor clock speeds, higher numbers are indeed better, but industry-wide problems with the transition to a 90-nanometer process caused problems for NetBurst, which on the whole relied on ever-increasing clock rates and ever-rising power consumption to maintain a performance edge over its rivals. As Intel ran into difficulties keeping up the regularly scheduled increases in the Pentium 4's clock rate, the processor's performance increases began to level off, even as its power consumption continued to rise.

Regardless of the drawbacks of the NetBurst architecture and its long-term prospects, the Pentium 4 line of processors has been successful from both commercial and performance standpoints. This is because the Pentium 4's way of doing things has advantages for certain types of applications—especially 3D and streaming media applications—even though it carries with it serious risks.

The General Approaches and Design Philosophies of the Pentium 4 and G4e

The drastic difference in pipeline depth between the G4e and the Pentium 4 reflects some very important differences in the design philosophies and goals of the two processors. Both processors try to execute as many instructions as quickly as possible, but they attack this problem in two different ways.

The G4e's approach to performance can be summarized as "wide and shallow." Its designers added more functional units to its back end for executing instructions, and its front end tries to fill up these units by issuing instructions to each functional unit in parallel. In order to extract the maximum amount of *instruction-level parallelism (ILP)* from the linear code stream, the G4e's front end first moves a small batch of instructions onto the chip. Then, its out-of-order (OOO) execution logic examines them for hazard-causing dependencies, spreads them out to execute in parallel, and then pushes them through the back end's nine execution units. Each of the G4e's execution units has a fairly short pipeline, so the instructions take very few cycles to move through and finish executing. Finally, in the G4e's final pipeline stages, the instructions are put back in their original program order before the results are written back to memory.

At any given moment, the G4e can have up to 16 instructions simultaneously spread throughout the chip in various stages of execution. As you'll see when we look at the Pentium 4, this instruction window is quite small. The end result is that the G4e focuses on getting a small number of instructions onto the chip at once, spreading them out widely to execute in parallel, and then getting them off the chip in as few cycles as possible. This "wide and shallow" approach is illustrated in Figure 7-2.

The Pentium 4 takes a "narrow and deep" approach to moving through the instruction stream, as illustrated in Figure 7-3. The fact that the Pentium 4's pipeline is so deep means that it can hold and work on quite a few instructions at once, but instead of spreading these instructions out more widely to execute in parallel, it pushes them through its narrower back end at a higher rate.

It's important to note that in order to keep the Pentium 4's fast back end fed with instructions, the processor needs deep buffers that can hold and schedule an enormous number of instructions. The Pentium 4 can have up to 126 instructions in various stages of execution simultaneously. This way, the processor can have many more instructions on chip for the OOO execution logic to examine for dependencies and then rearrange to be rapidly fired to the execution units. Or, another way of putting this is to say that the Pentium 4's instruction window is very large.

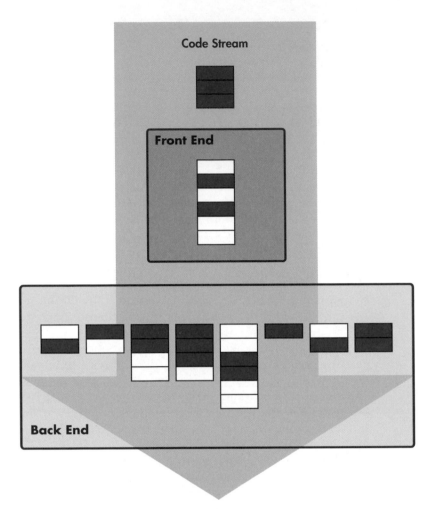

Figure 7-2: The G4e's approach to performance

It might help you to think about these two approaches in terms of a fast food drive-through analogy. At most fast food restaurants, you can either walk in or drive through. If you walk in, there are five or six short lines that you can get in and wait to have your order processed by a single server in one long step. If you choose to drive through, you'll wind up on a single long line, but that line is geared to move faster because more servers process your order in more, quicker steps. In other words:

1. You pull up to the speaker and tell them what you want.
2. You pull up to a window and pay a cashier.
3. You drive around and pick up your order.

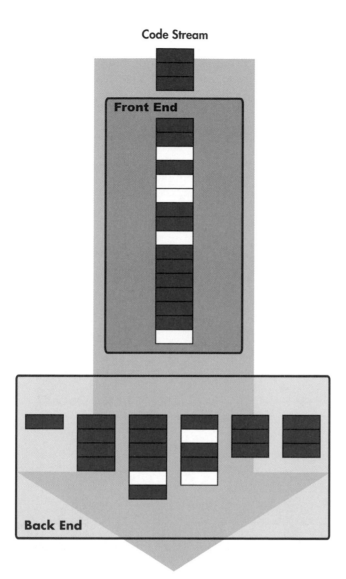

Figure 7-3: The Pentium 4's approach to performance

Because the drive-through approach splits the ordering process up into multiple, shorter stages, more customers can be waited on in a single line because there are more stages of the ordering process for different customers to find themselves in. The G4e takes the multiline, walk-in approach, while the Pentium 4 takes the single-line, drive-through approach.

As we've already discussed, the more deeply pipelined a machine is, the more severe a problem pipeline bubbles and pipeline fills become. When the Pentium 4's designers set high clock speeds as their primary goal in crafting the new microarchitecture, they had to do a lot of work to keep the pipeline from stalling and to keep branches from being mispredicted. The Pentium 4's enormous branch prediction resources and deep buffers represent a place where the Pentium 4 spends a large number of transistors to alleviate the negative effects of its long pipeline, transistors that the G4e spends instead on added execution units.

An Overview of the G4e's Architecture and Pipeline

The diagram in Figure 7-4 shows the basics of the G4e's microarchitecture, with an emphasis on representing the pipeline stages of the front end and back end. You might want to mark this page so you can refer to it throughout this section.

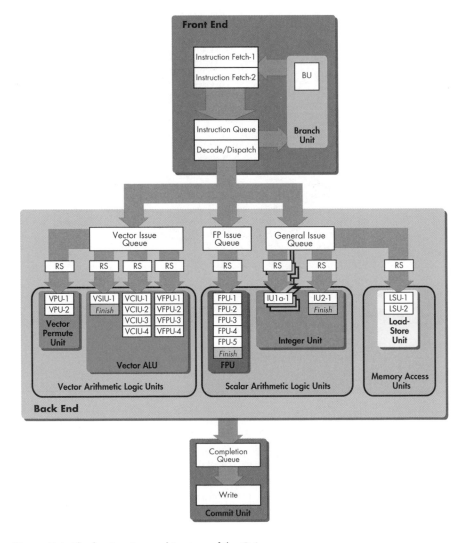

Figure 7-4: The basic microarchitecture of the G4e

Before instructions can enter the G4e's pipeline, they have to be available in its 32KB instruction cache. This instruction cache, together with the 32KB data cache, makes up the G4e's 64KB L1 cache. An instruction leaves the L1 and goes down through the various front-end stages until it hits the back end, at which point it's executed by one of the G4e's eight execution units (not counting the branch execution unit, which we'll talk about in a second).

As I've already noted, the G4e breaks down the G4's classic, four-stage pipeline into seven, shorter stages:

G4		G4e	
1	Fetch	1	Fetch-1
		2	Fetch-2
2	Decode/dispatch	3	Decode/dispatch
		4	Issue
3	Execute	5	Execute
		6	Complete
4	Write-back	7	Write-back (Commit)

Notice that the G4e dedicates one pipeline stage each to the characteristic issue and complete phases that bracket the out-of-order execution phase of a dynamically scheduled instruction's lifecycle.

Let's take a quick look at the basic pipeline stages of the G4e, because this will highlight some of the ways in which the G4e differs from the original G4. Also, an understanding of the G4e's more classic RISC pipeline will provide you with a good foundation for our upcoming discussion of the Pentium 4's much longer, more peculiar pipeline.

Stages 1 and 2: Instruction Fetch

These two stages are both dedicated primarily to grabbing an instruction from the L1 cache. Like its predecessor, the G4, the G4e can fetch up to four instructions per clock cycle from the L1 cache and send them on to the next stage. Hopefully, the needed instructions are in the L1 cache. If they aren't in the L1 cache, the G4e has to hit the much slower L2 cache to find them, which can add up to nine cycles of delay into the instruction pipeline.

Stage 3: Decode/Dispatch

Once an instruction has been fetched, it goes into the G4e's 12-entry instruction queue to be decoded. Once instructions are decoded, they're dispatched at a rate of up to three non-branch instructions per cycle to the proper *issue queue.*

Note that the G4e's dispatch logic dispatches instructions to the issue queues in accordance with "The Four Rules of Instruction Dispatch" on page 127. The only modification to the rules is in the issue buffer rule; instead of requiring that the proper execution unit and reservation station be available before an instruction can be dispatched, the G4e requires that there be space in one of the three issue queues.

Stage 4: Issue

The issue stage is the place where the G4e differs the most from the G4. Specifically, the presence of the G4e's three issue queues endows it with power and flexibility that the G4 lacks.

As you learned in Chapter 6, instructions can stall in the original G4's dispatch stage if there is no execution unit available to take them. The G4e eliminates this potential dispatch stall condition by placing a set of buffers, called issue queues, in between the dispatch stage and the reservation stations. On the G4e, it doesn't matter if the execution units are busy and their reservation stations are full; an instruction can still dispatch to the back end if there is space in the proper issue queue.

The six-entry *general issue queue (GIQ)* feeds the integer ALUs and can accept up to three instructions per cycle from the dispatch unit. It can also issue up to three instructions per cycle *out of order* from its bottommost three entries to any of the G4e's three integer units or to its LSU.

The four-entry *vector issue queue (VIQ)* can accept up to two instructions per cycle from the dispatch unit, and it can issue up to two instructions per cycle from its bottommost two entries to any two of the four vector execution units. But note that unlike the GIQ, instructions must issue *in order* from the bottom of the VIQ.

Finally, the single-entry *floating-point issue queue (FIQ)* can accept one instruction per cycle from the dispatch unit, and it can issue one instruction per cycle to the FPU.

With the help of the issue queues, the G4e's dispatcher can keep dispatching instructions and clearing the instruction queue, even if the execution units and their attached reservation stations are full. Furthermore, the GIQ's out-of-order issue ability allows integer and memory instructions in the code stream to flow around instructions that are stalled in the execute phase, so that a stalled instruction doesn't back up the pipeline and cause pipeline bubbles. For example, if a multicycle integer instruction is stalled in the bottom GIQ entry because the complex integer unit is busy, single-cycle integer instructions and load/store instructions can continue to issue to the simple integer units and the LSU from the two slots behind the stalled instruction.

Stage 5: Execute

The execute stage is pretty straightforward. Here, the instructions pass from the reservation stations into the execution units to be executed. Floating-point instructions move into the floating-point execution unit, vector instructions move into one of the four AltiVec units, integer instructions move into one of the G4e's four integer execution units, and memory accesses move into the LSU. We'll talk about these units in a bit more detail when we discuss the G4e's back end.

Stages 6 and 7: Complete and Write-Back

In these two stages, the instructions enter the completion queue to be put back into program order, and their results are written back to the register file. It's important that the instructions are rearranged to reflect their original ordering so that the illusion of in-order execution is maintained. The user needs to think that the program's commands were executed one after the other, the way they were written.

Branch Prediction on the G4e and Pentium 4

The G4e and the Pentium 4 each use both static and dynamic branch prediction techniques to prevent mispredictions and branch delays. If a branch instruction does not have an entry in the BHT, both processors will use static prediction to decide which path to take. If the instruction does have a BHT entry, dynamic prediction is used. The Pentium 4's BHT is quite large; at 4,000 entries, it has enough space to store information on most of the branches in an average program.

The earlier PIII's branch predictor had a success rate of around 91 percent, and the Pentium 4 allegedly uses an even more advanced algorithm to predict branches, so it should perform even better. The Pentium 4 also uses a BTB to store predicted branch targets. Note that in most of Intel's literature and diagrams, the BTB and BHT are combined under the label *the front-end BTB*.

The G4e has a BHT size of 2,000 entries, up from 512 entries in the original G4. I don't have any data on the G4e's branch prediction success rate, but I'm sure it's fairly good. The G4e has a 128-entry BTIC, which is twice as large as the original G4's 64-entry BTIC. The G4e's BTIC stores the first four instructions in the code stream starting at each branch target, so it goes even further than the original G4 in preventing branch-related pipeline bubbles.

Because of its long pipeline, the Pentium 4 has a *minimum misprediction penalty* of 20 clock cycles for code that's in the L1 cache—that's the minimum, but the damage can be much worse, especially if the correct branch can't be found in the L1 cache. (In such a scenario, the penalty is upward of 30 cycles.) The G4e's seven-stage pipeline doesn't pay nearly as high of a price for misprediction as the Pentium 4, but it does take more of a hit than its four-stage predecessor, the G4. The G4e has a minimum misprediction penalty of six clock cycles, as opposed to the G4's minimum misprediction penalty of only four cycles.

In conclusion, both the Pentium 4 and the G4e spend more resources than their predecessors on branch prediction, because their deeper pipelines make mispredicted branches a major performance killer.

The Pentium 4 and G4e do actually have one more branch prediction trick up their sleeves that's worth at least noting, even though I won't discuss it in any detail. That trick comes in the form of *software branch hints*, or extra information that a compiler or programmer can attach to conditional branch instructions. This information gives the branch predictor clues as to the expected behavior of the branch, whether the compiler or programmer expects it to be taken or not taken. There doesn't seem to be much information available on how big of a help these hints are, and Intel at least recommends that they be used sparingly since they can increase code size.

An Overview of the Pentium 4's Architecture

Even though the Pentium 4's pipeline is much longer than that of the G4e, it still performs most of the same functions. Figure 7-5 illustrates the Pentium 4's basic architecture so that you can compare it to the picture of the G4e presented in Figure 7-4. Due to space and complexity constraints, I haven't attempted to show each pipeline stage individually like I did with the G4e. Rather, I've grouped the related ones together so you can get a more general feel for the Pentium 4's layout and instruction flow.

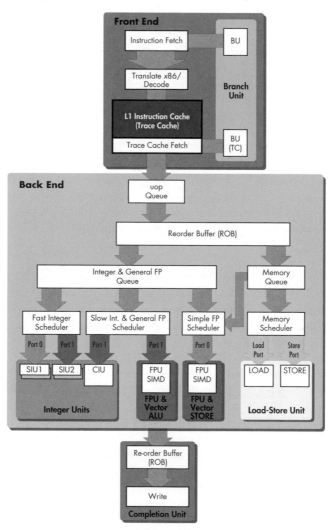

Figure 7-5: Basic architecture of the Pentium 4

The first thing to notice about Figure 7-5 is that the L1 instruction cache is actually sitting after the fetch and decode stages in the Pentium 4's front end. This oddly located instruction cache—called the *trace cache*—is one of the Pentium 4's most innovative and important features. It also greatly affects the Pentium 4's pipeline and basic instruction flow, so you have to understand it before we can talk about the Pentium 4's pipeline in detail.

Expanding the Instruction Window

Chapter 5 talked about the buffering effect of deeper pipelining on the P6 and how it allows the processor to smooth out gaps and hiccups in the code stream. The analogy I used was that of a reservoir, which can smooth out interruptions in the flow of water from a central source.

One of the innovations that makes this reservoir approach effective is the decoupling of the back end from the front end by means of the reservation station (RS). The RS is really the heart of the reservoir approach, a place where instructions can collect in a pool and then issue when their data become available. This *instruction pool* is what decouples the P6's fetch/decode bandwidth from its execution bandwidth by enabling the P6 to continue executing instructions during short periods when the front end gets hung up in either fetching or decoding the next instruction.

With the advent of the Pentium 4's much longer pipeline, the reservation station's decoupling just isn't enough. The Pentium 4's performance plummets when the front end cannot keep feeding instructions to the back end in extremely rapid succession. There's no extra time to wait for a complex instruction to decode or for a branch delay—the high-speed back end needs the instructions to flow quickly.

One route that Intel could have taken would have been to increase the size of the code reservoir, and in doing so, increase the size of the instruction window. Intel actually did do this—the Pentium 4 can track up to 126 instructions in various stages of execution—but that's not all they did. More drastic measures were required to keep the high-speed back end from depleting the reservoir before the front end could fill it.

The answer that Intel settled on was to take the costly and time-consuming *x*86 decode stage out of the basic pipeline. They did this by the clever trick of converting the L1 cache—a structure that was already on the die and therefore already taking up transistors—into a cache for decoded micro-ops.

The Trace Cache

As the previous chapter mentioned, modern *x*86 chips convert complex *x*86 instructions into a simple internal instruction format called a micro-operation (aka micro-op, µop, or uop). These micro-ops are uniform, and thus it's easier for the processor to manage them dynamically. To return to the previous chapter's Tetris analogy, converting all of the *x*86 instructions into micro-ops is kind of like converting all of the falling Tetris pieces into one or two types of simple piece, like the T and the block pieces. This makes everything easier to place, because there's less complexity to manage on the fly.

The older P6 fetches *x*86 instructions from the L1 instruction cache and translates them into micro-ops before passing them on to the reservation station to be scheduled for execution. The Pentium 4, in contrast, fetches groups of *x*86 instructions from the L2 cache, decodes them into strings of micro-ops called *traces*, and then fits these traces into its modified L1 instruction cache (the trace cache). This way, the instructions are already decoded, so when it comes time to execute them, they need only to be fetched from the trace cache and passed directly into the back end's buffers.

So the trace cache is a reservoir for a reservoir; it builds up a large pool of already decoded micro-ops that can be piped directly into the back end's smaller instruction pool. This helps keep the high-speed back end from draining that pool dry.

Shortening Instruction Execution Time

As noted earlier, on a conventional *x*86 processor like the PIII or the Athlon, *x*86 instructions make their way from the instruction cache into the decoder, where they're broken down into multiple smaller, more uniform, more easily managed instructions called micro-ops. (See the section on instruction set translation in Chapter 3.) These micro-ops are actually what the out-of-order back end rearranges, executes, and commits.

This instruction translation happens each time an instruction is executed, so it adds a few pipeline stages to the beginning of the processor's basic pipeline. Notice in Figures 7-6 and 7-7 that multiple pipeline stages have been collapsed into each other—instruction fetch takes multiple stages, translate takes multiple stages, decode takes multiple stages, and so on.

For a block of code that's executed only a few times over the course of a single program run, this loss of a few cycles to retranslation each time isn't that big of a deal. But for a block of code that's executed thousands and thousands of times (e.g., a loop in a media application that applies a series of operations to a large file), the number of cycles spent repeatedly translating and decoding the same group of instructions can add up quickly. The Pentium 4 reclaims those lost cycles by removing the need to translate those *x*86 instructions into micro-ops each time they're executed.

The Pentium 4's instruction cache takes translated, decoded micro-ops that are primed and ready to be sent straight out to the back end and arranges them into little mini-programs called traces. These traces, and not the *x*86 code that was produced by the compiler, are what the Pentium 4 executes whenever there's a trace cache hit, which is over 90 percent of the time. As long as the needed code is in the trace cache, the Pentium 4's execution path looks as in Figure 7-7.

As the front end executes the stored traces, the trace cache sends up to three micro-ops per cycle directly to the back end, without the need for them to pass through any translation or decoding stages. Only when there's a trace cache miss does that top part of the front end kick in order to fetch and decode instructions from the L2 cache. The decoding and translating steps brought on by a trace cache miss add another eight pipeline stages onto the

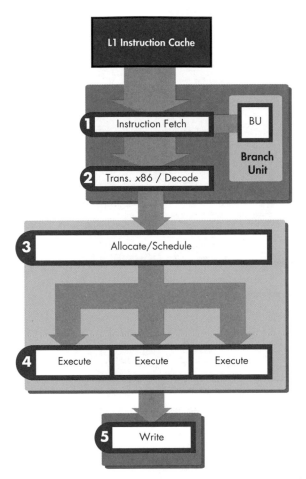

Figure 7-6: Normal x86 processor's critical execution path

beginning of the Pentium 4's pipeline. You can see that the trace cache saves quite a few cycles over the course of a program's execution, thereby shortening the average instruction execution time and average instruction latency.

The Trace Cache's Operation

The trace cache operates in two modes. *Execute mode* is the mode pictured above, where the trace cache feeds stored traces to the execution logic to be executed. This is the mode that the trace cache normally runs in. When there's an L1 cache miss, the trace cache goes into *trace segment build mode*. In this mode, the front end fetches *x*86 code from the L2 cache, translates it into micro-ops, builds a *trace segment* with it, and loads that segment into the trace cache to be executed.

Notice in Figure 7-7 that the trace cache execution path knocks the BPU out of the picture along with the instruction fetch and translate/decode stages. This is because a trace segment is much more than just a translated, decoded, predigested slice of the same *x*86 code that compiler originally produced. The trace cache actually uses branch prediction when it builds a

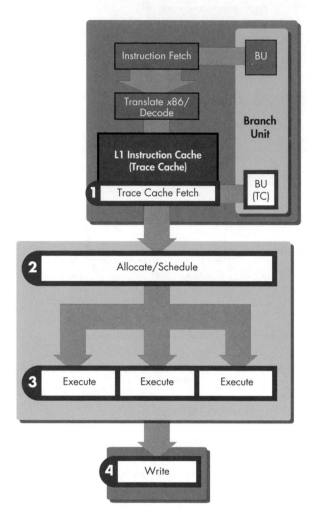

Figure 7-7: The Pentium 4's critical execution path

trace. As shown in Figure 7-8, the trace cache's branch prediction hardware splices code from the branch that it speculates the program will take right into the trace behind the code that it knows the program will take. So if you have a chunk of *x*86 code with a branch in it, the trace cache builds a trace from the instructions up to and including the branch instruction. Then, it picks which branch it thinks the program will take, and it continues building the trace along that speculative branch.

Having the speculative execution path spliced in right after the branch instruction confers on the trace cache two big advantages over a normal instruction cache. First, in a normal machine, it takes the branch predictor and BPU some time to do their thing when they come across a conditional branch instruction—they have to figure out which branch to speculatively execute, load up the proper branch target, and so on. This whole process usually

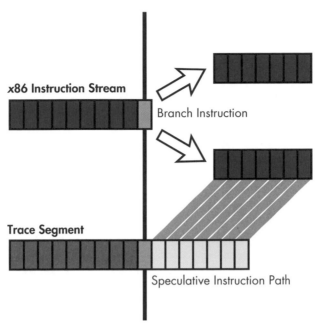

x86 Instruction Stream

Branch Instruction

Trace Segment

Speculative Instruction Path

Figure 7-8: Speculative execution using the trace cache

adds at least one cycle of delay after every conditional branch instruction, a delay that often can't be filled with other code and therefore results in a pipeline bubble. With the trace cache, however, the code from the branch target is already sitting there right after the branch instruction, so there's no delay associated with looking it up and hence no pipeline bubble. In other words, the Pentium 4's trace cache implements a sort of branch folding, like what we previously saw implemented in the instruction queues of PowerPC processors.

The other advantage that the trace cache offers is also related to its ability to store speculative branches. When a normal L1 instruction cache fetches a cache line from memory, it stops fetching when it hits a branch instruction and leaves the rest of the line blank. If the branch instruction is the first instruction in an L1 cache line, then it's the only instruction in that line and the rest of the line goes to waste. Trace cache lines, on the other hand, can contain both branch instructions and the speculative code after the branch instruction. This way, no space in the trace cache's six–micro-op line goes to waste.

Most compilers take steps to deal with the two problems I've outlined (the delay after the branch and the wasted cache line space). As you saw, though, the trace cache solves these problems in its own way, so programs that are optimized to exploit these abilities see some advantages from them.

One interesting effect that the trace cache has on the Pentium 4's front end is that x86 translation/decode bandwidth is for the most part decoupled from dispatch bandwidth. You saw previously how the P6, for instance, spends a lot of transistor resources on a three different x86 decoders so that it can translate enough clunky x86 instructions each cycle into micro-ops to keep the back end fed. With the Pentium 4, the fact that most of the time program code is fetched from the trace cache in the form of predigested micro-ops means that a high bandwidth translator/decoder isn't necessary. The Pentium 4's decoding logic only has to kick on whenever there's an L1 cache miss, so it was designed to decode only one x86 instruction per clock cycle. This is one-third the maximum theoretical decode bandwidth of the P6, but the Pentium 4's trace cache allows it to meet or exceed the P6's real-world average dispatch rate.

The trace cache's handling of very long, multi-cycle x86 instructions is worth taking a look at, because it's quite clever. While most x86 instructions decode into around two or three micro-ops, there are some exceedingly long (and thankfully rare) x86 instructions (e.g., the string manipulation instructions) that decode into hundreds of micro-ops. Like the P6, the Pentium 4 has a special microcode ROM that decodes these longer instructions so that the regular hardware decoder can concentrate on decoding the smaller, faster instructions. For each long instruction, the microcode ROM stores a canned sequence of micro-ops, which it spits out when fed that instruction.

To keep these long, prepackaged sequences of micro-ops from polluting the trace cache, the Pentium 4's designers devised the following solution: Whenever the trace cache is building a trace segment and it encounters one of the long x86 instructions, instead of breaking it down and storing it as a micro-op sequence, the trace cache inserts into the trace segment a tag that points to the section of the microcode ROM containing the micro-op sequence for that particular instruction. Later, in execute mode, when the trace cache is streaming instructions out to the back end and it encounters one of these tags, it stops and temporarily hands control of the instruction stream over to the microcode ROM. The microcode ROM spits out the proper sequence of micro-ops (as designated by the tag) into the instruction stream, and then hands control back over to the trace cache, which resumes putting out instructions. The back end, which is on the other end of this instruction stream, doesn't know or care if the instructions are coming from the trace cache or the microcode ROM. All it sees is a constant, uninterrupted stream of instructions.

Intel hasn't said exactly how big the trace cache is—only that it holds 12,000 micro-ops. Intel claims this is roughly equivalent to a 16KB to 18KB I-cache.

By way of finishing up our discussion of the trace cache and introducing our detailed walk-through of the Pentium 4's pipeline, I should note two final aspects of the trace cache's effect on the pipeline. First, the trace cache still needs a short instruction fetch stage so that micro-ops can be fetched from it and sent to the allocation and scheduling logic. When we look at the Pentium 4's basic execution pipeline, you'll see this stage. Second, the trace cache actually has its own little BPU for predicting the directions and return addresses of branches within the trace cache itself. So the trace cache doesn't eliminate branch processing and prediction entirely from the picture; it just alleviates their effects on performance.

An Overview of the Pentium 4's Pipeline

Now let's step back and take a look at the Pentium 4's basic execution pipeline. Here's a breakdown of the various pipeline stages.

Stages 1 and 2: Trace Cache Next Instruction Pointer

In these stages, the Pentium 4's trace cache fetch logic gets a pointer to the next instruction in the trace cache.

Stages 3 and 4: Trace Cache Fetch

These two stages fetch an instruction from the trace cache to be sent to the back end.

Stage 5: Drive

This is the first of two special *drive stages* in the Pentium 4's pipeline, each of which is dedicated to driving signals from one part of the processor to the next. The Pentium 4 runs so fast that sometimes a signal can't make it all the way to where it needs to be in a single clock pulse, so the processor dedicates some pipeline stages to letting these signals propagate across the chip. These drive stages are there because the Pentium 4's designers intend for the chip to reach such stratospheric clock speeds that stages like this are absolutely necessary.

At the end of these first five stages, the Pentium 4's trace cache sends up to three micro-ops per cycle into a large, FIFO *micro-op queue*. This in-order queue, which sits in between the Pentium 4's front end and back end, smoothes out the flow of instructions to the back end by squeezing out any fetch- or decode-related bubbles. Micro-ops enter the top of the queue and fall down to rest at the lowest available entry, directly above the most recent micro-op to enter the queue. Thus, any bubbles that may have been ahead of the micro-ops disappear from the pipeline at this point. The micro-ops leave the bottom of the micro-op queue in program order and proceed to the next pipeline stage.

Stages 6 Through 8: Allocate and Rename (ROB)

In this group of stages, up to three instructions per cycle move from the bottom of the micro-op queue and are allocated entries in the Pentium 4's ROB and rename registers. With regard to the latter, the *x*86 ISA specifies only eight GPRs, eight FPRs, and eight VPRs, but the Pentium 4 has 128 of each type of register in its rename register files.

The allocator/renamer stages also allocates each micro-op an entry in one of the two micro-op queues detailed in the next section and can send up to three micro-ops per cycle into these queues.

Stage 9: Queue

To implement out-of-order execution, the Pentium 4 flows micro-ops from its trace cache through the ROB and into two deep micro-op queues that sit between its instructions' dispatch and execution phases. These two queues are the *memory micro-op queue* and the *arithmetic micro-op queue*. The memory micro-op queue holds memory operations (loads and stores) that are destined for the Pentium 4's LSU, while the arithmetic micro-op queue holds all other types of operations.

The two main micro-op queues are roughly analogous to the G4e's issue queues, but with one crucial difference: the Pentium 4's micro-op queues are FIFO queues, while the G4e's issue queues are not. For the Pentium 4, this means an instruction passes into and out of a micro-op queue *in program order* with respect to the other instructions in its own queue. However, instructions can still exit the bottom of each queue *out of program order* with respect to instructions in the other queue.

These two micro-op queues feed micro-ops into the scheduling logic in the next stage.

Stages 10 Through 12: Schedule

The micro-op queues described in the preceding section are only part of the Pentium 4's dynamic scheduling logic. The other half consists of a set of four micro-op schedulers whose job it is to schedule micro-ops for execution and to determine to which execution unit the micro-ops should be passed. Each of these schedulers consists of a smaller, 8- to 12-entry micro-op queue attached to a bit of scheduling logic. The scheduler's scheduling logic arbitrates with the other schedulers for access to the Pentium 4's four issue ports, and it removes micro-ops from its in-order scheduling queue and sends them through the right port at the right time.

An instruction cannot exit from a scheduling queue until its input operands are available and the appropriate execution unit is available. When the micro-op is ready to execute, it is removed from the bottom of its scheduling queue and passed to the proper execution unit through one of the Pentium 4's four issue ports, which are analogous to the P6 core's five issue ports in that they act as gateways to the back end's execution units.

Here's a breakdown of the four schedulers:

Memory scheduler
Schedules memory operations for the LSU.

Fast IU scheduler
Schedules ALU operations (simple integer and logical instructions) for the Pentium 4's two double-speed integer execution units. As you'll see in the next chapter, the Pentium 4 contains two integer ALUs that run at twice the main core's clock speed.

Slow IU/general FPU scheduler
Schedules the rest of the integer instructions and most of the floating-point instructions.

Simple FP scheduler
Schedules simple FP instructions and FP memory operations.

These schedulers feed micro-ops through the four dispatch ports described in the next stage.

Stages 13 and 14: Issue

The P6 core's reservation station sends instructions to the back end via one of five issue ports. The Pentium 4 uses a similar scheme, but with four issue ports instead of five. There are two *memory ports* for memory instructions: the load port and the store port, for loads and stores, respectively. The remaining two ports, called *execution ports*, are for all the other instructions: execution port 0 and execution port 1. The Pentium 4 can send a total of six micro-ops per cycle through the four execution ports. This issue rate of six micro-ops per cycle is more micro-ops per cycle than the front end can fetch and decode (three per cycle) or the back end can complete (three per cycle), but that's okay because it gives the machine some headroom in its middle so that it can have bursts of activity.

You might be wondering how six micro-ops per cycle can move through four ports. The trick is that the Pentium 4's two execution ports are double-speed, meaning that they can dispatch instructions (integer only) on the rising and falling edges of the clock. But we'll talk more about this in the next chapter. For now, here's a breakdown of the two execution ports and which execution units are attached to them:

Execution port 0:

Fast integer ALU1 This unit performs integer addition, subtraction, and logical operations. It also evaluates branch conditionals and executes store-data micro-ops, which store data into the outgoing store buffer. This is the first of two double-speed integer units, which operate at twice the core clock frequency.

Floating-point/SSE move This unit performs floating-point and SSE moves and stores. It also executes the FXCH instruction, which means that it's no longer "free" on the Pentium 4.

Execution port 1:

Fast integer ALU2 This very simple integer ALU performs only integer addition and subtraction. It's the second of the two double-speed integer ALUs.

Slow integer ALU This integer unit handles all of the more time-consuming integer operations, like shift and rotate, that can't be completed in half a clock cycle by the two fast ALUs.

Floating-point/SEE/MMX ALU   This unit handles floating-point and SSE addition, subtraction, multiplication, and division. It also handles all MMX instructions.

In Figure 7-5, I've labeled the instruction flow paths going into each execution unit to show which dispatch port instructions must pass through in order to reach which execution unit.

Stages 15 and 16: Register Files

This stage is where the execution units, upon receiving the instructions, read each instruction's input operands from the appropriate register file. To return to the discussion from Chapter 1, this step is the read step in the read-execute-write cycle of computation.

Stage 17: Execute

In this stage, the instructions are actually executed by the back end's execution units. We'll take a closer look at the Pentium 4's back end in the next chapter.

Stage 18: Flags

If an instruction's outcome stipulates that it needs to set any flags in the PSW, then it does so at this stage.

Stage 19: Branch Check

Here's the stage where the Pentium 4 checks the outcome of a conditional branch to see if it has just wasted 19 cycles of its time executing some code that it'll have to throw away. By stage 19, the branch condition has been evaluated, and the front end knows whether or not the branch predictor's guess was right or not.

Stage 20: Drive

You've already met the drive stage. Again, this stage is dedicated to propagating signals across the chip.

Stages 21 and Onward: Complete and Commit

Although Intel only lists the last part of the execution phase—stage 20—as part of the "normal Pentium 4 pipeline," for completeness, I'll include the write-back phase. Completed instructions file into their pre-assigned entries in the ROB, where they're put back in program order before having their results update the machine's architectural state.

As you can see, the Pentium 4's 20-stage pipeline does much of the same work in mostly the same order as the G4e's seven-stage pipeline. By dividing the pipeline into more stages, though, the Pentium 4 can reach higher clock rates. As I've already noted, this deeply pipelined approach fits with the Pentium 4's "narrow and deep" design philosophy.

The Pentium 4's Instruction Window

Before I discuss the nature of the Pentium 4's instruction window, note that I'm using the terms *instruction pool* and *instruction window* somewhat interchangeably. These two terms represent two slightly different metaphors for thinking about the set of queues and buffers positioned between a processor's front end and its back end. Instructions collect up in these queues and buffers—just like water collects in a pool or reservoir—before being drained away by the processor's back end. Because the instruction pool represents a small segment of the code stream, which the processor can examine for dependencies and reorder for optimal execution, this pool can also be said to function as a window on the code stream. Now that that's clear, let's take a look at the Pentium 4's instruction window.

As I explaincd in the previous chapter, the older P6 core's RS and ROB made up the heart of its instruction window. The Pentium 4 likewise has a ROB for tracking micro-ops, and in fact, and its 126-entry ROB is much larger than that of the P6. The buffer functions of the P6's reservation station, however, have been divided among multiple structures. The previous section's pipeline description explains how these structures are configured.

This partitioning of the instruction window into memory and arithmetic portions by means of the two scheduling queues has the effect of ensuring that both types of instructions will always have space in the window, and that an overabundance of one instruction type will not crowd the other type out of the window. The multiple schedulers provide fine-grained control over the instruction flow, so that it's optimally reordered for the fast execution units.

All of this deep buffering, scheduling, queuing, and optimizing is essential for keeping the Pentium 4's high-speed back end full. To return yet again to the Tetris analogy, imagine what would happen if someone were to double the speed at which the blocks fall; you'd hope that they would also double the size of the look-ahead window to compensate. The Pentium 4 greatly increases the size of the P6's instruction window as a way of compensating for the fact that the arrangement of instructions in its core is made so much more critical by the increased clock speed and pipeline depth.

The downside to all of this is that the schedulers and queues and the very large ROB all add complexity and cost to the Pentium 4's design. This complexity and cost are part of the price that the Pentium 4 pays for its deep pipeline and high clock speed.

8

INTEL'S PENTIUM 4 VS. MOTOROLA'S G4E: THE BACK END

In this chapter, I'll explain in greater detail the back end of both the Pentium 4 and the G4e. I'll talk about the execution resources that each processor uses for crunching code and data, and how those resources contribute to overall performance on specific types of applications.

Some Remarks About Operand Formats

Unlike the DLW and PowerPC ISAs described so far, the *x*86 ISA uses a two-operand format for both integer and floating-point instructions. If you want to add two numbers in registers A and B, the instruction would look as follows:

```
add A, B
```

This command adds the contents of A to the contents of B and places the result in A, overwriting whatever was previously in A in the process. Expressed mathematically, this would look as follows:

```
A = A + B
```

The problem with using a two-operand format is that it can be inconvenient for some sequences of operations. For instance, if you want to add A to B and store the result in C, you need two operations to do so:

Line #	Code	Comments
1	mov C, A	Copy the contents of register A to register C.
2	add C, B	Add the numbers in registers C and B and store the result in C, overwriting the previous contents of C.

Program 8-1

The first instruction in Program 8-1 copies the contents of A into C so that A's value is not erased by the addition, and the second instruction adds the two numbers.

With a three-operand or more format, like many of the instructions in the PPC ISA, the programmer gets a little more flexibility and control. For instance, you saw earlier that the PPC ISA has a three-operand add instruction of the format

```
add destination, source1, source2
```

So if you want to add the contents of register 1 to the contents of register 2 and store the result in register 3 (i.e., r3 = r1 + r2), you just use the following instruction:

```
add 3, 2, 1
```

Some PPC instructions support even more than three operands, which can be a real boon to programmers and compiler writers. In "AltiVec Vector Operations" on page 170, we'll look in detail at the G4e AltiVec instruction set's use of a four-operand instruction format.

The PPC ISA's variety of multiple-operand formats are obviously more flexible than the one- and two-operand formats of x86. But nonetheless, modern x86 compilers are quite advanced and can overcome many of the aforementioned problems through the use of hidden microarchitectural rename registers and various scheduling algorithms. The problems with x86's two-operand format are much more of a liability for floating-point and vector code than for integer code. We'll talk more about this later, though.

The Integer Execution Units

Though the Pentium 4's *double-pumped* integer execution units got quite a bit of press when Netburst was first announced, you might be surprised to learn that both the G4e and the Pentium 4 embody approaches to enhancing integer performance that are very similar. As you'll see, this similarity arises from both processors' application of the computing design dictum: *Make the common case fast.*

For integer applications, the common case is easy to spot. As I outlined in Chapter 1, integer instructions generally fall into one of two categories:

Simple/fast integer instructions

Instructions like add and sub require very few steps to complete and are therefore easy to implement with little overhead. These simple instructions make up the majority of the integer instructions in an average program.

Complex/slow integer instructions

While addition and subtraction are fairly simple to implement, multiplication and division are complicated to implement and can take quite a few steps to complete. Such instructions involve a series of additions and bit shifts, all of which can take a while. These instructions represent only a fraction of the instruction mix for an average program.

Since simple integer instructions are by far the most common type of integer instruction, both the Pentium 4 and G4e devote most of their integer resources to executing these types of instructions very rapidly.

The G4e's IUs: Making the Common Case Fast

As was explained in the previous chapter, the G4e has a total of four IUs. The IUs are divided into two groups:

Three simple/fast integer execution units—SIUa, SIUb, SIUc

These three simple IUs handle only fast integer instructions. Most of the instructions executed by these IUs are single-cycle, but there are some multi-cycle exceptions to this rule. Each of the three fast IUs is fed by a single-entry reservation station.

One complex/slow integer execution unit—CIU

This single complex IU handles only complex integer instructions like multiply, divide, and some special-purpose register instructions, including condition register (CR) logical operations. Instructions sent to this IU generally take four cycles to complete, although some take longer. Note that divides, as well as some multiplication instructions, are not fully pipelined and thus can tie up the entire IU for multiple cycles. Also, instructions that update the PPC CR have an extra pipeline stage—called *finish*—to pass through before they leave the IU (more on this shortly). Finally, the CIU is fed by a two-entry reservation station.

By dedicating three of its four integer ALUs to the fastest, simplest, and most common instructions, the G4e is able to make the common case quite fast.

Before moving on, I should note that the finish stages attached to the ends of some of the execution unit pipelines are new in the G4e. These finish stages are dedicated to updating the condition register to reflect the results of any arithmetic operation that needs to do such updating (this happens infrequently). It's important to understand that at the end of the execute stage/start of the finish stage, an arithmetic instruction's results are available for use by dependent instructions, even though the CR has not yet been updated. Therefore, the finish stage doesn't affect the effective latency of arithmetic instructions. But for instructions that depend on the CR—like branch instructions—the finish stage adds an extra cycle of latency.

One nice thing that the PPC ISA has going for it is its large number of general-purpose registers (GPRs) for storing integers and addresses. This large number of architectural GPRs (32 to be exact) gives the compiler plenty of flexibility in scheduling integer operations and address calculations.

In addition to the PPC ISA's 32 GPRs, the G4e provides 16 microarchitectural general-purpose rename registers for use by the on-chip scheduling logic. These additional registers, not visible to the compiler or programmer, are used by the G4e to augment the 32 GPRs, thereby providing more flexibility for scheduling the processor's execution resources and keeping them supplied with data.

The Pentium 4's IUs: Make the Common Case Twice as Fast

The Pentium 4's integer functional block takes a very similar strategy to the G4e for speeding up integer performance. It contains one slow integer execution unit and two fast integer execution units. By just looking at the number of integer execution units, you might think that the Pentium 4 has less integer horsepower than the G4e. This isn't quite the case, though, because the Pentium 4's two fast IUs operate at *twice the core clock speed*, a trick that allows them to look to the outside world like four fast IUs.

The Pentium 4 can issue two integer instructions per cycle in rapid succession to each of the two fast IUs—one on the rising edge of the clock pulse and one on the falling edge. Each fast ALU can process an integer instruction in 0.5 cycles, which means it can process a total of two integer instructions per cycle. This gives the Pentium 4 a total peak throughput of four simple integer instructions per cycle for the two fast IUs combined.

Does this mean that the Pentium 4's two double-speed integer units are twice as powerful as two single-speed integer units? No, not quite. Integer performance is about much more than just a powerful integer functional block. You can't squeeze peak performance out of an integer unit if you can't keep it fed with code, and the Pentium 4 seems to have a weakness in this area when it comes to integer code.

We talked earlier in this book about how, due to the Pentium 4's "narrow and deep" design philosophy, branch mispredictions and cache misses can degrade performance by introducing pipeline bubbles into the instruction stream. This is especially a problem for integer performance, because integer-intensive applications often contain branch-intensive code that exhibits poor *locality of reference*. As a result, branch mispredictions in conjunction with cache latencies can kill integer performance. (For more information about these issues, see Chapter 11.)

As most benchmarks of the Pentium 4 bear out, in spite of its double-pumped ALUs, the Pentium 4's "narrow and deep" design is much more suited to floating-point applications than it is to integer applications. This floating-point bias seems to have been a deliberate choice on the part of the Pentium 4's designers—the Pentium 4 is designed to give not maximum but acceptable performance on integer applications. This strategy works because most modern processors (at least since the PIII, if not the PII or Pentium Pro) are able to offer perfectly workable performance levels on consumer-level integer-intensive applications like spreadsheets, word processors, and the like. Though server-oriented applications like databases require higher levels of integer performance, the demand for ever-increasing integer performance just isn't there in the consumer market. As a way of increasing the Pentium 4's integer performance for the server market, Intel sells a version of the Pentium 4 called the *Xeon*, which has a much larger cache.

Before moving on to the next topic, I should note that one characteristic of the Pentium 4 that bears mentioning is its large number of micro-architectural rename registers. The *x*86 ISA has only eight GPRs, but the Pentium 4 augments these with the addition of a large number of rename registers: 128 to be exact. Since the Pentium 4 keeps so many instructions on-chip for scheduling purposes, it needs these added rename resources to prevent the kinds of register-based resource conflicts that result in pipeline bubbles.

The Floating-Point Units (FPUs)

While the mass market's demand for integer performance may not be picking up, its demand for floating-point seems insatiable. Games, 3D rendering, audio processing, and almost all other forms of multimedia- and entertainment-oriented computing applications are extremely floating-point intensive. With floating-point applications perennially driving the home PC market, it's no wonder that the Pentium 4's designers made their design trade-offs in favor of FP performance over integer performance.

In terms of the way they use the processor and cache, floating-point applications are in many respects the exact opposite of the integer applications described in the preceding section. For instance, the branches in floating-point code are few and extremely predictable. Most of these branches occur as exit conditions in small chunks of loop code that iterate through a large dataset (e.g., a sound or image file) in order to modify it. Since these loops iterate many thousands of times as they work their way through a file, the branch instruction that is the exit condition evaluates to *taken* many thousands of times; it only evaluates to *not taken* once—when the program exits the loop. For such types of code, simple static branch prediction, where the branch prediction unit guesses that all branches will be taken every time, works quite well.

This description also points out two other ways in which floating-point code is the opposite of integer code. First, floating-point code has excellent locality of reference with respect to the instruction cache. A floating-point–intensive program, as I've noted, spends a large part of its execution time in relatively small loops, and these loops often fit in one of the processor caches. Second, because floating-point–intensive applications operate on large data files that are streamed into the processor from main memory, memory bandwidth is extremely important for floating-point performance. So while integer programs need good branch prediction and caching to keep the IUs fed with instructions, floating-point programs need good memory bandwidth to keep the FPUs fed with data.

Now that you understand how floating-point code tends to operate, let's look at the FPUs of the G4e and Pentium 4 to see how they tackle the problem.

The G4e's FPU

Since the G4e's designers have bet on the processor's vector execution units (described shortly) to do most of the serious floating-point heavy lifting, they made the G4e's FPU fairly simple and straightforward. It has a single pipeline for all floating-point instructions, and both single- and double-precision operations take the same number of cycles. (This ability to do double-precision FP is important mostly for scientific applications like simulations.) In addition, one single- or double-precision operation can be issued per cycle, with one important restriction (described later in this section). Finally, the G4e inherits the PPC line's ability to do single-cycle fmadds, and this time, both double- and single-precision fmadds have a single-cycle throughput.

Almost all of the G4e's floating-point instructions take five cycles to complete. There are a few instructions, however, that can take longer (fdiv, fre, and fdiv, for example). These longer instructions can take from 14 to 35 cycles to complete, and while they're executing, they hang up the floating-point pipeline, meaning that no other instructions can be done during that time.

One rarely discussed weakness of the G4e's FPU is the fact that it isn't *fully pipelined*, which means that it can't have five different instructions in five different stages of execution simultaneously. Motorola's software optimization manual for the 7450 states that if the 7450's first four stages of execution are occupied, the FPU will stall on the next cycle. This means that the FPU's peak theoretical instruction throughput is four instructions every five cycles.

It could plausibly be said that the PowerPC ISA gives the G4e a slight advantage over the Pentium 4 in terms of floating-point performance. However, a better way of phrasing that would be to say that the x86 ISA (or more specifically, the x87 floating-point extensions) puts the Pentium 4 at a slight disadvantage with respect to the rest of the world. In other words, the PPC's floating-point implementation is fairly normal and unremarkable, whereas the x87 has a few quirks that can make life difficult for FPU designers and compiler writers.

As mentioned at the outset of this chapter, the PPC ISA has instructions with one-, two-, three-, and four-operand formats. This puts a lot of power in the hands of the compiler or programmer as far as scheduling floating-point instructions to minimize dependencies and increase throughput and performance. Furthermore, this instruction format flexibility is augmented by a flat, 32-entry floating-point register file, which yields even more scheduling flexibility and even more performance.

In contrast, the instructions that make up the x87 floating-point extensions support two operands at most. You saw in Chapter 5 that the x87's very small eight-entry register file has a stack-based structure that limits it in certain ways. All Pentium processors up until the Pentium 4 get around this stack-related limitation with the "free" fxch instruction described in Chapter 5, but on the Pentium 4, fxch is no longer free.

So the Pentium 4's small, stack-based floating-point register file and two-operand floating-point instruction format put the processor at a disadvantage compared to the G4e's cleaner PowerPC floating-point specification. The Pentium 4's 128 floating-point rename registers help alleviate some of the false dependencies that arise from the low number of architectural registers, but they don't help much with the other problems.

The Pentium 4's FPU

There are two fully independent FPU pipelines on the Pentium 4, one of which is strictly for floating-point memory operations (loading and storing floating-point data). Since floating-point applications are extremely data- and memory-intensive, separating the floating-point memory operations and giving them their own execution unit helps a bit with performance.

The other FPU pipeline is for all floating-point arithmetic operations, and except for the fact that it doesn't execute memory instructions, it's very similar to the G4e's single FPU. Most simple floating-point operations take between five and seven cycles, with a few more complicated operations (like floating-point division) tying up the pipeline for a significantly longer time. Single- and double-precision operations take the same number of cycles, with both single- and double-precision floating-point numbers being converted into the x87's internal 80-bit temporary format. (This conversion is done for overflow reasons and doesn't concern us here.)

So the Pentium 4's FPU hardware executes instructions with slightly higher instruction latencies than the FPU of its predecessor, the P6 (for example, three to five cycles on the P6 for common instructions), but because the Pentium 4's clock speed is so much higher, it can still complete more floating-point instructions in a shorter period of time. The same is true of the Pentium 4's FPU in comparison with the G4e's FPU—the Pentium 4 takes more clock cycles than the G4e to execute floating-point instructions, but those clock cycles are much faster. So Pentium 4's clock-speed advantage and high-bandwidth front-side bus give it a distinct advantage over the Pentium III in floating-point–intensive benchmarks and enable it to be more than competitive with the G4e in spite of *x*87's drawbacks.

Concluding Remarks on the G4e's and Pentium 4's FPUs

The take-home message in the preceding discussion can be summed up as follows: While the G4e has fairly standard, unremarkable floating-point hardware, the PPC ISA does things the way they're supposed to be done—with three-operand or more instructions and a large, flat register file. The Pentium 4, on the other hand, has slightly better hardware but is hobbled by the legacy *x*87 ISA. The exact degree to which the *x*87's weaknesses affect performance has been debated for as long as the *x*87 has been around, but there seems to be a consensus that the situation is less than ideal.

The other thing that's extremely important to note is that when it comes to floating-point performance, a good memory subsystem is absolutely key. It doesn't matter how good a processor's floating-point hardware is—if you can't keep it fed, it won't be doing much work. Therefore, floating-point performance on both Pentium 4– and G4e-based systems depends on each system's available memory bandwidth.

The Vector Execution Units

One key technology on which both the Pentium 4 and the G4e rely for performance in their most important type of application—media applications (image processing, streaming media, 3D rendering, etc.)—is Single Instruction, Multiple Data (SIMD) computing, also known as *vector computing*. This section looks at SIMD on both the G4e and the Pentium 4.

A Brief Overview of Vector Computing

Chapter 1 discussed the movement of floating-point and vector capabilities from co-processors onto the CPU die. However, the addition of vector instructions and hardware to a modern, superscalar CPU is a bit more drastic than the addition of floating-point capability. A microprocessor is a *Single Instruction stream, Single Data stream (SISD)* device, and it has been since its inception, whereas vector computation represents a fundamentally different type of computing: SIMD. Figure 8-1 compares the SIMD and SISD in terms of a simple diagram that was introduced in Chapter 1.

As you can see in Figure 8-1, an SIMD machine exploits a property of the data stream called *data parallelism*. Data parallelism is said to be present in a dataset when its elements can be processed in parallel, a situation that most often occurs in large masses of data of a uniform type, like media files. Chapter 1 described media applications as applications that use small, repetitious chunks of code to operate on large, uniform datasets. Since these small chunks of code apply the same sequence of operations to every element of a large dataset, and these datasets can often be processed out of order, it makes sense to use SIMD to apply the same instructions to multiple elements at once.

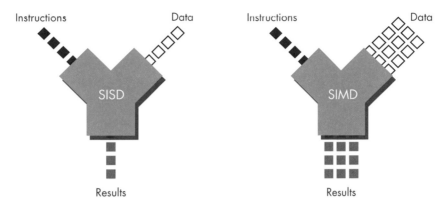

Figure 8-1: SISD versus SIMD

A classic example of a media application that exploits data parallelism is the inversion of a digital image to produce its negative. The image processing program must iterate through an array of uniform integer values (pixels) and perform the same operation (inversion) on each one. Consequently, there are multiple data points on which a single operation is performed, and the order in which that operation is performed on the data points doesn't affect the outcome. The program could start the inversion at the top of the image, the bottom of the image, or in the middle of the image—it doesn't matter as long as the entire image is inverted.

This technique of applying a single instruction to multiple data elements at once is quite effective in yielding significant speedups for many types of applications, especially streaming media, image processing, and 3D rendering. In fact, many of the floating-point–intensive applications described previously can benefit greatly from SIMD, which is why both the G4e and the Pentium 4 skimped on the traditional FPU in favor of strengthening their SIMD units.

There were some early, ill-fated attempts at making a purely SIMD machine, but the SIMD model is simply not flexible enough to accommodate general-purpose code. The only form in which SIMD is really feasible is as a part of a SISD host machine that can execute branch instructions and other types of code that SIMD doesn't handle well. This is, in fact, the situation with SIMD in today's market. Programs are written for a SISD machine and include SIMD instructions in their code.

Vectors Revisited: The AltiVec Instruction Set

The basic data unit of SIMD computation is the vector, which is why SIMD computing is also known as vector computing or *vector processing*. Vectors, which you met in Chapter 1, are nothing more than rows of individual numbers, or scalars. Figure 8-2 illustrates the differences between vectors and scalars.

A simple CPU operates on scalars one at a time. A superscalar CPU operates on multiple scalars at once, but it performs a different operation on each instruction. A vector processor lines up a whole row of scalars, all of the same type, and operates on them in parallel as a unit.

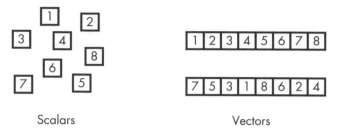

Scalars   Vectors

Figure 8-2: Scalars versus vectors

Vectors are represented in what is called a *packed data format*, in which data are grouped into bytes or words and packed into a vector of a certain length. To take Motorola's AltiVec, for example, each of the 32 AltiVec registers is 128 bits wide, which means that AltiVec can operate on vectors that are 128 bits wide. AltiVec's 128-bit wide vectors can be subdivided into

- 16 elements, where each element is either an 8-bit signed or unsigned integer or an 8-bit character;
- 8 elements, where each element is a 16-bit signed or unsigned integer;
- 4 elements, where each element is either a 32-bit signed or unsigned integer, or a single-precision (32-bit) IEEE floating-point number.

Figure 8-3 can help you visualize how these elements are packed together.

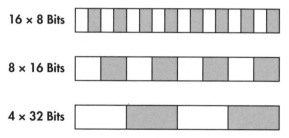

Figure 8-3: Vectors as packed data formats

AltiVec Vector Operations

Motorola's AltiVec literature divides the types of vector operations that AltiVec can perform into four useful and easily comprehensible categories. Because these categories offer a good way of dividing up the basic things you can do with vectors, I'll use Motorola's categories to break down the major types of vector operations. I'll also use pictures similar to those from Motorola's AltiVec literature, modifying them a bit when needed.

Before looking at the types of operations, note that AltiVec's instruction format supports up to four operands, laid out as follows:

```
AltiVec_instruction source1, source2, filter/mod, destination
```

The main difference to be noted is the presence of the *filter/mod* operand, also called a *control operand* or *control vector*. This operand specifies a register that holds either a bit mask or a control vector that somehow modifies or sets the terms of the operation. You'll see the control vector in action when we look at the vector permute.

AltiVec's four-operand format is much more flexible than the two-operand format available to Intel's SIMD instructions, making AltiVec a much more ideal vector processing instruction set than the Pentium line's SSE or SSE2 extensions. The *x*86 ISA's SIMD extensions are limited by their two-operand format in much the same way that the *x*86 floating-point extension is limited by its stack-based register file.

Motorola's categories for the vector operations that the AltiVec can perform are as follows:

- intra-element arithmetic
- intra-element non-arithmetic
- inter-element arithmetic
- inter-element non-arithmetic

Intra-Element Arithmetic and Non-Arithmetic Instructions

Intra-element arithmetic operation is one of the most basic and easy-to-grasp categories of vector operation because it closely parallels scalar arithmetic. Consider, for example, an intra-element addition. This involves lining up two or three vectors (VA, VB, and VC) and adding their individual elements together to produce a sum vector (VT). Figure 8-4 contains an example of intra-element arithmetic operation at work on three vectors, each of which consists of four 32-bit numbers. Other intra-element operations include multiplication, multiply-add, average, and minimum.

Intra-element non-arithmetic operations basically work the same way as intra-element arithmetic functions, except for the fact that the operations performed are different. Intra-element non-arithmetic operations include logical operations like AND, OR, and XOR.

Figure 8-4 shows an intra-element addition involving three vectors of pixel values: red, blue, and green. The individual elements of the three vectors are added to produce a target vector consisting of white pixels.

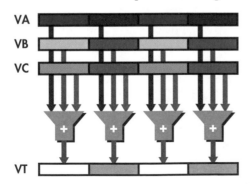

Figure 8-4: Intra-element arithmetic operations

The following list summarizes the types of vector intra-element instructions that AltiVec supports:

- integer logical instructions
- integer arithmetic instructions
- integer compare instructions
- integer rotate and shift instructions
- floating-point arithmetic instructions
- floating-point rounding and conversion instructions
- floating-point compare instructions
- floating-point estimate instructions
- memory access instructions

Inter-Element Arithmetic and Non-Arithmetic Instructions

Inter-element arithmetic operations are operations that happen between the elements in a single vector. An example of an inter-element arithmetic operation is shown in Figure 8-5, in which the elements in one vector are added together and the total is stored in an accumulation vector—VT.

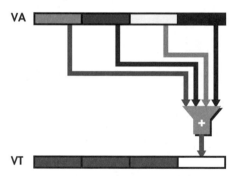

Figure 8-5: An inter-element sum across operation

Inter-element non-arithmetic operations are operations like vector permute, which rearrange the order of the elements in an individual vector. Figure 8-6 shows a vector permute instruction. VA and VB are the source registers that hold the two vectors to be permuted, VC contains the control vector that tells AltiVec which elements it should put where, and VT is the destination register.

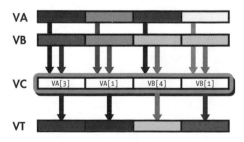

Figure 8-6: An inter-element permute operation

The following list summarizes the types of vector inter-element instructions that AltiVec supports:

- Alignment support instructions
- Permutation and formatting instructions
- Pack instructions
- Unpack instructions
- Merge instructions
- Splat instructions
- Shift left/right instructions

The G4e's VU: SIMD Done Right

The AltiVec extension to PowerPC adds 162 new instructions to the PowerPC instruction set. When Motorola first implemented AltiVec support in their PowerPC processor line with the MPC 7400, they added 32 new AltiVec registers to the G4's die, along with two dedicated AltiVec SIMD functional units. All of the AltiVec calculations were done by one of two fully-pipelined, independent AltiVec execution units.

The G4e improves significantly on the original G4's AltiVec implementation. The processor boasts four independent AltiVec units, three of which are fully pipelined and can operate on multiple instructions at once. These units are as follows:

Vector permute unit
This unit handles the instructions that rearrange the operands within a vector. Some examples are `permute`, `merge`, `splat`, `pack`, and `unpack`.

Vector simple integer unit
This unit handles all of the fast and simple vector integer instructions. It's basically just like one of the G4e's three fast IUs, except vectorized. This unit has only one pipeline stage, so most of the instructions it executes are single-cycle.

Vector complex integer unit
This is the vector equivalent of the G4e's one slow IU. It handles the slower vector instructions, like multiply, multiply-add, and so on.

Vector floating-point unit
This unit handles all vector floating-point instructions.

The G4e can issue up to two AltiVec instructions per clock cycle, with each instruction going to any one of the four vector execution units. All of the units, with the exception of the VSIU, are pipelined and can operate on multiple instructions at once.

All of this SIMD execution hardware is tied to a generous register file that consists of 32 128-bit architectural registers and 16 additional vector rename registers.

Intel's MMX

The story of MMX and SSE/KNI/MMX2 is quite a bit more complicated than that of AltiVec, and there are a number of reasons why this is so. To begin with, Intel first introduced MMX as an *integer-only* SIMD solution, so MMX doesn't support floating-point arithmetic at all. Another weakness of MMX is the fact that Intel jumped through some hoops to avoid adding a new processor state, hoops that complicated the implementation of MMX. I'll deal with this in more detail in "SSE and SSE2" on page 175.

Where AltiVec's vectors are 128 bits wide, MMX's are only 64 bits wide. These 64-bit vectors can be subdivided into:

- 8 elements (a packed byte), where each element is an 8-bit integer;
- 4 elements (a packed word), where each element is a 16-bit signed or unsigned integer;
- 2 elements (packed double word), where each element is a 32-bit signed or unsigned integer.

These vectors are stored in eight MMX registers, based on a flat-file model. These eight registers, MM0 to MM7, are *aliased* onto the *x*87's stack-based floating-point registers, FP0 to FP7. Intel did this in order to avoid imposing a costly *processor state switch* any time you want to use MMX instructions. The drawback to this approach is that floating-point operations and MMX operations must share a register space, so a programmer can't mix floating-point and MMX instructions in the same routine. Of course, since there's no *mode bit* for toggling the register file between MMX and floating-point usage, there's nothing to prevent a programmer from pulling such a stunt and corrupting his floating-point data by overwriting it with integer vector data.

The fact that a programmer can't mix floating-point and MMX instructions normally isn't a problem, though. In most programs, floating-point calculations are used for generating data, while SIMD calculations are used for displaying it.

In all, MMX added 57 new instructions to the *x*86 ISA. The MMX instruction format is pretty much like the conventional *x*86 instruction format:

```
MMX_instruction mmreg1, mmreg2
```

In this instruction, *mmreg1* is the both the destination and source operand, meaning that *mmreg1* gets overwritten by the result of the calculation. For the reasons outlined in the previous discussion of operand formats, this two-operand instruction format isn't nearly as optimal as AltiVec's four-operand format. Furthermore, MMX instructions lack that third filter/mod vector that AltiVec has. This means that you can't do those one-cycle, arbitrary two-vector permutes.

SSE and SSE2

Even as MMX was being rolled out, Intel knew that its 64-bit nature and integer-only limitation made it seriously deficient as a vector processing solution. An article in an issue of the *Intel Technology Journal* tells this story:

> In February 1996, the product definition team at Intel presented Intel's executive staff with a proposal for a single-instruction-multiple-data (SIMD) floating-point model as an extension to IA-32 architecture. In other words, the "Katmai" processor, later to be externally named the Pentium III processor, was being proposed. The meeting was inconclusive. At that time, the Pentium® processor with MMX instructions had not been introduced and hence was unproven in the market. Here the executive staff were being asked essentially to "double down" their bets on MMX instructions and then on SIMD floating-point extensions. Intel's executive staff gave the product team additional questions to answer and two weeks later, still in February 1996, they gave the OK for the "Katmai" processor project. During the later definition phase, the technology focus was refined beyond 3D to include other application areas such as audio, video, speech recognition, and even server application performance. In February 1999, the Pentium III processor was introduced.
>
> —*Intel Technology Journal, Second Quarter, 1999*

Intel's goal with SSE (Streaming SIMD Extensions, aka MMX2/KNI) was to add four-way, 128-bit SIMD single-precision floating-point computation to the *x*86 ISA. Intel went ahead and added an extra eight 128-bit architectural registers, called *XMM registers*, for holding vector floating-point instructions. These eight registers are in addition to the eight MMX/*x*87 registers that were already there. Since these registers are totally new and independent, Intel had to hold their nose and add an extra processor state to accommodate them. This means a state switch if you want to go from using *x*87 to MMX or SSE, and it also means that operating system code had to be rewritten to accommodate the new state.

SSE still had some shortcomings, though. SSE's vector floating-point operations were limited to single-precision, and vector integer operations were still limited to 64 bits, because they had to use the old MMX/*x*87 registers.

With the introduction of SSE2 on the Pentium 4, Intel finally got its SIMD act together. On the integer side, SSE2 finally allows the storage of 128-bit integer vectors in the XMM registers, and it modifies the ISA by extending old instructions and adding new ones to support 128-bit SIMD integer operations. For floating-point, SSE2 now supports double-precision SIMD floating-point operations. All told, SSE2 adds 144 new instructions, some of which are cache control instructions.

The Pentium 4's Vector Unit: Alphabet Soup Done Quickly

Now that you know something about SSE2, let's look at how it's implemented on the Pentium 4. In keeping with the Pentium 4's "narrow, deep, and fast" approach, the Pentium 4 does not sport any dedicated SSE2 pipelines. Rather, both FPU pipes double as VU pipes, meaning that the FPU memory unit also handles vector memory operations and the FPU arithmetic unit also handles vector arithmetic operations. So in contrast to the G4e's four vector arithmetic units, the Pentium 4 has one vector arithmetic unit that just does everything—integer, floating-point, permutes, and so on.

So, with only one execution pipeline to handle all vector and floating-point operations, you're probably wondering how the Pentium 4's designers expected it to perform competitively on the media applications for which it was obviously designed. The Pentium 4 is able to offer competitive SIMD performance based on a combination of three factors:

- relatively low instruction latencies
- extremely high clock speeds
- a high-bandwidth caching and memory subsystem

Let's take a look at these factors and how they work together.

The Pentium 4 optimization manual lists in Section C the average latencies of the most commonly used SIMD instructions. A look through the latency tables reveals that the majority of single- and double-precision arithmetic operations have latencies in the four- to six-cycle range. In other words, most vector floating-point instructions go through four to six pipeline stages before leaving the Pentium 4's VU. This number is relatively low for a 20-stage pipeline design like the Pentium 4, especially considering that vector floating-point instructions on the G4e go through four pipeline stages on average before leaving the G4e's vector FPU.

Now, considering the fact that at the time of this writing, the Pentium 4's clock speed is significantly higher than (roughly double) that of the G4e, the Pentium 4's ability to execute single- and double-precision vector floating-point operations in almost the same number of clock cycles as the G4e means that the Pentium 4 executes these operations almost three times as fast in real-world, "wall clock" time. So the Pentium 4 can get away with having only one VU, because that VU is able to grind through vector operations with a much higher instruction completion rate (instructions/ns) than the G4e. Furthermore, as the Pentium 4's clock speed increases, its vector crunching power grows.

Another piece that's crucial to the whole performance picture is the Pentium 4's high-bandwidth FSB, memory subsystem, and low-latency caching subsystem. I won't cover these features here, but I'll just note that the Pentium 4 has large amounts of bandwidth at its disposal. All this bandwidth is essential to keeping the very fast VU fed with data, and as the Pentium 4's clock speed has increased, bandwidth has played an even larger role in vector processing performance.

Increasing Floating-Point Performance with SSE2

I mentioned earlier that MMX uses a flat register file, and the same is true of both SSE and SSE2. The eight, 128-bit XMM registers are arranged as a flat file, which means that if you're able to replace an *x*87 FP operation with an SSE or SSE2 operation, you can use clever resource scheduling to avoid the performance hit brought on by the Pentium 4's combination of a stack-based FP register file and a non-free fxch instruction. Intel's highly advanced compiler has proven that converting large amounts of *x*87 code to SSE2 code can yield a significant performance boost.

Conclusions

The preceding discussion should make it clear that the overall design approaches outlined in the first half of this chapter can be seen in the back ends of each processor. The G4e continues its "wide and shallow" approach to performance, counting on instruction-level parallelism (ILP) to allow it to squeeze the most performance out of code. The Pentium 4's "narrow and deep" approach, on the other hand, uses fewer execution units, eschewing ILP and betting instead on increases in clock speed to increase performance.

Each of these approaches has its benefits and drawbacks, but as I've stressed repeatedly throughout this chapter, microarchitecture is by no means the only factor in the application performance equation. Certain properties of the ISA that a processor implements can influence performance.

9

64-BIT COMPUTING
AND x86-64

On a number of occasions in previous chapters, I've discussed some of the more undesirable aspects of the PC market's most popular instruction set architecture—the x86. The x86 ISA's complex addressing modes, its inclusion of unwieldy and obscure instructions, its variable instruction lengths, its dearth of architectural registers, and its other quirks have vexed programmers, compiler writers, and microprocessor architects for years.

In spite of these drawbacks, the x86 ISA continues to enjoy widespread commercial success, and the number of markets in which it competes continues to expand. The reasons for this ongoing success are varied, but one factor stands out as by far the most important: inertia. The installed base of x86 application software is huge, and the costs of an industry-wide transition to a cleaner, more classically RISC ISA would enormously outweigh any benefits. Nonetheless, this hasn't stopped many folks, including the top brass at Intel, from dreaming of a post-x86 world.

Intel's IA-64 and AMD's x86-64

As of this writing, there have been two important attempts to move mainstream, commodity desktop and server computing beyond the 32-bit *x*86 ISA, the first by Intel and the second by Intel's chief rival, Advanced Micro Devices (AMD). In 1994, Intel and Hewlett-Packard began work on a completely new ISA, called *IA-64*. IA-64 is a 64-bit ISA that embodies a radically different approach to performance from anything the mainstream computing market has yet seen. This approach, which Intel has called *Explicitly Parallel Instruction Computing (EPIC)*, is a mix of a *very long instruction word (VLIW)* ISA, *predication*, *speculative loading*, and other compiler-oriented, performance-enhancing techniques, many of which had never been successfully implemented in a commercial product line prior to IA-64.

Because IA-64 represents a total departure from *x*86, IA-64–based processors cannot run legacy *x*86 code natively. The fact that IA-64 processors must run the very large mass of legacy *x*86 code in emulation has posed a serious problem for Intel as they try to persuade various segments of the market to adopt the new architecture.

Unfortunately for Intel, the lack of backward compatibility isn't the only obstacle that IA-64 has had to contend with. Since its inception, Intel's IA-64 program has met with an array of setbacks, including massive delays in meeting development and production milestones, lackluster integer performance, and difficulty in achieving high clock speeds. These and a number of other problems have prompted some wags to refer to Intel's first IA-64 implementation, called *Itanium* and released in 2001, as *Itanic*. The Itanium Processor Family (IPF) has since found a niche in the lucrative and growing high-end server and workstation segments. Nonetheless, in focusing on Itanium Intel left a large, 64-bit sized hole in the commodity workstation and server markets.

In 1999, with Itanium development beset by problems and clearly some distance away from commercial release, AMD saw an opening to score a major blow against Intel by using a 64-bit derivative of Intel's own ISA to jump-start and dominate the nascent commodity 64-bit workstation market. Following on the success of its Athlon line of desktop processors, AMD took a gamble and bet the company's future on a set of 64-bit extensions to the *x*86 ISA. Called x*86-64*, these extensions enabled AMD to produce a line of 64-bit microprocessors that are cost-competitive with existing high-end and midrange *x*86 processors and, most importantly, backward-compatible with existing *x*86 code. The new processor architecture, popularly referred to by its code name *Hammer*, has been a commercial and technical success.

Introduced in April 2003 after a long series of delays and production problems, the Hammer's strong benchmark performance and excellent adoption rate spelled trouble for any hopes that Intel may have had for the mainstream commercial adoption of its Itanium line. Intel conceded as much when in 2004, they took the unprecedented step of announcing support for AMD's extensions in their own *x*86 workstation and server processors. Intel calls these 64-bit extensions *IA-32e*, but in this book we'll refer to them by AMD's name—*x*86-64.

Because *x*86-64 represents the future of *x*86 for both Intel and AMD, this chapter will look in some detail at the new ISA. As you'll see, *x*86-64 is more than just a 64-bit extension to the 32-bit *x*86 ISA; it adds some new features as well, while getting rid of some obsolete ones.

Why 64 Bits?

The question of why we need 64-bit computing is often asked but rarely answered in a satisfactory manner. There are good reasons for the confusion surrounding the question, the first of which is the rarely acknowledged fact that "the 64-bit question" is actually two questions:

1. How does the existing 64-bit server and workstation market use 64-bit computing?
2. What use does the consumer market have for 64-bit computing?

People who ask the 64-bit question are usually asking for the answer to question 1 in order to deduce the answer to question 2. This being the case, let's first look at question 1 before tackling question 2.

What Is 64-Bit Computing?

Simply put, the labels *16-bit*, *32-bit*, or *64-bit*, when applied to a microprocessor, characterize the processor's data stream. You may have heard the term *64-bit code*; this designates code that operates on 64-bit data.

In more specific terms, the labels *64-bit*, *32-bit*, and so on designate the number of bits that each of the processor's general-purpose registers (GPRs) can hold. So when someone uses the term *64-bit processor*, what they mean is a processor with GPRs that store 64-bit numbers. And in the same vein, a *64-bit instruction* is an instruction that operates on 64-bit numbers that are stored in 64-bit GPRs.

Figure 9-1 shows two computers, one a 32-bit computer and the other a 64-bit computer.

In Figure 9-1, I've tried my best to modify Figure 1-3 on page 6 in order to make my point. Don't take the instruction and code sizes too literally, since they're intended to convey a general feel for what it means to "widen" a processor from 32 bits to 64 bits.

Notice that not all of the data in memory, the cache, or the registers is 64-bit data. Rather, the data sizes are mixed, with 64 bits being the widest. We'll discuss why this is and what it means shortly.

Note that in the 64-bit CPU pictured in Figure 9-1, the width of the code stream has not changed; the same-sized machine language instruction could theoretically represent an instruction that operates on 32-bit numbers or an instruction that operates on 64-bit numbers, depending on the instruction's default data size. On the other hand, the widths of some elements of the data and results streams have doubled. In order to accommodate the wider data stream, the sizes of the processor's registers and the sizes of the internal data paths that feed those registers must also be doubled.

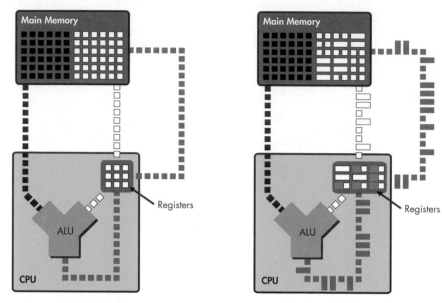

Figure 9-1: 32-bit versus 64-bit computing

Now look at the two programming models illustrated in Figure 9-2—one for a 32-bit processor and another for a 64-bit processor.

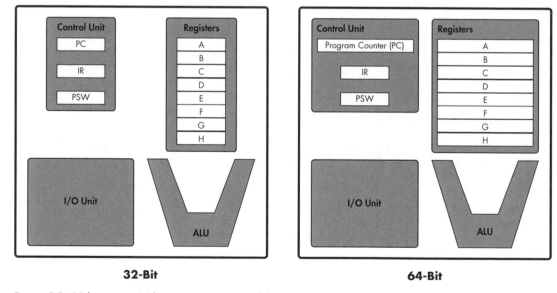

Figure 9-2: 32-bit versus 64-bit programming models

The registers in the 64-bit ISA pictured in Figure 9-2 are twice as wide as those in the 32-bit ISA, but the size of the instruction register (IR) that holds the currently executing instruction is the same in both processors. Again, the data stream has doubled in size, but the instruction stream has not. You might also note that the program counter (PC) has doubled in size. We'll talk about the reason for this in the next section.

The discussion up so far about widened instruction and data registers has laid out the simple answer to the question, "What is 64-bit computing?" If you take into account the fact that the data stream is made up of multiple types of data—a fact hinted at in Figure 9-1—the answer gets a bit more complicated.

For the simple processor pictured in Figure 9-2, the two types of data that can be processed are integer data and address data. As you'll recall from Chapter 1, addresses are really just integers that designate a memory address, so address data is just a special type of integer data. Hence, both data types are stored in the GPRs, and both integer and address calculations are done by the arithmetic logic unit (ALU).

Many modern processors support two additional data types: floating-point data and vector data. Each of these two data types has its own set of registers and its own execution unit(s). The following table compares all four data types in 32-bit and 64-bit processors:

Data Type	Register Type	Execution Unit	x86 Width (in Bits)	x86-64 Width (in Bits)
Integer	GPR	ALU	32	64
Address	GPR	ALU or AGU	32	64
Floating-point	FPR	FPU	80	80
Vector	VR	VPU	128	128

You can see from this table that the difference the move to 64 bits makes is in the integer and address hardware. The floating-point and vector hardware stays the same.

Current 64-Bit Applications

Now that you know what 64-bit computing is, let's look at the benefits of increased integer and address sizes.

Dynamic Range

The main thing that a wider integer gives you is increased *dynamic range*. Instead of giving a one-line definition of the term dynamic range, I'll just explain how it works.

In the *base-10* number system which you're all accustomed to, you can represent a maximum of 10 integers (0 to 9) with a single digit. This is because base-10 has 10 different symbols with which to represent numbers. To represent more than 10 integers, you need to add another digit, using a combination of two symbols chosen from among the set of 10 to represent any one of 100 integers (00 to 99). The formula you can use to compute the number of integers (dynamic range, or DR) you can represent with an *n*-digit base-10 number is

$$DR = 10^n$$

So a one-digit number gives you $10^1 = 10$ possible integers, a two-digit number $10^2 = 100$ integers, a three-digit number $10^3 = 1,000$ integers, and so on.

The base-2, or *binary*, number system that computers use has only two symbols with which to represent integers: 0 and 1. Thus, a single-digit binary number allows you to represent only two integers—0 and 1. With a two-digit (or two-bit) binary, you can represent four integers by combining the two symbols (0 and 1) in any of the following four ways:

Binary	Base-10
00	0
01	1
10	2
11	3

Similarly, a three-bit binary number gives you eight possible combinations, which you can use to represent eight different integers. As you increase the number of bits, you increase the number of integers you can represent. In general, *n* bits allow you to represent 2^n integers in binary. So a 4-bit binary number can represent $2^4 = 16$ integers, an 8-bit number gives you $2^8 = 256$ integers, and so on.

In moving from a 32-bit GPR to a 64-bit GPR, the range of integers that a processor can recognize and perform arithmetic calculations on goes from $2^{32} = 4.3e9$ to $2^{64} = 1.8e19$. The dynamic range, then, increases by a factor of 4.3 billion. Thus a 64-bit integer can represent a much larger range of numbers than a 32-bit integer.

The Benefits of Increased Dynamic Range, or, How the Existing 64-Bit Computing Market Uses 64-Bit Integers

Some applications, mostly in the realm of scientific computing and simulations, require 64-bit integers because they work with numbers outside the dynamic range of 32-bit integers. When the magnitude of the result of a calculation exceeds the range of possible integer values that the machine can represent, you get a situation called either *overflow* (the result was greater than the highest positive integer) or *underflow* (the result was less than the largest negative integer). When this happens, the number you get in the register isn't the right answer. There's a bit in the *x*86's processor status word that allows you to check to see if an integer arithmetic result has just exceeded the processor's dynamic range, so you know that the result is erroneous. Such situations are very, very rare in integer applications. I personally have never run into this problem, although I have run into the somewhat related problem of floating-point round-off error a few times.

Programmers who run into integer overflow or underflow problems on a 32-bit platform have the option of using a 64-bit integer construct provided by a high-level language like C. In such cases, the compiler uses two registers per integer—one for each half of the integer—to do 64-bit calculations in 32-bit hardware. This has obvious performance drawbacks, making it less desirable than a true 64-bit integer implementation.

In addition to scientific computing and simulations, there is another application domain for which 64-bit integers can offer real benefits: cryptography. Most popular encryption schemes rely on the multiplication and factoring of very large integers, and the larger the integers, the more secure the encryption. AMD and Intel are hoping that the growing demand for tighter security and more encryption in the mainstream business and consumer computing markets will make 64-bit processors attractive.

Larger GPRs don't just make for larger integers, but they make for larger addresses, as well. In fact, larger addresses are the primary advantage that 64-bit computers have over their 32-bit counterparts.

Virtual Address Space vs. Physical Address Space

Throughout this book, I've been referring to three different types of storage—the caches, the RAM, and the hard disk—without ever explicitly describing how all three of these types fit together from the point of view of a programmer. If you're not familiar with the concept of *virtual memory*, you might be wondering how a programmer makes use of the hard disk for code and data storage if load and store instructions take memory addresses as source and destination operands. Though this brief section only scratches the surface of the concept of virtual memory, it should give you a better idea of how this important concept works.

Every major component in a computer system must have an address. Just like having a phone number allows people to communicate with each other via the phone system, having an address allows a computer's components to communicate with each other via the computer's internal system of buses. If a component does not have an address, no other component in the system can communicate with it directly, either for the purpose of reading from it, writing to it, or controlling it. Video cards, SCSI cards, memory banks, chipsets, processors, and so on all have unique addresses. Even more importantly for our purposes, storage devices such as the hard disk and main memory also have unique addresses, and because such devices are intended for use as storage, they actually look to the CPU like a range of addresses that can be read from or written to.

Like a phone number, each component's address is a whole number (i.e., an integer), and as you learned earlier in our discussion of dynamic range, the width of an address (the number of digits in the address) determines the range of possible addresses that can be represented.

A range of addresses is called an *address space*, and in a modern 32-bit desktop computer system, the processor and operating system work together to provide each running program with the illusion that it has access to a flat address space of up to 4GB in size. (Remember the 2^{32} = 4.3 billion number? Those 4.3 billion bytes are 4GB, which is the number of bytes that a 32-bit computer can address.) One large portion of this *virtual address space* that a running program sees consists of addresses through which it can interact with the operating system, and through the OS with the other parts of the system. The other portion of the address space is set aside for the program to interact with main memory. This main memory portion of the address space always represents only a part of the total 4GB virtual address space, in many cases about 2GB.

This 2GB chunk of address space represents a kind of window through which the program can look at main memory. Note that the program can see and manipulate only the data it has placed in this special address space, so on a 32-bit machine, a program can see only about 2GB worth of addresses at any given time. (There are some ways of getting around this, but those don't concern us here.)

The Benefits of a 64-Bit Address

Because addresses are just special-purpose integers, an ALU and register combination that can handle more possible integer values can also handle that many more possible addresses. This means that each process's virtual address space is greatly increased on a 64-bit machine, allowing each process to "see" a much larger range of virtual addresses. In theory, each process on a 64-bit computer could have an 18 million–terabyte address space.

The specifics of microprocessor implementation dictate that there's a big difference between the amount of address space that a 64-bit address value could theoretically yield and the actual sizes of the virtual and physical address spaces that a given 64-bit architecture supports. In the case of *x*86-64, the actual size of the Hammer line's virtual addresses is 48 bits, which makes for about 282 terabytes of virtual address space. (I'm tempted to say about this number what Bill Gates is falsely alleged to have said about 640KB back in the DOS days: "282 terabytes ought to be enough for anybody." But don't quote me on that in 10 years when Doom 9 takes up three or four hundred terabytes of hard disk space.) *x*86-64's physical address space is 40 bits wide, which means that an *x*86-64 system can support about one terabyte of physical memory (RAM).

So, what can a program do with up to 282 terabytes of virtual address space and up to a terabyte of RAM? Well, caching a very large database in it is a start. Back-end servers for mammoth databases are one place where 64 bits have long been a requirement, so it's no surprise to see 64-bit offerings billed as capable database platforms.

On the media and content creation side of things, folks who work with very large 2D image files also appreciate the extra address space. A related application domain where large amounts of memory come in handy is in simulation and modeling. Under this heading you could put various CAD tools and 3D rendering programs, as well as things like weather and scientific simulations, and even, as I've already half-jokingly referred to, real-time 3D games. Though the current crop of 3D games (as of 2006) probably wouldn't benefit from greater than 4GB of address space, it's certain that you'll see a game that benefits from greater than 4GB of address space within the next few years.

There is one drawback to the increase in memory space that 64-bit addressing affords. Because memory address values (or *pointers*, in programmer lingo) are now twice as large, they take up twice as much cache space. Pointers normally make up only a fraction of all the data in the cache, but when that fraction doubles, it can squeeze other useful data out of the cache and degrade performance.

NOTE   *Some of you who read the preceding discussion would no doubt point out that 32-bit Xeon systems are available with more than 4GB of RAM. Furthermore, Intel allegedly has a fairly simple hack that it could implement to allow its 32-bit systems to address up to 512GB of memory. Still, the cleanest and most future-proof way to address the 4GB ceiling is a 64-bit pointer.*

The 64-Bit Alternative: x86-64

When AMD set out to alter the *x*86 ISA in order to bring it into the world of 64-bit computing, they took the opportunity to do more than just widen the GPRs. *x*86-64 makes a number of improvements to *x*86, and this section looks at some of them.

Extended Registers

I don't want to get into a historical discussion of the evolution of what eventually became the modern *x*86 ISA, as Intel's hardware went from 4-bit to 8-bit to 16-bit to 32-bit. You can find such discussions elsewhere, if you're interested. I'll only point out that what we now consider to be the "*x*86 ISA" was first introduced in 1978 with the release of the 8086. The 8086 had four 16-bit integer registers and four 16-bit registers that were intended to hold memory addresses but also could be used as integer registers. (The four integer registers, though, could not be used to store memory addresses in 16-bit addressing mode.) This gave the 8086 a total of eight integer registers, four of which could also be used to store addresses.

With the release of the 386, Intel extended the *x*86 ISA to support 32-bit integers by doubling the size of original eight 16-bit registers. In order to access the extended portion of these registers, assembly language programmers used a different set of register mnemonics.

With *x*86-64, AMD has done pretty much the same thing that Intel did to enable the 16-bit to 32-bit transition—it has doubled the sizes of the eight GPRs and assigned new mnemonics to the extended registers. However, extending the existing eight GPRs isn't the only change AMD made to the *x*86 register model.

More Registers

One of the oldest and longest-running gripes about *x*86 is that the programming model has only eight GPRs, eight FPRs, and eight SIMD registers. All newer RISC ISAs support many more architectural registers; the PowerPC ISA, for instance, specifies 32 of each type of register. Increasing the number of registers allows the processor to keep more data where the execution units can access it immediately; this translates into a reduced number of loads and stores, which means less memory subsystem traffic and less waiting for data to load. More registers also give the compiler or programmer more flexibility to schedule instructions so that dependencies are reduced and pipeline bubbles are kept to a minimum.

Modern *x*86 CPUs get around some of these limitations by means of a trick called *register renaming*, described in Chapter 4. Register renaming involves putting extra, "hidden," internal registers onto the die and then dynamically mapping the programmer-visible registers to these internal, machine-visible registers. The Pentium 4, for instance, has 128 of these microarchitectural rename registers, which allow it to store more data closer to the ALUs and reduce false dependencies.

In spite of the benefits of register renaming, it would still be nicer to have more registers directly accessible to the programmer via the *x*86 ISA. This would allow a compiler or an assembly language programmer more flexibility and control to statically optimize the code. It would also allow a decrease in the number of memory access instructions (loads and stores). In extending *x*86 to 64 bits, AMD has also taken the opportunity to double the number of programmer-visible GPRs and SIMD registers.

When running in 64-bit mode, *x*86-64 programmers have access to eight additional GPRs, for a total of 16 GPRs. Furthermore, there are eight new SIMD registers, added for use in SSE/SSE2 code. So the number of GPRs and SIMD registers available to *x*86-64 programmers has gone from eight each to 16 each. Take a look at Figure 9-3, which contains a diagram from AMD that shows the new programming model.

Notice that they've left the *x*87 floating-point stack alone. This is because both Intel and AMD are encouraging programmers to use SSE/SSE2 for floating-point code, instead of *x*87. I've discussed the reason for this before, so I won't recap it here.

Also notice that the PC is extended. This was done because the PC holds the address of the next instruction, and since addresses are now 64-bit, the PC must be widened to accommodate them.

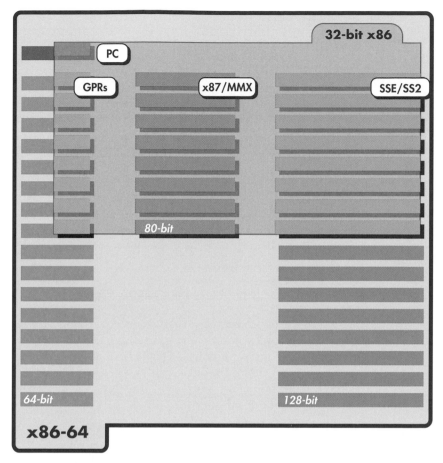

Figure 9-3: The x86-64 programming model

Switching Modes

Full binary compatibility with existing *x*86 code, both 32-bit and older 16-bit flavors, is one of *x*86-64's greatest strengths. *x*86-64 accomplishes this using a nested series of *modes*. The first and least interesting mode is *legacy mode*. When in legacy mode, the processor functions exactly like a standard *x*86 CPU—it runs a 32-bit operating system and 32-bit code exclusively, and none of *x*86-64's added capabilities are turned on. Figure 9-4 illustrates how legacy mode works.

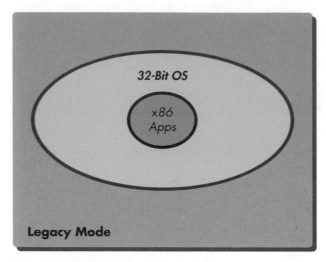

Figure 9-4: x86-64 legacy mode

In short, the Hammer in legacy mode looks like just another *x*86 processor.

It's in the 64-bit *long mode* that things start to get interesting. To run application software in long mode, you need a 64-bit operating system. Long mode provides two submodes—*64-bit mode* and *compatibility mode*—in which the OS can run either *x*86-64 or vanilla *x*86 code. Figure 9-5 should help you visualize how long mode works. (In this figure, x*86 Apps* includes both 32-bit and 16-bit *x*86 applications.)

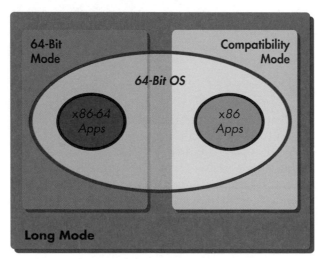

Figure 9-5: x86-64 long mode

So, legacy *x*86 code (both 32-bit and 16-bit) runs under a 64-bit OS in compatibility mode, and *x*86-64 code runs under a 64-bit OS in 64-bit mode. Only code running in long mode's 64-bit submode can take advantage of all the new features of *x*86-64. Legacy *x*86 code running in long mode's compatibility submode, for example, cannot see the extended parts of the registers, cannot use the eight extra registers, and is limited to the first 4GB of memory.

These modes are set for each segment of code on a per-segment basis by means of two bits in the segment's *code segment descriptor*. The chip examines these two bits so that it knows whether to treat a particular chunk of code as 32-bit or 64-bit. Table 9-1 (from AMD) shows the relevant features of each mode.

Table 9-1: x86-64 Modes

Mode		Operating System Required	Application Recompile Required	Defaults[1]			
				Address Size (Bits)	Operand Size (Bits)	Register Extensions[2]	GPR Width (Bits)
Long mode[3]	64-bit mode	New 64-bit OS	Yes	64	32	Yes	64
	Compatibility mode		No	32		No	32
				16			
Legacy mode[4]		Legacy 32-bit or 16-bit OS	No	32	32	No	32
				16	16		

[1] Defaults can be overridden in most modes using an instruction prefix or system control bit.

[2] Register extensions includes eight new GPRs and eight new XMM registers (also called SSE registers).

[3] Long mode supports only x86 protected mode. It does not support x86 real mode or virtual-8086 mode. Also, it does not support task switching.

[4] Legacy mode supports x86 real mode, virtual-8086 mode, and protected mode.

Notice that Table 9-1 specifies 64-bit mode's default integer size as 32 bits. Let me explain.

We've already discussed how only the integer and address operations are really affected by the shift to 64 bits, so it makes sense that only those instructions would be affected by the change. If all the addresses are now 64-bit, there's no need to change anything about the address instructions apart from their default pointer size. If a load in 32-bit legacy mode takes a 32-bit address pointer, then a load in 64-bit mode takes a 64-bit address pointer.

Integer instructions, on the other hand, are a different matter. You don't always need to use 64-bit integers, and there's no need to take up cache space and memory bandwidth with 64-bit integers if your application needs only smaller 32- or 16-bit ones. So it's not in the programmer's best interest to have the default integer size be 64 bits. Hence, the default data size for integer instructions is 32 bits, and if you want to use a larger or smaller integer, you must add an optional *prefix* to the instruction that overrides the default. This prefix, which AMD calls the *REX prefix* (presumably for *register extension*), is one byte in length. This means that 64-bit instructions are one byte longer, a fact that makes for slightly increased code sizes.

Increased code size is bad, because bigger code takes up more cache and more bandwidth. However, the effect of this prefix scheme on real-world code size depends on the number of 64-bit integer instructions in a program's instruction mix. AMD estimates that the average increase in code size from *x*86 code to equivalent *x*86-64 code is less than 10 percent, mostly due to the prefixes.

It's essential to AMD's plans for *x*86-64 that there be no performance penalty for running in legacy or compatibility mode versus long mode. The two backward-compatibility modes don't give you the performance-enhancing benefits of *x*86-64 (specifically, more registers), but they don't incur any added overhead, either. A legacy 32-bit program simply ignores *x*86-64's added features, so they don't affect it one way or the other.

Out with the Old

In addition to beefing up the *x*86 ISA by increasing the number and sizes of its registers, *x*86-64 also slims it down by kicking out some of the older and less frequently used features that have been kept thus far in the name of backward compatibility.

When AMD's engineers started looking for legacy *x*86 features to jettison, the first thing to go was the segmented memory model. Programs written to the *x*86-64 ISA use a flat, 64-bit virtual address space. Furthermore, legacy *x*86 applications running in long mode's compatibility submode must run in protected mode. Support for real mode and virtual-8086 mode are absent in long mode and available only in legacy mode. This isn't too much of a hassle, though, since, except for a few fairly old legacy applications, modern *x*86 apps use protected mode.

Conclusion

*x*86 wasn't the only consumer ISA to make the 64-bit leap in the first few years of the 21st century. IBM's 970, more popularly known as the G5, brought the PowerPC ISA moved into the same commodity 64-bit desktop and server space as AMD's Hammer. The next chapter will take an in-depth look at the G5, comparing it to the processors we've studied so far.

10

THE G5: IBM'S POWERPC 970

The last PowerPC processor to succeed the Motorola 74*xx* family as the heart of Apple's workstation line is the IBM PowerPC 970—the processor in Apple's G5 computer. This chapter takes an in-depth look at this processor, comparing it to Motorola's 7455 and, where appropriate, Intel's Pentium 4.

I'll begin by taking a look at the 970's overall design philosophy, and then I'll step through the stages of the 970's pipeline, much as we did in the previous two chapters on the Pentium 4 and G4e. Then we'll talk about instruction fetching, decoding, dispatching, issuing, execution, and completion, and we'll end with a look at the 970's back end.

At the outset, I should note that one of the most significant features of the 970 is its 64-bit integer and address hardware. If you want to learn more about 64-bit computing—what it can and cannot do, and what makes a 64-bit processor like the 970 different from 32-bit processors like the G4e and Pentium 4—make sure to read Chapter 9.

NOTE   *With the exception of the section on vector processing, most of the discussion below is relevant to IBM's POWER4 microarchitecture—the multiprocessor server micro-architecture on which the PowerPC 970 is based.*

Overview: Design Philosophy

In the previous chapters' comparison of the design philosophies behind the Pentium 4 and G4e, I tried to summarize each processor's overall approach to organizing its execution resources to squeeze the most performance out of today's software. I characterized the G4e's approach as *wide and shallow,* because the G4e moves a few instructions through its very wide back end in as few clock cycles as possible. I contrasted this approach to the Pentium 4's *narrow and deep* approach, which focuses on pushing large numbers of instructions through a narrow back end over the course of a many clock cycles.

Using similar language, the 970's approach could be characterized as *wide and deep.* In other words, the 970 wants to have it both ways: an extremely wide back end and a 14-stage (integer) pipeline that, while not as deep as the Pentium 4's, is nonetheless built for speed. Using a special technique, which we'll discuss shortly, the 970 can have a whopping 200 instructions on-chip in various stages of execution, a number that dwarfs not only the G4e's 16-instruction window but also the Pentium 4's 126-instruction one.

You can't have everything, though, and the 970 pays a price for its "more is better" design. When we discuss instruction dispatching and out-of-order execution on the 970, you'll see what trade-offs IBM made in choosing this design.

Figure 10-1 shows the microarchitecture's main functional blocks, and it should give you a preliminary feel for just how wide the 970 is.

Don't worry if all the parts of Figure 10-1 aren't immediately intelligible, because by the time this chapter is finished, you'll have a good understanding of everything depicted there.

Caches and Front End

Let's take a short look at the caches for the 970 and the G4e. Table 10-1 should give you a rough idea of how the two chips compare.

Table 10-1: The Caches of the PowerPC 970 and G4e

	L1 I-cache	L1 D-cache	L2 Cache
PowerPC 970	64KB, direct-mapped	32KB, two-way assoc.	512KB, eight-way assoc.
G4e	32KB, eight-way assoc.	32KB, eight-way assoc.	256KB, eight-way assoc.

Table 10-1 shows that the 970 sports a larger instruction cache than the G4e. This is because the 970's pipeline is roughly twice the length of the G4e's, which means that like the Pentium 4, the 970 pays a much higher performance penalty when its pipeline stalls due to a miss in the I-cache. In short, the 970's 64KB I-cache is intended to keep pipeline bubbles out of the chip's pipeline.

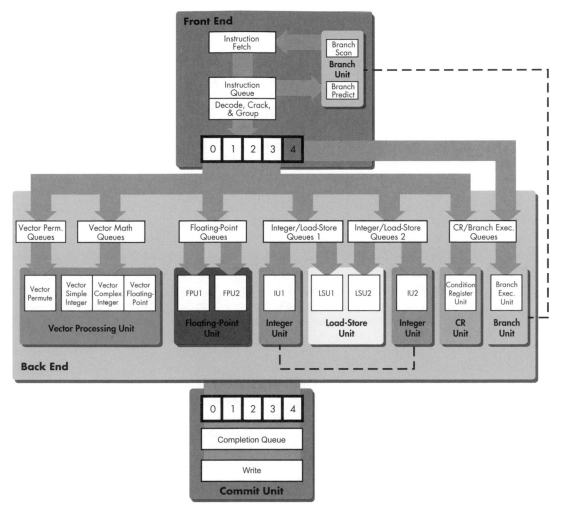

Figure 10-1: The IBM PowerPC 970

When you combine the 970's 32KB D-cache with its sizable 512KB L2, its high-speed double data rate (DDR) front-side bus and its support for up to eight data prefetch streams, you can see that this chip was made for floating-point- and SIMD-intensive media applications. This chip performs better on vector code than the G4e just based on these features alone.

Branch Prediction

Because of the depth of its pipeline and the width of its back end, the 970's designers spent a sizable chunk of the chip's resources on branch prediction. Like a high-hit-rate instruction cache, accurate branch prediction is essential if the 970 is to keep its pipeline full and its extensive execution resources in constant use. As such, the 970's extremely robust branch prediction unit (BPU) is one of its greatest strengths. This section takes a closer look at the top half of the 970's front end and at the role that branch prediction plays in steering that front end through the instruction stream.

The 970's instruction fetch logic fetches up to eight instructions per cycle from the L1 I-cache into an instruction queue, and on each fetch, the front end's branch unit scans these eight instructions in order to pick out up to two branches. If either of the two branches is conditional, the branch prediction unit predicts the condition's outcome (taken or not taken) and possibly its target address using one of two branch prediction schemes.

The first branch prediction scheme employed by the 970 is the standard BHT-based scheme first described in Chapter 5. The 970's BHT has 16 K entries—four times the number of entries in the Pentium 4's BHT and eight times the number of entries in the G4's BTIC. For each of these 16 K entries, a one-bit flag tells the branch predictor whether the branch should be taken or not taken.

The second scheme involves another 16 K entry table called the *global predictor table*. Each entry in this global predictor table is associated with an 11-bit vector that records the actual execution path taken by the previous 11 *fetch groups*. The processor uses this vector, which it constantly keeps up to date with the latest information, to set another one-bit flag for the global predictor table that specifies whether the branch should be taken or not taken.

Finally, there's a third 16 K entry table that's used by the 970's front end to keep track of which of the two schemes works best for each branch. When a branch is finally evaluated, the processor compares the success of both schemes and records in this selector table which scheme has done the best job so far of predicting the outcome of that particular branch.

Spending all those transistors on such a massive amount of branch prediction resources may seem like overkill right now, but when you've completed the next section, you'll see that the 970 can't afford to introduce any unnecessary bubbles into its pipeline.

The Trade-Off: Decode, Cracking, and Group Formation

As noted earlier, IBM's PowerPC 970 fetches eight instructions per cycle from the L1 cache into an instruction queue, from which the instructions are pulled for decoding at a rate of eight per cycle. This compares quite favorably to the G4e's four instructions per cycle fetch and decode rate.

Much like the Pentium 4 and its predecessor, the P6, the PowerPC 970 translates PowerPC instructions into an 86-bit internal instruction format that not only makes the instructions easier for the back end to schedule, but also explicitly encodes register dependency information. IBM calls these internal instructions *IOPs*, presumably short for *internal operations*. Like micro-ops on the Pentium 4, it is these IOPs that are actually executed out of order by the 970's back end. And also like micro-ops, cracking instructions down into multiple, more atomic and more strictly defined IOPs can help the back end squeeze out some extra instruction-level parallelism (ILP) by giving it more freedom to schedule code.

One important difference to note is that the architected PowerPC instructions are very close in form and function to the 970's IOPs, and in fact, the latter are probably just a restricted subset of the former. (That this is definitely true is not clear from the publicly available documentation.) The Pentium 4, in contrast, uses an internal instruction format that is significantly different in many important respects from the *x*86 ISA. So the process of "ISA translation" on the 970 is significantly less complex and less resource-intensive than the analogous process on the Pentium 4.

Almost all the PowerPC ISA instructions, with a few exceptions, translate into exactly one IOP on the 970. Of the instructions that translate into more than one IOP, IBM distinguishes two types:

- A *cracked* instruction is an instruction that splits into exactly two IOPs.

- A *millicoded* instruction is an instruction that splits into more than two IOPs.

This difference in the way instructions are classified is not arbitrary. Rather, it ties into a very important design decision that the POWER4's designers made regarding how the chip tracks instructions at various stages of execution.

Dispatching and Issuing Instructions on the PowerPC 970

If you take a look at the middle of the large PPC 970 diagram in Figure 10-1, notice that right below the *Decode, Crack, and Group* phase I've placed a group of five boxes. These five boxes represent what IBM calls a *dispatch group* (or *group*, for short), and each group consists of five IOPs arranged in program order according to certain rules and restrictions. It is these organized and packaged groups of five IOPs that the 970 dispatches in parallel to the six issue queues in its back end.

I probably shouldn't go any further in discussing how these groups work without first explaining the reason for their existence. By assembling IOPs together into specially ordered groups of five for dispatch and completion, the 970 can track these groups, and not individual IOPs, through the various stages of execution. So instead of tracking 100 individual IOPs in-flight as they work their way through the 100 or so execution slots available in the back end, the 970 need track only 20 groups. IOP grouping, then, significantly reduces the overhead associated with tracking and reordering the huge volume of instructions that can fit into the 970's deep and wide design.

As noted earlier, the 970's peculiar group dispatch scheme doesn't go into action until after the decode stage. Decoded PowerPC instructions flow from the bottom of the 970's instruction queue in order and fill up the five available dispatch slots in a group (four non-branch instructions and one branch instruction). Once the five slots have been filled from the instruction queue, the entire group is dispatched to the back end, where the individual instructions that constitute it (loads, stores, adds, fadds, etc.) enter the tops of their respective issue queues (i.e., an add goes into an integer issue queue, a fadd goes into a floating-point issue queue, etc.).

When the individual IOPs in a group reach their proper issue queues, they can then be issued out of program order to the execution units at a rate of eight IOPs/cycle for all the queues combined. Before they reach the completion stage, however, they need to be placed back into their group so that an entire group of five IOPs can be completed on each cycle. (Don't worry if this sounds a bit confusing right now. The group dispatch and formation scheme will become clearer when we discuss the 970's peculiar issue queue structure.)

The price the 970 pays for the reduced bookkeeping overhead afforded it by the dispatch grouping scheme is a loss of execution efficiency brought on by the diminished granularity of control that comes from being able to dispatch, schedule, issue, and complete instructions on an individual basis. Let me explain.

The 970's Dispatch Rules

When the 970's front end assembles an IOP group, there are certain rules it must follow. The first rule is that the group's five slots must be populated with IOPs in program order, starting with the oldest IOP in slot 0 and moving up to newest IOP in slot 4. Another rule is that all branch instructions must go in slot 4, and slot 4 is reserved for branch instructions only. This means that if the front end can't find a branch instruction to put in slot 4, it can issue one less instruction that cycle.

Similarly, there are some situations in which the front end must insert noops into the group's slots in order to force a branch instruction into slot 4. *Noop* (pronounced "no op") is short for *no operation*. It is a kind of non-instruction instruction that means "Do nothing." In other words, the front end must sometimes insert empty execution slots, or pipeline bubbles, into the instruction stream in order to make the groups comply with the rules.

The preceding rules aren't the only ones that must be adhered to when building groups. Another rule dictates that instructions destined for the conditional register unit (CRU) can go only in slots 0 and 1.

And then there are the rules dealing with cracked and millicoded instructions. Consider the following from IBM's POWER4 white paper:

> Cracked instructions flow into groups as any other instructions with one restriction. Both IOPs must be in the same group. If both IOPs cannot fit into the current group, the group is terminated and a new group is initiated. The instruction following the cracked instruction may be in the same group as the cracked instruction, assuming there is room in the group. Millicoded instructions always start a new group. The instruction following the millicoded instruction also initiates a new group.

And that's not all! A group has to have the following resources available before it can even dispatch to the back end. If just one of following resources is too tied up to accommodate the group or any of its instructions, then the entire group has to wait until that resource is freed up before it can dispatch:

Group completion table (GCT) entry
> The group completion table is the 970's equivalent of a reorder buffer or completion queue. While a normal ROB keeps track of individual in-flight instructions, the GCT tracks whole dispatch groups. The GCT has 20 entries for keeping track of 20 active groups as the groups'

constituent instructions make their way through the ~100 execution slots available in the back end's pipelines. Regardless of how few instructions are actually in the back end at a given moment, if those instructions are grouped so that all 20 GCT entries happen to be full, no new groups can be dispatched.

Issue queue slot

If there aren't enough slots available in the appropriate issue queues to accommodate all of a group's instructions, the group must wait to dispatch. (In a moment I'll elaborate on what I mean by "appropriate issue queues.")

Rename registers

There must be enough register rename resources available so that any instruction that requires register renaming can issue when it's dispatched to its issue queue.

Again, when it comes to the preceding restrictions, one bad instruction can keep the whole group from dispatching.

Because of its use of groups, the 970's dispatch bandwidth is sensitive to a complex host of factors, not the least of which is a sort of "internal fragmentation" of the group completion table that could potentially arise and needlessly choke dispatch bandwidth if too many of the groups in the GCT are partially or mostly empty.

In order to keep dispatch bottlenecks from stopping the fetch/decode portion of the pipeline, the 970 can buffer up to four dispatch groups in a four-entry *dispatch queue*. So if the preceding requirements are not met and there is space in the dispatch queue, a dispatch group can move into the queue and wait there for its dispatch requirements to be met.

Predecoding and Group Dispatch

The 970 uses a trick called *predecoding* in order to move some of the work of group formation higher up in the pipeline, thereby simplifying and speeding up the latter decode and group formation phases in the front end. As instructions are fetched from the L2 cache into the L1 I-cache, each instruction is predecoded and marked with a set of five predecode bits. These bits indicate how the instruction should be grouped—in other words, if it should be first in its group, last in its group, or unrestricted; if it will be a microcoded instruction; if it will trigger an exception; if it will be split or not; and so on. This information is used by the decode and group formation hardware to quickly route instructions for decoding and to group them for dispatch.

The predecode hardware also identifies branches and marks them for type—conditional or unconditional. This information is used by the 970's branch prediction hardware to implement branch folding, fall-through, and branch prediction with minimal latencies.

Some Preliminary Conclusions on the 970's Group Dispatch Scheme

In the preceding section, I went into some detail on the ins and outs of group formation and group dispatching in the 970. If you only breezed through the section and thought, "All of that seems like kind of a pain," then you got 90 percent of the point I wanted to make. Yes, it is indeed a pain, and that pain is the price the 970 pays for having both width and depth at the same time. The 970's big trade-off is that it needs less logic to support its long pipeline and extremely wide back end, but in return, it has to give up a measure of granularity, flexibility, and control over the dispatch and issuing of its instructions. Depending on the makeup of the instruction stream and how the IOPs end up being arranged, the 970 could possibly end up with quite a few groups that are either mostly empty, partially empty, or stalled waiting for execution resources.

So while the 970 may be theoretically able to accommodate 200 instructions in varying stages of fetch, decode, execution, and completion, the reality is probably that under most circumstances, a decent number of its execution slots will be empty on any given cycle due to dispatch, scheduling, and completion limitations. The 970 makes up for this with the fact that it just has so many available slots that it can afford to waste some on group-related pipeline bubbles.

The PowerPC 970's Back End

The PowerPC 970 sports a total of 12 execution units, depending on how you count them. Even a more conservative count that lumps together the three SIMD integer and floating-point units and doesn't count the branch execution unit would still give nine execution units.

In the following three sections, I'll discuss each of the 970's execution units, comparing them to the analogous units on the G4e, and in some cases the Pentium 4. As the discussion develops, keep in mind that a simple comparison of the types and numbers of execution units for each of the three processors is not at all adequate to the task of sorting out the real differences between the processors. Rather, there are complicating factors that make comparisons much more difficult than one might naïvely expect. Some of these factors will be evident in the sections dealing with each type of execution unit, but others won't turn up until we discuss the 970's issue queues in the last third of the chapter.

NOTE *As I cover each part of the 970's back end, I'll specify the number of rename registers of each type (integer, floating-point, vector) that the 970 has. If you compare these numbers to the equivalent numbers for the G4e, you'll see that 970 has many more rename registers than its predecessor. This increased number of rename registers is necessary because the 970's instruction window (up to 200 instructions in-flight) is significantly higher than that of the G4e (up to 16 instructions in-flight). The more instructions a processor can hold in-flight at once, the more rename registers it needs in order to pull off the kinds of tricks that a large instruction window enables you to do—i.e., dynamic scheduling, loop unrolling, speculative execution, and the like. In a nutshell, more instructions on the chip in various stages of execution means more data needs to be stored in more registers.*

Integer Unit, Condition Register Unit, and Branch Unit

In the chapters on the Pentium 4 and G4e, I described how both of these processors embody a similar approach to integer computation in that they divide integer operations into two types: simple and complex. Simple integer instructions, like add, are the most common type of integer instruction and take only one cycle to execute on most hardware. Complex integer instructions (e.g., integer division) are rarer and take multiple cycles to execute.

In keeping with the quantitative approach to computer design's central dictum, "Make the common case fast,"[1] both the Pentium 4 and G4e split up their integer hardware into two specialized types of execution units: a group of units that handle only simple, single-cycle instructions and a single unit that handles complex, multi-cycle instructions. By dedicating the majority of their integer hardware solely to the rapid execution of the most common types of instructions (the simple, single-cycle ones), the Pentium 4 and the G4e are able to get increased integer performance out of a smaller amount of overall hardware.

Think of the multiple fast IUs (or SIUs) as express checkout lanes for one-item shoppers and the single slow IU as a general-purpose checkout lane for multiple-item shoppers in a supermarket where most of the shoppers only buy a single item. This kind of specialization keeps that one guy who's stocking up for Armageddon from slowing down the majority of shoppers who just want to duck in and grab eggs or milk on the way home from work.

The PPC 970 differs from both of these designs in that it has two general-purpose IUs that execute almost all integer instructions. To return to the supermarket analogy, the 970 has two general-purpose checkout lanes in a supermarket where most of the shoppers are one-item shoppers. The 970's two IUs are attached to 80 64-bit GPRs (32 architected and 48 rename).

Why doesn't the 970 have more specialized hardware (express checkout lanes) like the G4e and Pentium 4? The answer is complicated, and I'll take an initial stab at answering it in a moment, but first I should clear something up.

The Integer Units Are Not Fully Symmetric

I said that the 970's two IUs execute "almost all" integer instructions, because the units are not, in fact, fully symmetric. One of the IUs performs fixed-point divides, and the other handles SPR operations. So the 970's IUs are slightly specialized, but not in the same manner as the IUs of the G4e and Pentium 4. If the G4e and Pentium 4 have express checkout lanes, the 970 has something more akin to a rule that says, "All shoppers who bought something at the deli must go through line 1, and all shoppers who bought something at the bakery must go through line 2; everyone else is free to go through either line."

Thankfully, integer divides and SPR instructions are relatively rare, so the impact on performance of this type of forced segregation is minimized. In fact, if the 970 didn't have the group formation scheme, this seemingly

---

[1] See John L. Hennessy and David A. Patterson, *Computer Architecture: A Quantitative Approach*, Third Edition (Morgan Kauffman Publishers: 2003).

minor degree of specialization might hardly be worth commenting on. But as it stands, group-related scheduling issues turn this specialization into a potentially negative factor—albeit a minor one—for integer performance for reasons that we'll discuss later on in this chapter.

Integer Unit Latencies and Throughput

The vast majority of integer instructions take one cycle to execute on the 970, while a few more complex integer instructions can take more cycles. Note that this one-cycle number signifies integer throughput. As a result, simple, non-dependent integer IOPs can issue and finish at a rate of one per cycle. Dependent integer IOPs, on the other hand, must be separated by a dead cycle, giving a latency of two cycles. Note that this two-cycle latency applies to operations in the same IU or in different IUs.

In the end, this unfortunate increase in latency is somewhat than mitigated by other factors, which I'll discuss shortly. Nonetheless, the two-cycle latency issue has turned out to have a non-trivial impact on the 970's integer performance.

The CRU

I haven't said all there is to say about the 970's integer-processing capabilities, so the preceding summary isn't quite complete. As I mentioned, the 970 divides up its integer resources in a slightly different way from that of the Pentium 4 or G4e.

Some of the operations handled by the integer units on the Pentium 4 and G4e are instead handled in different places by the 970. Specifically, there's one type of fixed-point operation normally handled by an integer unit that in the 970's case gets its own separate execution unit. The 970 has a dedicated unit for handling logical operations related to the PPC's condition register: the CRU. On the G4e these condition register (CR) operations are handled by the complex integer unit. Thus the 970, in giving these operations their own separate unit, takes some of the processing load off of the two integer units.

The PowerPC Condition Register

The CR is a part of the PowerPC ISA that handles some of the functions of the x86's processor status word (PSW), but in a more flexible and programmer-friendly way. Almost all PowerPC arithmetic operations, when they finish executing, have the option of setting various bits (or flags) in the PPC's 32-bit condition register as a way of recording information about their outcome for future reference (in other words, Was the result positive or negative? Did it overflow or underflow the register?). So you might think of the CR as a place to store metadata for arithmetic results. Subsequent instructions, like conditional branch instructions, can then check the CR's flags and thereby use that metadata to decide what to do.

The flag combinations that instructions can set in the condition register are called *condition codes*, and the condition register has room enough to store up to eight separate condition codes, which can describe the outcome of eight different instructions. Enabling the programmer to manipulate those condition codes are a collection of PowerPC instructions that perform logical operations (AND, OR, NOT, NOR, etc.) directly on the flags in the CR. The CRU is the execution unit that executes those instructions.

Preliminary Conclusions About the 970's Integer Performance

To summarize, the G4e dedicates the majority of its integer hardware to the execution of simple, one-cycle instructions, with the remainder of the hardware dedicated to the execution of less common complex instructions. In contrast, with two rare exceptions, all of the PPC 970's integer hardware can execute almost any type of integer instruction. Table 10-2 shows a breakdown of how the three types of integer operations we've discussed—simple, complex, and CR logical—are handled by the G4e and the 970.

Table 10-2: Integer Operations on the PowerPC 970 and G4e

	Simple Int.	Complex Int.	CR Logical	SPR
PPC 970	IU1, IU2	IU1, IU2[1]	CRU	IU1
G4e	SIU1-SIU3	CIU	CIU	CIU

[1] IU2 handles all divides on the 970.

As you can see from Table 10-2, the G4e has more and more specialized integer hardware at its disposal than the 970. Also, in terms of instruction latencies, the G4e's integer hardware is slightly faster for common, simple integer operations than that of the 970. Finally, as I hinted at earlier and will develop in more detail shortly, the 970's integer performance—as well its performance on other types of code—is fairly sensitive to compiler optimization and scheduling. All of this adds up to make 32-bit integer computation the place where the 970 looks the weakest compared to the competition.

Load-Store Units

Chapter 1 discussed the difference between instructions that access memory (loads and stores) and instructions that do actual computation (integer instructions, floating-point instructions, etc.). Just like integer instructions are executed in the IUs and floating-point instructions are executed in the FPUs, memory access instructions have their own specialized execution units in the form of one or more load-store units (LSUs).

Chapter 1 also discussed the fact that in order to access memory via a load or a store, it's usually necessary to perform an address calculation so the processor can figure out the location in memory that it should access. Even though such address calculations are just simple integer operations, they're usually not handled by the processor's integer hardware. Instead, all of the processors under discussion here have dedicated address generation hardware as part of their LSUs. Consequently, address generation takes place as part of the execution phase of the LSU's pipeline.

The G4e has one LSU that executes all of the loads and stores for the entire chip (integer, floating-point, and vector). As mentioned earlier, the G4e's LSU contains dedicated integer hardware for address calculations.

The 970 has two identical LSUs execute all of the loads and stores for the entire chip. This gives it literally twice the load-store hardware of the G4e, which it needs in order to keep all the instructions in its much larger instruction window fed with data. The 970's load-store hardware is more comparable to that of the Pentium 4, which also features a larger instruction window.

Front-Side Bus

A *bus* is an electrical conduit that connects two components in a computer system, allowing them to communicate and share data and/or code. If a computer system is like a large office building, then buses are like the phone lines that keep all the employees connected to each other and to the outside world.

The *front-side bus (FSB)* is the bus that connects the computer's CPU to the core logic chipset. If buses are the phone lines of a computer system, then the core logic chipset is the operator and switchboard. The *core logic chipset*, or *chipset* for short, opens and closes bus connections between components and routes data around the system. Figure 10-2 shows a simple computer system consisting of a CPU, RAM, a video card, a hard drive, and a chipset.

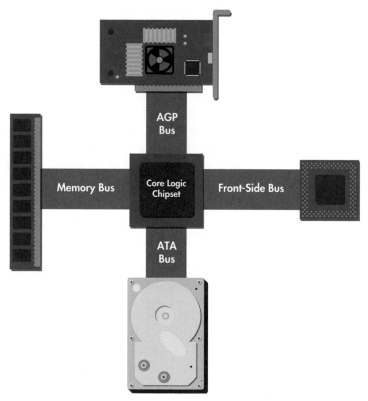

Figure 10-2: Core logic chipset

As you can see from Figure 10-2, the front-side bus is the processor's sole means of communication with the rest of the system, so it needs to be very fast.

A processor's front-side bus usually operates at a clock speed that is some fraction of the core clock speed of the CPU, and the 970 is no different. On the first release of Apple's G5 towers, the 970's front-side bus operates at half the clock speed of the 970. So for a 2 GHz 970, the FSB runs at 1 GHz DDR. (DDR stands for *double data rate*, which means that the bus physically runs at 500 MHz, but data is transferred on the rising and falling edges of the clock pulse.) The 970 can run at other multiples of the FSB clock, including three, four, and six times the FSB clock speed.

Because the 970's front-side bus is composed of two unidirectional channels, each of which is 32 bits wide, the total theoretical peak bandwidth for the 900 MHz bus is 7.2GB per second. Address and control information is multiplexed onto the bus along with data, so IBM estimates that the bus's total peak bandwidth for data alone (after subtracting the bandwidth used for address and control information) is somewhere around 6.4GB per second.

In the end, this high-bandwidth FSB is one of the 970's largest performance advantages over its competitors. The 970's two LSUs place high demands on the FSB in order to keep the 970's large instruction window full and its wide back end fed with data. When coupled with a high-bandwidth memory subsystem like dual-channel DDR400, the 970's fast FSB and dual LSUs make it a great media workstation platform.

The Floating-Point Units

The G4e's very straightforward floating-point implementation has a single FPU that takes a minimum of five cycles to finish executing the fastest floating-point instructions. (Some instructions take many more cycles.) The FPU is served by 48 microarchitectural floating-point registers (32 registers for the PPC ISA and 16 additional rename registers). Finally, single- and double-precision floating-point operations take the same amount of time.

The 970's floating-point implementation is almost exactly like the G4e's, except there's twice as much hardware. The 970 has two identical FPUs, each of which can execute the fastest floating-point instructions (like the fadd) in six cycles. As with the G4e, single- and double-precision operations take the same amount of time to execute. The 970's two FPUs are fully pipelined for all operations except floating-point divides, which are very costly in terms of cycles and stall both FPUs. And finally, the 970 has a larger number of FPRs: 80 total microarchitectural registers, where 32 are PowerPC architectural registers and the remaining 48 are rename registers.

Before moving on, I should note one peculiarity in the way that the 970 handles floating-point instructions. Some floating-point instructions—particularly the fused multiply-add series of instructions—are not translated into IOPs by the decode hardware, but instead are executed directly by the FPU. The reason for this is fairly straightforward.

Recall from Chapter 4 that the amount of die space taken up by the register file increases approximately with the square of the number of register file ports. The vast majority of PowerPC instructions specify at most two source registers and one destination register, which means that they use at most two register file read ports and one register file write port. However, there is a handful of PowerPC instructions that require more ports. In order to keep the size of the 970's register files to a minimum, the 970's designers opted not to add more ports to the register files in order to accommodate this small number of instructions. Instead, the 970 has two ways of keeping this small group of instructions from stalling due to the structural hazards that might be brought on by their larger-than-average port requirements:

- Non–floating-point instructions that require more than three ports total are dealt with at the decode stage. All of the 970's IOPs are restricted to read at most two registers and write at most one register, so instructions that do not obey this restriction are cracked into multiple IOPs that do obey it.

- There are a few types of floating-point instructions that do not fit the three-port requirement, the most common of which is the fused multiply-add series of instructions. For performance reasons, cracking a floating-point fused multiply-add instruction into multiple IOPs is neither necessary nor desirable. Instead, such instructions are simply passed to the FPU as decoded PowerPC instructions—not as IOPs—where they execute by accessing the register file on more than one cycle. Since these instructions take multiple cycles to execute anyway, the extra register file read and/or write cycles are simply overlapped with computation cycles so that they don't add to the instruction's latency.

As the preceding discussion indicates, the 970's floating-point hardware compares quite favorably with that of the G4e. Twice the hardware does not necessarily equal twice the performance, but it's clear that the 970 performs significantly better, clock for clock, on floating-point code. This performance advantage is not only due to the doubled amount of floating-point hardware, but also to the 970's longer pipeline and clock-speed advantage. Furthermore, the 970's fast front-side bus (effectively half the core clock speed), when coupled with a high-bandwidth memory subsystem, gives it a distinct advantage over the G4e in bandwidth-intensive floating-point code. Note that this last point also applies to vector code, but more on that in a moment.

Vector Computing on the PowerPC 970

The G4e's AltiVec implementation is the strongest part of its design. With four fully pipelined vector processing units, it has plenty of hardware to go around. As a brief recap from the last chapter, here's a breakdown of the G4e's four AltiVec units:

- vector permute unit (VPU)
- vector simple integer unit (VSIU)

- vector complex integer unit (VCIU)
- vector floating-point unit (VFPU)

All of this vector execution hardware is tied to a generous register file that consists of thirty-two 128-bit architectural registers and sixteen additional vector rename registers. Furthermore, each of the units is attached to a four-entry vector issue queue that can issue two vector ops per cycle to any of the four vector units.

NOTE   *The SIMD instruction set known as AltiVec was codeveloped by both IBM and Motorola, and it is co-owned by both of them. Motorola has a trademark on the AltiVec name, so in most of IBM's literature (but not all), the instruction set is referred to as VMX, presumably for Vector Multimedia Extensions. VMX and AltiVec are therefore two different names for the same group of 162 vector instructions added to the PowerPC ISA. This chapter uses the name AltiVec for both the G4e and the 970.*

The 970's AltiVec implementation looks pretty much like the original G4's—the MPC7400—except for the addition of issue queues for dynamic execution. The 970 has the following units:

- vector permute unit (VPU)
- vector arithmetic logic unit (VALU)
- vector simple integer unit (VSIU)
- vector complex integer unit (VCIU)
- vector floating-point unit (VFPU)

These units are attached to 80 vector registers—32 architectural registers and 48 rename registers.

Notice that the vector execution units listed here are essentially the same units as in the G4e, but they're grouped differently. This grouping makes all the difference. Take a look at the simplified diagram in Figure 10-3.

The 970 can dispatch up to four vector IOPs per cycle total to its two vector *logical issue queues*—two IOPs per cycle in program order to the 16-entry VPU logical issue queue and two IOPs per cycle in program order to the 20-entry VALU logical issue queue. (Each of these logical issue queues consists physically of a pair of interleaved queues that operate together as a single queue, but we'll talk more about how the logical queues are actually implemented in a moment.) Each of the two logical queues can then issue one vector operation per cycle to any of the units attached to it. This means that the 970 can issue one IOP per cycle to the VPU and one IOP per cycle to any of the VALU's three subunits.

As you can see, if you place the 970's vector unit and the G4e's vector unit side by side, the 970 and the G4e can issue the same number of vector instructions per cycle to their AltiVec units, but the 970 is much more limited in the combinations of instructions it can issue, because one of its two instructions must be a vector permute. For instance, the G4e would have no problem issuing both a complex integer instruction and a simple integer instruction to its VCIU and VSIU in the same cycle, whereas the 970 would only be able to issue one of these in a cycle.

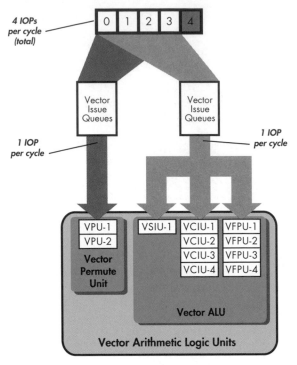

Figure 10-3: The 970's vector unit

Table 10-3 replicates a chart from Apple that compares the AltiVec execution unit latencies for the two G4s and the 970.[2]

Table 10-3: Vector Instruction Latencies for the G4, G4e, and 970

Hardware Unit	7400/7410	7450/7455	PPC 970
Vector simple integer unit (VSIU)	1	1	2^1
Vector complex integer unit (VCIU)	3	4	5^1
Vector floating-point unit (VFPU)	$4 (5)^2$	$4 (5)^{2,3}$	8^1
Vector permute unit (VPU)	1	2	2^4

[1] An extra cycle latency is required if the data is next used in VPU.

[2] The VFPU takes an extra cycle if Java mode is turned on. (It is off by default on Mac OS X, but on by default on Mac OS 9.)

[3] Some FP-related VSIU instructions were moved to the VFPU for later G4. These only take two cycles instead of the usual 4 (5).

[4] An extra cycle latency is required if the data is next used in VCIU/VSIU/VFPU.

Notice that the 970's vector instruction latencies are close to those in the G4e, which is an excellent sign given the fact that the 970's pipeline is longer and its issue queues are much deeper (18 instructions on the 970 versus 4 instructions on the G4e). The 970's larger instruction window and deeper issue queues allow the processor to look farther ahead in the instruction

---

[2] This is a truncated version of Apple's *AltiVec Instruction Cross-Reference* (http://developer.apple.com/hardware/ve/instruction_crossref.html).

stream and extract more instruction-level parallelism (ILP) from the vector instruction stream. This means that the 970's vastly superior dynamic scheduling hardware can squeeze more performance out of slightly inferior vector execution hardware, a capability that, when coupled with a high-bandwidth memory subsystem and an ultrafast front-side bus, enable its vector performance to exceed that of the G4e.

Floating-Point Issue Queues

Figure 10-1 shows the five dispatch slots connected to issue queues for each of the functional units or groups of functional units. Figure 10-1 is actually oversimplified, since the true relationship between the dispatch slots, issue queues, and functional units is more complicated than depicted there. The actual physical issue queue configuration is a bit hard to explain in words, so Figure 10-4 shows how the floating-point issue queues really look.

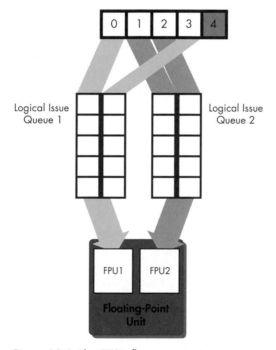

Figure 10-4: The 970's floating-point issue queues

Each of the floating-point execution units is fed by what I've called a logical issue queue. As you can see in Figure 10-4, each 10-entry logical issue queue actually consists of an interleaved pair of five-entry physical issue queues, which together feed a single floating-point execution unit.

Figure 10-4 also shows how the four non-branch dispatch slots each feed a specific physical issue queue. Floating-point IOPs that dispatch from slots 0 and 3 go into the tops of the two physical issue queues that are attached to them. Similarly, floating-point IOPs that dispatch from slots 1 and 2 go into the tops of their two attached physical issue queues. As IOPs issue from different places in the physical queues, the IOPs "above" them in the queue "fall down" to fill in the gaps.

Each pair of physical issue queues—the pair attached to slots 0 and 3, and the pair attached to slots 1 and 2—is interleaved and functions as a single "logical" issue queue. An IOP can issue from a logical issue queue to an execution unit when all of its sources are set, and the oldest IOP with all of its sources set in a logical queue is issued to the attached execution unit. This means that, as is the case with the G4e's issue queues, instructions are issued *in* program order from within each logical issue queue, but *out of* program order with respect to the overall code stream.

NOTE *The term* logical issue queue *is one that I've coined for the purposes of this chapter, and is not to my knowledge used in IBM's literature. IBM prefers the phrase* common interleaved queues.

It's important for me to emphasize that individual IOPs issue from their respective logical issue queues *completely independent of their dispatch group*. So the execution units' schedulers are blind to which group an IOP is in when it comes time to schedule the IOP and issue it to an execution unit. Thus the dispatch groups are allowed to break apart after they reach the level of the issue queue, and they're reassembled after execution in the group completion table (GCT).

Integer and Load-Store Issue Queues

The integer and load-store execution units are fed by issue queues in a similar manner to the floating-point units, but they're slightly more complex because they share issue queues. Take a look at Figure 10-5 to see how this works.

As with the floating-point issue queues, integer or memory access IOPs in dispatch slots 0 and 3 go into the two integer physical issue queues that are specifically intended for them. The twist is that this pair of queues is shared by two execution units: IU1 and LSU1. So integer or memory IOPs from slots 0 and 3 are sent into the appropriate issue queue pair—or logical issue queue—and these IOPs then issue to either IU1 or LSU1 as the integer scheduler sees fit. Similarly, integer or memory access IOPs from dispatch slots 1 and 2 go into their respective physical queues, both of which feed IU2 and LSU2. As with the floating-point issue queues, these four 9-entry interleaved queues should be thought of as being grouped into two 18-entry logical issue queues, where each logical issue queue works together with the appropriate scheduler to feed a pair of execution units.

BU and CRU Issue Queues

The branch unit and condition register unit issue queues work in a similar manner to what I've described previously, with the differences depending on grouping and issue restrictions. So the CRU has a single 10-entry logical issue queue comprised of two issue queues with five entries each, one for slot 0

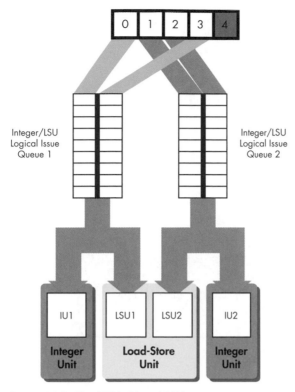

Figure 10-5: The 970's IU and LSU issue queues

and one for slot 1 (because CR IOPs can be placed only in slots 0 and 1). The branch execution unit has a single logical issue queue comprised of one 12-entry issue queue for slot 4 (because branch IOPs can go only in slot 4).

Vector Issue Queues

The vector issue queues are laid out slightly different than the other issue queues. The vector issue queue configuration is depicted in Figure 10-6.

The vector permute unit is fed from one 16-entry (four entries × four queues) logical issue queue connected to all four non-branch dispatch slots, and the vector ALU is fed from a 20-entry (five entries × four queues) logical issue queue that's also connected to all four non-branch dispatch slots. As with all of the other issue queue pairs, one IOP per cycle can issue in order from each logical issue queue to any of the execution units that are attached to it.

The Performance Implications of the 970's Group Dispatch Scheme

Because of the way it affects the 970's issue queue design, the group formation scheme has some interesting performance implications. Specifically, proper code scheduling is important in ways that it wouldn't normally be for the other processors discussed here.

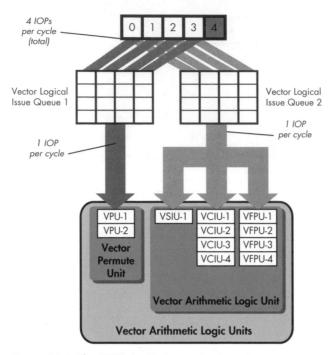

Figure 10-6: The 970's vector issue queues

Instead of trying to explain this point, I'll illustrate it with an example. Let's look at an instruction with few group restrictions—the floating-point add. The 970's group formation rules dictate that the fadd can go into any of the four dispatch slots, and which slot it goes into in turn dictates which of the 970's two identical FPUs executes it. As I explained in the previous section, if the fadd goes into slots 0 or 3, it is dispatched to the logical issue queue associated with FPU1; if it goes into dispatch slot 1 or 2, it is dispatched to the logical issue queue associated with FPU2. This means that the FPU instruction scheduling hardware is restricted in ways that it wouldn't be if both FPUs were fed from a common issue queue, because half the instructions are forced into one FPU and half the instructions are forced into the other FPU. Or at least this 50/50 split is how it's supposed to work out under optimal circumstances, when the code is scheduled properly so that it dispatches IOPs evenly into both logical issue queues.

Because of the grouping scheme and the two separate logical issue queues, it seems that keeping both FPUs busy by splitting the computation load between them is very much a matter of scheduling instructions for dispatch so that no single FPU happens to get overworked while the other goes underutilized. Normally, this kind of load balancing among execution units would happen at the issue queue level, but in the 970's case, it's constrained by the structure of the issue queues themselves.

This load balancing at the dispatch level isn't quite as simple as it may sound, because group formation takes place according to a specific set of rules that ultimately constrain dispatch bandwidth and subsequent instruction issue in very specific and peculiar ways. For instance, an integer instruction that's preceded by, say, a CR logical instruction, may have to move over a slot to make room because the CR logical instruction can go only in slots 0 and 1. Likewise, depending on whether an instruction near the integer IOP in the instruction stream is cracked or millicoded, the integer IOP may have to move over a certain number of slots; if the millicoded instruction breaks down into a long string of instructions, that integer IOP may even get bumped over into a later dispatch group. The overall result is that which queue an integer IOP goes into very much depends on the other (possibly non-integer) instructions that surround it.

The take-home message here is that PowerPC code that's optimized specifically for the 970 performs significantly better on the processor than legacy code that's optimized for other PowerPC processors like the G4e.

Of course, no one should get the impression that legacy code runs poorly on the 970. It's just that the full potential of the chip can't be unlocked without properly scheduled code. Furthermore, in addition to the mitigating factors mentioned in the section on integer performance (for example, deep OOOE capabilities, or high-bandwidth FSB), the fact that quantitative studies have shown the amount of ILP inherent in most RISC code to be around two instructions per clock means that the degenerate case described in the FPU example should be exceedingly rare.

Conclusions

While the 970's group dispatch scheme does suffer from some of the drawbacks described in the preceding section, it must be judged a success in terms of its impact on the processor's performance per watt. That this dispatch scheme has a significant positive impact on performance per watt is evidenced by the fact that Intel's Pentium M processor also uses a similar grouping mechanism to achieve greater power efficiency. Furthermore, Intel continues to employ this grouping mechanism more extensively with each successive revision of the Pentium M, as the company seeks to minimize power consumption without sacrificing number-crunching capabilities. Thus such grouping mechanisms will only become more widespread as microprocessor designers become ever more sensitive to the need to balance performance and power consumption.

Because the 970 can track more instructions with less power-hungry bookkeeping logic, it can spend more transistors on execution units, branch prediction resources, and cache. This last item—cache—is an especially important performance-enhancing element in modern processors, for reasons that will be covered in Chapter 11.

11

UNDERSTANDING CACHING AND PERFORMANCE

This chapter is intended as a general introduction to CPU caching and performance. Because cache is critical to keeping the processors described so far fed with code and data, you can't understand how computer systems function without first understanding the structure and functioning of the cache memory hierarchy. To that end, this chapter covers fundamental cache concepts like spatial and temporal locality, set associativity, how different types of applications use the cache, the general layout and function of the memory hierarchy, and other cache-related issues.

Caching Basics

In order to really understand the role of caching in system design, think of the CPU and memory subsystem as operating on a *consumer-producer model* (or *client-server model*): The CPU consumes information provided to it by the hard disks and RAM, which act as producers.

Driven by innovations in process technology and processor design, CPUs have increased their ability to consume at a significantly higher rate than the memory subsystem has increased its ability to produce. The problem is that CPU clock cycles have gotten shorter at a faster rate than memory and bus clock cycles, so the number of CPU clock cycles that the processor has to wait before main memory can fulfill its requests for data has increased. With each CPU clockspeed increase, memory is getting farther and farther away from the CPU in terms of the number of CPU clock cycles.

Figures 11-1 and 11-2 illustrate how CPU clock cycles have gotten shorter relative to memory clock cycles.

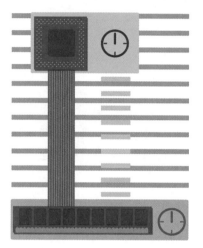

Figure 11-1: Slower CPU clock   Figure 11-2: Faster CPU clock

To visualize the effect that this widening speed gap has on overall system performance, imagine the CPU as a downtown furniture maker's workshop and the main memory as a lumberyard that keeps getting moved farther and farther out into the suburbs. Even if you start using bigger trucks to cart all the wood, it's still going to take longer from the time the workshop places an order to the time that order gets filled.

NOTE   *I'm not the first person to use a workshop and warehouse analogy to explain caching. The most famous example of such an analogy is the Thing King game, which is widely available on the Internet.*

Sticking with the furniture workshop analogy, one solution to this problem would be to rent out a small warehouse in town and store the most commonly requested types of lumber there. This smaller, closer warehouse would act as a cache that sits between the lumberyard and the workshop, and you could keep a driver on hand at the workshop who could run out at a moment's notice and quickly pick up whatever you need from the warehouse.

Of course, the bigger your warehouse, the better, because it allows you to store more types of wood, thereby increasing the likelihood that the raw materials for any particular order will be on hand when you need them. In the event that you need a type of wood that isn't in the nearby warehouse, you'll have to drive all the way out of town to get it from your big, suburban lumberyard. This is bad news, because unless your furniture workers have another task to work on while they're waiting for your driver to return with the lumber, they're going to sit around in the break room smoking and watching *The Oprah Winfrey Show.* And you hate paying people to watch *The Oprah Winfrey Show.*

The Level 1 Cache

I'm sure you've figured it out already, but the smaller, closer warehouse in this analogy is the *level 1 cache* (*L1 cache* or *L1,* for short). The L1 can be accessed very quickly by the CPU, so it's a good place to keep the code and data that the CPU is most likely to request. (In a moment, we'll talk in more detail about how the L1 can "predict" what the CPU will probably want.) The L1's quick access time is a result of the fact that it's made of the fastest and most expensive type of *static RAM,* or *SRAM.* Since each SRAM memory cell is made up of four to six transistors (compared to the one-transistor-per-cell configuration of DRAM), its cost per bit is quite high. This high cost per bit means that you generally can't afford to have a very large L1 unless you really want to drive up the total cost of the system.

In modern CPUs, the L1 sits on the same piece of silicon as the rest of the processor. In terms of the warehouse analogy, this is a bit like having the warehouse on the same block as the workshop. This has the advantage of giving the CPU some very fast, very close storage, but the disadvantage is that now the main memory (the suburban lumberyard) is just as far away from the L1 as it is from the processor. If data that the CPU needs is not in the L1— a situation called a *cache miss*—it's going to take quite a while to retrieve that data from memory. Furthermore, remember that as the processor gets faster, the main memory gets "farther" away all the time. So while your warehouse may be on the same block as your workshop, the lumberyard has now moved not just out of town but out of the state. For an ultra–high-clock-rate processor like the P4, being forced to wait for data to load from main memory in order to complete an operation is like your workshop having to wait a few days for lumber to ship in from out of state.

Check out Table 11-1, which shows common latency and size information for the various levels of the memory hierarchy. (The numbers in this table are shrinking all the time, so if they look a bit large to you, that's probably because by the time you read this, they're dated.)

Table 11-1: A Comparison of Different Types of Data Storage

Level	Access Time	Typical Size	Technology	Managed By
Registers	1–3 ns	1KB	Custom CMOS	Compiler
Level 1 Cache (on-chip)	2–8 ns	8KB–128KB	SRAM	Hardware
Level 2 Cache (off-chip)	5–12 ns	0.5MB–8MB	SRAM	Hardware
Main Memory	10–60 ns	64MB–1GB	DRAM	Operating system
Hard Disk	3,000,000–10,000,000 ns	20GB–100GB	Magnetic	Operating system/user

Notice the large gap in access times between the L1 and the main memory. For a 1 GHz CPU, a 50 ns wait means 50 wasted clock cycles. Ouch! To see the kind of effect such stalls have on a modern, hyperpipelined processor, see "Instruction Throughput and Pipeline Stalls" on page 53.

The Level 2 Cache

The solution to this dilemma is to add more cache. At first you might think you could get more cache by enlarging the L1, but as I said earlier, cost considerations are a major factor limiting L1 cache size. In terms of the workshop analogy, you could say that rents are much higher in town than in the suburbs, so you can't afford much in-town warehouse space without the cost of rent eating into your bottom line, to the point where the added costs of the warehouse space would outweigh the benefits of increased worker productivity. You have to fine-tune the amount of warehouse space that you rent by weighing all the costs and benefits so that you get the maximum output for the least cost.

A better solution than adding more in-town warehouse space would be to rent some cheaper, larger warehouse space right outside of town to act as a cache for the in-town warehouse. Similarly, processors like the P4 and G4e have a *level 2 cache* (*L2 cache* or *L2*) that sits between the L1 and main memory. The L2 usually contains all of the data that's in the L1 plus some extra. The common way to describe this situation is to say that the L1 *subsets* the L2, because the L1 contains a subset of the data in the L2.

A series of caches, starting with the page file on the hard disk (the lumberyard) and going all the way up to the registers on the CPU (the workshop's work benches), is called a *cache hierarchy.* As you go up the cache hierarchy towards the CPU, the caches get smaller, faster, and more expensive to implement; conversely, as you go down the cache hierarchy, the caches get larger, cheaper, and much slower. The data contained in each level of the hierarchy is usually mirrored in the level below it, so for a piece of data that's in the L1, there are usually copies of that same data in the L2, main memory, and hard disk's page file. Each level in the hierarchy subsets the level below it. We'll talk later about how all of those copies are kept in sync.

In Figure 11-3, the red cells are the code and data for the program that the CPU is currently running. The blue cells are unrelated to the currently running program. This figure, which will become even clearer once you read "Locality of Reference" on page 220, shows how each level of the cache hierarchy subsets the level below it.

As Table 11-1 indicates, each level of the hierarchy depicted in Figure 11-3 is controlled by a different part of the system. Data is promoted up the hierarchy or demoted down the hierarchy based on a number of different criteria; in the remainder of this chapter we'll concern ourselves only with the top levels of the hierarchy.

Example: A Byte's Brief Journey Through the Memory Hierarchy

For the sake of example, let's say the CPU issues a load instruction that tells the memory subsystem to load a piece of data (in this case, a single byte) into one of its registers. First, the request goes out to the L1, which is

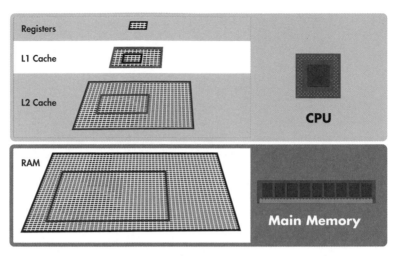

Figure 11-3: Code and data in the cache hierarchy

checked to see if it contains the requested data. If the L1 does not contain the data and therefore cannot fulfill the request—in other words, a cache miss occurs—the request propagates down to the L2. If the L2 does not contain the desired byte, the request begins the relatively long trip out to main memory. If main memory doesn't contain the data, you're in big trouble, because then it has to be *paged* in from the hard disk, an act that can take a relative eternity in CPU time.

Let's assume that the requested byte is found in main memory. Once located, the byte is copied from main memory, along with a bunch of its neighboring bytes in the form of a *cache block* or *cache line*, into the L2 and L1. When the CPU requests this same byte again, it will be waiting for it there in the L1, a situation called a *cache hit*.

Cache Misses

Computer architects usually divide cache misses up into three different types depending on the situation that brought about the miss. I'll introduce these three types of misses at appropriate points over the course of the chapter, but I can talk about the first one right now.

A *compulsory miss* is a cache miss that occurs because the desired data was never in the cache and therefore must be paged in for the first time in a program's execution. It's called a *compulsory* miss because, barring the use of certain specialized tricks like data prefetching, it's the one type of miss that just can't be avoided. All cached data must be brought into the cache for the very first time at some point, and the occasion for doing so is normally a compulsory miss.

The two other types of cache misses are misses that result when the CPU requests data that was previously in the cache but has been *evicted* for some reason or other. We'll discuss evictions in "Temporal and Spatial Locality Revisited: Replacement/Eviction Policies and Block Sizes" on page 230, and I'll cover the other two types of cache misses as they come up throughout the course of this chapter.

Locality of Reference

Caching works because of a very simple property exhibited to one degree or another by all types of code and data: locality of reference. We generally find it useful to talk about two types of locality of reference: *spatial locality* and *temporal locality*.

Spatial locality

> Spatial locality is a fancy label for the general rule that *if the CPU needs an item from memory at any given moment, it's likely to need that item's neighbors next.*

Temporal locality

> Temporal locality is the name we give to the general rule that *if an item in memory was accessed once, it's likely to be accessed again in the near future.*

Depending on the type of application, both code and data streams can exhibit spatial and temporal locality.

Spatial Locality of Data

Spatial locality of data is the easiest type of locality to understand, because most of you have used media applications like MP3 players, DVD players, and other types of applications whose datasets consist of large, ordered files. Consider an MP3 file, which has a bunch of blocks of data that are consumed by the processor in sequence from the file's beginning to its end. If the CPU is running iTunes and it has just requested second 1:23 of a five-minute MP3, you can be reasonably certain that next it's going to want seconds 1:24, 1:25, and so on. This is the same with a DVD file, and with many other types of media files like images, AutoCAD drawings, and 3D game levels. All of these applications operate on large arrays of sequentially ordered data that get ground through in sequence by the CPU again and again.

Business applications like word processors also have great spatial locality for data. If you think about it, few people open six or seven documents in a word processor and quickly alternate between them typing one or two words in each. Most of us just open up one or two relatively modest-sized files and work in them for a while without skipping around too much within the same file. These files are stored in contiguous regions of memory, where they can be brought quickly into the cache in a few large batches.

Ultimately, spatial locality is just a way of saying that related chunks of data tend to clump together in memory, and since they're related, they also tend to be processed together in batches by the CPU.

In Figure 11-4, as in Figure 11-3, the red cells are related chunks of data stored in the memory array. This figure shows a program with fairly good spatial locality, since the red cells are clumped closely together. In an application with poor spatial locality, the red cells would be more randomly distributed among the unrelated blue cells.

Spatial Locality of Code

Spatial locality applies to code just like it does to data—most well-written code tries to avoid jumps and branches so that the processor can execute through large contiguous blocks uninterrupted. Games, simulations, and media processing applications tend to have decent spatial locality for code, because such applications often feature small blocks of code (called *kernels*) operating repeatedly on very large datasets.

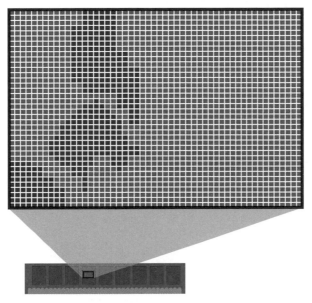

Figure 11-4: Spatial locality

When it comes to spatial locality of code for business applications, the picture is mixed. If you think about the way that you use a word processor, it's easy to see what's going on. As you create a document, most of you are constantly pressing different formatting buttons and invoking different menu options. For instance, you might format one word in italics, change the paragraph spacing, and then save the file, all in sequence. Each of these actions invokes a very different part of the code in a large application like Microsoft Word; it's not likely that the code for the File ▶ Save menu option is stored right next to the code that formats a font in italics. The way you use a word processor forces the CPU to jump around from place to place in memory in order to retrieve the correct code. However, the segment of the code stream that implements each individual action (i.e., saving a file, formatting a font, and so on) usually exists in memory as a fairly large, spatially localized chunk—very much like a little subprogram within the larger application. While the code for the File ▶ Save menu action might be quite far away from the code for the italics formatting option, both of these chunks of code exhibit good spatial locality as small programs in their own right.

What this means for a cache designer is that business applications need large instruction caches to be able to collect all of the most frequently used clumps of code that correspond to the most frequently executed actions and pack them together in the cache. If the instruction cache is too small, the different clumps get *swapped* out as different actions are performed. If the instruction cache is large enough, many of these subprograms will fit and there's little swapping needed. Incidentally, this is why business applications performed so poorly on Intel's original cacheless Celeron processor.

Temporal Locality of Code and Data

Consider a simple Photoshop filter that inverts an image to produce a negative; there's a small piece of code that performs the same inversion on each pixel, starting at one corner and going in sequence all the way across and down to the opposite corner. This code is just a small loop that gets executed repeatedly, once on each pixel, so it's an example of code that is reused again and again. Media applications, games, and simulations, because they use lots of small loops that iterate through very large datasets, have excellent temporal locality for code.

The same large, homogenous datasets that give media applications and the like good temporal locality for code also given them extremely poor temporal locality for data. Returning to the MP3 example, a music file is usually played through once in sequence and none of its parts are repeated. This being the case, it's actually a waste to store any of that file in the data cache, since it's only going to stop off there temporarily before passing through to the CPU.

When an application, like the aforementioned MP3 player, fills up the cache with data that doesn't really need to be cached because it won't be used again and as a result winds up bumping out of the cache data that will be reused, that application is said to "pollute" the cache. Media applications, games, and the like are big cache polluters, which is why they weren't too affected by the original Celeron's lack of cache. Because these applications' data wasn't going to be needed again any time soon, the fact that it wasn't in a readily accessible cache didn't really matter.

The primary way in which caches take advantage of temporal locality is probably obvious by this point: Caches provide a place to store code and data that the CPU is currently working with. By *working with*, I mean that the CPU has used it once and is likely to use it again. A group of related blocks of code and/or data that the CPU uses and reuses over a period of time in order to complete a task is called a *working set*. Depending on the size of a task's working set and the number of operations it takes the CPU to complete that task, spatial and temporal locality—and with them the cache hierarchy—will afford a greater or lesser performance increase on that task.

Locality: Conclusions

One point that should be apparent from the preceding discussion is that temporal locality implies spatial locality, but not vice versa. That is to say, data that is reused is always related (and therefore collects into spatially localized clumps in memory), but data that is related is not always reused. An open text file is an example of reusable data that occupies a localized region of memory, and an MP3 file is an example of non-reusable (or streaming) data that also occupies a localized region of memory.

The other thing that you probably noticed from this section is the fact that memory access patterns for code and memory access patterns for data are often very different within the same application. For instance, media applications have excellent temporal locality for code but poor temporal locality for data. This fact has inspired many cache designers to split the L1 into two regions—one for code and one for data. The code half of the cache is called the instruction cache, or I-cache, while the data half of the cache is called the data cache, or D-cache. This partitioning can result in significant performance gains, depending on the size of the cache, the types of applications normally run on the system, and a variety of other factors.

Cache Organization: Blocks and Block Frames

One way that caches take advantage of locality of reference is by loading data from memory in large chunks. When the CPU requests a particular piece of data from the memory subsystem, that piece gets fetched and loaded into the L1 along with some of its nearest neighbors. The actual piece of data that was requested is called the *critical word*, and the surrounding group of bytes that gets fetched along with it is called a cache line or cache block. By fetching not only the critical word but also a group of its neighbors and loading them into the cache, the CPU is prepared to take advantage of the fact that those neighboring bytes are the most likely to be the ones it will need to process next.

Cache blocks form the basic unit of cache organization, and RAM is also organized into blocks of the same size as the cache's blocks. When a block is moved from RAM to the cache, it is placed into a special slot in the cache called a *block frame*. Figure 11-5 shows a set of cache blocks stored in RAM and a cache with an empty set of block frames.

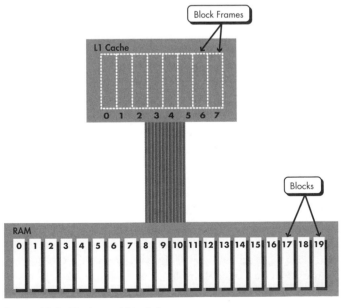

Figure 11-5: Blocks and block frames

Cache designers can choose from a few different schemes for governing which RAM blocks can be stored in which of the cache's block frames. Such a scheme is called a *cache placement policy*, because it dictates where in the cache a block from memory can be placed.

Tag RAM

When the CPU requests a byte from a particular block from RAM, it needs to be able to determine three things very quickly:

- whether or not the needed block is actually in the cache (i.e., whether there is a cache hit or a cache miss)
- the location of the block within the cache (in the case of a cache hit)
- the location of the desired byte (or critical word) within the block (again, in the case of a cache hit)

A cache accommodates all three needs by associating a special piece of memory—called a tag—with each block frame in the cache. The *tag* holds information about the blocks currently being stored in the frame, and that information allows the CPU to determine the answer to all three of the questions above. However, the speed with which that answer comes depends on a variety of factors.

Tags are stored in a special type of memory called the *tag RAM*. This memory has to be made of very fast SRAM because it can take some time to search it in order to locate the desired cache block. The larger the cache, the greater the number of blocks, and the greater the number of blocks, the more tag RAM you need to search and the longer it can take to locate the correct block. Thus the tag RAM can add unwanted access latency to the cache. As a result, you not only have to use the fastest RAM available for the tag RAM, but you also have to be smart about how you use tags to map RAM blocks to block frames. In the following section, I'll introduce the three general options for doing such mapping, and I'll discuss some of the pros and cons of each option.

Fully Associative Mapping

The most conceptually simple scheme for mapping RAM blocks to cache block frames is called *fully associative mapping*. Under this scheme, any RAM block can be stored in any available block frame. Fully associative mapping is depicted in Figure 11-6, where any of the red RAM blocks can go into any of the red cache block frames.

The problem with fully associative mapping is that if you want to retrieve a specific block from the cache, you have to check the tag of every single block frame in the entire cache because the desired block could be in any of the frames. Since large caches can have thousands of block frames, this tag searching can add considerable delay (latency) to a fetch. Furthermore, the larger the cache, the worse the delay gets, since there are more block frames and hence more block tags to check on each fetch.

Direct Mapping

Another, more popular way of organizing the cache is to use *direct mapping*. In a *direct-mapped cache*, each block frame can cache only a certain subset of the blocks in main memory.

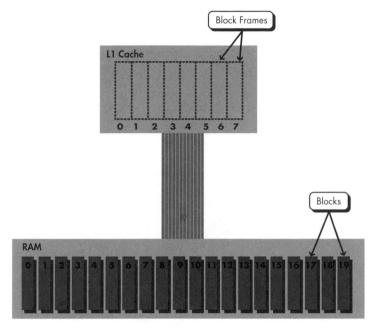

Figure 11-6: Fully associative mapping

In Figure 11-7, each of the red blocks (blocks 0, 8, and 16) can be cached only in the red block frame (frame 0). Likewise, blocks 1, 9, and 17 can be cached only in frame 1, blocks 2, 10, and 18 can be cached only in frame 2, and so on. Hopefully, the pattern here is apparent: Each frame caches every eighth block of main memory. As a result, the potential number of locations for any one block is greatly narrowed, and therefore the number of tags that must be checked on each fetch is greatly reduced. For example, if the CPU needs a byte from blocks 0, 8, or 16, it knows that it only has to check the tag associated with frame 0 to determine if the desired block is in the cache and to retrieve it if it is. This is much faster and more efficient than checking every frame in the cache.

There are some drawbacks to this scheme, though. For instance, what if blocks 0 to 3 and 8 to 11 combine to form an eight-block working set that the CPU wants to load into the cache and work on for a while? The cache is eight blocks long, but since it's direct-mapped, it can only store four of these particular blocks at a time. Remember, blocks 0 and 8 have to go in the same frame, as do blocks 1 and 9, 2 and 10, and 3 and 11. As a result, the CPU must load only four blocks of this eight-block set at a time, and swap them in and out as it works on different parts of the set. If the CPU wants to work on this whole eight-block set for a long time, that could mean a lot of swapping. Meanwhile, half of the cache is going completely unused! While direct-mapped caches are almost always faster than fully associative caches due to the shortened amount of time it takes to locate a cached block, they can still be inefficient under some circumstances.

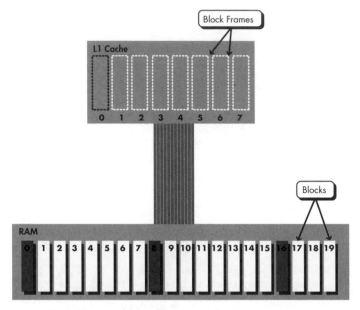

Figure 11-7: Direct mapping

Note that the kind of situation described here, where the CPU would like to store multiple blocks but it can't because they all require the same frame, is called a *collision*. In the preceding example, blocks 0 and 8 are said to collide, since they both want to fit into frame 0 but can't. Misses that result from such collisions are called *conflict misses*, the second of the three types of cache miss that I mentioned earlier.

N-Way Set Associative Mapping

One way to get some of the benefits of direct-mapped caches while lessening the amount of cache space wasted due to collisions is to restrict the caching of main memory blocks to a subset of the available cache frames. This technique is called *set associative mapping*, and a few popular implementations of it are described below.

Four-Way Set Associative Mapping

To see an example of what it means to restrict main memory blocks in a subset of available cache frames, take a look at the Figure 11-8, which illustrates *four-way set associative mapping*.

In Figure 11-8, any of the red blocks can go anywhere in the red set of frames (set 0) and any of the light yellow blocks can go anywhere in the light yellow set of frames (set 1). Think of the four-way associative cache like this: You took a fully associative cache and cut it in two, restricting half the main memory blocks to one side and half the main memory blocks to the other.

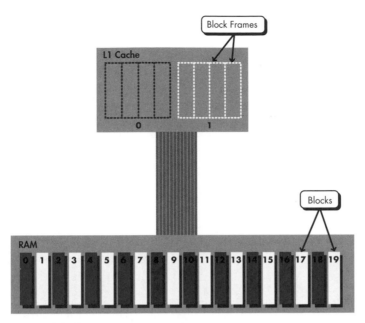

Figure 11-8: Four-way set associative mapping

This way, the odds of a collision are greatly reduced versus the direct-mapped cache, but you still don't have to search all the tags on every fetch like you did with the fully associative cache. For any given fetch, you need search only a single, four-block set to find the block you're looking for, which in this case amounts to half the cache.

The cache pictured in Figure 11-8 is said to be four-way *set associative* because the cache is divided into *sets* of four frames each. Since this cache has only eight frames, it can accommodate only two four-frame sets. A larger cache could accommodate more four-frame sets, reducing the odds of a collision even more.

Figure 11-9 shows a four-way set associative cache like the one in Figure 11-8, but with three sets instead of two. Notice that there are fewer red main memory blocks competing for space in set 0, which means lower odds of a collision.

In addition to its decreased odds of a collision, a four-way set associative cache has a low access latency because the number of frames that must be searched for a block is limited. Since all the sets consist of exactly four frames, no matter how large the cache gets, you'll only ever have to search through four frames (or one full set) to find any given block. This means that as the cache gets larger and the number of sets that it can accommodate increases, the tag searches become more efficient. Think about it. In a cache with three sets, only one-third of the cache (or one set) needs to be searched for a given block. In a cache with four sets, only one-fourth of the cache is searched. In a cache with one hundred four-block sets, only one-hundredth of the cache needs to be searched. The relative search efficiency scales with the cache size.

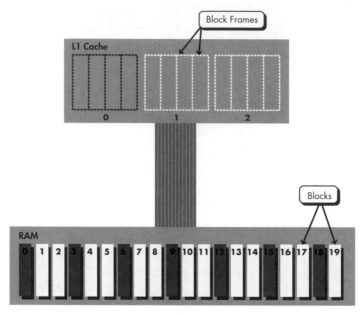

Figure 11-9: Four-way set associative mapping with three block frames

Two-Way Set Associative Mapping

Another way to increase the number of sets in the cache without actually increasing the cache size is to reduce the number of blocks in each set. Check out Figure 11-10, which shows a two-way set associative cache.

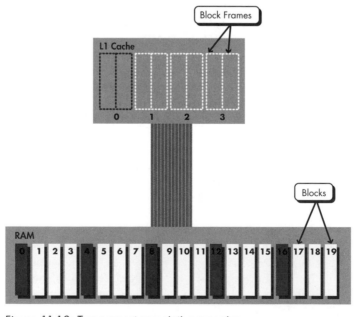

Figure 11-10: Two-way set associative mapping

To get a better idea of what's going on, let's compare the two-way associative cache to both the direct-mapped and the four-way cache. For the sake of comparison, assume that the cache size and the memory size both stay constant. And as you read the comparison, keep in mind that since each increase in the level of associativity (i.e., from two-way to four-way, or from four-way to eight-way) also increases the number of tags that must be checked in order to locate a specific block, an increase in associativity also means an increase in the cache's latency.

Two-Way vs. Direct-Mapped

With the two-way cache, the number of potential collisions (and hence the miss rate) is reduced compared to the direct-mapped scheme. However, the number of tags that must be searched for each fetch is twice as high. Depending on the relative sizes of the cache and main memory, this may or may not increase the cache's overall latency to the point that the decreased conflict miss rate is worth it.

Two-Way vs. Four-Way

Though a two-way cache's latency is less than that of a four-way cache, its number of potential collisions (and hence its miss rate) is higher. Just as with the preceding comparison, how a two-way associative cache compares to a four-way associative cache depends on just how much latency the four-way cache's increase in associativity ends up costing versus the decrease in conflict miss rate.

Associativity: Conclusions

In general, it turns out that when you factor in current technological conditions (the speed of tag RAM, the range of sizes that most caches fall into, and so on), some level of associativity less than or equal to eight-way turns out to be optimal for most caches. Any more than eight-way associativity and the cache's latency is increased so much that the decrease in miss rate isn't worth it. Any less than two-way associativity and the number of collisions often increases the miss rate to the point that the decrease in latency isn't worth it. There are some direct-mapped caches out there, though.

Before I conclude the discussion of associativity, there are two minor bits of information that I should include for the sake of completeness. First, though you've probably already figured it out, a direct-mapped cache is simply a one-way set associative cache, and a fully associative cache is an *n*-way set associative cache, where *n* is equal to the total number of blocks in the cache.

Second, the cache placement formula, which enables you to compute the set in which an arbitrary block of memory should be stored in an *n*-way associative cache, is as follows:

```
(block_address) MOD (number_of_sets_in_cache)
```

I recommend trying out this formula on some of the preceding examples. It might seem like a boring and pointless exercise, but if you take five minutes and place a few blocks using this simple formula in conjunction with the preceding diagrams, everything I've said in this section will really fall into place for you in a "big picture" kind of way. And it's actually more fun to do that it probably sounds.

Temporal and Spatial Locality Revisited: Replacement/Eviction Policies and Block Sizes

Caches can increase the amount of benefit they derive from temporal locality by implementing an intelligent *replacement policy* (also called, conversely, an *eviction policy*). A replacement policy dictates which of the blocks currently in the cache will be replaced by any new block that gets fetched in. (Or, another way of putting it is that an eviction policy dictates which of the blocks currently in the cache will be evicted in order to make room for any new blocks that are fetched in.)

Types of Replacement/Eviction Policies

One way to implement a replacement policy would be to pick a block at random to be replaced. Other possible replacement policies would be a FIFO policy, a LIFO policy, or some other such variation. However, none of these policies take into account the fact that any block that was recently used is likely to be used again soon. With these simple policies, you wind up evicting blocks that will be used again shortly, thereby increasing the cache miss rate and eating up valuable memory bus bandwidth with a bunch of unnecessary fetches.

The ideal replacement policy would be one that makes room for an incoming block by evicting the cache block that is destined to go unused for the longest period of time. Unfortunately, computer architects haven't yet devised a way of infallibly predicting the future, so there's no way to know for sure which of the blocks that are currently residing in the cache is the one that will go the longest time before being accessed again.

Even if you can't predict the future, you can make an educated guess based on what you know of the cache's past behavior. The optimal replacement policy that doesn't involve predicting the future is to evict the block that has gone the longest period of time without being used, or the *least recently used (LRU) block*. The logic here is that if a block hasn't been used in a while, it's less likely to be part of the current working set than a block that was more recently used.

An LRU algorithm, though ideal, isn't quite feasible to implement in real life. Control logic that checks each cache block to determine which one is the least recently used not only would add complexity to the cache design, but such a check would also take up valuable time and thereby add unwanted latency to each replacement. Most caches wind up implementing some type of *pseudo-LRU algorithm* that approximates true LRU by marking blocks as more and more *dirty* the longer they sit unused in the cache. When a new block is fetched into the cache, the dirtiest blocks are the first to be replaced.

Sometimes, blocks that aren't all that dirty get replaced by newer blocks, just because there isn't enough room in the cache to contain the entire working set. A miss that results when a block containing needed data has been evicted from the cache due to a lack of cache capacity is called a *capacity miss*. This is the third and final type of cache miss.

Block Sizes

In the section on spatial locality I mentioned that storing whole blocks is one way that caches take advantage of spatial locality of reference. Now that you know a little more about how caches are organized internally, you can look a closer at the issue of block size.

You might think that as cache sizes increase, you can take even better advantage of spatial locality by making block sizes even bigger. Surely fetching more bytes per block into the cache would decrease the odds that some part of the working set will be evicted because it resides in a different block. This is true to some extent, but you have to be careful. If you increase the block size while keeping the cache size the same, you decrease the number of blocks that the cache can hold. Fewer blocks in the cache means fewer sets, and fewer sets means that collisions and therefore misses are more likely. And of course, with fewer blocks in the cache, the likelihood decreases that any particular block that the CPU needs will be available in the cache.

The upshot of all this is that smaller block sizes allow you to exercise more fine-grained control of the cache. You can trace out the boundaries of a working set with a higher resolution by using smaller cache blocks. If your cache blocks are too large, you wind up with a lot of wasted cache space, because many of the blocks will contain only a few bytes from the working set while the rest is irrelevant data. If you think of this issue in terms of cache pollution, you can say that large cache blocks are more prone to pollute the cache with non-reusable data than small cache blocks.

Figure 11-11 shows the memory map we've been using, sitting in a cache with large block sizes.

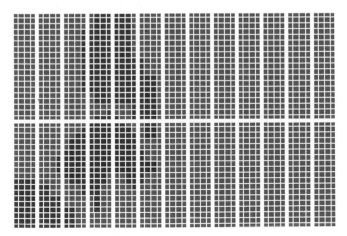

Figure 11-11: Memory map with large block sizes

Figure 11-12 shows the same map, but with the block sizes decreased. Notice how much more control the smaller blocks allow over cache pollution. The smaller cache blocks have a higher average ratio of red to blue in each block, which means that it's easier to keep the precise contours of the working set in the cache.

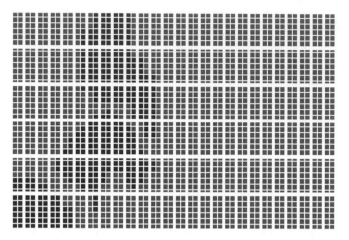

Figure 11-12: Memory map with small block sizes

The other problems with large block sizes are bandwidth related. The larger the block size, the more data is fetched with each load, so large block sizes can really eat up memory bus bandwidth, especially if the miss rate is high. A system therefore needs plenty of bandwidth if it's going to make good use of large cache blocks. Otherwise, the increase in bus traffic can increase the amount of time it takes to fetch a cache block from memory, thereby adding latency to the cache.

Write Policies: Write-Through vs. Write-Back

So far, this entire chapter has dealt with only one type of memory traffic: *loads*, or requests for data from memory. I've talked only about loads because they make up the vast majority of memory traffic. The remainder of memory traffic is made up of stores, which in simple uniprocessor systems are much easier to deal with. In this section, I'll explain how to handle stores in single-processor systems with just an L1. When you throw in more caches and multiple processors, things get more complicated than I want to go into here.

Once a retrieved piece of data is modified by the CPU, it must be stored or written back out to main memory so that the rest of the system has access to the most up-to-date version of it.

There are two ways to deal with such writes to memory. The first way is to immediately update all the copies of the modified data in each level of the cache hierarchy to reflect the latest changes. A piece of modified data would be written to both the L1 and main memory so that all of its copies are current. Such a policy for handling writes is called *write-through*, since it writes the modified data through to all levels of the hierarchy.

A write-through policy can be nice for multiprocessor and I/O–intensive system designs, since multiple clients are reading from memory at once and all need the most current data available. However, the multiple updates per write required by this policy can greatly increase memory traffic. For each store, the system must update multiple copies of the modified data. If there's a large amount of data that has been modified, this increased write activity could eat up quite a bit of memory bandwidth that could be used for the more important load traffic.

The alternative to write through is *write-back*, and it can potentially result in less memory traffic. With a write-back policy, changes propagate down to the lower levels of the hierarchy as cache blocks are evicted from the higher levels. An updated piece of data in an L1 cache block will not be updated in main memory until that block is evicted from the L1. The trade-off for write-back is that it's more complex to keep the multiple copies of the data in sync, especially in a multiprocessor system.

Conclusions

There is much, much more that can be said about caching; this chapter has covered only the basic concepts. As main memory moves farther away from the CPU in terms of CPU clock cycles, the importance of caching will only increase. For modern microprocessor systems, larger on-die caches have turned out to be one of the simplest and most effective uses for the increased transistor budgets that new manufacturing process technologies afford.

12

INTEL'S PENTIUM M, CORE DUO, AND CORE 2 DUO

In March 2003, Intel officially launched the Pentium M, a new *x*86 processor designed specifically for the mobile computing market. The Pentium M was a success from both performance and power efficiency perspectives, with the result that the immediate successor to the Pentium M, called Core Duo, made its way out of the portable niche and into desktop computers.

Core Duo's combination of high performance and low power consumption made it clearly superior to processors based on Intel's aging Netburst microarchitecture, and in the fall of 2005, Intel announced plans to unify its entire *x*86 product line, from portables all the way up to servers, on the follow-up to Core Duo: a brand new, power-efficient, 64-bit microarchitecture called Core. The desktop implementation of Core is the new Core 2 Duo processor line from Intel, while server products based on Core are sold under the venerable Xeon brand.

This chapter covers the major design aspects of the Pentium M, Core Duo, and Core 2 Duo, comparing the microarchitectures of these three related processors with the Intel processors covered in previous chapters. I'll talk about the major new features common to all three designs, like micro-ops fusion and the improved branch predictor, as well as each processor's individual innovations. Finally, I'll discuss memory instruction reordering, and I'll explain how a feature called memory disambiguation enables Core 2 to perform a kind of speculative execution on a processor's outgoing results stream.

Code Names and Brand Names

As far back as the launch of the Pentium 4 line, Intel began emphasizing the difference between microarchitecture and implementation. This difference, which is discussed in the section "Processor Organization and Core Microarchitecture" on page 247 has taken on new importance with the introduction of multi-core processors like the Core Duo. A particular processor from Intel might have three different names associated with it: a brand name for the processor itself (e.g., *Pentium 4*), a separate brand name for the microarchitecture that the processor implements (e.g., *Netburst*), and a commonly used code name that refers to a particular variant (e.g., *Prescott*) within a larger family of closely related microarchitectures that share a brand name. (*Willamette, Northwood, Prescott,* and *Cedar Mill* are all variants of Intel's Netburst microarchitecture that are used in different Pentium 4–branded processors.) The reader (and the author of computer books) is therefore forced to juggle three different commonly used names when referring to any one processor: the microarchitecture's code name, the microarchitecture's brand name, and the processor's brand name.

The processors described in this chapter are commonly known by the code names that Intel assigned to their microarchitectures prior to their launch. The first version of the Pentium M was called *Banias*, and a later revision was called *Dothan*; the code name for Core Duo was *Yonah*. The code name situation for Core 2 Duo is a bit complicated, and will be unraveled in the appropriate section. These code names are still used periodically by Intel and others, so you'll often need to be familiar with them in order to know which design is being discussed in a particular article or white paper.

Figure 12-1 should help you understand and keep track of the different names and codenames used throughout this chapter. Note that the related information for the Pentium 4 is included for reference.

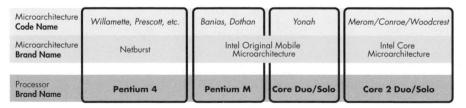

Figure 12-1: Code names and official brand names for some recent Intel architectures and implementations

To forestall any potential confusion, I have avoided the use of both the brand names and the code names for the microarchitectures under discussion. Instead, I typically employ the official brand name that Intel has given the *desktop* processor (as opposed to the mobile or server processor) that implements a particular microarchitecture.

The Rise of Power-Efficient Computing

Although the so-called "mobile revolution" had clearly arrived by the time Intel introduced the Pentium M in 2003, the previous years' rapid growth in portable computer sales wasn't the only reason Intel and other processor manufacturers had begun to pay serious attention to the power dissipation of their chips. As transistor sizes steadily shrank and designers became able to cram more power-hungry circuits into each square millimeter of a chip's surface area, a new barrier to processor performance loomed on the near horizon: the power wall.

Power wall is a term used by Intel to describe the point at which its chips' *power density* (the number of watts dissipated per unit area) began to seriously limit further integration and clockspeed scaling. The general idea behind the power wall is straightforward. Though the explanation here leaves out a number of factors like the effects of per-device capacitance and supply voltage, it should nonetheless give you enough of a handle on the phenomenon that you can understand some of the major design decisions behind the processors covered in this chapter.

Power Density

The amount of power that a chip dissipates per unit area is called its power density, and there are two types of power density that concern processor architects: dynamic power density and static power density.

Dynamic Power Density

Each transistor on a chip dissipates a small amount of power when it is switched, and transistors that are switched rapidly dissipate more power than transistors that are switched slowly. The total amount of power dissipated per unit area due to switching of a chip's transistors is called *dynamic power density*. There are two factors that work together to cause an increase in dynamic power density: clockspeed and transistor density.

Increasing a processor's clockspeed involves switching its transistors more rapidly, and as I just mentioned, transistors that are switched more rapidly dissipate more power. Therefore, as a processor's clockspeed rises, so does its dynamic power density, because each of those rapidly switching transistors contributes more to the device's total power dissipation. You can also increase a chip's dynamic power density by cramming more transistors into the same amount of surface area.

Figure 12-2 illustrates how transistor density and clockspeed work together to increase dynamic power density. As the clockspeed of the device and the number of transistors per unit area rise, so does the overall dynamic power density.

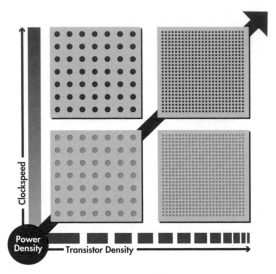

Figure 12-2: Dynamic power density

Static Power Density

In addition to clockspeed-related increases in dynamic power density, chip designers must also contend with the fact that even transistors that aren't switching will still leak current during idle periods, much like how a faucet that is shut off can still leak water if the water pressure behind it is high enough. This *leakage current* causes an idle transistor to constantly dissipate a trace amount of power. The amount of power dissipated per unit area due to leakage current is called *static power density*.

Transistors leak more current as they get smaller, and consequently static power densities begin to rise across the chip when more transistors are crammed into the same amount of space. Thus even relatively low clockspeed devices with very small transistor sizes are still subject to increases in power density if leakage current is not controlled. If a silicon device's overall power density gets high enough, it will begin to overheat and will eventually fail entirely. Thus it's critical that designers of highly integrated devices like modern *x*86 processors take power efficiency into account when designing a new microarchitecture.

Power density is a major, growing concern for every type of micro-processor, regardless of the type of computer in which the processor is intended to be used. The same types of power-aware design decisions that are important for a mobile processor are now just as critical for a server processor.

The Pentium M

In order to meet the new challenges posed by the power-efficient computing paradigm, Intel's Israel-based design team drew on the older, time-tested P6 microarchitecture as the basis for its new low-power design, the Pentium M. The Pentium M takes the overall pipeline organization and layout of the P6 in its Pentium III incarnation and builds on it substantially with a number of innovations, allowing it to greatly exceed its predecessor in both power efficiency and raw performance (see Table 12-1).

Table 12-1: Features of the Pentium M

Introduction Date	March 12, 2003
Process	0.13 micron
Transistor Count	77 million
Clock Speed at Introduction	1.3 to 1.6 GHz
L1 Cache Size	32KB instruction, 32KB data
L2 Cache Size (on-die)	1MB

Most of the Pentium M's new features are in its front end, specifically in its fetch, decode, and branch-prediction hardware.

The Fetch Phase

As I explained in Chapter 5, the original P6 processor fetches one 16-byte instruction packet per cycle from the I-cache into a buffer that's two instruction packets (or 32 bytes) deep. (This fetch buffer is roughly analogous to the PowerPC instruction queue [IQ] described in previous chapters.) From the fetch buffer, x86 instructions can move at a rate of up to three instructions per cycle into the P6 core's three decoders. This fetch and decode process is illustrated in Figure 12-3.

On the Pentium M and its immediate successor, Core Duo, the fetch buffer has been widened to 64 bytes. Thus the front end's predecode hardware can hold and examine up to four 16-byte instruction packets at a time. This deeper buffer, depicted in Figure 12-4, is necessary to keep the newer design's much improved decode hardware (described later) from starving.

A second version of the Pentium M, commonly known by its code name, *Dothan*, modifies this 64-byte fetch buffer to do double duty as a hardware loop buffer. This fetch/loop buffer combination is also used in the Pentium M's successor, the Core Duo.

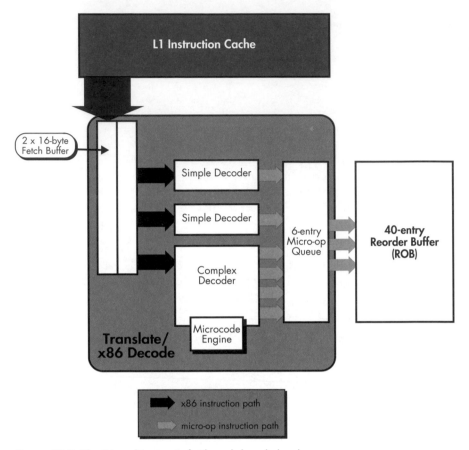

Figure 12-3: The P6 architecture's fetch and decode hardware

The Hardware Loop Buffer

A *hardware loop buffer* caches the block of instructions that is located inside a program loop. Because the instructions inside a loop are repeated many times, storing them in a front-end buffer keeps the processor from having to re-fetch them on each loop iteration. Thus the loop buffer is a feature that saves power because it cuts down on the number of accesses to the I-cache and to the branch prediction unit's branch target buffer.

The Decode Phase: Micro-ops Fusion

One of the most important ways that Intel's Pentium M architects were able to get more performance out of the P6 architecture was by improving on the predecessor design's decode rate.

You'll recall from Chapter 5 that each of the P6's two simple/fast decoders can output a maximum of one micro-op per cycle to the micro-op queue, for a total of two micro-ops per cycle. All instructions that translate into more than one micro-op must use the single complex/slow decoder, which can output up to four micro-ops per cycle. Thus, the P6 core's decode hardware can output a maximum of six micro-ops per cycle to its micro-op queue.

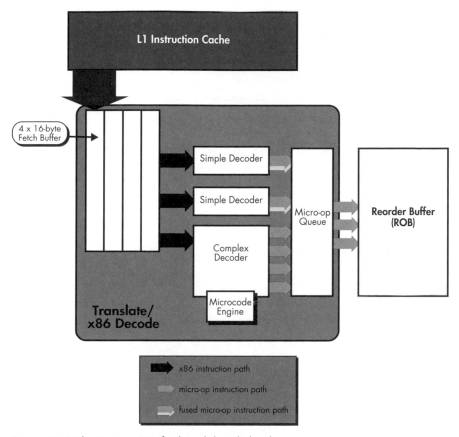

Figure 12-4: The Pentium M's fetch and decode hardware

For certain types of operations, especially memory operations, the P6's decoding scheme can cause a serious bottleneck. As I'll discuss in more detail later, *x*86 store instructions and a specific category of load instructions decode into two micro-ops, which means that most *x*86 memory accesses must use the complex/slow decoder. During bursts of memory instructions, the complex/slow decoder becomes backed up with work while the other two decoders sit idle. At such times, the P6's decoding hardware decodes only two micro-ops per cycle, a number far short of its peak decode rate, six micro-ops per cycle.

The Pentium M's redesigned decoding unit contains a new feature called *micro-ops fusion* that eliminates this bottleneck for memory accesses and enables the processor to increase the number of *x*86 instructions per cycle that it can convert to micro-ops. The Pentium M's two simple/fast decoders are able to take certain *x*86 instructions that normally translate into two micro-ops and translate them into a single fused micro-op. These two decoders can send either one micro-op per cycle or one fused micro-op per cycle to the micro-op queue, as depicted in Figure 12-5. Because both simple and fast decoders can now process these formerly two–micro-op memory instructions, the Pentium M's front end can actually achieve the maximum decode rate of six micro-ops per cycle during long stretches of memory traffic.

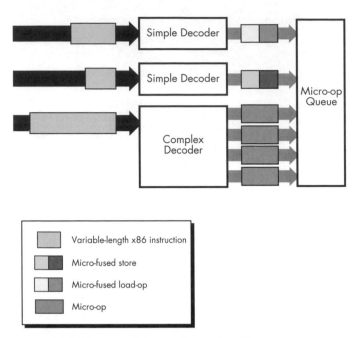

Figure 12-5: Micro-ops fusion on the Pentium M

From the micro-op queue, each fused micro-op moves on to the instruction window, where it is assigned to a single ROB and RS entry and tracked just like a normal micro-op through the rest of the Pentium M's pipeline. Note that the Pentium M's back end treats the two constituent parts of a fused micro-op as independent of each other for the purposes of issuing and execution. Thus the two micro-ops that make up a fused micro-op can issue in parallel through two different issue ports or serially through the same port, whichever is appropriate. Once the two micro-ops have completed execution, they're committed together as a single fused micro-op.

The two types of instructions that can be translated into fused micro-ops are the store instruction type and the load-op instruction type.

Fused Stores

Store instructions on *x*86 processors, including not only Intel processors but also those from AMD, are broken down during the decode phase into two micro-ops: a store-address micro-op and a store-data micro-op. The *store-address* micro-op is the instruction that tells the address generation hardware to calculate the address in memory where the data is to be stored. This micro-op is sent to the *store-address execution unit* in the back end's load-store unit (LSU) for execution. The *store-data* micro-op is the instruction that writes the data to be stored into the outgoing *store-data buffer*. From the store data buffer, the data will be written out to memory when the store instruction commits; this micro-op is executed by the *store-data execution unit*, which is also located in the LSU.

The Pentium M's instruction decoding hardware decodes the store operation into two separate micro-ops, but it then *fuses* these two micro-ops together before writing them to a single, shared entry in the micro-op queue. As noted earlier, the instructions remain fused until they're issued through an issue port to the actual store unit, at which point they're treated separately by the back end. Because the store-address and store-data operations are inherently parallel and are performed by two separate execution units on two separate issue ports, these two micro-ops can issue and execute in parallel—the data can be written to the store buffer at the same time that the store address is being calculated. When both micro-ops have completed execution, the core's commitment unit again treats them as if they are fused.

Fused Loads

A *load-op*, or *read-modify* instruction, is exactly what it sounds like: a two-part instruction that loads data from memory into a register and then performs an operation on that data. Such instructions are broken down by the decoding hardware into two micro-ops: a load micro-op that's issued to the load execution unit and is responsible for calculating the source address and then loading the needed data, and a second micro-op that performs some type of operation on the loaded data and is executed by the appropriate execution unit.

Load-op instructions are treated in much the same way as store instructions with respect to decoding, fusion, and execution. The load micro-op is fused with the second micro-op, and the two are tracked as a single micro-op in the processor's instruction window. As with the fused stores described earlier, the two constituent parts of the fused micro-op issue and execute separately before being committed together.

Note that unlike the store-address and store-data micro-ops that make up a fused store, the two parts of a fused load-op instruction are inherently serial, because the load operation must be executed first. Thus the two parts of the fused load-op must be executed in sequence.

The Impact of Micro-ops Fusion

Intel claims that micro-ops fusion on the Pentium M reduces the number of micro-ops in the instruction window by over 10 percent. Fewer micro-ops in-flight means that a larger number of instructions can be tracked with the same number of ROB and RS entries. Thus the Pentium M's re-order, issue, and commit width is effectively larger than the number of ROB and RS entries alone would suggest. The end result is that, compared to its predecessors, the Pentium M can bring out more performance from the same amount of instruction tracking hardware, a feature that gives the processor more performance per watt of power dissipated.

As you might expect, the Pentium M sees the most benefit from micro-ops fusion during sustained bursts of memory operations. During long stretches of memory traffic, all three of the Pentium M's decoders are able to work in parallel to process incoming memory instructions, thereby tripling the decode bandwidth of the older P6 core. Intel estimates that this improved memory instruction decode bandwidth translates into a 5 percent performance boost for integer code and a 9 percent boost for floating-point code, the former benefiting more from store fusion and the latter benefiting equally from store and load-op fusion.

NOTE   *You may have noticed that the Pentium M's micro-ops fusion feature works remarkably like the PowerPC 970's instruction grouping scheme, insofar as both processors bind translated instructions together in the decode phase before dispatching them as a group to the back end. The analogy between the Pentium M's micro-ops fusion feature and the 970's group dispatch feature isn't perfect, but it is striking, and both features have a similarly positive effect on performance and power consumption.*

Branch Prediction

As you learned in "Caching Basics" on page 215, the ever-growing distance (in CPU cycles) between main memory and the CPU means that precious transistor resources spent on branch prediction hardware continue to give an ever larger return on investment. For reasons of both performance and power efficiency, Intel spent quite a few transistors on the Pentium M's branch predictor.

The Pentium M's branch predictor is one place where the newer design borrows from the Pentium 4 instead of the P6. The Pentium M adopts the Pentium 4's already powerful branch prediction scheme and expands on it by adding two new features: a loop detector and an indirect predictor.

The Loop Detector

One of the most common types of branches that a processor encounters is the exit condition of a loop. In fact, loops are so common that the static method of branch prediction, in which all branches are assumed to be loop exit conditions that evaluate to *taken*, works reasonably well for processors with shallow pipelines.

One problem with static branch predictors is that they always make a wrong prediction on the final iteration of the loop—the iteration on which the branch evaluates to *not taken*—thereby forcing a pipeline stall as the processor recovers from the erroneous prediction. The other, more important problem with static prediction is that it works poorly for non-loop branches, like standard if-then conditionals. In such branches, a static prediction of *taken* is roughly the equivalent of a coin toss.

Dynamic predictors, like the Pentium 4's branch predictor, fix this shortcoming by keeping track of the execution history of a particular branch instruction in order to give the processor a better idea of what its outcome on the current pass will probably be. The bigger the table used to track the branch's history, the more data the branch predictor has to work with and the more accurate its predictions can be. However, even a relatively sizable branch history table (BHT) like that of the Pentium 4 doesn't have enough space to store all the relevant execution history information on the loop branches, since they tend to take a very large number of iterations. Therefore loops that go through many iterations will always be mispredicted by a standard dynamic branch predictor.

The Pentium M's *loop detector* addresses this problem by analyzing the branches as they execute, in order to identify which branches are loop exit conditions. For each branch that the detector thinks is a loop exit condition, the branch prediction hardware initializes a special set of counters in the predictor table to keep track of how many times the loop actually iterates. If loops with even fairly large numbers of iterations always tend to iterate the same number of times, then the Pentium M's branch predictor can predict their behavior with 100 percent accuracy.

In sum, the loop detector plugs into the Pentium M's P4-style branch predictor and augments it by providing it with extra, more specialized data on the loops of the currently executing program.

The Indirect Predictor

The second type of specialized branch predictor that the Pentium M uses is the indirect predictor. As you learned in Chapter 1, branches come in two flavors: direct and indirect. Direct branches have the branch target explicitly specified in the instruction, which means that the branch target is fixed at load time. Indirect branches, on the other hand, have to load the branch target from a register, so they can have multiple potential targets. Storing these potential targets is the function of the branch target buffer (BTB) described in Chapter 5.

Direct branches are the easiest to predict and can often be predicted with upward of 97 percent accuracy. Indirect branches, in contrast, are notoriously difficult to predict, and some research puts indirect branch prediction using the standard BTB method at around 75 percent accuracy.

The Pentium M's *indirect predictor* works a little like the branch history table that I've described, but instead of storing information about whether or not a particular branch was taken the past few times it was executed, it stores information about each indirect branch's favorite target addresses—the targets to which a particular branch usually likes to jump and the conditions under which it likes to jump to them. So the Pentium M's indirect branch predictor knows that a particular indirect branch in the BHT with a specific set of favorite target addresses stored in the BTB tends to jump to one target address under *this* set of conditions, while under *that* set of conditions, it likes to jump to another.

Intel claims that the combination of the loop detector and indirect branch predictor gives the Pentium M a 20 percent increase in overall branch prediction accuracy, resulting in a 7 percent real performance increase.

Improved branch prediction gives the Pentium M a leg up not only in performance but also in power efficiency. Because of its improved branch prediction capabilities, the Pentium M wastes fewer cycles and less energy speculatively executing code that it will then have to throw away once it learns that it mispredicted a branch.

The Stack Execution Unit

Another feature that Intel introduced with the Pentium M is the *stack execution unit*, a piece of hardware that's designed to reduce the number of in-flight micro-ops that the processor needs to keep track of.

The *x*86 ISA includes stack-manipulation instructions like pop, push, ret, and call, for use in passing parameters to functions in function calls. During the course of their execution, these instructions update *x*86's dedicated *stack pointer register*, ESP. In the Netburst and P6 microarchitectures, this update was carried out by a special micro-op, which was generated by the decoder and charged with using the integer execution units to update ESP by adding to it or subtracting from it as necessary.

The Pentium M's dedicated stack execution unit eliminates these special ESP-updating micro-ops by monitoring the decoder's instruction stream for incoming stack instructions and keeping track of those instructions' changes to ESP. Updates to ESP are handled by a dedicated adder attached to the stack execution unit instead of by the integer execution units, as in previous designs. Because the Pentium M's front end has dedicated hardware for tracking the state of ESP and keeping it updated, there's no need to issue those extra ESP-related micro-ops to the back end.

This technique has a few benefits. The obvious benefit is that it reduces the number of in-flight micro-ops, which means fewer micro-ops and less power consumed per task. Then, because there are fewer integer micro-ops in the back end, the integer execution units are free to process other instructions, since they don't have to deal with the stack-related ESP updates.

Pipeline and Back End

The exact length of the Pentium M's pipeline has never been publicly disclosed, but Intel has stated that it is slightly longer the older P6's 12-stage pipeline. One or two new pipeline stages were added to the Pentium M's front end phase for timing purposes, with the result that the newer processor can run at a higher clockspeed than its predecessor.

Details of the Pentium M's back end are also scarce, but it is alleged to be substantially the same as that of the Pentium III. (See Chapter 5 for details of the PIII's back end.)

Summary: The Pentium M in Historical Context

The Pentium M started out as a processor intended solely for mobile devices, but it soon became clear to Intel that this much-improved version of the P6 microarchitecture had far more performance-per-watt potential than the aging, high-clockspeed Netburst microarchitecture that was currently at the heart of the company's desktop and server offerings. This being the case, Intel's Israeli team began working on an improved version of the Pentium M that was intended for use outside the mobile market.

Core Duo/Solo

The successor to the Pentium M (almost as widely known in computing circles by its code name, *Yonah*, as by its official name, *Core Duo/Solo*) builds on the Pentium M's microarchitecture and brings it to new levels of performance and power efficiency (see Table 12-2). However, Core Duo is mainly an evolutionary, transitional design that sits between the Pentium M and the more radically improved Core 2 Duo described in the next major section of this chapter. This section will briefly cover the major ways that Core Duo improves on the Pentium M before moving on to the next section's more detailed coverage of Core 2 Duo.

Table 12-2: Features of the Core Solo/Duo

Introduction Date	January 5, 2006
Process	65 nanometer
Transistor Count	151 million
Clock Speed at Introduction	1.66 to 2.33 GHz
L1 Cache Size	32KB instruction, 32KB data
L2 Cache Size (on-die)	2MB
x86 ISA Extensions	SSE3

Intel's Line Goes Multi-Core

The Intel microarchitectures covered in previous chapters, especially the Pentium 4's Netburst microarchitecture, were designed so that their performance scaled primarily with clockspeed increases. But as you learned in the earlier section on power density, the viability of this approach has been rapidly diminishing in conjunction with shrinking transistor sizes. Instead of trying to run a single narrow instruction stream faster by increasing the processor's clockspeed, *multi-core processors* like Core Duo are designed to exploit Moore's Curves by integrating multiple copies of a microarchitecture onto a single piece of silicon in order to execute multiple instruction streams in parallel.

Processor Organization and Core Microarchitecture

Thus far, the discussions of microprocessor organization in this book have placed all of a processor's different components into a few basic categories. My descriptions and illustrations depict processors as being divided primarily into a front end and a back end, with each of these two main divisions consisting of various high-level functional blocks (decode unit, branch-prediction unit, integer unit, load-store unit, etc.), which are themselves made up of more specialized units (simple/fast decoders, complex integer execution unit, floating-point ALU, store-address unit, etc.).

All of these different levels of organization come together to comprise a processor's *core microarchitecture*, or simply *core*, for short. Note that a processor's core is typically understood to include the L1 cache, as well. Thus you'll often encounter references in computing literature to the *P6 core*, the *Netburst core*, the *Pentium core*, and so on, all of which are short-hand ways of referring to a particular combination of L1 cache, front-end, and back-end hardware as distinct from the other components on the processor die (for example, the L2 cache or less commonly integrated components like an L3 cache or a memory controller).

Figure 12-6 shows the floor plan of an Intel Pentium M processor. This is a picture of the actual processor die, with the core microarchitecture marked and distinguished from the L2 cache.

Figure 12-6: The floor plan of an Intel Pentium M processor

NOTE *The common use of the term core almost certainly explains Intel's decision to use the name Core in the branding of its new microarchitectures and their implementations.*

Often, it's also useful to draw a distinction between a microarchitecture—conceived more abstractly as a particular arrangement of front end and back end hardware—and one or more specific *implementations* of that microarchitecture. These implementations take the form of distinct microprocessor products that are either based on the same microarchitecture (as in the case of the Core 2 Duo E6300 [2MB of L2 cache] and Core 2 Extreme X6800 [4MB of L2 cache], both of which implement the Intel Core microarchitecture) or on closely related microarchitectures that can be grouped together into the same family (for example, the original Pentium 4 and the Pentium 4 with HyperThreading, both of which implement variants of the Netburst microarchitecture).

Multiprocessing and Chip Multiprocessing

For years, server, workstation, and even some consumer computers have used a technique called *multiprocessing* to increase the amount of execution hardware available to operating systems and applications. In a nutshell, multiprocessing is simply the integration of more than one processor core into a single computer system. In a traditional multiprocessor system, separate processor cores are implemented on separate pieces of silicon and are packaged as separate integrated circuits, as shown in Figure 12-7.

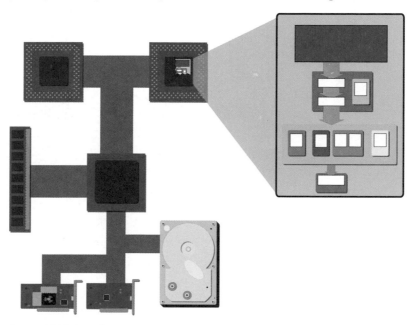

Figure 12-7: A multiprocessor computer

However, the semiconductor industry has now moved to a technique called *chip multiprocessing (CMP)*, where two or more processor cores are integrated onto the same silicon die. Under the CMP paradigm, the term *microprocessor* now refers to an integrated circuit that implements multiple copies of a core architecture on a single silicon die. Figure 12-8 is an abstract representation of a CMP computer containing what is commonly called a *dual-core processor*, a processor with two cores on the same die.

Different kinds of multi-core processors are often distinguished by their levels of integration. Some multi-core processors, like Intel's Netburst-based Pentium D, have cores that share only a silicon substrate—each core has a private L2 cache, and all inter-core communication buses are off-die. At the other end of the spectrum is a more highly integrated multi-core processor like the Core Duo, shown in Figure 12-9.

The two cores that make up the Core Duo each have a private L1 cache, but they share an L2 cache. The Core Duo also includes some arbitration logic that helps control access to the shared L2, so that neither core is able to soak up all the L2 bus bandwidth for itself.

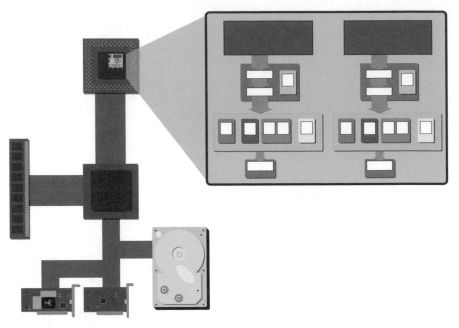

Figure 12-8: A chip multiprocessing (CMP) computer

NOTE   *The dual-core processors in the Intel Core Duo/Solo line are named Core Duo, while their smaller, cheaper, less powerful single-core counterparts are named Core Solo.*

The shared L2 offers a number of advantages, not the least of which is an increase in the ability of the two cores to share data without using a bus. If both cores are using the same working set of code and/or data, then that working set can be placed in the shared L2 where the cores can easily access it simultaneously. Core Duo's shared L2 also saves power, because both cores use a single, shared bus to access it.

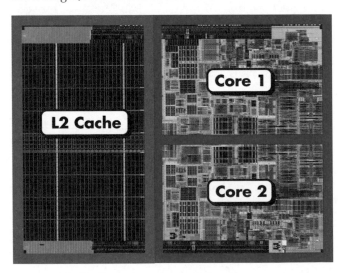

Figure 12-9: The floor plan of an Intel Core Duo processor

Core Duo's Improvements

Core Duo's architects took the basic microarchitecture of the second version of the Pentium M, codenamed *Dothan*, and made a number of improvements aimed at bringing the design to higher levels of performance and power efficiency. These improvements are described briefly in the sections here.

Micro-ops Fusion of SSE and SSE2 store and load-op Instructions

On the Pentium M, only *x*86 and *x*87 load-op and store instructions can be micro-fused. All SSE and SSE2 load-op and store instructions must therefore pass through the Pentium M's single complex/slow decoder, a situation that creates a serious bottleneck for 128-bit vector code with lots of memory traffic.

Intel fixed this bottleneck for Core Duo by enabling all three of the new processor's decoders to generate fused micro-ops for SSE and SSE2 load-op and store instructions. Thus Core Duo's decode phase can send up to three fused 128-bit load-op and/or store micro-ops per cycle into the micro-op queue. Because vector code is typically memory-intensive, Core Duo's ability to use any of its three decoders to process vector memory instructions is critical to the design's improved vector performance.

Micro-ops Fusion and Lamination of SSE and SSE2 Arithmetic Instructions

Even more significant for Core Duo's vector performance than micro-fused memory accesses is the fact that Core Duo also expands the use of micro-ops fusion to encompass 128-bit vector arithmetic instructions. For reasons that I'll explain in this chapter's discussion of Core 2 Duo, most SSE and SSE2 instructions decode into multiple micro-ops (typically from two to four) on the Pentium III, Pentium 4, Pentium M, and Core Duo. This means that SSE and SSE2 vector instructions have been bottlenecked at the decode phase on processors prior to Core Duo because they can only be decoded by the slow/complex decoder.

On Core Duo, 128-bit SSE and SSE2 vector instructions that decode into a pair of 64-bit micro-ops can be translated into a single fused micro-op by all three of the front end's decoders. Furthermore, vector instructions that decode into two micro-op pairs (for a total of four micro-ops per instruction) can be translated by the decoders into a single laminated micro-op. This *laminated micro-op* functions like a normal fused micro-op—it breaks apart into its four constituent micro-ops during the execute phase, but it's tracked and committed using a single ROB entry.

Core Duo's ability to generate fused and laminated micro-ops for SSE and SSE2 instructions is a crucial part of its superior vector performance. Not only do lamination and the extension of micro-ops fusion to the SSE family of instructions improve performance by eliminating a decode bottleneck, but these techniques also add to the design's power efficiency by enabling it to track more micro-ops using a smaller instruction window.

Micro-ops Fusion of Miscellaneous Non-SSE Instructions

Core Duo also supports micro-ops fusion of a few new types of instructions that had been forced to use the complex/slow decoder in previous designs. These new instruction types include indirect branch instructions, compare/test immediate and memory instructions, and some store immediate to memory instructions. Finally, a handful of other multi-micro-op instructions had the number of micro-ops into which they decode reduced, freeing up dispatch, issue, and retire bandwidth.

Improved Loop Detector

One of the problems with the Pentium M's loop detector is that it fails to detect loops that have a very low number of iterations. Core Duo's loop detector can detect loops with smaller iteration counts, a feature that saves power and improves performance by lowering the number of instruction fetches and BTB accesses.

SSE3

Core Duo introduces a new member into the SSE family of ISA extensions: SSE3. The SSE3 instruction set consists of 13 new instructions, which Intel's *Software Developer's Manual* summarizes as follows:

- One *x*87 FPU instruction used in integer conversion
- One SIMD integer instruction that addresses unaligned data loads
- Two SIMD floating-point packed ADD/SUB instructions
- Four SIMD floating-point horizontal ADD/SUB instructions
- Three SIMD floating-point LOAD/MOVE/DUPLICATE instructions
- Two thread-synchronization instructions

These new instructions fill in some gaps left in the SSE family and in the *x*87 extensions, mostly in the areas of byte shuffling and floating-point inter-element arithmetic. These are the areas in which the SSE family has been weakest when compared with AltiVec.

Floating-Point Improvement

When programmers use the *x*87 floating-point instructions to perform floating-point computations, they have multiple options available to them for dealing with the more complicated aspects of floating-point math like number formats and rounding behavior. The *x*87 FPU has a special register called the *floating-point control word (FPCW)*, which programmers can use to tell the FPU how they'd like it to handle these issues. In short, the FPCW holds configuration data for the floating-point unit, and programmers write new data into that register whenever they'd like to change the FPU's configuration.

All Intel designs prior to Core Duo have assumed that programmers very rarely write to the FPCW. Because of this assumption, Intel's chip architects have never associated any rename registers with the FPCW. As it turns out, however, some types of programs contain code that writes to the FPCW fairly frequently, most often to change the FPU's rounding control options. For such programs, a single copy of the FPCW is a significant bottleneck, because the entire floating-point pipeline must stall until that one register is finished being updated.

Core Duo is the first Intel processor to feature a set of microarchitectural rename registers for the FPCW. These four new rename registers enable Core Duo to extract more parallelism from floating-point code by eliminating false register name conflicts associated with the FCPW. (For more on false register name conflicts, data hazards, and register renaming, see Chapter 4.)

Integer Divide Improvement

Integer divisions are rare in most code, but when they do occur, they stall the complex integer unit for many cycles. The CIU must grind through the large number of computations and bit shifts that it takes to produce a division result; no other instructions can enter the CIU's pipeline during this time.

Core Duo's complex integer unit tries to shorten integer division's long latencies by examining each x86 integer divide instruction (idiv) that it encounters in order to see if it can exit the division process early. For idiv instructions that have smaller data sizes and need fewer iterations inside the ALU hardware to produce a valid result, the integer unit stops the division once the required number of iterations has completed. This technique reduces average idiv latencies because the ALU no longer forces every idiv, regardless of data size, to go through the same number of iterations. In some cases, an idiv that would take 12 cycles on Dothan takes only 4 cycles on Core Duo, and in others the latency can be reduced from 20 cycles (Dothan) to 12 cycles (Core Duo).

Virtualization Technology

The SSE3 instructions aren't the only new extensions added to the x86 ISA. Intel also used Core Duo to introduce its Virtualization Technology, called *VT-x*, along with a set of supporting ISA extensions called *Virtual Machine Extensions (VMX)*.

VT-x is worthy of its own chapter, but I'll summarize it very briefly here. In a nutshell, VT-x enables a single processor to run multiple operating system/application stacks simultaneously, with each stack thinking that it has complete control of the processor. VT-x accomplishes this by presenting a *virtual processor* to each operating system instance. A *virtual machine monitor (VMM)* then runs at a level beneath the operating systems, closest to the processor hardware, and manages the multiple operating system instances running on the virtual processors.

With virtualization technology, a single, possibly underutilized multi-core processor can be made to do the work of multiple computers, thereby keeping more of its execution hardware busy during each cycle. Indeed, VT-x can be thought of as a way to increase power efficiency simply by giving the processor more work to do, so that fewer execution slots per cycle are wasted due to idleness.

Summary: Core Duo in Historical Context

Core Duo's improvements on the Dothan design enabled Intel to offer a dual-core part with the power dissipation characteristics of previous single-core parts. Because it integrated two cores onto a single die, Core Duo could also offer a significant speedup for workloads involving multiple instruction streams (or *threads of execution* in computer science parlance). However, more radical changes to the microarchitecture were needed if Intel was to meet its goal of dramatically increasing performance on single instruction streams without also increasing clockspeed and power consumption.

Core 2 Duo

The Intel Core microarchitecture introduced in the Core 2 Duo line of processors represents Intel's most ambitious attempt since the Pentium Pro to increase single-threaded performance independently of clockspeeds. Because its designers took a "more hardware" instead of "more clockspeed" approach to performance, Core is bigger and wider than just about any mass-market design that has come before it (see Table 12-3). Indeed, this "more of everything" is readily apparent with a glance at the diagram of the new microarchitecture in Figure 12-10.

In every phase of Core's 14-stage pipeline, there is more of just about anything you could think of: more decoding logic, more re-order buffer space, more reservation station entries, more issue ports, more execution hardware, more memory buffer space, and so on. In short, Core's designers took everything that has already been proven to work and added more of it, along with a few new tricks and tweaks.

Table 12-3: Features of the Core 2 Duo/Solo

Introduction Date	July 27, 2006
Process	65 nanometer
Transistor Count	291 million
Clock Speed at Introduction	1.86 to 2.93 GHz
L1 Cache Size	32KB instruction, 32KB data
L2 Cache Size (on-die)	2MB or 4MB
x86 ISA Extensions	EM64T for 64-bit support

Core is wider in the decode, dispatch, issue, and commit pipeline phases than every processor covered in this book except the PowerPC 970. Core's instruction window, which consists of a 96-entry reorder buffer and a 32-entry reservation station, is bigger than that of any previous Intel microarchitecture except for Netburst. However, as I've mentioned before, bigger doesn't automatically mean better. There are real-world limits on the number of instructions that can be executed in parallel, so the wider the machine, the more execution slots per cycle that can potentially go unused because of limits to *instruction-level parallelism (ILP)*. Furthermore, Chapter 3 described how memory latency can starve a wide machine for code and data, resulting in a waste of execution resources. Core has a number of features that are there solely to address ILP and memory latency issues and to ensure that the processor is able to keep its execution units full.

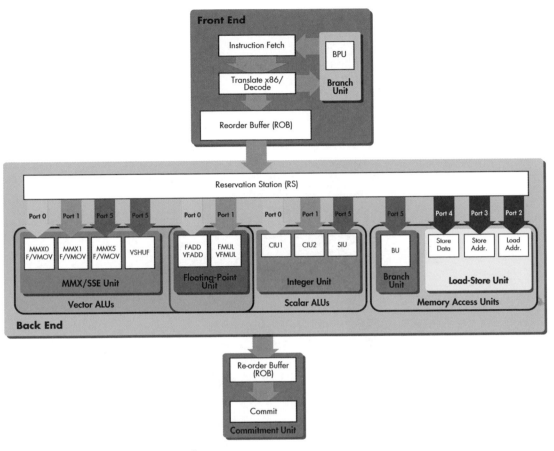

Figure 12-10: The Intel Core microarchitecture

NOTE   *The Intel Core microarchitecture family actually consists of three nearly identical microarchitectural variants, each of which is known by its code name. Merom is the low-power mobile microarchitecture, Conroe is the desktop microarchitecture, and Woodcrest is the server microarchitecture.*

In the front end, micro-ops fusion and a new trick called *macro-fusion* work together to keep code moving into the back end; and in the back end, a greatly enlarged instruction window ensures that more instructions can reach the execution units on each cycle. Intel has also fixed an important SSE bottleneck that existed in previous designs, thereby massively improving Core's vector performance over that of its predecessors.

In the remainder of this chapter, I'll talk about all of these improvements and many more, placing each of Core's new features in the context of Intel's overall focus on balancing performance, scalability, and power consumption.

The Fetch Phase

As I'll discuss in more detail later, Core has a higher decode rate than any of its predecessors. This higher decode rate means that more radical design changes were needed in the fetch phase to prevent the decoder from being starved for instructions. A simple increase in the size of the fetch buffer wouldn't cut it this time, so Intel tried a different approach.

Core's fetch buffer is only 32 bytes—the size of the fetch buffer on the original P6 core. In place of an expanded fetch buffer, Core sports an entirely new structure that sits in between the fetch buffer and the decoders: a bona fide instruction queue.

Core's 18-entry IQ, depicted in Figure 12-11, holds about the same number of *x*86 instructions as the Pentium M's 64-byte fetch buffer. The predecode hardware can move up to six *x*86 instructions per cycle from the fetch buffer into the IQ, where a new feature called macro-fusion is used to prepare between four and five *x*86 instructions each cycle for transfer from the IQ to the decode hardware.

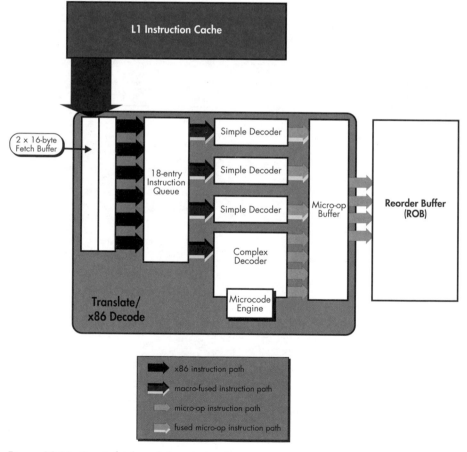

Figure 12-11: Core's fetch and decode hardware

NOTE *Core's instruction queue also takes over the hardware loop buffer function of previous designs' fetch buffers.*

Macro-Fusion

A major new feature of Core's front end hardware is its ability to fuse pairs of *x*86 instructions together in the predecode phase and send them through a single decoder to be translated into a single micro-op. This feature, called *macro-fusion*, can be used only on certain types of instructions; specifically, compare and test instructions can be macro-fused with branch instructions.

Core's predecode phase can send one macro-fused *x*86 instruction per cycle to any one of the front end's four decoders. (As we'll see later, Core has four instruction decoders, one more than its predecessors.) In turn, the decode phase as a whole can translate one macro-fused *x*86 instruction into a *macro-fused micro-op* on each cycle. (No more than one such macro-fused micro-op can be generated per cycle.)

All told, macro-fusion allows the predecode phase to send to the decode phase a maximum of either

- four normal *x*86 instructions per cycle, or
- three normal *x*86 instructions plus one macro-fused instruction, for a total of *five* *x*86 instructions per cycle.

Moving five instructions per cycle into the decode phase is a huge improvement over the throughput of three instructions per cycle in previous designs. By enabling the front end to combine two *x*86 instructions per cycle into a single micro-op, macro fusion effectively enlarges Core's decode, dispatch, and retire bandwidth, all without the need for extra ROB and RS entries. Ultimately, less book-keeping hardware means better power efficiency per *x*86 instruction for the processor as a whole, which is why it's important for Core to approach the goal of one micro-op per *x*86 instruction as closely as possible.

The Decode Phase

Core's widened back end can grind through micro-ops at an unprecedented rate, so Intel needed to dramatically increase the new microarchitecture's decode rate compared with previous designs so that more micro-ops per cycle could reach the back end. Core's designers did a few things to achieve this goal.

I've already talked about one innovation that Core uses to increase its decode rate: macro-fusion. This new capability has the effect of giving Core an extra decoder for "free," but remember that this free decoder that macro-fusion affords is only good for certain instruction types. Also, the decode phase as a whole can translate only one macro-fused *x*86 instruction into a *macro-fused micro-op* on each cycle. (No more than one such macro-fused micro-op can be generated per cycle.)

Intel also expanded the decode phase's total throughput by adding a brand new simple/fast decoding unit, bringing Core's number of simple/fast decoders up to three. The three simple/fast decoders combine with the complex/slow decoder to enable Core's decoding hardware to send up to seven micro-ops per cycle into the micro-op queue, from which up to four micro-ops per cycle can pass into the ROB. The newly expanded decoding unit was depicted in Figure 12-11.

Finally, Intel has increased Core's decode rate by making a change to the back end (described later) that now permits 128-bit SSE instructions to be decoded into a single micro-op instead of a fused micro-op pair, as in previous designs. Thus Core's new front end design brings the processor much closer to the goal of one micro-op per *x*86 instruction.

Core's Pipeline

Core's 14-stage pipeline is two stages longer than the original 12-stage P6 pipeline. Both of Core's new stages were added in the processor's front end. The first new stage was added in the fetch/predecode phase to accommodate the instruction queue and macro-fusion, and the second stage was added to help out with 64-bit address translation.

Intel has not yet made available a detailed breakdown of Core's pipeline stages, so the precise locations of the two new stages are still unknown.

Core's Back End

One of the most distinctive features of the older P6 design is its back end's issue port structure, described in Chapter 5. Core uses a similar structure in its back end, although there are some major differences between the issue port and reservation station (RS) combination of Core and that of the P6.

To get a sense of the historical development of the issue port scheme, let's take a look at the back end of the original Pentium Pro.

As you can see from Figure 12-12, ports 0 and 1 host the arithmetic hardware, while ports 2, 3, and 4 host the memory access hardware. The P6 core's reservation station is capable of issuing up to five instructions per cycle to the execution units—one instruction per issue port per cycle.

As the P6 core developed through the Pentium II and Pentium III, Intel began adding execution units to handle integer and floating-point vector arithmetic. This new vector execution hardware was added on ports 0 and 1, with the result that by the time the PIII was introduced, the P6 back end looked like Figure 12-13.

The PIII's core is fairly wide, but the distribution of arithmetic execution resources between only two of the five issue ports means that its performance can sometimes be bottlenecked by a lack of issue bandwidth (among other things). All of the code stream's vector and scalar arithmetic instructions are contending with each other for two ports, a fact that, when combined with the two-cycle SSE limitation that I'll outline in a moment, means the PIII's vector performance could never really reach the heights of a cleaner design like Core.

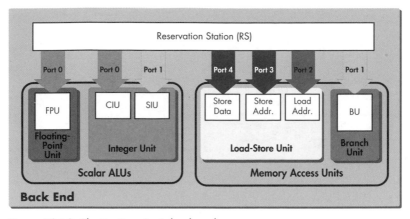

Figure 12-12: The Pentium Pro's back end

Almost nothing is known about the back ends of the Pentium M and Core Duo processors because Intel has declined to release that information. Both are rumored to be quite similar in organization to the back end of the Pentium III, but that rumor cannot be confirmed based on publicly available information.

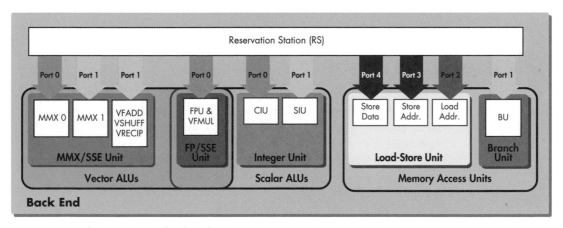

Figure 12-13: The Pentium III's back end

For Core, Intel's architects added a new issue port for handling arithmetic operations. They also changed the distribution of labor on issue ports 1 and 2 to provide more balance and accommodate more execution hardware. The final result is the much wider back end that is shown in Figure 12-14.

Each of Core's three arithmetic issue ports (0, 1, and 5) now contains a scalar integer ALU, a vector integer ALU, and hardware to perform floating-point, vector move, and logic operations (the F/VMOV label in Figure 12-14). Let's take a brief look at Core's integer and floating-point pipelines before moving on to look at the vector hardware in more detail.

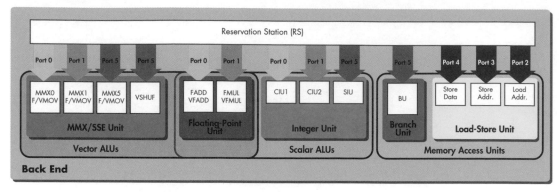

Figure 12-14: The back end of the Intel Core microarchitecture

Integer Units

Core's back end features three scalar 64-bit integer units: one complex integer unit that's capable of handling 64-bit multiplication (port 0); one complex integer unit that's capable of handling shift instructions, rotate instructions, and 32-bit multiplication (port 1); and one simple integer unit (port 5).

The new processor's back end also has three vector integer units that handle MMX instructions, one each on ports 0, 1, and 5. This abundance of scalar and vector integer hardware means that Core can issue three vector or scalar integer operations per cycle.

Floating-Point Units

In the P6-derived processors leading up to Core, there was a mix of floating-point hardware of different types on the issue ports. Specifically, the Pentium III added vector floating-point multiplication to its back end by modifying the existing FPU on port 0 to support this function. Vector floating-point addition was added as a separate VFADD (or PFADD, for *packed floating-point addition*) unit on port 1. Thus, the floating-point arithmetic capabilities were unevenly divided among the Pentium III's two issue ports as follows:

Port 0

- Scalar addition (*x*87 and SSE family)
- Scalar multiplication (*x*87 and SSE family)
- Vector multiplication

Port 1

- Vector addition

Core cleans up this arrangement, which the Pentium M and Core Duo probably also inherited from the Pentium III, by consolidating all floating-point multiplication functions (both scalar and vector) into a single VFMUL unit on port 0; similarly, all vector and scalar floating-point addition functions are brought together in a single VFADD unit on port 1.

Core's distribution of floating-point labor therefore looks as follows:

Port 0

- Scalar multiplication (single- and double-precision, *x*87 and SSE family)
- Vector multiplication (four single-precision or two double-precision)

Port 1

- Scalar addition (single- and double-precision, *x*87 and SSE family)
- Vector addition (four single-precision or two double-precision)

The Core 2 Duo is the first *x*86 processor from Intel to support double-precision floating-point operations with a single-cycle throughput. Thus, Core's floating-point unit can complete up to four double-precision or eight single-precision floating-point operations on every cycle. To see just how much of an improvement Core's floating-point hardware offers over its predecessors, take a look at Table 12-4, which compares the throughputs (number of instructions completed per cycle) of scalar and vector floating-point instructions on four generations of Intel hardware.

Table 12-4: Throughput numbers (cycles/instruction) for vector and scalar floating-point instructions on five different Intel processors

Instruction	Pentium III	Pentium 4	PentiumM/ Core Duo	Core 2 Duo
fadd[1]	1	1	1	1
fmul[1]	2	2	2	2
addss	1	2	1	1
addsd		**2**	**1**	**1**
addps	2	2	2	1
addpd		**2**	**2**	**1**
mulss	1	2	1	1
mulsd		**2**	**2**	**1**
mulps	2	2	2	1
mulpd		**2**	**4**	**1**

[1] *x*87 instruction

In Table 12-4, the rows with green shaded backgrounds denote vector operations, while those with blue shaded backgrounds denote scalar operations. The throughput numbers for all double-precision operations are bold. With the exception of the fadd and fmul instructions, all of the instructions listed belong to the SSE family. Here are a few SSE instructions interpreted for you, so that you can figure out which operations the instructions perform:

- addss: scalar, single-precision addition
- addsd: scalar, double-precision addition
- mulps: packed (vector), single-precision multiplication
- mulpd: packed (vector), double-precision multiplication

Core's designers were able to achieve this dramatic speedup in scalar and vector floating-point performance by widening the floating-point datapaths from 80 bits to 128 bits, as described below.

Vector Processing Improvements

One of Core's most significant improvements over its *x*86 predecessors is in the area of vector processing, or SIMD. Not only does Core feature the expanded vector execution resources described earlier, but the rate at which it executes the SSE family of 128-bit vector instructions has been doubled from one instruction every two cycles to one instruction per cycle. To understand how Core's designers achieved this throughput improvement, it's necessary to take a look at the limitations of Intel's previous implementations of the SSE family.

128-bit Vector Execution on the P6 Through Core Duo

When Intel finally got around to adding 128-bit vector support to the Pentium line with the introduction of streaming SIMD extensions (SSE), the results weren't quite what programmers and users might have hoped for. SSE arrived on the Pentium III with two disadvantages, both of which have continued to plague every Intel processor prior to Core 2 Duo that implements SSE and its successors (SSE2 and SSE3).

- On the ISA side, SSE's main drawback is the lack of support for three-operand instructions, a problem that was covered in Chapter 8.

- On the hardware implementation side, 128-bit SSE operations suffer from a limitation that's the result of Intel shoehorning 128-bit operations onto the 80-bit internal floating-point datapaths of the P6 and Pentium 4.

The former problem is a permanent part of the SSE family, but the latter is a fixable problem that can be traced to some specific decisions Intel made when adding SSE support to the Pentium III and the Pentium 4.

When Intel originally modified the P6 core to include support for 128-bit vector operations, it had to hang the new SSE execution units off of the existing 80-bit data bus that previous designs had been using to ferry floating-point and MMX operands and results between the execution units and floating-point/MMX register file.

In order to execute a 128-bit instruction using its 80-bit data bus and vector units, the P6 and its successors must first break down that instruction into a pair of 64-bit micro-ops that can be executed on successive cycles. To see how this works, take a look at Figure 12-15, which shows (in a very abstract way) what happens when the P6 decodes and executes a 128-bit SSE instruction. The decoder first splits the instruction into two 64-bit micro-ops—one for the upper 64 bits of the vector and another for the lower 64 bits. Then this pair of micro-ops is passed to the appropriate SSE unit for execution.

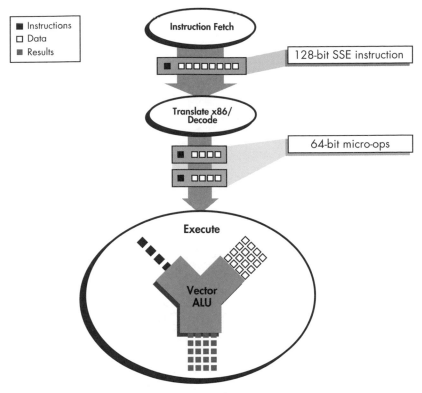

Figure 12-15: How the P6 executes a 128-bit vector operation

The result of this hack is that all 128-bit vector operations take a minimum of two cycles to execute on the P6, Pentium 4, Pentium M, and Core Duo—one cycle for the top half and another for the bottom half. Compare this to the single-cycle throughput and latency of simple 128-bit AltiVec operations on the PowerPC G4e described in Chapters 7 and 8.

128-bit Vector Execution on Core

The Core microarchitecture that powers the Core 2 Duo is the first to give *x*86 programmers a single-cycle latency for 128-bit vector operations. Intel achieved this reduced latency by making the floating-point and vector internal data buses 128 bits wide. Core's 128-bit floating-point/vector datapaths mean only a single micro-op needs to be generated, dispatched, scheduled, and issued for each 128-bit vector operation. Not only does the new design eliminate the latency disadvantage that has plagued SSE operations so far, but it also improves decode, dispatch, and scheduling bandwidth because half as many micro-ops are generated for 128-bit vector instructions.

Figure 12-16 shows how Core's 128-bit vector execution hardware decodes and executes an SSE instruction using a single micro-op.

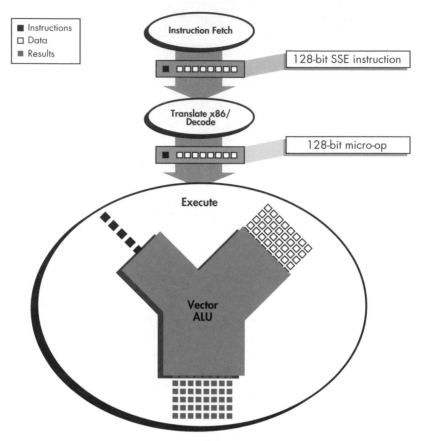

Figure 12-16: How Core executes a 128-bit vector operation

As you can see, the vector ALU's data ports, both input and output, have been enlarged in order to accommodate 128 bits of data at a time.

When you combine these critical improvements with Core's increased amount of vector execution hardware and its expanded decode, dispatch, issue, and commit bandwidth, you get a very capable vector processing machine. (Of course, SSE's two-operand limitation still applies, but there's no helping that.) Core can, for example, execute a 128-bit packed multiply, 128-bit packed add, 128-bit packed load, 128-bit packed store, and a macro-fused cmpjcc (a compare + a jump on condition code) all in the same cycle. That's essentially six instructions in one cycle—quite a boost from any previous Intel processor.

Memory Disambiguation: The Results Stream Version of Speculative Execution

As I explained previously, micro-ops fusion and the added simple/fast decoder give Core's front end the ability to decode many more memory instructions per cycle than its predecessors. Much of the benefit of this expanded capability would be lost, however, had Intel not also found a way to greatly increase the number of memory instructions per cycle that Core can execute.

In order to increase the number of loads and stores that can be executed on each cycle, Core uses a technique on its memory instruction stream that's somewhat like speculative execution. But before you can understand how this technique works, you must first understand exactly how the other *x86* processors covered in this book execute load and store instructions.

The Lifecycle of a Memory Access Instruction

In Chapter 3, you learned about the four primary phases that every instruction goes through in order to be executed:

1. Fetch
2. Decode
3. Execute
4. Write

You also learned that these four phases are broken into smaller steps, and you've even seen a few examples of how these smaller steps are arranged into discrete pipeline stages. However, all of the pipeline examples that you've seen so far have been for arithmetic instructions, so now it's time to take a look at the steps involved in executing memory access instructions.

Table 12-5 compares the specific steps needed to execute an add instruction with the steps needed to execute a load and a store. As you study the table, pay close attention to the green shaded rows. These rows show stages where instructions are buffered and possibly reordered.

As you can see from Table 12-5, the execution phase of a memory access instruction's lifecycle is more complicated than that of a simple arithmetic instruction. Not only do load and store instructions need to access the register file and perform arithmetic operations (address calculations), but they must also access the data cache. The fact that the L1 data cache is farther away from the execution units than the register file and the fact that a load instruction could miss in the L1 data cache and incur a lengthy L2 cache access delay mean that special arrangements must be made in order to keep memory instructions from stalling the entire pipeline.

The Memory Reorder Buffer

The P6 and its successors feed memory access instructions into a special queue where they're buffered as they wait for the results of their address calculations and for the data cache to become available. This queue, called the *memory reorder buffer (MOB)*, is arranged as a FIFO queue, but under certain conditions, instructions earlier in the queue can bypass an instruction that's stalled later in the queue. Thus memory instructions can access the data cache out of program order with respect to one another, a situation that improves performance but brings the need for an additional mechanism to prevent problems associated with *memory aliasing*.

Table 12-5: A comparison of the stages of execution of an arithmetic instruction and two memory access instructions.

	add	load	store	
Fetch	Fetch the add from the instruction cache.	Fetch the load from the instruction cache.	Fetch the store from the instruction cache.	
Decode	Decode the add.	Decode the load into a load-address micro-op.	Decode the store into store-address and store-data micro-ops.	
Issue	Wait in the RS to execute the add out-of-order.	Wait in the RS to execute the load-address out-of-order.	Wait in the RS to execute the store-address and store-data out-of-order.	
			store-address:	**store-data:**
Execute	Read the operands from the register file.	Read an address and possibly an index value from the register file.[1]	Read an address and possibly an index value from the register file.[1]	Read the data to be stored from the register file.
	Add the two operands using the ALU.	Calculate the source address using the address generation units (AGUs).	Calculate the destination address using the address generation units (AGUs).	
		Wait in the memory re-order buffer (MOB) for an opportunity to access the data cache.	Wait in the memory re-order buffer (MOB) for an opportunity to access the data cache.	
		Read the data from the data cache, using the address calculated by the load-address micro-op	Write the data to the data cache, using the address calculated in the store-data micro-op.	
Complete	Wait in the ROB to commit the add in order.	Wait in the ROB to commit the load-address in order.	Wait in the ROB to commit the store-address and store-data in order.	
Commit	Write the result into the register file, set any flags, and remove the instruction from the ROB.	Write the loaded data into the register file, set any flags, and remove the instruction from the ROB.	Set any flags, and remove the instruction from the ROB.	

[1] Depending on the type of address (i.e., register relative or immediate), this register could be an architectural register or a rename register that's allocated to hold the immediate value.

Memory Aliasing

I explained in Chapter 5 why out-of-order processors must first put instructions back in program order before officially writing their results to the programmer-visible register file: You can't modify an architectural register until you're sure that all of the previous instructions that read that location have completed execution; to do otherwise would destroy the integrity of the sequential programming model.

LOADS AND STORES:

TO SPLIT, OR NOT TO SPLIT?

You may be wondering why a load is decoded into a single load-address micro-op, while a store is decoded into store-address and store-data micro-ops. Doesn't the load also have to access the cache, just like the store does with its store-data micro-op? The load instruction does indeed access the cache, but because the load-address and load-data operations are inherently serial, there's no point in separating them into two distinct micro-ops and assigning them to two separate execution pipelines. The two parts of the store operation, in contrast, are inherently parallel. Because the computer can begin calculating a store's destination address at the same time it is retrieving the store's data from the register file, both of these operations can be performed simultaneously by two different micro-ops and two separate execution units. Thus the P6 core design and its successors feature a single execution unit (the load unit) and a single micro-op for load instructions, and two execution units (the store-address unit and the store-data unit) and their two corresponding micro-ops for store instructions.

The need for accesses to programmer-visible storage to be committed in program order applies to main memory just as it does to the register file. To see an example of this, consider Program 12-1. The first line stores the number 13 in an unknown memory cell, and the next line loads the contents of the red memory cell into register A. The final line is an arithmetic instruction that adds the contents of registers A and B and places the result in register C.

Program 12-1

Main Memory

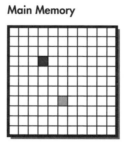

Program 12-1: A program with a load and a store, where the store's target is unknown.

Figures 12-17 and 12-18 show two options for the destination address of the store: either the red cell (Figure 12-17) or an unrelated blue cell (Figure 12-18). If the store ends up writing to the red cell, then the store *must* execute before the load so that the load can then read the updated value from the red cell and supply it to the following add instruction (via register A). If the store writes its value to the blue cell, then it doesn't really matter if that store executes before or after the load, because it is modifying an unrelated memory location.

When a store and a load both access the same memory address, the two instructions are said to *alias*. Figure 12-17 is an example of memory aliasing, while Figure 12-18 is not.

```
store 13,█           store 13,▨

load █,A             load █,A

add A,B,C            add A,B,C
```

Figure 12-17: An aliased
load-store pair

Figure 12-18: A non-aliased
load-store pair

Memory Reordering Rules

In order to avoid aliasing-related problems, all of the Intel processors prior to Core obey the following rules when reordering memory operations in the MOB:

1. Stores must always commit in program order relative to other stores.
2. No load can commit ahead of an aliased store-data micro-op.
3. No load can commit ahead of a store-data micro-op with an unknown target address.

Rule #3 dictates that no load is allowed to be moved (or "hoisted") above a store with an undefined address, because when that store's address becomes available, the processor might find that a load and store are accessing the same address (i.e., the load and store are *aliased*). Because of memory aliasing, this kind of *load hoisting* is not allowed on *x*86 processors prior to Core.

False Aliasing

As it turns out, the kind of load-store aliasing that rule #3 above is intended to prevent is exceedingly rare. The vast majority of the memory accesses in the MOB window do not alias, so they could theoretically proceed independently of one another. Thus the practice of preventing any load from committing until every last store in the MOB has a known target address unnecessarily restricts the number of memory instructions that the processor can commit each cycle.

Because most load-store pairs don't alias, processors like the P6 that play it safe lose quite a bit of performance to *false aliasing*, where the processor assumes that two or more memory accesses alias, when in reality they do not. Let's take a look at exactly where this performance loss comes from.

Figure 12-19 shows a cycle-by-cycle breakdown of how aliased and non-aliased versions of Program 12-1 execute on processors like the P6 and Pentium 4, which use conservative memory access reordering assumptions.

In both instances, the store-address micro-op must execute first so that it can yield a known destination address for the store-data micro-op. This destination address has to be available before any of the memory accesses that are waiting in the MOB can be carried out. Because the destination address of the store is not available until the end of the second cycle when the store-address micro-op has finished calculating it, the processor cannot execute either the store or the load until the third cycle or later.

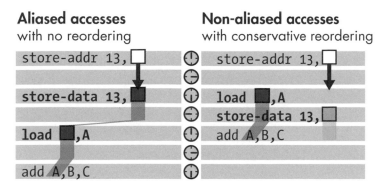

Figure 12-19: Execution without memory disambiguation

When the destination address of the store becomes available at the outset of cycle three, if it turns out that the memory accesses are aliased, the processor must wait another cycle for the store-data micro-op to update the red memory cell before it can execute the load. Then, the load executes, and it too takes an extra cycle to move the data from the red memory cell into the register. Finally, on the seventh cycle, the add is executed.

If the processor discovers that the accesses are not aliased, the load can execute immediately after the store-data micro-op and before the store-address micro-op. In other words, for non-aliased accesses, the processor will move the load up in the queue so that it executes before the less critical, "fire-and-forget" store instruction.

Memory Disambiguation

Core's *memory disambiguation* hardware attempts to identify instances of false aliasing so that in instances where the memory accesses are not aliased, a load can actually execute before a store's destination address becomes available. Figure 12-20 illustrates non-aliased memory accesses with and without the reordering opportunity that memory disambiguation affords.

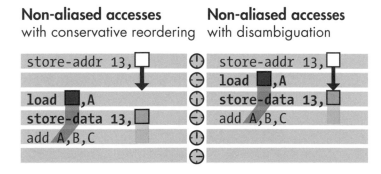

Figure 12-20: Execution with and without memory disambiguation

When the non-aliased accesses execute with memory disambiguation, the load can go ahead and execute while the store's address is still unknown. The store, for its part, can just execute whenever its destination address becomes available.

Re-ordering the memory accesses in this manner enables our example processor to execute the addition a full cycle earlier than it would have without memory disambiguation. If you consider a large instruction window that contains many memory accesses, the ability to speculatively hoist loads above stores could save a significant number of total execution cycles.

Intel has developed an algorithm that examines memory accesses in order to guess which ones are probably aliased and which ones aren't. If the algorithm determines that a load-store pair is aliased, it forces them to commit in program order. If the algorithm decides that the pair is not aliased, the load may commit before the store.

In cases where Core's memory disambiguation algorithm guesses incorrectly, the pipeline stalls, and any operations that were dependent on the erroneous load are flushed and restarted once the correct data has been (re)loaded from memory.

By drastically cutting down on false aliasing, Core eliminates many cycles that are unnecessarily wasted on waiting for store address data to become available. Intel claims that memory disambiguation's impact on performance is significant, especially in the case of memory-intensive floating-point code.

Summary: Core 2 Duo in Historical Context

Intel's turn from the hyperpipelined Netburst microarchitecture to the power-efficient, multi-core–friendly Core microarchitecture marks an important shift not just for one company, but for the computing industry as a whole. The processor advances of the past two decades—advances described in detail throughout this book—have been aimed at increasing the performance of single instruction streams (or *threads of execution*). The Core microarchitecture emphasizes single-threaded performance as well, but it is part of a larger, long-term project that involves shifting the focus of the entire computing industry from single-threaded performance to multithreaded performance.

BIBLIOGRAPHY AND SUGGESTED READING

General

Hennessy, John and David Patterson. *Computer Architecture: A Quantitative Approach.* 3rd ed. San Francisco: Morgan Kaufmann, 2002.

Hennessy, John and David Patterson. *Computer Organization and Design: the Hardware/Software Interface.* 3rd ed. San Francisco: Morgan Kaufmann, 2004.

Shriver, Bruce and Bennett Smith. *The Anatomy of a High-Performance Microprocessor: A Systems Perspective.* Los Alamitos, CA: Wiley-IEEE Computer Society Press, 1998.

PowerPC ISA and Extensions

AltiVec Technology Programming Environment's Manual. rev. 0.1. Motorola, 1998.

Diefendorff, Keith. "A History of the PowerPC Architecture." *Communications of the ACM* 37, no. 6 (June 1994): 28–33.

Fuller, Sam. "Motorola's AltiVec Technology" (white paper). Motorola, 1998.

PowerPC 600 Series Processors

Denman, Marvin, Paul Anderson, and Mike Snyder. "Design of the PowerPC 604e Microprocessor." Presented at Compcon '96. *Technologies for the Information Superhighway: Digest of Papers,* 126–131. Washington, DC: IEEE Computer Society, 1996.

Gary, Sonya, Carl Dietz, Jim Eno, Gianfranco Gerosa, Sung Park, and Hector Sanchez. "The PowerPC 603 Microprocessor: A Low-Power Design for Portable Applications." *Proceedings of the 39th IEEE Computer Society International Conference*. IEEE Computer Science Press, 1994, 307–15.

PowerPC 601 RISC Microprocessor User's Manual. IBM and Motorola, 1993.

PowerPC 601 RISC Microprocessor Technical Summary. IBM and Motorola, 1995.

PowerPC 603e RISC Microprocessor User's Manual. IBM and Motorola, 1995.

PowerPC 603e RISC Microprocessor Technical Summary. IBM and Motorola, 1995.

PowerPC 604 RISC Microprocessor User's Manual. IBM and Motorola, 1994.

PowerPC 604 RISC Microprocessor Technical Summary. IBM and Motorola, 1994.

PowerPC 620 RISC Microprocessor Technical Summary. IBM and Motorola, 1994.

PowerPC G3 and G4 Series Processors

MPC750 User's Manual. rev. 1. Motorola, 2001.

MPC7400 RISC Microprocessor Technical Summary, rev. 0. Motorola, 1999.

MPC7410/MPC7400 RISC Microprocessor User's Manual, rev. 1. Motorola, 2002.

MPC7410 RISC Microprocessor Technical Summary, rev. 0. Motorola, 2000.

MPC7450 RISC Microprocessor User's Manual, rev. 0. Motorola, 2001.

Seale, Susan. "PowerPC G4 Architecture White Paper: Delivering Performance Enhancement in 60x Bus Mode" (white paper). Motorola, 2001.

IBM PowerPC 970 and POWER

Behling, Steve, Ron Bell, Peter Farrell, Holger Holthoff, Frank O'Connell, and Will Weir. *The POWER4 Processor Introduction and Tuning Guide*. 1st ed. (white paper). IBM, November 2001.

DeMone, Paul. "A Big Blue Shadow over Alpha, SPARC, and IA-64." *Real World Technologies* (October 2000). http://www.realworldtech.com/page.cfm?AID=RWT101600000000.

DeMone, Paul. "The Battle in 64 bit Land, 2003 and Beyond." *Real World Technologies* (January 2003). http://www.realworldtech.com/page.cfm?AID=RWT012603224711.

DeMone, Paul. "Sizing Up the Super Heavyweights." *Real World Technologies* (October 2004). http://www.realworldtech.com/page.cfm?ArticleID=RWT100404214638.

Diefendorff, Keith. "Power4 Focuses on Memory Bandwidth: IBM Confronts IA-64, Says ISA Not Important." *Microprocessor Report* 13, no. 13 (October 1999).

Sandon, Peter. "PowerPC 970: First in a new family of 64-bit high performance PowerPC processors." Presented at the Microprocessor Forum, San Jose, CA, October 14–17, 2002.

Stokes, Jon. "IBM's POWER5: A Talk with Pratap Pattnaik." *Ars Technica*, October 2004. http://arstechnica.com/articles/paedia/cpu/POWER5.ars.

Stokes, Jon. "PowerPC 970: Dialogue and Addendum." *Ars Technica*, October 2002. http://arstechnica.com/cpu/03q2/ppc970-interview/ppc970-interview-1.html.

Tendler, J. M., J. S. Dodson, J. S. Fields, Jr., H. Le, and B. Sinharoy, "POWER4 System Microarchitecture." *IBM Journal of Research and Development* 46, no. 1 (January 2002): 5–25.

x86 ISA and Extensions

Granlund, Torbjorn. "Instruction latencies and throughput for AMD and Intel *x*86 processors" (working paper). Swox AB, September 2005. http://www.swox.com/doc/x86-timing.pdf.

Gwennap, Linley. "Intel's MMX Speeds Multimedia: Instruction-Set Extensions to Aid Audio, Video, and Speech." *Microprocessor Report* 10, no. 3 (March 1996).

Mittal, Millind, Alex Peleg, and Uri Weiser. "MMX Technology Architecture Overview." *Intel Technology Journal* 1, no. 1 (August 1997).

Thakkar, Shreekant and Tom Huff. "The Internet Streaming SIMD Extensions." *Intel Technology Journal* 3, no. 2 (May 1999).

Pentium and P6 Family

Case, Brian. "Intel Reveals Pentium Implementation Details: Architectural Enhancements Remain Shrouded by NDA." *Microprocessor Report* 7, no. 4 (March 1993).

Fog, Agner. "How to optimize for the Pentium family of microprocessors," 2004.

Fog, Agner. *Software optimization resources.* "The microarchitecture of Intel and AMD CPU's: An optimization guide for assembly programmers and compiler makers." 2006. http://www.agner.org/optimize.

Gwennap, Linley. "Intel's P6 Uses Decoupled Superscalar Design: Next Generation of *x*86 Integrates L2 Cache in Package with CPU." *Microprocessor Report* 9, no. 2 (February 16, 1995).

Keshava, Jagannath and Vladimir Pentkovski. "Pentium III Processor Implementation Tradeoffs." *Intel Technology Journal* 3, no. 2, (Q2 1999).

Intel Architecture Optimization Manual. Intel, 2001.

Intel Architecture Software Developer's Manual, vols. 1–3. Intel, 2006.

P6 Family of Processors Hardware Developer's Manual. Intel, 1998.

Pentium II Processor Developer's Manual. Intel, 1997.

Pentium Pro Family Developer's Manual, vols. 1–3. Intel, 1995.

Pentium 4

"A Detailed Look Inside the Intel NetBurst Micro-Architecture of the Intel Pentium 4 Processor" (white paper). Intel, November 2000.

Boggs, Darrell, Aravindh Baktha, Jason Hawkins, Deborah T. Marr, J. Alan Miller, Patrice Roussel, Ronak Singhal, Bret Toll, and K.S. Venkatraman, "The Microarchitecture of the Intel Pentium 4 Processor on 90nm Technology." *Intel Technology Journal* 8, no. 1 (February 2004).

DeMone, Paul. "What's Up With Willamette? (Part 1)." *Real World Technologies* (March 2000). http://www.realworldtech.com/page.cfm?ArticleID= RWT030300000001.

Hinton, Glenn, Dave Sager, Mike Upton, Darrell Boggs, Doug Carmean, Alan Kyker, Desktop Platforms Group, and Patrice Roussel. "The Microarchitecture of the Pentium 4 Processor." *Intel Technology Journal* 5 no. 1 (February 2001).

Intel Pentium 4 Processor Optimization Manual. Intel, 2001.

Pentium M, Core, and Core 2

Gochman, Simcha, Avi Mendelson, Alon Naveh, and Efraim Rotem. "Introduction to Intel Core Duo Processor Architecture." *Intel Technology Journal* 10, no. 2 (May 2006).

Gochman, Simcha, Ronny Ronen, Ittai Anati, Ariel Berkovits, Tsvika Kurts, Alon Naveh, Ali Saeed, Zeev Sperber, and Robert C. Valentine. "The Intel Pentium M Processor: Microarchitecture and Performance." *Intel Technology Journal* 7, no. 2 (May 2003).

Kanter, David. "Intel's Next Generation Microarchitecture Unveiled." *Real World Technologies* (March 2006). http://realworldtech.com/page.cfm? ArticleID=RWT030906143144.

Mendelson, Avi, Julius Mandelblat, Simcha Gochman, Anat Shemer, Rajshree Chabukswar, Erik Niemeyer, and Arun Kumar. "CMP Implementation in Systems Based on the Intel Core Duo Processor." *Intel Technology Journal* 10, no. 2 (May 2006).

Wechsler, Ofri. "Inside Intel Core Microarchitecture: Setting New Standards for Energy-Efficient Performance." *Technology@Intel Magazine* (March 2006).

Online Resources

Ace's Hardware   http://aceshardware.com.

AnandTech   http://anandtech.com.

ArsTechnica   http://arstechnica.com.

Real World Technologies   http://realworldtech.com.

sandpile.org   http://sandpile.org.

X-bit labs   http://xbitlabs.com.

INDEX

AMD. *See* Advanced Micro Devices (AMD)

and instruction, cycles to execute on PowerPC, 117

Apple. *See also* PowerPC (PPC)
  G3. *See* PowerPC 750 (G3)
  G4. *See* PowerPC 7400 (G4)
  G4e. *See* Motorola G4e
  G5, 193. *See also* PowerPC 970 (G5)
  Performas, 119
  PowerBook, 119

approximations of fractional values, 66

arithmetic
  coprocessor, 67
  instructions, 11, 12, 36
    actions to execute, 36–37
    binary code for, 21–22
    format, 12
    immediate values in, 14–16
  micro-op queue, 156
  operations, 67

arithmetic logic unit (ALU), 2, 5, *6*, 67–69
  multiple on chip, 62
  on Pentium, 88–91
  on Pentium 4, schedulers for, 156
  storage close to, 7

Arm, 73

assembler, 26

assembler code, 21

assembly language, beginnings, 26

associative mapping
  fully, 224, *225*
  n-way set, 226–230, *227*

Athlon processor (AMD), 72, 110

average completion rate, 52–53

average instruction throughput, 54
  pipeline stalls and, 56–57

B

back end, 38, *38*
  on Core 2 Duo, 258–270, *260*
  on Pentium, 87–91
    floating-point ALUs, 88–91
    integer ALUs, 87–88

on Pentium II, *108*

on Pentium III, *110*

on Pentium M, 246

on Pentium Pro, 94–100, 102–103, *103*

on PowerPC 603 and 603e, 119–121

on PowerPC 604, 123–126

on PowerPC 970, 200–203

backward branch, 30

bandwidth, and cache block size, 232

Banias, 236

base-10 numbering system, 183–184

base address, 16, 17

BEU (branch execution unit), 69, 85
  on PowerPC 601, 116

BHT. *See* branch history table (BHT)

binary code, 21
  for arithmetic instructions, 21–22

binary notation, 20

BIOS, 34

blocks and block frames, for caches, *223*, 223–224
  sizes of, 231–232

Boolean operations, 67

bootloader program, 34

bootstrap, 34

boot up, 34

BPU (branch prediction unit), 85

branch check stage, in Pentium 4 pipeline, 158

branch execution unit (BEU), 69, 85
  on PowerPC 601, 116

branch folding, 113
  by Pentium 4 trace cache, 153

branch hazards, 78

branch history table (BHT), 86
  on PowerPC 604, 125
  on PowerPC 750, 132
  on PowerPC 970, 196

branch instructions, 11, 30–34
  and fetch-execute loop, 32
  and labels, 33–34
  on PowerPC 750, 130–132
  on PowerPC 970, 198
  register-relative address with, 33
  as special type of load, 32–33
  in superscalar systems, 64

emulation, 72
encryption schemes, 185
EPIC (Explicitly Parallel Instruction Computing), 180
evicted data from cache, 219
eviction policy for cached data, 230–232
execute mode for trace cache, 151
execute stage of instruction, 37
  for G4e, 146
  in Pentium 4 pipeline, 158
  in Pentium pipeline, 84–85
  in Pentium Pro pipeline, 101
execution. *See also* program execution time
  phases, *39*
  time requirements, and completion rate, 51–52
execution ports, on Pentium 4, 157
execution units, 17
  empty slots, 198
  expanding superscalar processing with, 65–69
  micro-op passed to, 156
  on Pentium, 83
Explicitly Parallel Instruction Computing (EPIC), 180

F

fabs instruction, cycles to execute, 118
fadd instruction
  cycles to execute, 118
  on PowerPC 970, 212
  throughput on Intel processors, 261
fall-through, 114
false aliasing, 268
fast integer ALU1 and ALU2 units, on Pentium 4, 157
fast IU scheduler, on Pentium 4, 156
fdiv instruction, cycles to execute, 118
fetch buffer, on Intel Core Duo, 239
fetch-execute loop, 28–29
  and branch instructions, 32

fetch groups, on PowerPC 970, 196
fetch phase of instruction, 37
  for Core 2 Duo, *256*, 256–257
  for Pentium M, 239–240
Feynman, Richard, 3
fields in instruction, 12
FIFO (first in, first out) data structure, 88
file-clerk model of computing, 3–7
  expanded, 9–10
  refining, 6–7
FILO (first in, last out) data structure, 88
filter/mod operand, 171
finish pipeline stage, on PPC CR, 163, 164
FIQ. *See* floating-point issue queue (FIQ)
first in, first out (FIFO) data structure, 88
first in, last out (FILO) data structure, 88
fixed-point ALU, on PowerPC 601, 115
fixed-point numbers, 66
flags stage, in Pentium 4 pipeline, 158
flat floating-point register file, 88
flat register file, vs. stack, 90
floating-point ALUs, on Pentium, 88–91
floating-point applications, Pentium 4 design for, 165
floating-point control word (FPCW), in Intel Core Duo, 252
floating-point data type, on 32-bit vs. 64-bit processors, 183
floating-point execution unit (FPU), 68, 165–168
  on Core 2 Duo, 260–262
  on G4, 134
  on G4e, 166–167
  on Pentium, 69
  on Pentium 4, 167–168
  on PowerPC 601, 115–116
  on PowerPC 750, 130
  on PowerPC 970, 205–206

Electronic Frontier Foundation
Defending Freedom in the Digital World

Free Speech. Privacy. Innovation. Fair Use. Reverse Engineering. **If you care about these rights in the digital world, then you should join the Electronic Frontier Foundation (EFF). EFF was founded in 1990 to protect the rights of users and developers of technology. EFF is the first to identify threats to basic rights online and to advocate on behalf of free expression in the digital age.**

The Electronic Frontier Foundation Defends Your Rights!
Become a Member Today!
http://www.eff.org/support/

Current EFF projects include:

Protecting your fundamental right to vote. Widely publicized security flaws in computerized voting machines show that, though filled with potential, this technology is far from perfect. EFF is defending the open discussion of e-voting problems and is coordinating a national litigation strategy addressing issues arising from use of poorly developed and tested computerized voting machines.

Ensuring that you are not traceable through your things. Libraries, schools, the government and private sector businesses are adopting radio frequency identification tags, or RFIDs – a technology capable of pinpointing the physical location of whatever item the tags are embedded in. While this may seem like a convenient way to track items, it's also a convenient way to do something less benign: track people and their activities through their belongings. EFF is working to ensure that embrace of this technology does not erode your right to privacy.

Stopping the FBI from creating surveillance backdoors on the Internet. EFF is part of a coalition opposing the FBI's expansion of the Communications Assistance for Law Enforcement Act (CALEA), which would require that the wiretap capabilities built into the phone system be extended to the Internet, forcing ISPs to build backdoors for law enforcement.

Providing you with a means by which you can contact key decision-makers on cyber-liberties issues. EFF maintains an action center that provides alerts on technology, civil liberties issues and pending legislation to more than 50,000 subscribers. EFF also generates a weekly online newsletter, EFFector, and a blog that provides up-to-the minute information and commentary.

Defending your right to listen to and copy digital music and movies. The entertainment industry has been overzealous in trying to protect its copyrights, often decimating fair use rights in the process. EFF is standing up to the movie and music industries on several fronts.

Check out all of the things we're working on at http://www.eff.org and join today or make a donation to support the fight to defend freedom online.

ELECTRONIC FRONTIER FOUNDATION · 454 SHOTWELL STREET · SAN FRANCISCO, CA 94110 · 415.436.9333

WRITE GREAT CODE, VOLUME 2
Thinking Low-Level, Writing High-Level

by RANDALL HYDE

Today's computer science students aren't always taught how to choose high-level language statements carefully to produce efficient code. *Write Great Code, Volume 2: Thinking Low-Level, Writing High-Level* shows software engineers what too many college and university courses don't: how compilers translate high-level language statements and data structures into machine code. Armed with this knowledge, readers will be better informed about choosing the high-level structures that will help the compiler produce superior machine code, all without having to give up the productivity and portability benefits of using a high-level language.

MARCH 2006, 640 PP., $44.95 ($58.95 CDN)
ISBN 1-59327-065-8

THE TCP/IP GUIDE
A Comprehensive, Illustrated Internet Protocols Reference

by CHARLES M. KOZIEROK

Finally, an encyclopedic, comprehensible, well-illustrated, and completely current guide to the TCP/IP protocol suite for both newcomers and seasoned professionals. This complete reference details the core protocols that make TCP/IP internetworks function, as well as the most important TCP/IP applications. It includes full coverage of PPP, ARP, IP, IPv6, IP NAT, IPSec, Mobile IP, ICMP, and much more. It offers a detailed view of the TCP/IP protocol suite, and it describes networking fundamentals and the important OSI Reference Model.

OCTOBER 2005, 1616 PP. HARDCOVER, $79.95 ($107.95 CDN)
ISBN 1-59327-047-X

SILENCE ON THE WIRE
A Field Guide to Passive Reconnaissance and Indirect Attacks

by MICHAL ZALEWSKI

Author Michal Zalewski has long been known and respected in the hacking and security communities for his intelligence, curiosity, and creativity, and this book is truly unlike anything else out there. In *Silence on the Wire*, Zalewski shares his expertise and experience to explain how computers and networks work, how information is processed and delivered, and what security threats lurk in the shadows. No humdrum technical white paper or how-to manual for protecting one's network, this book is a fascinating narrative that explores a variety of unique, uncommon, and often quite elegant security challenges that defy classification and eschew the traditional attacker-victim model.

APRIL 2005, 312 PP., $39.95 ($53.95 CDN)
ISBN 1-59327-046-1

HACKING THE CABLE MODEM
What Cable Companies Don't Want You to Know

by DERENGEL

In the beginning there was dial-up, and it was slow; then came broadband in the form of cable, which redefined how we access the Internet, share information, and communicate with each other online. *Hacking the Cable Modem* goes inside the device that makes Internet via cable possible and, along the way, reveals secrets of many popular cable modems, including products from Motorola, RCA, WebSTAR, D-Link, and more. Written for people at all skill levels, the book features step-by-step tutorials with easy to follow diagrams, source code examples, hardware schematics, links to software (exclusive to this book!), and previously unreleased cable modem hacks.

SEPTEMBER 2006, 320 PP., $29.95 ($37.95 CDN)
ISBN 1-59327-101-8

THE DEBIAN SYSTEM
Concepts and Techniques

by MARTIN F. KRAFFT

The Debian System introduces the concepts and techniques of the Debian operating system, explaining their usage and pitfalls and illustrating the thinking behind each of the approaches. The book's goal is to give you enough insight into the workings of the Debian project and operating system that you will understand the solutions that have evolved as part of the Debian system over the past decade. While targeted at the well-versed Unix/Linux administrator, the book can also serve as an excellent resource alongside a standard Linux reference to quickly orient you to Debian's unique philosophy and structure. Co-published with Open Source Press, an independent publisher based in Munich that specializes in the field of free and open source software.

SEPTEMBER 2005, 608 PP. W/DVD, $44.95 ($60.95 CDN)
ISBN 1-59327-069-0

PHONE:
800.420.7240 OR
415.863.9900
MONDAY THROUGH FRIDAY,
9 AM TO 5 PM (PST)

FAX:
415.863.9950
24 HOURS A DAY,
7 DAYS A WEEK

EMAIL:
SALES@NOSTARCH.COM

WEB:
WWW.NOSTARCH.COM

MAIL:
NO STARCH PRESS
555 DE HARO ST, SUITE 250
SAN FRANCISCO, CA 94107
USA

COLOPHON

Inside the Machine was laid out in Adobe FrameMaker. The font families used are New Baskerville for body text, Futura for headings and tables, and Dogma for titles.

The book was printed and bound at Friesens in Altona, Manitoba in Canada. The paper is Weyerhaeuser 60# Husky Offset, which is an acid-free paper.

UPDATES

Visit **www.nostarch.com/insidemachine.htm** for updates, errata, and other information.

D-DAY, 1944

Voices from Normandy

OTHER TITLES BY ROBIN NEILLANDS

The Desert Rats (The 7th Armoured Division 1940–45)

By Sea and Land (Royal Marine Commandos 1942–82)

The Hundred Years' War

The Wars of the Roses

The Raiders (The Army Commandos 1940–45)

D-DAY, 1944

Voices from Normandy

Robin Neillands
and
Roderick de Normann

Weidenfeld & Nicolson
London

First published in 1993 by Weidenfeld and Nicolson
A division of The Orion Publishing Group Limited
Orion House, 5 Upper St Martin's Lane,
London WC2H 9EA

ISBN 0 297 81251 3

A catalogue record for this book is available from the
British Library

Chapter head drawings and maps by Terry Brown

Typeset by BP Integraphics Ltd, Bath, Avon
Printed and bound in Great Britain
by The Bath Press Ltd, Bath, Avon

The authors and contributors wish to dedicate this book to all those who fought along the coast of Normandy on D-Day 1944 and did not survive the day.

'Think not only upon their passing.
Remember the glory of their spirit.'

---

*US Military Cemetery
St Laurent, Normandy*

CONTENTS

CONTENTS

——ILLUSTRATIONS——

Juno Beach, D-Day (private collection)
4th US Infantry Division, Utah Beach (Imperial War Museum)
Commanders Montgomery, Eisenhower and Tedder (Imperial War Museum)
S/Sgt Wallwork, Glider Pilot Regiment (Wallwork, private collection)
Men of the Glider Pilot Regiment (R. A. Howard, private collection)
S/Sgt R. A. Howard, Glider Pilot Regiment (R. A. Howard, private collection)
Pfc John Robert Slaughter, 29th Infantry Division (J. R. Slaughter, private collection)
Captain H. A. Shebeck, 82nd Airborne Division (H. A. Shebeck, private collection)
Guillaume Mercader, Chef de la Résistance, with General Koëning (G. Mercader, private collection)
Preparations: the bombing of railways (Imperial War Museum)
US infantry train on Dartmoor, England (Imperial War Museum)
Transport aircraft and gliders in D-Day markings (Imperial War Museum)
Troopers of the 508th Parachute Infantry Regiment on a training jump in England, April 1944 (David Pike, private collection)
Aerial reconnaissance before D-Day over the beach obstacles near Arromanches (Imperial War Museum)
Bombardment warships sail for Normandy (Imperial War Museum)
Canadian infantry wait offshore (Imperial War Museum)
British tanks and infantry under fire, Sword Beach (Imperial War Museum)
Omaha Beach, 7 June 1944 (Imperial War Museum)
Troopers of 508th Parachute Infantry Regiment in Normandy (David Pike, private collection)

ACKNOWLEDGMENTS

A great many people and organisations helped us with this book. Our thanks go to everyone involved, including those whose accounts we were unable to include through lack of space. They serve all useful, either as a check or other information or as background to the story. We received nearly 1,000 contributions, stories, tapes, letters and photographs from all over the world, to support our own interviews. Without such assistance, this book could never have been written.

Within that broad framework, some particular thanks are due to: the Imperial War Museum, London; the Musée de la Libération, Cherbourg; the Army Museum, Ottawa, Canada; the Delta Museum, Portsmouth; the Airborne Museum, Ste-Mère-Eglise, Normandy; the Tank Museum, Bovington, and Major & Mrs Holt's Battlefield Tours, UK.

We would also like to thank the Americans, Royal British and Canadian Legions for publishing our appeal for help, or supplying lists of possible informants. Thanks go also to the D-Day and Normandy Fellowship and the Normandy Veterans Association, and to many Regimental Associations – especially the Queen's Own Rifles of Canada, the 29th Division Association, the Royal Marines Association, the 1st Division Association USA and the Retired US Officers Association – and to Stephen Ambrose of the Eisenhower Center, New Orleans; Blaine Abney of the US Military Academy, West Point, and Arthur Chute, Society of the First Division. Thanks also to Keith Howell for contacts among the Normandy veterans, and Toby Oliver of Bromley for his assistance with visits to France.

IN THE UNITED KINGDOM

Among a host of individuals – all of whom we thank – we would like to record a particular vote of thanks to: Colin Kitchen, RNVR, for permission to quote from his copyright account; the late Brigadier Peter Young, DSO, MC of No. 3 Commando; Croft Peters of the Para Wars; Kay Connell; Robin McDaniel-Groves, RM, Captain Desi Harden, MC, RM of 4 Commando; George Price of 12 Div, 1st Hampshire Regiment; Major Herman Frederick Hall, RASC, Brigadier Tony Gapton, CBE, Ken Hazell.

—ACKNOWLEDGEMENTS—

A great many people and organizations helped us with this book. Our thanks go to everyone involved, including those whose accounts we were unable to include through lack of space. They were all useful, either as a check on other information or as background to the story. We received nearly 1,000 contributions, stories, tapes, letters and photographs, from all over the world, to support our own interviews. Without such assistance, this book could never have been written.

Within that broad framework, some particular thanks are due to: the Imperial War Museum, London; the Musée de la Débarquement, Arromanches; the Army Museum, Ottawa, Canada; the D-Day Museum, Portsmouth; the Airborne Museum, Ste-Mère-Eglise, Normandy; the Tank Museum, Bovington, and Major & Mrs Holt's Battlefield Tours, UK.

We would also like to thank the American, Royal British and Canadian Legions for publishing our appeal for help, or supplying lists of possible informants. Thanks go also to the D-Day and Normandy Fellowship and the Normandy Veterans Association, and to many Regimental Associations – especially the Queen's Own Rifles of Canada, the 29th Division Association, the Royal Marines Association, the 1st Division Association USA and the Retired US Officers Association – and to Stephen Ambrose of the Eisenhower Center, New Orleans, Alan C. Aimone of the US Military Academy, West Point, and Arthur Chaitt, Society of the First Division. Thanks also to Keith Howell for contacts among the Normandy veterans, and Toby Oliver of Brittany Ferries for assistance with visits to France.

IN THE UNITED KINGDOM
Among a host of individuals – all of whom we thank – we would like to record a particular vote of gratitude to Colin Kitchen, RNVR for permission to quote from his copyright account; the late Brigadier Peter Young, DSO, MC of No. 3 Commando; Geoff Peters of the 2nd Warwicks; Colonel Robin McGarel-Groves, RM; Captain Dan Flunder, MC, RM of 48 Commando; George Price of 12 Bn, the Parachute Regiment; Albert Herring; Frederick Hall, RASC; Brigadier Tom Collins, CBE; Ken Beard,

RAF; Syd (Sticks) Lancaster, RM; Don Kelly of the Normandy Veterans Association; Warrant Officer 'Baron' Humphries, RAF; Jack Horsnell, RN; James Hinton, RN; Reg Bettis, RM; Norman Harris, 10th Beach Group, RN Commando; Lt Jim Booth, RN of COPP; Charles Lofthouse, 7 Squadron RAF; Geoff Riley, the Commando Association; Sidney Hoy, RN; Sidney Goldberg, RAF; Eric Downing, 22nd Dragoons; Tom Lovell of HMT *Glenroy*; Frank Haworth, RN; Noel Chaffey, RAF; Colonel Mike Morrison, the 8th King's Regiment; P.Finnegan, the 8th Bn, the King's Regiment; Lt John M. Moore, the 8th Bn, the King's Regiment; John Walford; Don Clarke, the Pathfinders Association; Roy Howard and James Wallwork, the Glider Pilot Regiment; Stuart Lasson; Kenneth McCaw, RNVR; Squadron Leader Douglas Millikin, RAF; Alan Schofield, 620 Squadron; Austin Prosser, RN; Peter Chambers, RN; Emlyn Jones, Signals Troop, 45 (RM) Commando; Ralph Rayner, Royal Engineers; Flt Sergeant David Swynne, Inns of Court Regiment; Bob Armit, RAF; Reginald T. Atkins, 1st Bn, Dorsetshire Regiment.

IN THE UNITED STATES

Commander Robert J. Erickson, USN; Harvy P. Newton, 508 Parachute Infantry Regiment; D. Zane Schlemmer of Hawaii, 508th PIR; John Robert Lewis, USN, of Yardley, Pennsylvania; A. A. Alvarez, 16th Infantry Regiment, 1st Infantry Division for his account of 'Omaha'; George M. Rosie, 101st Airborne Division Association; Anthony J. Di Stephano, 29th Infantry; Gene Owens, *Roanoke Times & World News*, Virginia; Milton Chadwick, 82nd Airborne; Leslie 'Bill' Kick of Westmoreland, New York, 82nd Airborne; David Pike for permission to reproduce extracts from *Airborne in Nottingham – the 508th PIR in England*; J. Robert Slaughter of Roanoke, Virginia, 116th Infantry Regiment, 29th Division for permission to reproduce extracts from his memoirs; Jack Schlegel of Shandaken, New York, 508th PIR; Jack Jones, 4th Infantry Division; Jack Capell, 4th Infantry Division, for his support and his account of D-Day and after; Fred Tannery, 4th Infantry; Anthony M. Jele, 4th Infantry; Frank P. Schroen of Hamburg, PA; Louis Siebel; Colonel 'Red' Reeder, 12th Infantry Regiment, for permission to reproduce extracts from his book *Born at Reveille*; Mario Porcellini, 29th Infantry Division; Colonel James H. Watts, 1st Infantry Division; Colonel Gerald K. Griffin, 1st Infantry Division; Phil Sykes, USS *Frankford*; Daniel S. Campbell, 82nd Airborne Division Association, for publishing our appeal in *Paraglide*, the Division's magazine; Commander J. M. Suozzo, USN; Howard L. Huggett, 82nd Airborne; Captain Warren L. Hooker, 4th Infantry; Lawrence J. Bour of Williamsburg, PA, 16th Infantry Regiment, 1st Infantry Division; Bill Garvin, 12th Infantry Regiment; Walter F. Schaad, 4th Infantry Division; Robert L. Sales of Madison Heights, Virginia, who has built his own memorial to

ACKNOWLEDGEMENTS

the men of Company 'B' who died on D-Day; Malcolm C. Williams Snr, 12th Infantry; Harold A. Shebeck, 325th Glider Regiment; Harper Coleman, 8th Infantry Regiment, Tucson, Arizona; Robert 'Bob' Salley, 326 Engineer Bn, 101st Airborne; Richard Willstatter, USN.

IN CANADA

Jack Jensen of Toronto, Ontario; Jane Fox of *The Legion*, the magazine of the Canadian Legion, Ottawa; Dorothy and William Ross, QORC; Lawrence A. Cornett, Port Credit, Ontario, QORC; P. C. Rea, QORC; Jack Martin of Scarborough, Ontario, QORC Association; S. W. (Wet Bird) Pawley, First Hussars Association; Alfie Hebbes of Rexdale, Ontario, Sherbrooke Fusilier Regiment (27th Canadian Armoured Regiment); Les Wagar of Red Deer, Alberta, QORC; Stanley Biggs, QORC; W. F. Lawson, 13th Canadian Field Regiment; Don Doner of Alliston, Ontario, QORC; Rolph W. Jackson, QORC.

IN FRANCE

Mlle M. Thomas of Caen; Henri Lamperière of Landelles et Compigny; M. and Mme Felix Reginensi of Condé-sur-Noireau, Normandy; André Heintz of Caen.

IN GERMANY

Annegret Hartmetz of Munich, for permission to reproduce the account of her late husband, Rainer Hartmetz; Oberst Helmut Ritgen, Panzer Lehr; Oberst Hans Von Luck, 21st Panzer; Herbert Muschallik, 352nd Infantry Division; Wolfgang Kittel, Deutsch Fallschirmjaeger.

Our thanks and appreciation are also due to Colonel E. G. Peters and Paul Reynolds for reading the manuscript, to Beverlie Flower for additional help with the correspondence, to Estelle Huxley for constant typing of the manuscript, and to Terry Brown for his work on the maps.

The D-Day Assault

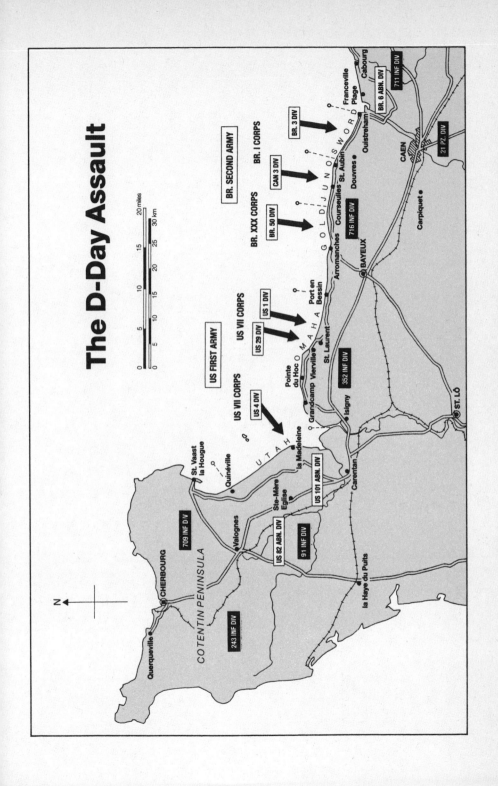

The D-Day Assault

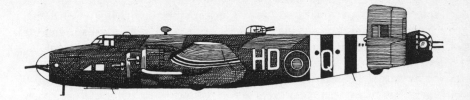

—CHAPTER ONE—
Dunkirk to D-Day 1940-1944

'Critics state that the strategy of World War
II was all wrong, that it would have been
better to have done this or that. Perhaps ...
but the fact remains, we did win the War.'
Omar N. Bradley
General of the Army

This is the story of one day, fifty miles of French coast and about 200,000
men. This is the story of Operation 'Overlord' and the most crucial day in
the long and painful history of the Second World War – the sixth of June
1944.

This is not an official history. It is a collection of stories, drawn from the
accounts of people who took part in Operation 'Overlord', of every nation,
rank and arm of service. The effect is to tell the story of D-Day in the words
of the men who were there.

This chapter will cover the years from the Dunkirk evacuation of 1940 to
the time in 1943 when the Allied commanders decided to launch Operation
'Overlord'. It will describe the difficulties encountered by the invasion
planners and how these problems were overcome.

To tell such a story in simple terms is difficult and the very size and
complexity of the D-Day operation is only one factor. All major operations
of war are complicated and a seaborne invasion is the most complicated of
all. What must be understood at the start of this story is the vital importance
of 'Overlord'.

1

On the success of 'Overlord' rested the outcome of the Second World War, the swift liberation of Western Europe and the ending of a tyranny that had stalked the civilized world for five long years. Had the landings failed Hitler would have employed his 'V2' rockets against Britain with lethal effect; the atomic bomb might well have been deployed in Europe and the Red Army could have advanced to the Rhine or beyond, with incalculable consequences when the war was over. D-Day, 1944, prevented all that.

The story of Operation 'Overlord', the Allied invasion of Europe on 6 June 1944, really begins on the night of 4 June 1940, when a Royal Navy destroyer sailed from Dunkirk with the last of the British Expeditionary Force. Over 225,000 men, French and British, had been brought back across the Channel during Operation 'Dynamo', but there would be a painful four-year gap before a British army again set foot in France. After Dunkirk, the Axis Powers alone controlled the Continent of Europe.

By June 1940, the German Führer, Adolf Hitler, was sure that Britain was out of the war. If possible, he would now reach some accommodation with the British in the West, as he had done with Soviet Russia in the East before attacking Poland in 1939. If he could not make peace with the British, then his U-Boats would see that they starved, and his Luftwaffe would pound them into submission. Hitler had viewed the British, or at least some of their politicians, at Munich and had formed his own opinion of the British as a nation. 'They are worms,' he stated.

The British were relieved, even delighted, by the 'miracle' of Dunkirk, and Winston Churchill, Britain's lion-hearted Prime Minister, soon saw a need to put the Dunkirk evacuation in perspective. 'It was a defeat,' he pointed out in Parliament, 'and wars are not won by evacuations.' What was left of the British Army was home again but the military might of Britain had been blighted in the débâcle at Dunkirk and future prospects looked bleak indeed.

Although most of the soldiers got back to England, almost all their weapons and equipment had been left behind. The defence of Britain now depended on the Royal Navy and the Royal Air Force, but the British have an irritating habit of not being able to see the writing on the wall until their backs are pressed against it. After the capitulation of France at the end of June 1940, spirits in Britain became almost lighthearted. The King, George VI, summed up the national mood when he wrote in his diary, 'I'm glad we no longer need be polite to our allies.' Indeed, other than those few who had made their way to England, Britain had no allies; Britain and her embattled Empire now stood alone. The whole country became an arsenal, devoted to producing guns, tanks and aircraft. Every man and woman strained their sinews to produce munitions and the weapons of war, while every able-bodied young man or woman went into one or other of the fighting services.

The one bright spot for the British in mid-June 1940 was that a drawn-out trench struggle on the 1914–18 pattern had been avoided. This meant, however, that to free Europe from Hitler the British and their Allies must one day invade Europe, but this course of action was still a long way off in the summer of 1940. A more immediate prospect was of German forces invading Britain.

To do that, the Luftwaffe had first to eliminate the fighters of the Royal Air Force and gain air superiority over the Channel, as they had already done over Poland, France and the Low Countries. With its larger and more experienced fighter arm, equipped in the main with superior machines, the advantage here seemed to lie with Germany, but by late June 1940, it had not yet come to that.

First, Hitler tried peace offers and blandishments. When these failed he tried threats. Only when the British flatly refused to negotiate did he decide to invade : 'As England, in spite of her hopeless military position, has shown herself unwilling to come to any compromise, I have decided to begin preparations for, and if necessary to carry out, the invasion of England . . .

'The English Airforce must be eliminated to such an extent that it will be incapable of putting up any substantial opposition to the invading troops.'

All military operations of any size have codenames. Hitler's planned invasion was codenamed Operation 'Sea-Lion' but Operation 'Sea-Lion' never took place. Throughout that long, hot summer of 1940, the skies over the English Channel and the south coast of England were ably defended by just 1,243 brave young men, the trained fighter pilots of the Royal Air Force, the famous 'Few', aided by pilots from the Commonwealth and Empire and American volunteer flyers of the two 'Eagle' Squadrons. Together these men fought the mighty German Luftwaffe to a standstill.

The full story of the Battle of Britain, the defeat of the Luftwaffe and the abandonment of Operation 'Sea-Lion' belong elsewhere, but the lessons of 1940 still held good in 1944; the first requirement for a successful cross-Channel invasion was *control of the air*.

If Hitler could not invade England and finish the war, then it followed that one day the British and their Allies must go back to France. The first step on the road back was quickly taken; on the night of 22 June 1940, just two weeks after the Dunkirk evacuation, a small party of British Commandos made a reconnaissance raid on the French coast near Boulogne.

The raid achieved very little but it was the start of a long series of amphibious landings, large and small, along the German-occupied coast of Europe, that would develop amphibious operational techniques to a high state of expertise and gain for the Allies a mass of knowledge about the defences of the enemy coast. Here were two more of the invasion requirements; *skill in amphibious techniques* and *knowledge of the enemy defences*.

It was to achieve these objectives that the British Commandos were

3

created, small units of men 'trained to act like packs of hounds', in the words of their creator, Winston Churchill. These Commandos came under the command of a new Headquarters, Combined Operations, and were only the first of several military innovations. Having seen the effect of parachute troops during the German 'Blitzkrieg' operations in France and Holland, Churchill also ordered the formation of parachute forces, initially a force of 5,000 men who could swiftly seize strategic points on the battlefield and hold them until the main force came up.

The employment of raiding forces soon revealed the need for another invasion requirement, a range of specialized landing craft. In 1939, the British Navy, then the largest naval force in the world, possessed exactly six landing craft. The best of these had a top speed of 5 knots and drew 4 feet of water. The US Navy had no landing craft at all. By the end of 1940, however, work had begun on both sides of the Atlantic on an expanding series of landing craft. These included the LCA (Landing Craft Assault) which carried a platoon of infantry, and the LCM (Landing Craft Mechanized) which could carry men, a couple of tanks or some transport. Both were in service by mid-1941, together with a most useful craft, the LCP(L), imported into Britain from the USA which by 1940 was already supplying Britain with a great quantity of war material.

Colin Kitchen, an RNVR officer, remembers them well: 'The letters LCP(L) stood for Landing Craft Personnel (Large) – the adjective seeming rather odd as the boat was a mere 37ft long; but there was an even smaller version, so there had to be some means of distinguishing between them. LCPs were made of seven-ply wood, with no armour protection. They were driven by a petrol engine and could do about 22 knots.

'These craft were built by a US firm named Higgins of New Orleans and the Americans called them "Higgins boats". The story goes that they were originally designed to run liquor from Cuba to the shores of Florida during Prohibition. With their overhanging bows the boats were reasonably well suited to the task of landing soldiers on beaches. They were the first craft to be acquired by the Royal Navy for that specific job, pending the introduction of purpose-designed landing craft.

'The LCP(L) flotillas' base was the aptly-named HMS *Tormentor* on the Hamble river at Warsash, between Portsmouth and Southampton. I joined the flotilla in March 1942 and six such flotillas took part in the costly raid on Dieppe in August 1942. My own flotilla carried the "floating reserve" of French-Canadian troops on that occasion, and at 7 o'clock on a brilliantly sunny morning we landed the soldiers on the central promenade at Dieppe in the face of massive German fire; with no armour protection we lost heavily in men and boats.

'As a consequence of this experience Combined Operations HQ decided (very sensibly) that LCPs were unsuitable for landing assault troops. Most of the flotillas were converted into specialist smoke-laying craft, while some became even more specialized navigation or survey vessels used for clandestine operations off the enemy coast.'

Meanwhile, from early 1941, Britain's parachute battalions were being raised and trained. Among the early volunteers who later served on D-Day was George Price, who volunteered for parachute training in 1943. 'My old pal Bill Worley and I volunteered for the Paras in August 1943. In a very short time indeed we were sent to Hardwick Hall near Chesterfield for selective training, where in three weeks we developed muscles we didn't know we had. Everything we did had to be done at the double. If we were caught walking, no matter where to, we were for the high jump. The hardest part was the ten-mile route march – run a mile, walk a mile, in full battle order. At the end of it our socks were covered in blood. It was a really tough course and a good many of the lads were RTU'd (Returned to Unit), but Bill and I got through and were duly graded as A1+.

'From Hardwick we were sent to Ringway near Manchester, where we did our parachute training. The hangar we used looked more like a circus – we rolled, tumbled, and jumped from heights on to mats. Then came the dreaded balloon drops. I can still hear the shout: "Up 800 – 4 men dropping!" We did two daytime drops and one night drop from the balloon. After that came the real thing, from a hole in the floor of a Whitley bomber. It was pretty good fun really and we enjoyed it, especially the extra shilling a day (5p) after we got our parachute wings. (I still have mine, which are promised to my grandson.)

'In September 1943 we were posted to the 12th (Yorkshire) Parachute Battalion, which was originally the 9th Bn, the Green Howards, and consisted mainly of Northerners. This was a bit strange for Bill and I, he being a Londoner and me coming from Slough. We had quite a dialect problem for a while, but we soon got used to it, which was just as well because I eventually married a lass from the North.

'The training was very hard. We did many exercises, including being dropped in Wales and having to mock-fight our way back to Larkhill. I think in all I must have done about twenty jumps from various types of aircraft: Halifax, Albemarle, Stirling and the American Dakota – the C47. We once had a visit from General Montgomery while we were digging a slit trench, and he asked us what we were doing. I thought that was a bit daft, coming from him.'

George Price jumped into France on D-Day, and this story will pick him up again later. Meanwhile, the war had spread across the world. In December 1941, Japan attacked the American Fleet at Pearl Harbor and the United States entered the war, but many American soldiers had already been drafted into the Army. Fred Tannery, from Brooklyn, New York, was called up in November 1941. 'I was inducted into the Army at Fort Bragg and assigned to the Signal Corps. I remember Sunday, December 7, 1941, the day of Pearl Harbor, and knew that we were in for some extended service in the Army. I was eventually assigned to the 4th Infantry Division and we spent a lot of time training at different camps along the eastern seaboard of the USA, until January 1944. On January 12 we set sail in the USS *George Washington* for England. The trip took twelve days in a tremendous convoy full of all kinds of ships, and after a lot of zig-zagging we arrived at Liverpool, England, and were sent to join the rest of the Division at Tiverton in Devon. We stayed there training until we sailed for "Utah" beach.'

In 1943, while George Price was doing his parachute training at Ringway and Fred Tannery was serving with the 4th Infantry Division in the United States, the 82nd American Airborne Division arrived in the UK fresh from the battlefields of Italy. Among them was Sergeant George Maruschak of Chicago, Illinois, then serving in the 32nd Glider Field Artillery.

'I will start my tale in an area around Leicester, England, where we were stationed prior to moving to the staging area for the invasion of Normandy. We were stationed in a farm area around Leicester – our location was about 15 miles away at Husbands Bosworth. There were many, many of us in Leicester daily, with two main objectives – finding pubs that were open, and meeting young females! Enjoying the pleasures took a setback when the Army located a battalion of black soldiers in a park in Leicester. It appeared that the "American Indians" (I don't know if the girls gave them that title or if the black soldiers said that is what they were) bought the girls fur stoles and other garments, and the girls preferred them to the paratroopers. Anyway, there were fights and knifings. All troops were warned and many passes to Leicester were abolished.

'I and two of my buddies were assigned to the Special Services Dept to work on a musical revue, "Together We Sing", to be presented to the troops and the people of Leicester. I spent most of my time with a Sergeant in the British ATS who, along with five other ATS girls and five civilian girls, was also in our revue. General Eisenhower and high-ranking British officers saw it and liked it so much that we were given permission to take it around RAF installations. We were also booked into the Scala Theatre in London and Cavendish Theatre in Nottingham. In London an air-raid alert was sounded and we heard the noise of a V1 – a buzz-bomb – but our tour was never completed. At the end of May 1944 we were ordered to report back to our units. That could only mean that the time for our next mission was not far away.'

Sergeant Maruschak's next performance would take place near Ste-Mère-Eglise, a small town in Normandy.

*

6

Between 1940 and 1943, while these men and millions like them were being recruited and trained, the war had spread. On 2 June 1941, violating the neutrality pact with the Soviet Union which had enabled him to rape Western Europe with impunity, Hitler invaded Russia and drove the Red Armies before him in defeat. Six months later, Hitler's ally, Japan, attacked the American Pacific Fleet at Pearl Harbor and the United States entered the war. A few days later, Britain declared war on Japan, and America and Britain then forged an alliance with the Soviet Union.

All these steps brought the cross-Channel invasion of Europe perceptibly closer. Soviet Russia began to demand help, a 'Second Front' in Western Europe. Specifically, they demanded a landing in the West, but this was, for the moment, impractical, though aid was sent to the Soviet Union in immense amounts. From mid-1941, first from Britain and later from the USA, munitions flowed to Russia in powerful convoys that fought freezing Arctic seas as well as German submarines and bombers to take Russia the weapons of war.

As soon as America entered the war, certain strategic decisions had to be taken between the Allies as to how the war should be fought. Two weeks after Pearl Harbor, on 20 December 1941, Britain's Prime Minister, Winston Churchill, and the American President, Franklin D. Roosevelt, met in Washington for what became known as the 'Arcadia' Conference. During this conference two decisions were arrived at which proved crucial to the future invasion of Europe.

The first step was the setting up of a unified Allied Command, the Combined Chiefs of Staff, to jointly direct the Anglo-American war effort and liaise with the Soviet Union. This was done in the light of the bitter experience of the Great War when the British and French Armies fought under separate commands until near defeat in March 1918. In this war there was to be unity from the beginning and, although not without strain, this unity held firm to the end.

The second major decision taken at 'Arcadia' was the 'Germany First' policy. It was decided that the Allied effort be directed first and foremost to the defeat of Germany, and that American armies were to go into action against the Germans as soon as possible, probably in Western Europe. This met with the full approval of the Soviet Union, which did not in fact declare war on Japan until the Second World War was practically over.

This 'Arcadia' decision was based upon the well-established article of strategic doctrine which states that a nation faced with an array of enemies should defeat the strongest first. This done, the weaker elements may collapse and will certainly be more easily overcome. Although strategically sound, this decision caused controversy. Some American commanders had deep misgivings about how far the Allies could go in excluding the Japanese in the Pacific from these calculations and Admiral King, Commander-in-Chief of the United States Navy, only agreed to the 'Germany First' policy with the greatest reluctance.

The American Pacific Fleet had suffered a major and infamous attack at Pearl Harbor and the Japanese were now swarming across the Pacific islands and the Philippines. Admiral King naturally wanted to hit back hard and fast, but revenge apart, he did not see how the Japanese could ever be defeated if they were given years to consolidate their conquests in the Pacific. Assurances of total commitment in the Pacific from all the British Empire and American forces immediately Germany was defeated quite failed to reassure him. The Pacific would also be primarily a naval theatre of operations, where Admiral King's fleets would dominate Allied strategy, and he naturally had no objection to that.

Admiral King's attitude to the European theatre was to have one unfortunate effect on the cross-Channel invasion plans. King controlled the allocation to theatres of the ships produced in the bustling American shipyards and the Pacific was a maritime and amphibious theatre which needed a great deal of shipping. As a result, the Allied cause in Europe and the Mediterranean suffered from a chronic shortage of landing craft and support vessels from 1942 until the end of the war. Britain's shipyards were already working flat out, producing or repairing warships and merchant vessels to fight the Battle of the Atlantic and support operations in the Channel, the North Sea and the Mediterranean. There was no spare capacity in Britain for massive landing-craft production.

The next disagreement was over European strategy. American agreement to the 'Germany First' policy was given on the understanding that the war was carried across the English Channel and on to the Continent as quickly as possible. The American intention was to build up an army in England in 1942, and then strike directly across the Channel into France. Roosevelt and his advisers originally proposed to reach this stage by the summer of 1942, just six months after entering the war. The British were more than a little dubious about the wisdom of such a venture and said so in unmistakable terms.

As American troops began to land in Britain in mid-1942, a stream of high-ranking American politicians and military men also began to arrive, urging the British into action. The Russians were also demanding an immediate 'Second Front' and General Marshall, the American Army Chief of Staff, conscious of the need to support Russia, proposed that the Allies might cross the Channel in the autumn of 1942 and establish a small bridgehead, perhaps in the Cotentin, the Cherbourg Peninsula. This they would maintain via the port of Cherbourg throughout the winter, emerge from this fortress in the spring of 1943 and advance into Germany. This operation bore the codename 'Sledgehammer'. Exactly what the Germans would be doing about this enclave during the winter of 1942–3 was hardly discussed, and the plan was soon seen to be unworkable.

Practical considerations alone made 'Sledgehammer' a non-starter. The Americans had entered the war with a very small army and instantly took on worldwide commitments. Thanks to the introduction of the draft of civilians for compulsory military service, the size of the American forces had been increasing steadily from 1940, but these forces had to be trained, equipped and transported overseas. All this could not be done overnight. Then the Battle of the Atlantic, the war against the U-Boat, was still being bitterly fought in 1942–3. The U-Boats were savaging the convoys and severely restricting the build-up of Allied strength in Britain. During the winter of 1942–3, German U-Boats operating in the North Atlantic sank over 800,000 tons of Allied shipping in one month alone.

Finally, the Luftwaffe were more than holding their own in the skies of France while the Allied air offensive against Germany had still to develop. When all these factors were taken into account, the invasion of France came some way down the list of immediate priorities.

Then, in August 1942, the impossibility of 'Sledgehammer' was bloodily underlined when the 2nd Canadian Division and three British Commandos, Nos 3, 4 and the Royal Marine 'A' Commando, together with a detachment of American Rangers, attempted a *coup-de-main* against the French port of Dieppe.

The Dieppe Raid has been described as a 'reconnaissance in force' and Lord Louis Mountbatten, then Chief of Combined Operations, stated later that the Battle of D-Day was won on the beaches of Dieppe, since the lessons learned there were crucial. This may well be true. The fact remains that the Dieppe Raid was a costly fiasco. Nearly half the men taking part were either killed or captured.

The Dieppe Raid taught the Allies several lessons. One was that they could not hope to capture an intact working port. To understand the lessons of Dieppe and the need for the prefabricated 'Mulberry' harbours of 1944 requires some knowledge of logistics, the branch of the military art concerned with supply.

The logistical problem is considerable for any army. Armies cannot function for long without large supplies of petrol, food, ammunition, medical supplies and men. For an invading army landing from the sea, the basic problem of delivering the right things in the right amounts to the right unit at the right time is compounded by the physical problem of getting them ashore, in all weathers and against a variety of opposition. This problem is greatly eased if the invading army enjoys the services of a functioning port. The enemy is equally aware of this fact and sees to it that all likely ports, as at Dieppe, are well defended and, if in danger of capture, extensively destroyed.

For the invasion to have a chance of success the Allies would need a port in good working order, through which their army could be supplied, the shipments safe from interruption by the weather. The big question to be answered was : was it possible to capture such a port by assault before the enemy has time to make it unusable ? The Dieppe Raid made it bloodily clear that it wasn't.

Having accepted that to seize a port was impossible, it was clear that the invading army must take a port with them. Eventually they took two, the floating, prefabricated ports known as 'Mulberry' harbours, each as big as the Channel ferry port of Dover, one for the Americans at 'Omaha' beach and one for the British and Canadians at Arromanches. Parts of the latter port still remain offshore fifty years later.

The slaughter of Canadian infantry on the beaches of Dieppe also pointed out the need for the employment of tanks in the initial assault waves, while the inability of the standard tank to cope with beach obstacles and break out from the landing area led directly to the development of specialized armour. This would eventually include mine-clearing tanks, bridge-building tanks, armoured bulldozers and tanks mounting heavy mortars to destroy concrete obstacles, but the main item of specialized armour was the DD (Duplex Drive) swimming tank, which all the Allied armies were to employ on D-Day. Launched from ships anchored beyond the range of coastal artillery, these tanks could sail in with the infantry landing craft and hit the beach at the same time.

Patrick Hennessey, MBE, trained on the first DD tanks : 'One lesson learned from the disastrous raid on Dieppe in 1942 was that infantry landing from the sea without the support of tanks were doomed. Our task was to get tanks on to the beach before or as the infantry arrived, and the problem was to do that without alerting the enemy. The solution was to launch the tanks into the sea and swim them ashore, but a tank does not float readily in water so a new type was invented.

'The DD tank was a normal Sherman tank weighing some 32 tons. A metal skirt was welded round the hull to which was attached a canvas screen. This could be erected around the tank, supported by pillars of compressed air and kept rigid by metal struts. When in the water the tank floated, but there was only about 3ft of freeboard above the surface. Two small propellers were fitted at the stern of the tank, driven by the tank's engine, and these gave us power and steering. Once on the beach, the screen was collapsed, and there stood a tank, ready to fight.'

Lance-Corporal Henry Jolly recalls his DD tank training : 'We started training for D-Day in the summer of 1943 on some Valentine tanks which had been converted for swimming purposes. I was just nineteen at the time.

'We had to learn the use of the Davis escape equipment, which was used in submarines. The training took place in a water tank 12–15ft deep, with the driving and turret compartments of a Valentine tank placed in the bottom. We then had to get into the Valentine tank and thousands of gallons of water poured down on us, and we were not allowed to use the Davis equipment until the water reached our chins. Breathing through the Davis equipment, we then had to stay in the Valentine until the outside tank was full. Only then, on an order from an instructor, could we escape from the Valentine. After this, and normal tank training, we started swimming and landing tanks from the sea on to the Isle of Wight.'

Meanwhile, in 1943, the tide of war was slowly turning against the Axis. Two months after Dieppe, in October 1942, the British Eighth Army in Africa, under General Montgomery, defeated Field Marshal Erwin Rommel's Afrika Korps at El Alamein. In November 1942, American troops went into action against the Germans for the first time when they landed in Morocco under the command of Major-General Dwight D. Eisenhower.

The North African campaign dragged on until the late spring of 1943, thereby effectively ruling out a cross-Channel invasion in that year. There was no time left to plan the attack, reorganize the troops and switch the landing craft to the Channel before the summer ended. To keep up the pressure on the Axis, Sicily and Italy were invaded in 1943, and the Italian government capitulated. The Germans, however, fought on in Italy and were still fighting there when the war ended in 1945.

Most significantly for the cross-Channel invasion in 1943, the U-Boat menace was finally controlled, if not defeated, in the Atlantic. With the decline of the U-Boats the naval, military and logistical strength necessary for the invasion of France could begin to gather in Britain, and by the end of 1943 there were nearly one-and-a-half million American servicemen in Britain. They joined hundreds of thousands of fighting men from all the free nations now assembling for the invasion. There were Canadian soldiers, Australian, New Zealand and South African airmen, and contingents from all over the Empire, plus thousands more from the occupied countries of Europe, the Free French, Dutch, Belgians, Norwegians and Danes. The invasion of Europe would be an international venture.

Among those arriving was Leslie W. Kick of the US 82nd Airborne Division, a unit which had already seen action in Sicily and Italy. 'Bill' Kick had been a paratrooper for just a year when he arrived in Britain. 'In September 1942 I took the four-week parachute course at Fort Benning, followed by a two-week parachute communications course. In late October or early November I was assigned to HQ Bty, 82nd Airborne Division artillery at Fort Bragg as a radio operator. We landed on the docks at Casablanca, Morocco on May 10, 1943. In July 1943, being one of thirteen from HQ Bty, I was on a plane heading for the invasion of Sicily. When we

11

flew over the US Navy ships laying offshore, we received heavy AA fire and both engines of our C-47 Dakota were knocked out. The pilot got over land and gave us the green light. We all got out without a scratch, but the pilot and co-pilot were killed in the crash.

'The division proceeded westerly along the south coast of Sicily to Trapani. We flew back to Africa in August, then back to Sicily in September. Then we took a trip from Palermo to Salerno by landing craft in late September. We entered Naples on October 1, 1943.

'In late November we took a three-week boat ride to Belfast, Ulster, where we stayed at Camp Ballyscullion, near Ballymena. About February 1944 we moved to Market Harborough, Leicestershire, in the English Midlands. Training from then until late May 1944 included a few weeks artillery firing in Wales.'

Another of those arriving in Britain from the USA at this time was J. Robert Slaughter of 1st Btn 116th Infantry, 29th Infantry Division, another unit destined for 'Overlord'. 'I joined the Virginia National Guard as a teenager in December 1940. On February 3, 1941 the Guard was inducted into Federal service and I was sent to Fort George G. Meade for one year's training. The attack on Pearl Harbor on December 7, 1941 changed our lives for ever. The song, "I'll Be Back In A Year, Little Darling" changed to "in for the duration!" We went overseas unescorted aboard the luxury liner, *Queen Mary* on Sunday, September 27, 1942.

'On Friday, October 2, a beautiful and calm day, 500 miles from our destination, Greenock in Scotland, the British Navy sent a light cruiser, HMS *Curacao* and a six-destroyer anti-submarine screen for our protection. *Curacao* zigged instead of zagging and we cut her in two, killing 320 British sailors. We limped into port the next day with a king-sized hole in the *Queen Mary*'s bow.'

Fifty years later, in a time when world travel is within most people's grasp, it is hard to imagine the impact the Americans had on the British people, or the curiosity the Americans felt about this war-weary little island. When the Americans arrived, the British people had been fighting Hitler for three long years and the strains were beginning to tell. Most of the men were in uniform, many of them abroad, and most of the women were in the services or working in the factories. Food rationing was in force and although most of the people were healthy enough, they were looking tired and thin. The centre of many of the cities had been reduced to rubble by German bombing, and the British people were in sore need of a little light relief. Into this scene erupted more than a million ebullient young Americans who seemed to have plenty of everything. Before long their trucks and troops filled the streets, and their music dominated the airwaves.

There were, inevitably, tensions. British reserve was frequently seen as sullenness, a resentment of America's wealth and power, while American enthusiasm was often taken as brashness and stupidity. British soldiers sourly remarked that the Yanks were 'over-paid, over-fed, over-sexed and over here'. The Americans replied that the British troops were 'under-paid, under-sized, under-sexed and under Eisenhower'. Relations between the Allied troops never became very friendly, though many American soldiers went to serve or train in British establishments. Robert Slaughter, for example, became a member of the 29th Ranger Battalion, which was trained by British Commandos at Achnacarry in Scotland.

Between the Americans and the British civilians – especially British girls – relations were much easier. Many Americans married British girls, and friendships were forged which endure to this day.

Fred Tannery, of 4th Infantry Division, remembers one of his English friends: 'In the five months before we went to France, I became very friendly with an English fellow, Gordon, who ran the Tiverton Theatre, the local movie house. He was the projectionist as well and I used to help him run the projector and take tickets in the lobby. We still keep in touch and I saw him on my visit to England long after the war. I met some very wonderful people in England, who I will remember as long as I live.'

Milton Chadwick arrived with a glider unit of 82nd Airborne: 'I loved England. Maybe the common language helped. I remember the flowers in the park at Market Harborough. I always used to swing the children in the park there and I was amazed that they remembered me when I came back from Normandy after six weeks' absence. The people treated us as their very own, and gave us a big welcome at the rail-road station upon our return from Normandy. I spent several pleasant Sunday afternoons with the Coleman family, who lived in Highfield Street in Market Harborough. I thought England was great, and if I could not have returned to the US after the war, I would have chosen England as my place to live.'

Jack Schlegel, now Chief of Police at Shandaken, New York, was then a twenty-year-old trooper in the 3rd Battalion of the 508th Parachute Infantry Regiment: 'After a few weeks in Portrush, Ireland, we came to our English base in Nottingham. English life and customs were strange to me, but I soon experienced the friendly warmth of the Nottingham people. Most of our time in Nottingham was taken up by training, but there were the lighter moments of pubs, romance, and rival fights between units. One incident always comes to mind; the killing of the King's deer in Wollaton Park. One day, a group of us decided deer steaks would be great, and since many of us were deer hunters in the USA, we felt the King would not miss a few. That night, several deer were shot, but the local constables got word of this, and several days after, a message from Col. Gavin's Headquarters put the 508th under base arrest with a warning that hunting deer was off limits in Nottingham. The deer steaks tasted great though!'

Alan Mitchell of Nottingham was a teenager when the American troops arrived : 'We used to hold dances in the youth club on a Saturday night, and as most of the local men were in the army, about four of us played in the band. It was really great playing such tunes as "You'll Never Know" and "My Devotion". The audience were mainly American paratroopers and the place was packed solid. Although I never heard them myself, the 508th had their own twelve-piece band, and they, too, used to play at the hall on numerous occasions. The stage was bedecked with different coloured parachutes.

'All in all, the GIs I met were a nice bunch, especially the Mexican boys. I used to walk home down Western Boulevard regularly with them as they walked back to Wollaton Park.'

Mary Hutton of Malmesbury in Wiltshire remembers another incident : 'My grandmother was a rather severe old lady and didn't approve of any girl going out with an American. Then one day, when she was going to the shops, a convoy went past full of American troops. One of them leaned out, gave a great wolf-whistle and called out, "Wish I was forty years older, Ma'am." The Americans could do no wrong in her eyes after that.'

The amazing thing is not that there were tensions but that, after the initial shock, the two peoples got on so well. Co-operation was necessary, for the day of decision was drawing closer.

The Allied leaders, Roosevelt, Churchill, Stalin, their Chiefs of Staffs and planners, were now meeting regularly, to plan overall strategy for the war, and in particular to plan the invasion of France. The decision to invade was finally taken by the Combined Chiefs of Staff in Washington in May 1943, with a provisional D-Day – the day of the actual assault – fixed for 1 May 1944.

In early 1943, the forthcoming invasion acquired a codename. They called it Operation 'Overlord', while the naval part was given another codename, Operation 'Neptune'. From the beginning there had been agreement that the Supreme Commander of 'Overlord' would be an American, for after the initial landing in France the bulk of the ground forces would be American, and the appointment of an American as 'Supreme Commander, Allied Expeditionary Force' was therefore inevitable.

The Anglo-American and Canadian troops were lucky in the man chosen to lead them to France. General Dwight D. Eisenhower had commanded the American forces in North Africa. He was, by any standards, a good soldier and a fine man, but was unequalled as a leader of disparate Allied armies. He could handle prickly Army Commanders tactfully, or slap them down hard if he had to, but without causing lasting rancour. He was universally liked and respected ; his smile alone was reputedly worth an Army Corps to the Allied cause.

Commanding a vast force drawn from many nations, Eisenhower was quite without nationalistic prejudice but, within limits, he could tolerate it in others, and his staff, following this example, worked together in an atmosphere remarkably free from friction. For internal disagreements among his officers, Eisenhower's rule was simple : 'If you disagree strongly with someone,' he said, 'you can call him a bastard if you have to. You may not, however, call him a Limey or a Yankee bastard.'

Eisenhower was not a fighting soldier. Before Operation 'Torch' (the American landings in North Africa at the end of 1942), Eisenhower had not even held an operational command. He was by profession a staff officer of considerable skill and experience and a protégé of General Marshall, the American Army Chief of Staff. This link with Marshall gave Eisenhower considerable political influence and a knowledge of how to get his views across to people in a position to help. Added to his universal popularity, this made him the perfect man for the job, while his staff experience proved invaluable for what was, in the end, a tremendous logistical task.

Eisenhower's appointment as Supreme Commander, Allied Expeditionary Force, was confirmed on Christmas Day 1943; from that moment Operation 'Overlord' was under way.

The Senior Command structure for 'Overlord' was as follows :

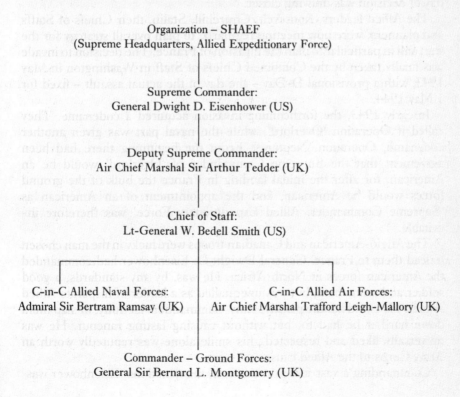

Organization – SHAEF
(Supreme Headquarters, Allied Expeditionary Force)

Supreme Commander:
General Dwight D. Eisenhower (US)

Deputy Supreme Commander:
Air Chief Marshal Sir Arthur Tedder (UK)

Chief of Staff:
Lt-General W. Bedell Smith (US)

C-in-C Allied Naval Forces: C-in-C Allied Air Forces:
Admiral Sir Bertram Ramsay (UK)   Air Chief Marshal Trafford Leigh-Mallory (UK)

Commander – Ground Forces:
General Sir Bernard L. Montgomery (UK)

As the diagram shows, the Army Field Commander for the invasion and build-up period was to be the British General, Sir Bernard L. Montgomery, the famous 'Monty', victor of El Alamein. His command would only endure for the invasion period or until sufficient American forces were ashore for Eisenhower to take up the Field Command.

Montgomery has had his critics, and not only in America, but you will not hear many critical voices among those who served under his command. 'With Monty, at least you knew what was going on . . . and that is not always the case in military matters,' is one typical comment.

General Montgomery, or 'Monty' as he was universally called, was Britain's most charismatic commander and a professional fighting soldier. Commissioned into the Royal Warwickshire Regiment, he had been wounded on the Western Front during the Great War, and commanded a division in France in 1940. These experiences had left Monty with two firm convictions. First, that his men's lives were precious ; no steps were too long or difficult if they saved lives. Second, that war was a chaotic business on which he must impose order by careful soldiering and meticulous tactics.

Monty's personality was often abrasive and he was undoubtedly arrogant. His attitudes brought him into conflict with his American colleagues who saw him as a cautious, even timid commander, while for his part Monty made little secret of his dislike of their bald-headed approach to battle. Monty's natural instinct to protect lives was compounded by the fact that by 1944 Britain's military resources, particularly in manpower, were almost at an end. He had to protect lives because his men were irreplaceable. Indeed, shortly after the D-Day landings it was necessary to break up one British division to supply reinforcements to other units ; no other reinforcements were available. Whatever the difficulties caused by his attitude, Montgomery was the acknowledged master of the planned, set-piece battle and, like Eisenhower, he was acknowledged as the best man for the job that had to be done on D-Day.

Eisenhower and Montgomery had their first look at the plans already prepared for 'Overlord' at Marrakech in Morocco on New Year's Eve 1943–4. They did not like what they saw. This plan had been in preparation since 1942 and was the work of a team under the direction of a British officer, Lt-General F. E. Morgan and his American assistant, Brigadier-General Barker. Morgan's appointment was entitled 'Chief of Staff to the Supreme Allied Commander (Designate)' or COSSAC for short, and his proposals were therefore known as the COSSAC plan.

The war itself had laid down many of the requirements necessary for a successful invasion ; air supremacy, surprise, adequate forces, specialized troops and armour, logistical support, the provision of ports. As more requirements became evident, so they were incorporated into the COSSAC plan. Now came the crucial problem of where the Allied armies should land

... and where the enemy's armies must be persuaded to *think* they would land. To these vital matters the planners now turned their minds.

Clearly, the invasion area must be within reach of Allied air cover. It must have weather-protected landing beaches which would also permit rapid deployment of the Allied armies inland after the invasion. The invasion area must be capable of being sealed off by bombing enemy communications, bridges, roads, and rail links, to delay the build-up of enemy counter-offensives, and have some reasonable port facility nearby that could quickly be captured, cleared of mines and obstructions, and brought into use. The planners spent hours and days poring over maps, seeking such a location on the French coast.

For the first requirement the Channel coast around Calais would be best. It was a bare twenty minutes' flying time away from the airfields in Kent and a beachhead there would give easy access towards Germany across northern France. It was so suitable that the enemy agreed with the Allies on this point and the defences along the coast around Calais were particularly strong. The Allied planners looked elsewhere. To the north of Calais the landing area was even more suitable, but a break-out would lead across the flood-plain of Flanders on to the fatal ground of the 1914–18 War, and this fact alone tended to eliminate that area. The COSSAC planners then turned their eyes south, across the Seine and, beyond that, to the Calvados coast of Normandy.

The coast of Normandy, and in particular the area between the Cotentin Peninsula and the Bay of the Seine, lay only 80 miles away from the south coast of England. This was just within fighter range in 1943, and fighter range was steadily increasing – Allied fighters ranged 75 miles into Normandy on D-Day. The beaches between the River Orne north of Caen and the River Vire at the foot of the Cotentin Peninsula were wide and gentle, and the Cotentin – or Cherbourg – Peninsula, apart from offering the port of Cherbourg, would give some protection from the full fetch of any Atlantic gales coming in from the west. Moreover, the area could be cut off by the tactical bombing of some thirty bridges leading in across the Seine, thus isolating the area from German reinforcements. Finally, on this sector the coastal fortifications were nowhere near as strong as they were along the Channel coast. COSSAC, therefore, chose Normandy for the 'Overlord' invasion, on a 30-mile strip running west from the mouth of the Orne, 6 miles north of Caen to the River Vire.

Eisenhower and Montgomery had many reservations about the COS-SAC plan and they wanted changes. With 1 May 1944 already set as the invasion date, they had only a few months to do much about it, but they did agree that the choice of a landing place was broadly correct. Thus the die was cast. Some time soon, in the coming year of 1944, the full weight of Allied arms would fall on the coast of Normandy.

——————CHAPTER TWO——————

The Defences of Normandy

'Rommel told me, "If the Allies will land
and we can't throw them back into the sea
within 24 hours, it's the beginning of the
end."'
Major Hans Von Luck
125 Panzer Grenadier Regiment
21st Panzer Division

Normandy, ancient dukedom of the English Plantagenet Kings, is the largest province in modern France. As in all French provinces, Normandy is sub-divided into a number of *départements*, of which two, Calvados and La Manche, were to be directly concerned with the invasion, which fell on their northern and eastern coasts.

The Calvados coast runs west from the mouth of the River Orne, north of the city of Caen, to the mouth of the River Vire, north of Isigny. Before the war this was a holiday and tourist area, noted for fine, safe, sandy beaches, for yachting and for the abundant and excellent local seafood. The coast west of Ouistreham, running through the little resort towns of Lion-sur-Mer, Luc-sur-Mer, Langrune and St Aubin, is referred to locally as '*Le Côte Nacré*', the Pearl Coast. Apart from some modern tourist developments, like caravan parks, it is still very much as it was fifty years ago, in the summer of 1944.

To the west, across the Vire, lies the *département* of La Manche, which runs west through the market town of Carentan and north up the Cotentin Peninsula, through the beautiful little town of Ste-Mère-Eglise, to Cherbourg on the tip of the peninsula. Cherbourg is the major port in this section of the coast and the nearest port to southern England, some eighty miles to the north. The beaches of Calvados and La Manche are very wide, flat and sandy, gently shelving and backed with drained salt marshes or low sanddunes. They do contain patches of mud and there are offshore sand-bars, but they are in general very suitable for amphibious operations.

These beaches are broken only once on the Calvados coast, between the River Vire and Arromanches, where steep cliffs, 100ft high, drop directly into the sea along twenty miles of coast. These cliffs are broken only twice, by the small harbour and town of Port-en-Bessin, and by 4 miles of beach below the villages of Vierville and St Laurent. This beach – codenamed 'Omaha' – was to be the scene of bloody fighting on 6 June 1944.

The country behind the beaches is very varied. Around Caen there are large open areas of arable fields interspersed with apple orchards and low wooded hills, land flat enough to contain the airfield at Carpiquet. South of the Cotentin Peninsula and Port-en-Bessin lie the close, irregular fields of the Normandy *bocage*. 'Bocage' is a Norman word meaning grove or copse ; the Normandy *bocage* consists of innumerable small, irregular fields, divided by high, thick hedges set atop earth banks. This was perfect defensive country if the enemy had the time and forces to occupy it. Overall, the country is not unlike Hampshire or the flatter areas of Vermont and Maine in the eastern United States. It is farming country, threaded with streams and rivers, home to an industrious rural population.

Large towns are few. The capital of the region is the university city of Caen, six miles up the Orne from Ouistreham. Caen and the city of St Lô, further to the west, would be the scene of bitter fighting later in the Normandy campaign. In the centre of Calvados, some ten miles inland from the coast, lies the ancient cathedral city of Bayeux, famous down the ages for that remarkable relic of another invasion, the Bayeux Tapestry, which depicts the landing of Duke William the Conqueror in England nine centuries ago in 1066. There are no other towns near the coast, with the exception of the sizeable fishing port of Ouistreham at the mouth of the Orne, with a population in 1944 of about 5,000. Then there is Courseulles at the mouth of the River Seulles, and over to the west, Carentan, a market town of the southern Cotentin also with a population of around 5,000. Another place to note is the village of Ste-Mère-Eglise in the centre of the Cotentin, which had a population of some 1,500 in 1944 and was noted for the breeding of horses.

When the COSSAC planners' eyes first turned upon it in 1943, Normandy was a backwater in the European war, quiet, peaceful and

19

relatively undisturbed. It had been that way since German forces overran France in 1940. Normandy was usually occupied by second-rank formations of the German Wehrmacht, units without motor transport or with obsolescent equipment, or by divisions resting after campaigns on the Russian Front. In late 1943 all that began to change.

The options open to generals are often limited. The Germans were able to predict when and where the invasion would probably take place simply by calculating what they would do in Eisenhower's place. By mid-1943 there was no doubt on either side of the Channel that an invasion was coming, and the Allied choice clearly lay between the Pas de Calais, which was favoured by General Von Rundstedt, the German Commander in the West, and most of the German High Command (the OKW), and Normandy, favoured for intuitive reasons by Adolf Hitler, the German Chancellor. Both parties felt that wherever the main invasion came in, there would be a major diversion in the other, to disperse the defenders and help the main assault. The main difficulty would be to decide which was the invasion and which the diversion.

Hans Von Luck, then a Major in the 21st Panzer Division, had served with General Rommel in the desert and was with him again in Normandy. 'Before, and on D-Day, I was commanding a Panzer Grenadier Regiment of the 21st Panzer Division, east of the River Orne. Our division was in Army Group "B" reserve and under strict orders not to move unless released by the Army Group on direct orders from Hitler's Headquarters.

'We didn't expect the invasion in Normandy because the distance was very long, there were a lot of cliffs, difficult to overcome, but we were training every night to get as familiar with the ground as possible. Rommel visited us several times, and he insisted that we had to take position and dig in, that the invasion might come in Normandy. General Marcks, who was the Corps Commander at that time, knew the British very well and he said, "I know the British. They will go to church on Sunday, they will land here in Normandy on Monday." So this was foreseen, only Eisenhower postponed the invasion for one day.'

The Germans had been building up their coastal defences, the so-called Atlantic Wall, since the invasion of Britain was abandoned in 1941. When completed, the Atlantic Wall was to run from Norway to the Spanish frontier, a thick belt of minefields, obstacles, strongpoints and artillery, the latter set in reinforced concrete blockhouses which could repel any invasion force. The snag was that even by the spring of 1944, the Atlantic Wall was not complete.

British Commandos and Allied agents crossed it with impunity night after night, and resources to complete it in terms of concrete, men or munitions were simply not available. The Pas de Calais was certainly strong enough and the Allied deception plans, which included stationing the American Third Army in Kent, fed the Germans the idea that this would be the area of the invasion, and that any attack in Normandy would only be a feint. However, Normandy needed much more attention before it could be considered secure. Hitler had some six months to prepare for the invasion, and clearly there was much work to be done. He did, however, have just the man to do it: Rommel.

Field-Marshal Erwin Rommel, infantry colonel, Panzer leader, some-time commander of the doughty Afrika Korps, the most charismatic general of the Second World War, was glad to be summoned to the Führer's Headquarters in December 1943. The previous twelve months had not been happy ones for him. Since his return from Africa in the spring of 1943 he had spent some time in hospital, recovering from jaundice and exhaustion following his efforts in the desert. He had kicked his heels for a while at Hitler's Headquarters, and in November 1943 was commanding an Army Group based in Bavaria and northern Italy.

This was not an active fighting command, and Rommel's time in office there was plagued with trouble from the SS, the soldiers drawn from the ranks of the Nazi Party. SS Divisions, while under Wehrmacht control for operations, were not under control in matters of discipline and the savage behaviour of SS troops toward the Italian civilian population proved a continuous source of trouble for Field-Marshal Rommel. His complaints about their behaviour were referred to political leaders such as Himmler, and then ignored. Though unpopular, SS units were nevertheless excellent fighting divisions, and through their political influence usually had the pick of manpower and equipment. Well trained, well equipped and often fanatical, SS troops, in particular the 12th SS Panzer Division, were to play a significant part in the early Normandy battles of 1944.

Rommel was glad to leave Italy and looked forward to the new appointment outlined by the Führer. His first task was to inspect all the defences of the Atlantic Wall, from Denmark to the Spanish frontier, and report on their ability to repel the coming invasion.

Rommel began his task with a series of whirlwind inspection tours along the entire length of the Atlantic Wall; he was horrified by what he found. In all but a few areas the Wall simply did not exist. The major ports and possible Allied landing areas, such as the coast of the Pas de Calais, were certainly well protected with heavy guns in concrete emplacements and adequate garrisons secure in intricate defence systems, but elsewhere there were long stretches of coast where the defences were no more than a few mines and some strands of barbed wire. The problem now was what to do about it in the short time available before the Allies came ashore.

By 1943 the shortage of war material for the German forces was becoming acute, but the main blame for the lack of defences along the coast lay with the Oberkommando Wehrmacht (OKW), the German High Command. The OKW had made the fundamental mistake of believing their own propaganda.

Following the bloody repulse of the Canadians at the Dieppe Raid of 1942, Goebbels, Hitler's Minister of Propaganda, had made great play with the impregnability of the Atlantic Wall, citing Dieppe as evidence of what would happen to any invader who dared put a foot in Fortress Europe, the Germans' *'Festung Europa'*. The German people and Army were bombarded with propaganda which seemed to bear out Hitler's claims that the Allies could never set foot in Europe until Hitler's long-promised V-weapons, the V1 and V2 rockets, were able to shatter Britain and end the war ... and these rockets and their launching sites were ready for deployment by the summer of 1944.

Since 1940 France had been listed low in the priority scale for men and equipment, and had become a rest area for divisions mauled on the Russian Front. The permanent garrison consisted largely of low-grade divisions, often containing Poles or Romanians, or elderly and unfit Germans, even renegade Russians. Some indication of the diversity in these divisions is indicated by the fact that in some of their battalions, eight different types of paybook were necessary, for Russians, Cossacks, Armenians, Georgians, Turkmen, Tartars, and so on.

The development of thick defences, especially of beach obstacles and strongpoints, was hampered by a shortage of steel, concrete and manpower, for the main German labour force, the Todt Organization, was kept busy repairing bomb damage to factories in the Ruhr. Rommel reported his dire findings to OKW and to Field Marshal Von Rundstedt, commanding Army Group West, but little was or could be done to rectify matters.

Rommel therefore decided to take a direct line in the affair. He went to Hitler and applied for command of Army Group B, which consisted of the German armies stationed between the Netherlands and the Loire. The invasion would certainly come somewhere in this area and Rommel would therefore be the Commander of the German anti-invasion forces. As Commander of Army Group B, Rommel was responsible directly to Von Rundstedt, the Chief of Oberkommando West, commanding all the troops in Western Europe. There might have been friction between the two men, since Rommel had gone over Von Rundstedt's head to obtain his command. Von Rundstedt was the doyen of the Offizier Korps, while Rommel was regarded in some Wehrmacht circles as an upstart who had gained his rapid promotion by the favour of Hitler. Fortunately, Von Rundstedt had little interest left in fighting the war and was happy to give Rommel his head.

In June 1944, Von Rundstedt had, at least on paper, 60 divisions, 11 of them Panzer divisions, to meet the Allied invasion, but these were deployed all down the western coast of Europe and their men and equipment varied widely; 24 of these divisions were deployed in Holland or Belgium, 11 were in the South of France and 6 south of the Loire. Some units had little or no transport, while the others relied heavily on horses, even for artillery haulage, a method which had long since been abandoned by the Allied armies.

Von Rundstedt's authority in the West was continually undermined by interference from Hitler and he was quite content to let Rommel have a free hand if he wanted one. Rommel's disputes with Von Rundstedt's head-quarters, Army Group West, were over supplies and tactics, and his main opponent here was not Von Rundstedt but the Commander of Panzer Forces in the West, General Geyr Von Schweppenburg. Their main dis-agreements centred on where the invasion would come and on what tactics should be employed to repel it.

Rommel's appreciation of Allied intentions fell somewhere between that of Hitler and the OKW. He felt that Normandy was more likely than the Pas de Calais, but decided that an assault around the mouth of the Somme was the most probable of all. It was therefore in this area and in Normandy that he concentrated his efforts, setting out to develop the coastal defences in depth, driving his men hard, using energy, ingenuity and his genius for improvisation to overcome a chronic shortage of material.

Rommel's intention was to halt the Allied invasion on the beaches. Here his views differed from those of Field Marshal Von Rundstedt, most of the General Staff, and certainly of Geyr Von Schweppenburg. Von Rundstedt felt that with over 1,500 miles of coast to defend and the Allied command of the sea and domination of the air, the invasion simply could not be pre-vented. Therefore he did not propose to try and prevent the Allies getting ashore. Rather, he proposed to concentrate on defending major ports and on building up a strategic reserve which, once the main invasion had been located, would move against it with overwhelming force and push the landing forces back into the sea.

This was a classic defensive strategy. Rommel appreciated the thinking behind it, while totally disagreeing with the concept. He felt that the Allied command of the air would be decisive and prevent the movement forward of any German strategic reserve. Such forces as were able to move would be shattered by Allied air strikes long before they got near the landing areas. He therefore intended to work well forward and defeat the invasion on the beaches, and on the first day – the 'longest day', as he called it. Within his own command he made preparations to do just that, but his preparations were constantly hampered by disagreements on this basic policy, particu-larly with Geyr Von Schweppenburg, who controlled the best equipped divisions in the West, the Panzer divisions of the Waffen SS. Rommel and his superiors were still arguing over the fundamental points of his policy when the Allied troops came ashore. There were only 18 German divisions in Normandy and Brittany, between the Seine and the Loire, and the disputes between Rommel and Von Rundstedt over the best invasion tactics led to a compromise in their deployment.

In the actual invasion area were two German armies, the Seventh to the south of the Seine and the Fifteenth to the north. The Seventh Army was to bear the brunt of the invasion, which fell on the three infantry divisions, the 709th, 91st and 243rd in the Cotentin, and two infantry divisions stationed along the Calvados coast, the 716th and 352nd. Of these, only the 352nd was a first-class, well-trained and properly equipped assault infantry division, although the 91st was up to strength and had been trained in anti-invasion tactics.

The only Panzer division near the coast was an ex-Afrika Korps formation, 21st Panzer, deployed between Caen and Falaise, and the only tactical reserve was the first-class 6th Parachute Regiment deployed around Carentan. Other formations available in support included the troops of 84th Corps deployed along the coast from the Orne to the Seine, and two more Panzer divisions, 12th SS Panzer, deployed around Bernay and Evreux, and Panzer Lehr, which was positioned further south, on the wide plains of the Beauce, near Chartres. The headquarters of the 1st SS Panzer Corps was at Rouen, while Rommel took up his headquarters at the château of La Roche Guyon, further up the Seine, near the base of the 116 Panzer Division.

Apart from the 21st Panzer Division, the 352nd and 91st Infantry Divisions, and the 6th Parachute Regiment, the troops along the Calvados and Cotentin coast were second-rank formations. Many of the soldiers had chronic complaints, stomach ailments or poor feet, or were Russian or Polish renegades, serving here to avoid forced labour. They lacked heavy weapons and motor transport, and got about on bicycles. Even at this stage in the war, most German infantry divisions in whatever state of readiness still used horse transport. Even so, these German formations were dug-in and prepared to make a fight of it when the day came. They had very little choice and could reflect that the normal attack : defence ratio, where one defending soldier was held to be worth three attackers was increased when the attackers had to land and attack from the sea.

Sergeant Rainer Hartmetz had arrived in Normandy from the Russian Front and was an experienced infantry NCO. 'When I came to Normandy I was stationed some kilometres east of Caen on the main road to Pont l'Evêque. It was different from those awful days in Russia, I remember the time the Russians assaulted us three times in one day, the last time with about 120 tanks. The company was stationed in Frénouville, a small village on the Caen–Lisieux road, with about 200 inhabitants. Each morning the company disappeared into the fields or forests for combat training by squads, platoons and companies. We practised with all our weapons, and the training became a kind of sport. We didn't know much about the other German troops in France. Our battalion came from Russia, and that was another world. We knew we would have to fight another adversary – the British. We didn't think of the Americans; they were not known to us. We had the feeling that fighting with the British would be a more human fight. We knew the British would be tough fighters but there would be humane rules.

'We never got the idea to surrender to the British, but there was a certain temptation to give up sooner than necessary, and that had been the problem of a lot of discussions between us and our officers. We fought this temptation with our feelings of honour and responsibility. Honour as a soldier, responsibility for Germany, but what was Germany? My parents, my teachers, my girlfriends, my younger friends in the Hitler Youth, the Nazi leader on the block, those fat guys in brown uniforms with big patriotic words in the mouth?

'What about Hitler? That simple soldier of World War I, four times wounded. He must have suffered like we did, but he couldn't have wanted what happened. We knew that there had been some things wrong and bad but he seemed, to us, sacrosanct. We fought for Germany against the Russians, and now we had to fight against the British, who helped them.

'After this war there would be a second one, to get rid of the Nazis. It was a very simple and primitive way of thinking, but it came out of our emotions, education, experiences and propaganda. Germany, our country, seemed to be strange to us, even our parents. We got furlough and felt alone at home. Being together with our parents, there was nothing to tell, and the things we wanted to talk of they didn't understand.'

Another of the German defenders was Herbert Muschallik, a soldier in the 352nd Infantry Division. 'I was not an NCO but an ordinary soldier. I was born in Buethen in Silesia in 1926, so I was just seventeen when I was sent to Normandy. We were shipped west in cattle trucks and I got there in September 1943, after just six weeks' infantry training at a place called Oppeln. I can't remember my company or regiment, but I was on an anti-tank gun crew, a Pak 38, and we trained with that a lot. We were stationed in a village near Bayeux, but we didn't go out much, and if we did, we had to be back by ten o'clock. We trained and trained and waited for the invasion, but when it came it was a surprise ... but I was only a soldier. Maybe the officers knew more about it.'

Oberst Helmut Ritgen was then serving with Panzer Lehr, a crack German armoured division. The word 'Lehr' means 'training', but Panzer Lehr was no training division. It was the demonstration division for the German Panzer Corps, equipped with the latest tanks and staffed by first-class men, including a high percentage of experienced officers and

NCOs. Panzer Lehr was deployed to the south of Caen and was one of the units which Rommel was eager to bring up towards the beaches.

Helmut Ritgen has left an account of the pre-D-Day period. 'All German field manuals on operations contained the phrase "Frictions and mistakes are commonplace phenomena". In 1944 such frictions thwarted the last possible effective counter-attack against the Allied landings in Normandy. This was to have been a violent and co-ordinated counter-attack by I SS Panzer Corps with three Panzer divisions within 48 hours of the landings. The beaches along the Calvados coast, on what were to be Gold, Juno and Sword, the British and Canadian beaches, were defended by 716th Infantry Division, a static division which was almost without any means of transport, even horses, and was made up of elderly soldiers who had no combat experience. It was insufficiently armed, mostly with captured French equipment.

'In the front line, on the dunes of "Juno", where the Canadians would land, two weak rifle battalions clung to a chain of pill-boxes and strong-points near the shore, partly armed with 50mm, 75mm or 88mm guns. Beach obstacles and minefields, some still under construction, had failed to delay the invaders landing even at ebb tide. The German coastal and divisional artillery, lacking any means of fire control, was only capable of firing single-battery, not multi-battery missions.'

Apart from a shortage of manpower the Germans needed to develop their coastal defences to a depth capable of bringing the invasion to a grinding halt under artillery and machine-gun fire. Rommel's defences therefore began well below high-water mark, in the area between the tides. Beams and tree trunks were driven deep into the sand, the tops projecting seawards and crowned with sharp steel cutters to rip open the hulls of landing craft. Other poles were draped with fused mines. Concrete tank obstacles, obsolete ashore, were dragged into the sea to hamper craft beaching, and naval mines were secured in the shallow coastal waters with lines attached to their horns. The obstacle which was to prove most difficult to overcome was called 'Element C'. This obstacle came in various forms but consisted of a heavy steel fence supported by wooden posts and mined. There were also steel girders welded together like enormous starfish, and wooden ramps, mines, barbed wire, and another barrier known as 'Belgian Gates' which consisted of concrete dragon's teeth and metal barriers, armed with fused shells.

Singly or in combination these obstacles offered a number of possible terrors. They might succeed in sinking landing craft outright, or in blowing the occupants sky high. They might impale the craft and expose them, stuck fast, to shell-fire from the shore. They might force the landing craft to disembark the troops too far out at low tide, well beyond the obstacles, where they could be machine-gunned as they waded or ran ashore. They might let craft in, but probably in the confusion the craft would not get out again to bring up reinforcements. At the very least, these underwater obstacles would disrupt the landings. The beaches themselves were sown with an assortment of anti-tank and personnel mines, screened with wire and covered by guns, anti-tank emplacements, flame throwers and machine-gun posts and artillery set in reinforced concrete bunkers.

Rommel made great use of mines. In the four months before June 1944, four million mines were laid along the Channel coast. Had time permitted, Rommel intended to lay between 50 and 100 million mines before his preparations could be considered complete. As with everything else, there was a shortage of mines, which Rommel partially overcame by employing old French shells attached to obstacles or buried on the beach, fused to explode on contact.

Unless they are covered by machine guns, minefields and barbed-wire entanglements can be rapidly cleared, so behind and above the beaches Rommel constructed pill-boxes and concrete emplacements for heavy machine guns, 81mm mortars and field artillery, notably the formidable 88mm anti-tank gun. These guns, and all the emplacements close to the shore, were usually sited to fire along the beach rather than out to sea. Their seaward wall was protected by reinforced concrete many feet thick, covered and camouflaged with earth and sandbags against naval gunfire, the slits positioned to enfilade troops and tanks crossing the beach and so deny the invaders any exit from the landing beach, which was converted into a killing ground.

Behind the beaches came more minefields and wire, and the trench lines of the defending infantry. Rommel instructed the coastal divisions to en-trench *everybody*, soldiers, cooks, clerks and drivers, all in deep dugouts linked by connecting passages to permit movement from one post to another under cover from enemy fire. All open fields inland considered likely spots for airborne landings, either by parachute or glider, were thickly studded with posts designed to smash the gliders as they came down. These became known as 'Rommel's Asparagus'. The posts were linked with barbed wire and many fields were mined with anti-personnel and anti-tank devices.

It was also possible to flood a number of tidal areas along the Normandy coasts and along the numerous rivers, notably around Ste-Mère-Eglise and Carentan, along the Vire and the Merderet, as well as in the flood plains east of Ranville along the River Dives, by destroying banks or breaking sluices, and in the east below the heights of Ranville, along the Orne and Dives. Both these areas were flooded, either by damming the rivers until the banks overflowed, or by breaking the banks themselves, allowing the water to flow out into the fields to a depth of between two and four feet. In the ditches, the water would be much deeper. The British, American and Canadian para-troopers would find these floods a considerable obstacle. Many men were to drown in them, trapped in their parachute harness, weighed down with their equipment and ammunition.

The flood waters quickly became covered with weed, and the floods were therefore invisible to Allied reconnaissance aircraft which by the spring of 1944 were making regular photographic flights over the invasion area. Many of these flights came in at wave-top height, to build up a 'soldier's eye' view of the invasion beaches for the assault craft coxswains and the invading troops.

Squadron Leader Jim Palmer flew many such sorties over the Normandy beaches. 'I was then an Army captain, an Air Liaison Officer (ALO), assigned to No. 239 Recce Squadron RAF. I was posted to No. 35 (Recce) Wing RAF, which comprised No. 4 Squadron equipped with the PR (Photo-Reconnaissance) Spitfire for high-level vertical photography; and with Nos 2 and 268 Squadrons equipped with American P-51 (Mustang) aircraft for low-level oblique and vertical photography and also visual recce backed up with photographs. I was assigned to No. 239 Squadron as ALO.

'We were employed in the main with taking low-level oblique photographs of the French coastline, covering not only the Normandy beaches which would eventually be used but also a much greater length of coastline in order to confuse the enemy as to our actual intentions. We paid quite a lot of attention to the Pas de Calais area where the Germans expected us to land. This supported the deception supposedly made by FUSAG, the 4th United States Army Group set up in South-East England and which actually consisted of only a handful of officers and men – mainly wireless operators who successfully hoaxed the German "Y" Service – their interception service.

'A great deal of the coastal cover was undertaken at low tide to show the obstacles erected in the sand below high-water mark as a deterrent to our landing craft. Most of these obstacles were steel sections welded into a tripod (in some cases old railway lines were used). Explosive mines were attached to these. Others were of reinforced concrete "Dragon's Teeth". The photographs were taken by a camera with very little depression, mounted behind the pilot's head. This meant that the pilots had to fly extremely low and were vulnerable to anti-aircraft activity. The main reason for flying so low was to obtain photographic cover of the beach obstacles, and to get a panoramic view of the landing beaches. These pictures were eventually used by the landing craft coxswains to guide their craft ashore as the church steeples and distinctive elevation of the beaches shown on these photographs were a far better guide than any map or chart.'

Other aircraft were engaged in aerial interdiction, sealing off Normandy from the rest of France. Ken Beard was then an RAF air gunner: 'I cannot recall air crews associating raids with any particular strategy for winning the war. In other words, we would go into briefing, be given a target and get on with the job. It must be realized that we lowly air gunners would attend the general briefing only, whereas navigators particularly would have their own additional briefing when, no doubt, they would be given more information regarding the target and its significance. Perhaps I ought to say that even at general briefings we would be given something of a background to the target, i.e., "electrical equipment for German fighters is manufactured here", or "lorries are made here".

'Air crews were very single-minded about their function in the war, and I have no recollection of anyone being particularly interested in the general aspects of what was happening elsewhere. For example, although obviously aware of newspapers screaming that it was time for the Second Front, that Russia was demanding it, and so on, I never recall air crew losing any sleep about the purpose of raids. We would have been stupid, on the other hand, not to have realized that as we did more and more raids on targets "nearer home" the Second Front was in the offing. As evidence of this I can itemize the raids in which my crew took part during the month of May 1944.

'1 May: Malines (Belgium) Railway Centre locomotive sheds. 7 May: Mantes-la-Jolie (on the Seine); stores depots and locomotive sheds. 10 May: Lens, Pas de Calais; railway yards. 22 May: mine-laying off enemy coast. 24 May: Aachen, two railway yards (442 aircraft involved – 25 lost – 14,800 people bombed out of their homes). Aachen was an important link in the railway system between Germany and France.'

The photo-reconnaissance aircrews noted, among other things, the construction of several battery positions, probably containing heavy guns, near the village of Merville, east of Ouistreham, and on the cliffs of the Pointe du Hoc on the west coast by the mouth of the Vire. These were thought to contain massive 155mm guns, with a range of 20 miles, enough to embarrass any anchored invasion fleet discharging troops off the Normandy coast. These positions, and a thousand more, were noted on the planners' maps and pondered over. This was a game of cat and mouse, of finding an obstacle and taking steps to eliminate it, each side attempting to gain a march on the other.

In this game, the Allied planners were greatly helped by the activities of the French Resistance. All along the coast of France, the men and women of the Maquis were taking note of the German defences as they developed and passing the information on to London. This activity was not without risk. On 6 June, even as the Allies came ashore, the Gestapo were shooting French patriots in the prison at Caen.

Mlle Thomas was a member of the Resistance. 'On 6 June 1944 we were at Caen, except for my sister Madeleine, who was still in the prison at Lisieux, from which she was eventually liberated by the bombing. Our father had been arrested and sentenced by a German Court Martial on the night of 9 November 1943, having been picked up by the Gestapo in early

October. We were part of the "Century" network, and gathered intelligence on enemy fortifications, movement of troops, and so on, right up to the moment of the invasion.'

Monsieur Reginensi was another Resistance fighter. 'I was not in the Normandy region at the time of the landings. I was with a unit of Maquisards in the centre of France, where we had tried to attack and immobilize the movement of German troops north towards the beachhead.'

In June 1944 the French Resistance could muster some 100,000 men and women, many of them well armed and trained. The German Army were already making sweeps against the Resistance, and the attacks mounted by Monsieur Reginensi and his comrades often led to savage reprisals, most notably when the 2nd SS Division surrounded the village of Oradour-sur-Glane in the centre of France and killed all the inhabitants, more than 600 men, women and children.

For defending the Normandy beaches, Rommel's main requirement was men. All these new positions demanded men, especially trained fighting infantry and artillery men, men who could hold their positions in spite of what came at them, as well as reserves to back them up and counter-attack when the first rush of the invasion subsided. Most of all, Rommel needed Panzer divisions close to the coast. More men were available in plenty, but Rommel could not move them to the Calvados.

North of the Seventh Army, lay the Fifteenth Army, which had 250,000 men in 20 infantry divisions and 4 Panzer divisions. Allied deception plans, plus the stubborn belief of the German High Command that Calais would be the real invasion area, would keep the Fifteenth Army out of the D-Day area until it was too late to intervene, and Rommel had to make do with what he had.

Normandy was now the scene of frantic activity. Throughout the spring of 1944 Rommel and his men worked and waited, while their defences grew and grew, becoming ever more secure. The morale of the men also improved as Rommel's constant badgering and inspection tours produced new equipment. Even as the Allied invaders were lucky to have Eisenhower, so were the German defenders of the Atlantic Wall lucky to have Field Marshal Rommel. Rommel was not quite the good chap of 'Desert Fox' legend and subsequent histories. He served Hitler loyally and well until he became convinced that Hitler was losing the war. His views were not noticeably liberal, nor was his information always accurate.

On 26 April, five weeks before the invasion, he wrote to his wife: 'In England morale is bad. There is one strike after another and the cries of "Down with Churchill and the Jews" are getting louder. These are bad omens for the coming offensive.'

Rommel had one other disadvantage; he was not lucky. He had the unfortunate knack of being away from his Headquarters when the crucial battles began. When the Alamein offensive began in 1942, Rommel was in Rome. When the Allies landed in Normandy, Rommel was in Germany. On the other hand, he was an inspiring general, who led his men from the front.

Rommel was never an easy man to work with, but he knew his job. The troops knew where they were with him and what he wanted. In case there was any doubt, Rommel spelt out his requirements in simple detail: 'I give orders only when necessary. I expect them to be obeyed at once, and to the letter. No order shall be ignored, changed, or delayed by lack of zeal or red tape.'

Rommel's declared intention was to defeat the Allies on the beaches. His men were to stay in their positions and carry out his intentions, whatever the problems and difficulties, and these were men of the German Army, products of the war machine which had conquered most of Europe. 'I've fought a lot of people,' said Brigadier Peter Young, DSO, MC and Bar, then a Lt-Colonel, who was to lead No. 3 Commando ashore on 'Sword' beach on D-Day, 'but if you haven't fought the Germans, then you don't know what fighting is.'

Although the defences of Normandy were nowhere near complete when the attack finally came, they were vastly improved from 1943 and manned by resolute troops. To overcome them would be a mighty task indeed.

CHAPTER THREE

COSSAC to 'Overlord'

'There it is ... it won't work. I know it
won't work, but you'll bloody well have to
make it work.'
General Alanbrooke
Chief of the Imperial General Staff

The basis for Operation 'Overlord' was the COSSAC plan. During 1942, an Allied Committee, the Combined Commanders' Committee, had drawn up a series of ever more gloomy forecasts for the forthcoming invasion of Europe. After the Casablanca Conference at the end of 1942, where Churchill and Roosevelt finally agreed to meet Marshal Stalin's demands for an invasion, the British Lt-General Frederick Morgan and his American assistant, Brigadier-General Barker, heading the COSSAC team, were handed the Combined Commanders' proposals. The Combined Commanders' Conference had concluded that a cross-Channel invasion, in sufficient strength to guarantee success, could only be made if there was enough shipping to lift ten divisions. There was only enough shipping available to lift five. 'Well, there it is,' said the British Chief of the Imperial General Staff (CIGS), General Alanbrooke, handing the Combined Commanders' proposals to General Morgan. 'It won't work. I know it won't work, but you will bloody well have to make it work.' Trying to make it work kept COSSAC busy until the end of 1943.

Apart from considering the options and selecting the area for the assault, COSSAC analysed most of the problems the invaders would have to face and had gone some way towards providing the answers long before Eisenhower and Montgomery took up their appointments. COSSAC decided on a landing between the Orne and the Vire, but when Morgan and Barker got down to detail they found that combat-loaded vessels, where the men and their equipment are loaded ready to go into battle as they come off, could only lift three infantry divisions, not five, and that the aircraft available could only lift two airborne brigades, far short of the number needed. COSSAC worked and reworked the plans, using the men, aircraft and shipping available, but when Eisenhower and Montgomery saw the final COSSAC plan in the New Year of 1944, they promptly rejected it.

Brigadier Tom Collins CBE had been appointed Director of Movements for Combined Operations in October 1943: 'I had a splendid American staff and I had to work with Admiral Ramsay on the details for mounting the invasion. When Montgomery arrived back from Africa at the end of 1943, he studied the COSSAC plan and asked the Joint Chiefs if they wanted the invasion to succeed. Not surprisingly they said they did. He then said that either the assault or the follow-up forces must be doubled. The original date for the invasion was 5 May 1944, but this request meant the date had to go back ... and he had the prestige and the backing to make his demands stick.' Montgomery relayed his doubts to Eisenhower, asking, 'Will you hurl yourself into the contest and get us what we want?'

The main disagreement that Eisenhower and Montgomery had with the COSSAC plan concerned the proposed weight of the assault. Three seaborne divisions and two airborne brigades were not sufficient to get ashore and stay ashore. As General Omar Bradley wisely remarked, 'You can almost always force an invasion but you can't always make it stick.' The size of the assault area, thirty miles of coast between the Orne and the Vire, meant that the landing would not be strong enough or wide enough to permit the build-up of Allied forces before the Germans could counter-attack.

This was no reflection on the ability or work of General Morgan. His COSSAC planners were fully aware of the limitations of their plan, but the size of the assault was necessarily restricted by a lack of suitable shipping. Shipping, transportation and supply played such a major part in 'Overlord' that it was treated as a separate operation and received a separate codename, Operation 'Neptune', which will be fully discussed in the next chapter. Eisenhower and Montgomery saw that 'Neptune' was simply not sufficient to ensure the success of 'Overlord', but unlike Morgan they had the authority to insist on changes. The invasion was Eisenhower's responsibility and he had the authority to get what he needed. The first things he needed were more men, more ships and more time.

After taking up his appointment at SHAEF, Eisenhower went directly to Washington to confer with Roosevelt and Marshall. He sent Montgomery ahead to London, instructing him to examine the COSSAC plan in detail and make proposals for the necessary changes. Montgomery decided that if 'Overlord' was to succeed, then whatever the difficulties, the whole invasion must be enlarged, both in strength and area.

The point at issue went far beyond the problems of getting men to the coasts of France and putting them ashore. It was necessary to examine the strategic objective of 'Overlord', the defeat of Germany, and the destruction of the Nazi regime, and then work back to the force necessary to achieve that end. The strategic objective of 'Overlord' was the liberation of France and the defeat of Germany. Montgomery's whole plan for the 'Overlord' operation had that strategy in mind from the first.

A tactical defeat on the beaches would stop 'Overlord' in its tracks, but even if the invasion force got ashore and stayed ashore, Montgomery considered that to achieve the strategic objectives of the plan, the landings must be on a much larger scale. He therefore proposed to enlarge the assault force to five seaborne divisions, backed with three airborne divisions supported by two Commando brigades (then called Special Service Brigades), and detachments of their American equivalent, the United States Rangers, plus as much armour, artillery, air and naval support as he could find.

He accepted the landing area along the Calvados coast but, to broaden the area of attack and as a step towards the capture of the vital port of Cherbourg, he suggested a parachute and coastal landing in the Cotentin. This, plus parachute landings east of the Orne at Ranville, would broaden the invasion front to about fifty miles. There would, of course, be gaps in this front, as dictated by the terrain, but the beaches could be quickly linked into one bridgehead by British Commando units and American Rangers making flank marches.

Eisenhower and the Combined Chiefs of Staff swiftly accepted these amendments. Montgomery then proceeded to prepare detailed plans for the actual landings, in his role as Commander-in-Chief, Ground Forces, for the invasion phase. In this he had the support of General Omar Bradley, commanding the American First Army.

Montgomery's plan called for the three airborne divisions, the British 6th, and the US 82nd and 101st, to drop after midnight on D-Day and seal off the flanks of the invasion area and seize certain vital features in the invasion area before the seaborne forces came ashore the following morning. The British 6th Airborne Division would seize two vital bridges over the Caen Canal and the River Orne at Bénouville and capture the high ground east of the Orne at Ranville, as well as the formidable Merville Battery which overlooked the invasion coast. The two American airborne divisions, the 82nd and the 101st, were to establish bridgeheads in the Cotentin Peninsula around Ste-Mère-Eglise and Carentan as a step towards seizing the Peninsula and capturing Cherbourg. They would also secure the causeways off the eastern beaches for the American 4th Infantry Division landing on the Cotentin coast around dawn. The 4th Infantry Division would land on a beach codenamed 'Utah'.

There would be four more assault areas along the Calvados coast. Two American Divisions, the 1st and 29th Infantry Divisions, would land two Regimental Combat Teams on that gap in the cliffs near Isigny-sur-Mer on a beach codenamed 'Omaha'.

One of the men who would go ashore on 'Omaha' was Robert L. Sales from Madison Heights in Virginia, who was serving in 'B' Company of the 116th Infantry Regiment, the 29th Infantry Division. 'I loved England and I have always wanted to get back there, though what with one thing and another it will have to be in 1994 for the 50th anniversary. I was a Staff Sergeant in "B" Company on D-Day, though I was just twenty-one years old, and I expected to go to France with the 29th Ranger Battalion. That was formed from picked ranks of the division when we were at Tidworth. We went to school at Achnacarry in Scotland, which was the training school for the British Commandos and the toughest battle school in the world. The discipline was unbelievable and we were on British rations up there ... if you didn't think you'd ever starve to death, you should try that! We started speed marches at seven miles and went on up and up, and if you fell out, you washed out. But I was young and fit and when I passed out I got a week's leave in London, where you just had to have a good time.

'The Ranger Battalion was broken up just before D-Day and the men sent back to their units. I really wanted to fight with that battalion, and when it broke up it near broke my heart. Anyway, I went back to "B" Company as personal bodyguard and radio man to Captain Ettore Zappacosta, and went ashore with him on "Omaha" beach.'

Further east, the British 50th Division would land at Arromanches on a beach codenamed 'Gold' and capture Bayeux. The Canadian 3rd Infantry Division would come ashore astride Courseulles, St Aubin and Bernières, on a beach area codenamed 'Juno'. Finally, the British 3rd Infantry Division would land on 'Sword' beach, link up with 6th Airborne and advance on Caen.

All these landings would be supported by air attacks, naval bombardment, artillery and armour, especially the swimming DD tanks. On the British and Canadian beaches, the specialized armour of the British 79th Armoured Division would play a vital part, but the great weight of the assault would rest on the shoulders of the infantry.

For the pre-invasion softening-up phase, Eisenhower had two Air Forces under his direct control, the American Ninth Army Air Force and the British Second Tactical Air Force. These were largely equipped with medium bombers like the American Mitchell and Boston, fighters like the Spitfire, Lightning and Typhoon, and fighter-bombers like the British Mosquito. These Tactical Air Forces were to provide pre-invasion bombing and interdiction of railway and road links, plus providing air cover and tactical support to naval and ground forces during the landing phase. Eisenhower also demanded and obtained, at least for the invasion period, operational control of the two strategic bomber forces operating out of Britain at the time, the American Eighth Army Air Force and RAF Bomber Command. The latter was obtained in the teeth of opposition from Air Marshal Sir Arthur Harris of the RAF. These air forces were equipped with long-range heavy bombers, the American B-17 and B-24, the British Lancaster and Stirling, and were busy at the time destroying German factories as part of the 'Pointblank' Directive, the long-term plan for paralysing German industry and thus ending the war.

In the spring of 1944, the heavy bombers switched their attacks to the marshalling yards and rail links between France and Germany, with a view to reducing the build-up of German forces and material in France before D-Day. In this task the air forces were highly successful. By mid-May 1944, rail traffic between France and Germany had fallen by 50 per cent; inside France it was down to 20 per cent of the January level. The tactical fighter and fighter-bomber forces then joined in, strafing train and troop convoys, shooting up stations and rail junctions. In the three months between March and June, over 1,500 French locomotives were destroyed, some 50 per cent of those available. Other rolling stock suffered in proportion.

Another air force task was to assist in sealing off the Normandy bridgehead by destroying the bridges across the Seine. Bridges are difficult targets and all were heavily defended, but the aircraft pressed home their attacks until by 1 June only 3 of the 26 bridges over the Seine were usable, and even these were damaged and under attack. This action was a vital part in the pre-invasion preparation, for the Germans would need these bridges either to pump reinforcements into Normandy, or for a speedy withdrawal to the east if the Normandy position became untenable.

Air force efforts in France were supplemented by the operations of the French Resistance, the Maquis. By June 1944, the French Maquis had a trained and equipped force of 100,000 men and women, ready to attack and disrupt German troop movements throughout France, reinforced by special parachuted teams of British and American soldiers, notably by men from the 2nd SAS Regiment. All this had a cumulative and debilitating effect on the German war machine. Damage that might have taken two days to repair in January was taking two weeks by June.

Henri Lamperière, a member of the French Resistance, was a gendarme in the village of Bretteville-sur-Laize on the outskirts of Caen. 'I joined the Gendarmerie to avoid forced conscription for work in Germany, but I was soon involved in resistance activity. I started by handing over to my friend, Foucu of the OCM (Organisation Civile et Militaire), the arms which the gendarmes had collected in 1940 and stored in a barn outside the city. I was also able to pass on information concerning the movements of German troops and German installations. My uniform enabled me to circulate freely by day and night and carry on my espionage work.

'I was able, for example, to penetrate the V1 rocket site at Quilly on the pretext of searching for a terrorist, but there was always danger from the Gestapo and their French auxiliaries, who were particularly dangerous, and did not spare the Gendarmerie. The complete brigade at St-Georges-du-Vièvre in the Eure, for example, was arrested and deported to the death camps for having given information and help to the Maquis Surcouf of Robert Leblanc at Pont Audemer. None of them returned.

'In April 1944, the OCM in our sector came under the orders of the Special Operations Executive and received two parachuted agents, Capitaine Jean Renaud-Dandicolle from Bordeaux, the leader, and his radio operator, Maurice Larcher, who came from Mauritius. On 3 June we received a parachutage of arms and explosives at Ste Claire and the drop zone was protected by the gendarmes of Pont-d'Ouilly. To give you some idea of the spirit of the gendarmerie I can give you two stories.

'One morning, two Germans from the *feldgendarmerie* at Falaise arrived at our station. They were seeking an evader who had been denounced to the Germans by a neighbour (that happened frequently, alas). I slipped out to a nearby café, phoned a friend and told him to pass the news on to the evader. When I got back to the station the adjutant, André, asked me simply, "Have you done the necessary?"

'On another day, André called me to his office and said, "I know you work for the Resistance, but it's none of my affair as long as you don't implicate me." André himself had difficulties with the Prefecture for having demanded the closure of a café which was popular with the Germans. He, alas, was killed in the bombardment of Bretteville on 10 June, together with his wife and two children.'

Heavy bombing and Resistance sabotage were augmented by low-level attacks from the RAF. 'Baron' Humphries was a British Mosquito fighter-bomber pilot flying sorties into France. 'I was sent to Lasham in Hampshire to join 613 Squadron, 2 Group, in the 2nd TAF, where I was overjoyed to find them converting to Mossies (Mosquito VIs), so I kept my old observer, Flt Sgt Joe Carroll.

'The squadron began operations in late December 1943, and my first effort was on 26 January 1944. We were then on "No Ball" ops, daylight low-level attacks on V1 rocket launching sites in the Pas de Calais. Joe and I did eight of these, collecting a bullet which starred the windscreen and on another trip a very tattered tailplane.

'By March we had to change to night flying. From then on 2 Group was given the job of low-level night intruder work, ready for D-Day, to bang away at anything we could find on the ground. On 11 April 1944, by which time I was a Warrant Officer, while six of our planes hit the Gestapo HQ in The Hague, the rest of us started three weeks of camping at Swanton Morley doing exercises with the Army. Then back to Lasham to continue intruding, mostly over France.

'About three days before 5 June we were given details of the invasion plan and a pep talk by Air Marshal Cunningham. After that we were confined to camp. 2 Group's task for the night of 4/5th June (later changed to 5/6th because of bad weather) and onwards was to search for and attack enemy ground movement in a patrol area inland from the beaches; 613 Squadron had the area roughly bounded by the towns St Lô, Argentan, Caen and Vire, with each aircraft in turn doing a spell of half to three-quarters of an hour over the land. At briefing I saw that my name was last on the list, due to return just before daylight on 6 June, as the Army boys went ashore.'

Thanks to all this activity, the Wehrmacht's ability to react to the invasion was severely crippled before the first invader set foot in France, yet to maintain security and spread doubt about the real invasion site, at least as many bombs were dropped around Calais as on the approaches to Normandy.

The main preoccupation of the planning staff of SHAEF during the winter and early spring of 1944 was to increase the weight of the assault and get the men safely ashore. This was the responsibility of the naval phase, code-named 'Neptune'. The 'Neptune' staff were soon in dire difficulties finding enough shipping for the extra divisions required by Montgomery's plan, and at the end of January 1944 it was decided that the invasion must be put back one month, to a date on or about 1 June. Careful consideration of tides and moon showed that the only days suitable for the invasion – with half-tide around dawn – were 5, 6 and 7 June. Thus 5 June was chosen as D-Day. Apart from giving the Anglo-American forces more time to build landing craft and train crews, this extra month would enable the invasion to coincide with the Russian summer offensive and prevent the Germans moving forces west. It also gave everyone a little more breathing space, for planning and training had now commenced on detailed aspects of the plan.

The hard lessons learned on the Dieppe Raid were now proving useful, in particular the necessity of giving the infantry armoured support in the actual moment of assault, and the need for various kinds of specialized armoured vehicles to get the tanks and other vehicles off the beaches, clear the obstacles and let the landing craft come in as the tide rose.

Montgomery's plan here was highly original. The traditional pattern for an assault was a bombardment followed by an infantry advance supported by tanks. Montgomery stood this concept on its head. He decided to land his tanks first, followed by the specialized armour, variously designed to deal with different types of beach opposition and obstacles, and so clear the way for the infantry in the assault landing craft. Then regular heavy infantry would land from LCAs or LCIs to mop up the beach defences. Finally, up to an hour later, the Commandos would come ashore, to deal with any strongpoints and begin the necessary flank deployment and link up the bridgeheads. This is almost exactly the opposite of the then accepted order, and shows a high degree of original thinking, with an ability to face facts, however unpalatable, and find solutions, however radical.

The seaborne landings were timed for half-tide on the flood, a compromise between giving the infantry too much open beach to cover and having all the obstacles exposed for the attention of the assault engineers. The DD tanks and armoured bulldozers would land in front of the beach obstacles and must clear them away before the tide could cover them.

Montgomery maintained that the tanks and specialized armour would have to clear a way through the beach defences for the infantry. Otherwise the infantry would be held up offshore in their craft or cut down in swathes by machine-gun fire from concrete emplacements as at Dieppe. He also saw that the tanks themselves would be neutralized by the defences unless some means could be found quickly to breach the various obstacles that Rommel had prepared to stop the assault on the beaches. Montgomery knew all about these obstacles, for parties of men were now swimming ashore on to the Normandy beaches every night to examine the defences.

One of the men swimming ashore was Jim Booth, then a Sub-Lieutenant in the RNVR. 'I joined the Royal Navy in 1939 and served on convoy escorts in the North Atlantic for a while. Then I thought I would try something different, so I volunteered for Chariots – human torpedoes – but I didn't get in, so I tried for COPP and got accepted.

'COPP – Combined Operations Pilotage Parties – was created after the Dieppe Raid. Dieppe was a disaster, partly because the tanks couldn't find the beach exits or get off the shingle, and the troops were unloaded in deep water – no beach survey beforehand, you see. Anyway, our job was pre-invasion recce and we did a lot of them, in Sicily and Italy. We went in big submarines which surfaced offshore and then we paddled in canoes to the beaches. There were always two men, a naval surveyor who did his stuff below the tide-line, and a Royal Engineers officer who did the beach above the low-water mark.

'We would put in a peg on the water-line and swim about, taking offshore depths at 25-yard intervals. I suppose the Army chap did the same on the beach. Then we'd paddle back and rendez-vous with the submarine and plot it all on a chart. I enjoyed it – jolly good fun.

'Now, when we came to do the Normandy beaches we had a problem. Big submarines were too big to go inshore, so we had to use midget submarines – X20 and X23 were allocated to COPP, and we had two COPP teams ; COPP 1 and COPP 9. We couldn't get our canoes into the midget subs and they were very slow, so a big sub would tow us into the mouth of the Bay of the Seine night after night, and then the midget sub took us to within 200 yards or so of the beach and we would swim in from there. My CO, Lt Jeff Lyne, surveyed a lot of the beach obstacles, and we did the gradients, while the REs took sand and beach samples, finding mud or quicksand and so on. All this was done well before D-Day. You didn't have to be a very good swimmer, incidentally, but I was twenty-three at the time and very fit. It was a good job and we didn't have many casualties – they wanted us back with the information, I expect, and took care to recover us.'

With this information, plans and equipment could be prepared to over-come and destroy the obstacles. Montgomery had one powerful answer to Rommel's obstacles in the wide range of specialized armoured vehicles contained in a unique British formation, the 79th Armoured Division. This unit had been raised in 1943 by Major-General Sir Percy Hobart, a pioneer of armoured warfare and a genius at training armoured forces. In the 1930s Hobart's ideas for the use of armour had been so revolutionary that the War Office rewarded him with desk jobs and an early retirement.

By 1940, after being sacked from command of the famous 7th Armoured Division in Egypt, General Hobart was serving his country in the only post open to him, as a corporal in the Home Guard. Hobart was rescued from this oblivion by Winston Churchill, who called on his ingenuity in the development of armoured devices for use in the forthcoming invasion. Hobart's machines, popularly known as 'The Funnies', were to play a vital part helping the British and Canadians ashore on the fire-swept beaches of Normandy. The 79th Division never fought as a unit, but was deployed in small groups to tackle obstacles located by beach reconnaissance.

The main item in Hobart's armoury was the Duplex Drive or DD swimming tank, which has already been described. The Germans sus-pected the existence of such a vehicle but until it appeared on the D-Day beaches they had no definite proof of its existence.

The big advantage of the DD tank, apart from surprise, was that it enabled tanks to land with the infantry and support them in places and at times where it was impossible or suicidal for the large tank-carrying vessels (LSTs or LCTs) to beach. The DD could be launched in deep water well offshore beyond the range of enemy artillery and plough ashore with the infantry landing craft (LCAs). Almost invisible till the tracks hit the sand, the DD was designed to give the defenders a very nasty turn when it lumbered out of the waves and opened fire. Around 900 DD tanks, mostly converted Shermans, were used by the British, Canadians and Americans on D-Day.

As well as the DDs, the 79th Division contained a wide variety of obstacle-clearing tanks. They had 'Crab' tanks bearing a huge flail that could beat a path through minefields for other tanks and infantry to follow. There were 'Bobbin' tanks which could unroll a carpet to make a path across mud or quicksand, and 'Petard' tanks, with a heavy gun, which could blast a hole in pill-boxes or through concrete sea walls. They had fearful 'Crocodiles', flame-throwing tanks, to scorch out machine-gun nests, and bridge-carrying tanks to mount walls or cross gaps, and 'Fascine' tanks, carrying a great bundle of logs to fill a shell or bomb crater, and many more. The British built these devices into their assault plans, combat-loading them into the ships in the order they would be needed ashore. They also had AVREs, armoured bulldozers, which could push or haul obstacles aside to let the landing craft in or the tanks deploy on the beaches. The AVREs gave the sappers of the Royal Engineers vital protection at their most vulnerable time.

The specialized armoured vehicles were combat-loaded to go ashore and tackle the difficulties revealed by beach reconnaissance. For example, the first obstacle might be a patch of tank-bogging mud, so the first tank out would be a 'Bobbin', to lay a path across it. Then came the minefield, so a 'Flail' followed to beat a path through the minefield to the sea wall, clearing the way for a bridge-building tank, which then helped to scale it, or a 'Petard' or 'Flame' tank to blast a gap or deal with the pill-box on top. Meanwhile, a 'Fascine' laid its logs to reduce the drop on the far side or filled in the anti-tank ditch. Behind them would come the other armour, the DDs supporting the assault infantry streaming through the breach, bursting through the Atlantic Wall with the minimum of casualties or delay.

Hobart's 'Funnies' were demonstrated and offered to the American assault forces, but General Bradley turned them down. This was partly because they were, in the main, based on the British Churchill tank, which might cause spares and maintenance problems, and partly because the two American beaches were more open and not backed with the small towns that lay along the British and Canadian front. He also considered the 'Funnies' a rather unnecessary frill. Bradley favoured a frontal assault by his infantry and combat engineers, and Montgomery could not order him to do otherwise. Bradley took the DD tanks, which were Shermans, and some armoured bulldozers, but he declined the rest. One thing Bradley did want which the British could not supply were 'Firefly' tanks, Sherman tanks mounting the British 17-pounder anti-tank gun. Only 'Fireflies' could match the powerful German 'Tiger' and 'Panther' tanks armed with the 88mm gun, but there were simply not enough of the 17-pounder guns to go round and equip all the tanks available. The British only had enough 'Fireflies' to supply one for every tank troop, but they proved very useful when the German Panzer divisions began to probe the invasion perimeter.

*

The outline of the invasion tasks now began to emerge from the original COSSAC plan. In military parlance an attack goes in phases, calculated from a precise time on the day and hour of attack. The day of attack is called 'D-Day' to separate it from other relevant days, which are set forward or back from D-Day as necessary. For example: before D-Day, D−1 (D minus 1), D−2, D−3, and so on, or following D-Day, D+1, D+2. In the same way, the hour of attack is H-Hour, and preparations taking place beforehand are timed for H−1, H−2, or afterwards to H+1, and so on.

The date and timing of D-Day was now set for 5 June 1944, but the timing of H-Hour varied from beach to beach because of the tide, which floods up the Channel from the Atlantic to the west. The assault would be undertaken by the First US Army and the Second British Army and the First US Army would deploy the VII Corps and the V Corps against 'Utah' and 'Omaha' beaches, landing at 0630 hrs while the Second British Army would deploy XXX Corps and I Corps against 'Gold', 'Juno' and 'Sword' about 0730 hrs. The seaborne landings would be preceded by airborne assault to secure the flanks astride the Orne and in the Cotentin.

Just after midnight (2359 hrs) on the night of 4/5th June, the three Airborne Divisions would land by parachute or glider, the British 6th Airborne Division astride the Orne, the American 82nd and 101st in the Cotentin. The invasion beaches, from 'Utah' to 'Sword', were subdivided into unit assault areas by a combination of the phonetic alphabet and naval port and starboard colours. 'Easy Red' and 'Easy Green' are still remembered from 'Omaha'; 'Mike Green' appears in the Canadian accounts; 'Queen White' saw much action on 'Sword'.

The seaborne landings would commence in the west when the US 4th Infantry Division, commanded by Major-General Raymond O. Barton, would land at 'Utah' on the east coast of the Cotentin. The 4th Infantry were to link up with 82nd Airborne around Ste-Mère-Eglise, while the 101st Airborne took Carentan. At the same time, twenty miles away on the Calvados coast, two Regimental Combat Teams, drawn from the 16th and 116th Infantry Regiments of the American 1st and 29th Infantry Divisions respectively, would go ashore on 'Omaha'.

At 'Omaha', 1st Infantry Division of the US V Corps were to swing east to link up with the British at Port-en-Bessin, while the 29th Division were to swing west and take Isigny by the evening of D-Day, aiming for a link-up with the 101st Airborne in Carentan. Between 'Utah' and 'Omaha', on the promontory of Pointe du Hoc, it was thought that a battery of heavy guns commanded the ship assembly areas for both beaches. This battery was to be heavily bombed and shelled, then assaulted by three companies of the 2nd US Rangers commanded by Lieutenant-Colonel James E. Rudder.

The fishing port of Port-en-Bessin was set as the dividing line between the Anglo-American armies and was to be captured by No. 47

(Royal Marine) Commando ; 47 Commando would land on the west flank of the British Second Army at Arromanches and make a ten-mile advance through enemy territory to attack Port-en-Bessin from the rear late on D-Day. Port-en-Bessin was important as it was a designated point for the petrol terminal of PLUTO, the Pipe Line Under The Ocean.

The British Second Army, commanded by General Sir Miles Dempsy, would land two corps on three beaches on a thirty-mile front between Arromanches and Ouistreham with an H-Hour of 0730 hrs on D-Day. On the western beach, codenamed 'Gold', the 50th (Northumbrian) Division of XXX Corps would land between Le Hamel and La Rivière, drive west to meet the Americans and inland to take Bayeux.

Next, on 'Juno', the Canadian 3rd Division, also of XXX Corps but later to form part of the Canadian Army, would land between Graye-sur-Mer and St Aubin, and proceed inland towards Caen. Also at St Aubin, No. 48 (Royal Marine) Commando would come ashore, behind the Canadians, turn east and clear defences along the coast, including the strongpoint at Langrune, and link up with No. 41 (Royal Marine) Commando, which would land on the west flank of the British 3rd Infantry Division at Lion-sur-Mer. The 3rd Infantry Division formed part of British I Corps which had 6th Airborne Division and 1 and 4 Special Service (Commando) Brigades under command for 'Overlord'.

The British 3rd Infantry Division's beach ran from Lion to the outskirts of Ouistreham, and was codenamed 'Sword'. The town of Ouistreham would be captured by No. 4 Commando from the 1st Special Service (Commando) Brigade. The remainder of 1st Commando Brigade would advance across country to link up with 6th Airborne in their positions astride the Orne and the Caen Canal at Bénouville where the bridges would have been taken by a glider force commanded by Major John Howard of the Oxfordshire and Buckinghamshire Light Infantry. The British paratroopers and the commandos would then hold the left flank of the invasion area on the heights of Ranville. Thus, the D-Day bridgeheads would run from the high ground around Ranville east of the Orne, to the floodwaters of the Vire around Isigny, then north to Carentan and the American drop zones, and finally to Ste-Mère-Eglise. This line should be complete on D+1, and embrace a front of 50 miles and a depth of up to 10 miles – if all went well.

In this, as in all plans, there were a large number of imponderables. First, there was the weather. An analysis of meteorological records for past years seemed to suggest that the May–June period, after the early spring gales, offered the best chance of fulfilling the necessary requirements for a successful landing. These were for at least four calm days, with the sea no rougher than a slight chop, good visibility of not less than 3 miles, a cloud base of more than 3,000 feet and, for the paratroopers, a surface wind of not more than 15 miles per hour. While the May–June period offered a chance of this, the odds were still calculated at 12 : 1 against. A further requirement for the paratroops was a late rising moon, so that the parachute aircraft had cover of darkness for the flight and moonlight during the drop. Finally, the optimum conditions for the seaward assault called for half-tide conditions around dawn, so that the beach obstacles could be avoided or destroyed, and the infantry would not be over-exposed as they crossed wide beaches.

At low tide, while most beach obstacles would be visible, the troops and tanks would have to advance up to 500 yards, over a quarter of a mile, across a flat beach under fire, before they got to cover in the dunes. On the other hand, at full tide the beach obstacles would be covered and difficult to locate and would certainly cause havoc among the assault craft. Beside this, the narrow strips of beach left above the high-water mark would be insufficient to let all the troops, tanks and vehicles deploy. Therefore half-tide was chosen as the optimum state, but speed was vital, for the beach must be captured and cleared of obstacles before the tide rose and covered them.

Because of the fifty-mile spread of the invasion beaches, it also followed that, to land at half-tide, the British forces in the east would have to land one hour later than the Americans in the west, as the incoming tide flooded up the Channel from the Atlantic. The next great imponderable was the reaction of the enemy. Allied Intelligence, with the advantage of the ENIGMA transcripts of German coded signals, was reasonably well informed about German troop movements, strengths and dispositions in Normandy, but the information on which their estimates were based was difficult to collect, delayed in transmission, and subject to change. Intelligence could never be fully up-to-date, and everyone was painfully aware that the unexpected appearance of even one Panzer Division in the wrong place could have a serious effect on the landing.

Brigadier Tom Collins, CBE, recalls Operation 'Overlord': 'The follow-up force in an operation of this type is usually the deciding factor of whether the beachhead can be held or not. Montgomery based his plan of maintaining the beachhead on the amount of armour that could be loaded by D+3. He came to my HQ in Fort Southwick above Portsmouth and went closely into our loading tables for those first days. Every assault brigade had a tank regiment. All guns in the assault and follow-up waves were 25-pounders mounted in Sherman chassis, and there were also two armoured divisions plus the 79th and the DDs.

'A further complication was waterproofing vehicles for the assault and follow-up. Any vehicle landing over open beaches had to have its engine protected against the possibility of having to wade through three feet of water. This had to be done in three stages because the final stage (water-tight) meant that the vehicle could only travel five miles before seizing up.

'In loading the follow-up forces, on which the long-term success of the operation depended, it was essential to keep the embarkation points filled with troops and vehicles so that returning ships and craft were never kept waiting. The organization consisted of concentration areas in the centre of England, from which units moved to marshalling areas, 15–20 miles from the coast. In these marshalling areas, units from the concentration areas were marshalled into the exact craft or ship loads in which they would be transported to the far shore. Once in a craft or ship they never moved out of it until arrival in Normandy.

'Once the loading commenced each area was filled from the one behind as it emptied, and a continuous process began in which the whole Allied Expeditionary Force, nearly 200,000 men, the tanks and guns, transport and equipment, ammunition and stores, began to move towards the South Coast. This gigantic movement began six days before D-Day and gave rise to one final complication, bigger than any previously tackled – the possibility of postponement which must require a halt and possibly even a reversal of the whole process.'

Apart from gradually concentrating forces in the South of England, opposite Normandy, the D-Day planners had to persuade the Germans that the invasion would come on some other part of the French coast. Knowing that the two best invasion areas, Normandy and the Pas de Calais, would be as obvious to the Germans as they were to the Allies, great pains were taken to hint discreetly, and apparently accidentally, at a large diversion in Normandy, followed a day or so later by the major assault in the Pas de Calais. This deception plan was known as Operation 'Fortitude'.

Obvious preparations for a landing were made in South-East England. Dummy landing craft were moved on the Thames and Medway, and dummy gliders appeared on the airfields of Essex and Kent. Montgomery's coded signals were sent by telephone to Kent and transmitted by wireless from there, creating a large volume of radio traffic for the Germans to monitor. General Patton's Third Army, one of the follow-up forces, assembled in Kent, and their massive tanks and field parks were clearly seen by German reconnaissance aircraft making quick darts across the Channel. This was a shrewd move, for Patton was recognized as a front-line field commander and he was, in fact, senior in rank to General Omar Bradley.

Meanwhile, in neutral capitals all over the world, German agents were receiving hints that the Pas de Calais would be the invasion area and any information to the contrary was part of a cunning Allied plot. Even the essential air attacks were made to contribute to this deception. For every ton of bombs dropped on Normandy, four tons went down in the Pas de Calais, where there were, in any case, many more targets. It all contributed to the massive all-out effort to confuse and disperse the German opposition.

Along with deception went security. From February 1944 the British Isles were sealed. No civilian traffic was permitted with neutral countries like Eire or Portugal, which swarmed with German agents. In April 1944 the coast of England was closed from the Wash to Land's End, for up to ten miles inland. Civilians were evicted from their homes in vital areas and military staging camps were set up to contain the invasion armies. Roads became clogged with military convoys, trains laden with tanks and guns and men rumbled by day and night, all heading in one direction – south. British civilians were then subjected to further restrictions in the use of the Post Office facilities and telephones in order to free the communications networks for military use. All overseas mail, even diplomatic bags, was either stopped completely or subjected to censorship.

Throughout the spring of 1944 the Allied armies were training, rehearsing their assault plans, exercising in landing craft, taking part in exercise after exercise, trying to get the plans just right, waterproofing vehicles and preparing their weapons, honing their skills.

'We also decided to beef up our fire-power,' said Peter Young, then CO of 3 Commando, a unit destined for 'Sword' beach. 'So we double-indented for Brens, magazines and ammunition. We got the extra guns in a few days. Things happened quickly in 1944, with no bloody red tape to worry about.'

Colonel 'Red' Reeder of the 12th Infantry Regiment in the American 4th Infantry Division also had problems getting more fire-power. 'I soon became acquainted with a worry of the regiment. The 12th Infantry lacked 4 .30-calibre machine guns and 8 Browning automatic rifles. Major Kenneth Lay, the regiment's supply officer, told me, "I try every day to get them but all we receive are promises. To give our men training we swap guns around, but this wastes time."

'I asked the General and he told me it was my problem, and when I got back to the barracks I met Major Lay and a lieutenant.

'"Sir," Lay said, "this lieutenant has a boyhood friend in a supply depot twenty-five miles from here. He called his pal, who's a master sergeant, and if we'll go up there tonight with a truck, he'll slip us those guns. Otherwise we may not get them until about June 1."

'"What the hell kind of army is this?" I asked. "*Slip* us the weapons? Get me Lieutenant Mills."

'William Mills, from North Carolina, was about 6 feet 2 inches tall, spoke with a drawl, and was one of the best officers in our regiment. In the regiments of 1944 a Colonel was allowed three liaison officers, who could be given almost any kind of duty. Lieutenant Mills was one of these.

'"Mills," I said, "you'll have to go with this lieutenant and get the weapons. I don't want to send Lay. I'm saving him for a real emergency. And don't get caught or we'll all be hanged."

'"I can't go," Mills said. "Tonight's the night of the Division Commander's map-reading exam."

'"Mills," I said, "I am going to examine you now in map reading. What's the declination of the compass in Nome, Alaska?"

'He looked puzzled. "Sir, I don't know."

'"Well, what is the exact distance in inches from San Francisco to Brisbane, Australia?"

'Mills gave me his wonderful smile. "I don't know, sir," he drawled.

'"Can you tell me the exact location of Hitler's headquarters?"

'"No, sir."

'"Well," I said, "you missed three questions. I know you know all the rest. I am awarding you a grade of 97 per cent. Now go get those guns!"'

At sea there was already plenty of action. K. G. Hancock was in the Channel, serving in the Hunt-class destroyer, HMS *Garth*. 'E-boats were the problem in the Channel. There was always a destroyer on patrol, escorting the small convoys of tramp steamers which sailed each night from London or Rosyth. There were never enough destroyers to go round, so we were usually at sea closed up at action stations throughout the night, breaking down to two watches at 0730 hrs. This would go on day after day until we became short of oil or ammunition, when we would return to Sheerness for a night before sailing again. We had a German Jew aboard working the radio, and he would try and pick up the German radio transmissions and hear what they were talking about. One night we beat off a real determined attack on a convoy. They sank two ships but we got one E-boat as she was blazing away and the skipper rammed her, cutting her in two. We picked up five Germans and two dogs.'

John Brown, a Royal Marine on an anti-aircraft landing craft, LCF(L) 19, recalls the final training phase in the Solent. 'LCF(L) 19 was the first of the Mark 4s fitted with eight Oerlikons and four Bofors anti-aircraft guns, and later the single Oerlikons were changed to twins. Two shipmates went ashore one night and were set upon by some American sailors. One was stabbed. The next night all the LCF (Landing Craft Flak) and LCG (Landing Craft Gun) crews went ashore to seek retribution. The result was satisfactory apart from the fact that we were then dispersed for a time. LCF 19 found herself on the "trots", the moorings at Bucklers Hard out on the Beaulieu River. Ever tried reaching a pub from the trots at Bucklers Hard?

'We spent much time on manoeuvres, gunnery practice and escort duties for smaller landing craft, but wherever we went along the south or south-west coast, it was noticeable that the Big Day was not too far away. We had one very bad scare off Bognor Regis when a severe storm blew up during the night. We sailed into the tide, took in a lot of water, but kept afloat. In spite of the earlier fracas with the Americans, we all tried to get on the big LSTs. They had limitless coffee, doughnuts, chocolate and ciggies. Every day we observed more and more landing craft wherever we went, with lots of troop movements ashore, so we went to Beaulieu and stored up.'

While the invasion forces were mustering ashore, the Channel was the scene of almost nightly engagements between the Royal Navy ships and German coastal forces. Stuart Lasson was an Able Seaman on board HMS *Rutherford*, an American-built frigate. 'In the months before 6 June, the Channel was split into patrol areas, all numbered numerically – omitting No. 13. The aim of our work was to clear the Channel of marauding German E-Boats, very fast and dangerous small craft which would strike at Channel convoys and coastal shipping. I was a submarine detector, operating the HFDF set, and we were able to discover and sink a number of E-Boats, taking the prisoners back to Harwich. We often set sail at night on patrol, and the information of exactly where we were and what we were doing was only known to the officers. I feel that this duty was a difficult, monotonous task, and we were very much in the dark, but on the whole we carried out our tasks successfully and must have played a vital part in the invasion.'

The German Navy was still active in the Channel as the nights grew longer, and sometimes the E-Boats got through. Throughout April and May 1944, at ports all over the country, the ships and landing craft were being loaded with vehicles and heavy equipment, and participating in large-scale landing exercises. Not all these were successful or free from enemy action. In 1944, on Exercise 'Tiger' off Slapton Sands, a force of landing craft carrying American troops was intercepted by German E-Boats, which sank several assault craft with great loss of life.

Kenneth McCaw was then a midshipman and First Lieutenant of LCT 974. 'This was a Mark IV Landing Craft which could take 13 three-ton lorries, or 8 Churchill tanks or other assorted loads. We were sent to the River Dart where the load turned out to be a USA tank support group of lorries, Jeeps and trailers, plus a one-star general. It transpired that our flotilla of 12 LCTs was to take part in Exercise "Tiger". After that we worked entirely with the Americans, subsequently landing on "Utah" and "Omaha" beaches, making about twenty Channel crossings in all.

'During "Tiger" we set sail for Torbay and landed our troops success-fully on Slapton Sands. Our route was inshore of the passing American LSTs, which were much faster than us. We could just about see the outlines of these big ships as they passed us to seaward, perhaps a mile away. I was on watch in the early hours when I saw flames break out on the two torpedoed LSTs. There was a red blaze across the water, reflected by the water.

'We were in convoy at the time and I think unescorted, and we just carried on. Had there been any communication (we had radio silence but kept in touch with Morse Light) it would have been simple for one of the lightly loaded LCTs to be despatched to pick up survivors. I never knew what had really happened until later, when we received our D-Day briefing. We had a full sack of instructions which we had to pore over (and burn those not required), and this disclosed the news of the E-Boat attack and that many men had put on their life-jackets upside down in the water and drowned.'

On 1 June 1944 the troops went into special holding camps near their embarkation points. There they received their final briefing, drew French money and were subject to complete security control. No messages, letters or phone calls could be made. The troops were only allowed out for route marches, closely flanked by Military Police. In the camps they were able to inspect models and aerial photographs of the Atlantic Wall, study maps, and see how and where they were to attack it, with every man and every tank playing a special part. Eisenhower, Montgomery, and many other dignitaries, including King George VI, visited many of the assault units, right down to battalion level, calling the men round their Jeeps to give them some orders or encouragement for the forthcoming attack.

Howard Huggett, then a 2nd Lieutenant, 2nd Platoon Company 'C' 326th Airborne Engineer Battalion, 101st Airborne Division, remembers this time. 'Ten officers were billeted on the upper floor of Basildon House in the village of Pangbourne, near Reading. On 28 May 1944 my platoon left Reading by rail for the marshalling area at Merryfield Airport in southern England to prepare for the invasion of Europe. The 2nd platoon was attached to the 501st Parachute Infantry Regiment to provide engineer support. Upon entering the marshalling area at Merryfield we were sealed in and not allowed to leave the area.

'The platoon was billeted in squad-size tents with cots for sleeping and all the comforts of home including latrines within walking distance. Once we were settled, Lt Jones and I briefed the platoon on our mission including where, when and how we were to participate in the invasion of Europe. Our mission was to prepare the bridge over the Douve river for demolition and destroy the bridge only on orders from the Regimental Commander. We calculated that approximately 600 lbs of C-2 explosives would destroy the stone, dirt and asphalt paved span of the bridge. During the next few days in the marshalling area we packed the parachute bundles with C-2 explosives, attached the equipment bundle parachutes, and continued to brief the platoon on their mission and combat duties.'

On 2 June the infantry went on board their assault ships and the naval bombardment forces, the battleships, cruisers and monitors, sailed south from their bases at Scapa Flow, Belfast and the Clyde. Everything was ready, but everything now depended on the weather and D-Day was still scheduled for Monday 5 June, the first date when both moon and tides would be favourable. The final command 'To carry out Operation "Overlord"' must come from SHAEF not less than 36 hours before H-Hour, so that every ship and aircraft had time to follow the plan. Then there was a pause, while it seemed that everyone in Britain held their breath. All that could be done had been done, and it only needed the word from General Eisenhower to set this juggernaut rolling into action. Then, on Saturday 3 June, only 48 hours before the assault, the weather broke.

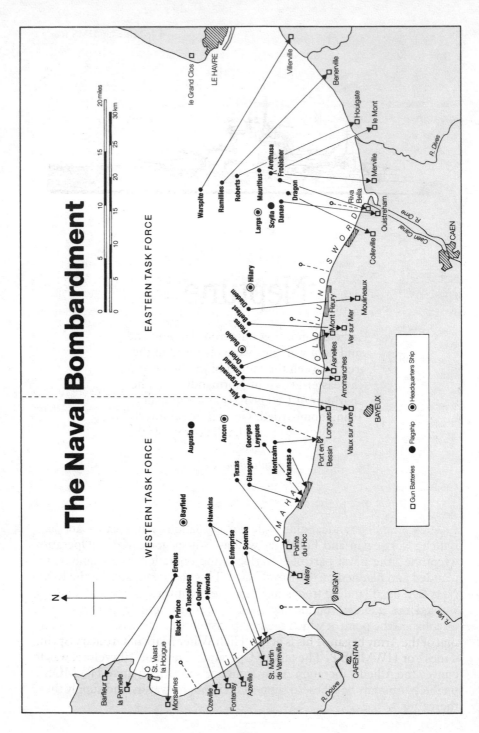

The Naval Bombardment

WESTERN TASK FORCE

EASTERN TASK FORCE

CHAPTER FOUR

'Neptune'

'Early this morning numerous landing craft
and light warships were observed in the
area between the mouth of the Seine and
the eastern coast of Normandy .... The
harbour of Le Havre is at the moment
being bombarded. German naval forces
have engaged enemy landing craft off the
coast.'
German broadcast
0700 hrs, 6 June 1944

Although warships and landing craft of many nations, American, Canadian, Dutch, Norwegian and Polish, as well as British, took part in Operation 'Neptune', the naval part of 'Overlord', the operation was mainly commanded and planned by the Royal Navy. This was fortunate, for the Royal Navy had been landing troops in France for centuries. They had long ago worked out a basic routine for such operations, and in particular had established the point at which their responsibility for the assault ended and that of the Army began. This is at the 'High Water Mark of Ordinary Spring Tides', or HWMOST. The task of Operation 'Neptune', therefore, was to convey the Allied Liberation Army from ports in Britain up to HWMOST on the Normandy beaches, to support them on the way in, and supply them thereafter.

51

To do this required an immense fleet of ships and landing craft and specialized vessels of all types. Of necessity most of these had to be British. To explain this, we must hark back to Admiral King, for the shortage of landing craft which had frustrated the COSSAC planners and was to perplex those of 'Overlord' was one of allocation, not of availability. Most of the larger landing craft then in service, especially the all-important LSTs, were American-built. The British shipyards were at the time fully engaged in repairing war-damaged vessels, building convoy escorts and merchant ships and, more particularly, in making the parts for the prefabricated 'Mulberry' harbours. There was little spare capacity for the construction of a varied fleet of landing craft, although of necessity many smaller craft, LCAs and LCGs, were constructed by temporary factories set alongside rivers as far inland as Reading, 60 miles from the sea.

There was a sufficiency of landing craft flowing from the American shipyards to meet all the Allied requirements, but as the allocation of craft to theatre depended on Admiral King, the European theatre tended to get very little. There is little need to debate this for the figures speak for themselves.

On 1 May 1944, the US Navy had in service some 10,000 landing craft of various types. Of these, only 1,400 were allocated to 'Overlord', the major Allied amphibious operation of the war, and Operation 'Anvil', the invasion of the South of France, planned as a concurrent and supporting operation. This shortage of landing craft had forced the 'Overlord' and COSSAC planners to make continual adjustments to their plan.

In the event, D-Day was put back a month to June, which allowed an extra month to produce craft and train crews, while 'Anvil' was delayed until enough craft could be spared from Normandy to take the armies ashore in the South of France.

The command structure for Operation 'Neptune' was as follows:

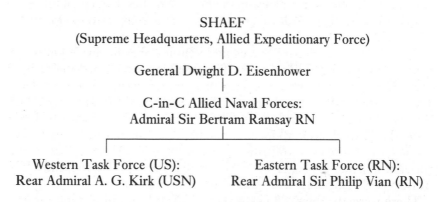

SHAEF
(Supreme Headquarters, Allied Expeditionary Force)
|
General Dwight D. Eisenhower
|
C-in-C Allied Naval Forces:
Admiral Sir Bertram Ramsay RN
|

Western Task Force (US):   Eastern Task Force (RN):
Rear Admiral A. G. Kirk (USN)   Rear Admiral Sir Philip Vian (RN)

The Western Task Force would take the Americans ashore on 'Omaha' and 'Utah', while Admiral Vian's force would escort the Canadians and

British to 'Gold', 'Juno' and 'Sword'. Under command of the two task forces were separate bombardment fleets, allocated to the various beaches, and therefore designated Force O (for Omaha), U, G, S and J, after their respective landing areas. Each beach area had a Headquarters Control vessel from which the commanding general controlled the battle until he could set up his HQ ashore, and there was a wide variety of landing and support craft available, firing rockets (LCRs) or guns (LCGs), or anti-aircraft guns (LCFs).

These various forces mustered a total of 1,213 warships, from battleships and heavy gun bombardment monitors to midget submarines. In addition to this there were 4,126 landing ships and landing craft. There were, in addition, another 1,000 vessels involved in supply and in the 'Mulberry' project, plus merchantmen, tugs, command and close support vessels. The combined fleets mustered for D-Day totalled over 6,000 ships and vessels of various types.

About 70 per cent of these vessels were British or Canadian. The rest came from the US Navy or the Free French, Norwegian and Dutch Navies. The D-Day invasion produced the largest fleet that ever put to sea, a vast armada fleet that filled every port, estuary, roadstead and bay in the South of England in the weeks before D-Day. The shipping for the American beaches gathered in the west, in Weymouth and Torbay, the ships destined for the British and Canadian beaches in the east, along the south coast from Poole to Newhaven.

The 'Neptune' invasion plan issued by Admiral Ramsay for the guidance of his captains ran, with all its various appendices, to some 700 closely typed foolscap pages, a sight which so jolted the sailors that a directive had to be issued advising them that they need only read, learn and inwardly digest those parts directly concerned with their own activities. Even so, it proved a lot to learn, and still provides a fair indicator of the complexity of Operation 'Neptune'.

For clarity here, the naval forces for 'Neptune' may be divided into two parts, warships and landing craft. The warships, which had the task of bombarding the beaches and counter-battery fire against shore artillery, included 6 battleships: the British HMS *Ramillies*, HMS *Rodney*, and HMS *Warspite*, and the US battleships USS *Arkansas*, USS *Nevada* and USS *Texas*. The British also produced 2 bombardment monitors, HMS *Erebus* and *Roberts*. There were 16 British cruisers, including HMS *Belfast*, now a museum ship moored in the Thames near the Tower of London, and 3 US cruisers, USS *Augusta*, USS *Quincey* and USS *Tuscaloosa*.

There were 30 American destroyers, 57 British destroyers and various destroyers from the French, Dutch and Norwegian Navies, including HNMS *Svenner*. Apart from the 4,126 landing ships and craft, there were

736 ancillary vessels and 864 merchant ships. There were 189 minesweepers and 2 midget submarines of the Royal Navy, X20 and X23. Next to air
power, naval gunfire support was to prove decisive in breaking up German
counter-attacks on the beachheads.

The landing craft were of wide variety. Largest and most important were
the LSTs, of which there were 236 in the assault, carrying the tanks and
specialized armour as well as soft-skinned transport and armour. They were
supported by 837 LCTs, the smaller Landing Craft Tank. The infantry
went ashore in a variety of craft, ranging from attack transports, Landing
Craft Personnel (LCPs), Landing Craft Assault (LCAs), Landing Ships
Infantry [Large] (LSI[L]), and Landing Craft Infantry [Small] (LCI[S]).
There were also the support landing craft, Landing Craft Rocket (LCRs),
Landing Craft Guns (LCGs), and Landing Craft Flak (LCFs), the latter
carrying quick-firing anti-aircraft guns. One of the more curious craft
employed was the LB, or Landing Barge. Among these was an LBB
(Landing Barge, Bakery), which cooked bread throughout D-Day for the
troops ashore. Everything had to be considered, from shells for the 15-inch
guns to bags of wooden pegs for hammering into bullet holes on the small
landing craft.

Jack Horsnell was on LBF Landing Barge (Flak) No. 2 in the 26th
Flotilla, heading for 'Gold' beach, the landing area of the 50th Northumbrian Division. 'These rather strange-looking craft were apparently
intended as the original landing craft, but some sane person had noticed
that in order to unload any cargo they would have to reverse before
discharge, with an obvious loss of timing and life. Each craft comprised a
naval crew and twelve soldiers of the Royal Artillery, who manned the two
static Bofors guns.

'After the signal to sail we met up with many different types of craft
assembling off Hayling Island and Portsmouth, appearing like corks out of a
bottle from the inlets round about. Our skipper, Sub-Lt Tilley, told us that
should anyone fall overboard, we would not be allowed to stop for rescue.
Other craft had been allocated to look for survivors.

'The sea was very rough and we had the experience of wallowing in a deep
trough and looking up at the propellers of a much larger vessel ahead, which
will always stay in my memory. During the crossing we claimed a "hit",
shooting down an enemy aircraft which was trying to fly the flag in that
atrocious weather. Our last-minute orders were that we were to land on the
beaches, the guns being used as air defence. What was to happen to us then
was anybody's guess.

'Surprisingly, fate took a hand. We tried to follow our leader, who was a
Lieutenant-Commander operating from a strengthened motor cruiser. He
decided not to land but to turn in close to "Gold" beach at Arromanches
and patrol up and down the coast. The reason that later reached us was that

this officer was trying to get a fix by locating the "Mulberry" harbour of sunken ships, which were, of course, not brought out until D+1. One of my first recollections of Normandy was being on watch in the wireless cabin late on D-Day, and of our skipper looking very agitated because the Beachmaster wanted to come aboard. The Beachmaster was "Dod" Osborne of the fishing boat *Girl Pat* fame.

'Osborne launched into his story of the landing and of entering a house and killing all the occupants. As he was talking about the German Army we found his story rather hard to believe, but such was the man. His progress afterwards was rather chequered. The harbour of sunken ships protecting the "Mulberry", the "Gooseberries", was later used as billets for spare crews who had lost their craft and were available as working parties. The story goes that on seeking men for a working party, Osborne found no sign of life and proceeded to stir the occupants by firing a Tommy-gun down the hatches. This was not appreciated.

'It was also alleged that Osborne, needing a trip inland, hailed an American lorry, and on being refused a lift decided to press the point home with his revolver. This was the last straw and he was supposed to have been sent packing back to the UK. Anyway, here we were on D-Day, just patrolling the coast, looking out for doodlebugs (V1 rockets), and although we were battered by the subsequent storm that created havoc, we found life fairly easy. A few of the flotilla found themselves in trouble when patrolling up local rivers, getting between opposing forces, but as far as I remember there were no casualties. One of my shore memories later was of walking through Arromanches and being halted by a naval medical officer and torn off a strip as I had the bottom button of my jacket undone!'

Had it not been for the decision to postpone the invasion for a month, it is doubtful if Admiral Ramsay could have found enough shipping to convey the assault forces ashore. Eisenhower's requirements called for the navies to land 175,000 men, 1,500 tanks, 3,000 guns and 10,000 assorted trucks, Jeeps and other vehicles in the first 24 hours. To put this in perspective, it might help to realize that the American infantry for the 'Utah' and 'Omaha' assaults alone filled 200 large troop trains. To make room for all the men and their equipment it was necessary to cut the transport requirements of the assault divisions to the bone, but even so, the amount of necessary stores was daunting. On to the ships, apart from troops, weapons, ammunition and transport, went everything the armies might need, including a million gallons of drinking water.

The Royal Navy was also responsible for the design and construction of the 'Mulberry' harbours. The 'Mulberries' were artificial harbours that could be floated across the Channel and sunk in position on the other side. Such ports were considered vital, and construction had been proceeding in prefabricated units, called 'Phoenix', all over the UK since the end of 1943.

The plan called for two 'Mulberries' to be positioned, one off 'Omaha' for the Americans, and one off Arromanches for the British. Each would enclose an area about the size of Dover Harbour and accommodate ships of medium tonnage. The unloading piers were arranged so that they could float up and down with the tides, which in the Channel have a rise and fall of 19ft. The outer breakwaters, or 'Gooseberries', were composed of sunken merchantmen, and these would, in addition, provide shelter for the landing craft in the event of sudden gales. Once constructed, it was calculated that 7,000 tons of supplies could be unloaded daily through each port.

The 'Mulberries' components came to 400 separate units, totalling one-and-a-half million tons with the concrete caissons of the inner harbour, the 'Phoenix', displacing 6,000 tons apiece. To this could be added an outer ring of sunken blockships, or 'Gooseberries'.

Marine Syd 'Sticks' Lancaster went to Normandy on one of these 'Gooseberries', a Greek merchant ship. 'We had joined a Greek ship, the SS *Agios Spyridon*, and we sailed under the Greek flag. She carried her meat live, with at least a dozen sheep on board. I remember the sheep well, for when we first went aboard they roamed all around the upper deck, so we penned them into one area and cleaned up the rest of the deck. The crew consisted of the Greek Skipper, 1st Mate, Steward, Engineer, and about a dozen others. Among the Greek crew there was one other, a Canadian seaman. These people had all volunteered for the job, all except the Greek cook and he had a suitcase packed ready to leave the ship.

'The RN party consisted of Sub-Lt Saunders RNVR, "Dolly" Gray of Naval Signals, one Corporal and five Marines. Before leaving we were issued with emergency kit – knife, fork, spoon, tin plate, etc., plus two toilet rolls, and I remember saying, "My God ... you've got some faith in us!"

'I remember the convoy going past Plymouth on Sunday 4 June, and saying to Lt Saunders, "The people on the Hoe who see us would have a fit if they knew where we were going." We received a signal to make for Arromanches – the signal being "Open Package A". The weather was pretty rough and very dark around midnight, and we were halfway across the Channel when Lt Saunders received another signal, "Open Package B", which was to "Abort and make for Poole Harbour". When we got to Poole it was crammed with ships, so we stayed outside.

'Our ships were to be used as "block ships" or "Gooseberries", to make a harbour for the landing craft, and should have been in place for the first wave to arrive, but owing to the postponement we sailed with the first wave.

'On the way across the Channel, the coal bunkers on the ship caught fire, so to put the fire out we signalled Commander Maude, the Beachmaster, for permission to take her in out of order. When we got in position, a boat came alongside to take off the crew and sink the ship, but as she was on fire and the charges were already in place, they were rather reticent. Lt Saunders said, "That's all right – my Marines will sink her." So the merchant crew was put ashore along with the sheep and hens (still alive) and we blew the charges and sank the ship. These ships did not sink out of sight, but left their upper deck above the water, forming a breakwater for the landing craft. As you can imagine, it was pretty chaotic on the beach that day and everyone forgot that we were still aboard.'

Albert Barnes was on a naval tug, towing one of the 'Mulberry' 'Phoenix' caissons. 'I was aboard HMRT *Storm King* on 6 June. We were one of the first blocks to arrive over there. The gale force winds and the high side of the block, plus the square bows and stern, made it one of the worst tows I had in seven-and-a-half years as a tuggie. We made many trips from Selsey Bill to Arromanches, towing blocks, landing stages and roadways, all in bad weather, until the harbour was complete.'

It took 160 tugs and 10,000 men to get the 'Mulberries' in position, and regrettably they lasted in full use for less than two weeks. On 19 June, a fierce three-day gale destroyed the American 'Mulberry' off 'Omaha' and severely damaged the British one at Arromanches. The American one was abandoned, and although the one at Arromanches continued to function, it was discovered that ships could be safely beached at 'Utah' and their cargo unloaded directly into trucks as the tide fell, the ships floating off again, empty, on the next tide. Although of limited use, the 'Mulberries' were vital while they lasted, and their existence gave confidence to the staff at SHAEF who knew, when planning the assault, that they would have no port available to supply the armies unless they took one with them.

Another necessary invention for D-Day was PLUTO, the Pipe Line Under The Ocean. A force that would contain 15,000 vehicles on D-Day alone and thousands more with every day that passed thereafter, would have a tremendous thirst for petrol. This thirst could hardly be quenched by the use of tankers operating through the 'Mulberries' or over open beaches, and the planners' answer to this problem was PLUTO.

As soon as Port-en-Bessin was captured by 47 (Royal Marine) Commando on 6 June, a fuel depot was to be established. Here, where the US and British landing areas met, it could supply both armies. An armoured pipeline, laid under the sea, would receive fuel pumped from the tankers lying offshore, and later on, the first cross-Channel pipeline was laid from the Isle of Wight to come ashore at Querqueville near Cherbourg. There were eventually four PLUTO pipelines, and their daily deliveries of 2,500 tons of petrol kept the armies moving until the Channel ports were cleared of obstacles and opened up towards the end of July.

The troops were divided into three broad groups; the 'assault' formations would board their assault craft and sail with the first fleet. The 'pre-loaded, follow-up formations' of first-line reinforcements would be on board their vessels in British ports, ready to follow ashore on D+1 or D+2 as the situation developed. Later forces, earmarked for deployment on D+3 or later, were in concentration areas close to the embarkation ports, and they would be fed in as space permitted and the situation required.

The Royal Navy had one other small but vital task during the landings – to mark the beaches. Two midget submarines, X20 and X23, were to mark the beaches of 'Juno' and 'Sword', surfacing as darkness fell and shining green lights seaward to bring the landing craft in at the right place. At midnight on 2 June, X20 and X23 sailed for their stations off the coast of Normandy.

Jim Booth, the COPP Sub-Lieutenant and beach surveyor, was now embarked on a midget submarine. 'As I remember it, I was on X23, which is now resting outside the Submarine Museum at Gosport. There were buoys to lead the landing ships into the bay of the Seine and our task was to put out a radio beacon in a dinghy just offshore to mark the eastern end of the beach at "Sword" – that would be west of the Orne. We went across under tow by a big submarine on 3 June, all according to plan, and lay on the bottom all that night and the next day, ready to come up and put out the beacon on the night of 4/5th. When we came up we got the message that the invasion had gone back 24 hours, so down we went again.'

The infantry marched on board their ships on 3 June, and the western invasion convoys set sail from places like Falmouth in Cornwall, rolling before a stiff westerly gale as they turned towards the assembly area – known as 'Piccadilly Circus' – in mid-Channel, south of the Isle of Wight; but as the day wore on the gales steadily increased.

Don Kelly, then a regimental policeman, recalls the last days before the invasion. 'As a regimental policeman, it was one of my duties each morning to unbar the cells and kick in the boots, braces and trousers which were left outside the cell, but this day I found they were missing, and on entering the cell found it was empty, and after opening the third cell door I realized that all the prisoners had gone! I ran off immediately to find the Guard Commander in his bed. He was highly amused, and it transpired that all the prisoners had been taken away at 3.00 a.m. to join an advance party for the Second Front.

'A newsagent's errand lad rode along the quayside before departure and he was pelted with money for his newspapers by the troops on board, who had no further use for it. Finally he had collected so much money that he tied his errand bike on to a rope and we took it to France with us. We sailed down the Thames and passed a large munitions factory, with the workers on the roof displaying a huge banner inscribed: "The war workers wish you a safe journey and a speedy return." This produced a loud chorus of boos from the troops on board.'

At Eisenhower's Headquarters on 3 June the atmosphere was becoming fraught. Weather forecasting was not then as sophisticated as it is today;

there were no satellites or computers to observe and predict weather patterns, but all the information available indicated that severe weather was sweeping in from the Atlantic and would hit the Channel hard on or about 4 June, just when the invasion craft were putting to sea. All that could be done had been done, but no one could control the weather.

All attention was now fixed on Group Captain Stagg, RAF, Head of the SHAEF Meteorological Unit. General Eisenhower had been getting Stagg's weather forecasts for months, in order to gauge their accuracy, and had built up a considerable respect for his ability. Stagg's forecast for the early hours of 4 June was of continuing bad weather for the next three days, with gales to disrupt the landing–craft fleets and very low cloud, which would certainly ground the air forces and paratroop aircraft. The latter was the critical factor since only air force interdiction could prevent the massive German counter-attacks that were sure to follow the landings.

Time for a final decision was now getting very short. At dawn on 4 June, Eisenhower reluctantly postponed the invasion by 24 hours, and recalled the vessels then at sea. One group of ships, Force U2, bound for 'Utah', could not be contacted by radio and had to be chased and turned back by destroyers. For the soldiers, crammed into the wet, stuffy troop decks, already apprehensive and seasick, the delay seemed unendurable.

The pressure on General Eisenhower was tremendous. Other people could offer advice but the decision to launch the D-Day attack was his alone. Because of the moon and tide requirements the invasion could not be long delayed; it had to go in on 5, 6 or 7 June. The next suitable date was weeks away and any long delay meant unpicking the entire operation, with a great risk of a breach in security. 'The question is,' said Eisenhower to his staff, 'how long can we leave this situation hanging there?'

The storm grew worse throughout Sunday 4 June, with heavy seas pounding the beaches on both sides of the Channel. At 2100 hrs that evening, Eisenhower and his staff met again, and Group Captain Stagg had one slight chance to offer; the possibility that after the present front had passed, in about 24 hours' time, there would be a short period of reasonable weather, with moderate cloud and lower winds, lasting until the evening of 6 June. It was a small chance and a great risk, but the alternatives were equally unpalatable. The ships were ready to sail and if this chance went by, there would be a delay of at least two weeks until the tides would again be favourable. By dawn on 5 June, when SHAEF met again for another forecast and a final discussion, the issue could no longer be postponed.

By this time Stagg had a slightly more optimistic forecast; the break in the bad weather was now confirmed, from the afternoon of 5 June, and it would probably last until the evening of Wednesday 7 June. A small chance it might be, but it was all Stagg could offer. 'OK,' said General Eisenhower. 'We'll go.'

*

Two hours later the convoys began to sail. By the evening of Monday 5 June the minesweepers were off the Normandy coast, close enough to distinguish houses on the shore. The gales had moderated but the wind was still coming in hard from the west, blowing at 15 knots and kicking up waves 6ft high, causing surf on the beaches. The cloud base was around 10,000ft, but some cloud was down to 1,000ft.

Marine Jim Wilde was on the battleship HMS *Rodney*, sailing for 'Sword'. 'At the time of the D-Day landings I was serving on HMS *Rodney*, which was the battleship for the "Sword" beachhead. We had 3 turrets of 3 by 16-inch guns, 6 turrets of twin 6-inch guns, and were bristling with AA 4-inch pom-pom, and others too numerous to mention. At dawn on 5 June 1944, I could already see the outline of France. The sea was a bit rough, too rough for landing craft full of seasick soldiers, and the whole fleet turned about; "Mission Off", so back to port. Later that night we put to sea again and as the day dawned the crossing was more like a mill pond, at least from HMS *Rodney*, a miracle compared with yesterday. The sky was full of aircraft, some towing gliders.

'On arriving off "Sword" beach, I looked at the small craft busily going about their tasks. All at once a huge plume of water appeared right in front of P-1 and the look-outs reported the same to starboard. We were a sitting duck for the 15-inch guns on the Le Havre battery. We had on board the C-in-C, also the Senior Army Officer co-ordinating naval fire power. In all, I think they were too valuable to sacrifice, so we moved out some three miles and started to shell Le Havre.'

Phil Sykes was a Communications Officer on board the USS *Frankford*, a Fletcher-class fleet destroyer and flagship for DesRon 18, a squadron of fourteen US destroyers heading for 'Omaha' beach. 'Our particular assignment was to escort a whole mess of troop-carrying vessels, and supply ships, landing craft . . . anything that could float to the Normandy beachhead, take up positions to provide screening and gunfire support. The seas were not in our favour and if you know anything about destroyers, they roll even tied up to dock. Everybody was affected by the seas.

'Since our ship was the flag ship, we were point ship for the squadron and took up a position somewhere between 500 and 1,000 yards off the beachhead. We were to give gunfire support to the landing parties, and being dead in the water and broadside to the beach, we had an overview of all activities. We were supposed to have communications with a beachhead landing party who would call in gunfire on targets, but unfortunately most of those people got blown out of the water, or simply didn't make it. If you take 14 destroyers all with 5-inch guns firing at one co-ordinated target, along with the 40mm and 20mm, you can create quite a stir. There was a lot of confusion, as everything was happening so fast. You can't imagine the amount of shipping that was present, but we were held up for a time due to several enemy gun emplacements on the high ground behind the beachhead raising hell with our forces.'

Apart from shelling, the 'Neptune' forces had to contend with mines. Denis Froment was an Able Seaman on HMML 185: 'Q-Queenie Mine-sweeping Flotilla left Portsmouth Harbour in the afternoon of the 4th. It was blowing a Force 8 gale, so we anchored off the Isle of Wight and remained there until Monday morning, 5 June. We left late afternoon and started to sweep until about 8 o'clock that evening. According to the wheelhouse chart we were in direct line for Port-en-Bessin. The first glimpse of the French coast came at about 0400 hrs and at 0430 hrs all hell let loose.'

Commander John Robert Lewis Jnr was then an Ensign in the United States Navy on the staff of Rear Admiral Don P. Moon, Commander of Force U, destined for 'Utah' beach. 'Admiral Moon was a very intense man who slept for only about four hours a night, and our ship, the USS *Bayfield*, had been one of the ships involved in Operation "Tiger" when several LSTs were sunk. On June 1, Admiral Moon and his staff boarded the *Bayfield*, and on June 3 we picked up Major-General J.Lawton Collins (Commander of the VII Corps) and his headquarters troops, and also Major-General Barton, Commander of the 4th Infantry Division, along with his Deputy Commander, Brigadier-General Teddy Roosevelt Jnr.

'We then assembled with other ships of Force U and began our trip across the English Channel. During the cruise across we all assembled on the deck of the *Bayfield* and sang the "Battle Hymn of the Republic" and "Onward Christian Soldiers". This was a very sobering time to sing the words, "... *as God died to make men holy, let us die to make men free* ...". We arrived off "Utah" beach at approximately midnight on June 5. At that same time, bombardment by our naval ships commenced, and we also disembarked our underwater demolition teams and rubber boats. They were to go on to the beach and clear the underwater obstacles.

'A few days after the landing the flag ships were visited by General Marshall, General Eisenhower, General Arnold and Admiral King. It was a great thrill to see these officers, and I will never forget shaking the hand of General Teddy Roosevelt Jnr, not too long before he died in action. For three weeks the *Bayfield* sat anchored off the "Utah" beach and the staff stood four hours on, four hours off watches during this entire time. Then, in early July, we sailed for Naples, to plan for the landings in the South of France. Just a few days before these landings, Rear Admiral Don Moon committed suicide aboard the USS *Bayfield*. He wrapped a towel around his .45 calibre pistol and shot himself during the night. It was later announced that Admiral Moon had taken his own life due to combat fatigue.'

Deryk Thomas, then aged twenty-two, was a telegraphist on board HMS *Bangor*, one of the 9th Minesweeping Flotilla. 'Our flotilla could not sweep the last two miles to the beaches and this task was taken over by the BYMS (Brooklyn Yard Mine Sweepers). We drew in sweeps and we had a huge mine in our wire which was being dragged inboard until the winches were stopped and the First Lieutenant grabbed an axe and cut the wire, first securing a buoy to mark the spot. D-Day was already over as far as we were concerned.'

The minesweepers were ignored by the German radar and no shells fell about them as they deployed their paravanes and began to sweep. The troopships began to arrive at their assembly points just after midnight, ten miles or more offshore, quietly and without lights. There was no confusion and in spite of the heavy seas the grouping of vessels at their various assembly areas went according to plan.

Tom Lovell was a Royal Marine LCA coxswain on the assault ship HMT *Glenroy*. 'As a young man of twenty-two I well remember the scene before me. Here I was, privileged to be present with the greatest invasion force the world had ever seen, and indeed was ever likely to see again. We talked to each other and expressed our fears about what was to come, and whether we would be returning. We were all highly trained, but it seemed to me that thoughts of wives, kids and so on were uppermost in the minds of everyone I met.

'When we reached the open sea the scene was incredible, with hundreds of ships, boats and tugs all going the same way. I well remember PLUTO, the oil line reels and the huge concrete harbour piers and cranes which were all heading for Arromanches. There were also huge rafts containing motor vehicles and guns. These were all bobbing up and down in the gale which by now had reached around Force 6. As night fell the Air Force began adding their bit to the scene and this went on all night with more and more bombers going our way.

'We went to our craft on the davits and all the necessary checks were made. We then took on board our charges – each LCA held some thirty men of the Royal Hampshire Regiment, whose goal was Bayeux. Like us, they were worried about what lay ahead, but seemed more concerned about whether we would reach the beach. I assured them that we would and that I would see that they went right up out of the water; this seemed to settle them down. Later I was pleased that I was able to keep my promise.

'The Navy lowered us into the water and we then experienced the swell. On the way in we were going with the sea and it was quite pleasant and fast, for which I was grateful. Our touch-down point was near to the village of Le Hamel, and I was consulting the panoramic strip photos (taken by aircraft prior to D-Day). Then we came up against the beach obstacles – huge ramps made from old railway lines set in concrete, all with mines. We negotiated all these and I then saw the opening I was seeking. I put the craft full ahead and hard to port and we were through. I beached and all hell was let loose. Down went the ramp and all my Hampshires got out safely. I know this because I saw them go right up the beach.'

Able Seaman Sidney Hoy was a twenty-one-year-old signalman in an LCPL. 'Our LCP was a small landing craft about 8 metres long, rather like a small speedboat and made entirely of plywood. Our flotilla consisted of about 12 boats commanded by a lieutenant and we had a crew of 6. I was more than pleased when we anchored off the French coast at dawn. We had been towed from Weymouth during the night by an LST, the rough seas had pounded our craft and we were taking in water. As soon as the LST anchored we tied up alongside it and went aboard up the scramble nets. This was not easy because of the rough seas.

'The ship was manned by Americans and I remember queuing up cafeteria style with a metal tray and being given some splendid food. I have to say that I only had a rough idea of what we were supposed to do, and we could not claim to be highly trained for the job. We were to go in first with the amphibious tanks, closely followed by the troops in the LCAs. Our task was to pick up survivors. By 0530 hrs all the DD tanks had been floated from the ramp of the LST and were taking up formation. The order came to attack and we started to make our way towards the beach, about three miles away. We were not the only group of floating tanks; many others had been launched from other LSTs. By this time the enemy had woken up and we came under heavy fire. About a mile off the beach some of the DD tanks were getting into difficulties. The sea tore their canopies and they sank, while others had been swamped by waves. Some of the crews had gone down with their tanks but others managed to get out and were floating in the sea.

'We had been instructed not to rescue anyone until the main body of tanks had made it to the beach. We finally got very close to the shore, where some of the tanks got caught on the beach traps, others were hit by enemy fire or blown up by mines. Once the tanks had landed, we were able to set about the task of rescuing the crews floating in the sea. Soon the first waves of landing craft were converging on the beach, and from where we were it looked like the landing had been a failure. We carried on making ourselves generally useful offshore for some time till we were hit by enemy fire. I was wounded in the neck and thrown into the sea. I was in the water for some time, and there were many men in the same situation. Finally I was picked up by a rescue ship and the following day I was taken back to England.'

Marine Ernie Knibbs was with 536 LCA Flotilla on board SS *Empire Cutlass*: 'We carried two assault companies of the East Yorks Regiment, and I slept quite well for a few hours on the way over. We arrived at our lowering position about ten miles offshore, and as we assembled at our LCAs I saw the trail of a torpedo pass across our bow. Not long after that a Norwegian destroyer was hit midships, her bow and stern sticking out of the water to form the letter "V". She held that position for quite some time before she sank, almost as though she was putting two fingers up in defiance. I later learned that she was HNMS *Svenner*.

'We were lowered away, nine tons of LCA plus the crew and troops. We were lucky and caught the swell as it came up and so were able to slip hooks first time. Some were less fortunate and took quite a hammering, as one minute they were afloat and the next they were high and dry, still on the hooks. Both hooks must be slipped at the same time or disaster overtakes and you are upside down.

'We circled round until all craft were clear of the ship. It was a good run-in, with plenty of LCTs around us. There was a heavy swell and sick-bags appeared to be "dress of the day" for the troops. With about five miles to go the LCA astern of us was taking in water fast, and her stern-sheets man had the semi-rotary pump going as fast as his arms would let him. He must have done a grand job as I saw them hit the beach later.'

Apart from the loss of the destroyer HNMS *Svenner* to a torpedo there was no German naval opposition off the beaches. The German E-Boats stayed snug in the harbours of Cherbourg and Le Havre, convinced that no invasion fleet would have sailed in such weather. Even Field Marshal Rommel thought the invasion so unlikely that he went home to Germany to visit his wife on her birthday, which fell on 6 June, and to try and persuade Hitler to move more Panzer units to the beach areas.

J. L. 'Les' Wagar was a rifleman in 'C' Company, the Queen's Own Rifles of Canada, and remembers the run-in to the beach. 'Before dawn on 6 June the Channel was black and drizzly, the ship rolling in the back swells of yesterday's storm, but this was truly a luxury trip. The last time our Company had been in the Channel was on an exercise, crammed into an LCI, and nearly everyone was sick, including the Navy.

'This time it was no flat-bottomed LCI – this was a real ship, an LSI, equipped to feed, billet and transport an entire beach assault group, ringed with scrambling nets and with LCAs slung from the davits. We had been aboard her since 4 June, waiting. She would carry us comfortably across the Channel and drop the first of us into our LCAs under cover of darkness, about three miles off the coast.

'Reveille was early on the 6th; it was still night and the LSI was still ploughing ahead into the darkness. I don't remember eating – the Navy may have ladled out some porridge and coffee. All we had were our compo-rations anyway, but they were for later. I recall lining up for rum ration, but only because somebody talked me into it. Since I was so queasy in the stomach, at least I could be a good pal and get an extra shot for a drinkin' man. The drinkin' man was smarter than I was. He poured both mine and his into his canteen, which was already half-full; a little something he was saving up for a party when the time was right.

'Then official noises began coming over the intercoms, people started giving orders and the engines slowed. We got into our gear and lined up on deck beside our designated LCAs. The sky was just beginning to lighten as the LCAs were dropped into the swell, and we climbed down the nets to get on board. At that point I don't remember anyone saying anything. Each man's job had been set and memorized days before, and there was really nothing to say. We knew the width of beach we had to cross, the mines we had to avoid, the bunkers, the gun positions, the wall we had to get over or through, the streets and the buildings of the town we had to take, the minefields, the possible enemy strength, the perimeter we had to establish for the next wave to go forward.'

The only sound that disturbed the night was the steady drone of aircraft engines. The bombers of the US Ninth Air Force and RAF Bomber Command began their attacks on the German batteries and beach defences soon after dark, which came late, at about 10 p.m. on 5 June. These raids had been going on for months now and caused no particular alarm ashore, and the sailors and soldiers on the invasion craft hardly looked up as the bombers flew over.

Kenneth Beard was flying in one of these aircraft. 'I was rear gunner in a Halifax "G-George", registration LV825, which took off from Melbourne (York) aerodrome at 0235 hrs on the morning of 6 June, and landed at 0425 hrs. Our target had been Mont Fleury, and I was flying with Squadron-Leader R. Kennedy, "A" Flight Commander, as pilot.

'We had been given no inkling of the nature of the mission, but as an experienced crew we suspected something special by virtue of the fact that we had an extra briefing prior to take-off. Even at the second briefing we were not told that this was the day we had all been waiting for, and the only luxury the Intelligence officer permitted himself was to announce, with typical British irony, "If you have to jettison any bombs please don't do it in the Channel as there will probably be a few extra ships around!"

'Weather to the target was good and there was no evidence of German fighters or flak, but what stands out in my memory is the sight of a vast armada of ships below us. Our aircraft intercom was swamped, for disregarding all intercom discipline we virtually shrieked our delight, but we had to confess to each other later on that we were aware of the odd tear trickling into the flying helmet, and this from a hardened, experienced air crew.

'This was a very special trip for us as a crew who had flown together for thirty operations, most of them against heavily defended targets, but this was our final flight of our tour, so as we taxied to dispersal we bandied plans for our forthcoming celebrations. We weren't at all surprised to find the Squadron Commander waiting for us at dispersal, as it was usual for him to greet a crew returning from a final operation. Imagine our dismay when, instead of the congratulations we had expected, we were told that Air Ministry had requested all squadrons to provide as many aircraft as possible to give assistance to the landing troops, and that he would appreciate our "volunteering" to do another flight.

'We understood that "volunteering" was something in the nature of a euphemism, and so 2230 hrs saw us taking off, with the rest of 10 Squadron, for a target further afield, namely St Lô.'

Squadron Leader Douglas Millikin was then a Lancaster bomber pilot in 50 Squadron of 5 Group. 'Any man who says he wasn't frightened during the war either has no imagination or is a bloody liar. We took off from Skellington at about 3.30 a.m. on 6 June. We came over Didcot and crossed the coast near Bournemouth to bomb a battery of 15-inch guns near Cherbourg. We were not told that this was D-Day, and the Met. men had made a balls of it, offering cloud over England and clear skies over the French coast. It was as clear as a bell over England and got thicker as we crossed the English coast.

'Our bombing speed was 150 knots and we broke through the cloud at 2,500ft and saw the target indicators going down dead ahead. The bomb aimer said, "Left, left," and then "Bombs gone." In that half minute we saw a Lancaster go down, and only waited for the flash of the photo before we got up into the cloud again. Over England we could see the lights of the glider aircraft going over – hundreds of them. On the next night, 6 June, we went to Argentan to crater the crossroads and fields around the town to stop the Panzers getting up to the beaches. I did 45 operations in all and 50 was *the* Squadron for me – a wonderful Squadron. My second son is now in the RAF and has two commendations for valuable service in the air; one for the Falklands and one for the Gulf.'

Corporal Bill Fox of the RAF was at sea with the men of his airfield construction unit, preparing to go ashore in Normandy and build landing strips. 'We sailed with the Canadians, many of whom had cut their hair like Mohican Indians and carried hunting knives in their boots, saying they wanted to avenge Dieppe. On the way to the dock we stopped in Fareham, where a lady came out of a house and offered me a bath, which I was very grateful for. We then boarded an LCT at Gosport, and I remember sailing past the Needles on the way to France. I did not sleep well and awoke to see ships everywhere, and then a coastline dimly ahead towards which the LST was steaming hard. Then the ramp went down and more orders came – "Follow the white tapes as anywhere else is mined." I found out later that this was "Juno" beach and we had landed near the village of Courseulles.'

Ron Colledge was a Flight Lieutenant Navigator in a Stirling bomber of 218 Squadron. 'My pilot was Flight Lieutenant John McAllister, an Australian, and we carried out one of the spoof invasions designed to make the Germans think that the real invasion would take place off Calais. For this operation each aircraft carried three navigators. One to operate the Gee-box, one to operate the GH, and the third to carry out the dead reckoning. We took off around midnight to a point in the English Channel east of the Isle of Wight.

'At that point the Gee-navigator was responsible for flying an accurate course towards Cap Gris Nez, while the GH operators were in charge of dropping bundles of "window" (radar distorting foil) out of the windows and chutes. The effect of this was to simulate a convoy approaching the French coast at a speed of five knots. I can't remember how many different GH co-ordinates had to be set to get the required effect, but it seemed a hell of a lot at the time. I see from my log book that it took four-and-a-half hours, and I can still hear the radio announcing that the invasion had started as we sat down to our bacon and eggs in the mess at about 6.30 a.m. on 6 June.'

The news of the landings had also spread to the French Resistance, as André Heintz recalls: 'I was a member of the Underground and had been warned of the approach of D-Day by hearing the first message, "*L'heure du combat viendra*" on the crystal set in my cellar on 31 May. I heard the last order, "*Les dés sont sur le tapis*" – "The dice are on the table", the signal for general sabotage, at 8.45 p.m. on 5 June. I was in Caen on D-Day, and after the second message I passed the word on and spent the rest of the night watching the Headquarters of the German 716th Infantry Division, which was near where I lived in Caen. The first despatch rider only reached the HQ at 3.30 a.m. We had heard many planes going overhead from 11.20 p.m. onwards, and after 3.30 a.m. the rumbling of intense shelling from the sea. I think the Royal Navy were destroying the defences, the positions and shapes of which I had sent over to England during the previous months.

'My mother had been unable to sleep because of the noise and said, "It must be the landings, André." I told her, "We had better get some bottles filled with drinking water because we don't know how long drinking water will be available." In fact, ten days later we were still drinking some of the water and it was still the best of our supply. My mother cooked some potatoes, because she said the gas would soon be cut off, and three days later it was, and not put on again for six months.'

Just before midnight there came another sound, deeper, more constant, ominous, the steady roar of countless aircraft flying over the darkened fleets, like a great swarm of bees. Hundreds of aircraft were coming over now, flying very low across the sea, but these were transport aircraft and they carried not bombs but men.

At midnight on the night of 5/6 June, by parachute or glider, 20,000 Allied soldiers from three Airborne Divisions began to land in Normandy. Operation 'Overlord' had started and D-Day had begun.

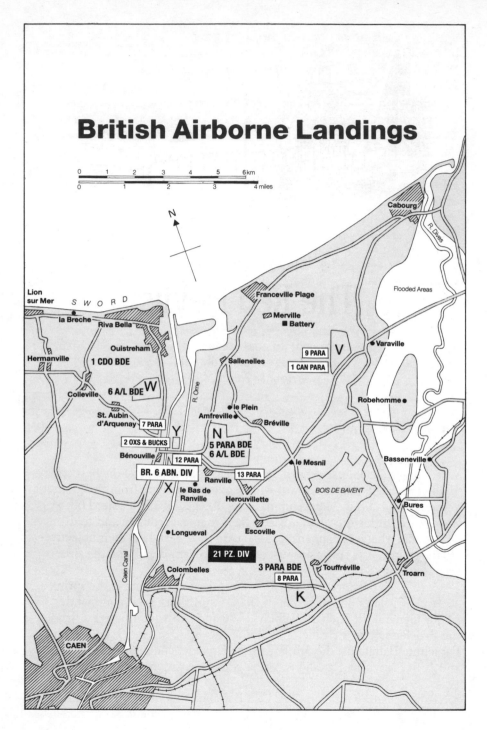

British Airborne Landings

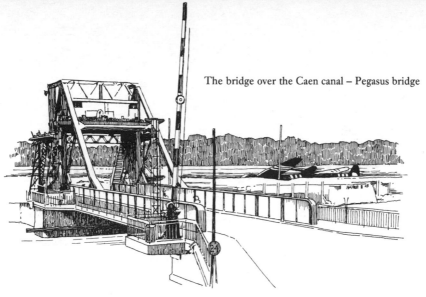

The bridge over the Caen canal – Pegasus bridge

CHAPTER FIVE

The Red Devils

'Gentlemen, do not be daunted if chaos
reigns: it undoubtedly will.'
Brigadier James Hill
3rd Parachute Brigade
6th Airborne Division

War is unpredictable. It is a sad fact but true, that in spite of the best efforts
of all concerned, matters in war will frequently go awry from the moment
the first shot is fired. Many commanding officers, like Brigadier Hill, were
well aware of this fact, had advised their men accordingly and told them
what to do; whatever happens, press on, do their best, take their objectives,
kill the enemy. As a rule plans just don't work in any detail, and the airborne
operations of D-Day went wrong from the start.

The British 6th Airborne Division was raised in England in the spring of
1943. A year later, in the spring of 1944, 6th Airborne was commanded by
Major General Sir Richard 'Windy' Gale and consisted of three brigades,
the 3rd Parachute Brigade, containing the 8th, 9th and 1st (Canadian)
Parachute Battalions; the 5th Parachute Brigade, containing the 7th, 12th
and 13th Parachute Battalions, and a glider formation, the 6th Airlanding
Brigade, made up of the 2nd Battalion, the Ox & Bucks, the 1st Battalion
the Royal Ulster Rifles, and the 12th Battalion the Devonshire Regiment.

An Airlanding Brigade consisted of three infantry battalions turned over to an airborne role and landing by glider. Allied glider formations at this time flew in three main types, the 'Horsa', a 24-seater, the 'Hamilcar', which could take 40 men, and the 'Waco', which was more popular with the Americans. For the airborne operations of the day the glider was essential. Only in gliders could guns, jeeps, scout cars, heavy ammunition and even tanks be transported. The glider needed no runway to land on, and was, on landing anyway, strictly expendable; most gliders crashed. They could stand up to very rough treatment but needed skilled handling. The British gliders were piloted by men of the Glider Pilot Regiment, a regiment of sergeants trained in infantry fighting and ready, once their passengers were landed, to join them in fighting the enemy.

The plan for 6th Airborne on D-Day called for the men to be dropped on the eastern flank of the seaborne landings. The drop zones (DZs) chosen were on the high ground around Ranville, between the Rivers Orne and Dives. Here they were given three main tasks: first, to secure the bridges over the River Orne and the Caen Canal at Bénouville and secure the Ranville heights to the east; second, to destroy the bridges over the flooded River Dives, 8km beyond the drop zone, at Bures, Robehomme, Troarn and Varaville, to seal off the bridgehead against counter-attacks; third, and perhaps most daunting of all, to destroy the 155mm guns of the Merville Battery at Franceville-Plage. The guns of Merville enfiladed the beachhead to the west and could easily sink the invasion shipping, destroying men and stores offshore.

This part of the Normandy coast was defended by the German 716th Infantry Division, commanded by Lt-General Wilhelm Richter. The 716th was a second-rank formation, up to strength but poorly equipped, especially regarding transport. To the east lay another German infantry division, the 711th, which was in a similar state of readiness. Far more formidable was the 21st Panzer Division which lay south of Caen and could be expected to move against the Allied flank as soon as the Allies were ashore.

The task for 6th Airborne, therefore, was a difficult and dangerous one. It exposed them to almost certain attack from an armoured division, the type of attack that lightly equipped paratroopers were least able to deal with, and if their heavy equipment and anti-tank guns should fail to arrive, or the seaborne link be delayed, they stood in considerable danger.

Most of the men of the 6th Airborne had not been in action before and were as untried as the division itself. They had, however, been intensively trained for their tasks and were confident in their ability to overcome any difficulty they might encounter. Their commander, General Gale, had spelt out their job in simple terms: 'What you get by stealth and guts,' he said, 'you must hold with skill and determination.'

The first task, the securing of the bridges over the Orne and the Caen Canal, was allocated to the 5th Parachute Brigade, landing to the north of

Ranville and clearing landing grounds for the Advanced Headquarters and anti-tank guns that would arrive later by glider. For the actual capture of the bridges they had under command a glider force of 180 men from the 2nd Oxfordshire and Buckinghamshire Light Infantry and from 249 Field Company Royal Engineers, commanded by Major John Howard. This force would take the bridges at midnight on 5/6th June by *coup-de-main*.

Major Howard's plan was to crash-land his glider force beside the bridges and overwhelm the defenders before the shock of their arrival wore off. This plan appeared to suffer a setback some days before the invasion when anti-invasion posts sprouted in the fields around the bridges, but his glider pilots were not a bit disconcerted. They considered they could use the posts to run the glider wings against and slow their landing speed.

Sergeant James Wallwork and his co-pilot, John Ainsworth, were selected as the crew of the first glider to land. They and the other five crews started training for this operation in March 1944, flying out of Netheravon in Wiltshire, and Sergeant Wallwork recalls the training: 'No word as to why, in the usual glider pilot style, but on arrival we were addressed by Colonel George Chatterton who pointed out a couple of triangles on the airfield marked with broad white tape. Not very big but apparently, in his judgement, big enough. "You will be towed," said the Colonel, "at one-minute intervals to 4,000 feet, which will take about one hour. You will then release three miles away at a point decided by your tug Nos 1, 2 and 3 will land in this one, making a right-hand circuit, and 4, 5 and 6 in t'other, from a left-hand circuit. Now, hop off for lunch. All gliders are ready and assembled on the towpath. Take-off 1300 hours."' All six crews landed within the taped-off areas.

Another of the six glider pilots involved was Staff Sergeant Roy Howard. 'For the next phase, a formation of trees close to the east side of Netheravon Airfield had been selected. Each day the 6 chosen glider crews, 3 from "B" Squadron and 3 from "C" Squadron, were towed from Tarrant on the same height and course and pull-off point to simulate the operation's requirements, of which we still knew nothing. Three gliders would land in two very small fields. RAF ground crews were there to get the "Horsas" back to Netheravon Airfield and service them, but we could only do one of these "Deadstick" landings each day.

'The operation required that the three gliders attacking the river bridge had to shed height as quickly as possible, whereas the three gliders attacking the canal bridge were to carry out a longer and more orthodox approach. Our three gliders had only about half the distance to fly, although from the same height of 6,000 ft, and in order to lose so much height in sufficient time, we had to apply full flap as soon as we released. As soon as we cast off, our Halifax tugs were to continue straight and drop bombs on Caen.

'By this time we were training at night, at first with a few lights on the ground, but as our landings became more precise these were removed and we were told to do spot-on landings in these small fields with no lights or aids of any kind. At first I thought that it could not be done, but after one or two hairy missions we found that it could.'

For the first of the practice landings the crews flew in empty gliders, but Sergeant Wallwork recalls how this changed: 'Air Vice Marshal Sir Leslie Hollinghurst, who exercised overall Group Command, had expressly forbidden any live-load or passengers on the "Deadstick" practice flights. We graduated to half-load and then full-load. The latter comprising a Bailey bridge which filled the "Horsa" and finished with a steel cross-beam directly behind the two pilots at neck level. We all flew very, very carefully that night, haunted by visions of Madame Guillotine and said, "No thanks." In all we practised our "Deadstick" routine 42 times, so we should have been – and were – bloody good at it by June 1944.'

At the end of May 1944, the glider crews met their passengers – Major John Howard and his small group of infantry. Roy Howard again: 'On 28 May we met our load of Major Howard and his Ox & Bucks Light Infantry, and in my case Lieutenant Fox and his men. Then followed the most intensive briefing on the military side of the operation, greatly aided by an elaborate sand-table model. This showed every detail of the terrain with all the trees, and of course, the river and canal with its bridges, though we did not know where it actually was until about two days before D-Day.'

Lieutenant David Wood, one of the platoon commanders, also recalls the briefings. 'The company was increased to six platoons by the addition of two from "B" Company and moved into a sealed transit camp on 27 May 1944. There the officers were briefed on 28 May and the men on the 30th. We had a really marvellous model on which every house, slit trench and even tree in the landing zone was shown. We even knew the name of the English-speaking café proprietor near the canal bridge. We were not told where the bridges were but an issue of francs in our escape kit gave us a clue to the country concerned!'

Like most other airborne operations that night, Howard's task did not go entirely to plan. Of the 6 gliders, 4 landed on target, close to the canal and river bridges. One landed half a mile away, and 1 beside a totally different river eight miles away. There were still enough men at Bénouville to do the job and James Wallwork describes the attack: 'We took off at 2245 hrs through low cloud and into the clear at 6,000ft over the Channel, avoiding the Navy – that most trigger-happy service – who had done their best to shoot us down on our way to Sicily the year before.

'The troops, encouraged by Major Howard, sang and (thank heaven) none was airsick. We were right on time and dead on target, thanks to our tug crew, and we saw the French coast in plenty of time to get set. Five, four, three, two, one, Cheers! Cast off! Up with the nose to reduce speed while turning to Course I. That's when the singing stopped. We came in on the final leg at 90 miles per hour and touched down, crashing through several fences in the process and coming to a final stop half way up the river embankment.

'We made an awful noise but it seemed not to have bothered the German sentries who perhaps thought that part of a shot-down bomber had landed. Exactly one minute later No. 2 arrived, followed by No. 3, justifying all those "Deadstick" training flights.

'There was only one casualty on landing. The Bren gunner in No. 2 glider was thrown out and drowned in the pond in our field, about which everyone seemed to have avoided asking daft questions during briefing. Johnnie and I revived in a few minutes and with the aid of a medic I managed to crawl free of the debris, but it required two of us to drag Johnnie out. Nothing was broken except an ankle and a badly sprained pair of knees for Johnnie. The medic took him to the ditch which had been designated the Regimental Aid Post. That was the last I saw of him until back in the squadron several weeks later. I had taken a header through the Perspex nose and was bleeding from a head cut. Blood had congealed quickly in my right eye socket and I thought all night that I had only one eye left.'

Sergeant Roy Howard, heading for the Orne bridge, also had a successful crossing. 'We were at 1,200 ft and there below us the canal and river lay like silver, instantly recognizable. Orchards and woods lay as darker patches on a dark and foreign soil. "It's all right now, Fred, I can see where we are," I said. I thought that it all looked so exactly like the sand-table model that I had the strange feeling I had been there before. I took off the flaps for a moment to slow our headlong descent and to ensure we had sufficient height. I put them back on as we shot towards the line of trees over which I had to pass, not by 50ft or we should overshoot and be crushed as we hit the embankment which I knew was at the end of our field.

'I had to just miss and scrape over the tree-tops as we deployed the parachute brake specially fitted to the rear of the glider in order to shorten our landing run to the minimum. Up with the nose and then the heavy rumble of the main wheels as we touched down a few minutes after midnight close to the river bridge. "You are in the right place, sir," I shouted to Lieutenant Fox, who seemed both happy and surprised at the same time. With a drumming and crash of army boots, he and his men disappeared into the night.

'It was only much later that we learned that No. 5 had undershot by some 400 yards, while No. 4, due to the tug navigator's error, was ten miles away, busy capturing a bridge on the wrong river. Realizing their error they were later to fight their way through the night to our bridge, an astonishing feat of skill and determination in itself.'

Major John Howard's small group scrambled out of their gliders and charged for the bridge. A white phosphorus grenade was thrown at the pill-box guarding the approaches, quickly followed by a grenade through a gun port. There was no time for the bridge guard to deploy fully, although the German NCO in charge did manage to get off a burst of machine-gun fire, killing Lt Brotheridge, the first British soldier to die on D-Day. The bridge was in Allied hands within minutes, the Royal Engineers then searching for and dismantling its demolition charges.

David Wood and his men flew in Glider No. 3. 'Quite suddenly, one of the pilots shouted, "Christ! There's the bridge," and we were descending for a rough and bumpy landing at about 90 m.p.h. with the skids throwing up sparks from flints in the ground. We thought they were rounds of tracer and that we were already under fire. The impact of landing broke the glider's back and I was pitched out through the side. I collected myself and my canvas bucket with its grenades still intact, which says something for the boys who designed the safety factor in those grenades. I reported to John Howard and pushed on across the road to clear the inner defences.

'The enemy had by this time come to life and Don Brotheridge was killed as he led his platoon on the far side of the Canal bridge. We were all a bit dazed but acted more or less automatically. There was a good deal too much firing and shouting, which is fairly typical of troops in action for the first time. I heard the success signals "Ham and Jam" on the radio before being sent for by my company commander. As I went towards him in the dark I was hit in the leg by a burst of fire, which also caught my platoon sergeant and my runner. I regret to say there were no heroics, although I had heard about folk who can run around on only one leg. I found I simply fell down and couldn't get up. My platoon medical orderly gave me a shot of morphia, applied a rifle splint and found my flask in my hip pocket. I always claim that I lasted 25 minutes in action, but I really cannot be sure how long it was.'

With both bridges in Allied hands, Major Howard and his small band dug in to await reinforcements. These were to come from Brigadier Nigel Poett's 5th Parachute Brigade. This brigade had been given the tasks of consolidating the capture of the two bridges and establishing a bridgehead both for further glider landings and against German counter-attacks. They were to be reinforced by Commando units from Lord Lovat's 1st Special Service (Commando) Brigade landing on 'Sword' beach, west of Ouistreham, six miles away, just after dawn.

Brigadier Poett hit the ground twenty minutes after midnight, but his brigade was well scattered. Strong westerly winds had carried 5th Parachute Brigade's pathfinders well away from their designated drop zone and over to the east. With no time to march back they set up their beacons where they were, with the result that the brigade main force, their aircraft harassed by anti-aircraft fire, landed well to the east and were unable to get back to the bridges before German infantry with armoured support began to probe Major Howard's defences. The battalion detailed to reinforce Howard's group, the 7th Parachute Battalion, could muster only 300 men to support the defenders at the bridges. This was just enough for the moment, and as the night wore on more 7th Battalion paratroopers arrived, trickling in alone or in small groups, obeying the old military dictum of 'when in doubt, head for the sound of the gunfire'.

One of those to drop with the 7th Battalion was Private Bill 'Ernie' Elvin, a member of 4 Platoon, 'B' Company. 'For me, D-Day started in the late afternoon of 5 June, when we boarded trucks at our concentration area on Salisbury Plain. As our convoy passed through the villages, groups of people waved us farewell. Some of the women were in tears; they had guessed that something big was about to begin. We arrived at Fairford in the early evening and were taken to our planes, which were four-engined Stirlings, twenty Paras to each plane. All our kit was unloaded and we then had parachutes issued.

'We looked like a lot of little Michelin men as we carried all our weapons and gear on our fronts. On our backs, of course, was a parachute. Being only 5ft 4in. I was as broad as I was long, carrying as much equipment as I weighed myself. With our faces blackened we settled down on the floor of the plane for the trip to France. If an officer had said to me, "You cannot go," I would have cried my eyes out, and so would many of my mates. We were all green, having never been in action before, but we all wanted to have a go.'

Another member of 'B' Company was Sergeant Bob Tanner: 'I joined the Parachute Regiment from the Royal Tank Regiment. Although an officer came round and explained what joining the Paras entailed, the hardships, training and relentless exercises, I did not catch on at the time. First and foremost was a desire to get away from ruddy Catterick Camp. My whole tank crew volunteered, and as far as I know, only two of us survived the war. I realized that I would be losing the protection of all that armour plating, but the horrors of seeing burned tanks and crews soon made me realize how lucky I was.

'Then came the day of reckoning – D-Day. The airfield, fitting chutes, checking equipment, last-minute instructions, the talk by our CO, Lt-Colonel Pine-Coffin, going to the toilets (they did a roaring trade). Some of us in "B" Company carried rubber dinghies for crossing the Caen Canal in the event of the bridge being blown. Last minutes to blacken faces and then emplane ... thinking about it all still gives me the willies! Engines started and finally we began to move. The plane seemed to be taking a long time before we lifted off. There was not much to see inside a darkened aircraft fuselage, and each man had his own thoughts. I remember deciding that I was going to come back. Although thoughts of death and injury cropped up, I made my mind up. I was coming back.'

The majority of the battalion was lifted to France in converted Stirling bombers. Joe Bedford was a Sergeant Rear-Gunner in a Stirling of 620 Squadron. 'Our aircraft for the night was coded QS-T. We took off from Fairford in Gloucestershire at 2330 hrs on the 5th with a load of twenty-four paratroops for a dropping zone near Caen. As we crossed the south coast the cloud was seven-tenths with a bright moon above. A few miles out in the Channel there was a gap in the clouds and I could see hundreds of ships heading towards France.

'We crossed the French coast, descending to about 800ft, and were met with a hail of light flak which continued all the way to the DZ. I fired back at quite a few but I don't know whether I hit anything. I saw one aircraft shot down which exploded on hitting the ground, and in the few seconds of light caused by the explosion, I saw paratroops going down all around us. One stick was just above my aircraft and just to starboard. I still don't know how we missed them. We made our drop at about 0130 hrs on 6 June, climbed away and made our way home without further incident, although we had to make deviations to avoid other aircraft as the sky was a bit congested that night. We landed back at Fairford after a four-hour trip.'

Private Elvin recalls his first operational jump: 'Stirlings were large and heavy planes and it was just like riding in a double-decker bus, only not so comfortable. To get out of the plane we had to waddle to the rear and drop out of a large hole shaped like a coffin. There was plenty of back-chat and we all had something to say – excitement and nervous tension, I guess.

'When we got near the dropping zone it was a case of "Red light on; Hook up; Get ready to jump." The engines throttled back and it was Green light on "Go" and we were out and floating down over France. It was so silent, only the noises of the plane's engines going away from us. Where was the war? Where were the Germans? Then I looked down ... Where was the land?

'All I could see below me was water. I panicked and set off the air-levers on my Mae-West jacket under my parachute harness. Suddenly there was I, being dragged over the water by my parachute, unable to release myself from the harness. Luckily one of my section was close by and he waded over and cut me free. I was then able to stand up waist-deep in water. We had landed in the flooded Dives valley.'

The flooding of the Dives valley had been noted by reconnaissance but the extent of it was not so easy to calculate once bushes and grasses had started to grow on the flooded plains. Many men, like Sergeant Tanner, found themselves totally alone when they landed. 'I didn't know where I was, apart from somewhere in Normandy. Although it was only minutes before I located our chaps, it seemed like eternity. I heard bugles going, then a noise, and I froze for a second or two. Was it ours or theirs? If theirs, I had to shoot them – would I be able to do it? I cocked my rifle in readiness and it seemed to me that the sound was deafening, till a good old Cockney voice bawled out, "What bleedin' unit are you in?" I can't explain the relief on hearing that voice. We eventually met up with others and finally made the Canal bridge, which by then was in our hands.'

Throughout that night small groups of paratroopers were roaming over the Ranville heights and the plain beyond, desperately looking for their own units, or setting off alone in search of their objectives. Having been released from his harness, Ernie Elvin found himself in just such a situation. 'There were six of us in the water, so we made our way to dry ground, which turned out to be a road. When we got there we had to make up our minds which way to go. We had no idea where we were or where the other members of our plane-load had dropped. It was pitch black and silent, like being in another world. We chose a direction and set off in file, not knowing where we were heading. We had not gone far when an order was given in German and two bursts of machine-gun fire and grenades were directed at us, then silence. I had dropped to the ground, my heart thumping, thinking that after all the hard training I had done I was now going to be killed without seeing a German. I had a grenade in my hand but did not throw it as the Germans had disappeared into thin air. I guess they were as startled as us and just as green.

'When we came to our senses there were only three of us left. Where the other three had gone we did not know; their bodies were not there so they must have scattered in the confusion. The three of us who were left, all privates, decided to head in the opposite direction from the one we had been following, away from where the Germans were going. Had we continued with our original plan we would have ended up at Cabourg and been either killed or taken prisoner. In the event, we carried on and came to a farm just off the road. The buildings were partly concealed and there was a faint light showing in a downstairs room. The occupants had, no doubt, been awakened by the firing. We now had a chance to find out where we were, so I knocked on the door and the two others kept me covered with their weapons in case a German came to the door. Nobody answered but a face appeared at the window. It was a man with a moustache and glasses and he shook his fist and gestured at us to go away. We did not argue.'

Alan Schofield of Tasmania was a Flight Sergeant with 620 Squadron and also recalls the drop. 'We dropped our paratroops at 0058 hrs. I remember fierce flak, a huge explosion lighting up the night sky, revealing aircraft everywhere and parachutes descending above and around us like falling snow. I expected to find remnants of parachutes in the aircraft but only found shell holes caused by fragments. I know that our Flight Commander, a Canadian, Squadron Leader Pettit, was shot down that night. His aircraft was coned by searchlights and seen going down in flames.' This heavy flak, combined with the high winds, dispersed the aircraft and gave many of the paratroopers a scattered drop.

The 5th Brigade suffered nearly 100 casualties in the drop alone, and over 400 men were missing when they assembled next day, though most of the missing trailed in later. While 7 Para were mustering at the bridges, 13 Para began clearing the drop zone of obstacles ready for the arrival of the Airlanding Brigade. They also cleared the enemy out of Ranville, while 12 Para, though 50 per cent under strength, made for the brigade concentration area, the high ground south of Ranville, where they dug in to await the inevitable German counter-attack.

Lance-Corporal George Price was one of those who jumped with the 12th (Yorkshire) Parachute Battalion: 'I had joined the 12th Battalion in September 1943, having volunteered from the Royal Armoured Corps. I was twenty years old and looking for some adventure and a bit of excitement and the prospect of parachuting appealed to me. I was a member of the Anti-Tank Section of Headquarter Company attached to "C" Company for D-Day. My main weapon was the "Projector Infantry, Anti-Tank", or PIAT. This was a heavy spring-operated weapon, firing a hollow-charge round. It was very heavy, cumbersome, and, like others in the brigade, I landed in the wrong place.

'Here I was, lying on my back in a field in Normandy, taking part in the liberation of Europe, with only a couple of hand grenades in my belt. In the drop I had lost all my equipment. My rifle and ammunition, my PIAT and food, were somewhere in the orchard behind me – and I was lost. I scrambled out of my harness, got to my feet and took stock of my surroundings. Although it was dark the sky to the west was aglow with light from the fires in the coastal towns that were being bombed by the RAF.

'I could see the orchard a short distance away and thought of my kit bag. I could see figures all around me and they all seemed to be going in the same direction, so I joined them hoping that I would eventually reach my allotted position. Dawn was just breaking when we approached Ranville, having been dropped some four miles from the drop zone.'

Also jumping with 'C' Company, 12th Parachute Battalion that night was Ron Dixon of the Signal Platoon: 'Fortunately, I dropped on the right drop zone at Ranville, but I appeared to be the only person on it. I hadn't a clue where I was, only that I was in France and for me the war had just begun. Luckily, I linked up with our Company Commander, Major Stephens, and within minutes we arrived at the battalion rendezvous. We moved off some time later with only half the battalion, the remainder having dropped some distance away by mistake. We reached our objective, the Bas de Ranville village, around dawn, where an elderly French lady came from her farmhouse, which was on the land where we were digging in. Not being able to understand the French language very well, I could only guess that she was asking who we were and what we were doing. In the little French I knew, I told her that we were British and this was the invasion. She went back into her house and minutes later came out with a jug of milk and some bread. I had a block of chocolate in my camouflaged denison smock, which I gave to her.'

The original rendezvous for this battalion was a quarry on the Cabourg–Caen road. Those who got there found that very few of the battalion had arrived and, not being able to wait, the commanding officer ordered those who were there to start out for their first objective, the village of Le Bas de Ranville.

At 0330 hrs Divisional Headquarters came in by 'Horsa' glider, bringing the Divisional Commander, Major General Gale, more ammunition and the all-important anti-tank guns. The German defenders were by now fully aware that a major parachute assault was taking place and began to send out fighting patrols and armoured cars.

Colonel Hans Von Luck of the 125th Panzer Grenadier Regiment recalls that night. 'Our position lay east of the River Orne and the Caen Canal. The bridges there were defended by a "second-rank" company, whose task was to make sure that Commandos or the French Resistance would not blow the bridge. Our division – 21st Panzer – was in reserve with a strict order not to move unless released by Army Group "B". However, I made a counter-attack on my own responsibility to support two companies of my regiment who were on a night exercise with dummy ammunition when airborne people dropped on their position.

'I am quite sure that had we been able to make a counter-attack at once, in the direction of the coast and Pegasus Bridge, it would have been successful.

'On D+2, part of my battle group met with Major John Howard – a very good friend of mine today – at Escoville, where he lost quite a large number of his company.'

Lieutenant David Wood recalls one of the first German probes: 'The enemy sent two armoured half-tracks down to the Canal bridge to find out what was happening; one was knocked out by a PIAT. There was a magnificent firework display as the ammo in it exploded and 7 Para thought we were still having a hell of a battle to capture the bridge. The commander of the local garrison, who had been out on the tiles for the night, returned across the river bridge in a staff car with an escort, which we shot up. Wounded and captured, he asked the MO to finish him off because his honour had been lost, but the MO would not oblige. Finally, the Germans sailed a gunboat down the Canal from Caen where it was swiftly despatched by a well aimed PIAT round.'

Some of the heavy equipment was now coming in and landing on the drop zones. Frank 'Snowy' May was a Flight Sergeant in 295 Squadron, flying an Albemarle tug towing a 'Horsa' glider. 'We were to tow a glider carrying a Jeep and field gun. Six aircraft took off half an hour before the main force to prepare the landing zone, but none of their gliders made it to the LZ. We took off at 0130 hrs on 6 June. As we approached the French coast I confirmed with the navigator that we were spot-on track. We verified our position by the mouth of the River Orne, and our LZ was on the east bank. There were no beacons to be seen, but thanks to the model of the LZ it was obvious we had arrived. I confirmed this with the glider pilot, and we all wished him luck as he cast off. As he neared the ground a beacon came on, so he must have been one of the first to land on that epic day.'

Another member of 295 Squadron was Flying Officer Ronald Sloan. 'My crew and I were not directly involved in the night-time operations of 6 June, and when we went into breakfast we knew the invasion had started, as a huge main glider force was waiting to be towed off later in the day. The main runway was crowded with stationary gliders, and at mid-day we were briefed to tow in these gliders to a landing ground in the Bréville and Ranville area.

'My glider was quickly airborne and in the "high tow" position before we were halfway down the runway, and we climbed away to take up a position about 100 yards behind and slightly to one side of the previous combination. Throughout the flight, which lasted about two hours, we were in constant conversation with our glider pilot through the telephone link in the tow rope, and we gathered their airborne infantry had a relatively smooth trip.

'We followed the glider stream across the French coast and saw for the first time the smoke and flashes of a battlefield. The glider pilots had their own maps and knew exactly when they proposed to release. Suddenly across the intercom came the farewell Irish message, "Thanks for a smashing tow – we're off now." Before I could say "Good luck" I felt 8EA surge forward as the rope trailed free. We flew forward another minute for the purpose of getting rid of our tow rope, away from gliders which were spiralling down like huge moths seeking a spot to land. Our rear gunner gave a call, "I think he's landed OK, but it's chaos down there." Some gliders had piled into each other, some were on top of each other, and there was smoke everywhere. Clear of the dropping zone I pulled the release handle and the rope fell free.

'Back at base the airfield looked different. It was almost empty of "Horsa" gliders which had been part of the scenery ever since we had arrived.'

By the time this glider force arrived on the afternoon of D-Day, the battle around Ranville was taking shape, but the 3rd Parachute Brigade, commanded by Brigadier James Hill, had been having problems from the moment they landed. This brigade had three main tasks. First, and most vital, was the elimination of the Merville Battery, a task given to the 9th

High tide on Juno Beach: the Canadians come ashore.

4th US Infantry Division land on Utah.

The Commanders. Left to right: Montgomery, Eisenhower, Tedder.

S/Sgt Wallwork, Glider Pilot Regiment.

The glider pilots. Left to right: Lofty Lawrence, No. 4 Glider; Roy Howard, No. 6 Glider; Len Guthrie (at back); 'Shorty' Shorter; Pete Boyle (at back); Stan Pearson, No. 5 Glider; George Chatterton (back to camera).

S/Sgt R. A. Howard DFM—
B Squadron, Glider Pilot Regiment.

Pfc John Robert Slaughter, Company D,
116th Regiment, 29th Infantry Division.

Captain H. A. Shebeck,
82nd Airborne Division.

Guillaume Mercader, Chef de la Résistance,
with General Koëning at Bayeux,
14 June 1944.

Preparations: the bombing of railways.

US infantry train on Dartmoor, England.

Transport aircraft and gliders in D-Day markings wait on an English airfield.

Troopers of the 508th Parachute Infantry Regiment on a training jump in England, April 1944.

Aerial reconnaissance before D-Day over the beach obstacles near Arromanches.

Bombardment warships sail for Normandy.

Canadian infantry wait offshore in LCAs (Landing Craft Assault).

*Sword Beach, 0830 hours. British tanks
and infantry under fire.*

'The Killing Ground': Omaha beach, with obstacles and bunkers, 7 June 1944.
3,000 men were killed here on D-Day.

Troopers of 508th Parachute Infantry Regiment in Normandy. Left to right, standing: Privates
W. L. Lamberson, A. J. J. Grindo, E. F. Wenzel, W. L. Ulrich, G. W. Womack; kneeling:
Privates S. Smith, H. Pubal.

Battalion. Second, they had to secure the high ground at Le Plein, a task given to the 1st Canadian Parachute Battalion. Third, they had to destroy the four bridges over the River Dives at Troan, Bures, Robehomme and Varaville. Having achieved all this the brigade was to concentrate close to Ranville in the area of the Bois de Bavant.

Among those to drop with the Brigade HQ was Gunner David King, a signaller with 53 Air Landing Light Regiment equipped with 75mm field guns. Like many others that night, David King had a very wet landing. 'I managed to jump but my kitbag was whipped away and I landed on my back in a couple of feet of water. I tried to keep my head above water and to release my parachute, and my Sten gun which was under my parachute harness, was swept away. I tried to feel for it for a while with no success and eventually managed to reach dry land. There I was, a twenty-year-old soldier, behind enemy lines, with eight magazines of Sten ammo in my pouches and no gun, no radio and no rations! After wandering about for what seemed like hours but was probably only minutes, I heard someone approaching. I was so relieved to hear him say the password for the drop, "Punch", I quickly replied, "Judy". This turned out to be an officer who carried a revolver and a Sten gun and he kindly gave me the Sten. Eventually we met other Paras, some heading for Le Mesnil – my target.

'We reached Le Mesnil without too much bother. There was no sign of my officer or fellow signaller and I was put as No. 2 on a Bren gun. My officer arrived that afternoon, followed by my fellow signaller, struggling in with the two heavy accumulators needed to operate our radio. He wasn't very pleased to discover that I had no radio to attach them to. However, a supply drop during the evening replaced the radio, and we were back in business.'

The Merville Battery still lies amid farmland south of the resort of Franceville-Plage. In June 1944 the concrete casements, 6ft thick, enclosed 4 heavy 155mm artillery pieces, with a garrison of 200 men entrenched to defend the guns. These were protected by minefields, barbed wire, and fixed-line machine guns, and their living quarters underground had concrete head cover against bombing. The task of destroying the battery was given to Lt-Colonel Otway and 600 men of the 9th Parachute Battalion.

Otway had found an area near Newbury in Berkshire that resembled Merville and, having had the landscape bulldozed into the appropriate contours, exercised his battalion endlessly in the assault plan. The battery would be bombed by a Lancaster force just before the assault. Then, the minefields having been gapped by Royal Engineer sappers, the battery would be assaulted by the entire battalion. As they went in, another volunteer force, 50 men in 3 gliders, would crash-land right on top of the battery position. Finally, if all else failed, the battery would be engaged by the guns of the fleet. This was a fine, if complicated, plan and it went wrong from the start.

The battalion had a terrible drop, being scattered widely across the flooded valley of the Dives, where many men were drowned. Some men fell thirty miles from their proper drop zone, though Lt-Colonel Otway and his batman landed right by a German headquarters and were nearly captured while still in their parachutes. When Lt-Colonel Otway reached the battalion rendezvous he found he had only 150 men and none of the special equipment he needed except a few Bangalore torpedoes for clearing wire. Even so, the Colonel decided to attack immediately.

One of those to jump with Lt-Colonel Otway was Private S.F.Capon, in 12 Platoon of 'C' Company. 'Our drop was set for 0030 hrs, 6 June. It wasn't long before we heard the order: "We are approaching the coast of France", and suddenly our aircraft was sent into a turmoil with German anti-aircraft fire raining on us. We were hurled from port to starboard before despatch, when a voice shouted, "Stand by the doors – Get ready! Red light . . . Green light . . . GO!" I had always jumped to perfection but this time I wondered what the hell was happening and fell out like a sack of coal. As I jumped I could see the amber glow from the shells exploding around the aircraft. After a disastrous exit I floated down to the best landing I had ever made.

'About a hundred yards further on a group of about six men, including Lieutenant Mike Dowling of "B" Company, were lying in a patch of stinging nettles trying to find their bearings. We moved on along a narrow road when suddenly the noise of a lorry was heard. It was full of Germans so we laid low. When the lorry had disappeared we crossed the road to be greeted by a Pathfinder, and we joined the few men who had arrived at the rendezvous. The final number reached 150.'

On arriving at the assembly area near the battery, Otway found that some of his men had already arrived and had cleared a few tracks through the minefields, crawling out in the dark to dig up the mines with their bayonets. The attack went in as timed, and the 9th Battalion took the Merville Battery by storm, capturing thirty of the garrison and killing the rest.

Private Capon again: 'We arrived at the outskirts of the Merville battery where all was very quiet. We advanced to the assembly point and laid low, facing the four gun emplacements that we could now see. My Platoon was to capture the No. 1 gun. The thirty-two men under the command of Lieutenant Alan Jefferson, who had trained day and night back in England for this task force, were now reduced to Alan Jefferson, Eric Bedford, Harold Walker, Frank Delsignore, Les Cartwright, me, and perhaps one other. Seven men to do the job of thirty-two. This left Mike Dowling with a group to take No. 2 gun, and another group to take No. 3, and likewise No. 4. However, all was not lost. We had three gliders with fifty men of "A"

Company, all parachutists, a *coup-de-main* force to land on the battery and cause havoc and maybe even take it.

'We laid low awaiting the gliders. The first one appeared, only to land well away from the target in an eleven o'clock position. The second glider hovered over the battery, and suddenly the German machine-gun tracer bullets raked the glider which veered behind us in a seven o'clock position, never to take part in the attack, though the survivors joined us later. The third glider never arrived at all.

'Our Colonel couldn't wait. Time was running out and the guns had to be silenced before the seaborne troops arrived. All eyes were facing the guns and awaiting the final words from Otway. He shouted, "Get in!" and Jefferson blew his little hunting horn, which he always did in training. Two blows on the horn and he fell wounded.

'I ran with my mates across the uneven ground, zig-zagging and firing as we ran. To my left I heard explosions and shouts of "Mines!" but I ran to my target. Within seconds I arrived with three others at the rear of the gun. Left standing with me were Eric Bedford, Harold Walker and Frank Delsignore – my mates, just four of us. Eric was now in charge and we threw grenades into the large emplacement. After the din and gunfire it seemed eerie, but after the exploding grenades, voices could be heard within the emplacement and the German prisoners pushed each other from the left-hand enclosure within the gun, across the corridor and out towards the opposite wing to us, with our guns pointing towards them. The last bespectacled German was shaking with fear.

'Colonel Otway arrived with some of the men he had kept in reserve and we proceeded out of the battery only to come under enemy fire from a machine-gun on the perimeter. After a few bursts, and on seeing the prisoners we had, the crew surrendered. Handing over the prisoners to Colonel Otway, we proceeded to pull out our wounded. The badly wounded were put on sledges, which I later learned were for pulling ammunition. We carried the less seriously wounded. In this my partner was Sergeant Paddy Jenkins and Frank Delsignore did the same with Harold Walker.'

While Lt-Colonel Otway and his men were taking the Merville Battery, Lt-Colonel Alistair Pearson and his men of the 8th Battalion were making for their objectives, the bridges over the River Dives.

Transported by Dakota aircraft, this battalion was widely scattered by high winds and enemy anti-aircraft fire. Lt-Colonel Pearson could only muster 150 men and had only one Royal Engineer instead of two troops of Sappers to blow the bridges, and it was not until 1000 hrs on D-Day that the last bridge at Troarn was put out of commission after a Jeep sortie behind enemy lines.

To support the troops of 8th Parachute Battalion, landing by parachute, heavier equipment had to be flown in by glider. Sergeant Watts had begun his military career in 1934 as a bandsman, and ten years later he was flying a glider on D-Day. 'At 11 p.m. on 5 June the six gliders took off from Blakehill Farm. The C-47 Dakota tug got us to the correct area, but there was no sign of the SAS lit cross. However, we released and glided down to about 30ft above the ground and then put the large landing light on to see clearly where the telegraph poles were. We landed safely at 1 a.m. on 6 June, only losing part of a wing. About five minutes later the parachutists landed and escorted the Jeep and trailer to Troarn to blow up the bridges.' Sergeant Watts stayed with 8 Para for two days, fighting alongside the paratroopers, before making his way back to the beaches.

The Canadian Parachute Battalion, making up the 3rd Parachute Brigade, was widely scattered in the drop. Of the 35 aircraft lifting the battalion, 16 dropped their parachutists more than two miles away from the planned drop zone. The plan for the Canadians on D-Day also involved prior *coup-de-main* operations to be mounted by their 'C' Company. 'C' Company was to seize and secure Varaville, especially the two pill-boxes and a trench system that overlooked Drop Zone V, the battalion's main landing area, and a 75mm gun on the far side of the DZ must also be destroyed. Once this had been done the company was to proceed to a bridge over the River Dives and destroy it.

This battalion too had problems in the drop, as John Madden of 'C' Company relates: 'In training we had encountered defective hatch catches for the cover of the jump hole on the Albemarle. The doors had a habit of falling shut in mid-stick, so before the "off" on D-Day, I spoke to the pilot and told him that he must not take any parachutists back to England. If the hatch slammed shut while we were jumping, he was to circle round and drop the rest. Well, after the first 6 got out, the hatch slammed down. The pilot subsequently dropped the last 4 of my men, but twenty miles from where he dropped me. Of the 4, 2 were killed and 2 were taken prisoner.

'At the time I was surprised by our wide dispersal. Never mind, enough men landed on target to achieve our objective, and those who dropped astray helped to create confusion in the minds of the enemy. I am the only officer of "C" Company still alive. Two were killed on D-Day, one was killed after the Rhine Crossing, one died about four years ago.'

After 'C' Company had secured the DZ at Varaville, the main battalion drop would take place, with 'A' Company protecting the left flank of the 9th Battalion taking the Merville Battery. 'B' Company would ensure the destruction of the Robehomme bridge and HQ Company would secure the drop zone itself. However, as with the other drops that night, the battalion was widely scattered. To compound their problems they were dropped at the same time as an RAF bombing force attacked the Merville Battery. These bombers over-shot the Merville Battery and dropped their bombs too far inland, catching the Canadian paratroopers as they landed. Despite all these setbacks the Canadians managed to complete their tasks before being reinforced by men of the 1st Commando Brigade coming from 'Sword' beach.

Captain John Madden again: 'As the wind dispersed the early-morning mist, I could see a faint line in the distance, which resolved itself into the Normandy coast. It was 0500 hrs and we were a mere 1,200 yards from the beaches. I knew we were caught on the coastal strip being prepared for the seaborne invasion, and could see the flashes of gunfire from the distant warships. Following this came the roar of aircraft, bombs showered in astride and behind us.

'The entire coastline was blotted out by clouds of smoke and we scratched pitiful little holes in the earth. Five minutes after the bomb line passed inland a new terror threatened. Low-flying fighters strafed our area. One of the men had a bullet pass through the stock of his rifle as he held it between his hands. Branches were cut down all around us, yet we survived.'

While the Canadians were completing their tasks, Ernie Elvin and his pals were still trying to get to the battalion rendezvous point, having hidden in a barn all night. Once it was daylight he and the other two set off again. 'We could see that each side of the road was flooded, but our only way was to go up the road and into the water. So up the road we went and after about a mile we could hear firing in the distance and knew that a battle was taking place. We then came to a driveway leading to a large house about 400 yards away. At the house we could see what appeared to be German soldiers on guard, so it was back into the water to make our way past, hoping that we had not been seen. Fortunately nothing happened, so we made our way back to the road. About five minutes later we came across a Frenchman and his wife coming down the road.

'The only thing we could understand was that there were no Germans in the direction we were going, so we carried on for a while until we saw men moving in the distance. We moved cautiously towards them until we saw that they were Paras. They turned out to be men of the 1st Canadian Para Battalion who were about to withdraw after blowing the Robehomme bridge and using it as a road block. So into the water we went again, and holding on to the debris of the bridge, we crossed to the other side of the river and withdrew with the Canadians.

'As we withdrew we could see signs of a battle; some Paras were hanging from the high-tension wires strung from pylon to pylon, their chutes caught in the wires from which they had been unable to free themselves, and so there they had died. Late that evening we ended up at the 3rd Para Brigade HQ at Le Mesnil and were put into defence positions around the HQ. It was a very noisy night, and by midnight on D-Day I had still not joined up with my battalion. On the morning of D+1 we were loaded onto a Jeep to take a very hairy journey to the 5th Para Brigade HQ. The two brigades had not yet joined up and there were still German positions between the two brigades.

'I got back to my unit, 4 Platoon "B" Company, 7th Battalion at Ranville at about 1130 hrs on D+1. They were dug-in opposite Ranville church. In the distance I could see the wrecked gliders and the Germans were beginning to infiltrate them. We were being shelled spasmodically. I shared a trench with Private Bushell, who told me what had happened on the west side of the bridges over the Orne and the Canal. Several men were missing from the platoon, but I was back where I should have been, having taken a roundabout route, and I felt safe with my old mates.'

Not every paratrooper was an infantryman. Among the men jumping were engineers, signallers and medics. One of the medics was Lewis 'Jack' Tarr, a member of 195 Para Field Ambulance, who jumped at 9 o'clock on the morning of 6 June. 'We landed near Ranville and what is now Pegasus Bridge in the second wave. We found the glider with our Jeep and trailer and started out for Longueval and our rendezvous. There were soldiers everywhere and, quite frankly, we were all like a herd of sheep.

'Our main problem was the snipers. We were right in their line. Close by was an officer manning a machine gun. He was wounded later and I was one of those who had to go and get him in. All those around him had been killed, picked off by the snipers. There was a wood nearby, giving them really good cover and they came in after dark, moving from tree to tree, well camouflaged. The only way to bring them down was to aim carefully directly at them, which one of our corporals did – shooting a sniper right through the forehead. The sniper was, like us, only about twenty-three or twenty-four years old.'

6th Airborne Division beat off an ever-heavier series of attacks by the Germans throughout D-Day. Luckily, most of the heavy equipment had arrived by glider during the day, and with their anti-tank guns and some help from naval gunfire they were able to hold on and even improve their defences until joined in the late afternoon by two more battalions of their third element, the 6th Airlanding Brigade. Lord Lovat's 1st Commando Brigade had also arrived in the early afternoon, fighting their way from 'Sword' to arrive just two-and-a-half minutes late for the rendezvous at what is now Pegasus Bridge at Bénouville.

Philip Pritchard of 6 Commando was one of the first seaborne troops across the Caen Canal bridge. 'We went through a coastal village into open country, until we came to the Canal bridges, which we doubled across as best we could with our heavy loads. I can remember the bullets striking the ironwork of both bridges, which were not too far apart. As I ran across one of the bridges, I stopped near a dead British officer who had a Colt .45 automatic pistol attached to his neck with a lanyard. I broke the lanyard by putting my boots on it and secured the pistol in an inner pocket of my BD blouse. The pistol came in very handy later on. This officer was one of the glider party that had landed during the night and did such good work in capturing the bridges intact.'

The airlanding battalions brought with them many of the division's heavy weapons, including field artillery, anti-tank guns and even Tetrarch light tanks. Lance-Corporal Price, who had lost his PIAT while landing with the 12th Battalion, was more grateful for the heavy equipment than most. 'I was given a PIAT and joined by the other two members of my section. So, fully equipped, we made our way to Le Bas de Ranville, and took up our positions in the corner of a wood. A PIAT and three men may not seem much of a deterrent to German Tiger tanks, but on the contrary this was quite capable of disabling a tank when used efficiently. However, the main object was for the three of us to make contact with the pilot and co-pilot of a glider which contained a Jeep, a 6-pounder anti-tank gun and limber, and within an hour of setting up our position, a Jeep, gun and limber joined us, and as a crew of five we became an even more efficient anti-tank section. In fact, after a while a Tiger tank came down the field in front of us and promptly received two shells from us – one in the belly and one in the turret.

'Things were pretty hot up until then, with machine-gun fire and mortar shells landing all around. A great many lads had been killed or wounded, but so far we had been lucky.'

Bill Higgs, another glider pilot, who flew an anti-tank gun in on D-Day, remembers the tank actions. 'There was still some action in Ranville and we managed to get our gun to it, and were dug-in and camouflaged by about 2 a.m. on 6 June 1944. We encountered a Frenchman at daybreak on a bike with a long loaf of bread under his arm. When he saw my 2nd Pilot and I, with black faces and helmets he thought we were Germans and started to pull out his pass to show us. I spoke the little bit of French I knew – "Je suis Anglais" – and he nearly died of fright and rushed away, cycling off to the village like a man possessed.

'I had been watching the skyline area towards Caen, from where we were expecting the enemy armour to come and eventually the enemy tanks and half-tracks crossed into our right angle of anti-tank guns, with infantry extended in front of them. This is something that will stick in my mind for ever. As if someone had blown a whistle, all the guns opened up, and in a short time all the armoured vehicles were blown up or on fire. I feel sure that the enemy had no idea that we had that sort of anti-tank defence on the ground from the night landing, and I think it must have made the Germans delay sending more armour in, thus giving us a chance to secure the bridges.

'After we attacked the infantry with our Brens, the enemy withdrew, but later, having located our positions, gave us a pounding with mortars. During the tank "shoot-out", one of our gun positions came under fire, and as the anti-tank gunner had been hit, "Chalky" White got to the gun and knocked a tank out, for which he received the DCM. Poor "Chalky" was later killed at Arnhem, and I got a Mention-in-Despatches.'

Glider pilot Sgt Roy Howard was also relieved to see the glider force landing: 'At 2100 hrs on 6 June the main glider force came into the Ranville area. Our task was complete and we decided to go home, our orders being to return to the UK as soon as practicable in order to be ready to fly in a further load if necessary. We took our leave of Major Howard and walked along the road to Ouistreham, snatching as much fitful sleep as the 15-inch shells which HMS *Warspite* was pumping into Le Havre would allow. As we arrived at the beach a Ju-88 was shot down, crashing some 30 yards from us, where it continued to explode and burn for some time. Later Colonel Murray and the glider pilots from the main landing force arrived. We all waded out to the LCIs and arrived back in Newhaven at 0630 hrs on 8 June.'

As well as bringing in heavy equipment, the airlanding battalions also brought in essential items such as fuel, water and rations. One of those bringing the Airlanding Brigade was Sergeant Sidney Dodd, flying a 'Hamilcar' glider. 'On D-Day, 6 June, I was second pilot to Staff Sergeant White in Glider No. LA636. We landed in support of the gliders that had taken the bridges over the Orne and the Canal outside Caen. We were one of three "Hamilcars" that carried petrol and ammunition, the tails painted yellow for recognition. We landed safely, having to cut through poles which the Germans had erected to stop us. We didn't encounter much trouble, joined up at the bridge and when the seaborne troops arrived we were pulled out.' Sidney went on to fly at both Arnhem and the Rhine Crossing, and says: ' . . . of the three operations, D-Day was the least demanding.'

The second wave of gliders flying in to the now secured landing zones carried 26 Tetrarch light tanks belonging to the 6th Airborne Reconnaissance Regiment. This was their first operation since formation in 1943, and here again D-Day did not go according to plan.

Corporal Charles Sheffield was with the Reconnaissance Regiment and recalls 6 June: 'We took off in the late afternoon, wondering what we were going to find over there. Most of us landed safely, and on leaving the glider I hitched up the three trailers to my tank. These contained petrol in the wheels and ammo in the large box between the wheels. We had very little opposition, just a few mortars a distance away, when suddenly the tank stopped. The driver did not know why so I slid out of the turret to the ground and found parachute cord and silk wound round the final drive. It was hard work cutting it off and, on moving forward, we came across the squadron leader having the same trouble.' So tangled with parachute cord were the tank tracks and sprockets that Corporal Sheffield was forced to use a blow-torch to burn it off before he could get away.

'At dawn on 7 June the regiment joined the 8th Para Battalion in the Bois de Bavent and set up a series of OPs watching the plain towards Troarn–Caen–Ranville–Escoville. We also sent bicycle patrols deep into enemy territory. Invaluable information was obtained and some very successful air strikes and bombardments by HMS *Mauritius* were directed on to enemy vehicle parks and armoured forming-up positions.'

Corporal A. Darlington was also in the Airborne Recce Regiment and recalls the preceding hours before embarking for France. 'We arrived at the airfield in the morning and were given a meal by the Air Force WAAF. We even had sugar in bowls and the best meal in years. WAAFs even refilled our water-bottles and gave us what, in the event, turned out to be a useless object – soap! This we termed the "Last Supper", and for many it was. We had been issued with a 48-hour emergency ration which when opened looked more like a child's compendium of games. Creamy-coloured dominoes turned out to be porridge with milk and sugar if reconstituted. The dice were tea, milk and sugar cubes.

'The landing was a roaring, twisting, bumping, skidding, from high speed to a dead stop, and we were all momentarily knocked out. The side door opened and the pilot looked in and shouted, "Sorry for the rough landing boys." I unstrapped, dashed out of the door to let the struts down for exit, only to find that the undercarriage no longer existed and parts of the wings were missing. The front was clear and the carrier engines were running. "All clear for exit, Sir, but the damned anchors are jammed!" I took the escape hatchet from the wall and after three or four good swipes, the carrier shot forward, the door opened and off they went. On leaving the glider, it settled down backwards and our Jeep anchor ropes were jammed also, so the hatchet came into action once more but the front edge of the exit had risen some two feet and the tail wheel was also torn off. The Jeep's front wheels could not reach the ground and we see-sawed on the edge with the chassis. I got out again, grasped the bumper so that the back wheels would drive the Jeep slowly forward, and then the front wheels would take over. I often wonder how I completed this feat of strength.'

As more and more heavy gliders swooped in, space on the landing zones ran out. Corporal Darlington continues: 'I saw two "Hamilcars" heading for the same space, and obviously they had seen each other because they tried to bank away from each other. One glider's wing tip turned the other over and it crashed sideways into the wood and the Tetrarch tank shot out of the front on impact. There was a mad dash over to it and the tank was upright, although it had somersaulted out of the glider. The crew was unstrapped and dragged out unconscious. They were strapped on the back of a passing tank's engine compartment with camouflage nets and retaining straps.

'The fields were hives of activity as gliders landed and unloaded. The problems, however, were not yet over, for as the tanks disembarked they made for cover, running over the parachutes left behind by the Paras. These 'chutes became a bigger hazard than the anti-invasion poles, for as the tanks ran over them, the tracks picked them up and they wrapped themselves tightly around the driving sprockets, bringing the tanks to a halt either by slewing the tank around or forcing it to a dead stop.'

Wally Grimshaw was present, with 6th Airborne Recce Regiment: 'I was the Troop-Sergeant of No. 1 Machine-Gun Troop in HQ Squadron. I rode a James motorcycle and led the way to the edge of the drop zone, dodging the mortar bombs which had started to fall on the DZ, as well as the odd bursts of MG fire.

'As we reached the shelter of the woods I saw one of the regiment's drop zone party, who explained that we were to rendezvous at the sawmills above Ranville. We cut through the woods until we met the main road and stopped for a quick "shuftie". We then came across a Jeep with four dead Gunners and saw they had caught a direct hit from one of the German mortar bombs. Further along the road we met some airborne medics who had some German medics working with them. I gave them the location of the bombed Jeep and a party went off to check.

'We drove through the woods and finally met up with the rest of my troop with the Troop Corporal and two pilots. I was then ordered to put out my guns as local protection, and within a few minutes engaged two six-wheeled armoured cars. After a few minutes' firing they retired down the hill, followed by one of "B" Squadron's recce troops. Our neighbours turned out to be the 1st Canadian Parachute Battalion, and I quickly liaised with them to make sure we did not receive any friendly "misses". A perimeter was being mapped out and after a few hours I went on a recce to a new position with one of the Para Battalions, the 12th I think, plus one of the Independent Para Companies. I had to select two front-line positions and one to cover the rear in case the position was overrun, because the Paras were a little thin on the ground and we had to hold this particular front.

'We used to have a "Hate Hitler" 30 minutes daily, when we fired all our weapons on our front, receiving a similar load of high explosive back in return. It was during one of these days I was wounded and back-loaded to England.'

By midnight on D-Day the 6th Airborne Division, reinforced by 1st Commando Brigade, was firmly in control of Ranville and the villages round about. Their introduction to Normandy had not been without difficulties. High winds and enemy anti-aircraft fire had broken up their aircraft and glider formations. Seven of the transport aircraft had been lost or shot down, and twenty-two gliders were missing, some having ditched in the sea. More than a third of the glider pilots had been killed or wounded and a third of the paratroopers were still missing, roaming the countryside looking for their units. The division suffered some 800 casualties, and many men had been captured.

On the other hand, all the divisional objectives had been achieved. The Orne and Caen Canal bridges had been taken, those over the Dives destroyed. The Merville Battery never fired a shot. The British Airborne and Commandos now held the heights above Ranville and had linked up with the seaborne troops. Though still thin on the ground, they were digging in to hold what they had taken against whatever enemy force would come against the eastern flank. Over to the west, in the fields and orchards of the Cotentin Peninsula, the parachute and glider troops of the two American airborne divisions were setting about the same tasks.

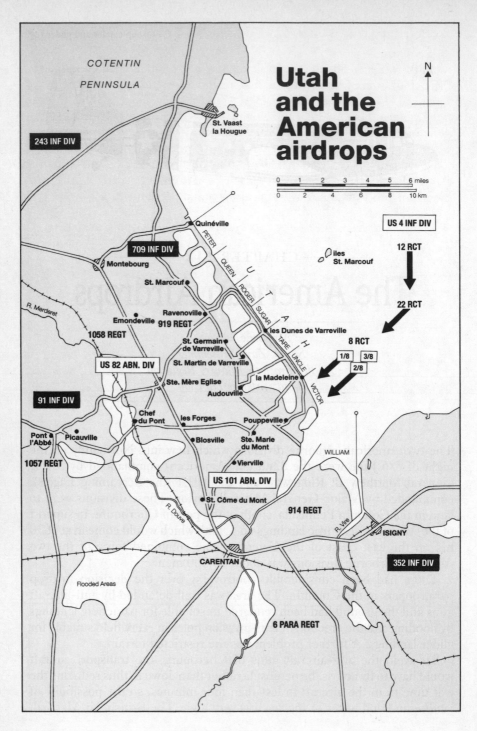

Utah and the American airdrops

N

COTENTIN PENINSULA

0 1 2 3 4 5 6 miles
0 2 4 6 8 10 km

St. Vaast la Hougue

243 INF DIV

US 4 INF DIV

iles St. Marcouf

12 RCT

709 INF DIV

Quinéville

Montebourg

St. Marcouf

22 RCT

R. Merderet

Ravenoville

Emondeville

919 REGT

8 RCT

les Dunes de Varreville

1058 REGT

St. Germain de Varreville

1/8   3/8

2/8

St. Martin de Varreville

US 82 ABN. DIV

Ste. Mère Eglise

la Madeleine

91 INF DIV

Audouville

Chef du Pont

les Forges

Pouppeville

Pont l'Abbé

Picauville

Blosville

Ste. Marie du Mont

WILLIAM

1057 REGT

Vierville

US 101 ABN. DIV

R. Douve

St. Côme du Mont

914 REGT

R. Vire

ISIGNY

6 PARA REGT

CARENTAN

352 INF DIV

Flooded Areas

PETER QUEEN ROGER SUGAR TARE UNCLE VICTOR

U T A H

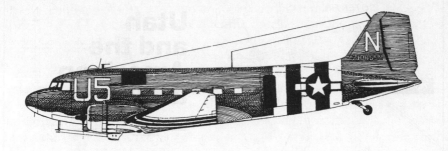

—————— CHAPTER SIX ——————

The American Airdrops

'Airborne, always.'
Sgt D. Zane Schlemmer
508th Parachute Infantry Regiment
82nd Airborne Division

The two American airborne divisions which flew into Normandy on the night of 5/6 June were the 82nd (All-American) commanded by Major General Matthew B. Ridgeway, and the 101st (the Screaming Eagles), commanded by Major-General Maxwell Taylor. These divisions were to land in the Cotentin Peninsula, south of the port of Cherbourg, in support of the American seaborne landings on 'Utah', which would come in at 0630 hrs on the east coast of the Cotentin. The combined force of the two American airborne divisions was about 13,500 men.

There had been considerable controversy over the decision to drop paratroopers in the Cotentin. The area was well defended by anti-aircraft guns and the ground had been rendered unsuitable for parachute landings by flooding and the erection of anti-invasion poles in every field suitable for glider landings. A further problem was the restricted terrain.

To avoid the anti-aircraft guns of Cherbourg, the transport aircraft would have to fly across the peninsula rather than down it, thus reducing the exit time from the aircraft to less than four minutes, so the possibility of landing in flood water or the sea was very high. The British Air Marshal,

93

Trafford Leigh-Mallory, objected to a drop in the Cotentin on the grounds that the losses would be too severe, perhaps up to 70 per cent of all the men dropped. He was eventually overruled, though the plan was modified in part to allow for at least some of the difficulties he anticipated. The wild card here as elsewhere was the weather.

Ideally, for a successful drop paratroopers require a flat, open plain, without rivers, trees or man-made obstacles. The aircraft have to fly across this plain below 1,000 feet, upwind and at as slow a speed as possible, certainly not faster than 120 m.p.h., while the troopers jump out as speedily as possible, one after the other. The faster they can get out of the aircraft and the slower the aircraft is going at a low height, then the closer the troopers will be when they arrive on the ground, enabling them to assemble quickly in orderly groups and set about their tasks. This close grouping is particularly important when the drop is made at night. A parachute drop is simply one way of getting an infantry battalion into action. It is not supposed to scatter individual soldiers all over the landscape.

Up to this time the two American airborne divisions had had quite a different war. The 82nd, which contained the 505th, 507th and 508th Parachute Infantry Regiments (PIR), had been in action in Sicily where they had been severely scattered in the drop and had a very bad time. They later fought at Salerno on the Italian mainland. The 82nd were an experienced and fully trained formation which had received plenty of reinforcements and had plenty of know-how to back their training. The 101st, or the 'Screaming Eagles' as they came to be called, were a new formation made up of the 501st, 502nd and 506th Parachute Infantry Regiments, and their men would be going into action on D-Day for the first time. Each division consisted of three regiments, each of three battalions, roughly the equivalent of a British brigade, supported by airborne artillery, engineers and medical units. Their heavy equipment was carried in American CG-4A 'Waco' gliders, or in British 'Horsa' gliders, for in the American as in the British airborne forces, men and equipment were delivered to the battlefield by glider as well as by parachute.

The German forces in the Cotentin Peninsula consisted of three infantry divisions, the 709th in the east, the 91st in the centre, and the 243rd on the west coast. The 709th and 243rd were second-rank formations, with plenty of men, although short of transport, but the 91st had received special anti-invasion training and equipment. The most formidable unit in the Peninsula was the German 6th Parachute Regiment, three battalions of tough and well trained young men whose average age was seventeen-and-a-half. These were commanded by a veteran paratroop officer, Colonel Friedrich August von der Heydte, hero of the German parachute assault on Crete in 1942. There was also a scratch tank formation, Panzer No. 100, equipped with obsolescent French tanks.

The 82nd's task on D-Day was to land around the small town of Ste-Mère-Eglise to seize and hold the crossroads there, and then seize or destroy the bridges over the River Merderet to secure the western flank of the invasion. The task of taking Ste-Mère-Eglise was given to the 505th Parachute Infantry Regiment of the 82nd, while the other two regiments were to drop on the flat plains beyond the Merderet. The Germans had broken dykes and sluices and allowed this river, like the Douve, to flood the surrounding fields to a depth of two or three feet, but surface weed had concealed this fact from the reconnaissance aircraft and from the invasion planners. The parachute drop would take place about 0100 hrs on 6 June and the gliders would arrive two hours later, bringing in field artillery and the vital anti-tank guns.

The 101st Division was to land further south, north and east of Carentan. Their task was to capture that town and seize four landward exits of the high causeways across the flooded ground behind 'Utah' beach. This belt of flooded land was some 2 kilometres wide and thickly planted with mines. Even with flail tanks, clearing paths through these minefields from the beach would take hours, if not days, so seizing the causeways was vital. This task was given to two of the 101st regiments. The other regiment, the 506th, was to advance on Carentan, seize the bridges over the Douve, and so secure the southern half of the Cotentin against enemy counter-attacks from the mainland of Normandy.

The American paratroopers would take off from airfields in southern England at about 2200 hrs on 5 June and fly a circle route to their drop zones, crossing the Channel to approach the narrow Cotentin from the west, flying in north of the Channel Islands and across, rather than down, the Peninsula. Britain was on Double Daylight Saving Time in 1944, so it was still broad daylight when their aircraft, the robust C-47 Dakotas, lurched heavily into the air and flew west towards Brittany.

Coming in from the west and flying across the Peninsula with the prevailing wind meant that the aircraft would be over the land for barely ten minutes and over their drop zones for less than four. The men knew that anyone jumping late stood a fair chance of landing in the sea. If the troops were scattered in the drop they might never find each other in the dark, enemy-held countryside on which they were to descend. Some confusion had been anticipated and every American trooper carried a small tin 'snapper', which made a 'click-clack' noise, rather like a cricket, to help them locate one another in the dark.

The Allied planners were well aware of these potential problems. Prior to D-Day the Americans held a series of night exercises, with mass parachute drops, to train the pilots in their duties and to rehearse all the pathfinding and drop-zone indicating techniques. All airborne divisions included pathfinder units, small bodies of highly trained men who would drop ahead of the main body to locate the drop zone and mark it accurately with lights and radio beacons in order to bring the main force in on their correct DZs. The exercises in England went reasonably well, and no real problems of drop-zone marking were expected on D-Day. Unfortunately, it is never possible to reproduce the nervousness and excitement generated by an operational drop, and the event itself was to confound all these hopes.

One problem the planners had anticipated on D-Day was the risk of aircraft collision. On D-Day there would be literally thousands of aircraft milling around in the skies over France, and it was far more likely that they would run into each other than into the much depleted Luftwaffe. A hundred thousand gallons of whitewash and twenty thousand paint brushes were supplied to ground crews in all the Allied air forces, and on 3/4 June three broad white bands were painted on the wings and fuselage of every bomber, fighter, parachute aircraft, transport plane and glider in the Allied command.

The delay in launching the invasion came as no surprise to the US airborne troops waiting on their air bases in southern England. They could see the wind bending the branches of the trees and whipping out the windsocks on the airfields. The wind was still blowing strongly at the North Witham Airfield, near Nottingham at 9 p.m. on 5 June, when the pathfinders of the 101st Division enplaned. The men were heavily loaded, carrying in addition to their normal equipment the pathfinding Eureka radios, beacons, lights and batteries. Some of these men had the additional task of reconnoitring routes from the drop zones to the various regimental objectives, which would make for swift deployment when the main force arrived. One example here will describe what happened to the majority of 101st's path-finders on 5/6 June.

The pathfinders for the 502nd Regiment, 101st Airborne, had to find a route for their regiment from their drop south of Ste-Mère-Eglise to a battery of coastal guns near 'Utah', which the regiment were to knock out before dawn. They took off at 2200 hrs on the night of 5 June and had a quiet, almost uneventful flight out to the west coast of the Cotentin. There they ran into the first difficulty. Low cloud and fog prevented the pilots from spotting any positive spot on the ground to check their navigation on crossing the French coast. The pathfinders were therefore dropped two miles from their correct location, which was, under the circumstances, not too bad. They duly set up their equipment in open fields near Ste-Mère-Eglise, and awaited the arrival of the main force. Time passed, and nothing happened.

For the next two hours the pathfinders waited in the darkness as aircraft streamed overhead, listening to bursts of machine-gun fire and watching the odd flight of tracer as the now-alert Germans began to investigate the appearance of groups of parachutists. Shortly after 1.00 a.m., however, the deep drone of hundreds of engines announced the arrival of the main force, and all eyes turned to the sky where confusion seemed to be reigning.

Aircraft were appearing over the drop zone from all points of the compass, and as the 101st's pathfinders ran out to meet the men landing, they were more than a little disconcerted to discover that the regiment now descending on their drop zone was not the 502nd of the 101st but the 505th Parachute Regiment of the 82nd Airborne Division. Something had gone seriously wrong.

Among those parachuting into Normandy that night was Leslie 'Bill' Kick, serving with the Headquarters of the 82nd US Airborne Division. 'About 200 of us, called "special troops", were directly under Brigadier-General James M. "Slim Jim" Gavin, the Assistant Division Commander. We were to go in with the 508th Parachute Infantry Regiment. The General got us together and gave us a quiet talk, after which I believe we would have gone to hell with him.

'On the evening of June 5, we were lined up by plane loads (sticks), getting ready to load into the C-47s. My stick was next to one from the division's engineer battalion. A friend, Bill Yeo, was next to me in that stick. Bill looked pretty bad, shaking and obviously not his cool, easy-going self. I asked him what was bothering him and he said something like, "I'm not going to get through this one." I told him to relax, that we were both going to get through it because we were both too mean to die. Several days later, his First Sergeant told me that he got it the first day, right between the eyes.

'The jumpmaster of our stick was Captain Whitley, whom I did not know, but he may have been a newcomer to the HQ staff. I was placed in the middle of the stick, with the job of hitting the strapped toggle switches to salvo the equipment bundles. It was still daylight when we took off, as Double British Summer Time was in effect, two hours ahead of Greenwich Time.

'Much of the flying time must have been used to get into the planned formation, and it was not a comfortable ride. In addition to the clothing, I had a .45 pistol with 3 clips, M-1 Garand rifle in 2 parts in a scabbard, trench knife on leg, 1 Gammon grenade, 1 'P' grenade, 2 fragmentation grenades, 2 bandoliers of rifle ammo, musette bag, pack harness, 3 days' D-rations, first-aid packet, canteen, switchblade knife, message book, pencil, escape kit, main and reserve chutes. All this was strapped, pocketed and tied on at take-off. There wasn't much room left for breathing. As a consequence there was some vomiting along the way, which gave us slippery footing. There was very little talking, no ditties were sung, no smart-ass remarks as were heard during practice jumps.

'As we approached the Normandy coast we were given the "Stand up and Hook up" order by Captain Whitley, so that we would be ready for any emergency. Shortly before we got the "Go" the tracers started going by the door and windows, but no lurching as at Sicily. It was quite a spectacle. Then we were going out, slipping on puke but keeping our balance by holding tight to the static line snap. There I was, hanging from a nicely opened 'chute, sharing the air with a whole lot of tracers and a whole lot more that weren't tracers. I remember thinking that I couldn't possibly get to the ground alive, so I kept slipping air front and back to hurry my descent.

'In the moonlight it looked like a nice smooth meadow to land in, but instead it was a splash. I couldn't get my leg straps unbuckled, so I cut them with my trench knife. The wind was blowing the 'chute and I took in a lot of water before I got myself cut loose. I was close to drowned and was having a tough time – standing in chest-deep water – getting my rifle together. A voice said, "Let me help you, Kick." I found out weeks later that the voice was that of Paul Wells.

'Several of us got to a railroad causeway which cut through the swamp, an inundated part of the Merderet river flood plain. We followed the railroad until we got to a road. At dawn, along came a German motorcyclist. Several of us fired, and we figured it would have taken three strong men to carry him to a grave with all that lead in him. He was being followed by a staff car which managed to turn around and get away. We sent a few rounds at it but there were no observable results. We had been unable to recover any of the equipment so all we had was our personal stuff. We were all soaked, and all that clothing held a lot of water for a long time.

'My first laugh of D-Day was seeing my buddy, Cliff Hieta, making a vest out of a piece of 'chute to help keep him warm. He had previously picked up malaria in Sicily, and I think a relapse was setting in then, because a few days later it hit him hard. We tried to take a German roadblock but didn't have much success. A few guys got hit. I helped a casualty out of the mess. Somehow he had got mixed up with us, as he was from the 505th in the other division. He had a nice clean hole in his leg and seemed happy about the whole thing. No shock there! Later we met up with our Divisional Commander, Major-General Matthew B. Ridgway, and Brigadier-General Gavin, who we had jumped with, and about a hundred others. The enemy got us pretty well located – they were good – and gave us a bit of hell with mortar and small-arms fire, including snipers. We had a few prisoners – as I remember, about twenty – including a few officers of field grade.

'I was given the job of setting up part of the perimeter defence, so I was kept busy. A sniper missed me with two rounds. I went looking for him but all I found was a makeshift ladder in a hedgerow tree that he had evacuated. Mortar fire came in hot and heavy that night, but the drainage ditches in the hedgerows gave good cover so the casualties were nil, as far as I knew.

'All in all, it wasn't a bad day for our plane-load. We all made it and I considered that a miracle of some sort.'

Leslie Kick was right. Many American paratroopers were not so lucky. Many men were not descending on marked drop zones at all but simply jumping blindly into the night. The 101st Division, instead of landing in four tight groups, were scattered over 300 square miles of Normandy and some troopers landed over 30 miles from their correct drop zones. Many, too many, jumped into the marshes or the sea. All over the Cotentin, poor visibility, high winds, anti-aircraft fire and bad luck combined to confuse the American airborne operation from the outset.

Jack Schlegel, now the Chief of Police in Shandaken, New York, was then with the 3rd Battalion of the 508 PIR. 'As D-Day approached, training took up almost all our time, and on June 4/5 we moved to an airport for the jump. I carried a carbine, tripod for the 30-calibre machine gun, grenades, Gammon bomb, ammo, shovel, gas mask, Mae West, C-rations and all the other items that were needed. We all needed help to get our 'chutes on, and two Air Force men assisted each trooper into the C-47. Our plane had 2 rows of 12 – putting 24 paratroopers, supply bundles and the air crew into the C-47. I cannot recall any laughter or joking on the flight except for the slop bucket being passed up and down the plane. Many threw up when the bucket was passed. I was the twenty-fourth man on our stick and sat next to the plane's radio man, who happened to live in the same area of the Bronx as I. He lived only three blocks from my house and we talked practically all the way over.

'As we approached our area to jump, some of the paratroopers from HQ 3rd Light Machine Gun Section were dozing when a line of tracer bullets cut through the length of the fuselage of the C-47 causing the men sitting on either side to pull their feet in closer. No one was hit, but it got their attention fast so that everyone was fully alert for the next surprise – a direct hit on the left engine. Immediately, Lt John Evans yelled, "Stand up and Hook up!" It didn't take any urging for the paratroopers to obey that order, as the plane was struggling to remain airborne. No sooner were we in place when a third hit took off part of the right wing. The plane tilted down and to the right. Lt Evans yelled, "GO!" and led the way. That was the last time anyone ever saw or heard from Evans. I recall that I was the twenty-fourth man and last to leave the plane, and remember how the plane was going down. I moved as fast as I could to get out and, after baling out, saw the plane go up in a ball of fire.

'I dropped in an open field amongst some cows and, with difficulty, shed my parachute and quickly found two or three other men of the 508th. Chick Miller remembered that I asked him to help read a map. We used a flashlight under a raincoat to study the map, but we could not get our bearings. Seeing a farmhouse with a faint light inside, we decided to seek information from the local Normans.

'I banged on the door until a frightened, elderly couple timidly opened it just enough to peep at the paratroopers outside. "*Je suis Americain*," I announced in schoolboy French, which was effective enough to calm the fears of the startled Normans, as they invited us inside. Using sign language, French, German and American English, we troopers learned we were near Picauville and our hosts were Monsieur and Madame Le Comte. The Le Comtes served bread and wine to the paratroopers as we sat around the dining table and planned our route. As a parting gesture I gave my para-trooper wings to Madame Le Comte as a remembrance.

'Our group started on our journey to find other members of our unit. A short while later, while walking along a road flanked by steep hedgerows and a farmhouse, we heard vehicles approaching. Two motorcycles with Germans approached and were killed by our unit. Upon hearing more sounds of approaching vehicles, we crossed a hedge and headed towards what we thought was Ste-Mère-Eglise. We were actually lost and walking in circles. About daylight, our group came upon a bullet-riddled German staff car rammed up against a stone wall and three dead Germans in the road. One of the dead was General Wilhelm Falley, CO of the 91st German Infantry Division, who had been killed earlier by Lt Malcolm Brannen of the 82nd. In examining the car, I found a package which contained a large swastika banner, the command flag of Gen. Falley which normally flew over his headquarters. This flag now hangs in the Airborne Museum at Ste-Mère-Eglise.

'Some time during the morning, Lt Bodak's group and my group came together, running into machine-gun cross-fire, when about nine of us made a break through a hedgerow. The group remaining with Bodak was totally surrounded. One of the paratroopers with Bodak translated the words of the German commanding officer: "You have three minutes to surrender or we will sweep the ditch from both ends, and there will be no chance of anyone surviving." Lt Bodak then gave the order to surrender.

'My group fled towards a barn. As we entered the barn door three Germans were trying to get out of the same door. The paratroopers grabbed the Germans and pulled them back inside as prisoners. While the prisoners were guarded in a small room, I slipped away alone to another part of the barn. I pulled up a loose board in the floor, stuffed my package of loot containing the German flag under the floor, replaced the loose plank and covered it with straw. I recovered this after the war.

'With our prisoners as insurance, we troopers left the barn safely. After travelling a few hundred yards, we came face to face with a German tank which fired its big gun. A shell exploded just behind the group, wounding many. One of the prisoners, although bleeding from his wounds, jumped up and waved cease-fire gestures to the tank commander. The insurance paid off. The tank commander decided to take prisoners rather than finish off the Americans.

'After capture I recall walking several miles to a château where there were about 250 prisoners – American, British and Canadians. The next day we were loaded on about ten unmarked German trucks with canvas covers and moved in convoy toward St Lô. About noon, Allied planes strafed the convoy and I estimate that 30 or 40 of our men were killed (many from the 508th). Over 80 were wounded. All of us pitched in to help with the dead and wounded. I remember moving three from my own company with the dead and placing Lt Bodak with the wounded. He was hit with a large-calibre shell in the spine and never walked again. So ended D-Day.'

One of the German soldiers now in action against the American para-troopers was Sergeant Rainer Hartmetz, whose battalion had been brought up from Brittany. 'Behind Pont l'Abbé we were stopped by a corporal of our Heavy Company, who directed us into an orchard. A half-track for our anti-tank guns was riddled with bullets and smeared with blood. The corporal was very excited and hurried us to make ourselves ready for combat. He hardly answered my question about the dead paratroopers we had seen hanging by their 'chutes on trees and poles and chimneys. "Hurry up," he said. "They are plastering each ten minutes this place with naval artillery, and the companies are in contact with them. They are 'Amis', you know." Crossing the road, I heard him shouting after me, "And take care!"

'A rifle squad had twelve men and our battalion had the machine pistol No. 43, which was issued in Russia and the soldiers were enthusiastic with that weapon. We had the rifle 98K for snipers and every soldier had hand grenades and additional ammunition for the Spandau. Magnetic mines and Panzerfausts had been distributed over the squad, but one of the most important pieces of outfit was the short infantry spade. Without the spade a German infantryman felt naked. We'd learned digging fox-holes in Russia, and you know the word, "Sweat saves blood". Besides that, the spade was an excellent weapon for man-to-man fighting, for it was sharp and handy.

'After some hundred metres we met about forty German soldiers along the road. They were very young – perhaps seventeen (I was nineteen) – some were wounded and supported by their comrades with a sergeant beside. When he saw us he addressed us. "They're recruits. We had a night training when they jumped into us. We had only blank cartridges." He had tears in the eyes and started sobbing.

'I never had interest to look at killed men, but this time we stopped to see our new adversaries. They had lost their helmets so we could see their uncovered heads with that crew-cut. We had been told that American troopers were convicts who had volunteered for the Airborne, but these couldn't be convicts, and when I saw that I felt better, knowing we had to fight against soldiers and not against criminals.

'The quietness became interrupted by the noise of rifle-fire and bursts of machine guns, and we could distinguish the American bursts from the

German Spandau and figure out the direction of it. We hardly started digging our fox-holes when a salvo of artillery shells exploded between us, and one of the riflemen was hit, and the next problem was to locate their snipers. I heard a noise like a slapping in the face, and Willy came down in the hole, the face covered with the hands, through which poured blood.

'We were sitting behind the hedgerows, not having seen an enemy soldier or fired a round, and had two casualties. I crawled over to Gottlieb, my assistant squad leader, and discussed how to tackle the snipers. This sniper was sitting in a tree, probably tied in, so I gave the order to some of our boys to observe the trees if there would be any movement, and we stayed there for two hours, but nothing happened. The night and the darkness came.'

Howard Huggett of North Carolina was in the 326th Airborne Engineer Battalion of the 101st Airborne Division. His aircraft had been hit by anti-aircraft fire soon after crossing the French coast and the 600lbs of C-2 explosive on board was now on fire. 'With the plane on fire, in a dive, the pilot and co-pilot slumped forward and the crew chief unable to determine our position, I gave the order to go. I estimated our altitude at between 350 and 400ft. When my 'chute opened it seemed I had two oscillations in the air and then I hit the ground hard somewhere in France, not sure of my location.

'While lying on my back in the middle of a field I readied my weapon, checked the direction of flight of the aircraft and removed my 'chute ready to engage the enemy – which turned out to be a big white horse. I could see that the plane had crashed approximately one kilometre away in a south-easterly direction. I collected my gear and proceeded to the edge of the field and started down the hedgerow to collect the jump stick. From the amount of firing it was obvious that a sizeable German force was between me and the men who had jumped with me and joining up was going to be a real problem. As I started down the hedgerow I saw an enemy patrol on the other side so I held my position to let them pass and then proceeded to get into position for a fire fight. I then back-tracked, hoping to find someone from my group and I even used my "cricket" to try and contact someone, but to no avail. I then surmised that the men in my stick had landed among enemy troops and I had landed on the fringe of the enemy bivouac.

'As daylight approached I could hear artillery to the north, and I started making my way towards the sound. I could hear German troops and vehicles moving around on roads and paths so I thought it would be safer to move in the hedgerows. It was now daylight and I was lost and alone, except for the enemy. By this time exhaustion was overtaking me. My cover was adequate in the hedgerow and I didn't resist the temptation to close my eyes and try to cat-nap.

'The sounds of battle seemed to have intensified so I decided to try and find some friendly troops in the area. When D-Day ended on 6 June 1944 I was lost and alone, not knowing if the beach landings had taken place, or even if I would be around for my twenty-second birthday just ten days away.'

John G. Kutz from Easton, Pennsylvania, was a demolition man. 'My assignment for D-Day was to destroy two wooden bridges over the Douve river north-east of Carentan. We were briefed for our mission at Exeter and prepared our equipment, which included in my case, 60lbs of C-2 explosive, a roll of primer, a roll of safety cord, 12 blasting caps, a Hawkins mine, plus rifle and so on. It took two men to get me into the plane, a zebra-striped C-47.

'We flew close to the water over the Channel and the plane pulled up to about 600–700ft over the coast of France when the flak and ground fire started coming at us. It looked like a giant Fourth of July celebration. I jumped out of the plane in the middle of all this, and landed in the Douve river.

'Fortunately, I landed close to shore, and pulled my equipment in. Then I took a rest for about five or ten minutes before carrying all my equipment through a flooded area, close behind three German soldiers moving a German artillery piece. Then I met my sergeant and six of my buddies. As we headed for the bridges we kept picking up more men and had a few fire fights, and we also blew up high-tension and underground cables on the way, getting to the bridges just before daylight.

'We could not prepare the bridges for demolition in the daylight because of enemy fire, but we prepared them as soon as it got dark, and the bridges were under mortar fire when we did it.'

George Rosie of Highland Park, Illinois, was with the 506 PIR in the 101st Airborne Division: 'Through broken clouds and a bright moon we headed for the coast. Over the Channel we could see hundreds of boats starting towards the south, and in every direction were planes. About 1.00 a.m. on June 6, one of the guys yelled, "There she is boys." We all knew what it was – the coast of France. About nine minutes to the drop zone. Flak and machine-gun tracers could be seen to the right and left. It looked like the Fourth of July. About that moment a plane on our right blew up, hit the ground in a large ball of fire – 18 to 20 men wiped out. This was no Fourth of July celebration. Welcome to the real war.

'The red light in the door came on. We stood up and hooked up. Then came the green light and we were out the door. Quite a struggle because of all our equipment. Someone fell down and had to be helped up and out the door. I don't know how high our plane was, but I'm sure it was very low because I remember swinging about twice and then landing in the middle of a road. I could see a man and a woman standing in the front yard of a house just beneath me. I took about two steps and went head first through a wooden fence, knocking out two teeth and cutting my lip. I rolled over, tried to get my carbine out, couldn't, sat up, and the man and woman were gone. I finally got out of my harness – those snap harnesses were a bugger to get out of – pulled my folding stock carbine out and could hear some soldiers coming down the road. I started up a hedgerow but it felt like someone was holding me by my belt. I stopped, tried to move again – same thing. I found the shroud lines from my parachute tangled up in the fence. I could hear the boots getting closer and closer. I finally got the shroud lines unhooked, climbed to the top of the hedgerow, fell over on the other side, and in about a minute 35 or 40 Germans came marching past. I could have reached out and touched them. Being alone behind enemy lines is a unique, indescribable feeling. You just feel so helpless, so alone that there is nothing in your life you can relate it to.

'After a while I ran into John Gibson, our medic, and Charles Lee, one of our 81mm mortar men. It was as if I had found a long-lost brother. It was the greatest feeling in the world. We could hear a German machine gun firing in our area and small arms a bit further away. Later I looked up and there was a C-47 at about 800ft with the left engine on fire and troopers baling out. Flames were streaming alongside the plane right by the door. The plane was flying in a kind of semi-circle, and at about 600ft it was coming straight at us and the troopers and the crew were still baling out. The last one baled out at not more than 200ft. The plane went right over the top of our heads, hit in the enjoining field and burst into a thousand flaming pieces that lit up the whole area. From the direction of the crashed plane four men came running towards us. When they got near the ditch we discovered they were from our plane: Phil Abbie, Francis Swanson, Leo Krebs, and Ronzani. The downed plane had hit right in the area where they were hiding and damn near got them.

'We now had a small army of seven. We decided to head for the river and the bridges which were part of our unit's objectives. We stuck to the ditches and hedgerows for concealment. When we got down near the river we had to cross a field. Abbie was our scout. As he came out on the road with Ronzani just behind him, daylight was breaking. There were approximately 100 Germans who were concealed in the field on the other side of the road. Fifteen or twenty of them stood up with their machine pistols and shot and killed Abbie and Ronzani. Seven men against a hundred was a hopeless position. In no time at all they had us surrounded and captured. Charles Lee crawled to the left and got away into a wooded area. A short time later they had four of us who were not wounded lying in a shallow ditch with our hands over our heads and a guard with a rifle on either side of us. Lee began shooting at the guards from about fifty yards away where he was hiding. I told Leo Krebs I had a hand grenade in my jumpsuit pocket the Germans had missed. I told Leo if Lee hit one of the guards, I was going to try and get away, but the Germans circled around Lee and killed him. Later, when they moved us out, I left the grenade lying in the ditch.

'All this took place years ago, but when you start thinking about the day you lost Abbie, Lee and Francis Ronzani it is still very difficult to talk about. After we were captured, Gibson and I had a chance to check out Ronzani. I don't know how many times he was hit through the chest – 3, 4, 5, 6. I'm sure he never knew what hit him. When I returned to the States after the war and visited his mother and father, one of the things that seemed to be of great relief to his parents was that Francis had not suffered.

'When we were first hit and pinned down in that field, strange things went through our minds. Bullets flying all over the place and Leo Krebs remarked, "God, these guys are lousy shots." During the short time we were exchanging fire with the Germans there was a German officer running, back and forth on the road in front of us. Krebs said, "What the hell is wrong with that guy? Is he nuts?" Leo and I both shot at him and he went down. Later, after we were captured they had us carry him on a shelter half back to the farmhouse where they were quartered. He was the first dead man I had ever touched. When we picked him up to put him on the shelter half, he broke wind and was making sounds like he was still breathing. As far as I could tell we had hit him several times in the chest area and I knew damn well he was dead, but those weird sounds really gave me the creeps.

'With my broken teeth and a swelling knee that I had injured when landing on the road and the sheer fear of being a prisoner, there was no sleep that night. I would open my mouth to breathe and the raw nerves from those broken-off teeth just killed me. In the morning, Leo Krebs, who could speak German, talked to one of the guards and an older soldier who might have been a cook or something came over. He had an old rusty pair of pliers. They sat me down on a bale of hay with Swanson and Krebs holding my arms and this old German started towards my mouth with these pliers. His hands were shaking and at the first grab he got the remaining portion of the first tooth and a hell of a chunk of my gum. I felt pain like I had never felt in my life. The second time his hand was shaking even harder. On his first attempt he didn't get the other stub out but did on the second try. It hurt like hell but at least the pain of the raw nerves was gone. Talking about this brings back memories that have been stored back in the furthest reaches of my mind that I haven't thought about in years.'

D. Zane Schlemmer, who now lives in Hawaii, was a nineteen-year-old sergeant in the 2nd Battalion, the 508th PIR, 82nd Airborne. 'I was a forward observer for an 81mm mortar platoon. My biggest memory of the night of June 6/7 was the struggle to stay awake. I had taken Benzedrine but the lack of sleep and constant staring at the grazing Normandy cows caused me to hallucinate – and I think that German patrols were roving out there. I spent the night swapping a hand grenade from hand to hand. How I slept when I finally got to sleep the next morning!

'Before the jump, my battalion assembled at Saltby airfield, under high security. We drew combat-scale ammunition and I had an M1 Garand 300-calibre rifle, for I was to be a front-line observer, and I was trying to look as inconspicuous as possible. I also had fragmentation grenades and a Gammon grenade – an English grenade that was a cotton sock filled with plastic explosive. These were ideal for attacking vehicles and we called them our hand artillery. However, they were also popular because the plastic explosive was ideal for lighting fires to brew coffee or K-rations in our fox-holes, so as time went on the grenade got smaller. We also had anti-tank mines. We were really loaded, but everyone drew more, as much ammo as we could carry.

'We cleaned and re-cleaned our weapons, sharpened and re-sharpened our knives, checked and re-checked our equipment. We then went into sand-table sessions showing our objective. We were told that we should jump regardless of circumstances, and were not under any circumstances to return with the aircraft. The places on the map eventually got their French names, like Pont l'Abbé, and we were finally told that our objective was Normandy, France, and that our task was to block all German advances onto the landing beaches.

'As you know there was a 24-hour delay, but finally about 8.30 p.m. on June 5 we assembled by our aircraft in "sticks". There were eight men in my "stick". We had a relief stop because once we had our equipment on it was impossible to relieve ourselves. We blacked our faces, donned our equipment and our chutes, and were pushed or hauled onto the planes. The mood was nervous chatter to real quiet, but camaraderie prevailed. I chewed an entire pack of gum after departing.

'June 6, 1944, 0001 hrs found us approaching the English Channel. After some time we banked left over two small islands, and then over the coast of France. We then ran into cloud which really concerned us. This suddenly cleared and we started to receive German flak and small-arms fire. When it struck the aircraft it was like gravel on a tin roof. I thought only of getting out of the plane as quickly as possible and of what I had done to get myself in this situation – then the green light came on and out went the stick.

'The sky seemed alive with tracer, red and green and pink, floating up and snapping past. In the distance to the east I could see a sizeable fire, a house in Ste-Mère-Eglise, though I didn't know it at the time. We had jumped anyway, and I hit in on an apple orchard and got some bruised ribs. I cleared my harness, put my rifle together, but I could not find any sign of life except some firing from down the road. Our stick leader had been immediately captured and was later killed by our own aircraft in a strafing attack. Another aircraft, flaring like a comet, crashed in a field nearby and I thought of the troopers on board. I later saw a C-47 down on the marshes of the Merderet river. The area into which we had jumped was occupied by the tightly disciplined 91st German Division, and they occupied most of the farms. We were also surprised at the immense size of the hedgerows. No one had told us about the flooded marshes. I had no idea where the hell I was and I could not find my stick, but I was alive.

'I laid my anti-tank mine and headed off in a southerly direction. Near the edge of the next field I came across a sergeant in the 101st, who was just as bewildered as I was as to where we were. We were both far from where we should have been. We then heard firing from the south-east and decided to head there and came across a road running east–west. We crossed a causeway to a masonry bridge and then to an intersection, so I knew we were near Chef du Pont, which meant I had landed some one-and-a-half miles south-east of our drop zone, which wasn't bad compared with others, but it meant I was on the wrong side of the Merderet river. The sergeant from the 101st decided to march on alone to find his division and I turned back to find mine.

'There was sporadic small-arms fire everywhere. As I reached the edge of the marsh I heard a glider crash into the trees nearby. Soon after, by using the "clicker" I met three troopers, two of whom were already hurt, one with a broken leg. We concealed the two wounded and the other came along with me.

'At dawn we left the road and kept to the fields, scouting the Germans like Indians in the West. I never entered a farmhouse during my time in Normandy. We eventually met other troopers waiting to ambush the enemy; every field was a separate battleground. The Normandy cows would stare at anyone in the fields and I still have a warm place in my heart for those big Normandy cows.

'By mid-morning on D-Day many more troopers had assembled and we found we had no mortars, few machine guns, little medical supplies, few medics for the wounded. However, we did have our personal weapons and we managed with them. We assembled on Hill 30 which overlooked the marsh I had crossed that morning, from which we could, theoretically, control the causeways across the Merderet. I was positioned in an outpost and I spent the time here with Lt-Colonel Shanley's group. I preferred the outpost as there were too many men we could not help inside the perimeter. It was difficult to listen to their cries. We had no re-supplies of any kind but the lack of medical supplies was felt by everyone. Later we could call up 75mm fire to break up German attacks on our position.

'June 6, 1944 at 2339 hrs found me very weary but very alive, dug-in with a parachute in my fox-hole, which was very warm and very luxurious. We did not know if the invasion had succeeded or not, but we stayed there for five days until the seaborne troops came up. Our Chaplain was killed while attending to our wounded. I was wounded in July and the fourth of July found me on a hospital ship bound for an English hospital. They had to cut off my bloody, stinking jumpsuit, which I had worn continuously for 29 days, but I insisted that they let me keep my jump boots.'

Of the 2,056 men of Zane Schlemmer's 508th Parachute Infantry Regiment who flew to Normandy on 5 June, only 995 returned to Nottingham on 14 July.

Scattered widely across the Cotentin countryside, the American paratroopers were making the best of a bad job. They cut telephone wires, ambushed enemy transport, attacked the Germans wherever they found them and slowly made their way towards their objectives, joining up with other paratroopers as the night wore on. None of this was easy and even the glider-borne forces suffered from the confusion.

The great advantage of gliders, apart from their ability to lift heavy equipment, lay in the fact that they could put down men in organized groups, but even here things went wrong. The first glider to land, carrying Brigadier-General Don Pratt, Assistant Commander of the 101st, landed perfectly on a well marked landing zone. Unfortunately the glider ran across the marking lights, totally destroying them, and crashed into a wall. General Pratt was killed, and the other gliders, landing in the pitch dark, also crashed, with heavy losses among the passengers and crews. General Pratt was the first American general to die in France.

Milton Chadwick was with the Glider Field Artillery of the 82nd Airborne. 'On June 6, 1944 I was a sergeant in charge of a howitzer section. We flew into Normandy in a British "Horsa" glider. We left England at 9 p.m. on June 6, but I cannot remember the name of the airport. We crash-landed at 11 p.m. near Ste-Mère-Eglise and our glider was literally torn to pieces. If we had not been well belted in I am sure some of us would have been killed but as it turned out all five of us walked away. Our equipment was salvaged although only 4 of the 6 howitzers were usable. It worked out well, however, as in the event there were only enough men left to man 4 guns anyway. During the battle our combat team was given the task of capturing Hill 95 and Hill 131, which are the highest points in that part of Normandy.'

Arley Goodenkauf of Table Rock, Nebraska, was a corporal in 'B' Battery, 377th Parachute Field Artillery Battalion, 101st Airborne Division: 'Our division had arrived in Liverpool, England in mid-October 1943 and were quartered in the little village of Wickham, near Newbury, Berkshire. We probably had the longest passage across the Atlantic of any army group, taking 45 days to make the journey from New York.

'I landed outside Montebourg, north of Ste-Mère-Eglise, instead of at St Martin de Varreville, just in from "Utah" beach, which was our designated drop zone. We had our first action just outside Le Ham early that morning, after we had stopped and destroyed three or four German ammunition trucks. During the next three days, we were involved in several skirmishes, usually against superior numbers and weapons. We had only carbines and grenades. Out of the twelve 75mm howitzers in the battalion, only one was ever recovered and put into action. On about June 9 I was wounded and taken prisoner, and remained in Germany until January 31 when I escaped during the POW evacuation. With several friends and with some assistance from the Russian Army, I made my way to Odessa on the Black Sea and eventually back to the American army at Naples.'

George Maruschak of Chicago, Illinois, who had performed in the airborne concert party in England, was a sergeant in the HQ Battery, 320th Glider Field Artillery, 82nd Airborne Division. 'My Army Serial Number was 36526691. It's funny that I still remember my ASN, because when I call one of my children I have to look up the number on our Rol-O-Dex!

'We were given an introduction to the "Horsa", a giant British glider, made completely of plywood, which made our "Waco" gliders look like toys. We left the airfield shortly after 2300 hrs on June 5. We sat a little behind the pilot's cabin, five on each side, directly above the single wheel of the three-wheel landing gear.

'We were cut loose and the glider was dropping quickly at a 45-degree angle – a great crash and the nose hit the large hedgerows – the single wheel broke through the bottom and separated the ten of us. We couldn't cut the six cables because the back was about 20ft in the air. Our main concern was how to get the Jeep and trailer out. An axe was part of the equipment on the glider, and one wing was touching the grass on the field. The other was way up, high over the road. The best place was at the door. We didn't want to chop, not knowing where the enemy was, but we had no choice. It took hours but we got the job done.

'We found another glider and the guys who were in it. It had one 105 howitzer and two rounds of ammunition. We put the howitzer on the road facing the direction we thought the enemy would be coming from. At dawn we met my major, who was happy to see us, but was worried as to what had happened to the rest of the battery, and he wanted me (from memory) to start making up our MIAs (Missing-in-Action).

'Looking around, we finally reasoned that we were on the wrong side of the church at Ste-Mère-Eglise. It was June 7 before we were reunited with the rest of the guys from the HQ Battery, and 28 days before we were replaced by infantry divisions. We moved back towards the beaches, and Boy! ... it sure was great to remove the impregnated underwear, to wash and shave, and to relax. The Red Cross was there to hand out just what most of us wanted most – a toothbrush and toothpaste. As for me, I would have preferred a beer and a shot of booze.'

'Stub' Storeby of Avenal, California, was in the 326 Engineering Battalion, 101st Airborne. 'As we started exiting the planes the sky was full of red tracer, and when my parachute opened I lost all my equipment, including my rifle. I landed in a bomb crater about 10ft deep, with only a trench knife strapped to my leg and some explosive caps taped to my armpit. Climbing out of the crater I was challenged by Harold Conway, who had a rifle pointed at my head, and I used my D-Day "cricket" to give the counter-sign. A few minutes later, Harold was hit in the groin by a bullet. I gave him sulpha powder and put him in some brush. He kept his grenades and gave me his rifle.

'I then located more of my platoon and we stayed in the hedgerows and watched the other paratroops and gliders land, while the Navy was shelling everything, especially towards our objectives at Carentan. We also found an equipment bundle with a machine gun and ammo, and at daylight my lieutenant told me to shoot up a farm where the enemy were holed up. After some corrections I managed to silence the Germans, and later that day I got another German on the far side of the hedgerow. I crawled over and examined him, taking his insignia and wallet. I still have his photos today but I saw his face every night for months. We spent the rest of D-Day assembling more and more troops for an assault on Carentan and waiting for the troops to come up from the beaches – and that was my D-Day.'

Captain Harold A. Shebeck of Minneapolis, Minnesota, was the Assistant Supply Officer and Graves Registration Officer with 325th Glider Regiment, 82nd Airborne Division: 'About May 27, the 82nd Airborne left our area around Leicester for the south of England. Of course, at this point we did not know when D-Day was, but we obviously knew it was imminent. When we left the train at a small town I noticed that the name of the town was Honiton in Devon, about ninety miles west of Southampton. At this time thousands of troops were making their moves to staging areas all over southern England.

'We were directed to our gliders and now began the job of loading. The glider to which I was assigned carried a Jeep, my driver, the Regimental Transportation Chief who was staff sergeant and myself as well as some assorted ordnance items. The gliders had to be loaded very carefully and heavy equipment lashed down very securely, because a shift of only four inches by a Jeep or cannon could send a glider into a dive, from which it could not recover. I sat in the Jeep and as we left the ground and began passing over the villages and towns of southern England, people filled the streets, waving from doorsteps or wherever they happened to be.

'My driver was now lying on the floor under the Jeep and vomiting as he suffered from a good case of air sickness. It might sound impossible to believe, but I soon began dozing, which I did intermittently once we were well underway. The Cherbourg Peninsula is only twenty-five miles wide, so it only took a short time to cross. Excellent timing, therefore, was vital in cutting the glider loose from the tow plane. Too early or too late and the gliders would land in the Channel.

'Now we began to see all the "welcoming" devices the Germans had erected in most of the fields in Normandy in anticipation of an airborne invasion. Poles, somewhat smaller than telephone poles, had been set up with wires strung between them, booby-trapped, to cause gliders to crash-land. Ditches had been dug about 6ft deep and 12ft across to cause a smash-up even if a glider was able to land in an open field.

'The Germans were aiming their fire at the tow planes, but were often late and were hitting the gliders. Machine-gun, artillery and small-arms fire was now coming up from barns, houses and German firing positions in scattered locations. In the glider we tried to make ourselves as small as possible, elbows close to the body, knees pulled up to chest and head bowed down. Now it was time for our pilot to cut loose from our tow plane. The pilot was desperately trying to slow the speed of the glider, which was now about 50 or 60 miles per hour. We came across the top of a hedgerow, knocked the wheels off the glider, crash-landed, and came to a stop about 4 miles inland from "Utah" beach, in the general vicinity of Ste-Mère-Eglise and the smaller village of Chef du Pont.

'Miraculously, no one was hurt. As we hit the ground I felt a terrible pain in my back and thought my back was broken, but I was able to move my legs and I knew I was lucky. I was concerned that the Jeep had been damaged, but luckily it was not, and we manhandled it out of the glider. My driver had recovered from his air sickness in a hurry what with the noise, dust, smoke, confusion and small-arms fire from snipers in the area. Our regimental mission was to assist in seizing and holding the main road up through the peninsula to Cherbourg.

'Here I think I should mention some of the things that led to the glider crack-ups in the landings. First, the fields were often smaller then they appeared on the photos and the sand-box models. The hedgerows which surrounded most of the fields in Normandy were often much higher than they appeared in the photographs, in some cases 20ft high. The result was that the pilots misjudged the height as they came in for a landing, and this caused a great many crashes, including ours. There were poles and ditches, and maps were not always accurate.

'Some gliders broke down before we even left England, and I was told that at least two came down in the Channel. I have been told that obstacles caused 50 per cent of the smash-ups in Normandy and enemy action the other 50 per cent. In all my time in Normandy, I only saw one glider that looked as though it could be used again, providing it could have been towed aloft – otherwise they were in various stages of destruction.

'Not long after our landing, I approached a smashed glider in which I saw the pilot slumped dead over the controls. No one else was around, and in the pilot's kit bag I found several oranges and a half-pound bar of chocolate, which I retrieved. The oranges were priceless in England and I savoured the chocolate for several days by eating a small square each day. It was permissible to take foodstuffs from the dead but everything else, obviously, was left for Graves Registration action.

'Shortly after I ran across the dead glider pilot, I found the Graves Registration Service people in a field where they were already in operation in a smashed glider. Bodies were gradually being collected and taken to a large field near Ste-Mère-Eglise, where the first American cemetery was being established. Here, row upon row of bodies were already being laid out. German bodies were being transported to their own cemetery which had been established by our GR people a few miles north-west of Ste-Mère-Eglise in the vicinity of Montebourg. I happened to be in this cemetery when a truckload of bodies arrived. Bodies were being hauled in GI two-and-a-half-ton trucks, with a couple of German prisoners to do the unloading. When the truck stopped, the front end was alongside what looked like a black, burned tree stump. As I looked at this "tree stump" more closely, I realized that it was the burned torso of a human body from mid-section to the knees, which had previously been brought in for burial.

'There were two things that were invariably found on nearly every German enlisted man, and these were a head of a partly eaten cabbage, and a loaf of dark rye bread.

'We had a young lieutenant in my regiment who was a company commander just promoted to captain a day or two before D-Day. He had not obtained captain's bars and had affixed two strips of white tape to the shoulder straps of his field jacket to denote his new rank. In my hurried travels an excited French farmer told me that there was a dead American officer in his barnyard. I found the body lying face down and I noticed the strips of tape on his shoulder straps before I turned him over.'

The more obvious landing zones had been quickly identified by the Germans, who added to the confusion on the drop zones by mortar fire and machine-gunning. All the 101st drops were from aircraft of the 9th US Airforce Troop Carrier Squadron and General Maxwell Taylor flew in the lead aircraft of his division to make his fifth parachute jump. On the way to France the general slept on the floor of the aircraft, a feat that was much admired by the other troopers in the aircraft, but as soon as his aircraft crossed the coast of France, the general led his men out into the night.

This sudden arrival of the American Airborne was a great surprise to the Norman villagers. André Heintz recalls one story: 'My great-aunt lived in what was going to be one of the drop zones for 101st US Airborne, at St Côme du Mont, near Carentan. The night before (5 June) the Germans asked the farmers in the area to bring in the cattle as they were going to have manoeuvres with live ammunition. That had happened before and the Germans always had manoeuvres in one part of the country or another to keep their men in shape.

'So when the family – my great-aunt over seventy, her son, and the old maid – heard quite a lot of noise during the night they didn't think at first about the Landing, but since more and more planes kept coming over and more noise could be heard towards the coast, they got scared. There were no shelters in the area so they chose the dark passage in the middle of the house on the first floor to take refuge.

'When, early in the morning, they dared at last to look through the windows, they saw an amazing sight. The fields there extend very far, as it is the open country by the marshes – that part was not flooded and there were no hedges to obstruct the view. There were parachutes all over the place, like huge flowers of all colours – red for ammunition, yellow for supplies, blue for medical supplies, white (very few) – the parachutist's second chance, a lap-pack parachute – and then the main camouflaged ones, mostly green, for the men.

'Unfortunately they also saw that a man whose white parachute had not opened had been impaled on the gate; the twisted white parachute lay beside him on the ground like a shroud, a trail of blood also came towards the front door, and probably a wounded soldier had tried to seek help. My family felt bad that from their dark passage, with all the noise outside, they had not been aware of him. A parachute was hanging from the roof, and obviously the man had slid down the ropes. Another one had apparently broken through the roof of the farm next door. Altogether eighteen men had dropped down in the grounds around the house.

'The battle lasted three days, sometimes with the Germans, sometimes with the Americans. Every time a new group of Germans came they would kick the corpse of the American killed in front of the house, turn him over and search his pockets.

'After the front door had been broken open with a hand grenade by an American Para, the family couldn't stay there any more. The Germans and the Americans chased one another through the house. It was a big place with two staircases, six different entrances, and it had become unbearable. The family couldn't even cook; every time they lit a fire (there was no gas or electricity then) the smoke through the chimney would bring a volley of shots through the windows. Whoever was outside, whether German or American, thought there were enemies inside. The family then decided to try and reach the tool shed at the end of the garden, but as they didn't have any helmets they wore copper saucepans on their heads and crawled across the garden with mattresses on their backs.

'When they came back to the house they found a dead German on one of the beds upstairs. He had written something with his blood on one of the mirrors, but it had dried off and could not be deciphered. The mother of the farmer next door had been killed and they had to bury her in the garden as no proper funerals could take place at this time.

'The day after the battle was over, Colonel Howard Johnson, who had been in charge of a special mission, holding a lock in the middle of the marshes, came and visited the house, explaining that he had fallen into the garden that night of 5/6 June. As he was coming down he had noticed, thanks to the tracer bullets, that he was being shot at by some Germans in the field opposite the house. Once on the ground he feigned death and then crawled towards the Germans and killed two in their slit trenches.'

On landing, General Maxwell Taylor of the 101st Airborne found himself commanding not 6,000 fighting men, but completely alone. The bulk of his division was dispersed over a wide area, generally south-east of Ste-Mère-Eglise. A further 30 per cent of his division fell outside this area, and most of these were quickly rounded up by the Germans. General Taylor's first encounter in Normandy was with a solitary trooper from the 501st Regiment. They were so pleased to see each other that general and GI hugged each other with delight in the darkness. The general and his sole subordinate then encountered Brigadier-General Anthony McAuliffe, who commanded the divisional artillery, but by dawn, only 1,100 of the 6,600 troopers in the 101st had rejoined their units.

The first organized group General Maxwell Taylor encountered was a small group from the 3rd Battalion of the 501st Parachute Infantry Regiment led by Lt-Colonel Ewell. Ewell had an uneventful jump, although his battalion was widely scattered, and like most of the other men, he didn't know where he was. General Maxwell Taylor took command of this detachment but it was some hours later before he located their position by the church at Ste Marie du Mont on the eastern Cotentin. This was near one of the causeway exits from 'Utah' beach, which was actually the objective of two battalions of the 506th Regiment, but since neither of these had been dropped on the right spot, General Taylor decided to lead his scratch formation to the attack, and capture the causeway exit.

The two battalions should have had 1,200 men for the job. General Taylor's force consisted of the 40 available men of the 3rd Battalion of the 501st, and 45 members of the Divisional Staff. Most of these were officers. The group contained two generals, a chief of staff, two colonels, a major, several captains and eight lieutenants. 'Never,' remarked General Taylor, wryly, 'have so few been commanded by so many.'

Lt-Colonel Ewell was placed in command, and the force made their way south, against light opposition, towards Pouppeville, collecting more men as they went. By the time they reached Pouppeville they had grown to about 150 men, from all parachute regiments and of both divisions. The group had 18 casualties in the fight for Pouppeville, but they took the village and

35 German prisoners, and so, just after dawn, secured the landward exit of the causeway.

On that wild and windy night in 1944, the US paratroopers were in action all over the Cotentin Peninsula of Normandy. The men might be dispersed, lost and confused, but they were not dismayed. They still had weapons and ammunition, and they were determined to make a fight of it. They cut telephone wires, shot up patrols and set up ambushes along the roads. One of these caught and killed General Falley, Commander of the German 91st Infantry Division, who was returning from an anti-invasion exercise in Rennes. In addition, using scratch forces like the one collected by General Maxwell Taylor and Lt-Colonel Ewell, they took their objectives. One of these was the small market town of Ste-Mère-Eglise, a target for the 82nd Airborne Division.

Ste-Mère-Eglise had been having a disturbed night even before the invasion began. A fire had started in the main square which called for the presence of the town fire brigade, while most of the town's population turned up as spectators. Thus distracted, the assembled French and Germans hardly heard the drone of engines as the parachute aircraft arrived overhead. It was the sight of descending parachutes, each lit red from the fire, each with a man dangling below, together with the sudden bursts of fire from the German garrison, that alerted the startled citizens to what was happening around and above their little town.

The men now descending on Ste-Mère-Eglise were from the 3rd Battalion, 505th Regiment of the 82nd Airborne, commanded by Lt-Colonel Edward Krause. The dropping of men on the town centre was another accident, for the drop should have been in the surrounding fields, and those who landed in the town paid for it with their lives. One actually fell into the fire, and others landed in the trees around the square or fell heavily onto the stones. One, the most famous paratrooper of all the D-Day men, landed on the church tower in the centre of the square, then slid down the roof to hang suspended by his parachute rigging lines from the edge of the tower.

This was John Steele, a trooper in the 3rd Battalion of 505th. Private Steele wisely decided to sham dead, and hung limply in his harness while gunfire whipped across the square below, some of the fire coming from a German machine gun set up on the church roof a few yards away. A member of this gun crew eventually suggested they haul up Steele's body and relieve it of chocolate and cigarettes, only to discover that Pfc John Steele was very much alive. Steele was taken prisoner about 0430 hrs, just as dawn was breaking, an hour before his comrades took the town. He spent the rest of the war in captivity, dying in Kentucky in 1969.

The 82nd Division had a generally better drop than the 101st. Most of the 505th Regiment landed on the drop zone near Ste-Mère-Eglise and by

4.00 a.m., with the assistance of men from the 2nd Battalion, 505th, under Lt-Colonel Ben Vandervoost, the 3rd Battalion of the 505th had taken Ste-Mère-Eglise and cut the Cherbourg–Carentan road. The 1st Battalion of the 505th had a much worse time during the drop, and most of their heavy equipment went astray. The 82nd were supposed to land astride the River Merderet and as the area around this river had been flooded, many men who dropped accurately fell into floodwater at least 2 to 3ft deep. Under normal conditions a fit man could simply stand up, wet but unhurt, but when carrying up to 100 lbs or more of equipment and ammunition and tugged over by the collapsing parachute, some found getting up too difficult, and therefore drowned.

Milton Chadwick of Upper Sandusky, Ohio, flew in with a glider formation of the 82nd Airborne. 'As for problems we had in the Normandy landings – they were many. My howitzer section and I flew in a "Horsa" glider. We had to land on a strange field since our original field was staked by the Germans. It was 11 p.m. and of course dark. Our glider hit the ground so hard that it disintegrated. After all the noise was over the first thing I heard was our pilot swearing. He was angry because he had made such a poor landing. Because of the condition of the glider we had trouble getting our equipment out – a Jeep and a howitzer.

'Our section had two axes as part of our equipment. In trying to unload I asked my corporal for an axe. He handed me one and I promptly broke the handle. I asked for the other axe and broke the handle on that one also. For the remainder of the war his favourite joke was, "Hand me that other axe."'

The 82nd had one great advantage in that they were quickly able to find their position in the ground, for the Cherbourg–Carentan railway line on its embankment above the Merderet made a perfect landmark. The Divisional Deputy Commander, Major-General James Gavin, dug his first fox-hole beside the road above the Merderet, where it remains to this day. He was then able to group the surviving troopers into sufficient strength to disperse or repel any counter-attack the Germans could make against them from beyond the river.

The German reaction to the paratroop landings was, in fact, surprisingly and mercifully slow. Had they reacted more quickly, the two American Divisions might have been severely mauled, but the scattered nature of the landings gave the Germans nowhere to aim at. The Americans were everywhere, and the paratroopers, facing up to the situation in which they found themselves, took the initiative and held on to it. When the Germans finally realized what was happening, they found it difficult to mount a co-ordinated counter-attack against the large but scattered forces now harassing their positions.

Fighting by squads, platoons and companies, the American paratroopers overran the Cotentin. This was fighting in which time was on the side of the

Americans, for at dawn the sea invasion must come, and by their guts and fighting ability they had already made its success certain. Soon after dawn, the men of Lt-Colonel Ewell's small force near Pouppeville saw a tank advancing towards them down the causeway. Playing safe, they greeted it with a few warning shots, at which it stopped and displayed a yellow recognition flag. Other men, infantrymen, then appeared from beside the causeway, also waving yellow flags, and the paratroopers were very glad to see them. These were men of the 4th Infantry Division, and they had come from the sea.

When they re-assembled in England after D-Day and counted the cost, it was found that the American airborne divisions had suffered about 20 per cent casualties on D-Day. Half of these were men killed or missing. This was bad, but nothing like as bad as the 75 per cent casualties forecasted by Leigh-Mallory. Only 20 parachute aircraft had been shot down out of more than 800 employed on the night of 5/6 June. The paratroops did not take all their D-Day objectives, for Carentan was not taken and the bridges over the Douve were still held by the Germans, but they had done very well. In spite of their misfortunes and the odds against them, the 82nd and 101st Airborne had given the 7th Corps of the US Army a foothold in France and a bridgehead in the Cotentin, from which Cherbourg could be quickly reduced, though there was a lot of hard fighting ahead before Cherbourg fell on 26 June. Above all, though, they had assured the success of the landings on 'Utah' beach. For 13,000 troopers, sorely harassed and scattered at the start of their adventure, that was an achievement indeed.

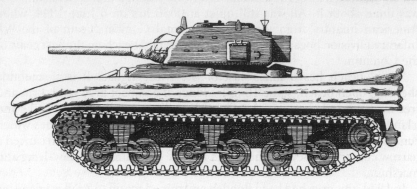

------CHAPTER SEVEN------

'Utah'

'We'll start the war right here.'
Brigadier-General Theodore Roosevelt
Deputy Commander, 4th Infantry Division,
Utah Beach, 6 June 1944

Midnight had come and gone. On the heights east of the Orne and in the close-knit fields of the Cotentin, men were fighting and dying, but elsewhere along the Normandy coast all was quiet. Had Field Marshal Rommel been at his headquarters at La Roche Guyon on the night of 5 June when reports began to come in of parachute landings astride the Orne and south of Cherbourg, his eyes would surely have strayed watchfully to the 40 miles of coast between the two. The image is so clear that it is possible to visualize him standing by the map-board, his hand moving over the surface and hardening into a fist which smites the Calvados coast as he says, 'Here!'

Rommel's action at the map-board is imaginary. Rommel was in Germany on 6 June 1944, celebrating his wife's birthday, waiting to see Hitler and get permission to move his Panzer divisions closer to the coast. He had been lulled into absence by the weather forecasts and the Channel gales. Those same forecasts had allowed some of his commanders to snatch some leave in Paris and others to attend an anti-invasion map exercise at Rennes. Even so, someone should have studied that map and drawn the obvious conclusion; that seaborne landings in the centre must surely follow these

118

widely separated airborne assaults. If anyone reached that conclusion, little was done about it. All was still quiet at 0630 hrs on 6 June 1944, when American infantry from the 8th Regimental Combat Team of the 4th Infantry Division began to come ashore on 'Utah' beach on the east coast of the Cotentin.

'Utah' beach lies 6 miles east of Ste-Mère-Eglise. It is a smoothly shelving, open beach, some 10 miles long, of compact grey sand, firm and free from natural obstacles. A mile offshore lies a small group of rocks and islands, the Iles St Marcouf. At the rear of the beach lie sand dunes which run up to 20ft high in places and behind them a low sea wall which carried a narrow coast road. Beyond the dunes and the road the land is low-lying and marshy.

In 1944, this area had been flooded and mined for up to 2 miles inland, as part of Rommel's anti-invasion preparations. Passage across this mined marsh depended on narrow causeways which, in peaceful times, give the villagers access to the beach. There were five of these, leading from the beach to the villages of Pouppeville, Hebert, Audouville, St Martin de Varreville and St Germain.

In the original plan, the inland exits from these causeways were to be seized by the airborne forces, and if they did their work well the beach defences could be quickly overwhelmed and the Americans rapidly debouch across the peninsula, well on the road towards the capture of Cherbourg.

The troops landing on 'Utah' were from the US 4th Infantry Division (the Ivy Leaves), commanded by Major-General Raymond O. Barton. This division formed part of General Lawton Collins's VII Corps. They were carried in a force of ships, Task Force 'U', commanded by Rear Admiral D. P. Moon, USN in the Force HQ ship, the USS *Bayfield*. This force contained, apart from troopships and landing craft, the US battleship *Nevada*, the 15-inch gun British monitor *Erebus*, 2 US cruisers, the USS *Tuscaloosa* and *Quincy*, and 3 British cruisers, HMS *Hawkins*, HMS *Enterprise* and HMS *Black Prince*, as well as 8 destroyers and the Dutch gunboat *Soemba*.

The Germans had three infantry divisions in the Cotentin, but 4th Infantry were to be chiefly concerned with the 709th and 243rd Infantry Divisions, which occupied defences on the east coast of the Cotentin. Fortunately, they were already engaged in attempting to swat the myriad bands of roving American paratroopers, and while they were thus distracted, 4th Infantry came ashore.

The infantry would be led ashore by the 8th Infantry Regiment (Colonel Van Fleet), with the 3rd Battalion of the 22nd Infantry attached, followed 75 minutes later by the 22nd Infantry (Colonel Tribolet), and on H+4 by the 12th Infantry (Colonel R. P. 'Red' Reeder). The assault would be supported by 32 DD tanks and a small amount of specialized equipment, mainly bulldozers, to clear the beach obstructions and deal with the beach defences.

The 709th and 243rd were composed largely of 'stomach' battalions, infantry considered fit only for coastal defence work, plus a small proportion of Russian and Georgian troops. The 243rd had, in theory, become an attack infantry division, when the men had been supplied with bicycles and some motor transport. There seemed to be no insurmountable problem to the Allies here, but early in June, Intelligence had reported that the formidable 91st Division, well trained in anti-invasion tactics, had arrived in the area and the possibility of some tough opposition grew stronger. The 91st Division had already suffered a major setback just after midnight when their Divisional Commander, Lt-General Wilhelm Falley, was ambushed and killed by Lt Malcolm Brannen of the 82nd Airborne.

Task Force 'U' sailed from ports in the west of England. Arthur McNeil was a nineteen-year-old signalman in LCT 2440, part of the British 104 LCT Flotilla, and recalls taking the Americans to France: 'I arrived in Brixham on the Saturday morning and from the railway station which stood above the harbour I looked down on an amazing sight. Both the inner and outer harbours were so full of LCTs that the water could hardly be seen. All the craft were covered with camouflage netting but it was obvious that they were all fully loaded. On reporting to the Flotilla Officer in his makeshift office on the quay, he asked me if I was ready to tackle the biggest job of my life, but before I could reply he had assigned me to LCT 2440 and I was aboard within the hour.

'My new craft was a Mark 5 LCT – American-built and shipped over the Atlantic in sections aboard cargo ships to be assembled in UK ports. The Royal Navy had 5 flotillas, each of 12 craft. Thus, it had 60 of the 500 which were built. It is possible that some "Overlord" planner felt that since we were American-built, we should have the honour of carrying American soldiers on the great day.

'Our ship, together with scores of others lying at Brixham, had loaded during the previous week at "hards" – man-made concrete "beaches" – on the River Dart above Dartmouth. Our Americans were part of a unit of US Army Assault Engineers and they were in three half-track vehicles and a Jeep. The vehicles were loaded with high explosive for clearing obstacles on the beach or further inland. There must have been about 20 GIs aboard and they outnumbered the ship's company by about 2 to 1. They took the view – rightly, I suppose – that this was what the craft had been built for, so they made full use of our messdeck and "heads" facilities – and later, when we were underway and most of us closed-up at defence stations, they used our bunks. Nothing was sacred ! They were quite the opposite of the archetypal

GI and we were all good friends – perhaps the fear of what might lie ahead brought us closer together.

'As we left Brixham in the late evening of the Saturday to form up in Torbay, I was on the bridge with the Skipper, Sub-Lieutenant Walter Webb RNVR, and an American officer. As we cleared the harbour, the Skipper called down the voicepipe to the Cox'n, "This is it, Cox'n, no exercise this time." He then gave me copies of the two Orders of the Day – one from General Eisenhower and one from the Naval C-in-C, Admiral Ramsay, RN – to distribute to the ship's company. The American officer did the same, handing copies of General Eisenhower's order to his soldiers. We were told that they were being handed personally to each member of the assault forces but that they would be read out to the follow-up waves. For that reason, I treasure my own copies.

'We formed part of Force "U", the assault force bound for "Utah" beach, the most westerly beach on the eastern side of the Cherbourg Peninsula. Force "U" had loaded at the Devon and Cornwall ports and had, therefore, the longest sea crossing by landing craft. The latter point is worth bearing in mind because many of the troops were carried in liberty ships and the similar victory ships which had been adapted as troopships for the invasion. The soldiers then transferred to landing craft a short distance from the beach. In leaving on the Saturday evening, we were scheduled to arrive at the assembly area off "Utah" after dark on the Sunday night. The crossing followed a dog-leg course at about six knots. LCTs were slow and cumbersome craft and not the best of sea boats.

'During Saturday night and Sunday morning the weather became steadily worse and, as we all know, H-Hour was postponed for 24 hours until Tuesday 6 June. For most of the Allied force this simply meant remaining in harbour for another 24 hours and nerve-wracking as that was, at least they had the relative comfort of calm water. Force "U" was already at sea and that made for problems – one of which was the formation of the convoy. Normal convoy formation consisted of a number of quite short columns of ships, never more than nine, although there could be a large number of columns. The object of this was to protect the flanks of the convoy against U-Boat attack. Because Force "U" had a vast number of craft, normal convoy formation would have led to an impossibly wide convoy, so we were in three long columns with a vanguard of minesweepers in an arc ahead of the convoy and escorts of every kind patrolling the flanks. Our craft was near the front of the centre column and as one looked astern, the columns seemed to merge into a solid line stretching right back to the horizon – an optical illusion, no doubt, but there were a lot of ships.

'When they landed, our GIs would have been at sea, a very rough sea, in a small craft, for over 60 hours. They had the longest and roughest sea crossing to Normandy of the entire assault force. Our hearts went out to them. At least we were more used to being at sea and we did not have to go ashore and fight.

'On the Monday afternoon, one of the GIs, a youngster of about my own age, lifted himself off the quarterdeck guardrail where he was trying to be sick. "Hey, Limey," he said. "Have you ever been in combat before?" I could only say that I had been in many air raids but I tried to reassure him by saying that the reality was not as bad as the apprehension. He said, "Well, I don't care how bad it is, it can't be any worse than this lousy boat and this lousy weather."

'We arrived at the assembly area east of the Cherbourg Peninsula after dark on the Monday evening and the weather seemed to be moderating – perhaps because we were now in the lee of the land. When dawn broke the sight was amazing. By now the heavy ships had arrived and the bombardment had begun. Battleships and cruisers were firing their main armament and they were being assisted by LCT(R)s – LCTs modified to launch thousands of rockets from launchers covering their tankdecks. The noise must have been deafening but our own engines and those of the craft all round us were noisy diesels, so the sound of the bombardment was rather dulled.

'As the LCTs of our flotilla formed a line abreast for the run into the beach, there seemed to be little opposition. As it turned out, "Utah" beach was indeed the quietest of all five Allied beaches – perhaps because it was over a mile south of where it should have been. The last thing I remember the American officer saying before he thanked us and left the bridge to join his men was that the run-in to the beach was quieter than some exercises he had taken part in. In any event, the only resistance was some mortar fire and light shelling. We could see the explosions in the water but none of our craft was hit. Just as well, in view of the explosives we were carrying! Neither were there any wrecked landing craft on the beach from earlier waves. We were quite proud of the fact that we gave our American friends a dry landing. The water barely reached their axles.

'When we started our approach to the beach, I hoisted our pennants – our number – and an additional White Ensign at the yard-arm (we always flew it at the gaff at sea). The additional one was our battle ensign and we explained to the American officer that it was customary in the Royal Navy, when going into battle, to fly as many battle ensigns as possible so that if one was shot away there would, hopefully, always be one still flying. The "battle" hardly seemed to justify our ardour. Having said that, I marvelled at the composure of our First Lieutenant, Sub-Lieutenant Jack Lathan RNVR. His beaching station was on the fo'c'sle to the right of the ramp down which the vehicles drove onto the beach. He had with him one of the able-seamen, "Dolly" Gray, whose task was to take soundings with a pole marked off in feet. These were relayed by the "Jimmy" to me by telephone and I called them over to the Skipper. The bridge was at the after end of the craft and the "Jimmy" and "Dolly" looked awfully exposed at the bow.'

Herb Stamer of Appalachin, New York, was then serving on LST 47, bound for 'Utah'. 'One hundred and seventy-three US-manned LSTs took part in the invasion, and only five were lost, and none on 6 June. On board our LST was a special service force of 40 underwater demolition men (UDT men). After the initial assault there were only 13 of the UDT men alive, and only 2 were uninjured. At H−2 we loaded the small boats with the demolition teams and they went ashore to do their jobs. Our H-Hour was set at 6 a.m. and proved to be everything it had been billed to be. The battleships began their barrage, minesweepers approached close to the shoreline, and the movements of troops landing in the heavy seas made it very difficult for the small boats. Two of ours breached-to and were swamped while landing. When the tide rolled back later we could see the red-iron railroad ties and crosses which made up the beach obstacles.

'We picked up 1,087 German prisoners, including a French woman who had been collaborating with the enemy. The crew members gave up their cots so the wounded could have a place to rest, and the officers gave up their quarters to the captured SS troopers, who were all tall, blond, tough as nails, and arrogant. In the tank deck, the majority of prisoners were kept with a clear space down the centre, where guards watched with machine guns.

'We returned to Normandy many times, perhaps 20 in all, before we left this area and sailed for Africa.'

Robin McGarel-Groves was a Royal Marine gunnery officer on one of the support ships, the cruiser HMS *Enterprise*. 'Back in mid-May, the Padre, the Rev. P. Husbands, had organized a sweepstake on which day was to be D-Day, and I had drawn 5 June ; but as I was sworn to secrecy I could only gloat privately over my potential winnings.

'Once we had rounded Land's End the weather got steadily worse and we felt sympathy for the unfortunate soldiery exposed to these unfamiliar elements. It also looked pretty tricky for those in small craft and particularly the Duplex Drive (DD) tanks, which had a canvas screen superimposed on them but with only a foot or so freeboard. It came as no surprise that all convoys were ordered to reverse course and that D-Day was postponed from 5 June. There went my sweepstake winnings.

'Eventually the signal was received that D-Day was to be 6 June. What a way to spend my twenty-fourth birthday ! We managed to arrive at our allotted bombardment position where we commenced firing just before 5.30 a.m. First a series of ranging shots to make sure we had found the target, and then a series of rapid broadsides, with small corrections to ensure that the whole length of the beach and village of St Martin de Varreville and its defences were covered. It all looked most effective.

Intelligence had indicated that there were two German 15-inch guns on the coast, within whose range we lay, and the plan was that these should be knocked out previously by the RAF or US Army Air Force. Fortunately this had happened, as we received no trouble from them. We ceased fire a short while before H-hour at 6.30 a.m. when the beach was engaged by LCRs using 1,000 2-pounder rockets fired in 3 salvos.

'The firing of these LCRs was most spectacular as the whole craft seemed to erupt. One did not envy the crew of these LCRs, who must have been mildly fried to say the least. The effect on the beach was equally spectacular as the entire area seemed to explode, literally drenching the beach with explosive, to the extent that it seemed hardly possible for anyone to survive.

'Due to all the smoke and dust from explosions on the beach, it was not possible to see much of what was happening. Anyway, even if we could have seen what was going on, we would have realized that the landing actually took place some mile and a half from the planned position. This was caused by casualties among the guiding craft. Landing on the wrong beach produced an immediate bonus as this beach was lightly held and the troops got ashore with very few casualties.

'Having carried out our pre-allotted task, we were now available for target opportunity with our fire controlled by aircraft spotting. I can still remember our call sign on radio. We were "Queen Easy Dawg" and our spotting aircraft, piloted by an American with a lovely Texan drawl, was "Nan Tare Rahger". Our Texan friend designated a target and ordered us to fire one round for him to apply the appropriate correction to get us on to his target. This being achieved he instructed us to "Fire for Effect". This meant a six-gun broadside, followed as quickly as we could by two similar broadsides. In order for him to spot we gave him the word just before the salvo was due to land. He dipped his wing so he could see and then gave us the appropriate instructions or correction. He and his successors kept us busy for the rest of that day and into the dusk. For once our own aircraft were everywhere, and on that first day we hardly sighted an enemy aircraft.

'One problem, however, did start to emerge. The Germans had laid a number of oyster acoustic mines, which exploded under a ship, triggered by the noise of its propellers. These mines lay on the bottom and were not swept by normal sweeping methods. Quite near us, the American destroyer the USS *Corry* struck one of the mines or was hit by shellfire, broke in two and sank quite quickly. Fortunately there were few casualties, and the survivors were picked up quickly by the many returning small craft, going back empty to fill up again. An American pilot vessel and several landing craft in our area suffered a similar fate and there were casualties on the other beaches from these mines, until a dead slow order was given for all movements in the immediate area of the beaches.'

*

The first men ashore were 132 men of the 4th and 24th Cavalry, who landed on the offshore Iles St Marcouf, which they found heavily mined but otherwise deserted. Meanwhile, as the troops trans-shipped into their landing craft, 247 Marauders of the 9th US Air Force began to bomb the beach and at about 0530 hrs the warships of Task Force 'U' began to fire on the shore defences and batteries.

The assault was supported by 33 LCRs or LCGs to give close support on to the beach, plus 32 DD tanks. The DD tanks were launched close in at only 3,000 yards from the beach, and 28 made it ashore, though they arrived 15 minutes after the infantry. The first infantry wave, of 2nd Battalion, 8th Infantry in 20 LCVPs, got ashore quite unopposed and, highly delighted, were waving their rifles in the air and cheering as they ran across the beach towards the dunes. They had not quite reached them when it became clear that something had gone wrong. The 4th Infantry Division had landed in the wrong place.

One of the ships going ashore that morning was commanded by Joseph Suozzo of Oceanside, California. 'I participated in the Normandy invasion as Officer in Charge of LCT 2310, beaching her on "Utah" beach at H Hour + 6 minutes. On May 10, 1944 I had been given command of LCT 2310, and went to Tilbury Docks to pick up the craft and crew. We became part of the Commander Gunfire Support Craft, Eleventh Amphibious Force. On June 1, 1944 we loaded three Sherman tanks and proceeded to Salcombe where we were berthed in mid-stream until getting underway for the invasion.

'Early on June 6, we arrived at the departure point. About 15 minutes before hitting the beach, Allied planes passed overhead and proceeded to saturate a strip of the landing beaches with bombs. Smoke, debris and dust obscured our view of the beach so badly that we couldn't see the beach for some time. We ended beaching some 300–400 yards further south than planned. It finally started to clear somewhat in the last 300 yards of our approach when we came under fire from an 88mm cannon in one of the pill-boxes on the beach. The profile of the beach was flat with no significant features and so we couldn't determine where the gunfire was coming from.

'Despite the gunfire, we did put the three Sherman tanks on the beach. They did not fire during the landing and I never did find out why. The wheel-house structure took one hit and both the helmsman and the engine man were wounded. Other damage was a hit to the winch, disabling it with 300ft of anchor cable out. Another hit the rudder cable, severing it with 30 degrees right rudder on and one hit in the engine room, disabling the starboard engine. We were able to back off after cutting loose our anchor cable and then jockeying the engines between forward and reverse to try and compensate for the loss of steering. All in all we took ten direct hits from 88mm and mortar fire. We were able to get a tow from a British LCF to the staging area five miles or so off the beach, where we remained until one of our LSTs towed us back to Portsmouth.' Joseph M. Suozzo was awarded the Silver Star for his action on D-Day.

Walter Schaad of Marietta, Ohio, went ashore on 'Utah' in a tank. 'On the morning of D-Day I woke up in the bottom of the tank, then I crawled on to the top and sat down to wait, and before long I was able to make out the beach. As we approached the shore we got down as low as possible in the tanks, and as the ramp dropped and we went into the water, our tank was hit with artillery at least four times. One shell hit right by my ear and cracked the side of the tank about a foot long. I still have loss of hearing because of that.

'Captain Warren was calling for someone to help him pull a Jeep from the water, and three sergeants ran to help him. Donald Schlemmer and I got off the tank, ran to the concrete wall, and got into a fox-hole, when we heard a shell coming. When the smoke, sand and water had cleared, the three sergeants lay there dead, and Captain Warren had a piece of shrapnel in his hand. We backed the tank to the edge of the water and pulled the Jeep onshore, and then we did the same thing with a half-track, jamming an opening in the sea wall, pulling it out of the way. Then we went through the wall into an open field, where our tank went into a shell hole and tore off a track. Our tank mechanic and two or three other boys started working on the track, but I felt it was safer in a fox-hole.

'After sitting there for nearly two hours, with shells dropping all around us, I had said every prayer I could think of. I begged the dear Lord not to let the next shell fall in the hole with us. After running out of prayers I started to think on all the bad things I had ever done and promised not to do them again.

'Believe it or not, I then heard a roaring noise from the west. Coming in were planes, planes and more planes, paratroopers and gliders. Unbelievable! You couldn't see the sky they were so thick. By that time our tank was fixed and we were able to get into a firing position.'

Among the first men ashore that morning was nineteen-year-old Anthony Jele from Albuquerque, New Mexico, then in Company 'C', 1st Battalion, 8th Infantry Regiment. Anthony Jele was carrying his rifle, some grenades, two bandoliers and a case of mortar ammunition for the heavy weapon crews that would follow him ashore. 'During part of the twelve-hour trip across the English Channel I stood guard and watched the five-pronged invasion. I saw water spouts shooting up next to our landing craft, but didn't know what they were. Somebody else said, "Hey, they're shooting at us."

'The French coast was calm when I got my first glimpse of Normandy just after dawn on June 6, 1944. When I looked at the beach it was all clear and quiet. It looked like a Sunday morning.

'The Germans weren't expecting a landing at "Utah" beach, so the first wave was able to scramble across the sand without many casualties, but Nazi artillery was alerted to the invasion soon after the first Americans waded ashore and the fifth wave nearly got wiped out. Our real baptism by fire came three days later, and on June 9 heavy enemy fire tore our unit apart. All the officers were killed and the rest of us struggled on for about a month with sergeants in command.'

The 8th Infantry should have landed opposite Exit 3, which led to Audouville. Instead they landed over a mile south, opposite Exit 1, leading to Pouppeville. One of the control vessels, which should have led them in, had struck a mine and been lost, and the strong set of the incoming tide sweeping up the Channel then carried their assault craft off course. This initial error could have been disastrous, but luckily landing in the first wave was the Assistant Commander of the 4th Infantry Division, Brigadier-General Theodore Roosevelt Jnr, son of the former American President, Teddy Roosevelt. Although fifty-seven years old at the time, he had persuaded his Divisional Commander to let him go ashore with the first wave.

This proved providential. General Roosevelt recognized the error, knew what to do, and had the authority to make his decision stick. He signalled out to the following waves of landing craft to ignore their original headings and follow in behind the initial wave. He then walked up and down the foreshore, waving his stick, cheering his men ashore, regardless of the machine-gun and artillery fire now beginning to sweep the beach. The 1st Battalion of the 8th Infantry pressed on towards Audouville, the 2nd Battalion continued towards Pouppeville. General Roosevelt died of a heart attack five weeks after the landings, but his action on D-Day won him the Congressional Medal of Honour.

Many men of the 4th Infantry Division recall seeing General Roosevelt on the beach; men like Jack Capell, then a radio wireman in the 8th Infantry Regiment. 'I spent five months in England before the invasion, and although I saw a lot of the towns in South Devon, I never got to London, which I really regret. One of my buddies did get a twenty-four hour pass to London and while he was there he got caught in an air raid and hit by a piece of shrapnel. He was the first man of the 4th Infantry Division to be wounded in Europe.

'We sailed from Dartmouth in South Devon. The landing craft we boarded was an LST and we were to be carried across on this and transfer to smaller landing craft ten or eleven miles offshore. Once at sea we saw more ships. The sea got rough and it began to rain. We were then told that we were to land in France, fight our way ashore and locate a road inland. Once inland we were to link up with our paratroopers somewhere between the beach and the village of Ste-Mère-Eglise.

'We trans-shipped to small landing craft late on June 5, though the seas were still rough. An LCT came up, the LST opened its doors and I was ordered to drive my Jeep from one to the other; all this while the two ships were rolling in the waves, out of phase with each other. I managed to do this but the transfer damaged our waterproofing.

'To starboard was the island of St Marcouf, and the battleship USS *Nevada* was firing on German gun positions and the shore batteries were firing back. Aircraft towing gliders were passing over, and obviously we would be hitting the beach in about an hour. I had a brief vision of being blown to pieces; some men became silent, others became boisterous. We filled in the time by breaking into the ship's stores and loading up with good Navy food.

'We – a sergeant, and Horace Cisk the Company clerk, and I – were ordered off in deeper water than there should have been, and after a few yards my Jeep engine began to misfire and then stopped. We were in deep water and neither of my passengers could swim. I swam for shore, touching bottom in the trough of each wave, left my equipment on the beach and swam back to bring the other two ashore. I got a rope from a DUKW and then towed the Jeep on to the sand. Artillery fire was falling on to the beach and we were strafed by a Messerschmitt. The wounded were already being taken off, many of the men had stepped on anti-personnel schu-mines, which damaged or blew off their feet. We eventually got the Jeep going and drove to the head of the beach. All our food had been lost and for two days we lived on fruit cocktail looted from the Navy; I have never cared for it since.

'By this time most of our rear echelon units had landed, including the artillery and anti-tank companies, military police, and so on. On leaving the beach to find the company we were confused because the terrain did not fit the features given in our briefing. This was because the 8th Infantry Regiment had been landed about a mile south of our intended position. General Theodore Roosevelt Jnr landed in the first wave, and he took charge on the beach where we landed. His words at the time were : "We'll start the war right here." Teddy Roosevelt was the most respected man in the unit and I believe his presence on the beach made the difference between success and failure on "Utah" beach. Unfortunately, he did not stay with us long and was to die in Normandy.'

Another man on the beach that day was a Combat Medic, Calvin Grose of the 22nd Infantry Regiment. 'When we boarded a transport for the invasion from Plymouth, we were told to stay below decks, but I sneaked top-side to watch the naval bombardment by such ships as USS *Nevada*, plus other cruisers and destroyers.

'We were about the first craft in, and the enemy fire was light until they found out what was going on. We reached the beach with Brigadier-General Theodore Roosevelt Jnr, and he told us not to lay there but to move in off the beach. We had never been under fire before and he walked from soldier to soldier and told us to move. We attacked some pill-boxes and I spent 55 days treating the wounded. I was then hit myself and shipped back to England to recover.'

Corporal Fred Tannery drove ashore in a Jeep. 'We could see the coastline of France as we went in. There was not too much activity, and when the battleships started bombarding the beach I thought this was going to be duck soup. Then the shells started splashing around and wounded soldiers were brought back on board our LST . . . so this was it. Our LST hit the beach, the ramp went down and "Pop" my driver, and I, got ashore without even getting our feet wet.

'We drove inland with just a little shell-fire going on, and that didn't bother us. We drove inland until we met a bunch of GIs and settled down with them for a while. My father had fought in France during the First War, and he told me about the red poppies in France, and the field next to the road where we stopped was full of poppies which reminded me of my father.

'Just after dark some German planes came over and every ship in the bay opened up on them – a sheet of red and green tracer; the most beautiful sight I have ever seen. One of the planes was hit and crashed nearby. I'll never forget that. Otherwise it was quiet – and that was my first day in France with the 4th Infantry Division.'

Colonel 'Red' Reeder was there, commanding the 12th Infantry Regiment. 'Before D-Day a conference on the Normandy Landings was held at a theatre in Plymouth, and the Corps Commander, Lt-General Collins, was explaining the missions of the different units in Normandy, indicating their objectives on the map with a long pointer. "Here is the 8th Infantry," he said, "Colonel Van Fleet commanding. I served in the 8th Infantry. It is a fine regiment of great traditions, and it will accomplish its mission. Here is the 22nd Infantry, Colonel Tribolet. I served in the 22nd Infantry. It is a fine regiment of great traditions, and it will accomplish its mission. Here is the 12th Infantry, Colonel Reeder commanding."

'Then he stopped and talked of the problems of the landing. I felt I could not let the General and his talk end there, for I had ten 12th Infantrymen with me in the room.

'When the General paused I stood up. "Sir," I said. "May I make a statement, sir?" "Certainly, Red. What is it?" "Sir, the 12th Infantry Regiment is a fine regiment, a regiment of great traditions, and it will accomplish its mission," I said. After the applause, Van Fleet howled, "Red, you looked like a West Point pleb correcting a first-classman."

'The four hours from 6.30 a.m. when the first troops landed till we went ashore at 10.30 a.m. were the longest four hours I ever spent. When I climbed down the cargo nets into the bucking LCVP, a young sailor said, "Colonel, sit up here on our perch with the coxswain and me. You can see better." "No thanks," I said. "I read in a book that a leader is supposed to be up front. I'll stand at the front ramp with Colonel Montelbano, battalion commander (Lt-Colonel Montelbano was killed on D+5) so I can be the first one out of this thing." That decision saved my life. When the boat grated on the Normandy shore, I stepped into waist-high water and ran up the beach while light artillery sprayed the sands with iron. A shell hit the LCVP and killed the young sailor, the coxswain, and the last 12th Infantryman leaving the boat.

'All along "Utah" beach 12th Infantrymen were wading ashore and running to the top of the dunes. "Mills," I said, "things don't look right to me. Where the hell are we?" Lieutenant Bill Mills took my map and in a moment justified his grade of 97 per cent on the map-reading exam. He said, "They've landed us about two miles south of where we're supposed to be." "It don't matter," I replied. "We know where to go! Get the word out we're two miles south of where we ought to be."

'At the top of the dunes I passed General Roosevelt, who had landed with Van Fleet's first wave. "Red, the causeways leading inland are all clogged up. Look at it! A procession of Jeeps and not a wheel turning. Something wrong." Roosevelt looked tired and the cane he leaned on heightened the impression. "We are going through the flooded area!" I yelled as loud as I could. Down the dunes I saw Lieutenant-Colonel "Chuck" Jackson of the 1st Battalion, and I gave him an arm signal. I knew the rest of the regiment coming ashore in the next wave would follow us.

'A mile across the flooded meadow lay the village of St-Martin-de-Varreville. Rising above it was a church steeple that looked like a friendly beacon. We waded through water in the German-made lake which varied in depth from waist to arm-pit and in a few spots was over our heads. We had the non-swimmers paired with the swimmers, and even so I was proud of the non-swimmers around me who were holding on to their weapons. The large groups of men in the water made a perfect target, but we waded the water safely.'

Louis Siebel was a Pfc serving in the Quartermaster Company of the 4th Infantry Division. 'I was inducted into the Army in 1942 and had three brothers in the armed services. My younger brother, a bombardier, was shot down over Germany the day I arrived in England. He later died of his injuries. We waited all day on our LST about 3,000 yards off "Utah". We watched a small destroyer go down and an ammunition dump blew up, and at about 5 o'clock in the evening the announcement came that we were about to land. About 170 men in 30 trucks rode on to "Utah" beach, where it was still daylight. We could see shell-holes and bodies covered by blankets, and there was still enemy fire, but we felt relieved because we had landed in France – and that was June 6 as I remember it fifty years afterwards.'

Dominic L. Alfano from Hamden, Connecticut was a member of 'B' Company, 1st Battalion, 8th Infantry. 'Needless to say we were anxious to set foot on land after the gales at sea, but prior to getting ashore we were shelled by the Germans and it seemed questionable whether we would get ashore without becoming casualties. However, we did get on to the beach, where we were strafed by enemy aircraft. Altogether, I spent seven years and four months in the service, being discharged on October 2, 1945, just one year after being wounded in Germany. As you may know, D-Day was not so difficult for us, but that was one of our easiest days. I learned from the accounting that by May 1945 the 4th Infantry Division had sustained a total of 34,000 killed and over 22,000 wounded, the most of any Division.'

Harper Coleman of Tucson, Arizona, was with Company 'H', 2nd Battalion, 8th Infantry Regiment and also recalls seeing General Roosevelt on the beach : 'We went in with the second wave of assault troops. Shortly after the larger ships came to a stop we were to go into the small LCVP. Being with the first waves had some advantage. We were not required to go over the sides of the ship but were put on the LCVP while it was still on the davits of the larger ship and let down in the water with the craft.

'As we started to move towards the beach in lines, we passed Rocket Launcher ships and as we were going past they were releasing many salvos of rockets on the beach. It must have been around 0530 hrs to 0600 hrs, as it was daylight and we were all standing up in the craft watching the show on the beach, which was still some distance ahead. The beach was almost hidden from view by smoke and shell bursts.

'I saw the craft in front of ours going up with some sort of direct hit, which left ours first at this time. Before we reached the shore something came through the side of our craft and tore quite a hole in it, in one side and out the other. It also tore a good sized piece out of my backpack. I don't recall how I replaced it but I did so quickly. Also, while on the way in, I recall seeing some sort of naval ship laying over with many people up on the side.

'The history books say we landed some distance to the left than we were supposed to, and that this was one of the easier landings. I don't know if this was good or bad. It did not seem good at the time. We went in the water somewhat more than waist deep and a good distance from dry land. When we came on shore we were greeted by Brigadier-General Theodore Roosevelt. How he got there, I do not know, other than that he was in one of the first landing craft, but there he was, standing on the beach, waving his cane and giving out instructions as only he could do. If we were afraid of the enemy, we were more afraid of him, and could not have stopped on the beach had we wanted to.

'My squad of six was down to four very early on ; we lost one on the beach and another when we came to the higher ridge just over the sandy area. Moving as fast as we could we came to a road that ran down to the beach, and this took us through the swamps that were behind the beach which had been flooded by the Germans. We came up on the small town of Pouppe-ville. This is where we began to see the results of our work – our first dead enemy. Shortly beyond the town we began to meet some of the airborne people. As I recall, they were rather glad to see us.

'I remember setting up for the first night. It was on a dirt road with a high hedge on either side. We dug in there for the night with a number of enemy dead laying in the roadway close to where we were. One of the remarks of the day was, "These ones won't hurt you." This was more or less the routine for the twenty-one days on the way to Cherbourg. We must have been a dirty and smelly bunch by the time we got there.'

Malcolm Williams was with the 2nd Battalion of the 12th Infantry Regiment and recalls another story of General Roosevelt. 'I once heard General Roosevelt asking Major O'Malley of "H" Company in our Bat-talion what his secret was for success in always being able to move forward in an attack. Major O'Malley's answer was, "Well, Sir, if my boys get pinned down and can't move, I just crawl a few yards out in front of them and holler for help. When they see and hear me, they think I'm in trouble, so they start moving up towards me. And once I get those boys moving, all hell can't stop them."

'On another day, the day when Colonel Montelbano was killed, I was sent back to regiment to report his death, and Major Burk told me to report to General Roosevelt. Colonel "Red" Reeder, our Regimental Commander, had been wounded that morning. The General asked me to have coffee to calm me. Then he asked what was going on up there. I told him about the Colonel getting killed. I was standing only 20 or 30ft away at the time. The General asked who was left in charge. I told him that Major O'Malley was in command. He said, "You go back and tell all those men that they have the best man in the whole Army." He then said, "Why, that black Irishman, I would trust him anywhere."

'On the day Major O'Malley was killed, we had been receiving a lot of artillery fire. A piece of shrapnel had torn off my gas mask but it didn't hit me. Boy, that was close! When Major O'Malley's body was brought back, I took his gas mask and used it for the rest of the war. All of us admired and respected Major O'Malley. He was a good soldier and I will never forget him. God rest his soul.'

After the infantry had secured the beach, the combat engineers and naval demolition teams came ashore and began to blast and clear away the beach obstacles. Quite apart from avoiding disastrous confusion, Brigadier Roosevelt's action in switching the landing had advantages. The defences to the south of the planned 'Utah' landing area were less strong than those in front of their original landing place, and more easily overcome. The beach obstacles here consisted of three lines of obstructions, mainly steel spikes and wooden posts crowned with fused Teller mines, steel caltrops, tetrahedra and 'hedgehogs', all designed to hole landing craft. All these obstacles were mined. The plan called for the combat engineers to clear a number of fifty-yard gaps in these obstacles to let landing craft in when the tide rose, and they did this quickly and well. By H+3 the beach had been largely cleared and the troops were pouring ashore, though German activity, mostly from artillery, was steadily increasing.

John Ausland, then aged twenty-four, was an Intelligence Officer with the 29th Field Artillery Regiment. 'The run into the beach was a bizarre experience. Most of us were happy to cower behind the little protection provided by the metal sides of the landing craft. One officer from Regimental Headquarters, however, insisted on sitting on a chair above us, where he was exposed to enemy fire. Arms folded, he announced that he did not want to miss a moment of this spectacular show. A few weeks later, under similar circumstances, he collapsed with a sniper's bullet through his head.

'When the landing craft hit the beach and the front ramp went down, I waded through some shallow water and ran to the shelter of the sea wall that ran along the beach, barely glancing at several soldiers who were lying on the sand as though asleep. I could hear rifle and machine-gun fire beyond the sand dunes, and some mortar shells fell not far away.

'My task, once ashore, was to guide our three artillery batteries to firing positions that we had selected in England from a detailed foam-rubber relief map of the beach. After crossing the sand dunes that lay just beyond the sea wall, I was unable to figure out where I was. When I asked an infantry officer to help me, he laughed and said that the Navy had landed the first wave several thousand yards south of where we were supposed to land. Fortunately, Brigadier-General Theodore Roosevelt Jnr had volunteered to go in with the first wave. He later told some of us how he had gone forward to reconnoitre the beach, and finding that Major-General Maxwell Taylor's Airborne Division, which had dropped during the night, had captured the causeways over the inundated area behind the beach, Roosevelt decided that to try to move the landing northward would only cause confusion.

'When I went back to the beach I told Colonel Thomason that I could find only two firing positions, not three, in the limited area between the sand dunes and the inundated area. He said, "It's all right. We'll only need two. B-Battery hit a mine on the way in and the landing craft sank." Before I could think too long about the sixty men on that boat, Thomason told me to get moving and guide the two other batteries to their firing positions.

'After the batteries were in position, Thomason suggested that we go inland to find the infantry. After crossing a causeway over the inundated area, we found ourselves in the middle of a field. We froze when we heard a soldier on the other side of the field shout, "Don't you fools know that you're in the middle of a minefield?" After discussing our predicament, we agreed to separate, so that if one of us stepped on a mine we would not both be blown up. It was a long way to the other side of that field.

'Late in the afternoon, after our batteries moved inland to support the infantry, the clear, blue sky was filled with coloured parachutes. From these were suspended boxes of supplies for the paratroopers. A colourful sight turned to horror, however, when gliders loaded with soldiers and equipment started to circle and land. Unnerved perhaps by German anti-aircraft fire, some of the pilots crashed their gliders into the hedgerows. Whenever I recall that scene, I can still hear the terrible screams of pain that filled the air around me. My last memory of that day is watching multicoloured tracer bullets arch through the sky over Ste-Mère-Eglise, which had been captured by our paratroopers but was still surrounded by German forces.

'I fell asleep well after midnight in a ditch by a road – a road that would lead us first north to the capture of Cherbourg and then south to the breakout from the bridgehead at St Lô.'

Girden 'Griff' Griffith came ashore with Company 'I' of the 12th Infantry. 'My battalion landed in the second wave of assault troops on "Utah" beach. Like everyone else, I recall D-Day as a time of saying my prayers and trying to stay alive. On the third day I was wounded by artillery fire near Emondeville and evacuated back to a hospital in England.'

The 4th Infantry Division had the easiest of all the D-Day landings, partly because of the southward shift on the beach, partly because the paratroopers had disrupted the German defences, partly because the landing plan worked. The entire 'Utah' beach area was captured at a cost of just forty-five men killed and injured. Initial opposition on the beach was fortunately light, because during the hour or so it took to clear the beach and the causeways and let the traffic off, the tanks and vehicles began to assemble in a manner that would have provided sitting targets for German artillery. In the main the opposition came in the form of undirected artillery fire from inland batteries and mortars, which were swiftly engaged by the big guns on the warships offshore.

The German infantry manning the coastal positions had first been shocked and dazed by the bombing, shelling and rocket fire, and startled by the sight of the DD tanks rearing out of the waves. Coastal strongpoints were soon reduced, and as more men came ashore, the chief problem on the 'Utah' beachhead was traffic congestion. Owing to the southward swing of the landings, only Exit 2 could be used by vehicles, and this was both mined and defended by pill-boxes. Behind the beachhead the fighting intensified, both along the causeways and across the flooded fields, as 4th Infantry got into its stride and began to force a passage inland.

William Garvin from Epping in New Hampshire was a Pfc in Company 'K' of the 12th Infantry Regiment. 'Three months after war was declared, I volunteered for Army service, foolishly choosing the infantry because I loved the outdoors and felt I could shoot a rifle well. I thought I could best serve Uncle Sam as a rifleman and foot soldier. After about two and a half years of rugged training at various Army installations in the US, our Division boarded the USS *George Washington* and set sail for Liverpool, England.

'On the night of June 5, we lifted anchor and pointed the ship's bows eastward, headed out into the night and the nervous unknown. It was required that all troops remain below decks for the crossing with the exception of Cpl John Delevan, the company radio operator, and his assistant, yours truly. We were to maintain radio transmission silence but to operate the SCR 300 radio set for message receiving only.

'Guns from some ships were lofting shells inland as the first wave of infantrymen hit the shores. Our turn came much later as we were scheduled for the ninth wave. We had transferred to LCIs (Landing Craft Infantry) and had rendezvous'd in a constant circle before our turn came to break out and head for the shore. The LCI pilot was kind enough to run the boat right up on to dry land before discharging his human cargo. This hardly proved beneficial to us, however, because the "shore" was but a mere sandbar which we quickly crossed before plunging into hip-deep water. Facing us was over two miles of inundated terrain with deep irrigation trenches about every two hundred yards. We had kept our Mae-West life-jackets on since debarking, which proved to be a tremendous aid in staying afloat while floundering across the flooded ditches, weighed down with heavy fighting gear.

'For us, the landing at "Utah" beach was a relatively pleasant adventure. There had been no visible casualties, though there were some light artillery shells exploding on the beachhead some distance away. After sloshing about and hand-paddling for about one and a half hours, we breathed easier on reaching above-water ground. We began to see the results of early-morning skirmishes as, with mixed feelings, we observed the corpses of the enemy. The regiment's mission was to push inland to relieve the paratroopers who earlier that morning had descended on the sleepy Normandy village of Ste-Mère-Eglise. Evidence of savage fighting grew as we neared the village and dead from both sides became commonplace. Torn parachutes hung from trees and buildings and broken branches and shattered buildings indicated fierce fighting had occurred.

'We accomplished our mission with little effort. Perhaps we were lulled into a feeling of complacency from having done little more than observe the countryside and the results of the actions of others. None of us in Company "K", to my knowledge, had fired a shot, but little did we realize how rapidly this scenario would switch to a frightful and costly nightmare. Before it was all over, my left arm received a bullet, my forehead a shell fragment, and my feet frostbite. I considered myself extremely fortunate to have emerged from the war with body and mind intact; many others were far less fortunate.'

By 1000 hrs on 6 June the seaborne forces were pushing inland hard from 'Utah', drawn on by the sound of firing up ahead, where mixed groups of paratroopers from both Airborne Divisions were striving to keep the landward exits clear. The first formation ashore, the 2nd Battalion of the 8th Infantry Regiment, was now heading fast for Pouppeville, harassed across the marshes by small-arms fire. On the way they found and recruited a DD tank, which then led their advance along the causeway until at the far end they were met with a hail of fire, which forced the tank to halt and the infantry to take cover in the water. The fire sounded familiar and stopped abruptly when yellow recognition flags were displayed by the tank and the infantry. Down the causeway to meet them, with wide grins spreading across their blackened faces, came the men of the 101st Airborne, and the first man they met was Captain George Mabry from South Carolina, the first seaborne soldier across the causeway.

By the evening of D-Day, 4th Infantry Division was well ashore, with the advance elements eight miles inland. Over 23,000 men had been landed on 'Utah', together with tanks and artillery, and they were now linking up with the paratroopers all along their divisional front. The 4th Infantry Division took only 210 casualties during the entire day and this included 60 men lost at sea. Although the 4th Infantry Division was to see much hard fighting in the following days as they pushed north to Cherbourg, their first day in battle had gone well.

Others were not so lucky. Just a few miles away, on the north coast of Calvados, two other American infantry regiments, from the 1st and 29th Divisions of General Gerow's V Corps, were being cut to pieces on 'Omaha' beach.

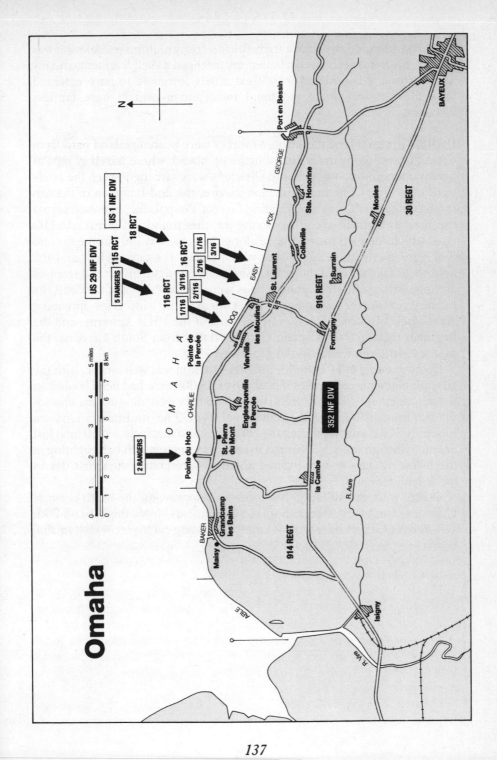

CHAPTER EIGHT
'Omaha'

'The only people on this beach are the dead
and those who are going to die – now let's
get the hell out of here.'
Colonel George Taylor
16th Infantry Regiment, 1st Infantry Division

Every campaign ever fought seems to involve at least one pounding match, some point on the battlefield where fine plans and well practised tactics dissolve into sheer murderous fighting. So far the invaders had done very well, or been very lucky. The airborne forces were at work on the flanks and the landing on 'Utah' had been very successful. A major setback somewhere was only to be expected and it came along the Calvados coast, on the beach codenamed 'Omaha'.

The USS *Ancon*, flagship of Admiral Hall, USN, commanding Task Force 'O' Headquarters ship for the V Corps, reached the transport area twelve miles off 'Omaha' about 0230 hrs on the morning of 6 June. Out there in the Bay of the Seine there was little shelter from the full fetch of the gales, and the laden men of the two assault divisions were in difficulties before they began to climb down the scrambling nets into their assault craft.

The two divisions of General Gerow's V Corps leading the assault on 'Omaha' were the 1st Infantry Division (the Big Red One) commanded by

138

Major-General Clarence R. Huebner, and the 29th Infantry Division (the Blue and the Grey) commanded by Major-General Charles Gerhardt. These two divisions had different origins. The 'Big Red One' was a regular infantry division, and although it contained many drafted men, the backbone of the division was made up of professional officers, NCOs and private soldiers, drawn from every state of the Union. The 29th Infantry Division (the Blue and the Grey), on the other hand, was a National Guard formation, the equivalent of a British Territorial Army unit.

The 29th Division recruited in the states of Virginia, Maryland and Pennsylvania, and many of the men in its ranks had joined up before the war in order to serve with their neighbours and buddies when the big war came. The 29th was drafted into Federal service in 1942 but had seen no action before D-Day. This local recruitment was to give the losses sustained by the 29th Infantry Division on 'Omaha' beach a particular poignancy when the casualty lists for D-Day arrived in the small towns back home. To give two examples, the town of Roanoke lost 18 men on D-Day and the town of Bedford lost 23 of its sons. Many of these men including three sets of brothers, were serving in 'A' Company of the 116th Infantry Regiment.

The assault formations for 'Omaha' were two Regimental Combat Teams (RCTs), the equivalent of a British brigade, made up from the 16th Infantry Regiment of 1st Infantry Division, landing on the left, or east, on 'Easy Red' and 'Easy Green', and the 116th Infantry Regiment of the 29th Division landing on the right, or west, on 'Dog Green, White and Red'. Both regiments, and their supporting assault engineers, DD tanks and artillery, came under General Huebner's command for the assault phase.

For support these regiments had 2 US battleships, the USS *Texas* and the USS *Arkansas*, the British cruiser HMS *Glasgow*, and 2 French cruisers, the *Montcalm* and the *Georges Leygues*, as well as 11 destroyers and squadrons of LCRs and some LCGs. The infantry were accompanied by special teams of combat engineers who, as at 'Utah', would land immediately after the assault waves to demolish and clear away the beach obstacles for the landing craft bringing in the follow-up waves. In this task they would be assisted by bulldozers as at 'Utah'. Unfortunately, 'Omaha' was not to be like 'Utah' at all.

'Omaha' beach is a wide, gently curving beach, some four miles long, which occupies the only gap in the 100-foot-high cliffs that run from the Pointe du Hoc north of Isigny, east towards Port-en-Bessin. 'Omaha' was an obvious point for a landing and the German defences here were therefore more developed than at many other points along the Calvados coast. In addition they were manned by the trained and resolute 352nd Infantry Division, the only full attack division on the Normandy coast. This division had only arrived in Normandy at the end of May and had moved to the Cotentin coast on an anti-invasion exercise in the first days of June. The presence of the 352nd was completely unknown to Allied Intelligence, and an unpleasant surprise for the assaulting infantry.

The defences at 'Omaha' were formidable and helped by the nature of the terrain. The beach shelves gently but leads up to a high shingle bank, along the top of which now runs a narrow road which rests on the sea wall. Behind the road is a shallow belt of sand, leading to high sand dunes and cliffs which provide visibility over the entire landing area.

There are only four exits through these cliffs and off the beach. In June 1944 these gaps, or 'draws', were protected by 35 pill-boxes full of infantry armed with rifles, machine guns and grenades. There were 8 concrete bunkers equipped with 75mm guns and no less than 85 machine-gun posts equipped with Spandaus. The heavy guns were sited in concrete emplacements to enfilade the beach, with the concrete on the roof and seaward side strong enough to withstand direct hits from bombs and heavy naval guns. Along 'Omaha' the Germans had laid out 18 anti-tank positions, mounting guns of between 37mm and 75mm, 6 Nebelwerfer (multiple-barrelled mortar) pits, 38 rocket batteries and 4 field artillery positions. To link all this together a network of trenches had been prepared, and the whole complex was manned by well trained infantry, including a good number of snipers. This combination of man-made defences and natural obstacles had turned 'Omaha' into a killing ground ... and there was more.

In addition to weaponry, the Germans had prepared a thick belt of beach obstacles. There were three rows of these set below the high-water mark consisting of mined posts and obstructions, the angular steel girders of 'Element C', 'Belgian Gates', and a variety of other obstructions, all mined and creating a complete barrier to any oncoming landing craft. Behind this was a further wide belt of mines and barbed wire laid along the shingle bank and in the strip between the bank and the dunes. All in all 'Omaha' was the most formidable German position along the Normandy coast. The task of overcoming it was committed to the enthusiastic troops of the 29th Infantry Division and their comrades of the Big Red One, the most experienced American division in Europe, veterans of the fighting in North Africa, Sicily and Italy.

During these early campaigns, 1st Infantry Division had established a great reputation in combat with the enemy at the front and – let it be admitted – an even greater one for combat with the military police in the rear areas. General Omar Bradley recalls in his memoirs that the 1st Infantry Division left 'a trail of looted bars and outraged mayors all the way from Arzew to Catania'. The Big Red One was a feisty, hard-fighting division, which needed careful handling in and out of combat.

After the conclusion of the Sicilian campaign, General Bradley decided that the time had come to find a new commander for the Big Red One, and he found just the man he wanted in Major-General Clarence R. Huebner, by repute the fiercest disciplinarian in the US Army. Huebner had enlisted as a private soldier in 1910, and had already served in the 1st Infantry Division, in every rank from private to colonel.

Clarence Huebner was a fighting soldier. During the Great War he had served with 1st Infantry in France and fought in the battles along the Aisne and Marne, at St Mihiel and in the Argonne. He had been wounded twice and received the Distinguished Service Medal, the Distinguished Service Cross and the Silver Star. General Huebner was not a man to mess about. He took firm command of 1st Infantry in North Africa and began to crack the whip, using methods which included the general officers' universal panacea for such situations, large amounts of close-order drill.

Major-General Charles H. Gerhardt of the 29th Infantry Division was another fighting man. Commissioned into the US Cavalry in 1917, he had served in France during the Great War and taken part in the fighting around St Mihiel and in the Argonne offensives. General Gerhardt took command of the 29th Infantry Division in May 1942.

General Huebner was in charge of both RCTs for the landing phase. Each RCT consisted of three battalions of a thousand men apiece, and these were to be supported by combat engineers, field artillery and DD tanks with further support from aerial bombardment and guns of the fleet.

Each regiment was to put ashore two battalions at H-Hour, 0630 hrs, to clear the beach defences. This done by H+3, the assault battalions would be followed by the reserve battalion, and then by the 18th and 26th Infantry Regiments, who would spread out inland to occupy a bridgehead six miles deep astride the Bayeux to Isigny road, by midnight. The 116th Infantry of 29th Division would also be responsible for capturing the German batteries on the Pointe du Hoc (or Hoe) to the west of the beachhead, for which tasks they had under command elements of the 2nd US Rangers commanded by Lt-Colonel James Rudder.

The most important job of the assault battalions was, as at 'Utah', to clear the exits from the beaches, through the cliffs and dunes to the villages behind – Vierville, St Laurent and Colleville. All these 'draws' were mined and wired, and covered by fire.

The assault began at H−50 minutes (0540 hrs) on 6 June, when 32 DD tanks of the 741 Tank Battalion entered the tossing Channel seas 6,000 yards offshore. Their waterproof screens could not withstand prolonged battering by the waves and soon collapsed. Only 5 tanks made it to the beach, and 3 of these were put ashore 'dry' by an LCT that could not lower its ramp at sea. Most of the DD tank crews drowned, trapped and entombed in their foundering vehicles. Had all the tanks got ashore it might have been very different. As it was, the defences and defenders of 'Bloody Omaha' gave the Allied armies the toughest fight of D-Day.

The defences at 'Omaha' were simply too strong for the forces sent against them, but the trouble began at the assembly point far offshore. The infantry went into their LCAs up to ten miles from the beach, and out there, in the middle of the great Seine bay, there was none of the protection from the weather that the Cotentin Peninsula offered to the landing craft off 'Utah'. The sea was very rough and many craft, especially the DUKWs (always known as 'Ducks'; a form of amphibious truck), carrying field guns, were swamped during the run-in. Most of the infantry were racked with seasickness.

An early account of the situation off 'Omaha' comes from a British Midshipman, Austin Prosser. 'I was the First Lieutenant of an LCT No. 1171, one of a flotilla of 12 LCTs allocated to the American Navy. We had long battles with the Americans over the rum ration served to the crews on British ships, because American ships are dry and they thought that as we were now part of their Navy we should be dry also. As there were signs of a Royal Navy mutiny the problem was resolved to our satisfaction.

'We loaded 6 Sherman tanks, 2 half-track ammunition lorries, and 2 half-track ambulances, and when the time came for us to sail we had a last party with the Americans, during which we drank every drop of alcohol on board. When the invasion was delayed for 24 hours there was great consternation, but one of the American officers produced a jar of medical alcohol from one of the ambulances and mixed this with orange juice. The result was not only lethal but revolting.

'After a very traumatic trip to the beaches we arrived at "Omaha" beach on time, at 0800 hrs. We reached the spot where we had to unload, but the beach was littered with wrecked assault craft and wounded and dead Americans. The Beachmaster was desperately looking for engineers to blow a way through the obstacles, and we were caught in a crossfire from the bunkers at either end of the beach, and lay off for a while as a destroyer sailed up and down firing its guns over open sights against the beach emplacements. About 10 o'clock, after pulling some of the broken-down assault craft off the beach, and removing some of the bodies, we put our tanks ashore, but I think very few of them ever got off the beach. We were then told to stand by to evacuate the troops as things were going badly and there were a lot of casualties ashore. I should mention that the skipper of our landing craft was just twenty-two years old.'

With their DDs sunk and all but one of the vital field guns lost at sea, their craft either flooded or destroyed by shell-fire or mines, the American infantry now approaching Omaha beach were without close support. Many of them were put out in the wrong place or on to an offshore sandbar, and had to abandon their equipment to swim across the deep-water channel to the beach. Enemy fire was smacking into the bow doors of the landing craft even before the ramps went down, and the killing began before the craft could beach. The infantrymen landing on 'Omaha' hardly had a chance.

Of nine infantry companies landing in the first wave at H-Hour that morning, three were swiftly decimated by machine-gun fire. Two clustered together under heavy fire near the Les Moulins exit in the 116th Regiment section. Elements of four companies of the 16th Infantry came to ground under fire below the cliffs before Colleville and one company's landing craft was swept so far to the east that they did not actually land for another hour and a half. The same thing was happening all along the beach, where a veteran now takes up the tale.

J. Robert Slaughter of Roanoke, Virginia, was a nineteen-year-old Heavy Weapons Sergeant, serving with 'D' Company, 1st Battalion, 116th Infantry, 29th Division. 'My thinking, as we approached the beach, was that if this boat didn't hurry up and get us in I would die from seasickness. This was my first encounter with this malady. Woosiness became stomach sickness and then vomiting. At this point death is not so dreadful. I used the first thing at hand – my steel helmet. I didn't care what the Germans had to offer, I wanted to get on dry land. Nothing is worse than motion sickness, except maybe 88mm's and MG-42 machine-guns.

'About 200 or 300 yards from shore we encountered the first enemy artillery fire. Near misses sent water skyward, and then it rained back on us. The British coxswain shouted to step back, he was going to lower the ramp and we were to disembark quickly. I was stationed near the front of the boat and heard Sergeant Norfleet counter, "These men have heavy equipment and *you will take them all the way in*." The coxswain begged, "But we'll all be killed!" and Norfleet unholstered his .45 Colt pistol, put it to the sailor's head and ordered, "All the way in!" The craft proceeded ashore, ploughing through the choppy water until the bow scraped the sandy bottom.

'About 150 yards from shore I raised my head despite the warning from someone to "Keep your heads down!" I could see the craft to our right taking a terrific licking from small arms. Tracer bullets were bounding and skipping off the ramp and sides as they zero'd in on the boat, which touched down a few minutes before we did. Had we not delayed a few minutes to pick up the survivors from a sunken craft, we might have taken the concentration of fire that boat took. Great plumes of water from enemy artillery and mortars kept spouting close by.

'We knew then that this was not going to be a walk-in. No one thought that the enemy would give us this kind of opposition on the water's edge. We expected "A" and "B" Companies to have the beach secured by the time we landed. The reality was that no one else had set foot in the sector where we touched down. This turned the boys into men. Some would be very brave men, others would soon be dead men, but all of those who survived would be frightened men. Some wet their breeches, others cried unashamedly, and many just had to find it within themselves to get the job done. This is where the discipline and training took over.

'As we approached the beach the ramp was lowered. Mortar and artillery shells exploded on land and in the water. Unseen snipers concealed in the cliffs were shooting down at individuals, but most havoc was from automatic weapons. The water was turning red from the blood. Explosions from artillery gunfire, the rapid-fire rattle from nearby MG-42s, and naval gunfire firing inland was frightening.

'I was stationed on the left side of the craft and about fifth from the front. Norfleet was leading the right side. The ramp was in the surf and the front of the steel craft was bucking violently up and down. As my turn came to exit, I sat on the edge of the bucking ramp, trying to time my leap on the down cycle. I sat there too long, causing a bottleneck and endangering myself as well as the men who followed. The one-inch steel ramp was going up and down in the surf, rising as much as 6 or 7ft. I was afraid it would slam me in the head. One of our men was crushed by the door, killing him instantly. There were dead men in the water and there were live men as well. The Germans couldn't tell which was which. It was extremely hard to shed the heavy equipment, and if one were a weak swimmer, he could drown before inflating his Mae-West. I had to inflate mine to get in, even though I was a good swimmer. I remember helping Private Ernest McCanless, who was struggling to get closer in, so he wouldn't drown under all the weight. He still had one box of precious 30 cal. One of the dead, Mae-West inflated, had turned a dark colour.

'There were dead men floating in the water and there were live men acting dead, letting the tide take them in. I was crouched down to chin-deep in the water when mortar shells began falling at the water's edge. Sand began to kick up from small-arms fire from the bluffs. It became apparent that it was past time to get the hell away from that killing zone and across the beach. I don't know how long we were in the water before the move was made to go. I tried to take cover behind one of the heavy timbers, and then noticed an innocent-looking mine tied to the top, so I made the decision to go for it. Getting across the beach became an obsession. The decision not to try never entered my mind.

'While lying half in and half out of the water, behind one of the log poles, I noticed a GI running from right to left, trying to get across the beach. He was weighted with equipment and looked as though he was having a difficult time running. He was probably from the craft that touched down about 50 yards to our right. An enemy gunner shot him as he stumbled for cover. He screamed for a medic. One of the aid men moved quickly to help him, and he also was shot. I will never forget seeing that medic lying next to that wounded GI and both of them screaming. They died in minutes.

'The tide was rushing in, and later waves of men were due, so we had to get across. I believe I was the first in my group, telling Pfc Walfred Williams, my Number One gunner, to follow. He still had his 51-pound machine-gun tripod. I had my rifle ready to fire, safety off, and had also fixed the bayonet before disembarking.

'I gathered my courage and started running as fast as my long legs would carry me. I ran as low as I could to lessen the target, and since I am 6ft 5ins I still presented a good one. I had a long way to run – I would say a good 100 yards or more. We were loaded down with gear and all our clothes were soaking wet. Can you imagine running with shoes full of water and wet wool clothing? As I ran through a tidal pool with about six or eight inches of water, I began to stumble. I finally caught my balance and accidentally fired my rifle, barely missing my foot. I continued on to the sea wall. This is the first time I have admitted the embarrassment of inadvertently almost shooting myself!

'Upon reaching the sea wall I looked back for the first time and got a glimpse of the armada out in the Channel. It was an awesome sight to behold. I also saw that Williams, Private Sal Augeri and Private Ernest McCanless were right behind. I didn't see Norfleet until later. Augeri had lost the machine-gun receiver in the water and I had got sand in my rifle. We still had one box of MG ammo but I don't believe we had a weapon that would fire. The first thing I did was to take off my assault jacket and spread my raincoat so I could clean my rifle. It was then I saw bullet holes in my raincoat. I didn't realize until then that I had been targeted. I lit my first cigarette. They were wrapped in plastic, as were the matches. I had to rest and compose myself because I had become weak in the knees. It was a couple of days before I had enough appetite to eat a K-ration.

'All the squad crossed the beach unscathed except Private Robert Stover and Medic Private Roland Coates, both of whom were killed. I don't know what happened to either of them. Stover was behind me in the boat and I didn't see him in the water or on the beach. (Records show Coates died of wounds on 7 June.) I didn't see Coates's fate, but knew Stover was a poor swimmer. A minor wound or accident could cause drowning in the rough surf.'

Alfred Lang of Linwood, New Jersey, came ashore with the Headquarters Battery of the 110th Field Artillery. 'British sailors manned the landing craft which brought our group ashore. They were good, they brought our landing craft right up on the sand and we didn't even have to wade through the water. We went across the beach in a weapons carrier which became bogged in the embankment on the sand, and the GIs laying about had to give us a hand to get us free. German artillery fire was pounding the area and snipers were holding out and taking pot shots at the invaders. We didn't get much chance to sleep for five days. Everyone was exhausted but we couldn't risk sleeping, and fear would keep you awake.'

Bob L. Sales of Madison Heights, Virginia, was then serving in 'B' Company of 116th Infantry. Like Robert Slaughter, he had previously served in the Ranger Battalion of 116th Infantry, a force trained at Achnacarry in Scotland by British Commandos. 'I really wanted to fight with the Ranger Battalion; they were picked men, all first class, but it was not to be. The Battalion was broken up and I returned to "B" Company, where I became bodyguard and radio man to our Company Commander, Captain Ettore Zappacosta. Anyway, on D-Day we thought we were just going to run up the beach and keep on going, but it wasn't going to be like that at all ...

'How did we feel going in? Difficult to explain.... You're so scared. Anyone who says he wasn't scared isn't telling the truth. But we knew what we had to do and we just did our best. On the way in I was standing up and watching, because I knew it was the only time I was ever going to do this. It was now getting light and the French coast was in sight, and we could see smoke where the big guns on the ships had been firing. Guns were going off ... the excitement was unreal ... it was unbelievable. The closer we got we could tell that there was trouble. We didn't see any of "A" Company, couldn't find them, and the coxswain said he couldn't go in any further. He dropped the ramp and when you open up the ramp on a landing craft, that's when the machine guns open up on you.

'Captain Zappacosta was the first man off and he was hit immediately. Machine-gun bullets were rattling off that boat. The next two men off were both hit and fell into the water, and I was the fourth man off. What saved my life was that the boat reared up and I went off the side of the ramp with that 30/40lb radio on my back, and went up to my neck in the water. I knew I couldn't keep the radio. Zappacosta came up and mumbled something – I think he said, "Help me!" and he went back down and we never saw him again. I tried to get in closer and kept looking back at the craft and who was following, and they were being cut down just like you wouldn't believe. No one have I ever met until this day who survived that boat. It was the command boat, with Captain Zappacosta on there, an officer from "C" Company was on there, the Forward Observer for the Artillery was on there, some of the radio operators were on there ... it was the Headquarters boat for "B" Company.

'This time I was in the water and shells were hitting all around and I could see we had a disaster on our hands. I didn't know how bad it was at that time. I met a fellow in the water I didn't know, and he helped me get rid of the radio, which was full of seawater anyway. A few minutes later a shell hit and knocked me groggy – I was almost out of it. I hung on to a log that had a mine on it and pushed it in front of me, moving as slow as possible because the Germans were sitting right up there and they could see all over the beach, and if you moved, well.... I finally made it to the beach and crawled up, and laying there was Dick Wright, Communications Sergeant. Dick raised up on his hands a little bit, and a sniper hit him in the head. He was not only my Sergeant, he was my friend for many years.

'I was really beginning to get uneasy at this point because there really wasn't anybody around to amount to anything, so I made my way along the beach a little at a time to a small wall where I found four or five other men, one of them a friend of mine, Max Smith from West Virginia. Max's eye was laying out on his face. I bandaged it up as best I could until a medic came along and bandaged up some of the other men. Max went on to recover from the war and died a few years ago of cancer in West Virginia.

'We had a little protection behind the wall. All day we dragged the dead and wounded in, slipping out to pull them up the beach as the tide was bringing them in. All day long shells were hitting that beach and tanks and men were landing. Some boats never got in at all but were blown up in the water. "Toad" Paget was one of the men who got his group ashore in pretty good shape. Lieutenant Williams, who later became Company Commander, was storming pill-boxes almost single-handed out there. These men were almost unbelievable.'

The experiences of Bob Sales and Robert Slaughter were endorsed by many other men trapped on the shrinking sands of 'Omaha' that day. The infantry of the 16th and 116th Regiments were trapped between the cliffs and the sea, unable to move forward or back and under heavy fire. Soldiers have a name for such a place; they call it a killing ground.

The 1st Battalion of the 116th Infantry landing on 'Dog Green' section of 'Omaha' beach suffered terrible casualties. Company 'A' landing at 0630 hrs had 91 men killed and almost as many wounded. Less than 20 men got across the beach. 'B' Company suffered a similar fate. Robert Slaughter's Company 'D', landing at 0710 hrs, had 39 men killed and 32 wounded. On D-Day they lost their Company Commander, 5 officers, the First Sergeant, and 10 other non-commissioned officers killed. Five other non-commissioned officers were wounded. In all, the 116th Regiment lost 800 men on D-Day.

The two right-flank companies, from the 2nd Ranger Battalion and Company 'A' of 116th Infantry, suffered even before they got ashore. One landing craft sank in the surf and another received direct hits by four mortar bombs. Company 'A' then lost about two-thirds of its strength to small-arms fire and half the Rangers were shot down as they waded ashore. Only half the regiment's supporting tanks – 8 out of 16 – made it to the beach, and all these came in on LCTs. There was a 1,000-yard gap between these right-flank companies and the rest of the battalion, and only two of the three rifle companies of the 2nd Battalion landed in the regimental area. One promptly lost 25 per cent of its men to small-arms fire just crossing the beach, which took 45 minutes.

Over on the left, the 16th Infantry of the 1st Infantry Division were not faring any better. Some squads of the 2nd/16th got across the beach below Colleville with the loss of only two men. The rest of the 2nd/16th battalion landed directly in front of the Colleville strongpoint and were immediately swept by enemy fire. Half of Company 'E' were killed there or wounded and later drowned by the incoming tide. Machine guns continued to sweep the beach as the rest of the companies came ashore.

Lawrence Bour of Williamsburg, Virginia, was in the 16th Infantry Regiment. 'Our slice of "Omaha" beach was codenamed "Easy Red". Maybe some staff officer's black sense of humour. It was red, but not easy. The run-in from the assembly area was rough. Three of our amphibious trucks went under with their howitzers. Three out of four of the amphibious tanks had their flimsy canvas skirts crumble and went to the bottom with their crews.

'We drove in in our LCVP, me on the left, Major Washington, the battalion exec., in the centre, and my communications sergeant on the right. I never saw the sergeant again, incidentally. I rolled over a body in the surf, thinking it might be he, but there wasn't much left of the face. Suddenly the growl from the engines died, but it wasn't dropping us on sand or shingle. We were fifty yards from the shoreline, just short of the obstacles, and due to touch down in the fourth wave at 0640 hrs, behind the assault waves. The assault waves would have cleared the beach of small-arms fire from the machine guns in the concrete bunkers, and we would take our chances with the shelling – a piece of cake!'

James Watts of San Diego, California, then a Lieutenant serving with a Mortar Unit with the 16th Infantry, came ashore on 'Easy Red'. 'My Company Commander, Captain Thomas P. Moundres, had a meeting with all the company officers, at which he wished us good luck and said goodbye. I think he had a premonition of impending death. He was killed by a mortar shell just as he reached the land, and is now buried in the American cemetery above the beach.

'The view of the beach from the landing craft showed the inferno that lay ahead. It was already a dull overcast morning. The explosions and the resulting smoke and debris laid a blackish pall over the beach. Survival that day was a matter of luck. You made it, the man next to you didn't.

'When the landing craft reaches the shore, the ramp is dropped and you exit the craft on the diagonal to avoid the craft broaching and catching you in the back. I went off the left side of the ramp into waist-deep water. Even so, the ramp swung left, knocked me off my feet and underwater. The sergeant coming off behind me said the water boiled with machine-gun fire just after I went under. I came up near the rear of the landing craft untouched.

'When we left the landing craft the leading elements of the infantry were just a few yards ahead, pinned down by fire from the top of the hill above (where the American cemetery is now). I have no recollection how long we were there before the infantry could clear the area at the top of the hill. We set up a mortar on the beach and tried to fire at the top of the hill. It was a futile effort because the distance to the top of the hill was under our minimum range of 600 yards. When the squads with the mortars landed, they used two hand-pulled carts per squad, one with the mortar, the other with the ammunition. This made them a very attractive target. Part of the squad was pulling by a handle and chains attached to the front of the cart. One man, Pfc Baumgartner, was behind pushing the cart. As I watched I could see his jacket puff from machine-gun rounds. He went to his knees, then got up and pushed for another step or two, then went down dead. The memory is still vivid, a brave, dedicated man trying to do his duty to the very end. The beach was full of such people that day.'

The underwater obstacles off 'Omaha' also took their toll. Craft sank or blew up, sending crews and occupants sky high, while from their vantage points high on shore the Germans flailed the oncoming craft with machine-gun and artillery fire. Within minutes the infantry assault of both RCTs was halted on the water's edge, the troops taking heavy casualties and unable to hit back, but still the infantry came on, adding more wounded, more dead, to the holocaust developing on 'Omaha'.

Other units coming in later did no better; the assault at 'Omaha' was stalled. Anthony J. Di Stephano came ashore about 0830 hrs with the guns of 'C' Battery, the 111th Field Artillery, part of the 116th RCT, and tells what happened to his unit. 'At H-Hour the tide had been low; now it was coming in fast, narrowing the flat expanse of sand, and as it came it swept the dead, the abandoned life-belts and the mess of wrecked equipment before it, tidying up the appalling scene like a huge broom. It also caught and drowned the wounded who were powerless to move. There was not much blood because the water was so cold and the sand acted as a blotter. The dead, looking as young and strong as ever in their brand-new uniforms and web equipment, began to form an irregular dark line at the waves' edge.

'The artillery forward observers and reconnaissance parties came in with the second wave. Lt-Colonel Thornton L. Mullins, our CO, was with them, already wounded. He didn't know that his batteries had lost all but four of his guns, but he saw immediately that the beach was no place for artillery. He began to put some fight back into the little knots of stunned, inert riflemen along the sea wall. Most of them had lost their weapons or dropped them in the sand. Lt-Colonel Mullins crept along, talking to one man after another. While he was urging one small group to clean their guns and start returning the fire from the bluffs, a sniper's bullet drilled through his hand. Mullins ignored this second wound as he had his first one, and started moving a pair of amphibious tanks into decent firing positions. He led one forward and showed its gunner a target. Then he looked for a mine-free site for the second tank. His search led him across a completely open patch of sand where a third bullet hit him in the stomach. Lt-Colonel Mullins fell forward on his face and died.

'Meanwhile, several thousand yards offshore, the "C" Battery DUKW right behind Captain Shuford's had caught a wave broadside and was sinking rapidly. Captain Shuford asked the coxswain of the guide LCVP to take off the gun crew in order to lighten the load and possibly save the howitzer; he left only the chief of section and the DUKW driver to carry on. The transfer was simple enough, but the Navy coxswain then decided to turn back and look for some place to deposit the twelve cannoneers. "Easy Green", he told Shuford, was straight ahead.

'About 1,000 yards from the shore the little procession ran into a bunch of other small craft, including a number of other DUKWs and the last two – "C" Battery's crewless DUKW and the "B" Battery DUKW with Dempsey in command – got separated from Shuford and Wilson. The crewless DUKW wandered in pretty close, its engine stalled.

'At about 9 o'clock, some 600 yards off Easy Green, Captains Shuford and Wilson lashed their boats together with a length of rope so they could talk over the situation. It was a fairly gloomy conversation. It would have been gloomier if they had known what was happening on the beach. Even without specific information, however, they could see mortar and artillery fire bursting on the beach. There was no sign of infantry activity, no movement of traffic towards the beach exit.'

To trace the cause of this state of affairs one must go back to the original assault plan. This left too much to the infantry. Little use was made of the available supporting arms and some planned support was less than fully effective. The aerial bombing, for example, had been moved well up the beach to avoid the risk of bombs falling among the landing craft. As a result, most of the bombs missed the beach entirely and fell up to three miles inland. The naval bombardment was also too light and too short to shatter the beach defences. Off-shore obstacles were virtually intact and still a barrier to the assault craft which were held out at sea under German gunfire.

The landings, supposedly at half-tide, were upset by the weather, but as the tide was flooding, it was clearly vital to clear the beach obstacles before the rising tide covered them, so that the big landing ships, the LSTs, could bring in more guns, more tanks and, above all, more men to secure the foothold. This task might have been much easier had the infantry had the support of the specialized armour used by the British and Canadians on the beaches further east.

The task of clearing away the obstacles on fire-swept 'Omaha' was left to the unprotected combat engineers of the US Army's demolition teams and they didn't have a chance. Their casualties were appalling. By nightfall on D-Day over 40 per cent of the assault engineers on 'Omaha' were dead or wounded. Most of their equipment had been lost during the run-in. A shell exploded the demolition charges being brought ashore by one team, blowing every man to pieces. Other engineers, working around the obstacles in the open, were picked off by snipers or cut down by the machine guns. When they could attach charges to obstacles they had to kick away the men hiding under them before they could pull the fuses. The gallantry of these combat engineers is beyond all praise.

John McAllister of Torrington, Connecticut, was a Lieutenant with Battery 'C' of 227th Field Artillery. 'We were assigned to "Omaha Dog Green" but I couldn't tell you where we actually landed. The water obstacles were still plentiful, indicating that the engineers assigned to clear the beach must have suffered heavy casualties. After an eternity the ramp was dropped and we jumped into the water, which came up to my waist. We instantly came under machine-gun fire and two of my small party were hit. My radio man and I went back for them and managed to drag them up to the sea wall where I gave them my canteen and a syrette of morphine.

'The radio man and I found some cover along the wall and began to reorganize to carry out our mission, recruiting two infantrymen who had become separated from their units to help carry our radio equipment. My first impression of "Omaha" was one of chaos. Smoke covered the ridge and a good part of the area between the sea wall and the top of the dunes, and the bodies of both German and American infantrymen were everywhere. I will never forget it.'

The Americans had taken bulldozers but only three out of sixteen got ashore. There they did sterling work, though the unprotected drivers were fully exposed to snipers' shells and machine-gun fire. Years after the war, Don Whitehead, an American war correspondent who landed on 'Omaha' that morning, recalled seeing Private Vinton Dove of Washington DC : '...he drove a bulldozer off his landing craft and began clearing the beach, as calmly as though grading his driveway back home ... he sat up there with only a sweatshirt and a helmet to protect him from bullets and shell fragments ... his name has stayed with me to this day.'

Until the obstacles were cleared, the follow-up craft could not get ashore. While waiting they milled about in the tossing seas offshore, still under shell-fire, the coxswains unable to find the gaps they had been promised. Meanwhile, the slaughter ashore went on.

The pitiless hail of fire went on for hours, until 'Omaha' beach was a shambles of dead men, burning tanks and wrecked landing craft. Only fragments of this story were getting back to USS *Ancon*, but more and more men were coming ashore where they could, simply adding to the carnage and confusion on the beach.

Peter Chambers was then a Royal Navy Petty Officer serving on USS *Ancon* as a 'Headache' operator. 'Our task was to maintain a listening watch in the radio room for German E-Boat transmissions, hoping to pick up any information regarding an E-Boat attack on the ships waiting offshore. When we weren't actually on duty we had no tasks to perform, so we stayed in our bunks or hung about on deck. I certainly had no idea of what was happening on "Omaha" beach. There was a battleship nearby firing salvos, but the atmosphere on board the *Ancon* was quite calm.'

At 0730 hrs the second group of assault troops, the reinforcement battalions of both regiments, came in at five separate points. This wave included more combat engineers and the rest of the assault regiments, including the vital heavy weapons companies. The rest of the 1st/116th were to land behind Company 'A' of the 1st/116th which had already been shattered, but the rest of the battalion did no better, meeting the same destructive fire as their craft came in to beach. The heavy weapons company was scattered at once and took two hours to assemble. Battalion HQ, including the Beachmaster who was charged with sorting out the chaos on shore, was pinned down by small-arms fire for much of the day.

Company 'C' was carried 1,000 yards to the east and landed in comparative safety covered by smoke from burning heather on the clifftops, and was able to cross the beach and re-group by the sea wall. The 5th Rangers followed by Company 'C' in and also got ashore without heavy loss, but two companies of the 2nd Rangers, landing on the right, lost between a third and a half of their men just crossing the beach.

Shortly after this, Brigadier General Norman 'Dutch' Cota, Assistant Divisional Commander of the 29th Infantry Division, came ashore near Les Moulins, but taking command was difficult. Most of the radios had been either lost or drowned and communication by runner was perilous or impossible. Brigadier Cota rounded up what men he could find and began to organize the fight back. All over the beach other men were doing the same.

Mario Porcellini was then a Private in Company 'E' of the 116th. 'I was Captain Madill's runner and radio man and was with him on D-Day when he was killed. Alongside him was our BAR man, Alex Bereski, who also got it – a day I can never forget. I just want to say that I was with one of the greatest outfits and I'm still proud to have been a member of the fighting 29th.'

At about 0930 hrs General Omar Bradley sent a staff officer, Colonel Benjamin Tallen, off in a DUKW to examine the situation and report back. Tallen returned an hour later, soaking wet, to report landing craft milling about in confusion off the beach, 'like a stampeding herd of cattle', chased by shellfire, while the 1st and 29th Infantry RCTs were pinned against the sea wall. Only in one section, 'Easy Red', had the beach obstacles been cleared and craft making for this area to unload were creating a monster traffic jam that provided wonderful targets for the Germany artillery. 16th Infantry were enduring heavy losses; all their companies and battalions were mixed up but fighting back in small groups.

At about 1000 hrs, some men managed to get across the beach and took shelter in the cover of the shingle bank. Here, in the few yards hard up against the shingle, they were comparatively safe from all but mortar- and shell-fire. As the morning wore on, more men arrived by the sea wall, wet, exhausted, frequently without equipment or weapons. Many who came in were wounded and they were the lucky ones. The wounded left out on the open beach were drowned as the tide came in. Many of the wounded came crawling up the beach with the tide, only their heads exposed above the waves, and even these were sniped at by Germans from their posts above the beachhead.

The American infantry did not just lie there and take it. They were firing back where they could, scrambling for positions, digging shell-scrapes, rescuing their comrades and attending to the wounded. John Pinder Tanon, a radio operator, was to receive the Medal of Honor for re-crossing the beach three times to recover the vital radios, and he was just one man among many, doing what he could on 'Omaha' beach. On his third trip into the surf John Tanon was shot and killed.

The losses were not all one-sided, for the German defenders were also taking casualties. The 916th Regiment, which occupied the centre of the beach, reported to the Divisional HQ that while they were holding the Americans on the beach, their own casualties, principally from naval gun-fire, were very heavy, and infantry reinforcements were urgently needed. Even so, they held on, flaying 'Omaha' beach with fire.

At noon, with the situation still critical, Bradley contemplated switching his follow-up forces to 'Utah' or the British beaches, and was about to order the evacuation of 'Omaha' when he received a message from V Corps: '*Troops formerly pinned down on beaches now advancing up heights behind.*' Somehow, here and there, the men of the 1st and 29th Infantry Divisions had pulled it off.

Many factors combined to halt the American assault at 'Omaha'. Many others combined to get it started again, but the main ingredient that turned disaster into success on 'Omaha' was simple human courage.

It takes courage to move out into the open, even from behind the elusive safety of a bullet-swept wall or a beach obstacle, but all along that beach, after hours of endurance, men found the courage to move. The advance seems to have begun in several places all around the same time. In one place an officer led a sudden rush over the shingle bank and found that the machine-gunning on the far side was less intense and movement possible. A combat-engineer sergeant moved up and down collecting explosives until he had enough to blow a hole in the sea wall and let other troops through. In some places, men simply decided they had had enough and it was time to move. They stood up and walked quietly across the shingle wall. Those who made it across gapped the minefields, often by hand, digging up the mines with bayonets. Losing men all the way, slowly and painfully, the 1st and 29th Infantry Divisions began to get off the beach.

Urged on by Brigadier Cota, on the west, Company 'C' of the 116th left the sea wall and crossed 150 yards of beach to the base of the cliffs. These they climbed, scrambling up shallow gullies, and found that the crumpled ground on the top gave them good protection. After them came men of the 5th Rangers, and together they began to snuff out the German machine-gun posts. At about the same time, over to the east the 3rd battalion of the 116th, in groups of 20 or 30 men, began to advance up the bluffs around Les Moulins. Company 'G' and Company 'E' of the 2nd/16th – the latter now down to 23 men – fought their way up the cliffs between Colleville and St Laurent. Second Lt John Spalding of Company 'E', 2nd/16th, attacked the maze of enemy positions defending the St Laurent draw, and after a two-hour battle with rifles and grenades, forced the garrison to surrender.

Shortly after 10.00 a.m. there was another welcome reinforcement when two landing craft, LCT 30 and LCT(L) 544, swept in to land and barged the obstacles aside to run hard on to the beach, all their guns firing on the German positions. Two destroyers also came in to 1,000 yards offshore to add the weight of their guns to the supporting fire. Slowly, painfully, the battle was tilting the Americans' way.

As at 'Utah', there were general officers ashore, men like Brigadier-General Cota, to get a grip on the fight and point the way. Most memorable of all was Colonel Taylor of the 16th Infantry, who declared: 'The only people on this beach, are the dead and those who are going to die ... now let's get the hell out of here.'

The 29th Infantry RCT had come ashore opposite Vierville and taken another thrashing there from the enemy guns. Here again, Brigadier-General Cota was around to point the way with his cry, 'They're murdering us here. Let's move inland and get murdered. 29th, Let's Go!' '29th, Let's Go!' remains the motto of the American 29th Infantry Division.

Scores of men were now on their feet and crossing the sea wall. Once the situation onshore became clear, General Huebner had acted fast to help his beleaguered troops. He called for naval help and destroyers were sent in close to shore to engage the German emplacements over open sights. He stopped the rear echelon support troops landing, sending more infantry instead, most notably the 115th Infantry Regiment which came ashore at H+4. He sent in engineers to blow the beach obstacles. Thanks to him, and those like him, and the courage of countless unnamed individuals, the American assault began to move forward again. In little groups and small companies the infantry began to infiltrate the enemy defences, to take them in the rear and, one by one, to eliminate them. There was much bitter fighting on the cliff heights behind 'Omaha', but by mid-afternoon the advance inland had begun.

German resistance at 'Omaha' came as an unpleasant shock to the American command. The Americans had expected to encounter second-rank troops but the battle-trained troops of the 352nd Division contested every step of the landing, even reporting back to Von Rundstedt at one point that they had thrown the invaders back into the sea. However, even as the 352nd were making this report, the battle was moving in the Americans' favour. The point of the American spearhead may have been blunted, but there was a lot of weight behind the shaft, and remorseless pressure, together with the naval gunfire and the constant arrival of fresh troops, gradually wore the Germans down. By 1500 hrs the situation seemed to warrant another close inspection, and General Omar Bradley again sent a staff officer ashore to check on the troops' progress.

He reported back with a story of a beach strewn with bodies and wreckage, but with the men fighting their way inland. The most pressing need now was for artillery and bulldozers. Bulldozers could clear away the beach obstacles and make a path for tanks through the shingle bank and into the dunes. These were sent in, together with men of the 18th Infantry Regiment. By nightfall, elements of this regiment had joined the 2nd Battalion of the 16th south and south-east of Colleville. The Americans had gained a shallow but secure grasp on the 'Omaha' beachhead, and during the night more infantry and seventeen tanks were moved in to reinforce the leading elements now digging in on the heights above 'Omaha'.

While 1st and 29th Infantry were slogging it out on Omaha, another vicious battle was going on a little to the west, on the Pointe du Hoc. The Pointe du Hoc, or Pointe du Hoe as it was called at the time, is a tall cliff or bluff jutting into the sea just west of 'Omaha'. Aerial reconnaissance had revealed that the Pointe du Hoc contained 155mm heavy guns in well protected concrete blockhouses – guns like those of the Merville Battery over to the east, which could wreak havoc among the shipping crowded offshore. These guns had been heavily bombed by the US Ninth Air Force and would be subjected from first light on D-Day to a heavy bombardment by the guns of the fleet, but in case all this failed, this battery, like the Merville Battery, was to be assaulted by infantry.

The men chosen for this venture came from the 2nd Ranger Battalion, three companies under the command of the CO, Lt-Colonel James Rudder. His men were to land at the base of the Pointe du Hoc and scale the 100-ft cliff on ropes fired on to the clifftop by grapnels. This force was to have been supported by the rest of the Ranger battalion and elements of

116th infantry, but in the event the follow-up force became involved at 'Omaha'. Colonal Rudder's 225 men were on their own.

The assault on the Pointe du Hoc was a most desperate venture. The Germans were alerted by the grapnels and quickly harassed the climbing men with grenades and rifle-fire, cutting the ropes and hurling the Rangers back into the sea. Only machine-gun fire from the British assault craft and LCAs kept the cliff edge clear, and only about half Rudder's force – some 150 men – made it to the top of the cliff. Once there they drove off the German infantry and stormed the blockhouses, only to find them empty.

The guns were eventually located 700 yards inland, well prepared and supplied with ammunition but totally deserted. Rudder's men blew them up and held the position for two days before the surviving 90 men of the original 225 marched on to join the battle beyond 'Omaha'.

General Gerow, Commander of V Corps, went ashore at 1930 hrs on the evening of 6 June, and set up his headquarters near Colleville. General Huebner found the atmosphere warmer when he joined the forward elements of his 1st Infantry Division on the evening of D-Day, while on the right flank the 29th Division were pushing hard towards the Pointe du Hoc to relieve the Rangers.

Behind them the tide was going out on 'Omaha' beach, uncovering the dead and an immense litter of equipment. Reinforcements were coming ashore and would come ashore all night and for days thereafter, the new arrivals awed by the evidence of battle. Guided by tired, wet men from the combat engineers, these reinforcements made their way slowly along the taped gaps in the minefields, up the 'draws' and past the blackened emplacements of the Atlantic Wall, scorched by shell-fire, littered with their dead defenders.

The Americans lost over 3,000 men, killed or wounded, along that three-mile strip of sand. Those who fought there have never forgotten that hard day on 'Omaha' beach.

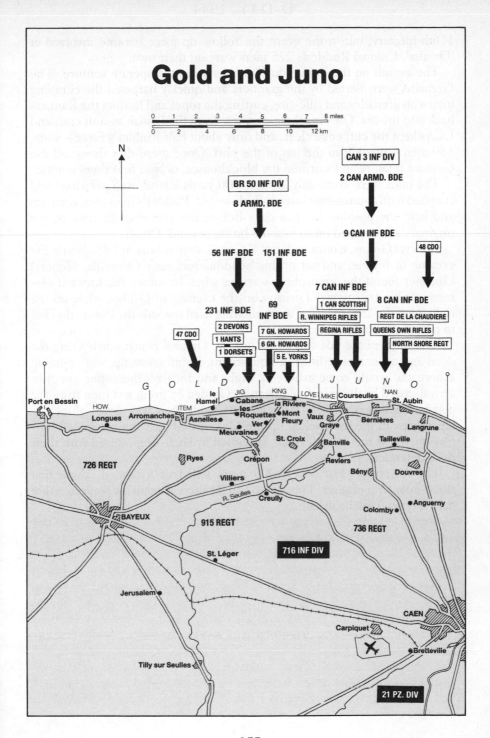

Gold and Juno

0 1 2 3 4 5 6 7 8 miles
0 2 4 6 8 10 12 km

N

CAN 3 INF DIV

2 CAN ARMD. BDE

BR 50 INF DIV

8 ARMD. BDE

9 CAN INF BDE

48 CDO

56 INF BDE   151 INF BDE

7 CAN INF BDE

69
INF BDE

231 INF BDE

8 CAN INF BDE

1 CAN SCOTTISH

47 CDO

R. WINNIPEG RIFLES

2 DEVONS

7 GN. HOWARDS

REGINA RIFLES

REGT DE LA CHAUDIERE

1 HANTS

6 GN. HOWARDS

QUEENS OWN RIFLES

1 DORSETS

5 E. YORKS

NORTH SHORE REGT

G O L D

le   JIG
Hamel

KING

LOVE MIKE

J U N O

NAN

Courseulles

St. Aubin

Port en Bessin

Cabane
les
Roquettes

la Riviere

Bernières

Langrune

ITEM

HOW

Longues   Arromanches

Asnelles

Ver

Mont
Fleury

Vaux
Graye

Meuvaines

St. Croix

Banville

Tailleville

726 REGT

Ryes

Crépon

Reviers

Bény

Douvres

Villiers

R. Seulles

Creully

Colomby

Anguerny

BAYEUX

915 REGT

736 REGT

St. Léger

716 INF DIV

Jerusalem

CAEN

Carpiquet

Bretteville

Tilly sur Seulles

21 PZ. DIV

CHAPTER NINE

'Gold'

'People of Western Europe: A landing was
made this morning on the coast of France
by troops of the Allied Expeditionary
Force...'
Communiqué No. 1
General Dwight D. Eisenhower
6 June 1944

To the east of 'Omaha', beyond the little harbour of Port-en-Bessin, lay the first of the British beaches. This was codenamed 'Gold', and the troops of the 50th Northumbrian Division began to come ashore here about 0730 hrs. Their task was to penetrate the German defences on 'Gold' beach between the resorts of La Rivière and Le Hamel, and press on inland to take the town of Bayeux. They also had to take the small port and spa of Arromanches as a step towards establishing the British 'Mulberry' harbour offshore. The Germans defending this sector came from the 352nd Infantry Division, which was now hammering the Americans at 'Omaha', and the 716th Division, which was deployed along the coast from here to the east. The 716th was another second-rank formation, but as the Americans had already discovered to their cost, the 352nd was an extremely formidable division.

The 352nd Infantry Division had been raised in the winter of 1943. It consisted of three Grenadier Regiments, Nos 914, 915 and 916, and supporting arms including an artillery regiment, an anti-tank regiment and an engineer battalion. The 352nd occupied the defences of Le Hamel, which proved a particularly hard nut to crack.

General Montgomery had anticipated that there might be problems along 'Gold' beach. This part of the coast was studded with strongpoints and well supplied with infantry, but the defenders also enjoyed cover in the small resort towns and scattered villas, which run east from Port-en-Bessin all the way to the mouth of the Orne at Ouistreham. These towns, and many of the villas, had been converted into strongpoints, the houses reinforced with concrete and transformed into machine-gun, light artillery and anti-tank positions. Minefields lay behind all the beaches and many of the streets had been blocked with barbed wire and anti-tank obstacles.

The Atlantic Wall here was strong and stoutly defended. The naval bombardment therefore began at 0510 hrs and continued until H-Hour, 0730 hrs, though this did not knock out as many strongpoints as the assault plan required. Most of the strongpoints were sited to fire along the beach rather than directly out to sea, their roofs and seaward walls reinforced against bombing and naval gun-fire. The German strongpoint on the beach at Le Hamel, for one, remained in action until noon and took a heavy toll of the infantry crossing the beach. The success of the landing on 'Gold' was largely due to the specialized armour of the 79th Armoured Division, which was able to breach the defences in various places and let the infantry and follow-up forces through.

It has to be remembered that the D-Day assault was made on a *flooding* tide. As time wore on, so the beaches got narrower and narrower, yet the invasion, once started, could not be stopped. More and more troops, tanks, guns, and vehicles kept pouring ashore on to an ever-smaller strip of beach, and without breaches in the Atlantic Wall these forces would have piled up on the foreshore, an easy target for the German guns. The troops landing on the D-Day beaches always had the tide pressing at their backs.

The plan for the British landings on 'Gold' beach was for the 50th Division to land with two brigades forward and one in reserve. The assault brigades were the 231st (Malta) Brigade on the left and 69th Brigade on the right. These brigades were to storm 'Jig' and 'King' beaches respectively and push inland as quickly as possible towards Bayeux. The beaches chosen for the landings consisted of low-lying sand dunes interspersed with patches of clay that could seriously hamper the movement of both the tracked and wheeled vehicles. 'Jig' beach was also dominated by heavily fortified strongpoints within the coastal villages of Le Hamel, Asnelles-sur-Mer and Les Roquettes. These positions were garrisoned by infantry companies amply supplied with machine guns and mortars, each company supported by at least two anti-tank guns.

H-Hour for the assault brigades was 0730 hrs. The 231st Brigade had two battalions in the first wave, the 1st Hampshires and the 1st Dorsets, who were met with heavy fire from a battalion of the 716th Division dug in around Le Hamel. Also landing with this brigade was 47 (Royal Marine) Commando, of whom we shall hear more later.

For support they had a squadron from the 6th Assault Regiment, Royal Engineers, and a squadron from the Westminster Dragoons, both equipped with specialist armoured vehicles, such as flail tanks, one of the many detachments of the 79th Armoured Division in action that day. Further support was given by the DD tanks of the Nottinghamshire Yeomanry and Centaur tanks of the First Royal Marine Armoured Support Regiment. Artillery support would be provided by 90 and 147 Field Regiments, RA, who opened fire on to the beaches from their landing craft during the run-in.

Corporal Lewis Richards was Signaller to the Commander of 231 Brigade, Sir Alexander Stanier. 'Wireless sets were to open at H−60 and wireless silence was not to be broken until H−30 unless any emergency arose. I was awakened at 0445 hrs and went on deck to see if anything was happening. Our ship was moving very slowly so I concluded that we were not far from our allotted position. The coast was now receiving the attentions of the Royal Navy and squadrons of planes and was soon covered by a pall of smoke. The cruiser HMS *Orion* was firing broadsides not far from us ... my brother was serving on that ship. The Brigadier came on deck and together we watched a rocket-firing LCT run in to the shore and discharge her salvo.

'H-hour was now rapidly approaching and the Navy was giving the coast all it had. Rocket-firing planes swept in towards the coast while the planes constituting our umbrella continued to weave and turn, but the enemy planes did not come to give battle.'

Reginald Rham was with the 9th Battalion, Royal Fusiliers. On 6 June he was his Colonel's driver and batman. 'I wondered what hell was awaiting us when we reached the beaches, and I was soon to find out. Such were the sea conditions that I don't think anybody cared about what lay in front of them, it could not be worse than what they were suffering from seasickness. For the moment the firing had quietened down, and I could see the coastline of Normandy. We were now coming under fire from German big guns and it was getting extremely uncomfortable. I saw that the infantry assault craft had dropped their ramps and the infantry were running ashore.'

The most westerly beach, 'Jig Green', was the target for the 1st Hampshires. The battalions' plan was in five phases with the object of capturing the eastern half of Le Hamel, with 'B' Company capturing Asnelles-sur-

Mer. Companies landing twenty minutes later at around 0745 hrs would take the western half of Le Hamel, while 'D' Company was directed on to a gun position near Cabane. Once all these initial objectives had been carried out, the next phase was the capture of a radar station just along the coast to the west.

This task was given to 'B' and 'C' companies with the support of a tank squadron. The battalion also had to secure the cliffs above Arromanches. Finally, Arromanches itself must be cleared and occupied. Those last two phases were very important, as Arromanches overlooked the area chosen by the planners for the British 'Mulberry' harbour.

To the left of the 1st Hampshires, the 1st Dorsets were also to land on 'Jig Green' east of Les Roquettes, subduing a machine-gun nest at Meuvaines, before advancing on Puits d'Harcot. This position covered Arromanches and its approaches.

Once the two lead battalions were ashore and secure, the 2nd Devons would land at H+40. They were to deploy south, around Asnelles, then press on to Ryes, several miles south of Arromanches, to deepen the assault area.

The success of the brigade plan clearly depended on the reduction of Le Hamel. Typhoons of the 2nd Tactical Air Force (2nd TAF) were to attack the German defences with rockets, and prior to this American Flying Fortresses – B17s – would bomb the beach defences. Unfortunately, the bombs fell inland and the strafing Typhoons failed to subdue the defenders. The rough seas prevented the DD tanks from being launched and they came ashore from landing craft arriving behind the infantry. The rough seas also took a toll of the RM Armoured Support Regiment tanks, whose landing craft had great difficulty in beaching. Of the 10 Centaurs that should have landed, only 5 made it, and those were knocked out almost immediately.

More specialist troops and vehicles came from 'B' Squadron, Westminster Dragoons and 82 Assault Squadron, Royal Engineers, who were detailed to clear six gaps in the beach defences. Due to the rough seas they landed late so, like the Americans on 'Omaha', the British assault infantry landing on 'Gold' went ashore without their close support.

Frank Wiltshire was a twenty-two-year-old mortarman with the 1st Dorsets. 'I jumped from the LCA straight into about 7 ft of water. I was the No. 1 of the mortar team and I had to jettison the base plate of my mortar as it weighed over 50 lbs and it would have kept me under. After wading ashore I made a dash across the sand to reach the bank before Le Hamel. Eventually we managed to assemble one mortar out of the six; the other five were lost. I got the mortar in a firing position but the barrel was full of sand and water because somebody had dragged it along the beach.

'After seeing my friends killed and injured around me, I thought it would be my turn soon, but I got off the beach after about two hours. The bloodshed was terrible and the Germans were tough fighters.'

The 1st Dorsets managed to get off the beach once the specialist armour, the mine-clearing flail tanks and the rest, had cleared suitable lanes through the minefields. Working through these man-made obstacles the engineers were further hampered by boggy patches of heavy clay and a salt marsh directly behind the beach road.

Edgar Lawrenson was in one of the flail tanks, or 'Crabs', from 'B' Squadron, the Westminster Dragoons. 'At dawn on 6 June we brewed up and the few who felt like eating had breakfast while the landing craft sailed for the beach. It was deathly quiet and my driver and co-driver were sealed in with a reminder that if we were hit the turret had to be traversed to enable them to undo their hatches and escape.

'During the final run-in I sat on top of our tank, giving a commentary to the three crew members inside. Captain Taylor was on the bridge checking landmarks for the lane we had to sweep through the minefields. Hostile shelling and small-arms fire had started and 16 LC(R)s opened fire over our heads.

'Our tank beached safely with the other flail tank. We blew off our water-proofing and, dodging between the beach obstacles, headed for the thick wire and sand-hills with the other flail tank slightly in front. We flogged through the heavy barbed wire into the minefield, while the other flail tank turned right and headed for Le Hamel and its second objective.

'My tank hit a mine which blew off the front bogey assembly and later we found the front driving sprocket had been hit by an AP round. Over 40 per cent of our chains had been blown off. The explosion had damaged the radio so I was sent back through the minefield to find Major Elfinston, who commanded our beaching party. He had been killed and the beach was now under heavy fire from strongpoints in Le Hamel.'

With gaps flailed through the minefields, the 1st Dorsets were able to get off the beach, and they found one of their initial objectives, Les Roquettes, in the hands of the 1st Hampshires. They left a company and battalion headquarters here and pressed on towards Puits d'Harcot.

Landing just behind the assault companies were the DD tanks of the Nottinghamshire Sherwood Rangers Yeomanry, officially known as the 'Notts Yeo' but more often called the Sherwood Rangers. One of the troop commanders was Lieutenant Stuart Hills. 'The original intention was to launch us 7,000 yards offshore for our swim to the beach. The problem that faced us was a difficult one – should we launch and risk sinking in the heavy seas, or take the landing craft inshore? The decision lay with our Squadron Leader, Major Stephen Mitchell, MC.'

The decision was made to bring the LCTs in as close as possible to the

shore and not trust the tanks to the rough seas. Lieutenant Hills continues :
'There seemed to be very little opposition coming back from the shore at
that time, except for a few odd shells which raised columns of water high in
the air. "B" Squadron, over on our right were up in line with us, and I saw
them drop their ramps to launch their DDs. Major Stephen Mitchell's craft,
which Bill Enderby and I were watching, never did, and later we learned
that during the night their craft had collided with another, damaging its
bows and ramp, so that they eventually had to beach. All I could hear over
the air was some other station netting in, and Stephen's furious cries of,
"Get off the air, I'm trying to fight a battle."

'Bill Enderby gave the order to move and we prepared to launch. We were
now about 700 yards from the shore and as the ramp was lowered I could see
two of the flails brewing up just to my front, and I could not help wondering
what had caused them to catch fire, and whether our tanks would meet the
same fate.

'Sure enough the shots soon came, one on the side of the ramp and the
other on our starboard beam, the latter wounding Sergeant Sidaway. Without more ado I gave my driver the order to go, and down the ramp we went.
As soon as we hit the water I knew something was very wrong. The screen
was very flimsy in the rough sea and water poured in everywhere. I gave a
few technical orders to try and save the day, but when I saw that things were
hopeless I gave the order to bale out. I can only imagine that the first shell
which landed was our undoing and that it must have holed one of the bottom
plates.

'Corporal Footitt pressed the button on our rubber dinghy, which inflated automatically, and Trooper Kirman, the only non-swimmer, put it
over the side. I scrambled inside the turret to get my map-case out, but we
were going down so fast that I didn't have time to retrieve it, and in my haste
to get out again I tore the headphones out of the set altogether. I followed
Troopers Reddish and Storey over the side and a few seconds later our tank
disappeared into the murky depths.'

The 1st Hampshires came ashore alongside the 1st Dorsets. The stormy
conditions and rising tides caused them to drift eastwards on their final
run-in, which brought them ashore opposite Les Roquettes, a 1st Dorsets'
objectives, which they quickly stormed and occupied.

1st Hampshires landed in the face of heavy machine-gun, mortar and
artillery fire, with some of the heaviest concentrations coming from Le
Hamel. Had they landed at the intended point, they would have had to
contend with even more problems, as the main German position at Le
Hamel, based in an old sanatorium, would have been directly in front of
them.

'A' and 'C' Companies of the Hampshires were pinned down on the beach, while 'B' Company took Les Roquettes, the 1st Dorsets objective, and pressed on towards Asnelles. Meanwhile 'D' Company came ashore and moved inland, again under heavy fire, to attack the gun position at Cabane.

It was fast becoming obvious that the immediate problem on 'Gold' beach was the village of Le Hamel, especially the seafront fortifications set in the sanatorium. The 1st Hampshires could not deal with it without tanks, and to compound their problems they lost their Commanding Officer, Lieutenant-Colonel Nelson Smith, who was wounded twice shortly after coming ashore.

Rescue came from the 'Funnies', the specialized armour of the 79th Division. One of their devices was the 'Petard' tank which mounted a huge mortar designed to shatter concrete pill-boxes, and it was one of these that came to the help of 1st Hampshires.

Trooper Joe Minogue was a twenty-year-old gunner in a flail tank of 'B' Squadron, the Westminster Dragoons. 'The scene on the beach is etched so deeply in my mind that I can hear it, feel it, smell it in fine focus so many years after the events of that summer day. We rolled off the tank landing craft into 4ft of water and hit "Jig Green" at 0725 hrs. Within seconds of landing, Major Elfinston was killed and Major Stanyon's tank was knocked out and set on fire, and some of his crew burned and wounded.

'It was a sobering sight as the Hampshires left their smaller infantry landing craft. German machine guns must have been firing along fixed lines, for men were dropping while still in the shallow water, to be dragged forward by their mates and left on the sand, while their comrades ran on in a purposeful steady jog trot, which betrayed no sign of panic.'

The flail tanks swept a path through the beach minefields and allowed an AVRE 'Petard' tank to get up to the Le Hamel strongpoint and deploy its weapon against the walls, firing two rounds into the enemy position. The 'Petard' then went on to engage and silence a large anti-tank gun emplacement. Once the strongpoint had been breached the infantry swarmed forward with grenades. This finally did the trick and the concussed German garrison surrendered about noon after five hours of stiff fighting, although the battle continued around Le Hamel throughout the day.

While the two assault battalions were battering their way off the beaches, the brigade's third battalion, the 2nd Devons, started landing just after 0800 hrs, closely followed by 47 (RM) Commando, which had to make a flanking march behind the German lines and attack Port-en-Bessin from the rear.

Private George Laity was a PIAT gunner with the 2nd Devons. 'I wondered what we were in for when we hit the beach. As we got nearer, shells began to burst around the landing craft and we hit the beach at half-tide, with the iron obstacles showing. The barrage, the noise, the infantry, the little LCAs ... it was all confusion and bewilderment. German

88s started pounding the beach. My company was pinned down for some time and it seemed endless.'

During the afternoon, with the main threat to the beaches now gone, traffic which had jammed up on the beaches was able to flow more smoothly to its allotted points inland. Among the units now advancing inland was 47 (RM) Commando, whose task was to capture Port-en-Bessin. Port-en-Bessin was defended by at least one company of German infantry, entrenched in pill-boxes overlooking the town and in strongpoints within the town itself. It was decided to take Port-en-Bessin from inland, which meant that 47 Commando had a march of ten miles through enemy territory to reach their assault positions.

Their troubles began as the Commando approached the beaches. Three LCAs were sunk on the way in, and on landing at Le Hamel, which should by then have been quiet, the Commando found the 1st Hampshires still fighting for a foothold. They found their intended assembly area held by a company of Germans and suffered 40 casualties before they cleared them out of it. They did, however, take 60 prisoners, whose weapons served to re-equip those men from the sunk LCAs who had had to abandon their own equipment and swim ashore. 47 Commando reached Port-en-Bessin at nightfall and attacked at dawn the next day, losing over 50 per cent of their strength before they took the town.

With the beaches taken and the Wall breached, the field artillery and more tanks could come ashore. Gunner Frank Topping was a driver and radio operator of a Sherman tank in 147 Field Regiment, Essex Yeomanry. 'A few yards from the beach the ramp flopped down with a crash. I thought we had hit one of the submerged mines we had been warned about, so I ducked, caught my waterproof trousers on a tank projection and ripped the suit. This meant that when I jumped into the sea – only about 3ft deep at that point – I touched bottom as my suit filled with water. The others had difficulty standing up as their suits were filled with air! We managed to get the obstacle out of the way, and the tanks landed without mishap.

'Soaked to the skin I ran up the beach to my tank, intent on climbing into the turret to get out of the way of mortar shells and snipers' bullets. Just as I reached it a shell exploded in a ditch alongside and I felt a blow between the shoulder blades. I was sure I had bought it, but the co-driver leaned down and picked a lump of dried mud off my back. Apart from subsequent bruises I wasn't even scratched.

'Once aboard we moved on towards the small hamlet of Le Hamel, and I was beginning to feel I had had enough excitement for one morning. It was not to be. We had not travelled many yards from the beach when an anti-tank gun opened up at one side and we received an armour-piercing shell in the engine. We all baled out and lay with the infantry at the side of the road. After hitting two other tanks, the German gun was knocked out by one of our SPs firing over open sights.'

Reginald Rham came ashore early, driving his Commanding Officer's Jeep. 'As I drove off the ramp into the sea, which was about 3ft deep, I saw one of these obstacles in front and I steered away from it but the wheel of the trailer caught it. I knew that some of these obstacles had mines attached to them and I yelled to the two radio operators to free the trailer from the towing socket. They were concerned about the rations that were on the trailer and I quickly replied, "Sod the rations ... if we don't move we won't be alive to eat them anyway!" Having released the trailer I was able to make the beach.

'There I lit a cigarette and surveyed the scene. My instructions were to meet up with the CO. He was on one of the landing craft controlling the run-in and had given me a map reference to rendezvous along with the Command Centre tank. While I was waiting for the tank to come ashore there was machine-gun and rifle fire coming from behind the dunes and we quickly dug some shallow trenches alongside the Jeep. I then saw the tank come ashore and drove along the beach to join up with it. The Second-in-Command was standing in the turret, and suddenly there was a sharp crack of a bullet and the officer disappeared. Sadly he had been hit by a sniper and died a few minutes later.'

Attention now turns to the 69th Brigade landing on 'King' beach, just to the west of La Rivière. Like 231 Brigade, 69 Brigade landed with two battalions in the first wave. The most easterly was the 5th Battalion, the East Yorkshire Regiment, while to their right was the 6th Battalion, the Green Howards. Armoured support for the first wave was provided by the DD tanks of the 4/7th Royal Dragoon Guards with the beach obstacles and mines being tackled by squadrons of 6 Assault Squadron, Royal Engineers and the Westminster Dragoons. The main German positions were in fortified strongpoints in La Rivière and around the high ground near Mont Fleury and its lighthouse. From La Rivière, after the third battalion of the brigade, the 7th Green Howards, had come ashore, they were to push inland towards Crépon and St Léger, enlarging the beachhead to allow the follow-up brigade, 151st Brigade, to land and deploy south. To complete this task, 69 Brigade were given just two hours.

5th East Yorks landed on the outskirts of La Rivière, and although initially pinned down by very heavy fire, managed to take their primary objectives with the judicial use of naval gun fire. The seas were too rough to swim the 4/7 Dragoon Guards' DD tanks ashore, so the Navy beached their LCTs, exposing themselves to direct fire from those batteries that had not succumbed to the bombardment.

Two 88mm guns and machine guns enfiladed the beach and these opened up on the LCAs as they beached and the infantry waded ashore. More fire came from houses in the village, and some LCAs were spiked or blown up on the beach obstacles, killing or maiming passengers and crew. Two 'Petard' tanks were hit immediately they came ashore and blew up, covering the infantry with a shower of debris. The survivors of the assault companies of the East Yorks had to crouch for shelter under the sea wall. Here they were joined by the reserve company, also harassed on landing by machine-gun and mortar fire.

Help, however, was at hand. A DD tank came along the beach to engage the machine guns, and under cover of the tank's guns two platoons crossed the wall and began to wipe out the machine-gun nests. Another tank of the Westminster Dragoons fired two shots which penetrated the slit covering the western 88mm gun, which then fell silent, while the one to the east was also knocked out. AVREs and DDs then forced a passage through the sea wall and La Rivière was captured by 0900 hrs after more than an hour of stiff, expensive fighting on the beach. This action on 'King' beach at La Rivière fully justified the specialized armour of the 79th Division. Tanks of the division were now in action all along the British and Canadian beaches, punching holes in Hitler's Atlantic Wall.

One of those who landed with 5th East Yorks was Frederick Ayliffe, a REME craftsman attached to 'S' Company's Mortar Platoon. Landing one hour after the initial assault troops, he recalls what it was like on the beach. 'Our carrier followed the rest down into the water, levelled out, and half submerged began to make our way to dry land. We had to avoid knocked-out vehicles and blackened bodies floating face downwards in the water.

'The beach in front of us was crowded and we came to rest in about two feet of water awaiting our turn to get into the taped-off lanes. The exit was over to our left near some houses down the beach. We slowly made our way in that direction, having to avoid a lot of wheeled vehicles that were stuck in the soft sand. The RAMC were attending to the wounded who were sheltering under the sea wall, where there were also groups of German prisoners. We had just reached the exit, which was between two houses, when enemy shells started coming in. A single-track lane led us off the beach, which was quite steep with a high wall on each side. When we reached level ground the column came to a standstill owing to a vehicle in front having a track blown off by a mine. We were stuck here for quite a while and most of us climbed out to put our feet on firm ground.

'I was standing with our driver, Corporal Johnson, Nobby Clark the batman, and Private Morrikin, the driver of the carrier in front, when there was a blinding flash followed by a terrific explosion and we were blown off our feet. I remember hitting the ground with the others falling on top of me. Nobby Clark was screaming for help with a gash in his thigh, Corporal Johnson was wounded in the chest and appeared to be unconscious, and I could not get up until some help came and moved Private Morrikin, who had been killed instantly, with one side of his face blown away. On getting to my feet I was thankful to find that my only injuries were temporary deafness and concussion.'

The 5th East Yorks made good progress once they got off the beach, capturing the Mont Fleury position and advancing towards Ver-sur-Mer, further south.

Another regiment from Yorkshire, the 6th Battalion, the Green Howards, also came ashore on 'King' beach. This battalion had studied the German defences in great detail and knew they had to face a series of six pill-boxes, containing machine guns with interlocking fields of fire. One of these pill-boxes mounted a 105mm gun. These pill-boxes were situated on the battalion's right flank, in front of a series of five trenches straddling the Meuvaines ridge. On the left flank was a formidable coastal battery containing four 150mm guns, protected by its own entrenched defence force.

The battalion landed on their allotted beach at 0737 hrs. There they encountered heavy mortar and machine-gun fire. 'A' Company lost several men drowned in the surf, but ran up the beach, led by their company commander and supported by a solitary DD tank, until they reached the sea wall. Here they paused, with the Germans throwing grenades on to them over the top of the wall. The Company Commander, Captain Honeyman, though wounded, then led an assault over the wall and drove the enemy back, an action for which he was awarded the Military Cross.

'D' Company also ran into trouble. Many men, including four of the NCOs were cut down by heavy fire as the company waded ashore, but the advance continued in the face of stiff opposition. Evidence of the hard fighting comes from the award of the Victoria Cross to Company Sergeant-Major Stan Hollis of the Green Howards. The official citation tells his story:

In Normandy, on June 6th, 1944, during the assault on the beaches and the Mont Fleury battery, C.S.M. Hollis's Company Commander noticed that two of the pill-boxes had been by-passed, and went with C.S.M. Hollis to see that they were clear. When they were twenty yards from the pill-box a machine-gun opened fire from the slit, and C.S.M. Hollis instantly rushed straight at the pill-box, recharged his magazine, threw a grenade in through the door, and fired his Sten gun into it, killing two Germans and making the remainder prisoner. He then cleared several Germans from a neighbouring trench. By his action he undoubtedly saved his Company from being fired on heavily from the rear, and enabled them to open the main beach exit.

Later the same day, in the village of Crépon, the Company encountered a field gun and crew, armed with spandaus, at a hundred yards range. C.S.M. Hollis was put in command of a party to cover an attack on the gun, but the movement was held up. Seeing this, C.S.M. Hollis pushed right forward to engage the gun with a PIAT from a house at fifty yards range. He was observed by a sniper who fired and grazed his right cheek, and at the same moment the gun swung round and fired at point blank range into the house. To avoid the falling masonry C.S.M. Hollis moved his party to an alternative position. Two of the enemy gun crew had by this time been killed, and the gun was destroyed shortly afterwards. He later found that two of his men had stayed behind in the house, and immediately volunteered to get them out. In full view of the enemy, who were continually firing at him, he went forward alone using a Bren gun to distract their attention from the other men. Under cover of his diversion, the two men were able to get back.

Wherever fighting was heaviest C.S.M. Hollis appeared, and in the course of a magnificent day's work he displayed the utmost gallantry, and on two separate occasions his courage and initiative prevented the enemy from holding up the advance at critical stages. It was largely through his heroism and resource that the Company's objectives were gained and casualties were not heavier, and by his own bravery he saved the lives of many of his men.

Archibald Cairns was a member of the Royal Signals. 'Battalion HQ was to land at H-Hour plus 20 minutes on "King Green" sector of "Gold" beach. I don't suppose many people have ever tried pushing or pulling a 22 set through 3 or 4 feet of water on top of sand laden with other equipment, but we were pretty fit in those days and we managed it, though I couldn't push my youngest grandchild up a 1 in 20 gradient nowadays.

'I could see spurts of sand on the beach where mortar bombs were landing and the road at the top seemed a long way away. I was not destined to get further than the road for about half way up some Germans dropped a mortar bomb which wounded me in the right leg. It also damaged the set. It was only a flesh wound, though nasty enough, and I made it to the top where my friend managed to summon the MO who dressed my leg. I think that excitement turned to apprehension as the mortar bombs kept falling. I lay there for a long time among other wounded and some German prisoners, before being carted back in an American LST.'

Lt-Colonel Richardson, commanding the 7th Green Howards, realized on reaching the beach that he was some 400 yards to the west of his planned landing point. He led his battalion along the beach and then south towards Ver-sur-Mer. Their initial objective, a coastal battery, had already been knocked out by naval gun fire, and they pressed on to Crépon supported by the 4/7th Dragoon Guards and their Field Battery.

Ken Calver was a Command Post Assistant with the 86th Field

Regiment, Royal Artillery. 'One clear recollection, which gave light relief to the lads, involved me conveying a message – a simple thing. I was instructed to take a map to an officer of one of the gun troops, and feeling that here was an opportunity of bringing an early end to the war, I hared off across a field which was bisected by a small river. I made a bee-line for a wooden bridge but as I was about to cross I had a flash of inspiration – the Germans would have mined all bridges! I moved a few yards down-stream, deciding to jump across. Half-way across, in mid-air, I had another flash of inspiration – that's just what the Germans would expect me to do and they will have mined the bank! I tried to stay airborne but gravity won and I landed in mid-stream, to the raucous cheers of the onlookers.'

The support battalions were now coming ashore behind the assault waves. Among the men landing was Lieutenant Frank Pearson, commanding the Assault Pioneer Platoon of the 2nd Devons. 'The 2nd Devons had already served in Sicily and Italy, where I had been wounded twice and contracted malaria. I was only twenty years old and still recovering from an attack of malaria but I would not have missed D-Day for anything. We were the support battalion to the 1st Hants and the 1st Dorsets in 231 Brigade, with the job of passing through these battalions and heading for the Longues Battery.

'My experiences had made me a realist and I thought our chances of surviving D-Day were small. The noise was tremendous near the beach with everything banging away, but I don't think much of it was coming from the Germans. Our LCA grounded on a sandbank, but it came off again and drifted ashore and we were able to wade ashore and reach the high-water mark without any casualties. One or two of the tanks were knocked out and beside one lay a Tommy without a head. It is strange to remember such details after all this time but they stay at the back of the mind like old photographs.

'There was a lot of fire coming from Le Hamel in the 1st Hampshires area, but only stray bullets and shrapnel were landing near us. We assembled our Bangalore torpedoes and pushed them through the wire and lit the fuses, but nothing happened. Everything was soaking wet and all we could do was lay the pieces on the sand and hope they would dry out. Our rifle companies had now landed and were joining us by the sea wall and trying to figure out what to do. I suggested that if we had any buckets, which we hadn't, we could make sand-castles.

'Meanwhile the tide was coming in as well as more and more troops, so the beach got smaller as the numbers on it grew. It seemed to me that the whole of 50th Division was pinned down on this beach and likely to remain so, and then the break-through came. A flail tank, one of the "Funnies", climbed the sea wall and began to flail a path across the minefield. We peered over the wall, holding our breaths, and watched it flail across. Then, to the best of my knowledge, and against all that the history books say, most of the 231 Brigade and the forward elements of 50th Division followed in the wake of that one flail tank. Perhaps it wasn't like that, but that's how it seemed to me.

'On the other side of the minefield it was very quiet, with no sign of friend or foe. There were some of our tanks around and we hurried to catch up with our rifle companies, coming to a French hamlet which I suppose was Asnelles. There was still nobody about, no Germans, no French, no 2nd Devons. Acting in the well tried Eighth Army tradition, "When in doubt, brew up", we halted in a back garden and made tea.

'Surprisingly I didn't feel too bad, but I remember thinking how I missed my friend Corporal Jewell. He had served with me in Sicily before being wounded and had always been a tower of strength. Most of my men were completely untried, and although they turned out to be absolutely splendid, I did not know that then. Then, suddenly, Corporal Jewell arrived. It seems he had landed separately as a reinforcement, and without his equipment, but the important thing was that he was back with me again.

'While we were brewing up, the rifle companies began to arrive and we pushed on towards our objective at the battery. Just before dark we halted with orders to dig in and attack the battery at first light. I remember there was quite a lot of optimism about – some felt that the Germans wouldn't make a fight of it but just let us walk in. What a pity they didn't.'

With the assault brigades ashore, more and more men and equipment began to pile up behind them. All over the beaches, teams of men were unloading much-needed supplies and vehicles. The task of controlling traffic on the beaches, bringing the follow-up landing craft ashore, and directing their passengers and contents to the right destination was entrusted to a number of Beach Groups. These were usually commanded by a naval officer, who had a group of Navy Commandos and sometimes a battalion of infantry under command, to provide local protection.

Able Seaman Norman Harris was a member of 10 Beach Group, landing just below the cliffs at Le Hamel. 'Our job as Naval Beach Commandos lay solely on the beach and its surrounding area, and had nothing to do with advancing inland. We had to secure the beach and defend it and get the rest of the invading force in with the least number of casualties as possible. We all had different jobs to do ; Taffy Williams and I had to get radio equipment ashore to a certain part of the beach. This was carried in a box with two handles back and front, just like a sedan chair without the top. We jumped out of the craft up to our waists in water and ran for the back of the beach, passing a pair of legs without a body on the way.

'Our next job was to erect a great big beach sign about 20 feet high and 8 feet wide. It consisted of two poles with a canvas sheet secured to them, painted bright green with a large letter 'J' on it denoting 'Jig Green Beach', and craft allocated to that beach could see it when out at sea, giving them a point to land on. Within minutes of erecting this sign the Germans started to concentrate their mortar and machine-guns on it, and we started exchanging fire with them. While this was going on the Germans had an 88mm gun dug in at Le Hamel, and this was knocking seven bells out of everything that beached. Something had to be done about it. LCT D28 beached about 30 yards away and within minutes it had more holes in it than a sieve. We saw one man staggering about on the stern of the craft, so Geordie Farrow and I waded out and got him ashore. He was a young Sub-Lieutenant from Manchester, and although he was covered in blood he wasn't seriously wounded, so we advised him to get down to the water's edge and jump on one of the landing craft which were disembarking, as we had no medical services with us.'

Sapper Ralph Rayner was one of the crew in an armoured bulldozer of the 149th Assault Squadron, Royal Engineers. 'We landed with our water-proof bulldozer on the left flank of "Gold" beach, just west of La Rivière. It was a frightening experience, because just as we came out of the water two AVRE tanks (Assault Vehicle Royal Engineers) exploded and disintegrated. They had been hit by an 88mm further up the beach, and this enemy gun was put out of action by Petard fire from another AVRE commanded by Captain King RE, who was awarded the Military Cross.

'Our task was to clear the beach of all obstacles and we worked with the Royal Navy Commandos. Their divers made safe the explosive charges attached to underwater obstacles and secured the bulldozer winch rope so that we could tow the obstacles ashore. It took five days to clear the beach of all obstacles, but we carried out a number of other duties. On D+1 a padre requested our assistance in recovering a number of bodies which were floating just offshore, and we recovered about 20 or 30, mostly from 47 (Royal Marine) Commando, whose landing craft had overturned during the approach to the beach.

'The highlight of our time was when we recovered two crates floating ashore from one of the sunken ships. One contained five-and-a-half gallons of 100 per cent proof Navy rum and the other contained two-and-a-half thousand Players cigarettes. I think I had better leave the consequences of this find to your imagination.'

Gunner Frank Davies came ashore with the 73rd Anti-Tank Regiment. 'Our Battery consisted of four Sherman M10s mounting 3-inch American naval guns, which, according to our BSM Silver, fired effectively round corners. Our officer, Lieutenant Brown, had a Bren gun carrier. I was his Gunner Signaller, and there was a driver and one other man who kept repeating at intervals, "We'll all get killed!"

'Following us were our four M10 Shermans plus a 3-tonner and a water cart, and so on. The "Rhino" raft we were on was driven by two outboard motors mounted on the rear corners, steered by switching the motors on or off as required. Progress to the beach was slow and we had time to study the amazing scene. To the left, to the right, and behind, were hundreds of ships, many of them sporting a barrage balloon which shimmered in the bright sun. There were multi-rocket firing-ships on the right and left of us. We couldn't see the one protecting us from behind but it put the fear of hell up us at intervals. To our right, supporting the Americans on "Omaha" beach and firing shells on to gun emplacements, was a British warship, the cruiser HMS *Ajax*.

'On the beach we made out carriers, mine-flailing tanks, bridging tanks, and so on. Infantry were dotted all over the place and occasionally an enemy shell landed on the beach. Suddenly we were looking to our "Rhino"'s left-hand outboard motor area which seemed to be out of commission, and we realized we were out of control and had become a lethal threat to the ships around us. The remaining outboard motor operator was soon doing a magnificent job, using the cross tide as the missing engine. Our hearts were in our mouths as our pilot, with great skill, weaved in and out and around the ships. I remember noticing open-mouthed faces looking down at us as we missed ships by yards. We grounded on the correct "Gold" beach, which I recall was divided into four colours, and I think we were only a few yards from the correct colour. A splendid effort, worth a VC we thought.'

Able Seaman Norman Harris and the 10th Beach Group were still having problems. 'To get back to that 88mm gun that was doing all the damage; Petty Officer Taffy Williams and Petty Officer Paddy Hodgetts took on the job of having a go at it, and ran along the beach under heavy fire and knocked it out with grenades. Taffy Williams was wounded in the legs in the process but Paddy Hodgetts got away without injury, a very courageous act that received no recognition, although the incident was reported.'

The beaches now had to be cleared of both obstacles and wreckage. Norman Harris again : 'One of the first jobs was to remove the steel girders and the mines on them. A few tanks had survived the landing, which we used to drag the girders out of the sand and pile them up, away from the water's edge.

'Between the beach and that road was a minefield full of Teller mines, so they had to be cleared before the beach became cluttered with the expected traffic. This was our next job. We didn't have mine detectors but used our daggers to feel for them. When we found one, we cleared the top away and felt underneath and around it for booby traps. All being well, we unscrewed the detonator which was in the centre of the mine, got hold of the handle and lifted it out. Eventually we had a pile of mines and detonators which needless to say we kept well apart.'

By mid-afternoon, with 'Gold' beach now in British hands, the follow-up brigades came ashore. These consisted of the 56th Infantry Brigade (the 2nd South Wales Borderers and the 2nd Battalions of the Gloucester Regiment and the Essex Regiment); and the 151st Infantry Brigade (the 6th, 8th and 9th Battalions of the Durham Light Infantry); for support they had the 8th Armoured Brigade, formed from the 4/7th Dragoon Guards and the Nottinghamshire Yeomanry. Their tasks now were to expand the bridgehead, take Bayeux, and occupy all the land up to and beyond the N13 road between Bayeux and Caen, and occupy the coast to the west as far as Port-en-Bessin, linking up with the Americans coming from 'Omaha'.

The 56th Brigade should have come ashore at 1000 hrs, but did not land until after midday, when their planned landing area, Le Hamel, was still in German hands. They therefore landed 1,500 yards to the east and were quickly ashore and heading down the La Rivière–Bayeux road.

Les 'Titch' Holden was a Private in the Pioneer Platoon of the 2nd Essex. He was one of a party of four chosen to act as an advance party and lead the battalion through the lanes cleared in the minefields. 'We had to liaise between the RE sappers clearing openings through the minefields, mark the routes as they were cleared, then convey the information by wireless to the incoming ships. Regimental banners were to be erected for quick recognition by the incoming troops and indicator signs fixed to assist in the rapid movement of troops off the beaches and through the minefields.

'Captain Chell told me to extend my area of watch while he went towards Le Hamel to find alternative exits for the battalion transport. It was almost midday when I saw what I had been waiting for, LCIs spilling out men of the 2nd Battalion, the Essex Regiment. They waded ashore and marched up the beach in single file led by their Colonel.

'It was my duty and honour to welcome my Colonel and fellow "Pompadours" and relay to them their marching orders which, if my memory serves me right were, "Black route is open, Sir." Colonel Higson slapped me on the back and said, "Well done – stay on the beach, recover your Jeep and rejoin us in due course." '

Lieutenant Bert Jalland was a platoon commander in 'B' Company, the 8th Durham Light Infantry. 'My recollection of the countryside that day is that it was pleasantly rolling, with numerous hedgerows and trees, scattered farmhouses and other buildings, and fields golden with ripening crops. There were plenty of cattle and other farm animals, but few people because most of the inhabitants had fled the bombardment or were in hiding where they hoped to be safe. It must have been a ghastly day for them.

'Our first major objective was the town of Bayeux, and we set off along the road leading towards it in single file and widely spaced, in order to limit possible casualties – a tactic that we had successfully adopted during the advance on Messina in Sicily. There was occasional enemy artillery and small-arms fire, but nothing that affected us directly.

'In the main, we did not know what was happening. Information was not getting down to the companies and certainly not to the platoons. We had to rely upon "news" given to us in passing by despatch riders and members of other units, gunners or tank crews, with whom we came in contact. The lack of any clear idea of what was going on is a very lasting impression of D-Day, but the absence of communication to the lower ranks was to be a feature of the whole of the Normandy campaign. Many of us had little idea of where we were, what action was taking place, or what we were supposed to do about it.

'We met few of the enemy on that first day, but those we did capture were infantry and gunners wearing German uniforms who claimed that they were Russians and were keen to surrender. They were obviously shocked by the ferocity of the bombing and the bombardment, but they received very little sympathy from our troops, who regarded them as traitors to the Allied cause.'

With the whole of 50th Division ashore, steady progress was made southwards. Joe Minogue of the Westminster Dragoons was now off the beaches with his flail tank, and his services were in great demand. 'Sergeant Poole was involved in a fierce argument between an irate major in the Royal Artillery and a subaltern in the Hampshires. For our next move, Sergeant Poole wanted to get into Le Hamel, as did the infantry officer, but the artillery major wanted us to flail a nearby field. The Major won, by virtue of his superior rank, and we began to clear mines for his guns, while Sergeant Poole went off on foot to try to get some new orders.

'There were few mines in that field but each time we struck one of them, the 75mm in the turret went off of its own volition. Neville Duell slammed another shell in the breech while at the same time trying to raise some of the squadron's other tanks. Eventually I had to bash him on the head to point out that the firing mechanism had gone wrong, probably knocked out of sequence by the mines as we came off the beach. By then it was time to change the flail chains, replacing them with the grease-covered spares kept in bins at the side of the tank.

'Although we had done it many times before, the crew never really became accustomed to the awkward moment when the chain, bolted to the flail drum, falls free, invariably to swing against one's shinbone to send a crew member hopping and cursing and wishing the 5-foot-long flail chain to the far depths of hell. We were sitting by the track, smoking and looking out to sea, where a stream of vehicles were using the lane we had cleared of mines. At that moment we felt proud that all the training we had undergone had been worthwhile and that the faith of the Commander of the 79th Armoured Division, Major-General Sir Percy Hobart, in his beloved "Funnies", had been justified.

'While we were having our smoke, Neville Duell was scrabbling about idly in the loose flailed earth. "What's this then?" he asked in alarm. It was a German box mine which the flail had missed. It was armed, with the wooden wedge that drove into a trip wire showing red side up. We shouted a warning, got back into the tank, and Sam Hardy turned the flail round and we went back to detonate the mine, resuming our interrupted smoke and watching in horror as the driver of a Bren gun carrier got down to pick up some object in his path, which turned out to be an anti-personnel mine that blew up in his hands. His screams as his hands were blown off put all the other noise in the shade.'

To George Laity, the PIAT man with 2nd Devons, 6 June was a mass of conflicting recollections. 'We moved off inland eventually, with no idea of time. I remember it being a very long day. I saw my first dead German laying in the road and also remember seeing dead cows in the fields, blown up like barrage balloons, on their sides with their legs sticking out.

'We advanced through Normandy, avoiding minefields and looking out for snipers. I assisted in knocking out a gun emplacement near Port-en-Bessin, after which we came under fire again in a cornfield and had to cross a large gap in a hedgerow. I ran like hell and the PIAT weighed a ton. A few of my mates didn't make it. By the end of the day, tired and hungry, having not eaten all day, the company consolidated and as it was getting dark we dug in. The presence of one of our tanks made us feel somewhat safer. We heard on the radio that the beachhead was secured and the invasion was successful, and I thought the worst was over – or was it? A week later I was a POW.' George Laity was captured at Tilly-sur-Seulles and remained a prisoner until April 1945.

Gunner Edwin Bartholemew was a despatch rider in the 102nd Anti-Tank Regiment, the Northumberland Hussars. 'Moving inland, a big French woman tugged at us and pointed to a burning barn, crying. We broke down the door thinking children were in there, and the biggest pig I have ever seen ran out. We seemed to come together as a regiment. Some were telling tales of meeting Germans but I hadn't seen any, only two Italians shouting that they were on our side – "German, son of a bitch." I remember thinking that war gives up strange bedfellows.'

Frank Davies of the 73rd Anti-Tank Regiment found little German tank action to the front of the division, and for the moment there was not very much for them to do. 'It was a great relief to be safely on *terra firma*. After exchanging greetings with Engineers and Pioneer Corps chaps and thanking them, we scurried off into the well worn tracks of the tanks, which had gone ahead of us. We saw a British Tommy flattened out in the right-hand track and this sight made us feel very hard towards the Germans, which was probably a good thing at the time.

'As we went through a village we passed German prisoners who had been told to make for the beach for transport to POW camps. A number of them had French girls still hanging on to their arms. Our Lieutenant, "Topper" Brown, was excellent and kept all his men up-to-date with the changing situation. We carried on and noted the various signs of battle, including hastily evacuated German camouflaged tents, cooking and eating utensils, and in a hedge a mobile anti-tank gun mounted on a tripod with straps for carrying it on the shoulders. This was new to me.

'Light was fading and we leaguered in a large pit. The sergeant removed the firing pins and placed rags into an ammo box lightly dug into the hedgeside. The officer and all the other men went off on a local recce, leaving me alone with four M10s, one Bren gun carrier and, of course, my own Sten gun. When they had left, a lone aircraft passed overhead, which I could only just make out. An eerie silence followed, which seemed a very long time, and I was relieved when they all arrived back. I asked Lieutenant Brown how long they had been and he said 20 minutes, but it was the longest 20 minutes I have ever known.'

Frederick Ayliffe, of the 5th East Yorks, had been in the thick of it all day. 'There was some hard fighting during the day and gaining ground was very slow. Knocked-out vehicles littered the roads, forcing us to take to the fields. Our objective was to capture Bayeux, but the enemy resistance hardened and it did not fall until midday on 7 June.

'It was early evening before we reached a road that was not under shell-fire and we were able to move forward about four miles. We passed farms on fire and scores of German prisoners who were being escorted to the rear. As night fell the gunfire lessened and we moved across a field to take cover in an area surrounded by trees. With darkness falling, tree roots everywhere, and everyone wanting to get their heads down, most of us gave up the digging, took a blanket and crawled under the vehicles. So ended a very long day.'

Enemy prisoners caused problems for the 10th Beach Group. Apart from Germans and Austrians, the prisoners also included conscripted soldiers from many East European nations. Norman Harris recalls them: 'During this time, German prisoners were being brought in and had to be contained. Some were very arrogant, some glad to be out of it. I remember one prisoner, a bomber pilot, very arrogantly saying that the German Air Force would blow us off the beaches and back into the sea, so I reminded him that very shortly he would be behind barbed wire in England and wouldn't be playing any part in it. The prisoners were a mixed bunch; Romanians, Poles, Czechs, and so on, but they gave us no problems except where to keep them as priority was given to our own wounded. As the landing craft emptied, the wounded were loaded aboard and taken back to the hospital ships moored off the beaches.'

Joe Minogue had an eventful evening. 'Our Colonel, Blair-Oliphant, came striding along, wearing white overalls and looking like an itinerant house-painter who had stumbled into the act by mistake. He had hitched a ride in one of the regiment's recovery vehicles and now he was asking us what had happened to our tank commander. Then, with a brief word of praise to the crew, he strode off again.

'Soon after this, our tank commander returned to tell us we were to join another of our flails on the road leading into Le Hamel, where we spent most of the afternoon, being cursed roundly by other drivers trying to squeeze past our 8-ft-wide jib. I reported the loss of my pistol to Sergeant Poole, who said he had seen a German rifle on the roadside and some ammunition. I recovered this, with his words following me : "You're going on about a lost pistol . . . just think of the poor bastards who have lost their lives."

'That night we moved to the small hamlet of Meuvaines, little realizing what a slender toe-hold we had in Normandy, and because we were only two scratch crews the Colonel joined me on our first night's guard in France.

'He thought he saw a German moving in the bedroom of a shell-shattered house. "Run and get me a Mills bomb from one of the flails, Trooper," he ordered. I did so and he threw it towards the bedroom window. Unfortunately, it hit the window sill and began to roll off. Although Colonel Blair-Oliphant was a tall man, we both made even time in diving for cover behind the low garden wall, which was destroyed, covering us both in stones and fragments of mortar.

'It turned into a lively night when two German fighters began to strafe the many ships still lying off the invasion beaches, which put up such a barrage of anti-aircraft fire that the night sky was lit by tracers, providing only a half-dark at the end of an exceptionally long day. After we were relieved we slept like dead men, realizing just how much we had yet to learn but satisfied that we had somehow survived a truly memorable day. Just glad, in fact, to be alive.'

For some men there was still no rest. Bert Jalland, with 8th Durham Light Infantry, having dug himself in for the night, was summoned to Battalion Headquarters. 'When I got there I found some confusion. Apparently Brigadier Senior had disappeared and our Commanding Officer had gone to HQ 151 Brigade to command the Brigade. Our Senior Company Commander, Major George Chambers, was temporarily commanding the Battalion. I was told that the Brigadier's Jeep had been ambushed, his jeep driver and signaller had been killed, and the Brigadier was missing. I was instructed to take out a patrol and endeavour to find him. I was to concentrate upon searching woods and copses. We were to use bicycles so that we could cover a wider area.

'I collected three volunteers from my platoon and we set off, having no map and no real idea of our location. The pass-words that day were "Bread and Cheese". If we came across anyone in the woods during our search, I was supposed to whisper "Bread" and the reply "Cheese" would be given to me. In the event the whole expedition became farcical. I challenged a number of people in the dark with the word "Bread" only to be met with profuse apologies, usually in broad Geordie dialect. It was clear that the people we were addressing had not been given the pass-word.

'We approached many woods during the night but they were all occupied by our own troops and we never found Brigadier Senior. We were told later that he had been taken prisoner but had escaped. Anyway, we arrived back with the battalion at "stand-to" (about 0400 hrs). I was utterly exhausted but even at that time I realized that it was highly unlikely that I would ever have to live through a more varied and adventurous day.'

During that night, many had time to reflect. Lewis Richards, signaller to the Commander of 231 Brigade, recalls : 'I arrived back from the last visit of the day in time to do "stand-to". It was getting dark and for the first time I saw German planes. They were attacking our shipping but the flak did not give them a very pleasant welcome and I saw two shot down in flames. After "stand-to" I ate the remainder of my box of rations and borrowed a box ready for breakfast. I borrowed some blankets as I had lost my own and all my kit had been in the Jeep which we had lost in the LCM.

'My clothes had dried on me during the day and I slept with them on. Before going to sleep the events of the day passed through my mind and I could not help thinking that at last we could say that the war was entering its final phase.'

Reginald Rham recalls his thoughts at the end of that day. 'My personal reflections at the time were that here I was, sitting in a slit trench, enjoying a cigarette in the fields of Normandy, and not all that long ago I had been enjoying a hot meal in the New Forest. Today, when I read the histories of D-Day and look at the photographs which have been published, I think to myself, "Christ, I was lucky."'

Norman Harris's 10th Beach Group recorded the final positions on D-Day in a news-sheet issued to the troops.

**10 Beach Group Intelligence Summary
and News No. 1 dated 7 June 1944**

50 Div. Situation a.m. 7 June

231 Bde occupying Longues.
56 Bde north of Bayeux, and moving into town, against slight opposition.
151 Bde across railway Bayeux–Caen, from Point 788078 – Nonant 8275.
69 Bde across road Bayeux–Caen as far as Port-en-Bessin 9072.

Prisoners : Total captured is not known, but some 500 have passed through 10 Beach Group area.

Casualties : Unknown on either side.

Booty :   (Apart from what has inserted itself into pockets.)
           Stocks of reserve ammo., grenades, rifles, LMGs, etc. are
           being counted. It is estimated that there are sufficient supplies
           for the whole Beach Group to blow itself up, if they go the right
           way about it.

General :
     After very hard fighting in the early stages, the operation has gone well
     and we are now firmly established. German retaliation after the opening
     phase has been slight, and it is likely that they are planning a large-scale
     armoured counter-attack. Tanks and A/Tk guns are coming ashore and
     getting forward in large enough numbers to deal with anything of this
     kind.

The fighting on 'Gold' beach cost the 50th Division about 1,000 casualties,
killed, wounded and missing. This total would have been much higher had
it not been for the gallant and resourceful men of the 79th Armoured
Division – the 'Funnies'. Many of them were going into action for the first
time in these strange and specialized machines, but thanks to their efforts in
breaching the Atlantic Wall, the infantry were able to get through and
advance towards Bayeux before the Germans had time to occupy it. Bayeux
is one Norman town which survived the fighting virtually intact, an enduring
tribute to the men who came ashore on 'Gold' beach.

 LCA431

CHAPTER TEN

'Juno'

'I don't care if there are 50 million
Germans on the beach; just let me off this
goddam boat !'
Corporal Hughie Rocks
The Queen's Own Rifles of Canada
off 'Juno', 6 June 1944

Three miles east of 'Gold' beach lay 'Juno', the landing area for the 3rd Canadian Division. This division was to assault the coast through a line of small resort towns, from Graye-sur-Mer just west of Bernières-sur-Mer along to St Aubin-sur-Mer further east. The Canadian beaches lay on either side of the oyster port of Courseulles, at the mouth of the River Seulles. This was the 'Mike' and 'Nan' section of the invasion coast and, from the west, the Canadian landing areas were codenamed 'Mike Green' and 'Mike Red', followed by 'Nan Green', 'Nan White', and at St Aubin, 'Nan Red'.

This entire coastline was, and still is, lined with houses and villas which virtually link the small resort towns together. The Germans had turned many of the towns into strongpoints, using reinforced concrete to fortify the cellars of the houses and villas, laying plenty of mines along the roads and in the gardens, while mazes of barbed wire covered by anti-tank and machine guns lay behind the beaches. The Canadians would be involved in street fighting from the moment they stepped ashore, and street fighting is both notoriously difficult to control and a great consumer of infantry. The German troops in this section came from the 716th Infantry Division, commanded by Lt-General Wilhelm Richter, and they were more than willing to make a fight of it.

The assault troops came from the 3rd Canadian Division of General Crerar's Canadian Army, under the command of Major-General R. F. Keller. General Keller's division had been attached to the British Third Army for the assault phase in Normandy and would return to the Canadian Army when sufficient Canadian divisions had come ashore.

General Keller decided to put his infantry ashore astride Courseulles, with close support from DD tanks of two Canadian tank regiments, the 6th Armoured Regiment (the 1st Hussars) at Courseulles, and the 10th Armoured Regiment, better known as the Fort Gary Horse, at St Aubin. The assault infantry would come from the Royal Winnipeg Rifles, the Regina Rifle Regiment, the Queen's Own Rifles of Canada (QORC) and the North Shore Regiment.

Follow-up waves in the assault brigades would consist of French Canadians from a famous Quebec Regiment, the Regiment de la Chaudière, and the 1st Battalion of the Canadian Scottish Regiment. The third brigade of the Division, the 9th Canadian Infantry Brigade, which contained the Highland Light Infantry of Canada (HLIC), the Stormont, Dundas and Glengarry Highlanders, and the North Nova Scotia Highlanders would come ashore later.

The Canadians would have the support of British units, the 8th Battalion of the King's Liverpool Regiment acting as the Beach Group and, landing at St Aubin, 48 (Royal Marine) Commando. This was the latest and last of the Royal Marine Commandos to form, and after landing at St Aubin had the task of taking a German strongpoint at Langrune-sur-Mer to the east and so linking up with 41 (RM) Commando coming west from 'Sword'. There would also be armoured support from 'C' Squadron of the Inns of Court Regiment and the 2nd Royal Marine Armoured Support Regiment in Centaur tanks.

The 3rd Canadian Division on D-Day actually consisted of 15,000 Canadian and 9,000 British troops. The main force would land at 0745 hrs while 48 Commando would come ashore at St Aubin at around 0830 hrs, after the beach had been taken by the North Shore Regiment and the tanks of the Fort Gary Horse. That, at least, was the plan; as usual on D-Day, it was not to work out like that.

Air cover would be provided by the 2nd Tactical Air Force and gunfire support would come from 2 British cruisers, HMS *Belfast* and HMS *Diadem*, and 11 destroyers, including the French *Combattant*, and 2 Canadian Tribal-class destroyers, HMCS's *Algonquin* and *Sioux*, as well as the

DD tanks and the 107mm mortars from the Cameron Highlanders of Ottawa. The Canadians were to capture all the coastal towns from Graye-sur-Mer to St Aubin and then advance inland as far as a defence line, codenamed 'Oak', which lay along the railway line running from Caen to Bayeux, some seven miles inland.

The accounts in this book all describe how most of the landings got off to a bad start, and the Canadian assault was no different. Bad weather delayed the landing craft and many of the obstacles were already covered by the tide before the craft reached the beach. Many craft were blown up on these obstacles. Others capsized in the surf or were driven onshore. At high tide the beach was far too narrow to let the men and their tanks and vehicles get organized, and an immense traffic jam soon built up on the narrow sand strip above the waterline, under German artillery and machine-gun fire.

Robert Pullin was a coxswain on an LCA and gives a vivid account of the 'Juno' landing. 'On the evening of 4 June we took on board six platoons of French Canadians (Regiment de la Chaudière) and proceeded into Cowes Road and anchored. We did not up-anchor till late evening on 5 June, and met up with the rest of the convoy to France, dropping anchor again eleven miles off the coast. We were then mustered and given our orders. The six LCAs, of which I was coxswain, were to head straight for the gun emplace-ments holding 88s, and were to land one platoon directly in front of them. We were given a course to follow on leaving the ship; I was given the spire of the church at Courseulles-sur-Mer. My oppo. was to land a mile up the coast at another pill-box – he had a water tower to aim for. Each craft had an LCR behind, blasting at the emplacement and any obstacles. Fortunately, there were none to be seen on arrival, as I had to go in on one engine. To make sure that we could get off the beach, I had to drop a kedge-anchor so that we could pull ourselves off.

'The 88mm was out of action and there were no casualties; the Canadian lads were lying in front of the pill-box. We were not so lucky. My seaman and signalman were in the water pulling on the kedge rope to get us off. They managed it, but on clambering on to the stern the enemy opened up with machine-gun fire and my seaman was shot through the knees. My signalman was hit in the shoulder. They were given morphia injections after we got back to the ship through mountainous seas. The next day my seaman was transferred to the hospital ship. Of the other five LCAs, four returned; the other had blown up on a mine, killing the seaman and wounding one CO and the coxswain.'

Royal Marine Corporal Lionel Long put his Canadians ashore at Ber-nières. 'We transferred our commandos and picked up 35 Canadian troops and put them ashore safely. On leaving the beach we were holed by an obstacle and started to sink. We were then picked up by a Canadian LCI and she was then hit by three bottle mines and began to sink. We were ordered by the crew to throw everything movable over the side to lighten her. We then went with the crew to the engine room with two pumps working and a chain of buckets. We were waist-high in water, but we managed to save her by applying large mats to stop the water coming in the holes in the engine room.

'We were then taken to our mother ship, which was anchored ten miles off the beaches. An LCA was sent across for us and a wounded Canadian seaman, who had been shot in the chest by a sniper. Our doctor operated on him and saved his life. I'm sad to say we lost 17 LCAs out of 20. Seven other ranks were killed and 6 wounded.'

The naval and air bombardment had clearly failed to knock out the beach defences, for the landing craft suffered severe losses getting ashore and the Canadian infantry suffered heavy casualties just getting off the beach. At Bernières the Queen's Own Rifles of Canada had a very bad time on landing, and only got off the beach with the help of DD tanks and flails of the 1st Hussars. When the reserve battalion, the Regiment de la Chaudière, came ashore half an hour later, they found 'Mike Green' and 'Mike Red' beach still under fire, strewn with dead and wounded and littered with the wreckage of landing craft and vehicles.

Major Mike Morrison, MC was then commanding 'A' Company of the 8th Battalion the King's Regiment, which landed at Graye-sur-Mer on the west flank of the Canadians. 'The sea was very rough with troughs so deep that our assault craft appeared to be the only one around although there were hundreds about. Thirty-five close combat soldiers and a crew of three Royal Marines were packed together aboard. We were trying to avoid seasickness but there was nothing to look at except the sea and all around seasick soldiers. Just on H-Hour (0730 hrs) the line of landing craft stormed the beaches. Underwater obstacles, mined angle irons slanted in close ranks, great pointed logs called "Belgian Gates", caused havoc.

'A craft to my left was blown sky high. We manoeuvred through the gap which had been created. Under heavy fire from the beach we landed head-on. I was first off and disappeared under the waves in 9ft of water. Needless to say no one followed. When I surfaced I told the commander to bring the craft further in while I made for the shore. I was the first to feel the dry sand of "Mike Green" beach; there was a feeling of tremendous elation and the seasickness vanished.

'Mortar and artillery fire saturated the beach area, a burst of machine-gun fire swathed through our small group, leaving six or more men killed or wounded. We reached the limited shelter of the sand dunes and established a command post. We moved back to help casualties and strangely we were not fired on. A formidable concrete German command post dominated our beach. Orders were quickly issued and grenades were hurled through the gun ports. Germans emerged with their hands up. I like to think that having witnessed the complete destruction of the machine-gun position they decided that enough was enough, but there was no time to linger. Germans appeared from everywhere, surrendering in droves, but we were still harassed by mortar fire from beyond the beach.

'The Canadians pushed on to deal with the artillery and I took a strong patrol to clear a large group of buildings just off the beach. It was another furious and hectic assault but we cleared the buildings with grenades and took many more prisoners.' For storming the command post and other actions on D-Day, Major Morrison was awarded the MC.

Lt John (Dinty) Moore was also in the 8th Battalion of the King's Regiment. 'Our task was to act as a Beach Group for the 3rd Canadian Division on the western part of the "Juno" landing, to disembark at the same time as the Royal Winnipeg Rifles west of Courseulles, to clear up any opposition on or near the beach and to protect the flanks while the Canadians moved forward.

'As we neared the Normandy coast, well before daylight, after a rough crossing, the shattering barrage on the coast started, first with bombers, then with a terrific bombardment from the Navy. The six Canadian self-propelled 105mm guns on the LCT opened up, blasting the beach area. Slowly the darkness gave way to light. Gradually the dim silhouettes of our landing area at Graye-sur-Mer, to the west of Courseulles, became discernible, with the dull green countryside rising slightly beyond. There were hundreds of landing craft firing at the coast, and behind them the cruisers HMS *Belfast*, *Diadem* and others. There were ships as far as the eye could see.

'Three Allied planes raced over towards the coast just at that moment, and the second one, hit by one of our own rockets, simply blew up in thousands of pieces. The coast, its forts, its obstacles, were now very close and clear. A German reinforced concrete pill-box fired a hail of 20mm shells at the landing craft just to our right, but the landing craft was a Landing Craft Gun (LCG) with two 4.7 inch guns, and having turned slowly around, it fired a salvo which blasted the pill-box to pieces.

'The small assault craft, the LCAs, were now slowly overtaking us, having been lowered from the troop-carrying ships well to our rear, the *Langibby Castle*, the HMCS *Prince Henry*, the *Mecklenburg* and others. These LCAs had been tossed about cruelly in the still rough sea and most of the troops packed in them were terribly seasick.

'We watched as the LCAs carrying the assault troops of the Royal Winnipegs and the Liverpool Irish tried to manoeuvre through the gaps in the obstacles. Some had the bottom of the landing craft torn off by the jagged obstacles, others were sunk or blown up by the exploding mines and shells. Almost a third of the assaulting landing craft were sunk or badly damaged.

'For the Germans to have survived the monstrous barrage was quite surprising, but several of their reinforced concrete gun-posts, buried in the sand dunes, were virtually intact, and the first troops ashore, two companies of the Royal Winnipegs, one company of the Regina Rifle Regiment together with "A" and "B" Companies of the Liverpool Irish, were met with machine-gun fire. German gun and mortar fire now started to rain down on the beach, the machine-gun fire sweeping the length of the narrow shore and catching the debarking troops in enfilade. Several men were killed or wounded while still in the water; others staggered limp, wet and seasick to the shore where bullets were kicking up spurts of sand.'

The Royal Winnipeg Rifles and Regina Rifles made good progress at Courseulles, and by mid-afternoon the Canadian armour had cut the Caen–Bayeux road, after a speedy advance inland of more than seven miles, but before this could be exploited the Germans counter-attacked.

The War Diary of the Queen's Own Rifles spells out their D-Day situation in detail:

0750 hrs
H-Hour postponed 30 minutes. DD tanks and AVREs behind schedule. Up to 0745 hrs no sign of action on beach but now anti-tank shells begin to drop around LCAs which makes heads go down in fast order.

Unfortunately postponement has definitely messed up support fire and all that is firing now is an LCF which cruised right in close to shore and let loose with a lot of tracers.

0805 hrs
Assault companies go in. As yet no DDs or AVREs can be seen which looks ominous.

0815 hrs
A & B Coys touch down. 'B' immediately catches a packet of trouble as they are landed in front of a heavily defended position. Several of the LCAs of both companies are blown up by mines but only the front two or three men are injured. 'A' Company are a little better off than 'B', able to get off the beach. As soon as they hit the railway they come under heavy mortar fire and are pinned down. Casualties mount; Lt Rea wounded, Sgt Charles Smith extricates platoon. Balance of 'A' Company get through. 'B' Company finally outflanks position.

0830 hrs
'C' and 'D' Coys and alternate Bn HQ touch down. Casualties among LCAs heavy. Almost one-half blown up by underwater mines. Personnel get ashore and pass through assault companies.

0900 hrs
The support all around has been very disappointing – none of the beach defences has been touched and this caused very high casualties among the assault companies.

0940 hrs
Bn HQ arrives. At this time it is noted that a café just 100 yards off the beach is opened up and selling wine to all and sundry.

Considerable delay as companies assemble. 'B' Coy casualties so heavy they gather first off the beach and try to sort themselves out. 'A' Coy moves to the forming-up place. Regiment de la Chaudière has now landed but are prevented from passing through us by the very accurate fire of a Battery of 88mm guns located just south of Bernières.

W. T. Jones of Peterborough, Ontario was with an artillery unit supporting the 7th Canadian Infantry Brigade. 'This is an honest account, years and memory permitting, of six Canadians who landed on D-Day. "G", "H" and "K" were three Troops of the 3rd Regt RCA, and had loaded on their LCT, Queen's Docks, Southampton. "G" was to support Regina Rifles, "H" Winnipeg Rifles, and "K" Canadian Scottish.

'Our Gun HI was to be the first towed gun of the regiment to land. We were to land on "Mike" sector of "Juno". This was the plan, but what action goes to plan? On our run-in to the beaches, about three miles from the shore we were ordered out of the landing order and fell back about five miles. Here we circled for hours, which seemed like days as the seas were rough and we weren't sailors. We had been told our beach exit was plugged and closed to vehicles.

'Finally, our turn came and in we went. The tide, however, was now not suitable for a direct landing, i.e., ramp down, drive off, as we had rehearsed for many months. Major Scott informed the Gun Sergeants we would be loading on a small "Rhino" raft. This was the first time we had heard about "Rhino" rafts and we sure weren't crazy about the word "raft". There were the usual derogatory remarks about the Canadian Brass. We were assured that four Bren gun carriers and guns could fit on these rafts "if properly handled". Out from the beach puttered our raft, a low-slung affair with steel decking and no railings, powered by two outboard motors and crewed by two REs who looked about forty years old. How they did it without loss of life or limb I'll never know, but they did.

'The Troop Commander had landed earlier, as planned, and had dropped off the Bombardier from H2, who was to guide us to Troop HQ. As we were hours behind schedule, we attempted to de-waterproof on the run. Splash shields were knocked off, life belts and waterproof covers removed from small arms, all tossed over the side. Bombardier Tom Grant (killed 8 June by 12 SS Panzer) was sitting by a wall, and when we halted, his first words to me were, "Where the hell have you been?" So much for rank respect in the Canadian Army this day.

'H Troop caught up to the Winnipegs and assumed our support role. A Captain in the "Pegs" wanted a house "taken out". Up went H1, un-limbered, put one up the spout and fired. What a commotion! In our eagerness and nervousness we forgot to remove the muzzle cover which sailed about 40ft down the road. The gun and road was enveloped in a huge cloud of blue smoke (grease not cleaned off breach and barrel). When the smoke cleared the gun sat alone and the crew had taken cover in a ditch. This was the first shot of H Troop, 14th Bty, 3rd Regt RCA. The rest of the day was spent performing the 3Ds of an Infantry division : Digging, Duck-ing, Dodging. At Creully, with the Royal Winnipeg Rifles, we dug in for the night. Our Troop Commander, Lt Reg Barker (killed 8 June by 12 SS Panzer) and Troop HQ and Major Scott caught up with us about 2300 hrs.'

The Canadians advanced further inland than any other troops on D-Day, threatening Caen. The Canadian 7th Brigade on their right flank linked up later that day with the 50th (Northumbrian) Division to give the Allies a beachhead 15 miles long and up to 7 miles deep on the east flank. So far, so good but as some of the above accounts indicate the 3rd Canadian Division was soon involved with heavy and extremely bitter fighting with the 12th (SS) Panzer Division, and these two divisions continued to slog it out for much of the subsequent Normandy fighting.

Courseulles was the main landing area for the Canadian 7th Infantry Brigade. The port was classified as a strongpoint, and apart from en-trenched infantry and concrete blockhouses, contained 3 75mm mortar positions and 12 machine-gun posts. Courseulles was the most heavily defended point along the Anglo-Canadian beaches and took a severe toll of the attacking force.

The 7th Infantry Brigade decided on a frontal assault by a mixed force of tanks and infantry, made up of two companies of the Regina Rifle Regiment which would land east of the mouth of the Seulles on 'Nan Green', supported by 'B' Squadron of the 1st Hussars in DD Shermans. The DDs were launched 4,000 yards offshore, in very heavy seas, but fourteen of them made it ashore and went straight into action against the beach defences.

'A' Company of the Reginas attacked the centre of Courseulles. They found it virtually untouched by bombs or shells and none of their tank support turned up, so 'A' Company took heavy casualties before the enemy was subdued. 'B' Company, with AVRE 'Petard' tanks and DDs, cleared the pill-boxes along the promenade east of the River Seulles and opened beach exits, freeing more DDs to enter Courseulles and assist 'A' Com-pany. The follow-up Regina Rifles companies, 'C' and 'D', had a mixed reception. 'C' got ashore virtually intact and went to the support of 'A', but 'D' Company's craft ran into mined obstacles, and only 49 of the Company got ashore. Still full of fight, they picked up some tanks and marched on their objective, the village of Reviers, three kilometres inland.

West of the Seulles was the province of the Royal Winnipeg Rifles, a regiment known in Canada as 'The Little Black Devils'. The Winnipeg battalion was commanded by Lt-Colonel John Meldrum, who had no tank or AVRE support on landing and had to take the enemy positions by infantry assault, with rifles, Bren guns and grenades. Fortunately, the DDs then arrived and began firing into the strongpoints and blockhouses, while the 6th Field Company, Royal Canadian Engineers, began the work of clearing away the mines and beach obstacles. This Field Company of 100 men was down to just 26 by the end of the day, sustaining one of the highest casualty rates on D-Day.

Fortunes could vary, even along a few yards of beach. 'A', 'C' and 'D' Companies of the Winnipegs got ashore without heavy loss and moved on Banville, west of Reviers, but 'A' Company then took losses at Ste Croix-sur-Mer, which was stoutly defended by a company of infantry from the 716th Division. The eastern part of this beachhead was the task of 'C' Company of the Canadian Scottish, which the Winnipegs had under command for the operation. This company had a successful day, taking their initial objective and the Château-Vaux, just outside Courseulles, where the three reserve companies of the Canadian Scottish came to join them. The Winnipegs' War Diary briefly covers these events:

0749 hrs
In spite of air bombardment failing to materialize, RN bombardment spotty, the rockets falling short and the AVREs and D.Ds being late, 'C' Company Canadian Scottish Rifles and Royal Winnipeg Rifles land.

0900 hrs
The bombardment having failed to kill a single German or silence one weapon, these companies had to storm their positions 'cold' and did so without hesitation.

1800 hrs
'D' Company had by this time gapped a minefield at La Valette and cleared Graye-sur-Mer. 'B' Company crossed the Seulles, cleared out four positions on the island. . . . 'A' Coy started inland 0805 towards Ste Croix pinned by six to eight MGs. 'C' Coy approached Banville, pinned down by three MGs on commanding ground.

The Battalion Diary carries a special note:

It is desired to make a special note of the services rendered to the Bn during the first day of Ops by our MO (Capt Robert M. Caldwell) and the Bn RAP Staff – and the assault sec. of 14 Canadian Field Ambulance u/c Capt. Harry Dixon. Not only were the wounded cared for with skill and despatch but confidence was developed and morale increased accordingly. A very special note, too, should be made about the general tone of the Bn during this day, called D-6 Jun. 44. Not one man flinched from his task, no matter how tough it was – not one officer failed to display courage and energy and a degree of gallantry. It is thought that the Little Black Devils, by this day's success, has managed to maintain the tradition set by former members. Casualties for the day exceeded 130.

The 'C' Squadron, Inns of Court Regiment, in armoured cars, landed in support of the Winnipegs at Graye-sur-Mer. David Swynne, then aged twenty-four, recalls the Graye beach area. 'The landings on the beach proved to be more difficult than had been expected, and on our arrival at first light at "Juno" beach (Graye-sur-Mer) the beach had not, in fact, been cleared and many of the Canadian infantry were still trying to negotiate the minefields at either side of the beach exit.

'Steel posts with mines on top could clearly be seen at the water's edge. At the time of our arrival the water was deeper than had been anticipated. We had been prepared for wading in about four-and-a-half feet of water; the car exhausts allowed only a few inches more than that. Our craft was the first to land but hit a mine which badly damaged the ramp, and by the time this had been dealt with the water was too deep for wading and we had to wait for the tide to recede. Our sister craft was able to unload and all that we could do was to watch.

'The Canadian infantrymen (the Winnipeg Rifles) 3rd Canadian Division, were finding the opposition more than had been anticipated and were having considerable problems with anti-personnel mines, which were profusely scattered in the sand hills either side of the beach exit. The mined areas were well marked with tapes and signs, but not the 88mm gun, which scored a direct hit on the first of our Daimler armoured cars to attempt to leave the beach. I could only sit and watch the driver, Trooper Dixon, a very good personal friend, burn to death.

'By the time the tide had receded, the beach exit had still not been fully cleared, and I and my car commander, Ewart Simms, were instructed to reconnoitre along the beach away from the exit, and to ascertain whether or not the next exit was clear. After about half a mile we were fired upon, and almost at the same time ran over a mine which caused no personal injury but completely destroyed the rear suspension. We were under small-arms fire at the time and so Ewart Simms and I hastily abandoned the car, lay on the ground and fired off a couple of magazines in the direction of the enemy.

'We then ran back to the beachhead, taking our Bren gun and personal arms with us. At the beachhead we joined the rest of the survivors. I think there were about a dozen of us. Some hours later we returned to our car to find that it had been completely burned out. We could find no trace of the remains of our personal kit or the ample supply of tinned food, etc., which we thought must have been removed prior to the car being fired upon.

'All the beach survivors of my own unit remained on the beach for the next three or four days. During this time our REME Sgt, Sgt Pratt, together with myself and one or two other members of the squadron, stripped down the engine of a "drowned" half-track which was then rebuilt; after which we all somehow managed to squeeze into it and so return to our unit. Sadly, in retrospect, we were the lucky ones. Many of those who managed to leave the beach early had been killed or badly wounded. Four of our armoured cars and one half-track vehicle were destroyed in an attack by American Thunderbolt aircraft.

'Because it was expected that some of us may have to operate at night, which indeed we did, all our armoured cars were painted jet black, with no corps signs or other means of identification, other than a yellow sheet which could be draped over the turret as a sign of recognition when required. Sadly, in practice, the Americans did not appear to understand this and many lives were lost, and particularly so at the Jerusalem crossroads when American Thunderbolts dropped a stick of bombs from rooftop level, which left four of our armoured cars and one half-track vehicle blazing furiously. It was thought that the entire population of the village had been killed, together with Lt Lofts RE, Lt Gwynne Jones and five other ranks. Lt Reeves and five ORs were wounded. In the event, a few civilians survived. I understand that a few of our veterans visited the rebuilt village some years later and were made very welcome.'

One of the German soldiers in action this day was Herbert Muschallik. 'I was on guard early in the morning and I remember an officer came running down the field, shouting, "They've landed! They've landed!" We moved all day towards the coast and ended up in a forest. We were all scared stiff and there were bullets ricocheting off the trees. I was on the crew of a Pak-38 anti-tank gun and we saw a tank, maybe British or Canadian. I don't know where we were but we were going to engage it and I was bringing up the ammunition when the tank fired and the explosion threw me into the ditch. We fled into a village and there was a lot of firing going on. About 10 o'clock I was hit by shrapnel in the right shoulder. I remember taking my helmet off and putting my face in it. I tried to get up but I couldn't and I stayed in the ditch all day long, getting hit again in the side.

'The next thing is a British or Canadian soldier prodding me with his bayonet. I remember he had a little spiked bayonet. They took me out of the ditch and made me put my hands up, and then a man came with a Red Cross and bandaged my shoulder and took me to a medical point, where I was given an injection and a cup of tea. Then I was put in a tent with four or five British soldiers, all wounded. They were talking to me but I didn't understand. They wanted to know how old I was, and I signalled "eighteen" with my hands, and suddenly cigarettes and biscuits were thrown on to my bed . . . that was something. I wish I could meet those men some time if they are still alive, and thank them.

'That night there was bombing, and next day I was put on a ship and ended up in a hospital at Epsom in England. I stayed there for five weeks before being shipped on a US transport, the USS *West Point* to Boston. I ended up picking peaches in South Carolina. I was sent back to England in 1947, a very hard winter shovelling snow, and one day I was given tea by a girl in the Land Army, who is now my wife. In 1952 an X-ray found a bullet in my back which was taken out in Maidenhead hospital, and I still have it.'

The Allied forces now coming ashore were meeting the men and women of the French Resistance, emerging to play their part in the battle. Henri Lamperière, the policeman from Bretteville, near Caen, had been out all night. 'As you know, the Germans were executing Maquis prisoners in Caen on the night of 5/6 June. Three of my comrades, Chef Caulet, Gendarme Ménochet de Vassy and Gendarme Guilbert, were shot by the Gestapo that night in the prison at Caen. We had already suffered a lot of arrests, deportations and executions before 6 June, but we had been able to inform the Allies about enemy positions and especially about the V1 and V2 rocket sites, which had then come under attack by the RAF.

'On 5 June, our group, which then belonged to the "F" Section of SOE, received the invasion message from the BBC : "*Le champ du laboureur dans le matin brumeux.*" Later on, even 30 kms from the coast we could hear the sound of the bombardment, and I returned at once to Bretteville. Monsieur Le Nevez, who was responsible for our sector as far as Thury-Harcourt, alerted all the men available and launched an attack on the railway line between Caen and Flers at the Grimbosq halt, making the line unusable. They also attacked a German column of 40 trucks full of soldiers at Meslay. Five officers and many Germans were killed before the Maquis had to withdraw. The Maquis Surcouf attacked the German *feldgendarmerie* post at Pont-Audemer.

'There were now many German troops and SS coming into the area and it was difficult to get news of all the attacks. Capitaine Danby of the SOE organized a system of communications with his radio officer, Maurice Larcher, but our main task was to hold up movement of German troops towards the invasion front. We multiplied our efforts to fell trees across roads and scatter tyre-piercing nails – *crève-pneus* – on all the roads. This last method was very effective. By these methods we created a number of road blocks and the German transport was attacked next day by British rocket-firing fighters.'

*

The second assault brigade, the 8th Canadian Infantry Brigade, were to land on the 'Nan' beaches to the east, running from Bernières to St Aubin. The weight of this assault was carried by two infantry battalions, the Queen's Own Rifles of Canada, landing in the centre at 'Nan White', and the North Shore Regiment on 'Nan Red'. These battalions were supported by the reserve companies of the QORC and the Regiment de la Chaudière.

Don Doner of Alliston, Ontario, was in the first wave ashore. 'We were 8 Section of 9 Platoon, "A" Company of the Queen's Own Rifles of Canada, and we were elected to be assault section for the platoon, which meant that we would be first to leap off the assault craft, carrying Bangalores, steel ladders, wire mesh and any other material that would assist us in scaling the sea wall and blowing holes in the barbed wire if necessary. We didn't particularly like the thought of being assault section, but not one of us ever thought that we couldn't do it, and we prepared ourselves accordingly.

'We lined up down the centre of the assault craft as follows : our little Corporal Hughie "Rockie" Rocks, a diminutive fellow of 5ft 3in, full of get-up-and-go and more fun than a picnic, aged thirty-eight and married to a girl he affectionately called Big Elsie. Next myself, then Ernie Cunningham of Toronto, a groaner like myself, who didn't like the army, and didn't mind telling everybody about it. Gill "Gabby" May sat in the next slot, and as his name implies, he was never lost for something to say. Then came the only guy in the section to admit that he was scared to death, and that was old John "Dinty" Moore.' (This was not the same John 'Dinty' Moore whose account is given earlier. 'Dinty' Moore was a cartoon character of the day and a popular nickname, but it is curious that two John 'Dinty' Moores, from two different regiments, landed on the same beach on D-Day.)

' "Dinty" had tried to evade all this, but now that he was into it he was readily admitting that he was scared out of his pants. Some of the guys teased him about it ; as for me, I kept my mouth shut. After all, how did I know how I would react ? As a matter of fact, how did any one of these guys know how they would act when they were staring death in the face ?

'When the guys would start in ragging "Dinty", old Buck Hawkins, our Bren gunner, used to drawl out, "I wouldn't get too mouthy, you guys, 'cause you're not kiddin' anybody. Every one of ya is just as scared as Dinty there, but ya haven't got the guts he has to admit it." Jackie "The Kid" Bland was next in line, and here was a kid who was liked by everybody. Jack had joined the army when he was fifteen and that was the reason why everybody called him "Kid". But he was no kid and had one of the levellest heads in the platoon, if not the whole company. Then there was big Harry "Buck" Hawkins, and he was the pride of the section. Buck was our Bren gunner and the greatest single factor in the success of the section. He was the guy everybody respected and looked up to. He was the guy you took advice from, the guy who slugged the Bren gun on twenty-mile route marches, and he was the guy we all had confidence in.

'For me to think that I would never see a lot of those guys again seemed impossible, and I looked forward to seeing them all at Hill 80, our consolidating point, after we had swept the beach clean and the Regiment de la Chaudière had passed through us.

'Well, the bombardment had started and it grew in intensity as we lurched and tossed the eight miles in to the beach. The big guns from the battleships and cruisers, Mosquitos and Spitfires all added to the roar of the rockets that crushed the sound of our own voices like matchsticks. Most of the guys were sick. The spray kept flying over the front into the craft, dowsing us to the skin and, standing up in the front, I cursed and swore until our officer, Lieutenant Raey, asked me if I would stop my groaning as it might affect the morale of some of the other boys whose morale was low enough as it was, being seasick and all. I was standing up in the front of the craft, not by choice, but because I knew if I sat down it would make me sick, and also because I have always had a desire to see where I'm going and what I'm heading into.

'We were right in close now and the Bren on our craft opened fire straight ahead and we weaved in and out between the ugly tripods standing in the water, with big black bottles full of explosive on the end. To hit one of those meant death or injury to most of the men on board. The last thing I saw before I ducked my head was one of the craft about a hundred yards down to our left blown sky-high from a direct hit. Just then two sharp cracks overhead sent all those still with heads scrambling for the bottom of the boat. A few seconds later we felt the scrape as the craft struck the sandy beach, and in no time the door was down and we were leaping into the foam.'

Les Wagar was a rifleman in 'C' Company, the QORC. 'H-Hour at Bernières was 0730 hrs. "A" and "B" Companies would take the beach and the wall. "C" and "D" would land twenty minutes later to take the town. Now we began to pick out the features of Bernières ahead. Support started up. Shells from battleships we couldn't see began hissing high overhead, exploding somewhere inland on targets we couldn't see. A line of four Spitfires swept low along the line of the coast, blazing away at God knows what. To our left, someone pushed the firing button on a long, converted LCT, bristling with bank after bank of heavy mortars. We watched nests of mortar shells lobbing up and over and down, and the town blowing up in slow motion. Someone – it had to be the CO, Major Nickson, cursed, "Damn! They're supposed to be hitting the beach."

'Now the Spitfires were coming back along the coast, higher up, and swinging out over us, heading home. The last one in line was on a collision course with the last nest of mortar shells lobbing up from the LCR. I watched their trajectories closing, and wondered if the guy would know what hit him. The plane exploded and fell into the water just offshore. The CO was trying to pick things out with his binoculars and suddenly blurted, "My God! There's a Frenchman in a boat out there, pulling the pilot out of the water."

'The unreality of things was creeping in. With our heads down as ordered, tucked safely behind the shelter of steel plates, and all hell breaking loose around us, here was a mere civilian who didn't know he was in a war – just knew that somebody had to get a man out of the water.

'Now we were maybe a quarter-mile off the beach, flanked by our other two LCAs, revved up on our final run-in, when the orders were changed. Our LCA turned, the CO waving the other two after us, and headed back to sea. I don't know where the message came from, or how it got to us, but now we were told that "A" and "B" hadn't landed. Our tank support had been slowed down by the heavy seas and hadn't arrived yet. "A" and "B" had been turned around about half an hour ago. H-Hour was now tentatively one hour later, and someone had forgotten to tell us. Forgot to tell the mortar ships, too, I was thinking. More cursing. About 1,000 yards offshore we turned again, and began doing slow circles, waiting. The odd shell began throwing up waterspouts nearby. Any help the earlier support fire had given us was rapidly disappearing.

'Now the order came to go; all the tanks hadn't arrived but we were going to have to go with what we had. The tide was coming in, and the higher the tide moved up the beach, the bigger the problem for the assault craft to keep clear of the mines. This time, over to the left, there were craft going in ahead of us. Our LCA revved up and we started in again.

'Some of the mines were in three or four feet of water. The coxswain was fighting surf to keep clear of them, trying to run a path that he'd also be able to back out of. The ramp dropped and we poured off in single file into waves up to our waists, running. Idiot orders were being shouted: "Off the beach! Off the beach! Get to the wall!" Relieved somebody's tension, I suppose, but I don't know anybody who had to be told what to do on that beach. As I hit the sand I was thinking, "Thank God for solid ground!" The world wasn't going up, down and sideways any more. In fact, that's all I was thinking. For the first minutes nothing else registered but relief.

'Company HQ set up beside the wall, near a jagged split where one man at a time could climb up to the waterfront road. Most of the company were already in the town when some sniper filtered back into the near houses and lined up on the road. There was a little panic in the rear until the sniper was taken out. Wounded were coming back with stories of snipers holding things up in town. I was thinking I didn't know most of these guys. I'd been in training away from the company for four months. For that matter, I'd never worked in Company HQ, so I hardly knew Major Nickson either –

and he'd only known me as an out-of-place kid in a rifle platoon. Word passed down that "A" and "B" Companies had a lot of casualties. "B" Company had landed in front of the main bunker. Compared to that, our beach was a cinch.

'Now a flail tank clanked ashore, rotary chains flailing the sand in front of it to explode the mines, clearing a path up the beach for another vehicle exit into town. A "step mine" blew its left track off and the crew baled out, minus the driver. Some engineers turned up from somewhere with their mine detectors, and started clearing a path the hard way.'

Rolph Jackson of Toronto was in 10 Platoon, 'A' company the QORC, landed on 'Nan White' beach at Bernières-sur-Mer. 'If you are familiar with the area, the half-timbered hotel which gets in all the D-Day photographs was to our right, and the sharp bend in the wall, with the pill-box, on our right front. My section was first from the LCA, and we were slaughtered.

'For some peculiar reason, as we approached the beach, our craft did an about turn, making a large loop, then came in for the landing. How long? Who can say, but the defences were manned as our craft grounded. Our Support Craft was knocked out so we had no heavy weapons. The DD tanks had not come ashore. My platoon, approximately 36 strong, went through what we believe was enfilade fire from 5 machine-guns.

'The official battalion killed in action figures on 6 June 1944 numbered 63, "B" Company, 34. I don't have figures for the platoon but I do know that only 9 men moved inland, 3 of whom were walking wounded. Of the 10 men in my section, 7 were killed and 2 wounded. Of these 10 men, 6 had been in the unit since June 1940. The one survivor, the latest replacement, had never done a "landing" in training.

'We landed in our proper area, but no specialized gear reached the wall. All our Assault Engineers were killed in action. We were still in the water when the section was cut down. Most of us had deflated the Mae-Wests we were wearing, and possibly those that died had drowned. I was a Lance-Jack, Bren crew, loaded with around a total of 300 rounds, plus 36s. The sea was red. One lad was hit in the smoke bomb he was carrying. Another, a human torch, had the presence of mind to head back into the water. Our flame-thrower man was hit and exploded, and we couldn't even find his body.

'I was asked by the Sergeant, acting CSM, to go back to the beach for Bren mags and grenades. 10 Platoon moved off the beach later, passing three burned-out self-propelled (SP) 25-pounders. 10 Platoon was under the command of an acting Sergeant – me – as one Bren and one other Junior NCO who had been hit in the legs, fell out earlier. The QORC did dig in at Hill 80, their objective. I was sent to the RAP by the A/CSM. The MO had also been hit but he stayed until replaced.

'I had smashed bones in my left hand, grenade fragments from a "potato masher" in one shoulder and minor flesh wounds to one leg. The platoon now consisted of one A/Sgt and five riflemen. The first Dressing Station had no room. The second took us in and we were into three groups : those who were OK to leave, those who could be treated, and the last sad group – "Don't waste time." Late the next day (7th) I went by DUKW out to an American LST with 300 stretcher cases plus the walking.

'A group of us, each 6 June, gather at Toronto's War Memorial to lay a wreath, and remember. We've been doing this since 1946. I belong to what was once a Regimental Legion and still see guys I knew so long ago. We have an annual dinner, and each year fewer stand for "Those who were on the Beach". In one section of Bernières-sur-Mer Canadian cemetery, I know half the graves by first name.'

Peter Rea was a Lieutenant commanding 9 Platoon, 1st Battalion QORC. 'I saw a Spitfire shot down by the rockets just offshore, but I am sure many men will tell you about that. I had the advantage of standing up, unlike my men who had to stay under cover and were very sick. As we approached the beach at Bernières, tracer bullets could be seen heading in our general direction from a supposedly empty pill-box about 200 yards on our right. We landed in 3ft of water, and I recall thinking that no matter what lay ahead, it was a great relief to be on dry land again.

'We reached shore safely and raced over the beach to the dunes. Sand had piled up against the sea wall, making it easily passable, but it was soon apparent that the pill-box on our right housed an 88mm gun which was firing on the landing craft and causing extreme damage. We were now coming under heavy mortar fire from inland. I moved to establish contact with No. 2 Section, and ordered the Section Leader to assault the pill-box. By this time I had been wounded twice, once by a mortar and once by a shell fragment which pierced my arm, rendering it useless. I then encountered the No. 2 Section Commander, who later died, and most of his men had already been wounded. I then went to a tank which had its turret closed, and tried banging on the armament with my Sten gun, without success, and it was at this time that, probably in shock and weakened by loss of blood, I collapsed to the ground.

'After the beach had been cleared, the remnants of my platoon, consisting of a sergeant and ten men, passed by, taking the maps from my pack and pressing on to join the company. I rejoined the regiment in October, and we were nearing Emden in Germany when hostilities ceased in May 1945. We returned to Canada in December 1945 and received a tremendous welcome from the City of Toronto.'

According to the Canadian Official History, the QORCs landing on 'Nan White' at Bernières had the toughest task of all the Canadian battalions. The DD tanks and AVREs arrived too late to help the initial assault waves, and one team of AVREs was put ashore a quarter of a mile from their intended position. 'B' Company of the QORC was landed directly in front of a strongly defended position they had intended to outflank, and took heavy casualties before the position was overcome.

Similar problems and the inevitable delays brought trouble to the Regiment de la Chaudière, which came ashore at 0930 hrs, when most of the beach obstacles were still intact and covered by the tide. Four of the five LCAs carrying 'A' Company of the 'Chauds' were damaged by mines on the way in, forcing most of the infantry to abandon their kit and swim ashore through the surf. Even so, by 1030 hrs all the QORCs and the Regiment de la Chaudière were ashore, where the local people, emerging from shelter, were amazed and delighted to meet French-speaking troops. Then the DDs and the self-propelled guns came up and the Regiment de la Chaudière led the 8th Brigade out of the landing area and south into Normandy.

The other Canadian battalion of the 8th Infantry Brigade was the North Shore Regiment landing on 'Nan Red' where, with support from the Fort Gary Horse, it was to take and clear the beach and take St Aubin before the Royal Marines of 48 Commando came ashore and swung east to capture Langrune.

Because of the heavy seas, the DDs of the Fort Gary Horse were not launched at their designated point 7,000 yards offshore but brought in by the LCTs to within a mile of the beach, which reduced their landing to what the Fort Gary War Diary calls 'a wet wade', though the screws had to be raised and the propeller engaged. At first they found 'Nan Red' 'fairly quiet except for sniping', but after 'A' Company of the North Shores left the beach for the town, German resistance began to stiffen.

Lt McCann, who commanded No. 6 Platoon of 'A' Company of the North Shores, recalls the situation on 'Nan Red': 'Our run-in was not bad and apart from small-arms fire and shelling we landed as per schedule and intact, but some of my fellow officers were not so fortunate. Lt Gerry Moran of 5 Platoon had been seriously wounded on the beach and I was left in charge of two platoons instead of one. I could have used six, for after cutting our way with Bangalore torpedos and wire cutters into the village, our communications broke down. During this period we found that the guns and emplacement that should have been put out of business by the Air Force were intact and very much in use.

'The Germans had a beautiful underground system of communicating with their pill-boxes. Perhaps it was as well we didn't know everything, for working on the assumption that we had a pushover, we went into the village in nothing flat. Now came the test. Things weren't going as planned and unless we captured those heavy guns the Germans were potting landing craft with, things were going to get worse – and worse they got. We had nothing heavier than Brens with which to attack heavily fortified enemy posts.'

Lt G. V. Moran of 5 Platoon has also left an account of the landing: 'Frank Ryan was the first man ashore from our craft, followed by his section of six men, then myself with Platoon Headquarters, and the other two sections. We were not too interested in looking around to see whether anyone else had landed but reached the doubtful shelter of the sea wall. It would be hard to estimate the width of the beach, but since the tide was well out I would hazard a guess of 300 feet at the time of our landing. Every square inch was under small-arms fire. The sea wall offered some protection from straight ahead but not from enfilade fire from the houses up and down the beach, and since there were no troops landing on our immediate left to keep the enemy occupied, they threw everything at us.

'Too many of us had bunched behind the sea wall and the second wave was now coming ashore. In order to get the men moving to their objective, I stood in the open and shouted at the top of my voice and, making vigorous motions with my arms, urged the sections around the wall and forward, standing with my back towards the upper beach and "A" Company's position. Apparently a sniper in the upper part of a house in "A" Company's area was watching for just such an indication of authority and laid a sight in the middle of my back. At the instant he squeezed the trigger fate invited me to turn, facing the water, so that I met the bullet with my left arm instead of my back. It passed through my arm, entered my chest under my armpit and ploughed on, coming out through the middle of my back. I didn't know that at the time because a mortar shell landed by at the same instant and I spun around and fell flat on my face. Rising again, I discovered my left arm was useless. Someone pulled me down and I didn't stand again for a month.'

The houses of St Aubin had been turned into fortresses and the streets were blocked with thick meshes of barbed wire. The North Shore Regiment and the Fort Gary Horse were still fighting for a foothold when 48 (Royal Marine) Commando came ashore.

48 Commando were to land at St Aubin from LSIs at 0930 hrs, two hours after the Canadians' first assault, and presumably over quiet beaches. After landing they would assemble, sort themselves out and proceed with their appointed task, taking the strongpoint at Langrune to the east. However, when the Commando's craft arrived off the 'Nan Red' beaches at St Aubin, they noticed that a considerable amount of firing seemed to be going on. Tanks were milling about on the beach and there seemed to be a lot of wreckage onshore. Orders were orders, though, and at the appointed time, 48 Commando went in to land.

The Commando Adjutant, Captain Dan Flunder, MC, gives his account of this time. 'As Adjutant, I was OC troops and spent the night with them in a cramped little mess-deck; almost everyone was sick. I had the men up on the superstructure early, because I thought the fresh air would restore them, and because men are always happier when they can see what is going on. Soon we were running into the beach, and I walked up and down the bows keeping an eye on the Navy people responsible for lowering the ramps. The sea was covered with craft as far as the eye could see. The shore was under bombardment, craft were sinking, and from where I stood, it certainly didn't look as if the Canadians had secured the beach – things didn't look good at all.

'I didn't realize we were under fire until I saw two men collapse and fall over the starboard side. By then it was too late to beat a retreat, and I later found three bullet holes in my map case ... they must have passed between my arm and body during that period. The tide was high and we had craft hitting the beach obstacles. The CO had our 2-inch mortars firing smoke from the bows, so at least we were not getting aimed fire. When we grounded, we got the starboard ramp down, which wasn't easy with the waves thrashing the stern about. I was halfway down when a big wave lifted the bow and somersaulted the ramp, with me on it, into the sea. I saw the great bows coming over me, and the next thing I remember is walking up the beach, soaking wet, with some of my equipment torn off, including my pistol. I was still clutching my stout ash walking stick. When I got to the top of the beach I was violently sick.

'The beach was covered with casualties, some Canadian, some British. The surf was incredible, with beached and half-sunken craft wallowing about in it. Offshore, other craft came steadily on. Some tanks struggled ashore and some bogged in the shingle. Those that were advancing had their turret lids shut and were heading for a large group of wounded. I was sickened to see one run over two of our wounded, and it was heading for our good padre, John Armstrong, who had been badly wounded in the thigh. I had spoken to him on the way up to the beach; typically, he had been vehement that I should not stop by him, exposed to enemy fire. I ran back down the beach and hammered on the turret, to try and get someone to put his head out. When this failed I stuck a Hawkins anti-tank grenade in the sprocket and blew the track off – that stopped it.'

Lt-Colonel Moulton, the Commanding Officer of 48 Commando, reached the assembly area, which was found to be under mortar fire, to discover that 48 Commando had already lost all its machine guns, all but one mortar, and 50 per cent of the troops. They had not yet fired a shot against the enemy. 'I began to realize', said Colonel Moulton later, 'that something very like disaster had overtaken 48 Commando. We were not aware that the Germans had built strongpoints right in the water here, and the naval and air support was inadequate and inaccurate. Look at that coast today – it is still lined with pre-war houses, virtually intact in 1944. You have to realize that if a shambles develops on the beach, there is no way of stopping the assault – craft keep coming in, men still push ashore. You have to sort yourself out and get on with the job.'

Like so many other units on D-Day, 48 (Royal Marine) Commando made the best of it and set out to accomplish their allotted task with what they had. After much fierce fighting and further casualties they took the strongpoint at Langrune and linked up with troops coming from 'Sword'.

By noon on D-Day, the 3rd Canadian Division was well ashore and they continued their advance until nightfall. 'C' Company of the North Shore's, with a troop of the Fort Gary Horse, fought their way out of St Aubin and took Tailleville, which contained a battalion headquarters and a full company of the German 716th Grenadier Regiment, finding that the naval bombardment which had missed St Aubin had totally wrecked Tailleville.

Brigadier Blackadder, commanding the Canadian 8th Brigade, had to hold back his troops because an 88mm gun and German infantry were still holding up the Regiment de la Chaudière in Bernières and the 9th Canadian Infantry Brigade, the last of the assault brigades, which had been supposed to land at St Aubin and advance swiftly on the airfield at Carpiquet, was held up by the turmoil ashore and afloat.

The continued fighting and congestion on the beach at St Aubin during the morning had forced the Navy to divert the 9th Brigade and the follow-up forces for 8th Infantry Brigade to the beach at Bernières. This proved of limited benefit as Bernières was still occupied by snipers and a massive traffic jam developed between the beach and the town centre.

At 1215 hrs, 8th Brigade radio'd to 'J' Force Headquarters on HMS *Hilary* and told General Keller that they were held up on their initial line, codenamed 'Yew', and needed naval gunfire support plus more infantry as soon as possible. It proved quite impossible to move anything or anyone through St Aubin or Bernières, which were now totally congested with troops and vehicles. The Official History recalls that in the centre of Bernières 'the entire 9th Canadian Infantry Brigade, complete with bicycles, were waiting, crowded in the streets.'

General Keller went ashore at 1245 hrs to sort out the situation, and by early afternoon the North Nova Scotias of the 9th Canadian Infantry brigade were on the march for the aerodrome at Carpiquet, and the Canadian D-Day beaches were secure. The QORC were at Anguerny, the 'Chauds' at Colomby-sur-Thaon, and the North Shores were around Tailleville.

Two years previously, at Dieppe, the Canadians had been the first to test the strength of the Atlantic Wall and taken heavy casualties in doing so. The sacrifices of Dieppe, tragic though they were, had provided the blueprint for the landings in Normandy. Although the Wall was stronger and the defenders tenacious, this time the Canadians won through. As D-Day ended,

German counter-attacks were developing and the German Panzer divisions, 21st Panzer, Panzer Lehr, and the 12th (SS) Panzer were moving forward to stem the Allied advance.

Over the next few weeks the Canadian infantry and the younger Panzer Grenadiers of the 12th SS were to take a bloody toll of each other's strength, but for the moment all was going well. Canadian casualties exceeded 1,000 men on the beaches of 'Juno', but their follow-up brigades were now ashore and pushing inland. When night fell on D-Day, the Canadian bridgehead was secure.

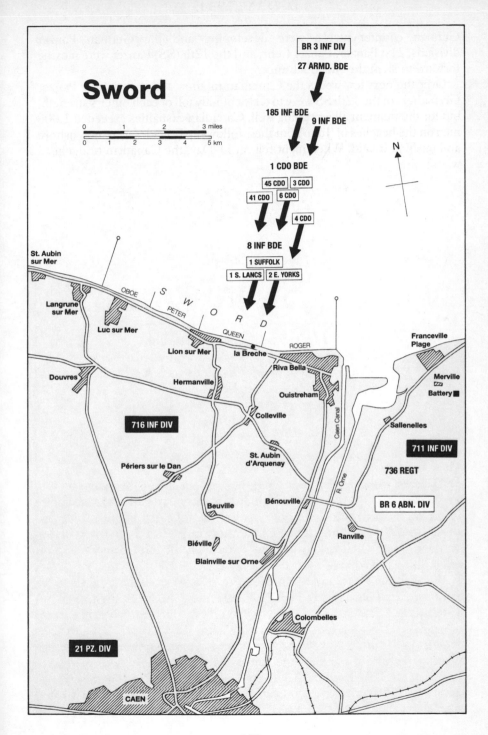

Sword

BR 3 INF DIV

27 ARMD. BDE

185 INF BDE   9 INF BDE

1 CDO BDE

45 CDO   3 CDO

41 CDO   6 CDO

4 CDO

8 INF BDE

1 SUFFOLK

1 S. LANCS   2 E. YORKS

0   1   2   3 miles

0   1   2   3   4   5 km

N

St. Aubin
sur Mer

Langrune
sur Mer

Luc sur Mer

Douvres

OBOE

PETER

QUEEN

S   W   O   R   D

Lion sur Mer

la Breche

ROGER

Riva Bella

Hermanville

Ouistreham

Colleville

716 INF DIV

St. Aubin
d'Arquenay

Périers sur le Dan

Beuville

Bénouville

Biéville

Blainville sur Orne

Ranville

Caen Canal

R. Orne

Franceville
Plage

Merville
Battery

Sallenelles

711 INF DIV

736 REGT

BR 6 ABN. DIV

Colombelles

21 PZ. DIV

CAEN

203

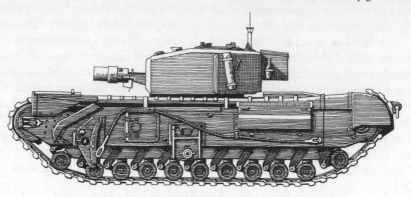

CHAPTER ELEVEN

'Sword'

*'Fire? Of course there was fire. The
Germans didn't want us there, you know.
We lost a lot of men crossing the beach at
La Brèche.'*
Lt-Colonel Peter Young, DSO, MC
No. 3 Commando

At 0725 hrs, while 6th Airborne continued to consolidate their gains on the
left flank around Ranville, the British 3rd Infantry Division started to come
ashore on 'Sword' beach, west of Ouistreham. The 3rd Infantry Division
was no stranger to France. It had fought there in 1940 and taken part in the
painful retreat to Dunkirk. Now, four years later, the 3rd Infantry Division
was back on the coast of France.

Although the British and Canadian divisions were supposed to land at
half tide, they found that the Channel gale, combined with the prevailing
westerly wind, had caused the sea to pile up over the beach obstacles and
run high on the beach itself. This caused many difficulties, but the British
landing on 'Sword' got off to a good start. The bombardment by Admiral
Vian's squadron of warships was made from close in and was therefore
accurate. The beaches were well marked, notably by the crews of the midget
submarines X20 and X23, who came gasping to the surface after a sub-
mersion that had lasted a whole day longer than they had expected. The DD

204

tanks were launched from close inshore and most of the landing craft hit the right beach at the right time. For all that, 'Sword' beach saw hard fighting, and stiff resistance from the men of the German 716th Infantry Division.

The landing areas of 'Sword' beach ran west from Ouistreham at the mouth of the Orne to Lion-sur-Mer. The 3rd Infantry Division, commanded by Major-General Rennie DSO, MBE, had the tasks of capturing Caen, nine miles inland, and forging a link with 6th Airborne astride the Orne, thereby bolstering the left flank of the bridgehead. For the assault the division would be supported by 2 battleships, HMS *Warspite* and HMS *Ramilles*, the monitor HMS *Roberts*, 5 cruisers, including the Polish *Dragon* and 13 destroyers including the Norwegian *Svenner*. Apart from the USS *Corry* off 'Utah', the *Svenner* was the only Allied warship to be sunk on D-Day.

Their German opponents, from the 716th Infantry Division, were dug-in on the beaches and in a series of defended strongpoints on the way to Caen. One of these strongpoints, codenamed 'Hillman', was to give the Suffolk Regiment a particularly stiff fight, but pegging out territory well inland was essential, for behind Caen, edging forward into the fight, was the most formidable German unit close to the Normandy coast, the 21st Panzer Division, which had been training and re-equipping on the plain south of Caen. Other German Panzer units were also alert and, although without orders from higher command, were beginning to make their way forward and engage the invading forces. Enemy shell-fire in particular increased throughout the day and resistance stiffened as the bridgeheads expanded inland.

The German defences were particularly intricate along 'Sword', and lay among a built-up area. All the houses in the resorts of Riva Bella, La Brèche and Lion-sur-Mer had been turned into fortresses, while the low country behind had been mined. The casino at Riva Bella proved a particularly hard nut to crack, but the open beaches further west were also mined, heavily wired, studded with concrete emplacements and pill-boxes, and protected with the usual array of underwater obstacles offshore. No. 3 Commando lost 10 per cent of its men crossing the beach at La Brèche.

The 3rd (British) Division comprised three infantry brigades, the 8th, the 185th and 9th, supported by 1st Special Service (Commando) Brigade (Nos 3, 4 and 6 Commandos and 45 (Royal Marine) Commando) under Brigadier Lord Lovat. No. 4 Commando had two troops of French Commandos and No. 41 (Royal Marine) Commandos attached for the landing phase.

The initial assault on the beach was made by the 8th Infantry Brigade Group, landing on the 'White' and 'Red' sectors of 'Queen' beach, with the task of securing the landing area. 4 Commando, with two French troops of No. 10 (Inter-Allied) Commando attached, were to take Ouistreham, while 41 (Royal Marine) Commando were to advance to the west towards

Lion-sur-Mer and link up with the Canadians. Lord Lovat's Commando Brigade, less 4 Commando, would make the six-mile dash to link up with the Airborne at Bénouville and while all this was going on, the 185th Infantry Brigade would advance through the secured beach area and take Caen. The taking of the city of Caen on the first day was an ambitious task for a single division.

The 8th Infantry Brigade consisted of three battalions : the 1st Battalion, South Lancashire Regiment, the 2nd Battalion, East Yorkshire Regiment, and the 1st Battalion, the Suffolk Regiment, with the Suffolks being charged with the reduction of two enemy strongpoints codenamed 'Hillman' and 'Morris'.

8 Brigade was to be preceded by the DD tanks of the 13th/18th Royal Hussars and AVREs of 5 Assault Regiment, Royal Engineers. The latter was to clear the beaches of obstacles and construct vehicle exits. 13th/18th Hussars, normally part of 27 Armoured Brigade, was attached to the division and would land two squadrons on 'Sword' seven minutes before the assaulting battalions. Their tasks were to dominate the beaches, thus covering both the sappers clearing beach obstacles and the arrival of the assault infantry. Once the beaches were secure they were to provide armoured support for the infantry as they pushed south for Caen.

Emlyn 'Taffy' Jones was an Army Commando serving in the Signal Troop of 45 (Royal Marine) Commando. 'We set sail for France about 9 o'clock on the evening of 5 June. Sailing down the Solent through an array of ships and craft that were at anchor was very impressive. As we passed by the crews stood on deck and gave us a remarkable send-off with their cheering and waving. It made one feel so proud, and above all this glorious noise we could hear the pipes, the bagpipes of Bill Millin, our Commando piper. It certainly made the heart beat that much faster.'

As dawn broke next morning, Naval Force 'S', conveying and supporting 3 Division, lay off the 'Queen' beaches. The medium bombers of the 2nd Tactical Air Force droned overhead on their way to targets just south of the beaches. Rear Admiral Sir Philip Vian, Commander of Force 'S', was flying his flag on HMS *Scylla*. The American 8th Air Force were also giving support along the British beaches.

Marshall J. Rahn of Fort Lauderdale, Florida, was then with the 306th Bomb Group. 'I was a pilot on a B-17 Flying Fortress. Our crew chiefs, or mechanics, were mostly older men, peacetime auto mechanics, who kept aloof from the twenty-year-old flight crews who were flying and (they thought) damaging their aircraft. They took great pride that their airplane was mechanically perfect and always sweated out the return of their baby. Our mission that day was a milk run, just across the French coast into Caen, and we went out to our aircraft about dawn.

'On one of the neighbouring B-17s the pilot shut the engines down and told his crew that one of his magnetos was running rough and he would not fly it. I saw the crew chief leaning over the stabilizer and crying like a baby because his aircraft was not making the most important raid of the war. Ninety-nine per cent of us would have flown with one magneto out. Each engine had two anyway and a mission to Caen counted as much as one to the Fatherland.'

Robin Fowler was a Petty Officer aboard LCI(L) No. 387. They had embarked 250 infantrymen from the King's Own Scottish Borderers (KOSB). 'I remember coming up on deck and marvelling at the number of ships which had joined us. Security on board was still maintained and even after we had sailed, we were told nothing other than that this was the Great Day and we were heading for France, but as the soldiers had maps of their landing sectors and we knew our compass course, we had a shrewd idea of our destination.'

Corporal Albert Smith, an anti-tank gunner in the 1st Norfolks, recalls lying off Sword beach. 'By 0530 hrs we were just off the Normandy coast, which was receiving a pounding from the RAF bombers. Then suddenly the guns of our own ships opened up to cover our approach to the beaches, and as the bombers wheeled away towards England, the German artillery opened up. The air cover supplied by the RAF fighters was superb. They ruled the sky, and not a German plane was to be seen . . . a far and different cry from the dark days of Dunkirk.'

Trooper Bob Knight was a Sherman tank driver in 'A' Squadron, the 1st East Riding Yeomanry, part of the 27th Armoured Brigade. 'I knew we were off during the early evening of 5 June, when I saw green-beret'd Commandos heading out in their LCIs. Maps were issued and at last we knew our destination. I remember a small cabin cruiser, maybe 30ft long, keeping station on our port side all the way across. I don't know if they felt as we did, but our ship was rolling with the high waves, and we all felt very seasick. As dawn arrived we were called over the Tannoy to collect our breakfast from the ship's galley – fried bacon floating in fat – and that really got things moving! However, at that precise moment we came under shell-fire from the shore, and that was the quickest cure for seasickness.'

Victor Kontzle was a signaller with 3rd Division Headquarters. 'Our prime function was to mark the route from our particular stretch of beach and establish where 3rd Divisional Signals HQ would be on D-Day. We also carried the spare wireless set for 3rd Division Signals in our "perambulator" contraption, for use in case of emergency. This meant that we would be landing at H-Hour plus 30 minutes, hard on the heels of the 8th Brigade.

'I awoke at just after midnight. The vessel was pitching and rolling, and most of the military personnel were suffering from seasickness. The moon had broken through the clouds and for a moment I had a strange feeling of quietness and tense expectancy. My comrades, Jimmy and Henry, were still asleep by our "perambulator", and making my way forward, I lay down on the deck and the beat of the LCT's engines sent me off to sleep again. It was already D-Day.'

While the ships were nearing the beaches just before dawn, the Allied Air Forces streamed over on the way to their targets. Victor Jones was a Royal Army Service Corps (RASC) Corporal attached to 9 Field Ambulance. 'I remember a most gallant action by the RAF pilot of a stricken bomber. The plane dropped down between our ship and the one next to us, obviously avoiding us, to crash into the sea behind. I can still see the face of the rear gunner looking at us, but no one survived the crash . . . that is still my most poignant memory of D-Day.'

After the aerial bombardment and heavy shelling from Admiral Vian's ships, the soldiers embarked in their landing craft and prepared to go ashore. Following Montgomery's plan, DD tanks of the 13th/18th Royal Hussars and assault engineers in bridging tanks and flails were to precede the assault brigade and clear a path for the infantry.

Sergeant Buck was a DD tank commander with 2 Troop, 'B' Squadron, 13th/18th Hussars. 'The code word to launch was "Floater". We launched successfully at 0615 hrs, despite a rough sea and heavy swell. The first one to one-and-a-half miles was uneventful, apart from the noise of shells from our warship and planes passing overhead, but as we approached closer to "Sword" beach, the shells from the German guns and machine-guns started to come closer. The rockets from our own rocket ships also started dropping among us and these caused many casualties among our DD tanks. Then the beach obstacles used by the Germans appeared. These consisted of Teller mines stuck on top of poles, together with triangular steel obstacles; fortunately the tide was still on the flood so these could be seen more clearly and enabled us to take avoiding action. We landed at 0720 hrs.'

Not far away from Sergeant Buck was nineteen-year-old Lance Corporal Patrick Hennessey, who also went ashore in a DD tank. 'The ramp at the bows of the LCT was lowered and one by one we drove down it. A strong wind was blowing and we shipped quite a lot of water over the top of the screen, so we had to work hard on the bilge pumps. Other DD tanks were launching all around us, and glancing to my right I saw one enter the water and start to make way. Behind it I could see the bulk of its LCT, and to my horror I realized that it was moving forward. Very soon it hit the DD tank, forcing it under the water. The tank commander escaped and was rescued, but the rest of his crew were lost.

'We battled on against the waves for about an hour until we felt the tracks meet the sand of the beach. We rose up out of the surf, dropped the screen, and there in front of us was the line of houses which was our target. By now we were under fire from several positions, so we brought our gun into action and fired our first shots. The infantry were now beginning to arrive, and we were able to provide the support and covering fire which they so badly needed.

'Once ashore we had to decide whether to move up the beach which we knew to be mined, or wait until the mines had been cleared. Suddenly, the problem was solved for us – we had landed on a fast in-coming tide, so the longer we stood still, the deeper the water became. One large wave hit the back of our tank, swamped the engine compartment, and the engine spluttered to a halt. With power gone, we could not move, so we stayed there, firing the guns until the tank was flooded and we had to give up. We took to the rubber dinghy and began to paddle for the shore through the water, which was by now quite deep.

'We had not gone far when we were hit by a burst of machine-gun bullets which capsized our little craft and wounded the co-driver in the ankle. Somehow, we swam and splashed our way to the beach and managed to drag our wounded comrade with us. The beach was a very noisy place with shells, mortars and bullets flying in all directions. Landing craft were coming in, depositing their troops, and backing out to sea again.

'Eventually we made our way inland, to the village of Hermanville, where we met up with other unhorsed tank crews and came together with what was left of our squadron and the five remaining serviceable tanks.'

In all, 31 DD tanks and AVREs reached 'Sword' beach with the assault waves. With the surviving DD tanks ashore and tackling the beach defences, the specialized armour of the Royal Engineers started to land and clear away the obstacles. Their Assault Sapper squadrons were divided into two groups, one to push lanes through the beach defences, the other to clear the beach of underwater obstacles. One of those who came ashore was Driver Beeton of 79 Assault Engineer Squadron, landing on 'Queen Red'.

'I was the driver of a Churchill AVRE tank in the first wave of the assault. Our tanks were fitted with special mortars called "Petards", which were used for destroying pill-boxes. There was a considerable amount of shellfire offshore and two of our ships were hit and went up in smoke. We watched as our own rocket-firing landing craft discharged their rockets at the enemy, but this was cut short by the order to crew the tanks. I was soon in position with my engine running, ready to leave for the beach. The first two tanks down the ramp were flails, but these were hit by gun-fire and burst into flames. It was not very pleasant seeing your own friends trying to leave their burning tanks. As I came down the ramp I could see German mines everywhere, fixed to cross-pieces on the obstacles about two feet above ground level. Further up the beach I could see the German pill-boxes.

'I was instructed by my officer to pick my way up the beach as best I could. My luck held and I was almost off the beach when we hit a mine which blew the bogey off. Fortunately the tank track held, but the officer and sergeant in our crew were killed. Over half the squadron was wiped out before we cleared the beaches.'

Closely behind the tanks and assault engineers came the infantry. The 1st South Lancs landed with two companies leading, the right-hand company to destroy the German defences on the beach and then move west, or right, for about a mile, clearing the enemy as it went. The left-hand company, having cleared the beach, was to move on and attack a strongpoint at La Brèche, codenamed 'Cod', in conjunction with 2nd Battalion East Yorks. Once captured, the battalion was to re-group and hold Hermanville on the right flank of the brigade beachhead.

The 2nd East Yorks, landing on the left of the 1st South Lancs, had similar tasks. The right assault company was to help capture 'Cod', while the left-hand company was to move east and move towards the outskirts of Ouistreham–Riva Bella. When the reserve companies came up it was then to assault two German strongpoints to the south-west of Ouistreham, codenamed 'Sole' and 'Daimler'. The latter was a heavily defended coastal battery, mounting four 155mm guns. The commanding officer of the East Yorks was further instructed to despatch one of his companies with a squadron of 13/18 Hussars tanks towards the Ranville area, now held by 5 Para Brigade. The battalion was also to secure St Aubin d'Arquenay and be prepared to assist 4 Commando in Ouistreham or 6 Commando as it moved forward to the Orne bridges.

The last battalion, the 1st Suffolks, were to land at H+60 minutes and move directly to La Brèche. From here they were to move south and secure the village of Colleville and a four-gun battery on its western outskirts known as 'Morris'. That secured, they were to move a further half-mile forward and capture a defended locality, known as 'Hillman'. From aerial photographs this appeared to be a major task. The position contained at least two 105mm and two 75mm guns, as well as numerous machine-gun positions. All these were linked by trenches and pill-boxes and surrounded by thick wire and minefield defences.

Lieutenant Edward Jones with the 1st South Lancs was suffering from seasickness as he boarded his landing craft. 'It was bad enough aboard a large vessel, but on board the smaller ships the conditions were intolerable. As far as we were concerned when the flat-bottomed, shallow-draft LCAs were launched, we bucked up and down unmercifully. Everyone was suffering from violent seasickness after a very short while. Yet this stormy weather was probably one of the causes of our salvation. I am sure the Germans looked out to sea and said, "They'll never land in that lot!"

'As we progressed towards the shore and the light increased, I was distinctly surprised to find ourselves moving towards a holiday resort, Luc-sur-Mer, which looked astonishingly like Blackpool. Instead of the promenade there was a low sea wall, but the gently shelving golden sands were there and the line of boarding houses, though the sands were covered with tripods with mines on top. The boarding houses were somewhat of a surprise, as we had gained the distinct impression that our aerial bombings and softening-up preliminary barrage would have flattened everything.'

'As I jumped out into about 3ft of water, the LCA lifted on a wave and lurched forward on top of me, crushing me into the sand. The Royal Marine coxswain swung the craft to one side and I emerged. We hastened ashore and got down on the beach above the tide to collect our bearings. DD tanks were supposed to land along with us, but there was no sign of these on our section of the beach. Directly ahead of us was a road leading from the beach, the exit choked with coils of barbed wire. While I was debating how to cope with this problem, an AVRE (Churchill) tank fitted with special equipment came waddling up the beach, ploughed through most of this wire and then lost a track on a mine.

'Shells were falling on the roofs of the boarding houses, and I directed my platoon towards a large house to the left of the beach exit. It was then I learned in action one of my first lessons of practical man-management. One of my section leaders, whom I had regarded highly, was a bright lad, a policeman in civilian life. I explained to him what I wanted his section to do, but got no reaction. I had just realized that he was too upset by the situation to comprehend what I was telling him, when another of my section commanders came over, an alert man, a regular soldier, whom I had previously believed to be rather slow, as at "O" Groups he always asked for a detailed repeat of orders. I realize now that he was only making quite certain what my instructions were. He said, "What are you asking him to do, Sir?" I explained that I wanted him to take his section into this house, while the other sections gave covering fire. He turned to his section, said, "Follow me!" and took them into the house. There was no opposition and the rest of the platoon followed – to find the Germans still in the cellars, waiting for the barrage to lift.

'This presented us with another problem. We had received no instructions on how to deal with prisoners at this early stage, so we disarmed them and locked them in the cellar, and moved on down the road.'

The defenders on 'Sword' appeared stunned by the Allied onslaught, but soon started to fight back. Return fire, coupled with a fast-moving tide and the myriad of beach obstacles made life very difficult, especially for the naval and Royal Marine crews of the landing craft. Dennis Osborne was the coxswain of LCT 1068, landing on 'Queen' beach. 'We beached between two mined tank obstacles, our troops disembarked and we made ready to move off. No such luck! We were stuck hard and fast, so there was nothing we could do but wait for the turn of the tide. We were about 200 yards from the road at the top of the beach with beached coasters and freighters all over the place. Amidst the confusion two soldiers were sheltering from enemy fire up against a coaster loaded with ammunition. Three DUKWs approached the beach in spearhead formation; the leading one hit a mine, injuring the driver who was covered with blood. I think he must have been fatally wounded. His passenger must have been blown out on to the beach for he was reeling about. Two stretcher bearers dashed across the beach with complete disregard for their own safety to rescue one of their comrades. They took him to the field hospital at the top of the beach which was shelled soon after. We saw our first POWs, who were set to clearing debris from the beach.

'We only saw one enemy aircraft, a fighter bomber who dropped his bomb further along the beach and hastily departed. A sniper was causing problems on the beach until a destroyer closed as near to the beach as possible and demolished the tower he was situated in.'

Corporal Rayson, of 9 Platoon, 'A' Company, the 1st Suffolks, recalls the landing. 'Have you ever got up in the morning and nothing goes right? Well, this was one of those days. As we approached the shore we were standing up. It was impossible to sit down because of the gear we were carrying. Morale was good but as we got nearer a few machine-gun bullets and some shells went over and we got down as far as we could. Then we ran on to one of those metal obstructions placed in the water by the Germans to tear the bottom out of the boat. The boat stopped, tilted slightly and the Royal Marine coxswain managed to get the ramp down. It didn't look very far to the beach so out went a naval officer, another officer and a corporal.

'Owing to the very heavy swell they disappeared but popped up after a while and swam ashore. No one else moved as a lot of fellows could not swim. I said to the Marine, "Pull back and go in again," and this he did. Still nobody moved, so I thought that if I went, they would follow. So off I went, but no one followed. I thought I was never going to touch the bottom, but I did and shot up again. On reaching the surface the LCA ramp was against my back and before I could move, the boat moved forward and I went under. I came up with the boat three yards in front of me. Eventually I got rid of all my stuff, including the Sten gun. I made a little progress but had to get rid of my steel helmet as it kept going over my face.

'At last I reached the shore, sat down and recovered. The beach seemed to be utter chaos. I took a steel helmet off a dead South Lancs soldier and picked up a Sten-gun magazine and a couple of grenades and put them in my pockets. On reaching the promenade I saw Harry Filby, one of "A" Company stretcher bearers, who said, "Can I do you up?" I replied, "What for?" and he pointed to my battle dress which was covered with blood. I had cut and broken my nose, and it was still bleeding heavily and, being wet through, I looked a sorry sight.'

Corporal Edwin Byatt of 'B' Company, 1st Suffolks, had been in the retreat from France in 1940; now, four years later, he was back. 'I could see a plane in the distance laying a smoke screen along the beach, and further back, HMS *Warspite* was busy firing. A lot of other ships were in action and shells were going over sounding like express trains. The "Success" signal went up from the South Lancashires on the beach and we were going in.

'LCAs were getting sunk and being hit from the shelling. Our LCA managed to get through and the doors went down and we were in the water up to our chests, but we were used to this anyway. I remember seeing bodies floating about, mostly South Lancs lads. Shells and small-arms fire were hindering us and the smell of cordite and smoke was everywhere.

'A Beachmaster was there with a towel round his head covered in blood; his job was to try and keep things moving, so we didn't hang about. I remember having to jump a very wide anti-tank ditch full of water. I just made the bank and was glad I was only carrying a Sten gun. I found I had lost one man in my section and later I found he had been wounded leaving the LCA and taken back to England. We got going fast inland, leaving snipers firing and pockets to be cleared up by follow-up troops. There was no stopping now.'

Eric Rowland, a Private with 'A' Company, 1st Suffolks remembers the chaos on the beaches. 'I remember bodies in the surf, and as I ran up the beach I passed a headless body. It was then I realized it was not an exercise and I was in the thick of it.

'We paused on the promenade to re-group, and as I looked out to sea, the sight that met my eyes was something I will never forget. There was an enormous mass of craft of all sizes, some on fire. More and more landing craft were beaching and discharging men.'

The beach obstacles were not the only problems the landing craft had to deal with. Bill 'Mac' Helas was aboard LCT 2433, transporting Royal Marines Centaur tanks. 'We did our landing as instructed, but while on the beach one of our own shells dropped short and almost blew our ramp off. Fortunately the crew had just moved aft, so we did not have any casualties, but a Landing Craft (Rocket) was alongside and had fired one salvo when it was hit. The LCR exploded and we did not see any survivors.'

Having managed to swim ashore, Lt Edward Jones and his platoon of the South Lancs joined the remnants of his Company. Their task was to clear the German defences to the west, in the village of Lion-sur-Mer. 'One of those occurrences which were to become so frequent now took place. Up to now the German shelling had been spasmodic and haphazard, but it began to increase and one of the places selected was obviously our crossroad. A shell exploded on the road close by and a fragment of shrapnel ploughed through the torch clipped on my webbing belt. I doubled up with pain and Bob Pearce rushed across and tore open my battledress blouse to reveal the piece of shrapnel which had only just broken the surface of the skin, having been slowed down by the torch. It was hot enough to burn my stomach, hence the pain.

'We now moved rapidly down the road towards Lion. There were no German soldiers about, only a number of French civilians, most of whom seemed too stunned to comprehend what was happening, though despite the bombardment some were still tilling the fields on the south of the road.

'Lion had been cleared of civilians and was occupied by German troops. Buildings had been converted into blockhouses and some streets had been completely blocked with coil upon coil of barbed wire, practically to roof level and 20–30ft in depth. As I reconnoitred cautiously down one of the few streets left open, two of my men, one on each side of me, were expertly picked off by hidden riflemen.

'We therefore moved round to the south of the village and entered farm buildings, which gave us a view across open country to the east. Here we made contact with 41 (RM) Commando and were able both to beat off a German counter-attack from the south and to give covering fire to the Royal Marines' advance to the west. We began to move further inland to the group of buildings from which the Germans had launched their attack. We lost one or two more men in this attempt, but as we reached the safety of a sunken lane with a stone wall on one side and a bank and hedge on the other, disaster struck. Without warning, a cluster of mortar-bombs landed in the middle of us, killing and wounding many of our men. Among the wounded was Lieutenant Pearce, who already held the MC and gained a bar for his D-Day actions. We took the wounded to the shelter of the stone wall and dressed their wounds. I remember we were joined here by a young French girl aged around ten or eleven, who kept repeating, "*J'ai peur*," – "I'm frightened", as well she might be !'

Lieutenant Jones lost many of his platoon in this attack, including his platoon sergeant, Sergeant West. While they were re-organizing, he realized that he was the only remaining 'A' Company officer on his feet. Re-grouping for another attack, a runner arrived with orders for the company to rejoin the rest of the battalion in Hermanville. 'We made our way back along the lateral road, which the Germans were now shelling constantly, and one of my platoon, a tall, thin young lad with sandy hair, was badly wounded by a piece of shrapnel in the neck. An Artillery captain emerged from a fox-hole alongside the road, expertly applied digital pressure to the wound and said, "You go on ! I'll look after him." We heard the officer calling for stretcher bearers as we left. Some weeks later one of my platoon showed me a photograph in a local newspaper depicting this lad, accompanied by a brief account of how he had been wounded on D-Day, and saying he was well on the way to recovery.'

While the 8th Infantry Brigade were advancing inland, 41 (Royal Marine)

Commando were battling their way to the west. Marine Raymond Mitchell was a despatch rider with the Headquarters Troop and went ashore on 'Sword' with a 'parascooter', a small collapsible motorbike. 'There was time for no more than a glance at the beach, a shambles of burning tanks, shattered landing craft and bodies floating in the shallows, as we queued to use the one usable ramp. It was bucking about like a cake-walk, so I had no option but to sit down, cradling the bike in my arms to stop it ending up in the drink. I needn't have worried about it because in trying to keep up with my troop, I found the machine too heavy to carry for very long, and its small wheels simply gouged a furrow in the soft sand when I tried to push it. Some tank men were crouching against their knocked-out Churchill tank. "Here mate !" I gasped to one of them. "Want a motorbike ?" Then I abandoned it and ran on.'

Having got rid of the bike, Marine Mitchell soon caught up with his troop. 'We doubled into Lion-sur-Mer, making very little noise in our rubber-soled "brothel creepers". Curious faces peered at us from the windows as we passed, until we stopped on the pavement in front of a small newsagent's shop, where I spent what was probably the very first "Invasion Money" used in France. I was persuaded to go inside to buy some matches for one of our number who had his soaked in the landing. We were left there while the Fighting (Rifle) Troops of the Commando went about their business, and my smattering of French enabled me to understand some French ladies who came to tell us that they had wounded men in their homes ; I sent two of our Sick Berth attendants back with them. Later, when mortar fire became intense, we moved into the church grounds to dig in. I was given a pushbike and did a few local trips, then was sent back on it to the beach to find some of our Jeeps. There was also a "Famous James" 125cc motorbike on the LCT, so I rode it back to HQ, leading the Jeeps, which were put to immediate use, evacuating wounded.'

To the east, Lord Lovat's 1st Special Services (Commando) Brigade was marching to link up with the paratroopers of 6th Airborne. 45 (RM) Commando was part of the brigade with Lieutenant John Day serving in 'E' Troop of 45 Commando. 'I had a specific task for the initial part of our operation ; to get ten inflatable dinghies to the River Orne. These would be required to get the brigade over the water if the bridges over the Orne or the canal at Bénouville had been destroyed. I had twenty men from "E" Troop allocated to me for this task and because of our heavy, awkward loads, dinghies, paddles, air pumps and ropes, in addition to our normal equipment, we would be the last to disembark from the LCIs.

'We were due to touch down at 0910 hours and we seemed to be just about on time. I did not even get my feet wet as I went ashore, and the rest of my group landed slowly but safely. Sadly, LCI(S) 517 sank as she withdrew from the beach, but the crew was saved.

'After a slight pause at the check-point while 6 Commando, which was leading the brigade's advance, dealt with some opposition, we moved off, my dinghy group moving slowly some distance behind the main body of the Commando. On arrival at Bénouville we dumped the dinghies by the Café Gondrée and were warned by an airborne soldier that the bridges were still under enemy fire. I sent my party off across the bridges in twos and threes and having seen them reach the far bank safely, I set off at a trot accompanied by Sergeant Hepper and my orderly. I was not conscious of being fired at, but Bob Hepper was hit in the neck as we were crossing the river bridge. Private Dunlop, RAMC, "E" Troop's medical orderly, came back to attend to him and he was then left with the Airborne. Bob Hepper survived his wound, though I did not meet him again until December 1991, at 45 (RM) Commando's first-ever reunion.'

The Commandos were supported by some of the special Royal Engineer tanks. One of these was driven by Driver Beeton. Having lost a bogey wheel from his AVRE on a mine but luckily not his track, he joined the Commandos in their dash for the Caen Canal. 'I managed to drive the tank behind some sand dunes where we unsealed the hatches and were joined by some Commandos. Our Major arrived and took charge of my tank as his had been knocked out, and I was instructed to drive off along a road. Here we immediately came under small-arms fire which my co-driver returned. We came to a bridge spanning a canal where we saw a pill-box and a number of Germans on the other side, but our mortar had only a short range and we were unable to hit the pill-box with it, so the Major decided to try and cross.

'I was then told to drive the tank on to an open space well clear of the houses and to remain there as the Major had to leave. By this time the engine was running hot, so I got on to the rear of the tank to unseal the engine covers and had just started my task when I heard the sound of an aircraft engine. When the plane first appeared, I thought it was a Mustang, but soon changed my mind when I saw it release a bomb which was coming straight at the tank. There was nothing I could do except to lay down flat on the engine covers and hope for the best. All my strength seemed to ebb away and it was utter relief when the bomb cleared the tank and exploded just in front.'

Major James Cuthbertson, commanding 90 Company RASC, attached to the 27th Armoured Brigade, had a special task on D-Day. His thirty-three trucks were to land at H+6 and move directly to the Orne bridges, taking up vital supplies of food, fuel and ammunition to the airborne soldiers. Major Cuthbertson and a despatch rider were to land on 'Sword' beach at H+2, reconnoitre a route to Ranville on motorbikes and make the initial contact with the Airborne.

Major James Cuthbertson recalls his day: 'The beach was complete chaos. Eventually we moved inland through Hermanville and made straight for the Orne, so off we went, out into open lanes, no hedges – an open, bare landscape. There was no one in sight. We just followed our maps and pressed on for five miles. It was very eerie – where were the enemy, or our own troops? We went along on our bikes and saw no one.

'At about 1130 hrs, having passed through two silent villages, we went down a steep little slope and around a sharp turn to the Orne bridges, at what is now Pegasus Bridge. We pulled up under some tall trees by a thick hedge and heard someone shout, "Get down, you're under enemy observation!" Looking more closely we saw half-a-dozen paratroopers in defensive positions about the bridge, but no liaison officers. We stayed "doggo" with the occasional recce to the bridge to see if the seaborne troops had arrived, and at about 1330 hrs, Lord Lovat and his Commandos arrived at the bridge, down the same road we had used. Apart from ourselves, these were the first seaborne troops to reach the bridge.'

By 1400 hrs, with no one arriving from the Airborne HQ, James Cuthbertson decided to ride back to the beaches to see if his vehicles had landed and, if so, to bring them back up with their much-needed stores.

'On the way down, I had the surprise of my life. Coming towards me were nine vehicles of my "B" Platoon. They were not scheduled to arrive until D+5 (11 June) and I just couldn't believe it. They had found room on an LCT and came on anyway.'

Having sorted out his men, Major Cuthbertson rode back to the bridges yet again, still not meeting anyone on the way. He got back there at 1700 hrs, where he took matters into his own hands and set out to find General Gale's Headquarters. His problem was to get across the bridges which the enemy had under heavy fire.

'The paratroopers laid down a protective smoke screen over the bridges, so I crossed in a fog and followed one of the lanes leading off on the other side. .... I eventually arrived at the Airborne HQ in a farm near Ranville, which was itself under sporadic mortar-fire.'

It transpired that both the Airborne officer guides he had been due to meet had been wounded, but General Gale ordered him to bring up his convoy after dark and off-load the stores in a nearby quarry.

'While I was with the Headquarters, at 1800 hrs we all listened to the King's speech, a most moving moment. Just as it finished, there was a mighty roar as hundreds of gliders and aircraft flew over, bringing the 6th Air Landing Brigade to reinforce the heavily pressed Airborne Division. There was an enormous cheer from everyone, immediately followed by a German mortar attack.'

Setting off yet again on his motorcycle, Major Cuthbertson raced back to his rendezvous at Colleville. That night he made his fifth trip along winding French lanes to the Caen Canal bringing up the much needed stores. For his efforts on D-Day, Major James Cuthbertson was awarded the Military Cross.

Not only fighting troops were involved on D-Day. The troops at the front had to be supplied with ammunition and fuel, and their wounded had to be evacuated, and these tasks depended on the men of the Royal Army Service Corps, like Major Cuthbertson's company. One of the men engaged in supply was Douglas Grey of the 27th Armoured Brigade. 'My job was to supply the tanks of the 27th Armoured Brigade with petrol, oil and lubricants. My personal transport was a motorcycle which was attached to the side of a Sherman tank of the East Riding Yeomanry, commanded by Sergeant East. There was little room on the landing craft and the only place I could find to try and sleep was between the two diesel engines. As we came to land at H+6 (approximately 1 p.m.) on "Sword" beach at Lion-sur-Mer, I was able to have a brief look out at the beaches from the top of the tank before Sergeant East asked me to return to the inside. Shells were passing overhead from the battleships and I was particularly astounded to watch the multiple rocket flak ships firing inland. I was more than glad we were not on the receiving end.

'My motorcycle was lowered from the tank and I said farewell to Sergeant East and his crew, who I never saw again. I then found, to my consternation, that it was impossible to steer the motorcycle as I had attached so much equipment to it. I set off in what I thought was the right direction for Brigade HQ, but was stopped by some of our infantry who told me not to proceed as the enemy was just round the corner. I thereupon retraced my steps and managed to negotiate all the traffic moving from the beaches and located Brigade HQ in Hermanville.

'My task until my trucks landed was to locate the "porpoises" which were loaded with ammunition and towed in by the tanks, and have their loads picked up. I might add that I was not very successful in finding them. Eventually my trucks arrived and we harboured up south of Hermanville. Conditions near the beaches and around the Sector Stores Dumps, whence all replenishment had to be made, were very difficult. There were only about two up and down routes and they were in use by all new units landing and all beach and DUKW transport. Congestion was very severe throughout the day. Bombings by day and night were frequent and even until D+2 isolated snipers remained in some houses behind the beaches.

'At about 2000 hrs some of the POL (Petrol, Oil and Lubricant) vehicles were sent forward with ammunition vehicles to replenish tanks in their forward positions. Throughout the night, which was one of considerable air activity, the work of replenishing the tanks went on, all vehicles then returning to the Sector Stores Dumps at "Queen" beach to refill. They arrived back at location as dawn was breaking.'

*

As more and more men came ashore, the assaulting battalions pushed inland, against increasing German resistance. Behind the assault battalions Lord Lovat's Commandos came ashore. The following accounts come from men of 45 (Royal Marine) Commando.

Emlyn Jones was in the Signal Troop. 'Only seconds to go now before we hit the beach, though naval ratings, both port and starboard were firing guns at the enemy targets oblivious of the fire that was coming back. This is it . . . ramp down . . . let's move. The Bren gunner has frozen at the top of the ramp and won't move. Then we found out that only one ramp could be used. While waiting those few minutes for my turn, I found myself quietly singing "Abide with me". Why? I don't know but it seemed appropriate at the time. If ever we needed God by our side, this was the time.

'At the foot of the ramp was a sailor lying prostrate with his face blown off. Poor devil, wish I had held my tongue about the Navy. Must push on. Mortars and shells raining down while struggling through the sand and dunes with the wounded and dead all around, but no time to stop. Medics following will attend to the wounded. Above all this bedlam we heard the skirl of the bagpipes. Bill Millin, Lord Lovat's piper, playing "Blue Bonnets". It was heart-stirring music, even to a Welshman.'

Despite all the briefings and planning, the anxiety of battle caused mistakes. John Day of 45 Commando recalls what happened later that day when his Commanding Officer took a wrong turn while moving up to the Merville Battery. 'The Commando set off at about 3 p.m., moving eastwards towards Sallenelles. I led "E" Troop immediately behind the CO's party. All was quiet and the countryside seemed peaceful, with no sign of Germans or civilians. Having passed through Sallenelles the two leading troops, quite correctly, turned right, up a narrow track leading to Merville. This move was not noticed by the CO's group which continued straight along the road, towards Franceville-Plage. When we were about 400 yards from Sallenelles I heard heavy small-arms fire ahead and saw the CO's group scatter off the road. The left-hand, seaward side of the road was completely open and as a few shots had come close to us, I moved "E" Troop back about 50 yards to a clump of trees by a track junction which provided some cover. As we took up position I saw about ten Germans, some 300 yards away to our left, running along a skyline towards a pill-box. An "E" Troop Bren gunner hurried them on their way.

'By now the firing ahead of us had ceased but I could see no sign of the CO's group, so I thought I should go forward to find out what was happening. Leaving the TSM in charge of the troop, I walked alone down the road. Suddenly, when I was about 150 yards from the troop position, I became the object of a great deal of unwanted attention, rifle-fire probably coming from the pill-box we had just spotted on the seaward side. The only nearby cover was a line of trees behind a wire fence on the other side of the road, so I dashed towards this haven and hurled myself at the fence.

'Unfortunately my rucksack caught in the fence but the whip-cracks of bullets were too close to permit a second attempt. I dropped to the ground and crawled along a shallow ditch until it seemed safe to get to my feet and run to rejoin "E" Troop. I had heard so often of men being killed before they had a chance to engage the enemy, and this had nearly happened to me. My Tommy gun being useless at the range required, I got behind a Bren gun and fired a couple of bursts at the pill-box. I could not claim to have hit anyone, but it made me feel better.'

Colin Fletcher was the machine-gun officer in the MG section of 'F' Troop, 45 Commando. 'On the run-in, only one man in my troop was wounded: Corporal Gooch, hit by shrapnel in the jaw. I do not think I was aware that he had been hit until after we were ashore, but I seem to remember being told that it was while we were still aboard. He stayed with us for quite some time – maybe two or three days, though I can't be sure just how long. I remember his being brought to me – probably by my medical orderly, L/Corporal Glidden – with a first-aid dressing still on his cheek, and the cheek swelling so badly that he clearly had to be sent back. We never saw him again.

'We had our first machine-gun action at Pegasus Bridge soon after noon in support of an attack on a pill-box by an airborne unit. We crossed the two bridges and moved on northward to a small quarry overlooking the river. There we came under command of Major Tony Lewis, commander of 6 Commando Heavy Weapons Troop, to form a little sub-unit composed of our MG section and that from 6 Commando. As far as I remember, the day ended for us when we dug in near the quarry.'

While the initial objectives on the beach were falling to the 8th Infantry Brigade, both the follow-up brigade, No. 185, and the support brigade, No. 9, were doing their best to get off the beaches and move inland towards Caen. The follow-up brigade consisted of the 2nd Battalion, the Royal Warwickshire Regiment, the Second Battalion, the King's Shropshire Light Infantry and the First Battalion, Royal Norfolk Regiment. Their armoured support was provided by the Staffordshire Yeomanry, equipped with Sherman tanks.

This brigade was to move south towards the 3rd Division objective for D-Day – Caen. 2nd Warwicks moved up behind Lord Lovat's Commando Brigade, and captured Blainville-sur-Orne, some kilometres south-east of the Orne bridges. The King's Shropshire Light Infantry and 1st Royal Norfolks in turn were to move right and left of 1st Suffolk from the 8th Brigade once the Suffolks had secured their objective, the strongpoint codenamed 'Hillman'. 1st Norfolks were to move to St Aubin d'Arquenay and then on to a second objective called 'Rover', south of 'Hillman'.

Corporal Edwin Byatt with 'B' Company, 1st Suffolks, recalls the attack on another strongpoint, codenamed 'Morris'. 'We went at the double from the beach, leaving snipers and other pockets of resistance to be mopped up by others following. "Morris" was still firing on the beach and with shells going overhead the noise was terrific. We managed to find some cover on the approach and got in position to attack. The Navy were to stop shelling when we were ready to go in and if we didn't send up the "Success" signal by a certain time, 30 minutes I think, they would start firing again, which would mean firing on us as well as on the Germans.

'The air photos we had studied had shown the trenches round the gun emplacements, so each section knew where to make for. I remember laying flat by the Bangalore torpedo team, ready to blow the wire, wondering what it was going to be like. The shelling stopped and we were just going to blow and attack when white flags were waved. We hoped it wasn't a trick, but they surrendered, 60 or 70 officers and men, which was just as well for us. Their positions were well covered and formidable, but the shelling and bombing had softened them up, although the emplacement looked intact. I think the speed with which we had got there also helped a lot. So the "Success" signal went up and our morale then was sky-high.'

'Morris' fell relatively easily; 'Hillman' was to prove much more difficult. This large dug-in complex was heavily defended and totally surrounded by two barbed-wire fences and mines. The 'Hillman' position was a mass of concrete emplacements and armoured gun cupolas removed from old French tanks, which were virtually impervious even to anti-tank gunfire. The defending German force comprised the Headquarters Company and infantry of the 736th Grenadier Regiment.

The task of taking 'Hillman' was given to 'A' Company of the 1st Suffolks, with a detachment of 246 Field Company, Royal Engineers to clear the mines and barbed wire, allowing the company to rush the first trenches and then fight their way through the position.

Eric Rowland of 'A' Company, 1st Suffolks takes up the story: 'A breaching party crawled through standing corn and managed to blow the first belt of wire with Bangalore torpedoes. A mine-clearing section of Royal Engineers then cleared a path through the mines and the second belt of wire was blown, but an attempt to rush the gap resulted in several casualties.'

Sapper Richard Ellis was one of those clearing the mines. 'We were told to tape a path through the minefield, where we came under machine-gun fire. I led the way into the minefield at the crouch and dived behind a small mound; the machine-gun rounds were bouncing off it and the third man of our team was hit in the chest. After lying there for a while I began to ease myself forward. Pinning marker tape around the mines, I picked up on the detector and crawled on until I reached a triple barbed-wire fence. I then crawled back down the tape, very aware of an extremely dry mouth and perspiration running down my face.'

With the mines pinpointed, another Bangalore team blew the final barbed-wire concertinas. Eric Rowland went forward again. 'I crawled forward so that I was lying on the path through the mines. Heavy machine-gun fire greeted every attempt at movement. Every now and again a bullet would ricochet off an angle-iron stake beside me. Eventually, word was passed back that we were to dash, one at a time, through the gap and into a small crater just inside the wire, and from there get into a trench. I relayed this message to the chap lying behind me and told him to pass it on – the rest of "A" Company being in among the corn. I then carried out the order and managed to get into the trench unharmed and joined the small party gathered there.'

Corporal Rayson of 9 Platoon remembers the move up to the outer defences of 'Hillman'. 'We crawled through a field of barley and waited till the Engineers lifted some mines and taped a track through. Another party got rid of the wire with Bangalore torpedoes. Then we went in. The first two, a corporal and a private, were killed as soon as they got through the gap. A machine gun in a tank turret was mounted right in front of the gap. The turret was made of what looked like glass. We all got down and he kept us down. Bullets whizzed above our heads. One hit the pick-axe on my back, one went through my gas cape rolled up on my belt . . . this proves my behind was higher than my head. The Bren gunner, lying behind me, had one hit his shovel, the bits going in his backside. After a while, things went quiet. We hit the turret twice, but didn't smash it, although we got rid of the gunner.'

Eric Rowland, now in a shell-hole on the German side of the wire, was ordered to move again. 'My platoon officer ordered me to crawl out of the trench as he needed someone to give covering fire for a Bren gunner he intended to send out. I did as I was ordered, feeling very vulnerable, but luckily I was not seen, probably due to the fact that vision was limited and the Germans concentrated on the gap in the wire. The officer then asked me if I could see anything that warranted a Bren. I said "No," so he told me to return to the trench. He then asked me what had happened to the rest of the company and why they hadn't joined us. He realized that our position was pretty hopeless and told us to get off the position as best we could – i.e., one at a time.'

Corporal Rayson was one of those who had entered the 'Hillman' position. 'Suddenly, along came the Company Commander. "Come on, Rayson," he said. I got up only to be knocked down by someone running behind him. I followed him only to be fired at as I got through the gap. I got down and then up again, and ran through a hole in the bank where the others had gone. I found myself in a deep trench. I couldn't see over the top, but following the trench to the left, then to the right, and so on, I eventually caught up with the others – although there weren't many of us left. As we were wondering what to do next, a runner came round the corner and told us to get out as quickly as we could. We didn't need encouraging. A flail tank then appeared from somewhere and made a large track through the mine-field, then up came three Sherman tanks, and in we went again.'

Eric Rowland takes up the story: 'This time we got in to the position with little trouble and proceeded to mop up. We took several prisoners, but we could not clear the objective properly because so much of it was under-ground. However, we neutralized it and withdrew to dig in for the night. I decided to make a cup of cocoa using a Tommy cooker and my enamel mug, and proceeded to burn my fingers. Considering what we had been through that day, I got off lightly! The next day the remainder of the German garrison surrendered, and that was the end of "Hillman".'

Corporal Rayson also found that he needed a brew after consolidating on the position. 'We couldn't get down into the position owing to some steel doors which we couldn't open, but to wake them up we put several grenades down the ventilation shafts, plus a few smoke ones. After this we dug in around the place. Things got quieter, so we opened the 48-hr ration packs and brewed up some tea in our tin mugs. The tea – tea, sugar and milk, looked like an Oxo cube, but at least it tasted like tea, although even the Naafi tea was better.'

With 'Hillman' neutralized the 1st Suffolks started to consolidate their position, holding the ground for 185 Brigade to push through towards Caen. Corporal Edwin Byatt was there with 'B' Company of the 1st Suf-folks. 'By now, 185 Brigade, with the 2nd Warwicks and so on, were going for Caen. They had been held up waiting for their tank support. The tanks had been held up getting off the beaches, so 185 had to go on their own, and they soon ran into trouble with 21st Panzer Division. I had placed my section for all-round defence. We dug two-man slit trenches. I shared mine with a very good young chap, George Jarvis, aged only 19 (I was an old man of 24). Unfortunately George Jarvis was killed three weeks later.

'Some self-propelled guns came to our position and started firing. I remember saying to George that they would draw fire down on us in return, so we dug deeper. To our left we could see 6th Airborne holding the bridges and firing going on there. They were doing a wonderful job and were reinforced by now. It was as well that we had moved away from the "Morris" position as the German artillery was ranged on to it and gave it a good shelling.'

While the 1st Suffolk were fighting their battle for 'Hillman' the 185th Infantry Brigade and the reserve brigade, the 9th Infantry Brigade, were making their way inland.

Geoff Peters was a twenty-four-year-old Corporal in the Signals Platoon of the 2nd Warwicks. 'We were landing between Ouistreham and Lion-sur-Mer in LCAs. We had about 80lbs of kit on our backs, and I had a wireless set added to all that. I didn't realize till later that the big aerial sticking up was attracting snipers. I was looking out from the boat and it was as if I were watching a war film. Our craft got hit about a hundred yards out, and hit again, and hit again, so we suddenly realized that all our careful plans were going to pot. The Signals Sergeant was killed as was one of the signallers. When we came to go ashore the ramp wouldn't go down so we finished up scrambling over the side. I was running behind a tank when it was hit as well. There was a lot of firing and shelling.

'We reached the forming-up position for the Warwicks. The Norfolks and the KSLI were in our brigade, and the job of the 185th Brigade was to push through and ignore some things and get to Caen on the first morning. Things started to go wrong because we had got our plans, but the Germans had got their plans.

'The KSLI were supposed to push up the road to Caen, riding on tanks. We were going on the right to knock out some strongpoints, with the Norfolks on the left. When it came to the push the Norfolks were so heavily engaged at some strongpoint, we hadn't got them. Then the tanks didn't turn up for the KSLI – they were bogged down on the beach. So within half an hour of landing all our plans were changed, and the Warwicks and the KSLI had to push on up the road to Caen on our own. When we got to Bénouville at Pegasus Bridge, the Airborne were expecting a counter-attack, and we sent a company of our lads to help them, so we were down to three-quarters of our strength, less what we had lost already. Then we started coming under quite a bit of fire, small-arms and shell-fire, and it was a plodding game then. There were villages . . . Beuville, Biéville, just villages that sounded nothing and looked just a dot on the map, but it was a big thing to us to take them. In fact, we never got into Caen that day.'

Major Eric Lummis of the 1st Suffolks was a witness to the problems that the soldiers suffered as they came ashore, mainly from German artillery. 'We managed to find a way through and at last arrived at what had been marked as the D-Day transit area. My Suffolk company was followed by the first reinforcement companies of the two other battalions in 8 Brigade and that of the 2nd Battalion of the King's Shropshire Light Infantry, who were the lead Battalion of the follow-up brigade – 185 Brigade. As I was nominally in charge of all these companies, I allocated areas and we settled down to dig slit trenches. To our surprise civilians started appearing. One offered me a glass of cider, another man and his wife invited me into their home and gave me a cup of tea.

'We had just about completed our trenches when further troops arrived. First some of the Beach Group, followed by vehicles of 9 Brigade headquarters with their commander in a Bren carrier. A few minutes later there were three or four bangs close by. The shells caught the HQ, wounding the Brigadier and his Intelligence Officer and killing three others, including the Canadian liaison officer from the Canadian Brigade on our right. We saw the Brigadier and his Intelligence Officer being taken off in a Jeep. In the brigade's place came a mortar detachment from a Royal Marine Commando who were still engaged in trying to clear a strongpoint on the beach in Lion.'

Corporal Albert Smith, a member of the Anti-Tank Platoon of the 1st Norfolks, continues the tale: 'It is strange how you remember the silly things, like seeing a barrage balloon brought ashore. The German guns quickly ranged in on it and began pin-pointing their fire on to the landing area. The last I saw of this balloon it was floating gently away down the coast.'

As the fighting moved inland, more and more of the local inhabitants ventured out of their shelters. Major Eric Cooper Key, commanding 'B' Company of 1st Norfolks that day, recalls a typically British incident. 'There was one piece of light relief shortly after we landed. Major Humphrey Wilson, the Battalion 2nd I/C, had a group of Frenchmen surrounding him, and most of them were jabbering at him. He turned to me and said, "Eric, these bloody fools don't understand their own language." He was replying in his best known foreign tongue – Urdu!'

Many a British soldier was to admire the stoicism of the French that day. Alfred Rampling, a Private serving with 'A' Company, 1st Norfolks, recalls a Frenchman he met, while all around the battle raged. 'We carried on and reached a small village. The residents were going about their daily tasks, and there was one old chap pushing a barrow full of cabbages, carrots and so on. He had just come back from his allotment. "*Bonjour, Monsieur*," he kept saying, and went on his way. All this time the Germans were getting within range of us and mortar bombs were cutting into our ranks.'

The Brigade Signals officer, Captain Philip, was also under pressure as 185 Brigade moved forward. With an impatient Brigadier desperately wanting to move forward to his battalions he had to try and find the necessary transport. 'We set off again, inland along the dusty road. Most of the roads in our area were only partially surfaced and all were dusty. After about a mile we arrived at the village rendezvous which was to be our first HQ. I felt at a complete loss. There was nothing I could do. Our small party had the wireless sets going and the IO had a map – and that was it. A horrible feeling of uselessness came over me and I wandered around somewhat aimlessly, wondering however on earth we were going to fight a battle on these slender resources. Then suddenly the miracle began to happen. Quite out of the blue one of my vehicles drove up. I can't even remember which one it was, but I fell on the necks of the crew as though they were long-lost brothers.

'And then another came, and another, and yet another. All the vehicles which I had seen distributed to various ports scattered along the south coast of England and which I thought I might never see again, were now all homing in on this tiny village in Normandy, picked off a map during the planning stage. I could hardly believe my eyes. It was a masterpiece of planning and organization, and we were back in business.

'There was only one fly in the ointment. The Brigadier was desperate to get up and see the battalions, but his command carrier had not arrived. There was no other transport available, and then I came across a French boy wheeling a bicycle. I spoke to the boy, borrowed the bicycle and wheeled it over to the Brigadier. It was much too small for him but that didn't matter. I can see him now, happily disappearing down the village street, compelled to pedal with his knees coming up outside the handlebars. I suppose he must have been the only senior British commander ever to have cycled into battle ! I subsequently found the carrier a few days later in a drowned vehicle park just behind the beaches, but by that time the crew had rejoined the section and were running the replacement carrier that quickly appeared.'

By midday the 3rd Infantry Division was ashore on 'Sword' beach and staking out claims inland. Lord Lovat's No 4 Commando had taken Ouistreham and the other Commando units were linking up and reinforcing the paratroops on the Ranville heights above Bénouville. The 9th Infantry Brigade had landed and pushed out from Hermanville, 185th Brigade were in front of Biéville, 8th Brigade were at Bénouville supporting 6th Airborne Division across the bridges at Ranville. The only trouble spot was the stretch of coast between St Aubin and Lion-sur-Mer and stretching back inland through Douvres and Périers to Caen, which was still in German hands. The two Royal Marine Commandos, 41 and 48, were now fighting to close this gap and link up the Canadian 'Juno' beach with 'Sword'.

The last brigade of 3rd Division to come ashore on 'Sword' was the 9th Infantry Brigade. This comprised the 2nd Battalion, the Lincolnshire Regiment, the 1st Battalion, the King's Own Scottish Borderers and the 2nd Battalion, the Royal Ulster Rifles. Armoured support was provided by Sherman tanks of the East Riding Yeomanry attached from 27th Armoured Brigade. 'Sword' beach was under artillery fire as this brigade came ashore.

Trooper King was with 'B' Squadron of the East Riding Yeomanry. 'The morning of the 6th began with a clear dawn. As soon as it became light, the "Rhino" raft was brought round and the task of transferring began. The big lorry which was the last on was the first off, and finally we headed for the French shore. A great ball of black smoke began to rise and fill the sky, and at its base huge flashes from the naval shelling and rockets from the special boats. Between us and land there were great water spouts, as the German guns returned fire. We approached "wading depth", when streams of machine-gun tracer riddled the lorry and the crew jumped out and ran behind the tanks.

'With bullets all over us we got up the beach and into a small excavation with infantry huddled around and under the tanks. We could not see or hear or know who was shelling who. Eventually the shelling eased and in the lull a group of prisoners with an escort ran down the beach to a boat. Just before they made it came two bright flashes and mines exploded among them, leaving a tangled heap of grey and khaki.'

Corporal Jack Hodgson was with 'A' Company, 9th Field Ambulance, and landed with 9th Infantry Brigade. 'Our Medic Section consisted of eighteen men. We were trained in first aid and our job was looking after the wounded in the forward areas and evacuating them to the rear. The rest of the troops on our craft were from the 2nd Battalion, the Lincolnshire Regiment.

'Our landing area was "Sword" beach at Hermanville–La Brèche. I was soon stepping around dead soldiers and at our assembly point we were relieved to find we had all arrived safely. In single file we moved off with the infantry towards Hermanville-sur-Mer, then took a left turn to Lion-sur-Mer. Near the outskirts of this village we medics stopped at a small stone building, which was to be our Regimental Aid Post, and the infantry carried on into the village. After only ten minutes or less we received our first casualty, a young infantryman with a severe flesh wound on his right forearm. He was quickly dealt with. Our next wounded soldier, a German, was carried in on a stretcher. The third was British. He was dead and we buried him under an apple tree. The tree was still there in 1990.'

Captain Philip, the Signals Officer with 185 Brigade Headquarters recalls the airborne reinforcements coming in by glider on the evening of 6 June. 'There were several incidents, but undoubtedly the most important was the landing of the Air Landing Brigade on our left. To refer to it as impressive is almost an understatement. The first indication we had was the sound of aircraft engines. Then suddenly we saw the beginning of a vast armada of some 250 four-engined bombers each towing a glider. In next to no time the sky was full and the stream seemed never-ending, though I guess the whole operation could not have lasted more than an hour at the most. The aircraft flew in at around 2,000 to 3,000 feet. The gliders cast off over the beaches, though this was too far away for us to see in detail and we only knew it had happened when the distance between glider and tug began to increase.

'I had always assumed that a glider's descent was by a gentle downward path. I soon learned that I was wrong. The pilot brought the aircraft over the landing zone without losing much height, presumably to stay above small-arms fire and to pick out a suitable landing spot. Then suddenly they would go into a horrifying steep dive, flatten out just above the ground and skid to a halt, though I must admit that from where we were we couldn't see the actual touchdown. The tugs had turned slightly to starboard and were flying directly over us, their tow ropes still dangling below. As they approached we could see the bomb doors open and the supply containers neatly grouped in the bomb racks.

'Suddenly they were all released simultaneously and descended amid a flutter of brightly coloured parachutes, each identifying the contents of its container. In a few instances the parachute failed to open and the container plunged earthwards at an alarming speed. Finally, the aircraft dropped the dangling tow rope and headed for home. To add to the spectacle the heavy German AA guns around Caen were banging away merrily, filling their part of the sky with black blobs. The Halifax bombers turned away too soon to come within effective range and, as far as I could see, none was hit.'

Geoff Peters of the 2nd Warwicks has another memory of this glider landing. 'Later on D-Day, 185 Brigade had reached the Bénouville–Beuville area and I was with "D" Company, the forward company. When the gliders came in one of them slid across a field and hit two of our signallers who were operating a set in the ditch. They had their earphones on and didn't hear it coming ... one of them was decapitated.

'We dug in that night in a small village and I was lucky in that place. We just had a 24-hour pack ... bits of cheese and stuff. The first big trench I sat down in for the night was in somebody's back garden, with onions all round me, and I was able to eat my little bit of cheese with some spring onions.

'Although it seemed a long way from home, it was homely from the fact of being in a battalion like the Warwicks ... they were all local Birmingham lads, and in between the shells falling and the general noise of war, you could hear a heated argument going on about the merits of Villa and Birmingham City football clubs in a couple of slit trenches just behind you, and it seemed then as if you weren't so far from home.'

For the 3rd British Infantry Division, D-Day was one of mixed success. All the brigades managed to get ashore and inland with less casualties than was initially anticipated, but they did not secure their objective, Caen. In the face of growing resistance from the enemy, particularly 21st Panzer Division, their advance slowed in the early afternoon. Nevertheless, the men who got ashore were happy to be alive and content with their achievement. Four years after Dunkirk, the British Army was back again in France.

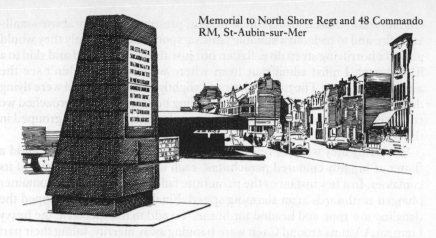

Memorial to North Shore Regt and 48 Commando RM, St-Aubin-sur-Mer

——— CHAPTER TWELVE ———
After D-Day

'It had always been difficult to imagine
D+1.'
Norman Scarfe
3rd (British) Infantry Division

The men involved in planning and fighting Operation 'Overlord', had always found it hard to think beyond D-Day. Plans were drawn up with future operations in mind, but D-Day was so important, the issue so vital and the battle so finely balanced that just to get ashore and stay ashore would seem victory enough.

Total Allied casualties on D-Day amounted to some 10,000 men killed, wounded and missing. According to the US Official History, published by the US Department of the Army in 1951, the 101st Airborne lost 1,240 men, including 182 definitely killed and 501 missing, presumed captured or killed. The 82nd Airborne lost 1,259, including 156 definitely killed and 756 missing, presumed captured or killed. Casualties on D-Day along 'Utah' beach were mercifully low, but the heaviest of all fell on 'Omaha', where some 2,000 men were killed, wounded or missing at the end of the day. The initial figures came to 1,190 for the 1st Infantry, 743 for the 29th Infantry, and 441 for Corps troops. These figures were later revised downwards slightly as men rejoined their units, but the accurate figures are still not known. Casualties along the British and Canadian front amounted to about 1,000 men per beach.

German casualties were very high, especially among the 352nd and 91st Infantry Divisions, where the men fought stubbornly. Total German casualties on D-Day have never been accurately established but certainly ran into thousands, with many thousands more wounded or taken prisoner.

The accounts in this book have concentrated on the events of D-Day and end at midnight, 2359 hrs in military parlance, on 6 June. This chapter takes the story on a little and describes what happened to some of the people met in these preceding pages.

Two days after the landings, General Montgomery wrote his appreciation of the post D-Day situation in a private letter to his friend and colleague, General Dempsy.

8-6-44

My dear Simbo

You may like the following news of our battle.

1. There is no doubt that the Germans were surprised, and we got on shore before they had recovered. The speed, power, and violence of the assault carried all before it.

2. Generally, the beach obstacles presented no difficulty; where they were troublesome it was because of the rough weather – and on some beaches it was pretty rough.

3. DD Tanks
   (a) Used successfully on UTAH beaches.
   (b) Failed to reach the shore on OMAHA beaches and all sank – too rough.
   (c) Were not launched on 50 Div front as it was too rough; were landed 'dry' behind the leading flights; casualties to AVRE sappers high as a result, and to leading infantry.
   (d) Landed 'dry' on Canadian front.
   (e) Used successfully on 3 Div front.
   Generally it can be said that the DD tanks proved their value, and casualties were high where they could not be used.

4. As a guess, prisoners about 6,000 so far. They consist of Germans, Russians, Poles, Japanese, and two Turks.

5. British casualties about 1,000 per assault Division.
   American casualties not known.
   High proportion of officer casualties, due to sniping behind our front.

Two Bde Cmds wounded :
  Cunningham   9 Bde
  Senior   151 Bde
Good many COs killed, including Herdon, OC 2 Warwicks.
No general officers are casualties.

6. The Germans are fighting well; Russians, Poles, Japanese, and Turks, run away, and if unable to do so, surrender.

7. Our initial attack was on a wide front, and there were gaps between landings. The impetus of the assault carried us some way inland and many defended localities were by-passed; these proved very troublesome later. In one case a complete German Bn, with artillery, was found inside 50 Div area ; it gave some trouble but was eventually collected in (about 500 men). There is still one holding out – the radar station west of Douvres; it is very strong and is held by stout-hearted Germans.

8. Snipers in beach areas have been very troublesome, as a result of para 7. The roads have been far from safe and we have lost several good officers. I have been all right myself, though I have toured the area all day. There have been women snipers, presumably wives of German soldiers ; the Canadians shot 4 women snipers.

9. The Germans are doing everything they can to hold on to CAEN. I have decided not to have a lot of casualties by butting up against the place, so I have ordered Second Army to keep up a good pressure at CAEN, and to make its main effort towards VILLERS-BOCAGE and EVRECY and thence SE towards FALAISE.

10. First US Army had a very sticky party at OMAHA, and its progress at UTAH has not been rapid.
I have therefore ordered it to join up its two lodgement areas and to secure CARENTAN and ISIGNY. It will then thrust towards LA HAYE DU PUITS and cut off the Cherbourg peninsula.

11. The two armies have now joined hands east of BAYEUX.

No time for more.

Yrs ever

B. L. Montgomery

P.S.
The country here is very nice ; green fields ; very good crops ; plenty of vegetables ; cows and cattle ; chickens, ducks, etc.
    The few civilians there are appear well fed, the children look healthy, the people have good boots and clothing.
    The locals did not believe the British would ever invade France or

come over the Channel; they say that the German officers and men thought this also – which may account for the tactical surprise we got.

B.L.M.
0900 hrs
9 June

That was the view of the Commanding General, written fifty years ago. Other people have their own memories.

André Heintz, the young French Resistance worker, kept an account of what happened in Caen after the landings. 'I kept a short diary of the period – in fact 36 pages for the first day only – which I wrote afterwards from a few notes – but afterwards I gave up! That "longest day" – so long awaited for – was in fact a grand day and a most wonderful experience; not much hope of living through it and yet we did, but we were happy at the idea it would bring freedom to others at last.

'A man who was found dead in the ruins of the city after the battle when they started clearing the cellars had kept a diary until the end. That diary was found beside him in the cellar where he had been trapped. His strength was failing as he wrote the last line and he must have given up hope by then, and yet he said: "I feel that I am dying and it's terrible to think that I shall never see that day of the liberation I have been so long waiting for but I know that because of my death others will be liberated; so long live France, long live the Allies."

'This is a poor translation from French into English of what that man was writing, but it is a fair statement of what we were feeling at the time.

'I could also tell you how my sister and I made the first red cross in the city with the blood of the wounded that day. My sister was a nurse in the improvised hospital, a former lunatic asylum where Beau Brummell had been confined. My sister helped the surgeons who were operating on British soldiers as well as civilians. She had seen several bombs falling on one of the wards near her, killing some people, and she was conscious that something had to be done to warn the Allies that so many wounded were being gathered and tended in that spot. By then, two other hospitals had been hit; all the firemen in the city had been killed, with all their equipment lost. The only place where coffins could be made had been destroyed, so we wanted to do something quickly.

'Painting red crosses on the buildings would have taken too long and finding paint itself was a problem. We decided to look for the red carpets that were usually laid in the church for weddings but we could not find the key nor anyone who could help us. So my sister decided to take four of the big sheets that had been used in the operating theatre, already smeared with blood. We dipped them into the pails of blood that stood there and went to spread them on the forcing frames of the hospital garden. We thought that the reflection of the glass would help in spotting this international sign, but as we were spreading the fourth sheet, making the fourth side of the cross, a small plane came down and we thought it was going to strafe us.

'Although tempted to abandon the job and run into hiding, we still decided to risk it and finish our red cross. We did not know much about British planes then, as the battle was just beginning, but we noticed that it was moving its wings, rocking slightly, and soon we realized it was a spotter plane. It was obvious that it had spotted the red cross and was trying to let us know. The next day, however, when we went back to the huge vegetable garden to check if the red cross still lay as it should on the forcing frames, we realized that it was not red any more but had turned a dark brown, so we added some mercurochrome – though this was scarce – to the blood before we dipped the sheets again in order to stain them more efficiently.

'When I was told later by the surgeons to clear the mess and empty those pails, as I was throwing the blood from one of the pails, a severed hand fell out. I must confess that it took me years before I could admire again any of Dürer's or Rodin's studies of hands or even look at a painting representing hands. We were still sensitive then; I was twenty-four in 1944.'

Jack Capell was still with the wire section of the 8th Infantry Regiment, 4th Infantry Division. 'On 7 June the regimental command post was near Ste-Mère-Eglise and that was where Cisk and I rejoined the company. On 9 June the command post moved to Fréville. On the 10th we encountered heavy fighting south of Montebourg. We remained in or near that location for the next nine days. One night the German counter-attack was so intense that I felt our position would be overrun by morning. I wondered about the rest of the wounded men I had been unable to take back to the aid station, as I had previously taken wounded men back in my Jeep. I was so tired that I fell asleep in my fox-hole. In the morning I found the Germans had not continued their advance either because they were in no condition to do so or because they didn't realize how weak we were. We remained at something of a stand-off with the Germans from 10 June through 19th.

'One morning I was taking a nap beside my fox-hole when one of my men told me the General was coming. I thought this must be Teddy Roosevelt because he was the only General who regularly inspected the front line. I shall never forget Teddy Roosevelt – he was truly the soldier's friend. Teddy Roosevelt died in Normandy of exhaustion on the night of 12 July.

'We were cheered one day by the arrival of nine American tanks in our sector; by nightfall six of them had been knocked out. The situation appeared grim again. We hoped that if the D-Day landings were successful and a good beachhead established, the German defences would collapse. By the time we got to Cherbourg we realized there was going to be a long war ahead.

'Thus we began to value the "Million-dollar wound". This meant a wound serious enough to get a man to hospital but not serious enough to kill or permanently maim him. Atterbury, of our wire section, was hit by shrapnel in the buttocks area. It did not appear to be serious but was enough to get him evacuated. We congratulated him as he lay on the ground smiling, awaiting evacuation to a hospital in England. Next day we asked the medic who attended to him if he was indeed on his way to England. The medic informed us that Atterbury had died at the aid station.

'Self-inflicted wounds began to occur more frequently after mid-June. One day I was sitting in my fox-hole, when I noticed a man put his foot on the edge of his hole, aim his rifle at it and blow the end off. This was the most common self-inflicted wound at the time.

'Some men took to drinking heavily since there was abundant liquor available in evacuated farmhouses and towns. There was as much brandy as anyone could drink. Nearly every farm in Normandy had an apple orchard and at least one vat of hard cider. Whenever a GI drank too much in combat he was usually killed or wounded after a short time. In some cases this led to acts of foolish bravery. A fellow in our company who drank too much strapped grenades around his waist, grabbed his rifle and raced for the enemy lines, announcing he was going to kill every German he could find. We found him dead the next day.'

By 7 June the German Army were hurling themselves in force against the bridgehead. Colonel Helmut Ritgen of Panzer Lehr Division takes up the story. 'From 6 June onwards, 21st Panzer had been thrown piecemeal into battle to counter the British airborne landings. This armoured attack towards the shore was halted prematurely when British paratroopers landed in our rear. On D-Day night the British I Corps had captured a coastal strip six miles long though not yet very deep. In vain the exhausted German defenders looked for reinforcements but all local reserves had been used up.

'C-in-C West had ordered increased readiness to move for Panzer Group West, which included 12th SS Panzer, Panzer Lehr, and the 17th SS Panzer Grenadier Division. 12th SS Panzer was put under command of Army Group "B" and Kurt Meyer led them towards a sector of the 711th Infantry Division east of the Orne. Movement was difficult because of air strikes and too many failures of the radio sets. Marching at night turned out to be reasonably safe and Panzer Lehr made their way to the Flers–Vire area on previously reconnoitred routes.

'My battalion was attacked by aircraft during a supply halt near Alençon. Bomb and gun bursts set tanks and POL trucks on fire, soldiers were killed and wounded. Similar incidents happened to all columns. Some mushroom clouds of smoke were guiding the fighter bombers to their targets. In spite of increased vehicle distances and dispersion to small groups, marching in daylight under repeated air attack was a risky venture, costing time and losses.

'While the columns of Panzer Lehr Division headed for their objectives under rolling air interdiction, General Bayerlein was severely cut up when his car was attacked from the air. His aide and his driver were killed. He himself got away, slightly wounded but violently shaken.'

Back on the British and Canadian beaches, men and equipment were still pouring ashore. Harold Addie, Royal Navy Seaman came into 'Juno' beach on an LCT and gives an account of the scene. 'On landing we hit a mine which damaged the stern, screws and rudder, but we were not holed, but when the tide receded we were not able to get off the beach. The beach was being tidied up now and the dead were being dragged along and placed in stacks for collection. As we were high and dry, a Geordie friend and myself asked permission to go ashore. We found a hole in the Atlantic Wall and went through it. There were still dead Germans in the bunkers, and we collected some souvenirs lying about, namely belts and tin hats. We went into the town of Bernières and were amazed to find a shop open selling newspapers and German magazines, but our progress was stopped by the troops in one street, because a sniper was still holed out in a church steeple. The railway station was deserted and we returned across the field to the craft.

'That night the fighting was still going on in the town and along the coast to St Aubin. During the next day LCT 530 came alongside. It had been hit and was sinking. We tried to use our generators to pump out the water but it was a losing battle and we had to let it go. It was not until 10 June that we were finally towed back across the Channel.'

Over in the Cotentin, the 4th Infantry Division was butting its way towards Cherbourg. On D+5 Colonel 'Red' Reeder of the 12th Infantry Regiment was hit by shell-fire near Montebourg. 'I stopped to talk a moment to some replacements sitting behind a hedgerow, who had just arrived from England. I felt sorry for them because they looked frightened. I said, "Great to have you fellows with us. You're joining a winning outfit. The 12th Infantry has been beating the Germans for six days."

'When we walked across an open field, a single shell cracked over my head and I went down. My left leg was on fire. I sat up and looked at it and saw that it was horribly mangled above the ankle. My left elbow was torn open. I screamed and could not help it. Bill Mills, who was wounded and stunned in the same explosion, recovered quickly and placed a tourniquet on my leg. His blood splashed on me as he gave me a shot of morphine from his paratrooper's first-aid kit. I was thankful for Bill Mills. I lay there in the dirt for maybe fifteen minutes, then a Jeep rolled up carrying six wounded on a stretcher, and I saw the top man being removed for me. "Oh, no, you don't," I called. "Take those men to the Aid Station, then come back for me."

'When I woke up I was in a huge black tent, the wounded on stretchers lay in neat rows. Two shadows appeared. One I recognized in the dim light as the head of the beach hospital. The other, who wore a steel helmet, knelt on one knee.

' "Red," he said, "this is General Collins." He fumbled with my shirt. "I am pinning on you the Distinguished Service Cross. Brad – General Bradley – said to tell you he was sorry that he could not come himself, and he wants you to know he sent an aviator to London to get this. This is the first DSC to be awarded in Normandy."

'General Collins stood up. "Red, is there anything I can do for you ?"

' "Make Van Fleet a General," I said.

' "The recommendation is already in," he replied, "but what can I do for you ?"

' "Tell the regiment it won the first DSC," I said, "and that I will be back." '

Another man wounded was George Nicolson with 'D' Company, the 7th Green Howards. 'I survived until 13 August, when I was wounded in the head by shrapnel. By then I was the last surviving member of the platoon that came ashore on D-Day. The officer and two men were killed on D-Day, and the rest were wounded ... so they got the lot of us in the end.

'At the time of the 40th Anniversary of D-Day I was interviewed by a teacher from a local secondary school, whose class was studying the Second World War. She asked me if the Army put us up in hotels during the fighting, and if hot food came up every day in lorries ; the more you write about how war really was, the better.'

Inland from 'Juno', the Canadians were getting locked into their bitter fight with 12th SS Panzer Division. The 25th SS Panzer Grenadier Regiment of 12th SS Panzer was commanded by Standartenführer Kurt Meyer and on 7 June 1944 this regiment shot twenty-three Canadian prisoners at Buron, a village north-west of Caen. 12th SS continued to shoot its prisoners throughout the Normandy campaign, and there was certainly retaliation for these atrocities. In December 1945 a Canadian Military Court Martial found Kurt Meyer guilty of murder and sentenced him to be shot. The sentence was later commuted to life imprisonment and he was released in 1954.

S.J.Dann was a soldier in No. 6 Commando, holding the Ranville heights. 'We had been briefed to expect a German counter-attack four days after the landing. Facing us at the time was the 744th Infantry Regiment, and we expected an attack from the 857th and 858th Infantry Regiments backed up by 21st Panzer. During the night of 9/10 June we could hear a lot of movement from the enemy as there was only a cornfield between us. The night passed quietly though we could hear tracked vehicles which we assumed were mobile 88s. Just after "Stand-to", I was shaving when the Brigadier, Derek Mills-Roberts, came along (Lord Lovat had by then been wounded by shell fire and evacuated), and gave us his "Not a step back, fight to the last man, the last drop of blood" routine. It looked like being a lousy day.

'At 0800 hrs all was still and quiet, and then all hell broke loose. Mortar shells and machine guns, but all the fire fell on the edge of the orchards. We held our fire and waited until we saw the helmets of the German infantry as they advanced through the corn. They came at a steady pace and penetrated several yards into the orchard, where they stopped and looked about. By all the rules we should have occupied the leading edge and looking down the forward slope to their positions. Instead the CO had us dig in at the back of the orchard. Very crafty. On a given word we opened up with everything. These included a Bren, a Vickers K gun, an American Browning, and a German MG-34. The Germans were lifted off the ground by the weight of fire.

'The next attack came in from our right flank but this was a weak affair which soon died out. Then, at about 1100 hrs, it was our turn again with a barrage of mortars and shells, and this time their shelling was accurate. Their infantry crawled through the corn and fired on us from the hedgerow, and when they thought we had been softened up enough, they charged. They made half the distance before faltering and falling back. Then they hit the right flank again and there was the danger of a break-through. Our TSM took one man from each trench and got them across to 4 Troop. A stick of mortar bombs landed near me and a man behind was killed and three others wounded. I dived into the first slit trench I found but got out a lot quicker. The two occupants had been hit. One was very dead and the other had a serious back wound. I met him again thirty-five years later, still paralysed from the waist down.

'The attack died down. The German troops had infiltrated into the small wood on our right and brought up a self-propelled 88mm gun. We had a stalemate situation. We could not move out and were down to our last magazine for the Bren. Then came one of my lasting memories of the war, one I remember when I go back to Normandy each year for the D-Day pilgrimage and walk down that road. The Germans were behind a low wall and one of them suddenly jumped over the wall and ran towards us, firing from the hip with a Schmeisser. He had 50 yards to go and stood no chance. A short burst stitched his chest and he fell. Later on we moved down and I turned him over. He was a tall blond, pure German, wearing an Iron Cross 2nd Class, the Afrika ribbon and several other campaign ribbons. I thought what a terrible waste, what a way to finish his career and life. We picked up the two German wounded and flushed out a couple of poor specimens hiding in the bushes and returned to the farm.

'About 1800 hrs the Germans had had enough and withdrew. Peace reigned over our little piece of Normandy. We had been engaged by three battalions, we were now about 350 in number, but I think we did a good job. We had about one-third of the unit as casualties.'

No. 6 Commando were still in action eleven months later in May 1945, when the war came to an end. They were then deep in Germany, had fought many battles, and overrun the concentration camp at Belsen. When the German Field Marshal Milch surrendered his baton to the Commando Brigadier, Derek Mills-Roberts, the Brigadier, disgusted with the sights uncovered at Belsen, broke the baton over the Field Marshal's head.

Over on the western flank, the American airborne troops were still in action and continued to fight in Normandy until mid-July, when they were withdrawn to the UK. The 508th PIR returned to a tumultuous welcome from the people of Nottingham, and David Pike, a local historian, has left an account of this time. 'The troopers were very, very weary, some were even in a state of shock. They had been in action continuously for 31 days and of the 2,056 young men who had landed on D-Day only 995 were returning back to England. The rest were missing or casualties, and 307 had been killed.

'The 508th landed at Southampton to a hero's welcome. People were waving and cheering as the troopers left the LSTs and boarded trains for Nottingham. The welcome at Southampton was greatly appreciated by the troopers, but it was nothing compared with the welcome they got when the train pulled in at Nottingham. There were two ATS bands and hundreds of people waiting to welcome the 508th back "home".

'As the bands played "Over There", there were shouts of "God bless you, Yank." The troopers walked slowly through the crowd, the tiredness plainly visible on their faces. People were crying and it was at this moment that the 508th came to realize that Nottingham was indeed their second home. In fact the 508th's History stated that one trooper had suggested that the regiment should not have received foreign service pay at all during their stay in Nottingham, such was the bond of friendship that was felt between the 508th and the citizens of Nottingham.

'After reaching Wollaton Park 50 per cent of the regiment was immediately given a seven-day furlough, the other 50 per cent would have the same the following week. Just how fierce the fighting had really been suddenly hit the troopers the minute they returned to their tents. They could tell by looking at the empty cots how high the casualties were. In fact, on more than one occasion, a trooper would find that he was the lone survivor from his eight-man tent, and it has been brought to my notice that on discovering this, many a trooper simply sat on a bed and cried his eyes out for his missing buddies.'

AFTER D-DAY

Howard Hughes from California says: 'The only sad time I had in Wollaton Park was when we came back from Normandy. We left with about 130 of the finest men I have ever met and when we returned five weeks later only 30 of us came back. I remember someone singing "Danny Boy", the tears came down my cheek when I looked around and saw all the men who were no longer with us. It was a sad day, I lost so many good buddies. We had been like one big family.'

Two months later, in September 1944, the American Airborne were in action again, parachuting into Holland as part of the 'Market Garden' operation, taking bridges on the road to Arnhem, where the British 1st Airborne Division made a memorable stand.

The D-Day landings of 1944 were a glorious victory, but war is not glorious. If the accounts in this book have not already made that clear, this final account will do so.

Sergeant Rainer Hartmetz was fighting the American paratroopers when he was wounded. 'I was on the left flank of my squad with Gottlieb's squad 150 metres away on the right. Machine-gun fire was coming from that flank and my boys could not move, for they were pinned down by the machine-gun fire. Then soldiers began to pass me by shouting that Gottlieb was hit, and by the loss of him my machine gun wasn't any more protected. If now the American infantry would assault along our hedgerow they could roll up our line and fight down our riflemen one after the other. My squad would be lost and the big dying begin.

'I had only one thought – to replace Gottlieb. I had 150 metres to run towards the American hedgerow, and the apple tree half way had the leaves and the branches flying away, hit by bullets. It was a run like the 100 metres in High School, with only my magazines and the machine pistol in my hand. I crashed into Gottlieb's fox-hole. He was pale in the face, eyes wide open. I fired a magazine into the hedgerow to keep the Americans down, then I turned back to Gottlieb. He was hit in the hip and I said, "Now let's see ..." when I got a push in the right shoulder.

'It was like a hit from a mighty hammer. All seemed to be smashed and torn apart. I let the weapon fall and tried to grip my arm with my left hand, but I couldn't find it. Blood ran out of the sleeve, over my hand and soaked my pants. Gottlieb got up and started firing to give me cover. I crawled out of the fox-hole into the next fox-hole, where a man cut my blouse away and dressed my shoulder. I hardly dared to look at the wound but I did. It seemed to be as large as the palm of the hand, a deep, bloody crater, surrounded by a lot of small holes. Two bandages were soaked, so he took a third one. I became tired and leaned my head on the wall of the fox-hole.

'I wanted to close my eyes and repose a little. All energy was gone. Lutz

239

got me awake and my energy came back again. "You can't stay here. If they start cleaning the position they'll kill you," he said, and he helped me out of the hole. I ran, the rest of the field jacket hanging on the left shoulder, the upper part of my body naked. They were firing and I had the feeling they were using me for target practice. I passed my machine-gun position, and saw the gun crew fall down like they were swept away by a hand. One of them cried in pain. It was a cry like an animal. They died. All of the boys died.

'I walked and walked, each step became harder. The bandages wouldn't stop the blood. I saw suddenly big drops of blood on my dusty boots. My neck became stiff and I became tired. I wanted to sit down in the ditch and sleep a little, but I knew I would never wake up again. Then it all became black before my eyes and I couldn't stay on my legs. I let myself fall into the ditch and as I fell I thought, "That's it! They will never know how it happened."

'I felt that someone kept me in a sitting position, and I could see again. First I couldn't figure out what was going on. It was two men in khaki, one of them lit a cigarette and gave it to me. It was a Camel. The two khakies were Americans. At first I thought they had caught me, but then I could see they were wounded themselves and had no weapons. After a while we got up and they supported me. We reached a crossroad with a German first aid station.

'It was a dreadful night, tired, pain, and not able to sleep. In the morning hours they put us on trucks and brought us to the south in the region of St Lô. Another castle, another ambulance place. We lay lined up in a long tent. Paratroopers, infantrymen, tank crews, and between us some Americans. The end of the tent was parted by a curtain of a tent sheet. Behind that the surgery room. From time to time a doctor appeared. Around his waist was a blood-spotted apron. He had shadows under the eyes. Passing our line he chose the men for operations. They carried me on a stretcher behind the curtain. There were two tables. On the other one worked an American surgeon who had been taken prisoner.

'The German doctor cut off my bandages. "We have to cut clean the lip of the wound, boy. It doesn't hurt much." The doctor cut and the pain was terrible. Then it was over. I couldn't have stood it a minute longer. I was exhausted. They brought me back and gave me something to drink. Then I was placed by the exit of the tent. Beside me was a small table. Two Paymasters were sitting there and talked while having a meal. I heard that since the morning hours England was bombed by "V" weapons, the new German rocket bombs. They talked of that with satisfaction. I thought of the boys in the hedgerows.

'They prepared us for the transport, to clear the place for newcomers. A dozen of us were lying on stretchers in the middle of the courtyard, waiting for the trucks. The sky was grey and it started raining. First some drops, then very strong. The ambulance personnel took cover in the entrance of the castle. Nobody took any notice of us. The rain splashed on our faces and soaked the rest of our uniforms and the bandages were full of water. We felt like forgotten dogs.'

BIBLIOGRAPHY

Stephen Ambrose, *The Supreme Commander*, New York, 1970.

Stephen Ambrose, *Pegasus Bridge*, Allen & Unwin, 1984.

General Omar Bradley, *A Soldier's Story*, Eyre & Spottiswoode, 1951.

Canada's Battle in Normandy, 1944, Dept of Defense, Ottawa, 1946.

Paul Carell, *Invasion – They're Coming*, London, 1962.

D-Day, accounts by The Eisenhower Foundation, University Press of Kansas, 1971.

W. F. Dawson, *The All-American (82nd Airborne)*, privately printed, 1950.

Kenneth Edwards, *Operation Neptune*, Collins, 1947.

General Dwight D. Eisenhower, *Crusade in Europe*, Heinemann, 1949.

Major L. F. Ellis, *Victory in the West* (Vol. 1), HMSO, 1962.

Bernard Fergusson, *The Watery Maze*, Collins, 1956.

General Sir Richard Gale, *With the 6th Airborne Division in Normandy*, London, 1948.

Frederick de Guingand, *Operation Victory*, Collins, 1960.

George Harrison, *Cross Channel Attack*, US Dept of the Army, 1951.

Max Hastings, *Overlord*, Michael Joseph, 1984.

Gordon Holman, *Stand by to Beach*, Hodder & Stoughton, 1944.

David Howarth, *Dawn of D-Day*, Collins, 1959.

John Keegan, *Six Armies in Normandy*, Pan Books, 1982.

B. H. Liddell Hart (ed.), *The Rommel Papers*, London, 1953.

Brigadier the Lord Lovat, *March Past*, Weidenfeld & Nicolson, 1978.

Oberst Hans von Luck, *Panzer Commander*, Prager, 1992.

Captain J. R. Madden, 'Ex Coelis', *Canadian Army Journal*

Field Marshal Sir Bernard L. Montgomery, *Normandy to the Baltic*, World Publishing, 1958.

Jacques Mordel, *Dieppe – The Dawn of Decision*, Souvenir Press, 1962.

General Sir Fredrick Morgan, *Overture to Overlord*, Hodder & Stoughton, 1950.

Maj.-General James Moulton, *Haste to the Battle (48 Commando)*, Cassell, 1963.

Ross Munro, *Gauntlet to Overlord*, Macmillan, 1945.

Robin Neillands, *By Sea and Land (The Royal Marine Commandos)*, Weidenfeld & Nicolson, 1987.

Robin Neillands, *The Raiders (The Army Commandos)*, Weidenfeld & Nicolson, 1989.

General Matthew B. Ridgeway, *Soldier*, Harper & Row, 1956.

Cornelius Ryan, *The Longest Day*, Simon & Schuster, 1959.

Hilary St George Saunders, *The Green Beret*, Michael Joseph, 1949.

Hilary St George Saunders, *The Red Beret*, Michael Joseph, 1951.

Norman Scarfe, *Assault Division*, Collins, 1952.

The 79th Armoured Division, privately published, London, 1950.

Hans Speidal, *We defended Normandy*, London, 1951.

Jack Thomson and others, *First Infantry Division*, privately published, New York, 1947.

Warren Tute, *D Day*, Pan Books, 1974.

George Weller, *The Story of the Paratroops*, Random House, 1958.

Chester Wilmot, *The Struggle for Europe*, Collins, 1952.

David Young, *Four-five (45 Commando, Royal Marines)*, Leo Cooper, 1972.

Brigadier Peter Young, *Storm from the Sea*, William Kimber, 1959.

INDEX